Concepts in Composition

Concepts in Composition

Theory and Practice
in the Teaching of Writing

Irene L. Clark, Ph.D.
California State University, Northridge

with Contributors
Betty Bamberg
Darsie Bowden
John R. Edlund
Lisa Gerrard
Sharon Klein
Julie Neff Lippman
James D. Williams

LAWRENCE ERLBAUM ASSOCIATES, PUBLISHERS
2003   Mahwah, New Jersey   London

Senior Acquisitions Editor: Naomi Silverman
Textbook Marketing Manager: Marisol Kozlovski
Editorial Assistant: Erica Kica
Cover Design: Kathryn Houghtaling Lacey
Textbook Production Manager: Paul Smolenski
Full-Service Compositor: TechBooks
Text and Cover Printer: United Graphics Incorporated

This book was typeset in 10/12 pt. ITC New Baskerville,
Italic, Bold, Bold Italic.
The heads were typeset in ITC New Baskerville Bold.

Lawrence Erlbaum Associates, Inc., Publishers
10 Industrial Avenue
Mahwah, New Jersey 07430

Library of Congress Cataloging-in-Publication Data

Clark, Irene L.
    Concepts in composition : theory and practice in the teaching of writing /
Irene L. Clark ; with contributors, Betty Bamberg . . . [et al.].
        p.   cm.
    Includes bibliographical references and index.
    ISBN 0-8058-3820-1 (pbk. : alk. paper)
    1. English language—Rhetoric—Study and teaching.   2. English
language—Composition and exercises—Study and teaching.   3. English
language—Study and teaching—Foreign speakers.   4. Report writing—Study
and teaching.   I. Bamberg, Betty.   II. Title.
PE1404 .C528   2003
808′ .042′071—dc21   2002011661

For my husband, Bill, my growing family, and the many colleagues whose insights have influenced my concept of Composition.

Brief Contents

Contents

Preface

At the beginning of each semester, at colleges and universities throughout the country, writing program directors and department chairs grapple with two important lists. One is a schedule of first-year composition classes; the other contains the names of teaching assistants and faculty members, both full- and part-time, who are available, willing, and sometimes eager to teach these classes. Generically referred to as First-year Writing or Freshman Comp, such classes at some institutions comprise more than one hundred sections, and the question of who should teach them and what sort of preparation Composition teachers should have remains a perplexing one.

At one time, not too long ago, it was believed that pretty much anyone who could write or who had studied literature was, by definition, qualified to teach first-year writing. In fact, in my first academic job, the Chair of the English department assumed that my Master's degree in English Literature rendered me perfectly capable of teaching three sections of Composition per semester. I recall being handed a sample syllabus, a book that explained traditional rules of grammar, and a collection of exemplary essays, including "Once More to the Lake," which, at that time, was my first visit to that well-traveled shore. Then I was left on my own to plan and teach my classes—to construct writing topics, provide feedback to students, and assign grades. No one asked if I had been given any sort of preparation for teaching writing, if I had any notion of what a Composition course was supposed to be, or even if I had ever taken such a course, myself. Miraculously, though, with the help of sympathetic colleagues and generous students, I managed to get through that first semester without doing too much harm. Cheerfully, I blundered my way from class to class, relying on my youth, enthusiasm, and determination to carry me through.

That was the way it used to be. More recently, scholarship in the developing field of Rhetoric and Composition has brought the recognition that teaching writing requires not only willingness, enthusiasm, an interest in texts as a subject of study, and the ability to write and "relate" to students, but also an understanding of the "concepts" of Composition on which effective several ideas associated with the field of second language acquisition that can help composition teachers work effectively with ESL students. These include theories of language acquisition, insights from contrastive rhetoric, and the role of grammar and error correction. Chapter 10, written by Sharon Klein at California State University, Northridge, is concerned with theories of language and language variation, focusing on the highly politicized controversy over Ebonics. Chapter 11, written by Lisa Gerrard at the University of California at Los Angeles, presents an overview of the association between computers and writing pedagogy, examines the issue of computer literacy, and suggests possibilities for incorporating computers into classroom teaching.

For all of us, the most daunting challenge in writing this book was figuring out how to address each multifaceted and complex concept in Composition within the confines of a single chapter. Composition scholarship is extensive; the question of what to include and what to omit was the subject of many conversations among my contributors, all of whom were concerned about simplifying, but who also recognized the paradox of teaching composition: that teachers need to know a little about each concept to plan their courses effectively, but that it is only through classroom experience that they will really be able to understand the interaction of theory and pedagogy. It is a credit to my contributors that they all managed to find a middle ground between too much and too little information, presenting sufficient information for beginning teachers while pointing the way to further exploration and research, in the section titled "For Further Exploration." Still, I expect that some readers of this book will be concerned about this necessary limitation.

Too frequently, classes aimed at preparing writing teachers tend to separate theory from practice, and, in fact, many new teachers, anxious about how to fill class time, are often impatient with courses that address theory at all. "Just tell me what I need to teach," they implore. "Give me a syllabus and I'll follow it." *Concepts in Composition: Theory and Practice in the Teaching of Writing* aims to help such teachers find the answers for themselves by establishing the interconnection between theoretical concept and classroom lesson. Only when prospective writing teachers understand that relationship will they be able to teach effectively.

ACKNOWLEDGMENTS

I would like to thank my colleagues for their generous contributions. Their breadth of scholarship and hard work has brought this book to fruition and greatly improved it. I am also grateful to Lori Hawver and the editorial staff at Lawrence Erlbaum, and especially to my editor, Naomi Silverman, whose initial recognition of the possibilities of this book enabled its publication and whose insights and straightforward suggestions helped me shape each chapter. I would also like to acknowledge my research assistant, Anne Thorpe, who has evinced a consistently strong interest in the subject matter and goals of this book, locating new material with genuine excitement and cheerfully undertaking even tedious tasks, such as converting the end of chapter references from MLA to APA style. Finally, I would like to thank my husband, Bill, and my children, Lisa, Louisa, Clif, and Justin, who have always supported my publishing efforts and encouraged me in all my endeavors.

Process

Irene L. Clark

> This chapter traces the history of the process movement within
> the emerging discipline of rhetoric and composition, discusses
> several competing views or theories of composing, and suggests
> assignments that will enable prospective teachers to understand
> their own writing process.

When I first began teaching writing, the hallway outside my office displayed
a cartoon-like picture depicting a classroom of 100 years ago or more. In the
center of the scene was a stereotypical professor, caricatured with pointed
gray beard, wire spectacles, bushy gray eyebrows, and censorious expression,
who was doggedly pouring knowledge through an oversized funnel into the
head of a student, a sulky, somewhat plump young man. Obviously intended
to be humorous, the picture ironically suggested that successful teaching involves transferring knowledge from professor to student, the professor active
and determined, the student passive and submissive, perhaps uninterested,
even unwilling.

I often recall that picture when I think about the term "process" in the
context of composition pedagogy, because the outmoded concept of teaching it portrays constitutes the antithesis of current ideas about the teaching
of writing. Over the past 30 years, the discipline of rhetoric and composition
has emphasized the importance of helping students become active participants in learning to write, because, as the learning theorist Jerome Bruner
(1966) has maintained, "to instruct someone in [a] discipline is not a matter
of getting him to commit results to mind. Rather, it is to teach him to participate in the process that makes possible the establishment of knowledge....
Knowledge is a process, not a product" (p. 72).

Because students do not learn to write by having knowledge poured into their heads, one of the most important goals of a writing class is to enable students to develop an effective writing "process," so that they can continue to learn after the class has ended. The term "process" is, therefore, of key importance for anyone entering the field of composition, both as a teacher and a researcher. This chapter traces the history of the process movement within the emerging discipline of rhetoric and composition, discusses several competing views or theories of composing, and includes several assignments that will enable teachers to understand their own writing process. These insights will enrich their teaching.

THE WRITING PROCESS MOVEMENT: A BRIEF HISTORY

In the long sweep of history, it is only recently that serious consideration has been given to writing in colleges and universities. The field of written rhetoric, which came to be called "composition," grew during the 19th century from an older tradition of oral rhetoric, which has been traced back to 500 B.C.. However, during the 19th century, several political and technological developments had the effect of focusing academic attention on writing in English, instead of in Latin and Greek, as had previously been the case. The establishment of the land grant colleges in 1867 brought a new population of students to the university, students from less-privileged backgrounds who had not studied classical languages and who, therefore, had to write in the vernacular—that is, English. Then, a number of inventions had the effect of making writing more important in a variety of settings. The invention of the mechanical pencil (1822), the fountain pen (1850), the telegram (1864), and the typewriter (1868), plus the increasing availability of cheap durable paper, paralleled and aided the increasing importance of writing at the university.

As writing became more important, the task of teaching writing was assumed by various educational institutions. The writing classes developed were viewed as "a device for preparing a trained and disciplined workforce" and for assimilating "huge numbers of immigrants into cultural norms, defined in specifically Anglo-Protestant terms (Berlin, 1996, p. 23). In 1874, Harvard University introduced an entrance exam that featured a writing requirement; when the English faculty received the results, they were shocked by the profusion of error of all sorts—punctuation, capitalization, spelling, and syntax. In 1879, Adam S. Hill, who was in charge of the Harvard entrance examination for several years, complained that even the work of good scholars was flawed by spelling, punctuation, and grammar errors and urged that a required course in sophomore rhetoric that had been offered at

Harvard for several years be moved to the first year. Thus, was a literacy crisis born, and when Harvard instituted a first-year writing course, a number of institutions did likewise.

The First-Year Course and the Use of Handbooks

First-year writing courses abounded. However, it was soon realized that the course not only failed to provide an instant solution to the problem but also that it created a great deal of work for faculty who undertook or were assigned the task of reading and responding to student texts. Yet by the turn of the century, a presumed method of addressing this situation was devised—the creation of a new sort of textbook called the "handbook," in which all of the rules and conventions of writing could be written and to which teachers could refer in the margins of student papers. The idea behind the development of the handbook was that teachers would no longer have to read and mark student papers in detail. Instead, they could skim the papers for errors, circle those errors in red, and cite rule numbers, which students could then look up in their handbooks. Handbooks became very popular, and soon every publisher had developed one, followed by a workbook of exercises that students could use to practice. Presumably, these handbooks and workbooks would lighten the teacher's load and solve the problem of teaching students to write. Yet, not surprisingly, the problems continued, and student writing did not improve.

The difficulties experienced by those attempting to teach students to write at the beginning of the 20th century were described in the lead article of the first issue of the *English Journal,* published in 1912. The title of that article was "Can Good Composition Teaching Be Done Under Present Conditions?"and the first word of the article was "No." Then, after a few sentences, the article went on as follows:

> Every year teachers resign, breakdown, perhaps become permanently in-valided, having sacrificed ambition, health, and in not a few instances even life, in the struggle to do all the work expected of them. (Hopkins, p. 1)

Certainly, this was not an encouraging portrait of an emerging field!

Moreover, the composition course was often a brutal experience for students as well. Lad Tobin (1994), in his essay "How the Writing Process Was Born—and Other Conversion Narratives," recalled it like this:

> Once upon a time, in an age of disciplinary darkness and desolation . . . writing students were subjected to cruel and inhuman punishments. They were assigned topics like "Compare Henry Fleming from *The Red Badge of Courage* to one of the characters in the *Iliad;* make sure to consider the definition of an anti-hero" or "Write about your most humiliating moment." They were told, with a straight face, that no decent person ever wrote without outlining

first, that there is a clear distinction between description, narration, exposition, and argument; that grammatical errors were moral and mortal sins, and that teachers' evaluations of student essays were always objective accurate and fair....

In that dark period of our disciplinary history, teachers rarely explained anything about the process of writing (unless you count "outline, write, proofread, hand in" as the student's process ... Or they would explain some of the rules governing good writing. But they would say nothing about invention, how to get started, what to do in the middle, or what to do when the middle turned back into the start, and so on. (pp. 2–3)

Of course, this picture constitutes a generalization, and it is likely that at least some teachers, intuitively understanding what was helpful to beginning writers, did not adhere to this model of "teaching" writing. Yet, that this model did indeed exist, I can attest to from my own college experience, where essays topics were assigned regardless of whether students knew or cared much about them, and where few, if any, process-oriented activities—prewriting strategies, multiple drafts, collaborative groups, student–teacher conferences—were encouraged or even mentioned. When I submitted a paper as a college student, I would wait with trepidation for the teacher to return it, which he or she would eventually do, usually without having written anything other than a grade or perhaps a brief evaluative comment on the front cover.

In a recent review essay titled, "Of Pre- and Post-Process: Reviews and Ruminations," Richard Fulkerson (2001) characterizes first-year writing as "like riding a bicycle. If you knew how to do it, then you could demonstrate your ability on demand; hence the idea of in-class and time-limited writing" (p. 96). Fulkerson (2001) describes his own experience in a "pre-process program" as follows:

In the fall quarter, we had an anthology of readings, a handbook of grammar, and the 2nd edition of McCrimmon's *Writing with a Purpose*. We wrote at least five papers. One assigned topic was "My First day at School." Another was "any philosophical issue." A third was a limited research paper about some historic person, who we were to argue was or was not "great" based on several readings in the anthology. Dr. Staton would assign *the* topic orally, and we would have about a week to write. Then he marked the paper, put a grade on it, and a brief comment. (p. 95)

Learning to write in those days meant being able to figure out what the teacher wanted in order to create an acceptable "product," and apparently, few teachers thought that helping students acquire a workable writing "process" was part of their job. Whatever process students used, they had to manage on their own.

This lack of attention to the process writers engage in when they write reflected a concept of creativity that to some extent persists in our culture—that is, that a "good" writer is someone who can produce an excellent text as quickly, independently, and effortlessly as a bird learns to fly. This idea suggests that those of us who struggle, for whom writing is a laborious, time-consuming, and often painful process (i.e., most, if not all of us) are not, by definition, "good" writers. One could either write, or one couldn't. Such was the fantasy of that time, and even now, our culture continues to value speed and ease of production, particularly in reference to the speaking ability of our politicians, who are deemed "good speakers" if they can think on their feet.

In ancient times, however, classical rhetoricians were aware of how much thought and preparation went into the production of a seemingly effortless speech. In ancient Greece and Rome, rhetoricians envisioned the composing process as consisting of five stages—invention (the discovery of ideas), arrangement (putting ideas in a persuasively effective order), style (finding the right language in which to present the ideas), memory (memorizing the speech), and delivery (using voice and gesture to present the speech effectively). Apparently, no one at that time was under the impression that a "gifted" speaker did not have to engage in an elaborate process before he could deliver an effective speech.

The Birth of the Process "Movement"

This product-oriented view of writing continued through the 1950s and 1960s. Then, in 1963, at the Conference of College Composition and Communication, it is reported that there was a different feeling in the air, a feeling that the field had changed. That conference signaled a renewal of interest in rhetoric and composition theory, a revival that generated the "process" approach to composition and a new research area that focused on understanding how people write and learn to write. This interest in writing as a process led to the development of a number of process-oriented methods and techniques—staged writing, conferencing, strategies of invention, and revision—activities that are now considered essential components of a writing class. Suddenly, all over the country, writing teachers began to embrace a "process" approach to writing, tossing out their handbooks and grammar exercises in order to focus on process-oriented teaching. The sentence "Writing is a process, not a product" became a mantra. "Process" was in; "product" became almost a dirty word.

Can this interest in writing as a process and the emergence of composition as a research discipline be called a "movement?" Richard Fulkerson suggests that we refer to this interest in process-oriented writing as a political party, "with members frequently willing to vote together for the same candidates, and more or less united around certain slogans lacking in nuance and short enough for bumper stickers. 'Teach process not product.' 'Down with Current-Traditional Rhetoric.' 'Say no to grammar'" (pp. 98–99).

Influences on the Concept of Process Teaching

Whether one characterizes the concept of process teaching as a movement or a political party, the notion that "writing is a process" became a slogan for the enlightened. However, like all movements (or political parties), one can retrospectively note antecedent influences. One particularly important influence on the development of process teaching in the early 1960s was what has been referred to as the New Education Movement often associated with the ideas of the psychologist Jerome Bruner. Bruner viewed learning as a process that reflected "the cognitive level of the student and its relation to the structure of the academic discipline being studied" (Berlin, 1990, p. 207), and emphasized the role of student participation and individual discovery in the learning process. In the context of writing pedagogy, Bruner's ideas translated into an emphasis on students engaging in composing activities so as to discover their own composing process—rather than in analyzing someone else's text—and on teachers creating a facilitative learning environment to enable students to do so—rather than focusing on assigning grades or correcting grammar.

Another important influence on the emerging writing process movement was the Dartmouth conference of 1966, a meeting of approximately 50 English teachers from the United States and Great Britain to consider common writing problems. What emerged from the conference was the awareness that considerable differences existed between the two countries on how instruction in English was viewed. In the United States, English was conceived of as an academic discipline with specific content to be mastered, whereas the British focused on the personal and linguistic growth of the child (Appleby, 1974, p. 229). Instead of focusing on content, "process or activity. . .defined the English curriculum for the British teacher" (Appleby, 1974, p. 230), its purpose being to foster the personal development of the student. As Berlin (1990) noted, "The result of the Dartmouth Conference was to reassert for U.S. teachers the value of the expressive model of writing. Writing is to be pursued in a free and supportive environment in which the student is encouraged to engage in an act of self discovery" (p. 210). This emphasis on the personal and private nature of composing was also manifested in the recommendations of Ken Macrorie, Donald Murray, Walter Gibson, and Peter Elbow.

The re-emergence of interest in rhetoric and composition is often referred to as the "new rhetoric," although the term "rhetoric" was absent from early publications. However, in 1971, James Kinneavy published *A Theory of Discourse,* which established "the relation between composition and classical—specifically Aristotelian—rhetoric" (Williams, 1998, p. 30). This work helped legitimize composition as a genuine research field and suggested that anyone who is serious about teaching writing should be studying rhetoric. Providing a theoretical grounding for the new rhetoric, Kinneavy's work was also notable for its reminder that writing is an act of communication between writer and audience.

What does it actually mean to view writing as a process? Broadly speaking, a process approach to writing and the teaching of writing means devoting increased attention to *writers* and the activities in which writers engage when they create and produce a text, as opposed to analyzing and attempting to reproduce "model" texts. Reacting against a pedagogy oriented toward error correction and formulaic patterns of organization, the process approach, as it evolved during the 1960s and 1970s, was concerned with discovering *how* writers produce texts, developing a model of the writing process, and helping writers find a process that would enable them to write more effectively and continue to improve as writers. Although to many writers and teachers, the concept of a writing "process" was not news, the increased emphasis in the classroom on helping students acquire an effective process and on finding out what successful writers did when they wrote, constituted a new pedagogical approach and a potentially exciting research direction.

FOR WRITING AND DISCUSSION

Reflecting on Your Own Writing Process

The goal of this assignment is to enable you to gain conscious awareness of the process you use to write papers that are assigned in classes (and the extent to which that process might be different when you write for other purposes). Such consciousness will help you not only to evaluate the effectiveness of your writing process and make adjustments to it but also to formulate your own "theory" of writing.

To Prepare for Writing

Think about a paper you have written recently for a college class. Describe the writing assignment and class for which it was intended. How did you feel about the assignment? Were you interested in it immediately? Did you find it difficult or confusing?

List as many activities associated with that writing as you possibly can recall. Some questions to consider:

- What was the first action you performed to complete the writing task? What actions followed?

- Did you think about the writing when you were involved in other activities (driving a car, for example)?
- Did you talk with anyone about the topic?
- What sort of revision did you do?
- Were these behaviors typical of what you usually do when you are given a writing assignment?
- Do you feel your writing process is effective?
- Do you use a different process when you are working on something that you, yourself, have decided to write? If so, how is it different?

Writing Task

Describe in detail the process you use when you are assigned to write a paper for a class. Use as many details as possible to enable the reader to understand fully what you do and gain insight into your writing process.

Length: Two full pages (but it is okay if you write more)

THE STAGES OF WRITING

One perspective that gained prominence during the early days of the process movement was that the writing process consisted a series of sequenced, discreet stages sometimes called "planning, drafting, and revising," although today they are often referred to as "prewriting, writing, and rewriting." An article by Gordon Rohman (1965), "Prewriting: The Stage of Discovery in the Writing Process," published in *College Composition and Communication,* emphasized the importance of invention and providing students with models of how writing is actually done. Articles published during this period strongly emphasized prewriting; however, what many of them also suggested was that writing occurred in a linear sequence; each stage following neatly upon the other; the "prewriting" phase preceding the "writing" phase, which then precedes the "revising" phase. Such a model was based on the idea that writing is a reflection of what already has been formulated in the mind of the writer and, by implication, suggested that writing can occur only after the main ideas are in place. According to this model, discovery and creativity entered the process only in terms of the writer's decisions about *how* to say what has been discovered, not in discovering and selecting *what* to say.

The problem with this linear view of writing as a series of discreet stages is that it does not reflect what writers actually do, because writers frequently discover and reconsider ideas during, as well as before they write, moving back and forth between the prewriting, writing, and revision stages as the text emerges. For example, when I wrote this chapter, I began with a set of points I planned to discuss, but I modified them many times as I wrote, often revising sentences and generating additional material as new ideas occurred to me. Moreover, because every person's writing habits are different, an insistence on a lock-step sequence of stages can prove inhibiting, sometimes paralyzing, to beginning writers. Those who believe that writing cannot occur until every thought is clarified often delay actually writing until the paper is fully outlined and developed—or until time has run out and the due date forces the writer to begin. For some students, the idea that a writer must know exactly what he or she is going to say before beginning to write can create a writer's block that actually *prevents* effective writing from taking place. Although the idea that writing occurs in stages was a more helpful one than the previous emphasis on grammatical correctness, when it was interpreted rigidly, this idea did not provide sufficient insight into the composing processes of actual writers; nor was it always useful in the classroom.

EARLY RESEARCH ON COMPOSING

Observational Studies

In an overview of early research concerned with the writing process, Sandra Perl (1994) noted 1971 as the year when the field of composition moved from an almost exclusive focus on written products to an examination of composing processes. This was the year (1971) that Janet Emig published "The Composing Processes of Twelfth Graders," which Perl describes as the first study to ask a process-oriented question, "How do 12th-graders write?" and the first to devise a method to study writing processes as they unfolded. Emig observed eight 12th-graders who spoke aloud as they composed, and from her observations, called into question the absoluteness of the stage-model theory of composing. Noting that these students did not create outlines before they composed, Emig characterized the composing process as recursive, rather than linear, noting that writers move back and forth between various phases of the process as they compose.

Although the validity of having students speak aloud as they compose can be questioned, Emig's study was important because it showed the oversimplification of the writing process inherent in the stage model, which was, and to some extent still is, reinforced in textbooks. Moreover, it generated a number of observational studies that shed further light on the composing process, among them the work of Linda Flower and John Hayes (1980), discussed later in this chapter, that linked the development of writing ability to cognitive development and the studies by Sondra Perl (1979) and Nancy Sommers (1980) who provided valuable insight into revision.

FOR FURTHER EXPLORATION

Faigley, L., & Witte, S. (1981). Analyzing revision. *CCC, 32,* 400–414.

Flower, L., & Hayes, J. (1981). A cognitive process theory of writing. *CCC, 32,* 354–387.

Kroll, B., & Schafer, J. (1978). Error analysis and the teaching of composition. *CCC, 29,* 242–248.

Matsuhashi, A. (1981). "Pausing and planning: The tempo of written discourse production. *Research in the Teaching of English, 15,* 113–134.

Perl, S. (1979). The composing process of unskilled college writers. *Research in the Teaching of English, 13,* 317–336.

Perl, S. (1981). Understanding composing. *CCC, 31,* 363–369.

Pianko, S. (1979). A description of the composing processes of college freshmen writers. *Research in the Teaching of English, 13,* 5–22.

Sommers, N. (1980). Revision strategies of student writers and experienced adult writers. *CCC, 31,* 378–388.

FOR WRITING AND DISCUSSION

Compare Nancy Sommers' "The Revision Strategies of Student Writers and Experienced Adult Writers" included at the end of Chapter 3 in this volume, with Muriel Harris' essay "Composing Behaviors of One- and Multi-Draft Writers" at the end of this chapter. Note the similarities and differences between their perspectives on the writing process. What are the implications of these perspectives for working with students in a writing class?

The Role of Cognitive Psychology

Early studies of the composing process were strongly influenced by ideas associated with cognitive psychology, particularly those of Jerome Bruner, previously, discussed, and those of Jean Piaget and Lev Vygotsky. The underlying idea of cognitive psychology is that to understand an observable behavior (such as writing), one must understand the mental structures that determine that behavior. Conceiving of language and thought as the primary mental structures that influence writing, cognitive psychologists maintain that to understand how students learn to write, one must understand how these structures develop as an individual matures and acquires knowledge of the world.

Cognitive psychology perceives linguistic and intellectual ability as developing in a natural sequence, and it is this concept that has had the most significant impact on the study of writing acquisition and on how a writing teacher can utilize that sequence in the classroom. Emig (1971), for example, maintained that the ability to write personal, expressive writing precedes the ability to write on literary or academic topics. She, therefore, urged teachers to use more of what she referred to as "reflexive"—that is, personal, writing in the classroom, based on students' own experiences and feelings. Beginning with personal topics before addressing more abstract topics, Emig claimed, fosters students' cognitive development.

Developmental Models

This notion that the development of writing ability correlates with human linguistic and intellectual development resulted in a number of publications that suggested that the English curriculum should parallel the sequence in which that development was presumed to occur. Deriving from Piaget's notion of cognitive development, James Moffett's *Teaching the Universe of Discourse* (1968) outlined a theory by which a sequential curriculum in language arts could be based. Moffett's system consisted of a progression that moved from the personal to the impersonal and from low to high levels of abstraction based on two horizontal scales. The first, the audience scale, organized discourse according to the distance between the writer and his or her audience, according to four categories (Moffett, 1968):

Reflection (interpersonal communication within the self)

Conversation (interpersonal communication between two people within communication distance)

Correspondence (interpersonal communication between remote individuals)

Publication (impersonal communication between unconnected individuals, unknown to one another). (p. 33)

Moffett's second scale, the subject scale, categorized discourse by how far away the writer or speaker is from the subject being considered. For example, a person may be sitting at a table in a cafeteria eating lunch, noting what is happening at the given moment. Later on, he or she might report on what happened in the cafeteria during lunch, generalize about what usually happens in the cafeteria at lunch, or argue that something might or should happen in the cafeteria at lunch. These two scales, the audience scale and the subject scale, Moffett suggested, can be used to help students recreate their experience through language, enabling them to develop facility in writing. Moffett's concept of a language arts curriculum based on this sequence was explained in considerable detail in his textbook *A Student-Centered Language Arts Curriculum* (1968).

A British study, *The Development of Writing Abilities (pp. 11–18)* published in 1975 by James Britton, Tony Burgess, Nancy Martin, Alex McLeod, and Harold Rosen also included the notion of sequential development. Aimed at creating a model that would "characterize all mature written utterances and then go on to trace the developmental steps that led to them" (p. 6), this system of Britton and his colleagues categorized all student writing by function—the transactional, which communicates information to an unknown audience, the expressive, which communicates information to a known audience, and the poetic, which deals only tangentially with any form of audience. Britton et al. characterized most school writing as transactional, but argued that because students are most engaged in expressive writing, this is the type of writing that is most likely to foster the development of writing ability.

Both Moffett's work and the work of Britton et al., evolving from the theories of Jean Piaget, addressed the question of how children learn to move beyond their early egocentricism to reach out to an audience, a topic addressed by Linda Flower in her seminal article, "Writer-Based Prose: A Cognitive Basis for Problems in Writing" (1979). According to Flower, novice writers often have difficulty transcending their own egocentric perspective to consider the needs of their intended audience. As a result, their texts are often characterized by what she refers to as "writer-based prose"—that is, texts in which information is omitted or inadequately explained, definitions unclarified— in other words, texts that reflect what might be in their writers' minds at the time of writing but that have not been sufficiently contextualized or modified for a reader. Often reflecting the order in which the writer first generated ideas, writer-based prose may be clear to the writer, but a reader may have difficulty understanding it. Awareness of writer-based prose in the writing class can be used to help novice writers transform "writer-based" to "reader-based" prose, enabling them to develop a better understanding of the concept of audience.

Pursuing a similar direction, Andrea Lunsford, in an article titled "Cognitive Development and the Basic Writer" (1979), claimed that the difficulties novice or "basic" writers have with writing is because of their not having reached a level of cognitive development that would enable them to form abstractions. To remedy this problem, Lunsford suggested a variety of workshop activities focusing on analysis and active thinking. During that same year (1979), Sharon Pianko published "A Description of the Composing Processes of College Freshman Writers," in which she claimed that the composing process of basic writers is less developed than that of more skillful writers.

The Work of Flower and Hayes

Several articles by Flower and Hayes continued to explore the writing process based on theories of cognitive psychology. Concerned with avoiding models that suggest that the writing process is linear, Flower and Hayes (1981) set up a cognitive theory based on four points:

1. The process of writing is best understood as a set of distinctive think processes that writers orchestrate or organize during the act of composing.

2. These processes have a hierarchical, highly embedded organization in which any process can be embedded within any other.

3. The act of composing itself is a goal-directed thinking process, guided by the writer's own growing network of goals.

4. Writers create their own goals in two key ways: by generating both high-level goals and supporting subgoals that embody the writer's developing sense of purpose, and then, at times, by changing major goals or even establishing new ones based on what has been learned in the act of writing. (p. 366)

Flower and Hayes also focused on the role of problem definition in the writing process, noting in their article "The Cognition of Discovery: Defining a Rhetorical Problem" (1980) that although a teacher may give "20 students the same assignment, the writers themselves create the problem they solve" (p. 23). Using the technique of "protocols" (having students speak aloud as they compose), Flower and Hayes constructed a model of the rhetorical problem itself, which consisted of two major units: the rhetorical situation, which consists of the "writer's given," including the audience and the assignment, and the set of goals that the writer creates for himself. The four goals they noted involved the reader (creating a persona or voice), building a meaning, and producing a formal text, which, as they point out, "closely parallel the four terms of the communication triangle: reader, writer, world, word" (p. 25).

EXPRESSIVISM AND THE CONCEPT OF PERSONAL VOICE

The initial phase of the process movement has often been associated with an emphasis on the importance of students being able to "express" their thoughts and feelings through writing, a perspective that is often referred to as "expressivism." Teachers adhering to an expressivist philosophy tended to assign essays concerned with personal experience and self-reflection, the goal being to enable students to discover their own personal "voice" that would result in "authentic" writing and self-empowerment. Ken Macrorie, in his 1970 textbook *Telling Writing*, insisted on the importance of truth telling by avoiding what he refers to as "Engfish," which he defines as institutional language, or language that conceals rather than reveals a personal self. In the preface to that work, Macrorie (1970) defined composition teaching in the following terms:

Enabling students to use their own powers, to make discoveries, to take alternative paths. It does not suggest that the world can best be examined by a set of rules ... The program gives the student first, freedom to find his voice and let

his subjects find him . . . for both teacher and student, a constant reading for
truth, in writing and commenting on that writing. This is a hard requirement,
for no one speaks truth consistently. (pp. vii–viii)

For Macrorie, good writers speak in honest voices and tell some kind of truth,
a perspective similar to that of Donald Stewart (1972) for whom the most
important goal of a writing course was for students to engage in a process of
self-discovery, manifested in the student's text by the appearance in the text
of an authentic voice; Donald Graves (1983) also referred to voice as infusing
a text with the writer's presence. Perhaps the best-known proponent of the
concept of voice, Peter Elbow (1986), although acknowledging the difficulty
of defining voice, nevertheless viewed the discovery of voice as a necessary
prerequisite of growth. "I can grow or change," Elbow maintained, but "not
unless I start out inhabiting my own voice or style. . . . In short, I need to
accept myself as I am before I can tap my power or start to grow" (p. 204).
Voice, for Elbow, constitutes both a motivating force and a source of power.
In its emphasis on empowering the inner self, the expressivist approach
to writing is sometimes referred to as the "romantic" school of writing, in
contrast to the "classical" or "cognitive" school, which view writing in terms
of intellectual development as manifested in problem solving.

Of course, there is no reason that the "process" approach should be so
closely connected to expressivist writing. Certainly, as Lad Tobin (1994)
points out, "a teacher could assign a personal essay but ignore the writing
process or assign a critical analysis yet nurture the process." (p. 6). Nevertheless, process and personal or expressivist writing were often associated
with one another in the early days of the process movement, and today the
expressionists remain "a force in rhetoric and composition studies. Such figures as Peter Elbow, Donald Murray, Ken Macrorie . . . continue to explore
writing as a private and personal act. It is this group that continues to insist
on the importance of the individual against the demands of institutional
conformity, holding out for the personal as the source of all value" (Berlin,
1990, pp. 218–219).

SOCIAL CONSTRUCTIONISM

Although cognitive and expressivist approaches to composition dominated
scholarship during the 1970s and 1980s, during the mid-1980s, publications
began to appear that questioned both the validity and the utility of focusing
on individual writing processes. Patricia Bizzell's "Cognition, Convention,
and Certainty: What We Need to Know About Writing" (1983) argues that
writers are not autonomous individuals, distinct and removed from culture, but, rather, that individual consciousness is shaped by culture through
language. This perspective implies that all writers, even when they are

presumably composing only for themselves or writing notes for a subsequent piece of writing, are mentally influenced by the "inner speech," as Vygotsky (1978) refers to it, that develops in response to a particular culture's concept of language and thought. From this perspective, then, writing is *socially constructed* because it both reflects and shapes thinking, a position that in composition studies is known as *Social Constructionism*. Social constructionist approaches to composition emphasize the role of community in shaping discourse and the importance of understanding community expectations when working with students. Bizzell's article (1983), for example, points out that although Flower and Hayes' cognitive-based model describes how writing occurs, it focuses too strongly on the individual writer and does not help composition teachers "advise students on difficult questions of practice" (p. 222).

Social constructionist approaches to composition derive from perspectives in philosophy, as well as other fields that emphasize the importance of community consensus in determining knowledge. This view is based on the idea that individuals perceive the world according to the shared beliefs and perceptions of the community or communities to which they belong; it is one that writers in fields such as history or ethnography have supported for some time. The philosopher, Richard Rorty, for example, in *Philosophy and the Mirror of Nature* (1979), maintains that knowledge is a "socially constructed belief," a viewpoint that straddles a middle position between absolute relativism, in which an individual may choose to believe anything, and the positivist notion of objective truth derived from an absolute reality. The anthropologist, Clifford Geertz (1983), similarly argues that modern consciousness is an "enormous multiplicity" of cultural values, and Charles Bazerman (1981) has emphasized the role of the scientific community in shaping the writing of scientists.

In composition, social constructionist approaches are associated with the work of David Bartholomae, Kenneth Bruffee, Patricia Bizzell, and James Berlin, who all focus on the social context of writing and the role of community in determining the appropriateness and effectiveness of a text. Kenneth Bruffee's "Collaborative Learning and the Conversation of Mankind" (1984) maintains that every person is born into the "conversation of mankind" and that it is this conversation that gives meaning and value to what we do, influencing both thinking and writing. "We can think because we can talk, and we think in ways we have learned to talk" (p. 87), Bruffee explains. For writing teachers, it is important to realize (Bruffee, 1984):

> ...that our task must involve engaging students in conversation among themselves at as many points in both the writing and the reading process as possible and that we should contrive to ensure that students' conversation about what they read and write is similar in as many ways as possible to the way we would like them eventually to read and write. The way they talk with each other determines the way they will think and the way they will write. (p. 89)

Collaborative Learning

Social constructionism is often associated with collaborative learning, although this pedagogical approach has been around for some time. Bruffee's
work acknowledges the use of collaborative learning in teaching medical
students through group diagnosis, and Albert DeCiccio (1988) has noted
its association with progressive education and the educational approach of
John Dewey. Moreover, as Bruffee (1984) has noted, the uses of collaborative
learning in the composition class in the 1970s derived more from practical
need than from a particular philosophical or theoretical perspective on
learning. Because open admission policies brought a large number of students to the university who were educationally disadvantaged, collaborative
learning developed as a means of enabling students to assist one another.
As Bruffee (1984) points out, "For American college teachers, the roots of
collaborative learning lie neither in radical politics nor in research." Rather
it was based primarily on "a pressing educational need." (p. 637)

Whatever its roots, the concept of collaborative learning has significant
implications for what occurs in the writing class. Most important, it implies
a decentering of the writing class, a balancing of authority between students
and teacher, so that students can participate in their own learning through
peer editing and writing groups. This idea, as Bruffee points out, is actually
quite similar to the work of the early process theorists such as Peter Elbow,
who has long advocated the effectiveness of the "teacherless" classroom
and the necessity of delegating authority to writing groups. According to
this perspective, students learn only when they have assumed responsibility
for their own learning. They do not develop writing skills by listening to a
teacher lecture about the writing process. Rather they must engage fully in
that process themselves, working together with peers.

Collaborative Learning in the Classroom

Although the concept of collaborative learning is easy to endorse in the
abstract, successful implementation in the classroom requires the teacher
to plan carefully all activities involving group work, whether they be peer
editing sessions, group discussions, or team research projects. All of us who
have blithely assumed that simply telling students to work together or putting
them into pairs or groups without providing specific instructions can attest
to the problems that often occur. Unless collaborative activities are carefully
orchestrated by the teacher, students may not take group work seriously,
socializing instead of working, allocating most of the work to one member,
completing the activity superficially, and generally not engaging fully in the
process. Sometimes they will offer innocuous compliments to one another
such as "I liked your paper. I could relate to it." Or "It flowed." Or else they

will complete the group activity quickly so that they can leave the class early. The following are suggestions for maximizing the value of collaborative activities in the writing class:

- Model the activity by first engaging in it yourself in front of the class. Before putting students into groups for peer editing, ask students to volunteer a paper to be edited, or use one from another class. Make copies for the class and demonstrate how you expect students to proceed.
- Determine the procedures for group work, such as whether students should read papers silently or aloud, how many copies of the paper students should bring in, how much time should be allotted for each paper, and the sort of comments that should be encouraged.
- Assign the groups yourself through random selection. If students choose their own groups, they may spend the time socializing instead of working. To enable the groups to develop a productive working relationship, keep the groups constant throughout the semester, unless there is a good reason for changing them.
- For peer editing, develop assignment specific questions (see the following "For Writing and Discussion" for an example).
- When possible, require students to report their discussion results to the class. This works well when students engage in group research because it requires them to take responsibility for their work. They should be aware that they will be standing in front of the class and that inadequate preparation will be apparent to everyone!

FOR WRITING AND DISCUSSION

The following assignment is provided as an example of how peer questions should be oriented toward a specific assignment. Work through this process by writing a response to the assignment, bringing your response to class, and working in groups to respond to the questions. By completing the process yourself, you will gain insight into how to use it in your writing class.

WRITING ASSIGNMENT

One important insight arising from research into the composing process is that no approach or strategy is appropriate for all writers and that, as Muriel Harris points out, "there is a very real danger in imposing a single 'ideal' composing style on students." In fact, the more we engage in research about the composing process, the more we realize how much more we need to learn.

As a writer and a student of writing, you have learned a great deal about the writing process from your own experiences, some of them useful, some less so, and it is your writing background that will serve as the primary resource for this assignment. Think about your own history as a writer—your classroom successes and failures, teachers and writers who have influenced you, assignments you have completed, and strategies you have developed as you grappled with various types of writing assignments throughout your academic career. Then in an essay of **three to five pages,** respond to the following question:

Based on your experience as a writer and a student, what insights into the composing process do you consider to be the most important?

In discussing insights you have gained, please enliven your prose with specific examples and anecdotes.

First draft: 3 copies due in class on___. First drafts must be typed.
Final draft due on___.

Peer Editing Question Sheet

Name of Writer_____ Feedback Provided by_____

1. Does the essay respond to the prompt—that is, what insights into the composing process does the writer consider most important?
2. Examine the introduction. What function does it serve? To attract attention? To indicate a direction for the essay? How does the introduction prepare the reader for other sections in the essay?
3. Examine the essay for support. What are the main ideas or themes? What specific examples, anecdotes, or explanations are used to support these ideas or themes?
4. Examine the essay for coherence. What strategies are used to connect each paragraph with the next?
5. Examine the essay for style and sentence structure. What specific words does the writer use to illustrate main points? What kind of person do you sense behind the prose? How does the writer make this person seem real? How does the writer use sentence structure to develop the essay? Is the essay's style sufficiently varied? Are the sentences choppy?
6. What has the writer done to make the essay interesting? What did you learn from this essay? What did the writer do to enhance the audience appeal of this essay?

FOR FURTHER EXPLORATION

Social Constructionism

Bartholomae, D., & Petrosky, A. (1986). *Facts, artifacts, and counterfacts*. Portsmouth, NH: Heinemann.

Bazerman, C. (1981). What written knowledge does: Three examples of academic discourse. *Philosophy of the Social Sciences, 11,* 361–387.

Bruffee, K. Social construction, language and the authority of knowledge. *College English, 48,* 773–790.

Geertz, C. (1983). *Local knowledge*. New York: Basic Books.

Harris, J. (1989). The idea of community in the study of writing. *CCC, 40,* 11–22.

Rorty, R. (1979). *Philosophy and the mirror of nature*. Princeton, NJ: Princeton UP.

Vygotsky, L. (1978). *Mind in society* (M. Cole, V. John Steiner, S. Scribner, & E. Souberman Eds.) Cambridge, MA: Harvard University Press.

Collaborative Learning

Bizzell, P. (1983). Cognition, convention, and certainty: What we need to know about writing. *PRETEXT, 3,* 213–243.

Brooke, R. (1991). *Writing and sense of self: Identity negotiation in writing workshops*. Urbana, IL: NCTE.

Brooke, R., Mirtz, R., & Evans, R. (1994). *Small groups in writing workshops*. Urbana, IL: NCTE.

Bruffee, K. A. (1984, November). Collaborative learning and the 'conversation of mankind.' *College English, 46,* 635–652.

Elbow, P. (1973). *Writing without teachers*. New York: Oxford University Press.

Forman, J. (Ed.). (1992). *New visions of collaborative writing*. Portsmouth, N.H.: Boynton/Cook.

George, D. Working with peer groups in the composition classroom. *CCC, 35,* 320–326.

Gere, A. R. (1987). *Writing groups: History, theory, and implications*. Carbondale, IL: Southern Illinois University Press.

Lunsford, A., & Ede, L. (1990). *Singular texts/plural authors: Perspectives on collaborative writing*. Carbondale, IL: Southern Illinois University Press.

Mason, E. (1970). *Collaborative learning*. London: Ward Lock.

Smith, D. (1989). Some difficulties with collaborative learning. *Journal of Advanced Composition, 9,* 45–57.

Spellmeyer, K. (1994). On conventions and collaboration: The open road and the iron cage. In J. Clifford & J. Schilb (Eds.), *Writing theory and critical theory*. New York: MLA.

Trimbur, J. (1989, October). Consensus and difference in collaborative learning. *College English, 51,* 602–616.

CRITICISM OF THE PROCESS MOVEMENT

The process movement resulted in important developments in the teaching of writing, notably a flowering of interest in composition pedagogy, the creation of an established research discipline concerned with writing and the teaching of writing, the realization that people learn to write by actually writing and revising, rather than by completing decontextualized exercises, and a renewed attention to individualized instruction. However, although recognizing its pedagogical importance, some critics maintain that because "the process model focuses on writers and their psychological states . . . it offers little insight into the relationship between writers and audience" (Williams, 1998, p. 45). Other critics have pointed out that the process model does not address the issue of how gender, race, class, and culture influence writers' goals, standards, and methods, or even the concept of literacy itself. Recently, scholars such as Denny Taylor and Catherine Dorsey-Gaines examined how the concept of "process" is influenced by race, and Nancie Atwell (1988) and Julie Neff (1994) wrote about how a process approach must be specially tailored to the needs of the learning disabled. Mike Rose, in *Lives on the Boundary: The Struggle and Achievements of America's Underprepared* (1989), and Shirley Brice Heath in *Ways with Words: Language, Life, and Work Communities and Classrooms* (1983), discussed the impact of social class on the acquisition of literacy.

Another critical perspective focuses on the extent to which the process model addressed the literacy crisis. Some scholars noted that it neither provided a magic solution to student writing problems, nor influenced the writing class as drastically as has sometimes been claimed. Lad Tobin (1994) characterized the movement as a type of "fairy tale," not because "it is false or childish or naïve," but, rather, because its "disciples" tended to oversimplify the problems inherent in composing and in the teaching of writing. Tobin argued that although we can appreciate the usefulness of the process model, we also "need to acknowledge and confront the extent of the difficulties we face . . to stop pretending that we have everything under control, that everything is proceeding according to plan." (pp. 144–145)

In a similar vein, Joseph Harris noted that "while it seems clear to me that the process movement helped establish composition as a research field, I am not nearly so sure it ever transformed the actual teaching of writing as dramatically as its advocates have claimed" (1997, p. 55). Harris also pointed out that although "the older current-traditional approach to teaching writing focused relentlessly on surface correctness, the advocates of process focused just as relentlessly on "algorithms, heuristics, and guidelines for composing" (p. 56). No system, Harris argued, should be adopted without qualification.

Post-Process Theory

Recently, criticism of the process movement has been manifested in literature concerned with "post-process theory," a term that refers to the idea that the process movement is no longer pertinent, either theoretically or pedagogically. In *Post-Process Theory: Beyond the Writing-Process Paradigm* (1999), Thomas Kent asserts that because every communication act requires the writer to "guess" how a text will affect a reader, it is impossible to model communication, and, therefore, there is no writing process that can be presented in the classroom. "No single course can teach a student how to produce or analyze discourse," Kent maintains, "for the hermeneutic guessing required in all discourse production and analysis can be only refined; it cannot be codified and then taught" (p. 39). In his essay in that collection, Gary Olson (1999) takes this position further, asserting not only that writing cannot be taught but also that it cannot even be adequately described. To construct a model of the writing process, Olson states, is to be in conflict with the postmodern rejection of certainty and the corresponding emphasis on assertion as a valued academic skill. For Olson, "the vocabulary of process is no longer useful" (p. 9), and, therefore, compositionists must move away from "a discourse of mastery and assertion toward a more dialogic, dynamic, open-ended, receptive, nonassertive stance" (p. 14). Olson, however, does not suggest how this perspective can benefit students or be applied in a pedagogical context.

Another criticism of the process movement focuses on the emphasis on formula with which the writing process has been presented in the classroom. Joseph Petraglia and David Russell both reject the rigidity of a "prewrite, write, revise, edit" model, Petraglia noting in "Is There Life after Process?" (1999) that composition scholarship seems to be increasingly irrelevant to working effectively with students. Russell, embracing an activity theory orientation, emphasizes that there are many writing processes. Instead of teaching one process, Russell (1999) maintains, compositionists study those various processes to "(re)classify them, commodify them, and involve students with (teach) them in a curriculum" (p. 88) that acknowledges that some writing activities can be performed mechanistically, whereas others cannot. As yet, post-process theory does not lend itself to effective classroom teaching. However, for an excellent and enjoyable review of post-process scholarship, read Richard Fulkerson's "Of Pre- and Post-Process: Reviews and Ruminations" (2001).

Genre Theory and the Concept of Process

Although the original goals of the process "movement" focused on promoting student literacy, a number of scholars associated with recent notions of genre theory have maintained that process pedagogy in its most rigid manifestations has resulted in only limited success for the groups that it was originally intended to help. This perspective emphasizes that the progressive classroom, with its focus on individual expression and personal voice, has not resulted in writing improvement in those groups who were most in need of improvement. In fact, according to several critics associated with the genre-based curriculum in Sydney, Australia, the process-oriented classroom, despite its original goal of validating culturally marginalized groups, has actually served "to sustain the powerlessness of children and preserve the class divisions in western culture" (Richardson, 1994, p. 55). According to Cope and Kalantzis, 1993, those involved in implementing the Australian curriculum argue that:

> Many working-class, migrant and Aboriginal children have been systematically barred from competence with those texts, knowledges, and 'genres' that enable access to social and material resources. The culprits, they argue, are not limited to traditional pedagogies that disregard children's cultural and linguistic resources and set out to assimilate them into the fictions of mainstream culture. But the problem is also located in progressive 'process' and 'child-centered' approaches that appear to 'value differences but in so doing leave social relations of inequity fundamentally unquestioned. (p. vii)

Contributors to Cope and Kalantzis' book *The Powers of Literacy: A Genre Approach to Teaching Writing* (1993), which is intended to explain the Australian genre approach to non-Australians, have maintained that the emphasis on personal voice and the corresponding reluctance of teachers to intervene directly in changing students' texts has, ironically, promoted a situation in which only the brightest middle-class children, those whose voices are already in tune with those in power and whose backgrounds include acquaintanceship with the genres of privilege, will be able to learn what is needed for social, and, ultimately, economic success. Noting that "by the 1980s it was clear that the new progressivist curriculum was not producing any noticeable improvement in patterns of educational attainment" (Cope & Kalantzis, 1993, p. 1), Cope and Kalantzis also pointed out that such a curriculum "encourages students to produce texts in a limited range of written genres, mostly personalised recounts" (p. 6).

It is clear that the process movement has not solved every problem associated with helping students to learn to write. Nevertheless, it was characterized by an intellectual and moral energy that generated an exciting new discipline and an important ideological focus that continues to influence composition pedagogy at various levels. Although in many institutions, the concepts of expressive writing and personal voice have been superceded by other academic emphases, the idea that writing is a recursive process and that teaching writing means helping students develop a process that works effectively for them now constitutes a basis for writing curricula across the country.

FOR FURTHER EXPLORATION

Process

Bartholomae, D. (1980). The study of error. *College Composition and Communication, 31,* 253–269.

Daniell, B. (1994). Theory, theory talk, and composition. In J. Clifford and J. Schilb (Eds.), *Writing theory and critical theory* (pp. 127–140). New York: MLA.

Dyer, P. M. (1990). What composition theory offers the writing teacher. In L. A. Arena (Ed.), *Language proficiency: Defining, teaching, and testing* (pp. 99–106). New York: Plenum.

Elbow, P. (1973). *Writing without teachers.* New York: Oxford UP.

Elbow, P. (1981). *Writing with power:* Techniques for mastering the writing process. New York: Oxford UP.

Elbow, P. (1981). *Embracing contraries:* Explorations in learning and teaching. New York: Oxford UP.

Elbow, P. (1991). Reflections on academic discourse. *College English, 53,* 135–155.

Faigley, L. (1986). Competing theories of process: A critique and a proposal. *College English, 48,* 527–542.

Hairston, M. (1982). The winds of change: Thomas Kuhn and the revolution in the teaching of writing. *College Composition and Communication, 33,* 76–86.

Knoblauch, C. H., & Brannon, L. (1984). *Rhetorical traditions and the teaching of writing.* Upper Montclair, NJ: Boynton Cook.

Scardamalia, M., Bereiter, C., & Goelman, H. The role of production factors in writing ability. In M. Nystrand (Ed.), *What writers know: The language, process, and structures of academic discourse* (pp. 173–210). New York: Academic.

Selzer, J. (1984). Exploring options in composing. *College Composition and Communication, 35,* 276–284.

WRITING ASSIGNMENT

Understanding Yourself as a Writer[1]

Although all writers engage in planning, drafting, and revising, they do so in a variety of ways and no writer approaches every writing task the same way. One way to move away from writing habits that have not worked well for you in the past is to understand what type of writer you are. Think about the models of writers described here. In the space provided, indicate the extent to which this description pertains to your own writing habits.

Writers Who Plan in Advance. These people tend to think about their ideas and plan their writing in their minds or on paper before they begin to write.

---

[1] This form is based on a discussion of various types of writers in Lisa Ede. (1995). *Work in Progress* (3rd ed.). Boston/New York. St, Martin's Press.

As a result, their first drafts are usually better than most first drafts often are, even though these drafts will probably still need additional revision before they can be submitted. People who plan in advance use spare moments of their time to think—while they eat lunch, drive, and wait in line. When they start fo write, they usually have at least some idea about what they want to say.

Writers Who Discover Ideas Through Writing.   Although every writer discovers ideas through writing, at least sometimes, these writers use writing to find out what they want to say, planning and revising while they write. They begin by writing whatever comes into their minds and then reconsider and rewrite again and again. Writers who discover ideas through writing may even throw out a whole first draft and begin again.

Writers Who Spend Equal Time on Planning, Writing, and Revising.   Some writers divide the writing task into stages, a method that is probably the most effective in writing a college essay as long as adequate time is allowed for each stage of the process. However, it is important to keep in mind that an effective plan involves more than a few notes scratched on a sheet of paper, that sufficient time must be allowed for drafting, and that a revision means a great deal more than correcting a few sentences.

Writers Who Delay.   This is a familiar type of writer —those who delay writing until right before the paper is due. These writers sometimes stay up all night, trying to write a complete draft of a paper, and, thus, when they submit their work, they are really submitting a first draft, not usually their best work. Of course, for various reasons, all writers probably procrastinate sometimes. But those who always write first drafts under conditions of pressure or panic are unlikely to do as well as they could.

WRITING ASSIGNMENT

Assessing Your Own Writing Process

This self-assessment will enable you to look at your own writing process, to evaluate the strategies you use when you write. Please answer each question as fully as possible.

1. Mark the scale below to indicate how easy or difficult you find the process of writing.
    Easy_____Difficult
    Please explain your selection, indicating the reasons for your response.

2. Describe how you usually write your papers.

3. What practices or "rules of writing" do you find to be useful? Which do you find to be phony or not useful?

4. Which of the following problems have you experienced?
   - Beginning the paper
   - Knowing what you want to say
   - Writing an introduction
   - Getting a first sentence
   - Finding a thesis
   - Organizing the paper
   - Deciding how to structure your ideas
   - Writing an outline
   - Addressing the needs of your audience
   - Knowing what your reader wants
   - Deciding what information to include
   - Working on coherence and style
   - Connecting each paragraph to your overall point
   - Writing sentences that connect with one another
   - Making your writing lively and interesting to read
   - Finding the right words

5. Based on your responses to the previous questions, what changes would you like to make in your writing behavior?

WRITING ASSIGNMENT

Writing Class Observation

If you currently attend a college or university where writing classes are taught, arrange to observe at least three classes over a 2-week period. Then, based on your observations, write a two-part report of 5–7 pages that addresses the following:

Part I. Describe the writing class you observed, including many specific details such as the name of the teacher, the level of the class, how often the class meets, the number of students, the textbook used, the assignment the students are working on, the handouts that were used, the chair arrangement—any details that will enable a reader to understand what the teacher and students were doing during various segments of the class.

Part II. Discuss how observing these classes has provided you with information that you will use to plan your own writing class. Specific points to address in this section include the teacher, students, classroom dynamics, methodology, and materials. What did you learn in this class from both the teacher and the students that will be helpful to you?

Note that your purpose is NOT to evaluate the teacher or the methods in any way, but rather to reflect on what you have learned and can apply to your own teaching.

Classroom Observation Guidelines

1. Select the "teacher volunteer" whose class you plan to observe.
2. Plan to observe at least three successive class meetings, or a total of four class meetings over a 3-week period.
3. Contact the teacher (via telephone, e-mail, or mail) and make certain that you will be the only observer in class on the days of your visits. Request that he or she provide you with a copy of the course syllabus and any other important handouts when you observe your first class.
4. Find out if the teacher has any preference regarding your "role" as observer in his/her class. For example, should you get up and walk around if group work is in progress or remain in your seat and listen-in on the closest group?
5. During your first observation, take as many notes as you feel are necessary to provide you with a full record of your experience.
6. During your second and subsequent observations, focus on what you consider to be the most informative and important insights you have gained.
7. If possible, have a short "debriefing" session with the instructor when you have finished the sequence of observations.
8. Be sure to arrive on time for the class. Do not leave until the class has ended.

Points to Note When Observing Composition Classes

Physical Arrangement of Class. How seats are arranged and placement of teacher.

Atmosphere in Classroom/Classroom Dynamics. Formal? Informal? Friendly?

The Lesson. The day's agenda, the day's topic, specific skills to be taught, activities planned (group work, writing/thinking activities, revision, invention, & exercises), sequencing of activities, materials used, quality of discussion, and applicability of lesson to student writing/language skills.

Student Behaviors.

- What kind of writing are the students doing?
- How many students are participating?
- What are students doing who are not participating?
- Are students reading their work aloud?
- Are students speaking to one another?
- Are students working in groups?
- How are students reacting to the day's agenda and topic?

Teacher Behaviors.

- What sort of voice does the teacher use?
- Has the teacher engaged the students?
- What kind of working relationship does the teacher have with the students?
- What is the evidence that suggests that kind of working relationship?
- What does the teacher do when students participate or ask questions? Characterize the teacher's strategies for listening and promoting dialogue.

Teacher Activities.

- Presenting the assignment/lesson.
- Modeling a particular writing strategy.
- Teacher addressing class as a whole.
- Teacher addressing a small group.
- Teacher speaking with an individual student.
- Teacher presenting the lesson.

Overall, you should be aware of how writing and reading are addressed in the class, how students are engaged, with the instructor and with each other, how the lesson has been planned, and how much student participation drives and supports the action of the class.

WRITING ASSIGNMENT

Keeping a Reflective Writing Journal

A useful strategy for gaining insight into your own writing process is to keep a Reflective Writing Journal. A Reflective Writing Journal will enable you to recall writing experiences in your past, from which you can develop your own "theory" of writing. Insights fostered by this means will be useful for helping your students to develop an effective writing process. The following are some suggestions for entries into your Reflective Writing Journal:

1. Discuss your history as a writer, focusing on particular highlights.
2. Describe your own writing process.
3. Write about one of your best teachers.
4. Find some examples of what you feel is "good writing." What makes this writing good?
5. Why have you chosen to study rhetoric and composition?

REFERENCES

Appleby, A. N. (1974). *Tradition and reform in the teaching of English: A history.* Urbana IL: NCTE.

Atwell, N. (1988). A special writer at work. In T. Newkirk and N. Atwell (Eds.), *Understanding writing: Ways of learning, observing, and teaching K–8* (2nd ed.). Portsmouth, NH: Heinemann.

Berlin, J. (1990). Writing instruction in school and college English. In J. Murphy (Ed.), *A short history of writing instruction.* Davis, CA: Hermagoras Press.

Berlin, J. (1996). *Rhetorics, poetics, and cultures: Refiguring English studies.* Urbana, IL: NCTE.

Bizzell, P. (1983). Cognition, convention, and certainty: What we need to know about writing. *PRETEXT, 3,* 213–243.

Britton, J., Burgess, T., Martin, N., McLeod, A., & Rosen, H. (1975). *The development of writing abilities 11–18.* London: Macmillan Education Ltd.

Bruffee, K. A. (1984, November). Collaborative learning and the 'conversation of mankind.' *College English, 46,* 635–652.

Bruner, J. (1966). *Toward a theory of instruction.* Cambridge, MA: The Belknap Press of Harvard University Press.

Cope, B., & Kalantzis, M. (Eds.). (1993). *The powers of literacy: A genre approach to teaching writing.* Pittsburgh, PA: University of Pittsburgh Press.

De Ciccio, A. (1988). *Social constructionism and collaborative learning: Recommendations for teaching writing.* CCCC paper: ERIC ED 282212.

Elbow, P. (1986). *Embracing contraries: Explorations in learning and teaching.* New York: Oxford University Press.

Emig, J. (1971). *The composing process of twelfth graders. Research report No. 13.* Urbana: NCTE.

Flower, L. (1979, September). Writer-based prose: A cognitive basis for problems in writing. *College English, 41,* 19–38.

Flower, L., & Hayes, J. (1980). The cognition of discovery. *College Composition and Communication, 31,* 21–32.

Flower, L., & Hayes, J. (1981). A cognitive process theory of writing. *College Composition and Communication, 32,* 365–388.

Flower, L. S., & Hayes, J. (1980, February). The cognition of discovery. *CCC,* 31, 21–32.

Fulkerson, R. (2001). Of pre- and post-process: Reviews and ruminations. *Compostiion Studies, 29* (2), 93–119.

Graves, D. (1983). *Writing, teachers & children at work.* Portsmouth: Heinemann.

Harris, J. (1997). *A teaching subject: Composition since 1966.* New Jersey: Prentice Hall.

Harris, M. (1989, February). Composing behavior, of one- and multi-draft writers. *College English, 51* (2), 174–190.

Heath, S. B. (1983). *Ways with words: Language, life, and work communities and classrooms.* Cambridge: Cambridge University Press.

Hopkins, L. T. (1912, January). Can good composition teaching be done under present conditions? *English Journal, 1,* 1–12.

Kent, T. (1999). *Post-process theory: Beyond the writing-process paradigm.* Carbondale: Southern Illinois UP.

Kinneavy, J. (1971). A theory of discourse. Englewood Cliffs, N.J.: Prentice Hall. (Reprinted 1980. New York: Norton).

Lunsford, A. (1979). Cognitive development and the basic writer. *College English, 41,* 38–46.

Macrorie, K. (1970). *Telling writing.* Rochelle Park, NJ: Hayden.

Moffett, J. (1968). *Teaching the universe of discourse.* Portsmouth, New Hampshire: Boynton/Cook.

Neff, J. (1994). Learning disabilities and the writing center. In J. A. Mullin & R. Wallace (Eds.), *Intersections: Theory-practice in the writing center* (pp. 81–95). Urbana. IL: NCTE.

Olson. G. (1999). Toward a post-process composition: Abandoning the rhetoric of assertion. In T. Kent (Ed.), *Post-process theory: Beyond the writing-process paradigm* (pp. 7–15). Carbondale: Southern Illinois UP.

Perl, S. (1994). Writing process: A shining moment. In S. Perl (Ed.), *Landmark essays on writing process* (pp. xi–xx). Davis, California: Hermagoras Press.

Petraglia. J. (1999). Is there life after process: The role of social scientism in a changing discipline. In T. Kent (Ed.), *Post-process theory: Beyond the writing-process paradigm* (pp. 49–64). Carbondale: Southern Illinois UP.

Pianko, S. (1979). A description of the composing processes of college Freshman writers. *Research in the Teaching of English, 13,* 5–22.

P. Medway (Eds.), *Learning and teaching genre* (pp. 117–142). Portsmouth, N.H.: Boynton/Cook Publishers.

Rohman, D. G. (1965). Pre-writing: The stage of discovery in the writing process. *College Composition and Communication, 16,* 106–112.

Rose, M. (1989). *Lives on the boundary: The struggles and achievements of America's underprepared.* New York: Free Press.

Russell, D. (1999). Activity theory and process approaches: Writing (power) in school and society. In T. Kent (Ed.), *Post-process theory: Beyond the writing-process paradigm* (pp. 80–95). Carbondale: Southern Illinois UP.

Stewart, D. C. (1972). *The authentic voice: A prewriting approach to student writing.* Dubuque, IA: William C. Brown.

Tobin, L. (1994). How the writing process was born and other conversion narratives. In T. Newkirk & L. Tobin (Eds.), *Taking stock: The writing process movement in the '90s.* Portsmouth: Boynton/Cook.

Williams, J. D. (1998). *Preparing to teach writing: Research, theory, and practice* (2nd ed.). Mahwah, NJ: Lawrence Erlbaum Associates.

Readings

THE NEW ABOLITIONISM: TOWARD A HISTORICAL BACKGROUND*

Robert J. Connors
University of New Hampshire

Since the required course in freshman composition was conceived at Harvard in 1885 and quickly adopted by most U.S. colleges and universities, it has been at the heart of a continuing series of arguments about its worth and standing. Arthur Applebee (1974) characterized the history of English teaching in the United States as being marked by periods of tradition and reform, and in this chapter I want to borrow one of his terms and, changing its meaning rather seriously, claim that the history of American higher education in composition over the last century has been marked by alternating periods of what I call *reformism* and *abolitionism*. During reformist periods, freshman comp, although problematical, is seen as the thin red line protecting the very life of literacy. Abolitionist periods are times during which at least some English teachers call for the end of freshman composition, declaring the large sums expended on this all-but-ubiquitous course a gross waste.

There is a sense in which these arguments about the required comp course are metonymic representations of other more general questions facing American culture. We see reformist periods of deep interest in improving composition—some of which are called literacy crises—and abolitionist periods, when some teachers declared it too hopeless to reform, repeat themselves several times

---

*This chapter is a longer and more fully developed version of a paper given at the 1993 Crisis and Change conference at Miami University of Ohio. A condensed version of the essay appears in the volume of papers from that conference, *Composition in the Twenty-First Century: Crisis and Change*, edited by Lynn Z. Bloom, Donald Daiker, and Edward White.

across the last 10 decades. Each reformist or abolition period is to some degree unique, of course, but they do have certain elements in common, and they ebb and flow according to patterns that we may learn from. As this volume suggests, we are now involved in the end of a reformist period and in a new period of abolitionist sentiment. Contributors to this anthology represent a growing number of writing professionals asking us to reconsider the theoretical integrity and practical utility of required composition as manifested in general writing skills instruction (GWSI) for over the last century. By way of introducing the collection gathered here, it may be worthwhile to ask how or whether this New Abolitionism is like the older ones, and whether the current movement will go the way of the older ones. To understand the New Abolitionists in context, we need to look back.

Required Freshman Composition: The First Reform and its Antagonists

The required freshman composition course itself is the product of a reformist period. It was created in direct response to the literacy crisis of the period 1875 to 1885. This is a story that has been told many times by historians, and we need only outline it here. Harvard College, roused by popular debates on literacy and linguistic correctness, had by 1870 become uncomfortably aware that students entering from the academies that served as its feeders were having problems with its demanding classical courses. In response, Harvard instituted its first entrance examinations in written English in 1874. To the horror of professors, parents, and the American intellectual culture as a whole, more than half the students taking the exam failed it. What had been a vague disquiet crystallized into a sharp alarm. Large numbers of American boys from the best schools were incapable of correct writing, and something had to be done. This first crisis might be called the "Illiteracy of American Boys" crisis, after the best known article written about it.

The Harvard exam and the continuing problems students had with it (and with the host of similar writing examinations quickly set up by the many colleges that took Harvard for a model) created the first American college literacy crisis and the first experiments in basic writing instruction on the college level. The Harvard examiners began quickly to agitate for better training on the secondary level and for more effective writing instruction on the college level.

A. S. Hill, Boylston Professor of Rhetoric, had argued strongly as early as 1879 that the sophomore rhetoric course be more oriented toward correctness and composition and be made a required course for freshmen: "The next best step [after improving secondary schools] would be to give to English two hours or more a week during the Freshman year. Could the study be taken up at the threshold of college life, the schools would be made to feel that their labors in this direction were going to tell upon a pupil's standing in college" (Hill, 1896, p. 12). At first no room could be found for such a requirement during freshman year, but the exam results kept the pressure on and in 1885 a basic freshman course, "English A," was offered at Harvard. Its structure solidified quickly. By 1894 the only required courses for freshmen were English A and a modern language (Rudolph, 1962). By 1897 the only required course at Harvard for any student was English A. Many other colleges took Harvard's lead on all educational issues, and by 1890 the majority of U.S. colleges and universities had established required freshman composition courses. The formation of these courses nationwide was a great paroxysm of reformist work, a large-scale curricular endeavor that has no parallel in U.S. college history.

Yet it was very soon after 1890 that the first widespread movement to disestablish these new course requirements arose. This first group of abolitionists consisted primarily of literature teachers in what were then newly established English departments. Their dislike of required composition courses was based in their affiliation with Arnoldian idealism, but their essential rationale for abolishing freshman requirements was based on two more practical claims about college composition: First, the required freshman course was never meant as a permanent English offering, but was instead a temporary stop-gap until the secondary schools could improve; and second, the teaching of required composition was tiresome, labor intensive, and a bad use of trained literary scholars.

That the early freshman course was considered a temporary remedial measure and was bitterly resented by college faculty members is clear from the few published comments that exist on it. "The instruction in English which we are forced to give to Freshmen and perhaps to Sophomores should all be finished in the preparatory schools," wrote Hurlbut (1896). "It is absurd that a college should be obliged to teach spelling, pronunciation, grammar, construction of sentences and of paragraphs" (p. 49). Only if reforms were made on the elementary and secondary levels, argued Hurlbut, would the student acquire there "the training in English composition which is now given in college, and the college student will be able to devote himself to university work" (p. 53). Up until the mid-1890s, in other words, it was assumed by many that freshman composition courses were a stop-gap remedial measure, a temporary aberration, to be dispensed with after the great propaganda war in favor of more secondary school composition had been won.

We see a good deal of this attitude in William Morton Payne's (1895) interesting collection, *English in American Universities,* which contains 20 reports on the teaching of college English at different institutions that had originally appeared in *The Dial* in 1894. Although most of the reports detail both literature and composition courses being offered, several are fervid in their triumph at having dispensed with required freshman writing altogether. Payne himself, the editor of *The Dial,* was entirely sympathetic to this movement, and his introduction makes clear why; he was a classic exponent of literature teaching who was in favor of the most stringent entrance requirements possible. He was very doubtful about the Eastern colleges' reliance on the freshman course. "As we go West, we do better and better" (p. v) he said, noting that Indiana, Nebraska, and Stanford had all abolished freshman composition in favor of strong entrance requirements.

Examining the reports from those schools, however, it was clear that liberal culture is not the only reason for the abolition. Martin Sampson (1895) of Indiana wrote that "There are no recitations in 'rhetoric.' The bugbear known generally in our colleges as Freshman English is now a part of our entrance requirements" (p. 93). Melville Anderson's (1895) report on English at Stanford gives us a genuine feel for the earliest abolitionist sentiments. Stanford, he said, had abolished Freshman English: "Had this salutary innovation not been accomplished, all the literary courses would have been swept away by the rapidly growing inundation of Freshman themes, and all our strength and courage would have been dissipated in preparing our students to do respectable work at more happily equipped Universities" (p. 52). We see here the expected liberal culture attitudes, of course, but more strongly we see pure self-protection on the part of the tenured faculty. They did not want to teach theme writing, and killing the requirement was the easiest way out of it. Anderson wrote a bit later that Stanford would be hiring two "instructors" the following year to give the two unfortunate composition professors a break, because "however great a man's enthusiasm for such work may be, it is incident to human nature that no man can read themes efficiently for more than three hours at a stretch" (p. 52).

Thomas Lounsbury and Liberal-Culture Abolitionism

The first wave of abolitionism ebbed after 1900, and Anderson's attitude gives us a key to the reasons why: the growing willingness of universities and colleges to draw on lecturers, instructors, and graduate students to teach their required freshman courses. As discussed in more detail in Connors (1991), the rise of academic specialization and the modern hierarchy of ranks in English departments meant that between 1880 and 1900 most tenured professors were gradually relieved of composition duties by younger and less powerful colleagues or by graduate students. Thus the earliest wave of abolitionism, which had been caused by overwork panic among faculty members, receded because the Andersons and Sampsons no longer had to worry themselves about having to teach freshman composition. This was fortunate for these senior professors, because the requirement of the course had hardly been touched by their arguments in most places (Stanford, for example, reinstituted English A in 1907; Greenbaum, 1969). The years between 1885 and 1915 saw a tremendous number of critiques of the freshman course launched, but most of them were oriented toward reforming the course. Not until the end of that period was there a resurgence of the abolitionist sentiment, in the famous article "Compulsory Composition in Colleges" by Thomas Lounsbury (1911). David Russell (1988) did groundbreaking work on Lounsbury and some of the attitudes that have underlain the early forms of abolitionist argument. Russell described Lounsbury's abolitionist sentiment as a product of a specific kind of educational idealism that sounds today like liberal culture literary elitism, tinged throughout by Lounsbury's thinly concealed opinion that undergraduate students were ignorant barbarians.

To Lounsbury, the idea that expression could be taught was idiotic, the conception that college students could know anything worth writing about silly, and the position that writing teachers could respond usefully to student writing unlikely. Wrote Lounsbury (1911), "I [am] thoroughly convinced that altogether undue importance is attached to exercises in English composition, especially compulsory exercises; that the benefits to be derived from the general practice in schools is (sic) vastly overrated" (p. 869). His answer to the problem of literacy was more or less to let it take care of itself, to make composition completely elective, thus making certain that only those students who wanted to write—a minority compared to that "large body of students who have not the slightest desire to write a line" (p. 876)—took it. The enthusiasm of the students would make the course so much more satisfying to teach that it would again attract experienced and effective teachers.

Despite his romantic elitism, Lounsbury (1911) made some telling points against compulsory composition. He was correct in his assessment that "the average student loathes it," that "under the compulsory system now prevailing the task of reading and correcting themes is one of deadly dullness," in which "more and more does the business of correcting and criticizing themes tend steadily to fall into the hands of those who ... have themselves little experience in the practice of composition" (pp. 870–871). But Lounsbury was an outsider. His claim to have 25 years' experience correcting themes had never actually included required freshman composition, which Yale did not have, and he was senior enough to have avoided the most punishing junior composition teaching assignments. Thus his sympathy for teachers was mostly forced, because he considered most of them "incompetent to do anything much better," and for students hardly existent; they are "crude," "thoughtless and indifferent," "immature," and clearly in need of a stiff dose of Milton. Lounsbury presented an early but completely recognizable version of E. D. Hirsch's cultural literacy argument: Writing could not be taught as pure practice-based skill without content. His real and obvious sympathy was with those who had a "cultivated taste begotten of familiarity with the great masterpieces of our literature" (p. 876), and until students' minds were thus furnished, they need not apply, to him at least.

This article caused a small sensation in the English teaching world, and especially in the still-active circle of composition enthusiasts. Lounsbury had repeated several times in his essay that his was an unpopular minority position, but it was taken very seriously. His article was not followed up in *Harper's*, but it created a long discussion in the *Educational Review (ER)* in 1913, and we see here the whole modern reformist-abolitionist debate for the first time.

Although some of the *ER* correspondents agreed with Lounsbury, the majority did not. Some commentators saw no problem in the freshman course at all, and they actively praised the course as they had experienced it. We also see in this discussion the first wave of what might be called status quo or modern reformism. These correspondents took the position, as all reformists later would, that the course was imperfect but necessary, and that it would be much improved by the author's suggestions. N. A. Stedman (1913) of the University of Texas admitted that freshman English was useful and yielded some good results, but he saw that its "technical" nature created in students "a distaste for English" (p. 53), and proposed that the course be reformed to create more interest in English. Lucile Shepherd (1913) of the University of Missouri believed that "the course on the whole is admirable," and that with more humanism and a few tinkerings it would be better still (p. 189).

Lounsbury had some clear allies. Carl Zigrosser (1913) of Columbia wrote that, "in my estimation prescribed work in English is unnecessary" (p. 188), and George Strong (1913) of North Carolina huffed that, "My own experience with these courses was profitless. It was, in fact, enough to discourage me from continuing the study of English. I failed to derive any benefit whatever from them.... Away with such work! I should rather live an ignoramus all my life than to endure again such a burden as I did in English I and English II" (p. 189). We begin in these responses to Lounsbury to see proposals for that brand of abolitionism later called *writing across the curriculum*. Preston W. Slosson (1913) proposed that "The real way to make sure that every Columbia graduate, whatever his other failings, can write whatever it may be necessary for him to write as briefly, logically, and effectively as possible, is not to compel him as a freshman to write stated themes on nothing-in-particular but to insist on constant training in expression in every college course" (p. 408).

Finally, the Lounsbury-based discussion petered out sometime around 1915, after having never attained a solid enough base of agreement from the abolitionists Charles G. Osgood (1915) writing in *English Journal,* titled his article "No Set Requirement of English Composition in the Freshman Year," and suspected that the suggestion made by his title "is not a popular opinion, and that in holding it I am one of a small minority" (p. 231). Osgood went on to make a case for literature rather than composition in the freshman year, and to praise the small-group preceptorial system used at Princeton, but his attitude was that of a man who did not expect to win. Reformism began to dominate the professional discussion.

At least part of the reason for the failure of abolitionism and the segue into a clearly reformist period during the mid-1910s had to do with the growing influence of the ideas of John Dewey. Some of the more widely read teachers of composition were beginning to realize that freshman composition could be more than a mere enforcement of mechanical rules. Helen Mahin (1915), one of Fred Newton Scott's graduate students, wrote that she was moved to action by Lounsbury. "Stirred to an indignant curiosity by the vigorous denunciation of compulsory composition in colleges by a learned professor of English," she asked her freshman students if they would take the course without the requirement. Their answers made her realize that "nearly two-thirds of these Freshmen, many of who had entered the course unwillingly, realized before the end of the first semester that their lives had grown in some way broader and fuller then they had been before" (p. 446). This result, Mahin said, controverted Lounsbury's claims. Required composition could be taught, and should be taught, in such a way that students realize that "writing means simply living and expressing life":

> From the testimony of the Freshmen themselves and from the actual results shown in their work the conclusion is very well justified that the student of writing who does not in the course of his study, if that study is rightly guided, become a happier, bigger, and more socially efficient being is the student who, unless he is subnormal in intellect, deliberately sets himself against progress. (p. 450)

This concept of "English for life skills" and the "more socially efficient being" is instantly recognizable as based in Dewey's ideas. This concept, that writing skills were humane learning and inherently broadening, was to become a staple claim of reformism for decades.

The reformist movement was set even more strongly on the road by the victory in Europe in World War I and the millennial ideas many intellectuals held immediately after the war. The United States had lost thousands of men, but it had not been ravaged as Europe had, and many educators saw the war victory as the gateway into a shining new world. Horace Ainsworth Eaton (1919) looked forward to a new birth of democratic spirit in the world, to be created by committed teachers: "The war is won—marvelously and completely won—and we stand on a new Pisgah looking into the future.... In composition we must, I believe, even more than in literature, work in the new spirit. The first and most important thing is to awaken the pupil to think and then to help him to express his thought effectively.... Ideas come first, ideas expressively and effectively phrased; impeccable spelling and faultless punctuation are sorry substitutes" (pp. 310–312). Used to seeing the postwar era through the eyes of Dos Passos and Hemingway, we can sometimes forget that for many Americans it was a glorious time of dreaming world rebirth. In this atmosphere, and abetted by Dewey's educational ideas, many English teachers began to work hard toward reforming the freshman course in the direction of more social experience, more practical kinds of writing, and more creative expression.

The period following the war was, then, a classic period of reformism that saw the end of Lounsburian grousing and a halt to talk of abolitionism. The Central Division Modern Language Association (Fred N. Scott's home base) commissioned a Special Committee on Freshman English in 1916, and the report of this committee (which was made up of Scott's former students) gave no credence at all to abolishing the course. It proposed that there were two ways of thinking about freshman composition, "merely elementary drill" or "a subject in which the student is given a maturer and more largely significant training in thinking and in expression," and, not surprisingly, came out strongly for the latter. "The present committee ... when it remembers the increasing number of students whose contact with a liberal type of training is virtually confined to this one course, does not doubt that the second and more ambitious conception of Freshman English is the only one which a university can afford to adopt" (Scott, Thomas, & Manchester, 1918, p. 592). The committee recommended, in fact, a second required composition course for those students who did not do well in the first.

The reformist period that began after World War I lasted throughout the 1920s. Examining the professional articles of that period, one finds any number of proposals for improving the required course but none that make any version of the abolitionist case. This is not to say that reform periods contain no grumbling or that no teachers existed during them who wished to see freshman composition done away with. However, abolitionism is submerged during reform periods because the mission of the course comes to seem so important that more of value would be lost than gained by cutting the requirement altogether, and so it was during the 1920s. The 1920s were filled with criticism of the course itself, which by that time had become a standardized institution immediately recognizable to anyone who had ever attended college. Many agreed with Bernard DeVoto (1928), who had taught at Northwestern, that "nothing in the colleges is more grotesquely taught.... It is universally loathed by those who teach it and those who take it.... And yet, for all this, it generally gets results. Students do usually write a little better when they have finished it than they did when they began" (pp. 205–206). DeVoto was no friend of English composition, but like many critics he did not feel it could be done away with.

A Decade of Debate: The 1930s

By the end of the 1920s, college demographics were shifting strongly. Enrollments had almost doubled between 1920 and 1930, from 598,000 students to more than 1.1 million, and they were beginning to place a strain on the single course that had to serve all students (*Digest of Educational Statistics,* 1974, p. 84). As so often occurs, demographic changes in the student body seemed to create strains leading to powerful proposals—either radical reformism or some kind of abolitionism. When abolitionism appeared again after the 1920s, however, it came from a place that Scott would not have suspected: the educational research community, which by 1930 was finding a serious voice within English studies. The debate erupted at the National Council of Teachers of English (NCTE) meeting of 1931, in which Alvin C. Eurich (1932) of the University of Minnesota reported findings of a study conducted there in the late 1920s. In one of the earliest horse race experiments conducted of freshman composition, pretest and posttest compositions were required of 54 freshmen passing through the Minnesota course. These essays were rated using the Van Wagenen English Composition Scales (one of the many rating scales devised during the first three decades of this century in the attempt to make essay grading "scientific"), and the results showed that "no measurable improvement in composition was apparent after three months of practice" (p. 211).

Eurich's essay looks surprisingly "modern" in the context of *English Journal* composition essays of the period, which were often informal, personal, and pedagogical. Eurich's was a research report, written with a complete footnoted literature survey, and he reported his conclusion, which was simply the fact that the problem with freshman composition rested on "the inadequacy of the administrative arrangement which is based upon the assumption that the life-long habits of expression can be modified in a relatively short time" (p. 213). To solve this problem, Eurich proposed a different form of writing across the curriculum, a sophisticated system in which English teachers would work with teachers in other fields on writing-based assignments—one of the most serious early writing across the curriculum programs.

Eurich's paper at NCTE was answered by one written by Warner Taylor (1932). Taylor's essay was an archetype of reformist objection to abolitionism. Should the course be abolished, he asked. It is problematical, he said, but, "As for me, I do not consider the course futile. I do consider it, in general, open to several changes for the better" (pp. 301–302). Taylor went on to discuss a survey he had done that showed freshman courses relying overwhelmingly on handbooks and rhetorics and making a claim that such methods were themselves to blame for the poor showing the course made in Eurich's research. Taylor really believed in the freshman course, rejecting Eurich's contention that cross-curricular writing was a good answer and claiming that it would make teachers mere grading assistants: "Is it to be a course correlated with history or economics? If so, watch your rights! Historians and economists are in the saddle now, riding hard and confidently. You may call in a partner only to find him your boss" (p. 311). He proposed instead a course that got rid of rhetorics and handbooks and mixed composition with literature.

In the spirited discussion following the delivery of these two papers there was no consensus of opinion, although in general Eurich's writing across the curriculum-based plan was looked on as radical. The discussion was joined by such major figures as Charles C. Fries, Edwin M. Hopkins, and Joseph V. Denney, but although the general tenor of the discussion was reformist, Eurich held his own. The short reports of the discussion make clear the degree to which the composition teachers and scholars of the early 1930s identified themselves with the freshman course and were much more willing to make claims for its potential and to work at reforming it than to abandon it for less specific teaching situations (Davidson, 1932). No one could say that Eurich's findings were false, but they were interpreted in widely different ways, usually based, like Taylor's, in a claim that the freshman course did not work because it needed reform.

This willingness to admit problems and propose reforms rather than agree to abolitionist ideas has been a continuing entropic strand in composition discourse from that time forward. It represents a sort of argumentative jujitsu, using the strength and cogency of any abolitionist argument against abolitionism as a position. "The freshman course is problematical, is hated, is boring, does not work? Absolutely true," reformists typically say, "and proof positive that it needs reform—needs, specifically, the reform I am about to propose." There is, of course, a certain amount of vested interest on the part of composition reformers. Even as early as 1930, there were teachers and scholars whose careers were primarily concerned with writing pedagogy, and these people associated freshman composition as a course very clearly with "their discipline." It would be almost unnatural for them to admit that the course that was their primary responsibility and interest was so hopelessly compromised and ineffective that abolishing it was the best solution. There is no doubt that reform rather than abolition served the professional needs of most composition specialists best.

The decade of the 1930s saw more lively discussion of reform and abolition than had ever occurred before. The great lions of *fin de siecle* composition, Scott, Genung, and Wendell, were all dead by 1930, but the edifice they had raised had become a huge industry, and the profession of English was filled with their intellectual descendants. The decade of *English Journal* numbers from the 1930s is filled with debates that sound almost incredibly contemporary—proposals for English as training for social experience, for Marxist critique in the classroom, for writing across the curriculum, for research-based reforms of various kinds, for more or less literary influence on composition, and for better conditions for teachers. When *The Teaching of College English,* the report of the NCTE Committee on College English (1935) appeared, for example, it strongly condemned the freshman composition course and recommended that required writing be delayed until the sophomore year. The release of this report set off a "symposium" of different opinions in *English Journal* that year, most of which agreed that the report was admirable and that the freshman course was a serious problem—but not one of which agreed with the Committee's recommendation. "Shall we kill Freshman English? Certainly not!" harrumphed Frank Clippinger (1935, p. 575) in the Symposium before going on to propose how turning the course into a modern literature course would solve its problems. Outside the pages of the journal, the Committee's recommendations fell on even stonier ground.

Oscar J. Campbell chaired that critical committee, and in 1939, the strong liberal culture side of the abolitionist argument popped up again in his now well-known article, "The Failure of Freshman English." D. Russell (1988) dealt very effectively with the major part of Campbell's position, and here we might merely note that literary elitism was not the entirety of Campbell's (1939) position. He, too put forward a writing across the curriculum agenda, at least tacitly, saying that:

> What your students need is not more instruction in writing but a few teachers of geology who are capable of describing not only geological phenomena but also of teaching their students how to think consecutively and logically about geology.... Since most teachers of geology, history, or economics find themselves incapable of it, they conceal the incompetence from themselves by shifting the responsibility of their failure upon the harried instructor in Freshman English, who labors valiantly to accomplish the impossible. (p. 181)

As Russell described, Campbell also made the familiar claim that composition cannot be taught apart from content, that it is intellectually dishonest as well as futile. He blamed freshman composition for teacher disaffection and for the blunting of the impact of literary education.

Campbell's position, although probably sympathetic to most literature teachers, received far less support than Lounsbury's had 25 years before. Unlike Lounsbury, Campbell was facing a composition establishment that was already entrenched and was even building the beginnings of a scholarship and a discipline. Although Campbell was respected, he was not agreed with, and all the responses to his essay were essentially reformist. Only a few months after Campbell's essay, Fred A. Dudley (1939) replied to it: "Accepting much of what Professor Campbell so vigorously says in his essay by that title, we yet believe that Freshman English is succeeding—not perfectly, but better this year than five years ago; and we expect it to succeed still better five years from now" (p. 22). Andrew J. Green's (1941) "The Reform of Freshman English" took Campbell's arguments on directly, stating squarely that "Freshman English is ubiquitous, inevitable, and eternal" (p. 593).

Campbell also found himself in the unfortunate position of opening a battle immediately before the nation's attention became caught up in an all-consuming World War II. Instead of the debate that Campbell had no doubt hoped to produce, the entire issue of the worth of freshman composition slipped away, as did what had been other consuming issues of the 1930s—experience curriculum, social conditions, Marxism—in the intellectual conflagration that was the war effort. After 1941, his complaints seem to have been forgotten, and reformism itself was almost blunted for the duration of the war as the needs of the military came to the fore and stressing any U.S. problems seemed somewhat defeatist. Throughout the war years, overt criticism of the course almost disappeared as scholars betook themselves to serve the war effort by keeping up morale.

Postwar: The Triumph of Reformism

The postwar world was a different place, one in which the debate that had been damped down during the war emerged in many forms. Particularly hotly debated was the question of the mission and purpose of liberal arts colleges, a question that was always tied in powerfully to the issue of required freshman composition. Ironically, it was not the abolition sentiment of the Campbells but a kind of accelerated reformism that had the greatest abolitionist effect after World War II. The General Education movement, which proposed that college curricula after the introduction of the elective system had become too specialized, was first widely enunciated in the Harvard Report of 1945, and, gaining power rapidly after 1948, it produced widespread withdrawal from the traditional freshman composition course.

The General Educationists wished to meld the "heritage" model of traditional education with the more recent pragmatic insights of the followers of Dewey and James (Harvard Committee, 1945, pp. 46–47), and to do so they proposed that the specialized introductory courses of the freshman and sophomore years be supplanted by much broader general courses, one each in the humanities, the social sciences, and the sciences. The Harvard Committee specifically proposed that the traditional course in freshman composition be replaced by more emphasis on writing in these new general education courses: "Since the responsibility for training in written communication is vested in the staff of English A, the other members of the faculty too often feel that they have little if any responsibility for the development of skill and facility in writing. This seems to us a serious weakness" (p. 199). In 1949, the proposed change was made. English A, which had been taken by Harvard freshmen since 1885, was dropped. Other schools followed similar lines, and the static acceptance of required freshman composition courses that had for so long been tacit educational policy was suddenly shaken as "communication" courses replaced the older composition model.

The Communication movement, which was the working out of General Education ideas in an English context, proposed to unify what had been separate fields of English and speech by rolling together all four of the "communications skills"—speaking, listening, reading, and writing—and creating a new course around them, the communication course. This movement began to take hold in earnest in the late 1940s and prospered through the mid-1950s, when it lost momentum. During that time, however, many traditional freshman writing courses were converted into communication courses, often team-taught by English and speech professors.

It is important to note several things about these communications courses. First, they were not part of anyone's abolitionist agenda. The General Education movement itself was not at all against required courses; it was essentially about widening and adding requirements, especially during the first 2 years of college. Although the communications movement proposed to add to the charge of the traditional composition course, the requirement was still there for freshmen. This was a specifically successful brand of reformism, perceiving the freshman course in need of change, rather than abolitionism, which perceived the course as hopeless or its change as impossible. Second, the changes that came down during these years came down from on high as part of a sweeping mandate reaching all the way from Harvard to the federal government. Traditional freshman courses were not transformed by liberal culture romantics of the old literary sort or even by the sort of writing across the curriculum-oriented attitude of Eurich, but rather by a temporary enthusiasm for a new sort of reform. It was a reform that changed the name and some of the methods of the traditional freshman composition class in many places but removed not a jot of requirement anywhere.

Throughout this postwar period, there continued a steady drumbeat of dissatisfaction with the freshman course in its various forms. Most faculty members outside of English continued in their optimistic belief that a semester or a year of composition (or communication) early in a student's career would inoculate him or her from any viral illiteracies. English teachers responded to these critiques with their traditional protests that no one course could accomplish all that the critics asked but that the freshman course was an invaluable training ground in the humanities even if it could not guarantee inviolate literacy. Despite the critiques, freshman composition and communications courses flourished throughout the early and mid-1950s. Only at the end of the decade did abolitionism resurge.

The most famous recent abolitionist statement was made in 1959 by Warner G. Rice, Chair of the Michigan Department of English, at the NCTE Convention of that year. Rice's (1960) essay, "A Proposal for the Abolition of Freshman English, As It Is Now Commonly Taught, from the College Curriculum," was a classic statement of its period; the late 1950s were for colleges a low-stress time during which fewer but much better prepared students were seeking admission. We might think of the period as the antithesis of a literacy crisis: There was no press of new student populations, test scores were rising every year, and there were fewer bachelor's degrees conferred in 1960 than in 1950 (*Digest of Educational Statistics,* 1974, p. 84). The postwar GI boom had not quite been succeeded by the baby boom in colleges, and thus at that moment the need for a required course to remedy freshman literacy problems seemed to many less pressing.

Rice's (1960) stance is by now familiar. He made the same claims that abolitionists had always made: Basic literacy should be a prerequisite for college; freshman composition in a semester or a year tries to accomplish the impossible and does not really "take"; students are ill motivated; the course is a financial drain on colleges; English teachers will be happier teaching other courses (pp. 361–362). What is surprising to someone reading Rice's essay in the historical context of other abolitionist essays is its aridity of spirit, its open English department self-concern, and its lack of interest in seeking creative answers to the problem of underprepared students. Rice was an almost direct throwback to the very first generation of abolitionists 70 years earlier; his attitude was that literacy issues were the responsibility of the high schools and that college should not be bothered. He did not wish to replace required composition with literature. Although he thought that all disciplines should take over their own responsibilities for correct writing, he did not believe that English professors should be involved in any sort of writing across the curriculum-based program. He was not overly concerned with students who simply could not "make the grade" and get into colleges. "It will be asked what will replace the Freshman English now taught if, by various expedients, it proves possible to get along without it. The answer must be firm and emphatic: Nothing. College requirements should simply be reduced by whatever number of hours Freshman English now absorbs" (p. 365). Rice's was the voice of literary professional self-interest.

As Eurich had been answered by reformist Taylor at the NCTE Convention 28 years earlier, Rice was answered by reformist Albert R. Kitzhaber in 1959. Kitzhaber's (1960) essay, "Death—Or Transfiguration?" admitted immediately that "no one would want to make an unqualified defense of the present Freshman

English course" (p. 347), and went on to catalog its shortcomings: overambitious aims, lack of agreement about course content, poor textbooks and methods, and impossibility of proving success. However, Kitzhaber then went on to state positive aspects of the course: It subsidized graduate study, let young teachers gain experience, and often got clearly positive results. He also believed that a writing-based course was worthwhile in and of itself. Kitzhaber contested Rice's main points, arguing that abolishing freshman composition would not be cheaper to colleges, that faculty in other disciplines would not take up any great part of literacy responsibilities, that the high schools were not equipped yet to handle the responsibilities themselves, and that a more rhetorically oriented Freshman English course would help solve the problem.

Strangely, Kitzhaber's reply to Rice sounds to today's reader almost as hopeless about the course as Rice's attack. In Kitzhaber's rejoinder, reformism gets as far away from concern with students as we ever see it; Kitzhaber was concerned with college finance, teacher morale, English departments, and high school curricula— but only tangentially, it seems, with college students. A large part of his essay was taken up with proposals for improving high school English. Except for his admission that "there must be some value in requiring all Freshman to take at least one course that has writing as its focus," Kitzhaber found little to be cheered by in the possibilities of freshman composition, and those seeking any sort of humanistic defense of writing as learning in his essay will be disappointed. Perhaps it was the period; except for the New Rhetoric that he hoped would arrive (as it did, on schedule, 3 years later), he had little sanguinity about required composition in the form it usually took. Perhaps it was Kitzhaber's own historicism; he had read too deeply in composition history to be cheerily hopeful about course reform proposals.

Reformism and Abolitionism in the Modern Era

With the eruption of the New Rhetoric in the early 1960s and the gradual growth of composition studies as a scholarly discipline with its own books and journals, its own disseminative and reproductive mechanisms, we enter a new era. It is an era in which reformism is immensely strengthened—becomes, indeed, the backbone of an ever-larger professional literature. Improving the freshman course (through the New Rhetoric, or invention, or classical rhetoric, or Christensen paragraphing, or sentence combining) becomes the essential purpose of the books and essays that appear in always greater numbers.

Abolition sentiment, however, does not die easily, and there was a short period during the late 1960s when the iconoclasm of that time caused the usual reformist consensus to be disrupted again by arguments against the required freshman course. Several of these are familiar liberal culture arguments that took advantage of the ferment of the times. Robert Russell (1968), chair of English at Franklin and Marshall, wrote of pressuring his faculty to vote against teaching

demographic sector into college classrooms, and the resulting "literacy crisis" of the middle 1970s. There is nothing like a new population or a perceived problem of lack of student preparation to put energy back into a composition requirement, and by 1976 we had both in plenty. The "Johnny Can't Write" furor of 1976 was at least as potent as the "Illiteracy of American Boys" furor had been 90 years before, and any chance that abolitionist ideas might have had in the early 1970s was swamped by mid-decade. The "Back to the Basics" movement, the rise of basic writing as a subdiscipline, even the writing process movement all presumed a required freshman course.

Just as important to the decline of abolitionism, I believe, was the maturation of the discipline of composition studies and its increasing ability to turn out doctoral specialists who could direct and defend programs. The natural tendency early on was for such specialists to talk reform and defend the course, but their very existence tempered the conditions that had made some literary specialists argue for abolition. The liberal culture abolitionists of the 1890s had largely lost interest in the battle when they themselves had been relieved of the duty of teaching required composition by graduate students and instructors. This left literary specialists only with the duty of overseeing the toilers in the writing vineyard, and nearly all liberal culture abolitionists had been either freshman directors or departmental chairs. With the increasing availability of a class of tenure-track composition specialists to handle oversight of the course, literary members of English departments could rest increasingly secure from ever having to do anything associated with composition unless they chose to. Those overseeing required courses had an increasing professional stake in them, and thus reform ideas came hard and fast—but not proposals for abolition. So things went, through the later 1970s and most of the 1980s.

The New Abolitionism

This dearth of abolitionist sentiment, by now lasting almost 20 years, makes the historian with even a slight tinge of Toynbeeism begin to expect that the wheel must turn again, and turn again toward abolitionism. True to form, we now must consider the New Abolitionism. A founding statement of the New Abolitionism was made by Sharon Crowley (1991), in her "A Personal Essay on Freshman English."

Crowley's thoughtful essay is something that had not been seen in the literature for many years: a nonreformist argument from a composition insider. It details her gradual realization, by way of her immersion in the creation and ongoing attempt at implementation of the Wyoming Resolution, that required freshman composition courses implicated her and all composition specialists with any program oversight in structures that could not be significantly reformed. The course is simply too tied up with institutional and professional baggage to be amenable to serious reform. "In short," she wrote, "I doubt whether it is possible to radicalize instruction in a course that is so thoroughly implicated in the maintenance of cultural and academic hierarchy" (p. 165). Crowley's solution was abolition, not of the course but of the requirement. "Please note," she wrote, "that I am NOT proposing the abolition of Freshman English. I am not so naive as to think that the course can be abolished. But it can be made elective. To deny the supposition that all students need to jump over the hurdle of Freshman English is to begin chipping away at the course's historical function as a repressive instrument of student (and teacher) legitimation" (p. 170). Crowley went on to argue that eliminating the requirement would get rid of admissions exams, prevent any sort of indoctrination of first-year students, offer administrative control over enrollment freshman courses, and control teaching assistantships more effectively. She then took on what she considered good arguments—that is, student needs-based—and bad arguments—that is, institutionally or ideologically based—that could be made against her position.

Crowley's deliberately provocative essay led to the proposal of a roundtable session at the 1993 Conference on College Composition and Communication (CCCC) in San Diego titled "(Dis)missing the Universal Requirement" From the quick sketch I have given here of traditional responses to abolitionist arguments over the last century, we might have expected the standard response: reformism; reformism of a very high standard, no doubt, but, still, reformism: protests that the freshman requirement does more good than harm, or that its methods must be changed to fill-in-the-blank so that it can reach its potential, or that fill-in-the-blank will certainly arrive soon and make it all worthwhile.

But no. No Mahin or Taylor or Kitzhaber stood forth to disagree with Crowley. Instead, three of the most respected composition scholars and theorists rose and each one, in his or her own way, agreed with Crowley that the universal requirement should be rethought. Lil Brannon of SUNY–Albany reported that her university had abolished the standard freshman course in 1986 because "a group of faculty from across the curriculum successfully made the case that a 'skills' concept of writing—the very idea of writing that caused the faculty to re-quire Freshman Composition—had no professional currency" (p. 1). David Jolliffe (1993) making an argument based on his historical study, asked whether such a "skills"-based course was a reflection of late 19th-century perceptions: "I wonder if freshman composition isn't a metaphor for a time long passed. I wonder if we shouldn't rethink the position of requiring all incoming students to be 'skilled' in this anachronistic fashion" (p. 1). Calling regular freshman courses "literacy calisthenics," Jolliffe went on to argue that they should be replaced with a writing-based sophomore-level elective course that would concentrate on writing about content of their choice. Charles Schuster (1993) spoke from the point of view of a practicing composition administrator, saying that freshman composition is the third world of English studies, "a bleak territory within which students have little power to choose" (p. 6), and in which faculty are underpaid and overworked. Teaching writing is foundational, said Schuster, but "either Freshman Composition has to matter to our departments, or we have to get rid of it—or get rid of our colleagues" (p. 6).

The discussion that followed these three presentations was spirited, and although there was by no means unanimity of opinion, many session attenders agreed with the central points made by the presenters. Within a few weeks, the grapevine of hallway conversations, telephone calls, workshop and presentation discussions, and electronic mail was buzzing with word of the session, and the issue even had its name: the New Abolitionism. The following year saw the predictable rejoinder from the reformist camp in a session at the Nashville CCCC called "Dissing Freshman Composition," at which Marjorie Roemer, Russell Durst, and several other University of Cincinnati teachers criticized the claims of Crowley, Jolliffe, and Brannon. Two full-scale debates on the subject took place at the 1995 CCCC in Washington, and this continuing conversation bids fair to become a prime dialectic in the field.

We have come a long way from 1893 to 1993, from the oldest to the newest abolitionism movements. Are there any conclusions we can draw from what we have learned? Can our understanding of the past inform our sense of the present, or even the future? Is the New Abolitionism any different from previous similar arguments?

The observer of abolition arguments cannot help noting some salient similarities. The New Abolitionism is like previous versions in its condemnation of the required course as often futile, as a disliked hinterland of English studies, as expensive to run, exhausting to teach, and alienating to administer. Some New Abolitionists are present and former course administrators, as were a large number of abolitionists throughout history. The alternatives proposed by many of the New Abolitionists are not too dissimilar to alternatives proposed by Slosson in 1913 and Eurich in 1932 and Campbell in 1939 and Rusell in 1968: Make writing instruction the responsibility of the whole faculty.

The differences between the New Abolitionism and the older movements are, however, even more striking than the similarities. Most obviously different is the professional forum in which the argument is playing itself out. The New Abolitionism is a product of a newly scholarly and professionalized discipline of composition studies, one with many national journals and a constant and ongoing conversation. Writing specialists today are not just course administrators or pedagogy enthusiasts but are increasingly visible in English departments as scholars and researchers with their own claims to respect. The change of the discipline is revealed most clearly in the fact that this abolition conversation is not between liberal culture literary specialists and embattled teachers, as previous abolition conversations have been, but between serious and prepared experts on writing issues. Since the institutional beginning of the required composition course, the greatest number of abolition arguments have come from outsiders who despised the course as useless and mechanical—nearly always from what D. Russell (1988) called "romantics," people who did not believe that writing could be taught at all. The New Abolitionism is the work of insiders—people trained as writing specialists from an early point in their careers—and it is based on exactly the opposite conclusion: that the development of writing abilities can be facilitated within different situational contexts, and that experts can assist the student writer in navigating through these contexts, but that the required freshman course is not the most effective forum for attaining the ends we seek.

The intellectual and pedagogical backgrounds for the argument have shifted dramatically as a result of these changes in institutional and disciplinary cultures, and it is this background shift that may be the most important element in any success the New Abolitionism may have. From a very early point, abolitionists have been claiming that freshman composition should be replaced with one or another system that would take responsibility for literacy off English teachers and place it on all faculty members. These were voices crying in the wilderness through much of this century, however. There were no institutional structures that would have helped faculty members in other disciplines make writing more central to their courses, and there was no extant part of English studies with enough credible expertise to do such outreach work. All that has now changed radically with the advent of the writing across the curriculum movement. For the last decade and longer, writing professionals have, with the blessing and help of administrators, been forging professional links that never existed before with extradisciplinary colleagues, bringing contemporary knowledge of writing issues to content-area courses. This is a strong and broadly respected movement, one that is unlikely to go away, and it provides a practical base for the ideas of the New Abolitionism that no previous such movement had (witness the arguments presented by Brannon, chap. 12; Freedman, chap. 6; Petraglia, chap. 4; and Russell, chap. 3, all this volume). Writing across the curriculum has made R. Russell's (1968) challenge to other faculty members who wanted students trained in writing papers, "Then assign them!" something more than bad-tempered buck-passing.

The arguments we hear from proponents of the New Abolitionism are qualitatively different from those to be heard in previous avatars of the movement. New Abolitionists typically appeal first to student interests, and only secondarily to the interests of teachers, departments, and colleges. Even when previous abolitionists transcended liberal culture arguments, their calls for the end of the required course were often based in issues of self-interest—getting rid of the composition underclass, or allowing professors to teach courses they liked, or avoiding the criticism of colleagues who felt the course was ineffective. Today's abolitionists are arguing from their scholarly as well as their practical knowledge of writing issues that students are not as well served by the required freshman course as they could be by other kinds of writing instruction. They are ideologically informed in ways that even 1960s radicals like Greenbaum were not, and they are certainly sympathetic to both students and teachers in ways that few abolitionists have ever been. Most importantly, this change in the institutional base of the argument means that we may see fewer reformist claims based in the need to safeguard jobs, turf, and respectability.

Finally, and perhaps most importantly, the New Abolitionists are in positions to make their critique stick. Because most of them are administrators or advisors to administrators, they know the institutional situation surrounding composition programs, writing across the curriculum, and literary studies. They know what is possible, and they know how to get things done—not just whether they should be done. Because they are respected scholars and teachers, they can and do counter the predictable response from traditionalists and reformists by taking a position of informed sympathy mixed with telling argumentation. Because they are composition insiders, they can make their case from within the discourse of the field rather than complaining scornfully from without, as most abolitionists have done in the past.

It may just be, then, that the New Abolitionism will come to have a real effect. It may be that after a century we will begin to see some actual abolition of the required freshman course in favor of other methods of writing instruction. But as Eliot's Gerontion says, "Think now/History has many cunning passages, contrived corridors/And issues, deceives with whispering ambitions,/Guides us with vanities." None of our historical knowledge can really predict the outcome of the New Abolitionism movement. What we can learn, however, is what may promote or block such changes in entrenched curricular practices. My own position, if I have not already tipped my hand, is one of sympathy for the New Abolitionism. I still believe that we have more of a chance today than ever before to rethink in a serious and thoroughgoing way the best methods for working on student literacy issues, and that we can do so without harming the best interests of either our students or our colleagues. I look forward to a continuation of the debate and even—could it be?—to real changes in our world of teaching and thinking about writing.

References

Anderson, M. B. (1895). The Leland Stanford, Junior, University. In W. M. Payne (Ed.), *English in American universities* (pp. 49–59). Boston: D. C. Heath.

Applebee, A. N. (1974). *Tradition and reform in the teaching of English: A history.* Urbana, IL: National Council of Teachers of English.

Brannon, L. (1993, March). *(Dis)missing freshman composition.* Presentation given at CCCC, San Diego, CA.

Campbell, O. J. (1939). The failure of freshman English. *English Journal, 28,* 177–185.

Committee on College English, NCTE (1935). *The teaching of college English.* New York: Appleton-Century.

Connors, R. J. (1991). Rhetoric in the modern university: The creation of an underclass. In R. Bullock & J. Trimbur (Eds.), *The politics of writing instruction: Postsecondary* (pp. 55–84). Portsmouth NH: Boynton/Cook.

Crowley, S. (1991). A personal essay on freshman English. *Pre/Text, 12,* 156–176.

Davidson, H. C. (1932). Report of the College Section meeting. *English Journal, 21,* 220–223.

DeVoto, B. (1928). Course A. *American Mercury, 13,* 204–212.

Digest of educational statistics. (1974). Washington, DC: U.S. Department of Health, Education, and Welfare, Education Division.

Dudley, F. A. (1939). The success of freshman English. *College English, 1,* 22–30.

Eaton, H. A. (1919). English problems after the war. *English Journal, 8,* 308–312.

Eurich, A. C. (1932). Should freshman composition be abolished? *English Journal, 21,* 211–219.

Green, A. J. (1941). The reform of freshman English. *College English, 2,* 593–602.

Greenbaum, L. (1969). The tradition of complaint. *College English, 31,* 174–187.

Harvard Committee on the Objectives of a General Education in a Free Society. (1945). *General education in a free society.* Cambridge, MA: Harvard University Press.

Hill, A. S. (1896). An answer to the cry for more English. In A. S. Hill (Ed.), *Twenty years of school and college English* (pp. 6–16). Cambridge, MA: Harvard University Press.

Hoover, R. M. (1974). Taps for freshman English? *College Composition and Communication, 25,* 149–154.

Hurlbut, B. S. (1896). College requirements in English. In A. S. Hill (Ed.), *Twenty years of school and college English* (pp. 46–53). Cambridge, MA: Harvard University Press.

Jolliffe, D. (1993, March). *Three arguments for sophomore English.* Presentation given at CCCC, San Diego, CA.

Kitzhaber, A. R. (1960). Death—Or transfiguration? *College English, 21,* 367–378.

Lounsbury, T. R. (1911, November). Compulsory composition in colleges. *Harper's Monthly, 123,* 866–880.

Mahin, H. O. (1915). The study of English composition as a means to fuller living. *English Journal, 4,* 445–450.

Osgood, C. G. (1915). No set requirement of English composition in the freshman year. *English Journal, 4,* 231–235.

Payne, W. M. (1895). *English in American universities.* Boston: D. C. Heath.

Rice, W. G. (1960). A proposal for the abolition of freshman English, as it is now commonly taught, from the college curriculum. *College English, 21,* 361–367.

Rudolph, F. (1962). *The American college and university: A history.* New York: Knopf.

Russell, D. R. (1988). Romantics on writing: Liberal culture and the abolition of composition courses. *Rhetoric Review, 6,* 132–148.

Russell, R. (1968). The question of composition: A record of a struggle. *College English, 30,* 171–177.

Sampson, M. W. (1895). The University of Indiana. In W. M. Payne (Ed.), *English in American universities* (pp. 92–98). Boston: D. C. Heath.

Schuster, C. (1993, March). *Toward abolishing composition.* Presentation given at CCCC, San Diego, CA.

Scott, F. W., Thomas, J. M., & Manchester, F. A. (1918). Preliminary report of the Special Committee on Freshman English. *English Journal, 7,* 592–599.

Shaw, P. W. (1974). Freshman English: To compose or decompose, that is the question. *College Composition and Communication, 25,* 155–159.

Shepherd, L. (1913). Discussions: Prescribed English in college. *Educational Review, 46,* 188–190.

Slosson, P. W. (1913). Discussions: Prescribed English in college. *Educational Review, 45,* 407–409.

Smith, R. (1974). The composition requirement today: A report on a nationwide survey of four-year colleges and universities. *College Composition and Communication, 25,* 138–148.

Stedman, N. A. (1913). Discussions: Prescribed English in college. *Educational Review, 46,* 52–57.

Strong, G. (1913). Discussions: Prescribed English in college. *Educational Review, 45,* 189.

Symposium on *The teaching of college English.* (1935). *English Journal, 24,* 573–586.

Taylor, W. (1932). Should freshman composition be abolished? *English Journal, 21,* 301–311.

Zigrosser, C. (1913). Discussions: Prescribed English in college. *Educational Review, 45,* 187–188.

COMPOSING BEHAVIORS OF ONE- AND MULTI-DRAFT WRITERS

Muriel Harris

A belief shared by teachers of writing, one that we fervently try to inculcate in our students, is that revision can improve writing. This notion, that revision generally results in better text, often pairs up with another assumption, that revision occurs as we work through separate drafts. Thus, "hand in your working drafts tomorrow and the final ones next Friday" is a common assignment, as is the following bit of textbook advice: "When the draft is completed, a good critical reading should help the writer re-envision the essay and could very well lead to substantial rewriting" (Axelrod and Cooper 10). This textbook advice, hardly atypical, is based on the rationale that gaining distance from a piece of discourse helps the writer to judge it more critically. As evidence for this assumption. Richard Beach's 1976 study of the self-evaluation strategies of revisers and non-revisers demonstrated that extensive revisers were more capable of detaching themselves and gaining aesthetic distance from their writing than were non-revisers. Nancy Sommers' later theoretical work on revision also sensitized us to students' need to re-see their texts rather than to view revision as an editing process at the limited level of word changes.

A logical conclusion, then, is to train student writers to re-see and then re-draft a piece of discourse. There are other compelling reasons for helping students view first or working drafts as fluid and not yet molded into final form. The opportunities for outside intervention, through teacher critiques and suggestions or peer evaluation sessions, can be valuable. And it is equally important to help students move beyond their limited approaches and limiting tendency to settle for whatever rolls out on paper the first time around. The novice view of a first draft as written-in-stone (or fast-drying cement) can preclude engaging more fully with the ideas being expressed. On the other hand, we have to acknowledge that there are advantages in being able, where it is appropriate, to master the art of one-draft writing. When students write essay exams or placement essays and when they go on to on-the-job writing where time doesn't permit multiple drafts, they need to produce first drafts which are also coherent, finished final drafts. Yet, even acknowledging that need, we stil seem justified in advocating that our students master the art of redrafting to shape a text into a more effective form.

The notion that reworking a text through multiple drafts and/or visible changes is generally a beneficial process is also an underlying assumption in some lines of

Reprinted from *College English*, Volume 51, Number 2, February 1989. Used with permission.

research. This had been particularly evident in studies of computer-aided revision, where counts were taken of changes in macrostructure and microstructure with and without word processing. If more changes were made on a word processor than were written by hand, the conclusion was that word processors are an aid to revision. Such research is based on the premise that revision equals visible changes in a text and that these changes will improve the text.

Given this widely entrenched notion of redrafting as being advantageous, it would be comforting to turn to research results for clearcut evidence that reworking of text produces better writing. But studies of revision do not provide the conclusive picture that we need in order to assert that we should continue coaxing our students into writing multiple drafts. Lillian Bridwell's 1980 survey of revision studies led her to conclude that "questions about the relationship between revision and qualitative improvement remain largely unanswered" (199), and her own study demonstrated that the most extensively revised papers "received a range of quality ratings from the top to the bottom of the scale" (216). In another review of research on revision. Stephen Witte cities studies which similarly suggest that the amount of re-drafting (which Witte calls "retranscription") often bears little relation to the overall quality of completed texts ("Revising" 256). Similarly, Linda Flower and John Hayes, et al., citing studies which also dispute the notion that more re-drafting should mean better papers, conclude that the amount of change is not a key variable in revision and that revision as an obligatory stage required by teachers doesn't necessarily produce better writing. (For a teacher's affirmation of the same phenomenon, see Henley.)

Constricting revision to retranscription (i.e., to altering what has been written) also denies the reality of pre-text, a composing phenomenon studied by Stephen Witte in "Pre-Text and Composing." Witte defines a writer's pre-text as "the mental construction of 'text' prior to transcription" (397). Pre-text thus "refers to a writer's linguistic representation of intended meaning, a 'trial locution' that is produced in the mind, stored in the writer's memory, and sometimes manipulated mentally prior to being transcribed as written text" (397). Pre-texts are distinguished from abstract plans in that pre-texts approximate written prose. As the outcome of planning, pre-text can also be the basis for further planning. In his study Witte found great diversity in how writers construct and use pre-text. Some writers construct little or no pre-text; others rely heavily on extensive pre-texts; others create short pre-texts; and still others move back and forth between extensive and short pre-texts. The point here is that Witte has shown us that revision can and does occur in pre-texts, before visible marks are made on paper. In an earlier paper, "Revising, Composing Theory, and Research Design," Witte suggests that the pre-text writers construct before making marks on paper is probably a function of the quality, kind, and extent of planning that occurs before transcribing on paper. The danger here is that we might conclude that the development from novice to expert writer entails learning to make greater use of pre-text prior to transcribing. After all, in Linda Flower's memorable phrase, pre-text is "the last cheap gas before transcribing text" (see Witte, "Pre-Text" 422). But Witte notes that his data do not support a "vote for pre-text" ("Pre-Text" 401). For the students in Witte's study, more extensive use of pre-text doesn't automatically lead to better written text. Thus it appears so far that the quality of revision can neither be measured by the pound nor tracked through discreet stages.

But a discussion of whether more or fewer drafts is an indication of more mature writing is itself not adequate. As Maxine Hairston reminds us in "Different Products, Different Processes," we must also consider the writing task that is involved in any particular case of generating discourse. In her taxonomy of writing categories, categories that depict a variety of revision behaviors that are true to the experience of many of us, Hairston divides writing into three classes; first, routine maintenance writing which is simple communication about uncomplicated matters; second, extended, relatively complex writing that requires the writer's attention but is self-limiting in that the writer already knows most of what she is going to write and may be writing under time constraints; and third, extended reflective writing in which the form and content emerge as the writing proceeds. Even with this oversimplified, brief summary of Hairston's classes of writing, we recognize that the matter of when and if re-drafting takes place can differ according to the demands of different tasks and situations as well as the different skills levels of writers.

Many—or perhaps even most—of us may nod in agreement as we recognize in Hairston's classes of writing a description of the different types of writing we do. But given the range of individual differences that exist among writers, we still cannot conclude that the nature of effective revision is always tied to the writing task, because such a conclusion would not account for what we know also exists—some expert writers who, despite the writing task, work at either end of the spectrum as confirmed, consistent one-drafters or as perpetual multi-drafters. That writers exhibit a diversity of revising habits has been noted by Lester Faigley and Stephen Witte in "Analyzing Revision." When testing the taxonomy of revision changes they had created. Faigley and Witte found that expert writers exhibited "extreme diversity" in the ways they revised:

> One expert writer in the present study made almost no revisions; another started with an almost stream-of-consciousness text that she then converted to an organized essay in the second draft; another limited his major revisions to a single long insert; and another revised mostly by pruning. (410)

Similarly, when summarizing interviews with well-known authors such as those in the *Writers at Work: The Paris Review Interviews* series, Lillian Bridwell notes that these discussions reveal a wide range of revision strategies among these writers, from rapid producers of text who do little revising as they proceed to writers who move along by revising every sentence (198).

More extensive insights into a variety of composing styles are offered in Tom Waldrep's collection of essays by successful scholars working in composition, *Writers on Writing*. Here too as writers describe their composing processes, we see a variety of approaches, including some writers who plan extensively before their pens hit paper (or before the cursor blips on their screens). Their planning is so complete that their texts generally emerge in a single draft with minor, if any, editing as they write. Self-descriptions of some experienced writers in the field of composition give us vivid accounts of how these one-drafters work. For example, Patricia Y. Murray notes that prior to typing, she sees words, phrases, sentences, and paragraphs taking shape in her head. Her composing, she concludes, has been done before her fingers touch the typewriter, though as she also notes, she revises and edits as she types (234). William Lutz offers a similar account:

> Before I write, I write in my mind. The more difficult and complex the writing, the more time I need to think before I write. Ideas incubate in my mind. While I talk, drive, swim, and exercise I am thinking, planning, writing. I think about the introduction, what examples to use, how to develop the main idea, what kind of conclusion to use. I write, revise, rewrite, agonize, despair, give up, only to start all over again, and all of this before I ever begin to put words on paper. . . . Writing is not a process of discovery for me. . . . The writing process takes place in my mind. Once that process is complete the product emerges. Often I can write pages without pause and with very little, if any, revision or even minor changes. (186–87)

Even with such descriptions from experienced writers, we are hesitant either to discard the notion that writing *is* a process of discovery for many of us or to typecast writers who make many visible changes on the page and/or work through multiple drafts as inadequate writers. After all, many of us, probably the majority, fall somewhere along the continuum from one- to multi-drafters. We may find ourselves as both one- and multi-drafters with the classes of writing that Hairston describes, or we may generally identify ourselves as doing both but also functioning more often as a one- or multi-drafter. Just as we have seen that at one end of the spectrum there are some confirmed one-drafters, so too must we recognize that at the other end of that spectrum there are some confirmed multi-drafters, expert writers for whom extensive revising occurs when writing (so that a piece of discourse may go through several or more drafts or be reworked heavily as the original draft evolves.) David Bartholomae, a self-described multi-drafter, states that he never outlines but works instead with two pads of paper, one to write on and one for making plans, storing sentences, and taking notes. He views his first drafts as disorganized and has to revise extensively, with the result that the revisions bear little resemblance to the first drafts (22–26). Similarly, Lynn Z. Bloom notes that she cannot predict at the outset a great deal of what she is going to say. Only by writing does she learn how her content will develop or how she will handle the structure, organization, and style of her paragraphs, sentences, and whole essay (33).

Thus, if we wish to draw a more inclusive picture of composing behaviors for revision, we have to put together a description that accounts for differences in levels of ability and experience (from novice to expert), for differences in writing tasks, and also for differences in the as yet largely unexplored area of composing process differences among writers. My interest here is in the composing processes of different writers, more particularly, the reality of those writers at either end of that long spectrum, the one-drafters at one end and the multi-drafters at the other. By one-draft writers I mean those writers who construct their plans and the pre-texts that carry out those plans as well as do all or most of the revising of those plans and pre-texts mentally, before transcribing. They do little or no retranscribing. True one-drafters have not arrived at this developmentally or as a result of training in writing, and they should not be confused with other writers who—driven by deadlines, lack of motivation, insufficient experience with writing, or anxieties about "getting it right the first time"—do little or no scratching out of what they have written. Multi-drafters, on the other hand, need to interact with their transcriptions in order to revise. Independent of how much planning they do or pre-text they compose, they continue to revise after they have transcribed words onto paper. Again, true multi-drafters have not reached this stage developmentally or as a result of any intervention by teachers. This is not to say that we can classify writers into two categories, one- and multi-drafters, because all the evidence we have and, more importantly, our own experience tells us that most writers are not one or the other but exist somewhere between these two ends of the continuum.

However, one- and multi-drafters do exist, and we do need to learn more about them to gain a clearer picture not only of what is involved in different revising processes but also to provide a basis for considering the pedagogical implications of dealing with individual differences. There is a strong argument for looking instead at the middle range of writers who do some writing in single drafts and others in multiple drafts or with a lot of retranscribing as they proceed, for it is very probable that the largest number of writers cluster there. But those of us who teach in the individualized setting of conferences or writing lab tutorials know that we can never overlook or put aside the concerns of every unique individual with whom we work. Perhaps we are overly intrigued with individual differences, partly because we see that some students can be ill-served in the group setting of the classrooms and partly because looking at individual differences gives us such enlightening glimpses into the complex reality of composing processes. Clinicians in other fields would argue that looking at the extremes offers a clearer view of what may be involved in the behaviors of the majority. But those who do research in writing also acknowledge that we need to understand dimensions of variation among writers, particularly those patterned differences or "alternate paths to expert performance" that have clear implications for instruction (Freedman et al. 19). In this case, whatever we learn about patterns of behavior among one- and multi-drafters has direct implications for instruction as we need to know the various trade-offs involved in any classroom instruction which would encourage more single or multiple drafting. And, as we will see when looking at what is involved in being able to revise before drafting or in being able to return and re-draft what has been transcribed, there are trade-offs indeed. Whatever arguments are offered, we must also acknowledge that no picture of revision is complete until it includes all that is known and observed about a variety of revision behaviors among writers.

But what do we know about one- and multi-drafters other than anecdotal accounts that confirm their existence? Much evidence is waiting to be gathered from the storehouse of various published interviews in which well-known writers have been asked to describe their writing. And Ann Ruggles Gere's study of the revising behaviors of a blind student gives us a description of a student writer who does not redraft but writes "first draft/final draft" papers, finished products produced in one sitting for her courses as a master's degree candidate. The student describes periods of thinking about a topic before writing. While she doesn't know exactly what she will say until actually writing it, she typically knows what will be contained in the first paragraph as she types the title. Her attention is not focused on words as she concentrates instead on images and larger contexts. A similar description of a one-drafter is found in Joy Reid's "The Radical Outliner and the Radical Brainstormer." Comparing her husband and herself, both composition teachers, Reid notes the differences between herself, an outliner (and a one-drafter), and her husband, a brainstormer (and a multi-drafter), differences which parallel those of the writers in *Writers on Writing* that I have described.

The descriptions of all of the one- and multi-draft writers mentioned so far offer a fairly consistent picture, but these descriptions do little more than reaffirm their existence. In an effort to learn more, I sought out some one- and multi-drafters in order to observe them composing and to explore what might be involved. Since my intent was not to determine the percentage of one- and multi-drafters among any population of writers (though that would be an interesting topic indeed, as I suspect there are more than we may initially guess—or at least more who hover close to either end of the continuum). I sought out experienced writers who identify themselves as very definitely one- or multi-drafters. The subjects I selected for observation were graduate students who teach composition or communications courses, my rationale being that these people can more easily categorize and articulate their own writing habits. From among the group of subjects who described themselves as very definitely either one- or multi-drafters, I selected those who showed evidence of being experienced, competent writers. Of the eight selected subjects (four one-drafters and four multi-drafters), all were at least several years into their graduate studies in English or communications and were either near completion or had recently completed advanced degrees. All had received high scores in standardized tests for verbal skills such as the SAT or GRE exams; all had grade point averages ranging from B+ to A in their graduate courses; and all wrote frequently in a variety of tasks, including academic papers for courses and journal publications, conference papers, the usual business writing of practicing academics (e.g., letters of recommendation for students, memos, instructional materials for classes, etc.), and personal writing such as letters to family and friends. They clearly earned their description as experienced writers. Experienced writers were used because I also wished to exclude those novices who may, through development of their writing skills, change their composing behaviors, and also those novices whose composing habits are the result of other factors such as disinterest (e.g., the one-drafter who habitually begins the paper at 3 a.m. the night before it's due) or anxiety (e.g., the multi-drafter who fears she is never "right" and keeps working and re-working her text).

The experienced writers whom I observed all confirmed that their composing behaviors have not changed over time. That is, they all stated that their writing habits have not altered as they became experienced writers and/or as they moved through writing courses. However, their descriptions of themselves as one- or multi-drafters were not as completely accurate as might be expected. Self-reporting, even among teachers of writing, is not a totally reliable measure. As I observed and talked with the eight writers, I found three very definite one-drafters. Ted, Nina, and Amy; one writer, Jackie, who tends to be a one-drafter but does some revising after writing; two very definite multi-drafters, Bill and Pam; and two writers, Karen and Cindy, who described themselves as multi-drafters and who tend to revise extensively but who can also produce first draft/final draft writing under some conditions. To gather data on their composing behaviors, I interviewed each person for an hour, asking questions about the types of writing they do, the activities they engage in before writing, the details of what happens as they write, their revision behaviors, the manner in which sentences are composed, and their attitudes and past history of writing. Each person was also asked to spend an hour writing in response to an assignment. The specific assignment was a request from an academic advisor asking for the writers' descriptions of the skills needed to succeed in their field of study. As they wrote, all eight writers were asked to give thinking-aloud protocols and were videotaped for future study. Brief interviews after writing focused on eliciting information about how accurately the writing session reflected their general writing habits and behaviors. Each type of information collected is, at best, incomplete because accounts of one's own composing processes may not be entirely accurate, because thinking-aloud protocols while writing are only partial accounts of what is being thought about, and because one-hour writing tasks preclude observing some of the kinds of activities that writers report. But even with these limitations I observed patterns of composing behaviors that should differentiate one-draft writers from multi-draft writers.

Preference for Beginning with a Developed Focus vs. Preference for Beginning at an Exploratory Stage

Among the consistent behaviors that one-drafters report is the point at which they can and will start writing. All of the four one-drafters expressed a strong need to clarify their thinking prior to beginning to transcribe. They are either not ready to write or cannot write until they have a focus and organization in mind. They may, as I observed Jacky and Ted doing, make some brief planning notes on paper or, as Amy and Nina did, sit for awhile and mentally plan, but all expressed a clearly articulated need to know beforehand the direction the piece of writing would take. For Nina's longer papers, she described a planning schedule in which the focus comes first, even before collecting notes. Ted too described the first stage of a piece of writing as being a time of mentally narrowing a topic. During incubation times before writing, two of these writers described some global recasting of a paper in their minds while the other two expressed a need to talk it out, either to themselves or friends. There is little resorting of written notes and little use of written outlines, except for some short lists, described by Ted as "memory jogs" to use while he writes. Amy explained that she sometimes felt that in high school or as an undergraduate she should have written outlines to please her teachers, but she never did get around to it because outlines served no useful purpose for her. Consistent throughout these accounts and in my observation of their writing was these writers' need to know where they are headed beforehand and a feeling that they are not ready to write—or cannot write—until they are at that stage. When asked if they ever engaged in freewriting, two one-drafters said they could not, unless forced to, plunge in and write without a focus and a mental plan. Ted, in particular, noted that the notion of exploration during writing would make him so uncomfortable that he would probably block and be unable to write.

In contrast to the one-drafters' preference for knowing their direction before writing, the two consistent multi-drafters, Pam and Bill, explained that they resist knowing, resist any attempt at clarification prior to writing. Their preference is for open-ended exploration as they write. They may have been reading and thinking extensively beforehand, but the topic has not taken shape when they decide that it is time to begin writing. Bill reported that he purposely starts with a broad topic while Pam said that she looks for something "broad or ambiguous" or "something small that can grow and grow." As Bill explained, he doesn't like writing about what he already knows as that would be boring. Pam too expressed her resistance to knowing her topic and direction beforehand in terms of how boring it would be. Generally, Bill will do about four or five drafts as he works through the early parts of a paper, perhaps two to four pages, before he knows what he will write about. He and Pam allow for—and indeed expect—that their topic will change as they write. Pam explained: "I work by allowing the direction of the work to change if it needs to. . . . I have to allow things to go where they need to go." When

I observed them writing, Pam spent considerable time planning and creating pre-texts before short bursts of transcribing while Bill wrote several different versions of an introduction and, with some cutting and pasting, was about ready to define his focus at the end of the hour. He reported that he depends heavily on seeing what he has written in order to find his focus, choose his content, and organize. Pam also noted that she needs to see chunks of what she has transcribed to see where the piece of discourse is taking her.

The other two writers who characterized themselves as multi-drafters, Karen and Cindy, both described a general tendency to plunge in before the topic is clear. Karen said that she can't visualize her arguments until she writes them out and generally writes and rewrites as she proceeds, but for writing tasks that she described as "formulaic" in that they are familiar because she has written similar pieces of discourse, she can write quickly and finish quickly—as she did with the writing task for this study. Since she had previously written the same kind of letter assigned in this study, she did not engage in the multi-drafting that would be more characteristic, she says, of her general composing behaviors. Cindy, the other self-described multi-drafter, almost completed the task in a single draft, though as she explained with short pieces, she can revert to her "journalistic mode" of writing, having been a working journalist for a number of years. For longer papers, such as those required in graduate courses, her descriptions sound much like those of Bill, Pam, and Karen. All of these writers, though, share the unifying characteristic of beginning to write before the task is well defined in their minds, unlike the one-drafters who do not write at that stage.

Preference for Limiting Options vs. Preference for Open-ended Exploring

Another consistent and clearly related difference between one- and multi-drafters is the difference in the quantity of options they will generate, from words and sentences to whole sections of a paper, and the way in which they will evaluate those options. As they wrote, all four of the one-drafters limited their options by generating several choices and then making a decision fairly quickly. There were numerous occasions in the think-aloud protocols of three of the four one-drafters in which they would stop, try another word, question a phrase, raise the possibility of another idea to include, and then make a quick decision. When Ted re-read one of his paragraphs, he saw a different direction that he might have taken that would perhaps be better, but he accepted what he had. ("That'll do here, OK... OK" he said to himself and moved on.) Nina, another one-drafter, generated no alternate options aloud as she wrote.

As is evident in this description of one-drafters, they exhibited none of the agonizing over possibilities that other writers experience, and they appear to be able to accept their choices quickly and move on. While observers may question whether limiting options in this manner cuts off further discovery and possibly better solutions or whether the internal debate goes on prior to transcribing, one-drafters are obviously efficient writers. They generate fewer choices, reach decisions more quickly, and do most or all of the decision-making before transcribing on paper. Thus, three of the four one-drafters finished the paper in the time allotted, and the fourth writer was almost finished. They can pace themselves fairly accurately too, giving me their estimates of how long it takes them to write papers of particular lengths. All four one-drafters describe themselves as incurable procrastinators who begin even long papers the night before they are due, allowing themselves about the right number of hours in which to transcribe their mental constructs onto paper. Nina explained that she makes choices quickly because she is always writing at the last minute under pressure and doesn't have time to consider more options. Another one-drafter offered a vivid description of the tension and stress that can be involved in these last minute, all-night sessions.

While they worry about whether they will finish on time, these one-drafters generally do. Contributing to their efficiency are two time-saving procedures involved as they get words on paper. Because most decisions are made before they commit words to paper, they do little or no scratching out and re-writing; and they do a minimum of re-reading both as they proceed and also when they are finished. The few changes I observed being made were either single words or a few short phrases, unlike the multi-drafters who rejected or scratched out whole sentences and paragraphs. As Nina wrote, she never re-read her developing text, though she reported that she does a little re-reading when she is finished with longer papers. The tinkering with words that she might do then, she says, is counterproductive because she rarely feels that she is improving the text with these changes. (Nina and the other one-drafters would probably be quite successful at the kind of "invisible writing" that has been investigated, that is, writing done under conditions in which writers cannot see what they are writing or scan as they progress. See Blau.)

In contrast to the one-drafters' limited options, quick decisions, few changes on paper and little or no re-reading, the multi-drafters were frequently observed generating and exploring many options, spending a long time in making their choices, and making frequent and large-scale changes on paper. Bill said that he produces large quantities of text because he needs to see it in order to see if he wants to retain it, unlike the one-drafters who exhibit little or no need to examine their developing text. Moreover, as Bill noted, the text he generates is also on occasion a heuristic for more text. As he writes, Bill engages in numerous revising tactics. He writes a sentence, stops to examine it by switching it around, going back to add clauses, or combining it with other text on the same page or a different sheet of paper. For the assigned writing task, he began with one sheet of paper, moved to another, tore off some of it and discarded it, and added part back to a previous sheet. At home when writing a longer paper, he will similarly engage in extensive cutting and pasting. In a somewhat different manner, Pam did not generate as many options on paper for this study. Instead, her protocol recorded various alternative plans and pre-texts that she would stop to explore verbally for five or ten minutes before transcribing anything. What she did write, though, was often heavily edited so that at the end of the hour, she, like Bill, had only progressed somewhat through an introductory paragraph of several sentences. Thus, while Bill had produced large amounts of text on paper that were later rejected after having been written, Pam spent more of her time generating and rejecting plans and pre-texts than crossing out transcriptions.

Writing is a more time-consuming task for these multi-drafters because they expect to produce many options and a large amount of text that will be discarded. Both Bill and Pam described general writing procedures in which they begin by freewriting, and, as they proceed, distilling from earlier drafts what will be used in later drafts. Both proceed incrementally, that is, by starting in and then starting again before finishing a whole draft. Both writers are used to re-reading frequently, partly to locate what Pam called "key elements" that will be retained for later drafts and partly, as Bill explained, because the act of generating more options and exploring them causes him to lose track of where he is.

Because both Bill and Pam seem to be comfortable when working within an as-yet only partially focused text, it would be interesting to explore what has been termed their "tolerance for ambiguity," a trait defined as a person's ability to function calmly in a situation in which interpretation of all stimuli is not completely clear. (See Budner, and Frenkel-Brunswick.) People who have little or no tolerance for ambiguity perceive ambiguous situations as sources of psy-chological discomfort, and they may try to reach conclusions quickly rather than to take the time to consider all of the essential elements of an unclear situation. People with more tolerance for ambiguity enjoy being in ambiguous situations and tend to seek them out. The relevance here, of course, is the question of whether one-drafters will not begin until they have structured the task and will also move quickly to conclusions in part, at least, because of having some degree of intolerance for ambiguity. This might be a fruitful area for further research.

For those interested in the mental processes which accompany behaviors, an-other dimension to explore is the Myers-Briggs Type Indicator (MBTI), a measure of expressed preferences (i.e., not performance tasks) in four bi-polar dimensions of personality. The work of Geroge H. Jensen and John K. DiTiberio has indicated some relationships between the personality types identified by the MBTI and writ-ing processes. Of particular interest here is that Bill, who had independently taken the MBTI for other reasons, reported that he scored highly in the dimensions of "extraversion" and "perceiving." Extraverts, say Jensen and DiTiberio, "often leap into tasks with little planning, then rely on trial and error to complete the task" (288), and they "often find freewriting a good method for developing ideas, for they think better when writing quickly, impulsively, and uncritically" (289). Perceivers, another type described by Jensen and DiTiberio, appear to share ten-dencies similar to those with a tolerance for ambiguity, for perceivers "are willing to leave the outer world unstructured. . . . Quickly made decisions narrow their field of vision" (295). Perceiving types tend to select broad topics for writing, like a wide range of alternatives, and always want to read one more book on the subject. Their revisions thus often need to be refocused (296). The similarities here to Bill's writing behaviors show us that while the MBTI is somewhat circular in that the scoring is a reflection of people's self-description, it can confirm (and perhaps clarify) the relationship of writing behaviors to more general human behaviors.

The Preference for Closure vs. Resistance to Closure

From these descriptions of one- and multi-drafters it is readily apparent that they differ in their need for closure. The one-drafters move quickly to decisions while composing, and they report that once they are done with a paper, they prefer not to look back at it, either immediately to re-read it or at some future time, to think about revising it. Ted explained that he generally is willing to do one re-reading at the time of completing a paper and sometimes to make a few wording changes, but that is all. He shrugged off the possibility of doing even a second re-reading of any of his writing once it is done because he says he can't stand to look at it again. All of the one-drafters reported that they hardly, if ever, rewrite a paper. This distaste for returning to a completed text can be the source of problems for these one-drafters. Forced by a teacher in a graduate course who wanted first drafts one week and revisions the next week, Nina explained that she deliberately resorted to "writing a bad paper" for the first submission in order to submit her "real" draft as the "revised" paper. Writing a series of drafts is clearly harder for one-drafters such as Nina than we have yet acknowledged.

These one-drafters are as reluctant to start as they are impatient to finish. Although they tend to delay the drafting process, this does not apply to their preparation which often starts well in advance and is the "interesting" or "enjoyable" part for them. With writing that produces few surprises or discoveries for any of them because the generative process precedes transcription, drafting on paper is more "tedious" (a word they frequently used during their interviews) than for other writers. Said Ted, "Writing is something I have to do, not something I want to do." Even Jackie, who allows for some revising while drafting in order to develop the details of her plan, reported that she has a hard time going back to revise a paper once it is completed. She, like the others, reported a sense of feeling the paper is over and done with. "Done, dead and done, done, finished, done," concluded another of these one-drafters.

On the other hand, the multi-drafters observed in this study explained that they are never done with a paper. They can easily and willingly go back to it or to keep writing indefinitely. Asked when they know they are finished, Bill and Pam explained that they never feel they are "done" with a piece of discourse, merely that they have to stop in order to meet a deadline. As Pam said, she never gets to a last draft and doesn't care about producing "neat packages." Understandably, she has trouble with conclusions and with "wrapping up" at the end of a piece of discourse. Asked how pervasive her redrafting is for all of her writing, Pam commented that she writes informal letters to parents and friends every day and is getting to the point that she doesn't rewrite these letters as much. Bill too noted that he fights against products and hates to finish. As a result, both Bill and Pam often fail to meet their deadlines. Cindy, bored by her "journalistic one-draft writing," expressed a strong desire to return to some of her previously completed papers in order to rewrite them.

Writer-Based vs. Reader-Based Early Drafts

One way of distinguishing the early drafts produced by the multi-drafters for this study from the drafts produced by the one-drafters is to draw upon Linda Flower's distinction between Writer-Based and Reader-Based prose. Writer-Based prose, explains Flower, is "verbal expression written by a writer to himself and for himself. It is the working of his own verbal thought. In its *structure,* Writer-Based prose reflects the associative, narrative path of the writer's own confrontation with her subject" (19–20). Reader-Based prose, on the other hand, is "a deliberate attempt to communicate something to a reader. To do that it creates a shared language and shared context between writer and reader. It also offers the reader an issue-oriented rhetorical structure rather than a replay of the writer's discovery process" (20). Although Flower acknowledges that Writer-Based prose is a "problem" that composition courses are designed to correct, she also affirms its usefulness as a search tool, a strategy for handling the difficulty of attending to multiple complex tasks simultaneously. Writer-Based prose needs to be revised into Reader-Based prose, but it can be effective as a "medium for thinking." And for the multi-drafters observed in this study, characterizing the initial drafts of two of the multi-drafters as Writer-Based helps to see how their early drafts differ from those of the one-drafters.

One feature of Writer-Based prose, as offered by Flower, is that it reflects the writer's method of searching by means of surveying what she knows, often in a narrative manner. Information tends to be structured as a narrative of the discovery process or as a survey of the data in the writer's mind. Reader-Based prose, on the other hand, restructures the information so that it is accessible to the reader. Both the protocols and the written drafts produced by the two confirmed multi-drafters, Bill and Pam, reveal this Writer-Based orientation as their initial way into writing. Bill very clearly began with a memory search through his own experience, made some brief notes, and then wrote a narrative as his first sentence in response to the request that he describe to an academic counselor the skills needed for his field: "I went through what must have been a million different majors before I wound up in English and it was actually my first choice." Pam spent the hour exploring the appropriateness of the term "skills."

In distinct contrast, all four of the one-drafters began by constructing a conceptual framework for the response they would write, most typically by defining a few categories or headings which would be the focus or main point of the paper.

With a few words in mind that indicated his major points. Ted then moved on to ask himself who would be reading his response, what the context would be, and what format the writing would use. He moved quickly from a search for a point to considerations of how his audience would use his information. Similarly, Amy rather promptly chose a few terms, decided to herself that "that'll be the focus," and then said, "OK, I'm trying to get into a role here. I'm responding to someone who ... This is not something they are going to give out to people. But they're going to read it and compile responses, put something together for themselves." She then began writing her draft and completed it within the hour. Asked what constraints and concerns she is most aware of when actually writing, Amy said that she is generally concerned with clarity for the reader. The point of contrast here is that the search process was both different in kind and longer for the multi-drafters. Initially, their time was spent discovering what they think about the subject, whereas the one-drafters chose a framework within a few minutes and moved on to orient their writing to their readers. Because the transformation or reworking of text comes later for the multi-drafters, rewriting is a necessary component of their writing. The standard bit of advice, about writing the introductory paragraph later, would be a necessary step for them but would not be a productive or appropriate strategy for one-drafters to try. For the one-drafters, the introductory paragraph is the appropriate starting point. In fact, given what they said about the necessity of knowing their focus beforehand, the introductory paragraph is not merely appropriate but necessary.

Because the early stages of a piece of writing are, for multi-drafters, so intricately bound up with mental searching, surveying, and discovering, the writing that is produced is not oriented to the reader. For their early drafts, Bill and Pam both acknowledged that their writing is not yet understandable to others. When Pam commented that in her early drafts, "the reader can't yet see where I'm going," she sighed over the difficulties this had caused in trying to work with her Master's thesis committee. If some writers' early drafts are so personal and so unlikely to be accessible to readers, it is worth speculating about how effective peer editing sessions could be for such multi-drafters who appear in classrooms with "rough drafts" as instructed.

Conclusions

One way to summarize the characteristics of one- and multi-drafters is to consider what they gain by being one-drafters and at what cost they gain these advantages. Clearly, one-drafters are efficient writers. This efficiency is achieved by mentally revising beforehand, by generating options verbally rather than on paper, by generating only a limited number of options before settling on one and getting on with the task, and by doing little or no re-reading. They are able to pace themselves and can probably perform comfortably in situations such as the workplace or in in-class writing where it is advantageous to produce first-draft, final-draft pieces of discourse. Their drafts are readily accessible to readers, and they can expend effort early on in polishing the text for greater clarity. But at what cost? One-drafters are obviously in danger of cutting themselves off from further exploration, from a richer field of discovery than is possible during the time in which they generate options. When they exhibit a willingness to settle on one of their options, they may thereby have eliminated the possibility of searching for a better one. In their impatience to move on, they may even settle on options they know could be improved on. Their impulse to write dwindles as these writers experience little or none of the excitement of discovery or exploration during writing. The interesting portion of a writing task, the struggle with text and sense of exploration, is largely completed when they begin to commit themselves to paper (or computer screen). Because they are less likely to enjoy writing, the task of starting is more likely to be put off to the last minute and to become a stressful situation, thus reinforcing their inclination not to re-read and their desire to be done and to put the paper behind them forever once they have finished. And it appears that it is as hard for true one-drafters to suspend the need for closure as it is for multi-drafters to reach quick decisions and push themselves rapidly toward closure.

Multi-drafters appear to be the flip side of the same coin. Their relative inefficiency causes them to miss deadlines, to create Writer-Based first drafts, to produce large quantities of text that is discarded, and to get lost in their own writing. They need to re-read and re-draft, and they probably appear at first glance to be poorer writers than one-drafters. But they are more likely to be writers who will plunge in eagerly, will write and re-write, and will use writing to explore widely and richly. They also are more likely to affirm the value of writing as a heuristic, the merits of freewriting, and the need for cutting and pasting of text. They may, if statistics are gathered, be the writers who benefit most from collaborative discussions such as those in writing labs with tutors. Their drafts are truly amenable to change and available for re-working.

Implications

Acknowledging the reality of one- and multi-drafting involves enlarging both our perspectives on revision and our instructional practices with students. In terms of what the reality of one-drafting and multi-drafting tells us about revision, it is apparent that we need to account for this diversity of revision behaviors as we construct a more detailed picture of revision. As Stephen Witte notes, "revising research that limits itself to examining changes in written text or drafts espouses a reductionist view of revising as a stage in a linear sequence of stages" ("Revising" 266). Revision can and does occur when writers set goals, create plans, and compose pre-text, as well as when they transcribe and re-draft after transcription. Revision can be triggered by cognitive activity alone and/or by interaction with text; and attitudes, preferences, and cognitive make-up play a role in when and how much a writer revises—or is willing to revise—a text.

Yet, while recognizing the many dimensions to be explored in understanding revision, we can also use this diversity as a source for helping students with different types of problems and concerns. For students who are one-drafters or have tendencies toward single drafting, we need to provide help in several areas. They'll have to learn to do more reviewing of written text both as they write and afterwards, in order to evaluate and revise. They will also need to be aware that they should have strategies that provide for more exploration and invention than they may presently allow themselves. While acknowledging their distaste for returning to a draft to open it up again, we also need to help them see how and when this can be productive. Moreover, we can provide assistance in helping one-drafters and other writers who cluster near that end of the spectrum recognize that sometimes they have a preference for choosing an option even after they recognize that it may not be the best one. When Tim, one of the one-drafters I observed, noted at one point in his protocol that he should take a different direction for one of his paragraphs but won't, he shows similarities to another writer, David, observed by Witte ("Pre-Text and Composing" 406), who is reluctant to spend more than fifteen seconds reworking a sentence in pre-text, even though he demonstrates the ability to evoke criteria that could lead to better formulations if he chose to stop and revise mentally (David typically does little revision of written text). This impatience, this need to keep moving along, that does not always allow for the production of good text, can obviously work against producing good text, and it is unlikely that such writers will either recognize or conquer the problem on their own. They may have snared themselves in their own vicious circles if their tendency to procrastinate puts them in a deadline crunch, which, in turn, does not afford them the luxury of time to consider new options. Such behaviors can become a composing habit so entrenched that it is no longer noticed.

As we work with one-drafters, we will also have to learn ourselves how to distinguish them from writers who see themselves as one-drafters because they are not inclined, for one reason or another, to expend more energy on drafting. Inertia, lack of motivation, lack of information about what multiple drafts can do, higher priorities for other tasks, and so on are not characteristic of true one-drafters, and we must be able to identify the writer who might take refuge behind a label of "one-drafter" from the writer who exhibits some or many of the characteristics of one-draft composing and who wants to become a better writer. For example, in our writing lab I have worked with students who think they are one-drafters because of assorted fears, anxieties, and misinformation. "But I have to get it right the first time." "My teachers never liked to see scratching out on the paper, even when we wrote in class," or "I hate making choices, so I go with what I have" are not the comments of true one-drafters.

With multiple-drafters we have other work to do. To become more efficient writers, they will need to become more proficient planners and creators of pre-text, though given their heavy dependence on seeing what they have written, they will probably still rely a great deal on reading and working with their transcribed text. They will also need to become more proficient at times at focusing on a topic quickly, recognizing the difficulties involved in agonizing endlessly over possibilities. In the words of a reviewer of this paper, they will have to learn when and how "to get on with it."

Besides assisting with these strategies, we can help students become more aware of their composing behaviors. We can assist multi-drafters in recognizing that they are not slow or inept writers but writers who may linger too long over making choices. For writers who have difficulty returning to a completed text in order to revise, we can relate the problem to the larger picture, an impatience with returning to any completed task. Granted, this is not a giant leap forward, but too many students are willing to throw in the towel with writing skills in particular without recognizing the link to their more general orientations to life. Similarly, the impatient writer who, like Ted, proclaims to have a virulent case of the "I-hate-to-write" syndrome may be a competent one-drafter (or have a preference for fewer drafts) who needs to see that it is the transcribing stage of writing that is the source of the impatience, procrastination, and irritation. On the other hand, writers more inclined to be multi-drafters need to recognize that their frustration, self-criticism, and/or low grades may be due to having readers intervene at too early a stage in the drafting. What I am suggesting here is that some writers unknowingly get themselves caught in linguistic traps. They think they are making generalizations about the whole act of "writing," that blanket term for all the processes involved, when they may well be voicing problems or attitudes about one or another of the processes. What is needed here is some assistance in helping students define their problems more precisely. To do this, classroom teachers can open conferences like a writing lab tutorial, by asking questions about the student's writing processes and difficulties.

In addition to individualizing our work with students, we can also look at our own teaching practices. When we offer classroom strategies and heuristics, we need to remind our students that it is likely that some will be very inappropriate for different students. Being unable to freewrite is not necessarily a sign of an inept writer. One writer's written text may be just as effective a heuristic for that writer as the planning sheets are for another writer. Beyond these strategies and acknowledgments, we have to examine how we talk about or teach composing processes. There is a very real danger in imposing a single, "ideal" composing style on students, as Jack Selzer found teachers attempting to do in his survey of the literature. Similarly, as Susan McLeod notes, teachers tend to teach their own composing behaviors in the classroom and are thus in danger either of imposing their redrafting approaches on students whose preference for revising prior to transcribing serves them well or of touting their one- or few-draft strategies to students who fare better when interacting with their transcribed text. Imposing personal preferences, observes McLeod, would put us in the peculiar position of trying to fix something that isn't broken. And there's enough of that going around as is.

Works Cited

Axelrod, Rise B., and Charles R. Cooper. *The St. Martin's Guide to Writing*. New York: St. Martin's, 1985.

Bartholomae, David. "Against the Grain." Waldrep 1:19–29.

Beach, Richard. "Self-Evaluation Strategies of Extensive Revisers and Non-revisers." *College Composition and Communication* 27 (1976): 160–64.

Blau, Sheridan. "Invisible Writing: Investigating Cognitive Processes in Composition." *College Composition and Communication* 34 (1983): 297–312.

Bloom, Lynn Z. "How I Write." Waldrep 1:31–37.

Bridwell, Lillian S. "Revising Strategies in Twelfth Grade Students' Transactional Writing." *Research in the Teaching of English* 14 (1980): 197–222.

Budner, S. "Intolerance of Ambiguity as a Personality Variable." *Journal of Personality* 30 (1962): 29–50.

Faigley, Lester, and Stephen Witte. "Analyzing Revision." *College Composition and Communication* 32 (1981): 400–14.

Flower, Linda. "Writer-Based Prose: A Cognitive Basis for Problems in Writing." *College English* 41 (1979): 19–37.

Flower, Linda, John R. Hayes, Linda Carey, Karen Shriver, and James Stratman. "Detection, Diagnosis, and the Strategies of Revision." *College Composition and Communication* 37 (1986): 16–55.

Freedman, Sarah Warshauer, Anne Haas Dyson, Linda Flower, and Wallace Chafe. *Research in Writing: Past, Present, and Future*. Technical Report No. 1. Center for the Study of Writing. Berkeley: University of California, 1987.

Frenkel-Brunswick, Else. "Intolerance of Ambiguity as an Emotional and Perceptual Personality Variable." *Journal of Personality* 18 (1949): 108–43.

Gere, Ann Ruggles. "Insights from the Blind: Composing Without Revising." *Revising: New Essays for Teachers of Writing*. Ed. Ronald Sudol. Urbana, IL: ERIC/NCTE, 1982, 52–70.

Hairston, Maxine. "Different Products, Different Processes: A Theory about Writing." *College Composition and Communication* 37 (1986): 442–52.

Henley, Joan. "A Revisionist View of Revision." *Washington English Journal* 8.2 (1986): 5–7.

Jensen, George, and John DiTiberio. "Personality and Individual Writing Processes." *College Composition and Communication* 35 (1984): 285–300.

Lutz, William. "How I Write." Waldrep 1:183–88.

McLeod, Susan. "The New Orthodoxy: Rethinking the Process Approach." *Freshman English News* 14.3 (1986): 16–21.

Murray, Patricia Y. "Doing Writing." Waldrep 1:225–39.

Reid, Joy. "The Radical Outliner and the Radical Brainstormer: A Perspective on Composing Processes." *TESOL Quarterly* 18 (1985): 529–34.

Selzer, Jack. "Exploring Options in Composing." *College Composition and Communication* 35 (1984): 276–84.

Sommers, Nancy. "Revision Strategies of Student Writers and Experienced Adult Writers." *College Composition and Communication* 31 (1980): 378–88.

Waldrep, Tom, ed. *Writers on Writing*. Vol. 1, New York: Random House, 1985. 2 vols.

Witte, Stephen P. "Pre-Text and Composing." *College Composition and Communication* 38 (1987): 397–425.

_____. "Revising, Composing Theory, and Research Design." *The Acquisition of Written Language: Response and Revision*. Ed. Sarah Warshauer Freedman. Norwood, NJ: Ablex, 1985, 250–84.

2

Invention

Irene L. Clark

This chapter presents an overview of invention, tracing its origins in classical rhetoric and discussing a number of invention strategies, both formal and informal, that prospective teachers can practice in their own writing and then adapt for their students.

"I don't know what the teacher wants."
"I'm totally confused by this assignment."
"I can't think of anything to write about."

These are statements that students often make when they receive a writing assignment. Sometimes they are so anxious about their writing that they will even put off thinking about the assignment until the night before the paper is due, procrastination compounding anxiety. Then they will stay up all night, staring at a blank screen, tossing unsatisfactory drafts into an already overflowing waste basket, and still not be able to write anything they are proud to submit. Or they may manage to write a draft or part of a draft but then discover that it doesn't fulfill the requirements of the assignment because they didn't engage with it seriously. Because students often experience problems with generating ideas, developing effective invention strategies is an important part of the writing class.

As a concept in composition, "invention" refers to the process writers use to search for, discover, create, or "invent" material for a piece of writing. Invention can (and usually does) occur throughout the writing process, but when it happens before a writer has produced any actual piece of text, the process is sometimes called "prewriting." Invention can be both a conscious and unconscious process, and for a few writers, it seems to happen effortlessly, involving little more than thinking about the topic and jotting down scraps of inspiration. But for most writers, generating ideas, particularly for a topic that has been assigned and about which they haven't thought much about, involves considerable effort, often accompanied by stress. Even people who write frequently in their professional lives say that they have at least some difficulty with invention, and for students, who have had little experience with the composing process and who often don't allow sufficient time for ideas to percolate, a writing assignment can be formidable.

This chapter presents a brief overview of invention, focusing on its origins in classical rhetoric, and discusses a number of invention strategies, both informal and formal. Although some writers may be suspicious of formalized invention strategies, finding them artificial, limiting, and perhaps a bit mechanistic, students frequently find them helpful, particularly those who have experienced problems in completing writing assignments. The discussion will be framed in the context of the following questions:

1. How does invention reflect its heritage in classical rhetoric?
2. What controversies are associated with the concept of invention?
3. Why do people experience writing block?
4. What strategies of invention are useful in the writing class?

THE HERITAGE OF INVENTION

In considering the role of invention in the writing process, both as a writer and prospective teacher, it is important to understand the following concepts:

1. Current approaches to and debates about invention have their roots in the past, particularly in classical rhetoric.
2. What is deemed an "appropriate" subject is strongly influenced by societal values.
3. The process of invention is strongly influenced by the subject and rhetorical situation being addressed.

For invention to occur, a writer must have the capacity to invent, that is, he or she must have a store of experience and/or knowledge that is sufficient enough to generate ideas, either through the imagination or a quest for information. This statement seems self-evident, but it raises the question of how writers develop this capacity and what should be done in the writing class to aid in the process. Does any person, simply on the basis of being human, have the ability to invent material for a piece of writing? Or is invention the province of only highly educated, intelligent, or imaginative people?

Debate on this issue has occurred for a long time and has implications for how writers should be educated and for how writing should be approached in the classroom..

Robert Connors (1987), in his article "Personal Writing Assignments," notes that throughout the history of rhetoric, a true "rhetor' (anyone who composes discourse that is intended to affect community thinking or events) was supposed to know everything, so as to be able to write on any possible subject. Cicero (106–43 B.C.) in *De Oratore* (1942) asserted that "no one can be an absolutely perfect orator unless he has acquired a knowledge of all important subjects and arts" (I, 4, 20), and Quintillian (35–95 A.D.), although not stating this idea so forcefully, nevertheless, in *Institutio Oratorio* (1920), recommends a complete literary and philosophical education as preparatory to the learning of rhetoric, "for there is nothing which may not crop up in a cause or appear as a question for discussion" (II, 21, 22). Thus, one position in the debate about invention maintains that, to have anything worthwhile to say, speakers or writers must be highly educated and possess such a wealth of knowledge that ideas will flow from them as easily and effortlessly as water in a stream.

On the other hand, more practical or realistic rhetoricians recognized that although it might be desirable for writers and speakers to be so broadly educated, in actuality, this level of knowledge is impossible for most people to acquire. Epitomized in the works of Aristotle, this more realistic and practical approach acknowledges that many writers and speakers need specific invention strategies to investigate a subject and generate ideas. According to Aristotle's perspective, potential writers and orators can prepare by familiarizing themselves with argumentative approaches and text structures that will enable them to respond to any rhetorical situation.

Another debatable issue addressed during classical times concerns the question of where ideas come from, a question that is of interest today as well. Are ideas "created" through the active mind, and generated, fresh and new from within? Or are ideas "out there," waiting to be discovered? In the ancient world, the term "invent" was almost synonymous with "discover," and the focus was on where ideas could be discovered. Tracing the origins of this issue, W. Ross Winterowd points out that the concept of invention took two directions, one associated with Plato, the other with Aristotle, and he refers to this split as "the idealist-empiricist dialectic" (Winterowd & Blum, p. 2). For Plato (428 B.C.–348 B.C.), ideas existed independently and were available through the mind, the goal of invention being the discovery of truth obtained through an inner-directed search. But for Aristotle, ideas were "out there," waiting to be discovered, their purpose being to convince an audience of the persuasiveness of a concept of belief. Winterowd maintained that Plato's conception of ideas as being "inner directed" was the source of the "transcendental tradition," which provided the basis for the romantic view of composing associated with Peter Elbow and Donald Murray, whereas Aristotle was the founder of the "empirical tradition."

| **FOR WRITING AND DISCUSSION** |

Briefly describe the invention strategies you use to generate ideas for assigned essays, indicating the extent to which you are satisfied with the process you use. How do you feel about teaching students particular invention strategies? Share your response in small groups.

Invention in Classical Rhetoric

Historians usually locate the classical period in rhetoric from the 5th century B.C. to around the 5th century A.D., the period that saw the flowering of rhetorical scholarship in Athens and Rome. To clarify a few terms, the word "rhetoric" does not refer to empty or deceptive words, as a modern reader might think; rather, it refers to the art that helps people compose effective discourse. For ancient rhetoricians, rhetoric was an important means of helping "people to choose the best course of action when they disagreed about political, religious, or social issues" (Crowley, 1994, p. 1), and "invention" (*heuresis* in Greek, *inventio* in Latin) was a significant division of rhetoric. It referred to the means of discovering possible arguments, providing "speakers and writers with sets of instructions to help them find and compose proofs appropriate for any rhetorical situation" (Crowley, 1990, p. 30). The word "invenire" meant "to find" or "to come upon" in Latin, and the Greek equivalent, "heuriskein," also meant "to find out" or "discover," a word that has given us "heuristic," which means "an aid to discovery." To Plato and Aristotle, "rhetoric" was oriented toward the construction of "proofs"—that is, any statement or statements that could be used to persuade an audience to think or act in a certain way, because ancient rhetoricians were concerned primarily with persuasion. Those studying rhetoric at that time became familiar with many invention strategies, which they could then apply to any rhetorical situation that arose. Usually those situations occurred in a public context, growing out of the life of the community.

The idea of community was inextricably linked to invention in the ancient world because knowledge was located in communal learning. In fact, according to rhetorical theorist Sharon Crowley, the idea that knowledge exists outside of people and has to be taken in or absorbed and then transferred to others by speaking and writing is a modern one. Ancient rhetoricians defined knowledge as the collected wisdom of those who are knowledgeable. Thus, they would have had difficulty understanding the problem students have with finding something to write about, because they assumed that anyone who wanted to compose would have had a clear reason for doing so. They would not be grappling with a topic such as "The Problem With My Roommate" or "Describe a Moment When You Learned Something About Yourself." Rather, they would be addressing issues of public interest that had generated some disagreement or dispute.

In ancient Greece, the need to train orators gave rise to two traditions: the techne, which prescribed how to structure an oration, and the sophistic, which "offered set speeches that students of oratory could memorize, analyze, and imitate" (Covino & Jolliffe 1995, p. 39). Plato questioned both of these traditions as being too mechanistic and not sufficiently concerned with the discovery of truth, which he saw as absolute. Plato had this same criticism of a group known as the "sophists," who conceived of "rhetoric as epistemic, that is, as an art that creates rather than reflects knowledge" (Covino & Jolliffe [1995], p. 84). Plato distrusted the sophists for believing in the relativity of truth and for being manipulators of language; he was concerned that the linguistic facility obtained through the teaching of the sophists was a trick that could be used for ignoble purposes, such as influencing young people to believe what is false. He would, no doubt, have had great difficulty with the language of advertising.

It must be noted here, however, that although the term "sophist" today suggests a person who uses language to deceive, sophists in 5th century B.C. Athens were initially professors who "lectured on the 'new learning' in literature, science, philosophy, and especially oratory. The Sophists set up small private schools and charged their pupils a fee for what amounted in many cases to tutoring" (Corbett & Connors 1999, p. 491). In 392 B.C., Isocrates set up a school of oratory, which was apparently quite lucrative, enabling him to amass "a considerable fortune from his teaching" (Corbett & Connors 1999, p. 491). Plato, however, held the sophists in low esteem, arguing in the *Gorgias* and the *Phaedrus,* quoted in Covino and Joliffe (1995) that:

> Rhetoric could not be considered a true art because it did not rest on universal principles. Moreover, rhetoricians, like poets, were more interested in opinions, in appearances, even in lies, than in the transcendental truth that the philosopher sought. They made the "worse appear the better reason." They were mere enchanters of the soul, more interested in dazzling their audiences than in instructing. (p. 492)

These objections to those who use language to manipulate still pertain today; often we disdain the "sophistry" of politicians or advertisers.

FOR WRITING AND DISCUSSION

Plato's criticism of the sophists is based on their ability to manipulate language to suit particular audiences and situations as well as on their belief in the relativity and contingency of truth. To what extent do you agree with Plato's criticism? Consider the following questions:

1. Is it ethical to teach persuasive strategies if they can be used to manipulate?
2. Are the means of persuasion simply a *knack,* a trick of language that anyone can learn?
3. When students write an essay in which they are asked to express and support an "opinion," must they really believe what they write?
4. Is it ethical to write an essay that expresses an opinion that the author does not really hold?

Aristotle

Aristotle's *The Art of Rhetoric,* composed between 360 and 334 B.C., is an important source of information about how invention was conceived of in the ancient world. Born in 384 B.C., Aristotle went to Athens to study with Plato in 367 B.C. and then, at Plato's death in 347 B.C., stayed on as a teacher, where he eventually taught rhetoric, dividing it into five parts: invention, arrangement, style, memory, and delivery, although only the first three are considered important in the context of writing. Aristotle is associated with two important overall claims that pertain to invention: that rhetoric is an art that can be taught (thus, students can be "taught" to invent), and that subject matter can be discovered in the world. Seeking to rescue rhetoric from Plato's low opinion of it, Aristotle asserted that although individual "rhetors" (those who attempt to influence an audience through speaking or writing) might use rhetoric for unscrupulous ends, it is a skill, like a number of others, such as physical strength or the ability to decipher codes, that can be used for either noble or ignoble purposes. In fact, he argued, the study of rhetoric would enable people to understand and evaluate the quality of ideas, thereby helping them to assess their own beliefs and recognize poor or fallacious arguments.

For Aristotle, rhetoric was a system that enabled a "rhetor" to perceive the available means of persuasion or "proofs" (pisteis), which he classified as either "artistic" or "non-artistic." As Corbett and Connors (1999) explained:

> Non-artistic proofs are unimportant to the concept of invention because they consisted of appeals to physical evidence, such as contracts or testimony. These are not invented by the speaker because they involve the interpretation of already existing material such as "laws, witnesses, contracts, tortures, oaths. Apparently, the lawyer pleading a case in court made most use of this kind of proof, but the politician or the panegyrist could use them too. (p. 18)

However, "artistic" proofs (called "artistic" because they are part of the "art" of rhetoric) could be discovered, and these constituted the subject matter of *The Art of Rhetoric,* which focused on three types of artistic proofs or appeals which still have validity today. The first was *ethos*, usually translated as the character of the speaker as it comes across in a speech. According to Covino and Jolliffe (1995), "theorists in ancient Greece and Rome did not agree among themselves whether ethos exists solely in the text a *rhetor* creates, or whether the *rhetor* must evince *ethos* in his or her life as well as in his or her texts" (p. 15). But Aristotle believed that "a rhetor could not depend . . . on the audience's knowing more about the rhetor's ethos than the text itself established" (Covino & Joliffe, p. 15). In other words, the text must speak for itself—that is, it must demonstrate that the rhetor is a person of good sense, virtue, and will. In the context of the composition class, *ethos* refers to a writer rather than a speaker, but the principle is the same, because a writer who has established trustworthiness and good will in a text will be more convincing than one who has not. All of us are more likely to accept another person's ideas if we think of that person as knowledgeable, trustworthy, logical, and fair, as opposed to ignorant, untrustworthy, illogical, and biased.

The second type of proof Aristotle discussed was *pathos*, which is sometimes called the emotional or pathetic appeal. The main idea behind pathos was that an effective discourse will appeal to or move an audience, and Aristotle's (333 B.C.) *Rhetoric* contains a list of emotions that could be used for this purpose, such as pity, fear, indignation, or anger. Aristotle also categorized potential audiences into character types such as the young, the old, aristocrats, and the wealthy, assigning various emotions to each character type. This type of appeal also has relevance to the composition class, in that an effective text will take into consideration what is likely to move an intended audience. Moreover, a consideration of audience can serve as an effective invention strategy that can aid in discovery. Later in this chapter, I will discuss an audience-based invention strategy that can be useful in the classroom.

Aristotle's third and most important proof was *logos*, the appeal to reason, which in ancient Greece did not refer simply to logic, but rather to "thought plus action." As Covino and Jolliffe (1995) explained, "just as *ethos* moves an audience by activating their faith in the credibility of the rhetor and *pathos* stimulates their feelings and seeks a change in their attitudes and actions, so *logos*, accompanied by the other two appeals, mobilizes the powers of reasoning." (p. 17)

The Topoi

In addition to discussing the types of proofs that can be used to develop a more persuasive text, Aristotle also referred to places in the memory, or topoi, where ideas can be stored and retrieved. These topoi can be considered types of argumentative strategies and reasons that can be useful in various rhetorical situations, and his idea was for orators to ask themselves questions that the topoi generated, thereby developing content. The most frequently used and most usable topics deriving from Aristotle's system are definition, comparison, cause-and-effect, and authority. Aristotle was the first rhetorician to introduce the topics, but others such as Cicero and Quintilian developed them further, often describing "the places as though they were hidden away." Quintilian (1994), for example, defined the topoi as "the secret places where arguments reside and from which they must be drawn forth." (p. 50)

It must be clarified here, however, that the word "topic" as it was conceived of in ancient times, is not synonymous with the way in which the term is used today. When a teacher asks a class to list "topics" they would like to write about, he or she means a subject, drawn either from books, general knowledge, or personal experience. Ancient rhetoricians, however, thought of topics as existing in "the structures of language or in the issues that concerned the community. That is why they were called common places—they were available to anyone who spoke or wrote the language in which they were couched and who was reasonably familiar with the ethical and political discussions taking place in the community" (Crowley, *Ancient Rhetorics* [1994], p. 50).

Emphasis on Community in Classical Rhetoric

Classical invention was directed outward, based almost entirely on logos, rather than on ethos, concerned with the community, and focused on questions that were of concern to all members of society. As Connors (1987) phrases it:

> Rhetorical exercises mirrored the classical belief that the world—the brute facts of it, the doings of the persons in it, the nature of their feelings, judgments, beliefs—was the grist for the mill of rhetoric. From the earliest age, students were to be trained to see the world, to know what has been thought and said about it, and to hammer that knowledge into discourse that could change it. (p. 167)

THE HERITAGE OF PERSONAL WRITING

Given the public orientation of classical rhetoric, argument that was based on personal opinion or that used personal experience as its main subject was considered self-centered and unconvincing. Yet many composition classrooms today focus on, or at least include, assignments concerned with personal writing, invention being directed toward individual recollection, feeling, and opinion. Given the emphasis on argumentation and corresponding de-emphasis on personal opinion in classical and neo-classical rhetoric, how did personal writing gain such a position of importance in the writing class today?

Connors (1987) traced the beginnings of this trend to the 17th century, in which the individual—personal tastes, feelings, experiences—began to be considered important to public life, epitomized in the "rise of novels, books of personal essays, travel books, realistic narrative and overly personal poems" (p. 169). This emphasis on the individual gained importance in the latter part of the 18th and early 19th centuries, with the shift from a classical outlook to a romantic one, with the individual writer beginning to occupy a position of greater prominence in education. The focus of George Campbell's *The Philosophy of Rhetoric* (1776), was on the thoughts and perceptions of the individual, and, according to Winterowd and Blum (1994), "moved invention to the ivory tower of the individual mind" (p. 20), placing a new emphasis on creativity (genius, imagination, fancy). Invention in this context did not mean "discovering" content; it meant "creating" something completely new. Sharon Crowley (1990, p. 32) noted that with the publication of Campbell's *The Philosophy of Rhetoric* (1776), "for the first time in the history of rhetoric, the inventional process was focused solely on the individual creative mind of a rhetor working in relative isolation." This tendency was further emphasized in the writing of Hugh Blair, whose influential Lectures on Rhetorical and Belles Lettres (1783) focused attention on individual understanding as the goal of knowledge, culminating in the development of creativity and taste. The dissemination of what Winterowd referred to as "romantic rhetoric" thus resulted in the exaltation of self-expression, and the privileging of imagination and inspiration over invention.

Personal Writing in the Early Phase of the Process Movement

Emphasis on the personal also characterized the initial phase of the process movement of the 1960s and 1970s, when the need to provide "at-risk" student populations with successful writing experiences led to an emphasis on simple writing assignments concerned with topics with which students were presumably familiar—that is, assignments concerned with their own lives. An important goal at this time was to enable students to develop self-confidence by accessing their own personal voice and to validate their experiences. As expressed by Ken Macrorie (1970) in *Telling Writing:*

> The New English Movement has begun. . . . The program gives the student first, freedom, to find his voice and let his subjects find him; and second, discipline, to learn more professional craft to supplement his already considerable language skills. (Preface, pp. vii–viii)

In this context, personal topics were considered more relevant than academic ones, enabling students to write about what they know so that they could focus on the "craft" of writing.

STRATEGIES OF INVENTION

Whether the emphasis on personal writing during the early phases of the process movement was really helpful to at-risk students can be debated, but, certainly, scholars of that time devoted significant attention to invention, considerably more than they do today. Ken Macrorie and Peter Elbow emphasized the importance of freewriting as a means of helping students find a voice in writing. Janice Lauer (1970) in "Heuristics and Composition," set up criteria for judging the effectiveness of heuristic procedures, which, she maintains, have both generative and evaluative powers. Such procedures, she emphasizes, must be distinguished both from trial and error methods, which are non-systematic and, hence, inefficient, and from rule-governed procedures, which are overly rigorous. Lauer's article also establishes the criteria of transcendency, flexibility, and generative capacity for judging the effectiveness of a heuristic procedure. Translated into questions, these characteristics may be perceived as follows:

1. Transcendency
   How can writers transfer this model's questions or operations from one subject to another?
2. Flexible Order
   Is the model flexible so that a thinker can return to a previous step or skip to an inviting one as the evolving idea suggests?
3. Generative Capacity
   Is the model generative so that it involves the writer in various operations—such as visualizing, classifying, defining, rearranging, and dividing?

Lauer's attempt to develop useful strategies for composition students, however, was criticized by Ann Berthoff (1971) who condemned heuristics as being overly mechanical in an article titled "The Problem of Problem Solving." Berthoff's criticism was then countered by Lauer (1972) who argued that heuristics were, by definition, open ended, not rigid, flexible, and not oriented toward finding a "right" answer.

The Lauer–Berthoff debate over heuristics is indicative of the interest in invention that characterized the process movement in the 1960s and 1970s. In "Pre-Writing: The Stage of Discovery in the Writing Process," D. Gordon Rohman (1965) claimed that engaging in prewriting enabled students to produce writing that "showed a statistically significant superiority to essays produced in control sections" (p. 112). Richard Young, Alton L. Becker, and Kenneth L. Pike (1970) in their book, *Rhetoric: Discovery and Change,* devised an elaborate invention scheme derived from tagmemic linguistics, which approached composing in terms of a complex invention strategy that requires a writer to examine a subject from nine different perspectives. The tagmemicists maintained that because people conceive of the world in terms of repeatable units that are part of a larger system, understanding those units can enable writers to investigate and, thus, generate material for a wider range of subjects. The tagmemic system is quite complicated, and only a few writers use it on a regular basis, but it became the subject of significant scholarship during the 1970s. Those who are interested in this approach to invention can find additional information in the following publications.

FOR FURTHER EXPLORATION

Kenupper, C. W. (1980). Revising the tagmemics heuristic: Theoretical and pedagogical consideration. *CCC, 3,* 161–167.

Odell, L. (1978). Another look at tagmemic theory: A response to James Kinney. *CCC, 29,* 146–152.

Young, R. E., & Becker, A. L. "Toward a modern theory of rhetoric: A tagmemic contribution. *Harvard Education Review, 35,* 50–68.

WRITER'S BLOCK[1]

Because the initial phase of the process movement focused on the needs of marginalized, at-risk student writers, scholarly attention at that time addressed the problem of writer's block, a phenomenon that occurs when writers are unable to generate material for a text, even when they possess the necessary skill and desire to do so. Writer's block has come to be recognized as extremely common, not only among students, but also among professional writers and acclaimed authors. In fact, Mike Rose (1984) began his ground-breaking, *Writer's Block: The Cognitive Dimension,* with a quotation from Flaubert that describes the agony of staying "a whole day with your head in your hands, trying to squeeze your unfortunate brain so as to find a word." Rose's study suggested that at least "10% of college students block frequently, and the boom of 'writer's block' workshops stands as a reminder

---

[1]Some of the material on writer's block is also discussed in Irene L. Clark. *Writing in the Center,* 3rd Edition. Dubuque, IA: Kendall Hunt, 1998.

that writer's block is a problem outside of the classroom as well" (p. 1). Rose (1984) cites the following factors as contributing to writer's block:

1. The rules by which students guide their composing processes are rigid, inappropriately invoked, or incorrect.
2. Their assumptions about composing are misleading.
3. They edit too early in the composing process.
4. They lack appropriate planning and discourse strategies or rely on inflexible or inappropriate strategies.
5. They invoke conflicting rules, assumptions, plans, and strategies.
6. They evaluate their writing with inappropriate criteria or criteria that are inadequately understood.

Rose maintained that students who block seem to be depending on rules and plans that impede rather than aid the composing process. He cited the example of "Ruth," who believed that every sentence she wrote had to come out grammatically correct the first time around. This belief led Ruth to edit each sentence before she proceeded to the next, thus closing off the flow of ideas. Another example was "Martha," who spent days developing a complex plan for her paper, leaving her little time to actually write.

In terms of invention, Rose asserted that people who suffer from writer's block are more likely to generate material if the strategies they use are well-structured. Nonstructured techniques, such as freewriting and brainstorming, can be useful, Rose (1984) maintained; however, the resulting morass of ideas "can sometimes lead to more disorder than order, more confusing divergence than clarifying focus" (p. 91).

Another work concerned with writer's block that was prominent during the early days of the process movement was James Adams' *Conceptual Block-busting* (1974), which suggested that most of us, but particularly anxiety-ridden students, are prevented from exploring ideas freely because of emotional blocks that inhibit us from doing so. A few of these blocks contribute to the problem students have in generating ideas for papers, in particular:

1. **The fear of taking a risk.** Adams pointed out that because most of us have grown up rewarded when we produced the "right answer" and punished when we made a mistake, we tend to avoid risk whenever possible. Yet exploring ideas for papers means taking risks, to some extent. To come up with anything new means considering, at least for a short time, a notion that has not been mentioned before, a notion that one may later reject as inappropriate in some way. Because students fear the rejection associated with risk taking, they are often unable to entertain new ideas and will reject even a glimmer of

creative thought, which may prove to be unsuitable and subject them to ridicule.

2. **No appetite for chaos.** Because the fear of making a mistake is rooted in insecurity, most of us tend to avoid ambiguity whenever possible, opting for safety over uncertainty, a condition Adams (1974) referred to as "having no appetite for chaos." Thus, because they are uncomfortable with the "chaos" that characterizes the stage in the writing process that exists before one generates an idea or focuses a topic, many students reach for order before they have given the topic sufficient exploration. Thus, they find themselves "stuck" with dead-end or uninteresting topics.

3. **Preference for judging, rather than generating ideas.** This emotional block, according to Adams, also has its root in our preference for safety, rather than for risk, producing in students a tendency to judge an idea too early or indiscriminately. Adams (1974) stated, "If you are a compulsive idea-judger, you should realize that this is a habit that may exclude ideas from your own mind before they have had time to bear fruit" (p. 47).

4. **Inability to incubate.** There is a general agreement that the unconscious plays an important role in problem solving, and it is, therefore, important for students to give their ideas an opportunity to incubate, to wrestle with a problem over several days. Yet students often procrastinate, putting off work on their papers until the day before they are due. They often find themselves blocked before they can even get started.

5. **Lack of motivation.** Students are often asked to write about topics in which they have little interest; their motivation lies only in the grade they hope to receive. Yet, as Adams pointed out, it is unlikely that students can come up with an interesting idea for a paper if they aren't motivated, at least somewhat, by the topic.

FOR WRITING AND DISCUSSION

Write a short paper discussing rules of composing that you find most useful when you write. Include in your paper responses to the following questions:

1. What rules of writing do you think about when you compose?
2. Do any of these rules make writing more difficult for you?
3. Have you ever experienced writer's block?
4. Share your responses in small groups.

Invention and the Writing Task

In the conclusion to his study on writer's block, Rose (1984) emphasized the importance of selecting an invention strategy that is suited to the writing task. This means that the kind of essay being written (e.g., a personal essay or an academic argument) and the subject being addressed strongly determine the type of invention strategy that is most appropriate for generating material. Heuristics direct writers' attention in particular directions, encouraging them to approach a topic from one direction or perspective as opposed to another. Thus, instructors should consider the effects of using one heuristic instead of another, helping students understand their differences.

INVENTION STRATEGIES FOR THE COMPOSITION CLASSROOM

Ancient rhetoricians recognized that to "invent" material for a discourse, a rhetor had to be familiar with the subject under consideration, an idea that seems obvious. Yet in presenting assignments to students, many teachers do not seem to recognize the importance of this basic concept. Scribbling a writing assignment on the board or handing it out hastily in class, they send students home to write an essay, or, even more unrealistically, to generate an essay right on the spot. A fundamental invention concept derived from ancient rhetoricians, then, is that it is important to familiarize students with the topic they are going to be writing about, help them feel comfortable with the subject, and make sure that they understand what is expected of them. This is true whether the essay is concerned with a public controversy or with students' own personal experiences.

An Invention-Oriented Classroom Atmosphere

In introducing a writing topic in the classroom, it is helpful to foster a classroom atmosphere that invites experimentation and exploration so that students will be able to entertain possibilities without fear of ridicule or negative evaluation. To create a classroom atmosphere that is "invention-oriented," it is useful to share your own invention process with students and encourage students to try out new ideas. Assure them that everyone finds invention difficult, and help them understand that discovery of a main topic or subtopic can occur at any stage of the writing process, not only at the beginning. An important goal of the writing class is to enable students to explore new ideas—even in a half-written draft—and to investigate directions not previously considered.

An invention-oriented writing class also means stressing the importance of developing ideas *actively*. Although for some writers, "invention" means sitting at a desk and waiting for an idea to strike like a bolt of lightening, most people find it useful to explore a subject by engaging in preliminary exploratory writing activities. Such activities enable writers to assess what they already know about the subject, although there is no guarantee that something wonderful will be discovered immediately; in fact, writers often reject a significant portion of what they have written at this stage. But even if this is the case, it is likely that the process will stimulate the discovery of something that is useful or, at least, bring the realization that additional information is needed.

Helping Students Understand the Assignment

Fostering an invention-oriented atmosphere in class means that teachers should allot adequate time to helping students understand and engage with their assignments, because students don't often read assignments carefully and spend too little time thinking about them. They often wait until the night before a draft is due to examine it seriously. It is important, then, for teachers to prepare students for a writing assignment by familiarizing them with necessary background and holding relevant discussion in class. When the assignment is first distributed, the teacher should read it aloud to the class and then students should reread it on their own. They can also use the following worksheet (see Fig. 2.1), to be completed either at home or in class, to help them understand what is required.

INVENTION POSSIBILITIES
FOR THE WRITING CLASS

Unstructured Strategies for Generating Ideas
(Particularly Suitable for Personal Topics)

Class and Group Discussion

The most useful method of helping students generate ideas for a writing assignment is to have them discuss the topic in pairs, small groups, or with the whole class. Sharing ideas will enable students of all levels to engage with a topic, fostering insight that will stimulate the imagination. This is a principle that seems self-evident; yet it is often overlooked. In 1969, however, Robert Zoellner, in his article "Talk Write: A Behavioral Pedagogy for Composition," asserted that students will be able to write more clearly and expansively if they approach writing through another behavior (speaking) that has already proven at least reasonably successful. Zoellner based this

---

THINKING ABOUT YOUR ASSIGNMENT: A WORKSHEET

This worksheet will enable you to learn as much as possible about your assignment, so that you will be able to write your essay with greater insight. Follow each of the steps below, writing your response in the space provided.

1. Read the assignment aloud to yourself, paying particular attention to the place where the **writing task** is discussed.

2. List the **key terms** in the assignment that give directions.

List any terms that need to be defined.

3. Summarize in your own words the type of writing task that the assignment requires. Remember that most college writing assignments require a thesis or main point and that although you may not know yet what that thesis will be, eventually you will have to formulate one.

4. What type of information does this paper require? Will the information be based primarily on personal experience or opinion? Will you need to find information from the library or the Internet?

5. Locate any requirements of the assignment that may not be directly stated, but which are necessary in order for the assignment to be completed satisfactorily.

   Does this assignment require you to define terms? If so, which ones?

   Does this assignment require you to develop a relationship between ideas? If so, which ideas must be connected?

   Does this assignment require you to take a position on a controversial subject? If so, list two opposing views. Does this assignment require you to consider questions of degree or make a judgment (does it say "to what extent" for example)?

6. Who is the audience for this paper, aside from your teacher? What sort of knowledge about the topic do you assume your audience has?

   Respond to the following questions about audience:

   Before the people in my audience have read this paper, they are likely to have the following beliefs about this topic:

   After the people in my audience have read this paper, I would like them to have the following beliefs about this topic:

7. Why does this topic matter? Why would anyone care about it? Why is it important to think about? Are there implications or consequences that should be addressed?

8. A possible thesis or main point for this paper might be ____

FIG. 2.1.   A Worksheet for Thinking About an Assignment.

"principle of intermodal transfer" on two assumptions:

1. Students are better at talking than writing because they have had more pratice.
2. Students have the ability to improve their writing because, in trying to do so, they are already using a learned skill: talking.

Although Zoellner's ideas have not been tested rigorously, a number of years ago, George Kennedy conducted some research that suggested the validity of Zoellner's work. Kennedy divided a group of basic writers into two groups: the experimental "Speakwrites" and the control "Writeonlys," and both groups watched a film, which was used as the stimulus for a writing assignment. The Speakwrites were interviewed individually on the subject of the film and were then asked to write a 30-minute essay on a general topic generated by the film. The Writeonlys had no opportunity to discuss the film and were asked only to write the 30-minute essay. When the essays were graded by independent evaluators, the Speakwrites' essays received significantly higher scores than did the Writeonly's. Kennedy's research, therefore, highlighted the importance of "talking" to the invention process and the necessity of preparing students before they begin to write.

Journals

Journals are another unstructured source of ideas for an essay, and students often enjoy writing them. For journals to be useful to the invention process, though, it is important to explain that a journal in a composition class is not a diary of daily events, but, rather, a place for grappling with ideas or responding to readings. Students will be able to distinguish between journals and diaries if you prompt journal entries with specific questions, at least in the beginning of the class, and to ask those whose entries are particularly well developed if you might share them with other students. In my advanced writing class for teachers, If often ask students to address the following questions in their journals:

1. Describe how you usually write papers for your classes.
2. What teachers have you found particularly influential on your attitude toward writing?
3. In your own writing process, on which stage do you spend the most amount of time?
4. Describe an experience in writing paper for a class that you found particularly difficult or frustrating.
5. How did you learn to write?
6. How important is it to develop a strong personal voice in writing?

Freewriting and Brainstorming

Many students find that writing freely about a topic enables them to generate preliminary ideas about it, particularly if the topic has affected them personally. Jotting down ideas or brainstorming about a topic can thus be extremely helpful both as a classroom exercise or as a homework assignment. Images that come to mind can suggest other images, and frequently students find that they can then generate ideas that they didn't even know they had.

Clustering

Clustering is similar to freewriting and brainstorming in that its aim is to elicit as many ideas as possible. Clustering, however, enables students to group ideas visually and to see possible connections between ideas. Clustering is done as follows:

The writer places the central idea or topic in the center of the paper and circles it. Around this circled word, he or she writes other words that are associated with this central idea and puts circles around them as well. Then they write other words that are associated with these other ideas and use lines to connect them either to each other or to other words on the page. Clustering helps writers develop details and find connections that might not have been discovered otherwise.

Structured Strategies For Generating Ideas

The Points to Make List

Brainstorming is usually just the first step in generating an interesting and well-thought out essay, with ideas that go beyond the superficial. A useful invention strategy that follows brainstorming and precedes the drafting of an essay is the *Points-to-Make List,* which enables a writer to sort and narrow ideas. Although different writers do this in individual ways, most good writers will take time to write down, examine, and revise their ideas in an informal list that is not as rigid as an outline. It is also an important tool to help develop an effective rough plan and thesis statement (see Fig. 2.2).

Exploring a Topic Through Questioning

Learning to ask oneself questions about a topic is a useful invention strategy, loosely derived from Aristotelian Rhetoric. Responding to questions enables writers to reflect on experiences, facts, opinions, and values they already have about the topic, determine what they *don't* know about the topic, decide what they need to find out, and then evaluate the material they find. Several of the following strategies are based on the use of questions.

THE POINTS TO MAKE LIST[2]

Procedure:

1. Create a preliminary list:

Review your brainstorming notes and readings. It might be useful to do this with a highlighter or different-colored pen so that you can clearly mark the ideas that you think might be effective in your essay. At this stage, don't worry if you're interested in a number of different (and possibly unrelated) ideas. In fact, be as inclusive as you can. Just develop a primary list of points (ideas and/or opinions you have about this topic) and evidence (facts, examples, and quotes) that you like for your essay. Then in the space provided below, list out those points.

_____   _____

_____   _____

_____   _____

Reminder:
The above list will probably include many different kinds of ideas, some broad, some narrow, some opinions, some explanations. Don't be concerned about this variety of ideas, and don't try to jump to a thesis statement too soon. Sometimes you need to work with ideas for a while before you finally arrive at what you "really want to say." Especially be aware of the trap that many students fall into–A MERE LIST OF POINTS IS *NOT* A THESIS STATEMENT.

2. Re-read the writing task for this assignment, comparing your list to the actual question you are supposed to address. In any writing situation, you need to compare your brainstorming with the assigned task, because it is very easy to move in other directions.

3. Examine, narrow and reorder your list. Decide which points you like best, listing them below.

_____   _____

_____   _____

_____   _____

_____   _____

4. Look over your list and see if you can find a preliminary thesis statement or argument that responds to the assignment prompt. List that preliminary thesis below:

Possible Thesis:

---

[2] The Points to Make List was developed by Jack Blum at the University of Southern California.

FIG. 2.2.   The Points to Make List.

EXPLORATION QUESTIONS

(Useful for developing ideas for an essay concerned with a controversy)

1. Is there a controversy associated with this topic? If so, briefly outline the nature of the controversy.

2. What was your opinion on this controversy when you were growing up? What opinion did your family and community have on this topic?

3. How did your school experiences influence your conception of the topic? Did your teachers and classmates feel the same way about it as did your family? Were there any points of disagreement?

4. Can you think of at least two people who hold differing views about this topic? If so, describe these people and summarize what you believe were their points of view.

5. Has your opinion changed about this topic in any way? Why or why not?

6. Do you think that this topic is important for people to think about? Why or why not?

FIG. 2.3.   Exploration Questions.

Exploration Questions.   Exploration questions are useful for exploring a topic that is concerned with a controversy, one that requires the writer to develop a thesis or position (a characteristic of most college writing assignments). Responding in writing to these questions enables the writer to understand a controversy in terms of background and issue, insight that helps writers construct a point of view. A sheet that can be used for this purpose appears in Fig. 2.3.

Topical Questions.   Another questioning strategy, loosely based on Aristotle's *On Rhetoric* (1991), uses the idea of "topics" as a means of discovering material for an argument, a strategy that was developed by Edward Corbett (1981) in *The Little Rhetoric and Handbook*. Corbett's questions are listed below:

Questions about concepts.

1. How has the term been defined by others?
2. How do you define the term?
3. What other concepts have been associated with the term?
4. In what ways has this concept affected the lives of people?
5. How might this concept be changed?

Questions about a statement or proposition.

1. What must be established before a reader will believe the proposition?

2. What are the meanings of key words in the proposition?
3. By what evidence or argument can the proposition be proved or disproved?
4. What counterarguments must be confronted and refuted?
5. What are the practical consequences of the proposition?

Journalistic Questions. The five questions journalists frequently ask to generate information about a topic can be used effectively as an invention strategy. They are particularly useful in writing about a problem, a focus that characterizes a number of writing assignments, but they can also be adapted to other situations or experiences. The following are the five questions, phrased in the context of a problem.

WHAT is the problem?
WHO finds this a problem?
WHEN is this a problem?
WHERE is this a problem?
HOW can this problem be solved?

The Pentad. The author/scholar/rhetorician, Kenneth Burke, contributed many ideas to the field of rhetoric, but in terms of invention, he is best known for the strategy known as the "pentad." The pentad is a scheme for investigating pretty much anything, and, indeed, Burke regarded the field of rhetoric as inclusive of almost all human actions, defining it as "the use of language in such a way as to produce a desired impression on the reader or hearer" (1953, p. 165). Thus, Burke, like Aristotle, conceived of rhetoric in terms of audience, claiming in *The Rhetoric of Motives* (1950) that meaning always involves an element of persuasion. The pentad was first introduced in *A Grammar of Motives* (1952) as a device for analyzing literature, and, indeed, it is well suited for this purpose. However, it can also be used to investigate other subjects.

The pentad consists of five terms that can be used to "invent" material. These terms are as follows:

Act (What does it say? What happened? What sort of action is it?)
Agent (Who wrote it? Who did it? What kind of agent is it?)
Agency (How was it done? What were the methods of accomplishing it?)
Scene (Where did it happen? What background is necessary to understand? When did it happen?)
Purpose (Why did it happen? What is its purpose?)

Whatever questioning strategy you recommend to your students, it is important to demonstrate it by working with it in class on the board. Only when students have observed how an invention strategy functions—to see it in action—will they be ready to work with it on their own.

FOR WRITING AND DISCUSSION

Read Mike Rose's article at the end of this chapter, "Rigid Rules, Inflexible Plans, and the Stifling of Language: A Cognitivist Analysis of Writer's Block." This article was written in 1980, over 20 years ago, before many of the seminal ideas and approaches explored through the writing process movement had been incorporated into composition pedagogy. We are now in the beginning of a new century, and it is worth examining whether Rose's article is relevant to the writing scene today.

In this context, consider whether Rose's ideas pertain to experiences with writing that you personally have encountered, either in school or elsewhere. Discuss these ideas in small groups. Then write an essay that addresses the following question:

To what extent is Rose's position on writer's block still relevant?

In developing ideas for this assignment, work with at least one invention strategy previously described.

FOR FURTHER EXPLORATION

Coe, R. M. (1981, October). If not to narrow, then how to focus: Two techniques for focusing. *CCC, 32,* 272–277.

Connors, R., & Glenn, C. (1999). *The new St. Martin's guide to teaching writing.* Boston: Bedford/St/Martin's.

Emig, J. (1977, May). Writing as a mode of learning. *CCC, 28,* 122–128.

LeFevre, K. B. (1987). *Invention as a social act.* Carbondale: Southern Illinois University Press.

Witte, S. (1987). Pre-text and composing. *CCC, 38,* 397–425.

REFERENCES

Adams, J. L. (1974). *Conceptual Blockbusting: A pleasurable guide to better problem solving.* San Francisco, CA: W. H. Freeman.

Aristotle. (1991). *Aristotle on Rhetoric: A Theory of Civic Discourse.* Ed & trans. George A Kennedy. New York: Oxford University Press.

Aristotle. (1991). *On rhetoric: A theory of civic discourse.* (G. A. Kennedy, trans. & ed.). New York: Oxford University Press.

Berthoff, A. (1971). The problem of problem solving. *College Composition and Communication,* *22,* 237–242.

Blair, H. (1966). Lectures on Rhetoric & Belles. Lettres. H. Harding, ed. Carbondale: Southern Illinois University Press.

Burke, K. (1950). *A rhetoric of motives.* Englewood Cliffs, NJ: Prentice Hall.

Burke, K. (1952). *A grammar of motives.* Englewood Cliffs, NJ: Prentice Hall.

Burke, K. (1953). *Counterstatement.* Los Altos, CA: Hermes.

Campbell, G. (1963). *The Philosophy of Rhetoric.* Lloyd Bitzer, ed. Carbondale, Southern Illinois University Press.

Cicero. (1942). *De Oratore.* (E. W. Sutton & H. Rackham, Trans.). Cambridge, MA: Harvard UP.

Connors, R. (1987, May). Personal writing assignments. *College Composition and Communication,* *38,* 166–183.

Corbett, E. P. (1981). *The little rhetoric and handbook.* New York: John Wiley.

Corbett, E. P., & Connors, R. J. (1999). *Classical rhetoric for the modern student* (4th ed.). New York: Oxford University Press.

Covino, W. A., & Jolliffe, D. A. (1995). *Rhetoric: Concepts, definitions, boundaries.* Boston: Allyn and Bacon.

Crowley, S. (1990). *The methodica l memory: Invention in current-traditional rhetoric.* Carbondale IL: Southern Illinois University Press.

Crowley, S. (1994). *Ancient rhetorics for contemporary students.* New York: Macmillan.

Kennedy, G. E. (1983). The nature and quality of compensatory oral expression and its effects on writing in students of college composition. *Report to the National Institute of Education.* Washington State University.

Lauer, J. (1970). Heuristics and composition. *College Composition and Communication, 21,* 396–404.

Lauer, J. (1972). Response to Anne E. Berthoff, "The problem of problem solving." *College Composition and Commuication, 23,* 208–210.

Macrorie, K. (1970). *Telling writing* (4th ed.). Upper Montclair, NJ: Boynton/Cook.

Ong, W. (1975, January). The writer's audience is always a fiction. *PMLA, 90,* 9–21.

Quintillian. (1920). *Institutio oratoria.* (H. E. Butler, Trans.). Cambridge: Harvard UP.

Quintillian. (1994). Ancient rhetorics. In S. Crowley, (Ed.), *Ancient Rhetorics for Contemporary Students.* New York: Macmillan.

Rohman, D. G. (1965). Pre-writing: The stage of discovery in the writing proccess. *College Composition and Commuication, 16,* 106–112.

Rose, M. (1980). Rigid rules, inflexible plans, and the stifling of language: A cognitivist analysis of writer's block. *College Composition and Communication, 31,* 389–401.

Rose, M. (1984). *Writer's block: The cognitive dimension.* Carbondale, IL: Southern Illinois UP.

Winterowd. W. R, & Blum, J. (1994). *Composition in the rhetorical tradition.* Urbana, IL: NCTE.

Young, R. E., Becker, A. L., & Pike, K. L. (1970). *Rhetoric: Discovery and change.* New York: Harcourt.

Zoellner, R. (1969). Talk-write: A behavioral approach to writing. *College English, 30,* 267–320.

Reading

RIGID RULES, INFLEXIBLE PLANS, AND THE STIFLING
OF LANGUAGE: A COGNITIVIST ANALYSIS
OF WRITER'S BLOCK

Mike Rose

Ruth will labor over the first paragraph of an essay for hours. She'll write a sentence, then erase it. Try another, then scratch part of it out. Finally, as the evening winds on toward ten o'clock and Ruth, anxious about tomorrow's deadline, begins to wind into herself, she'll compose that first paragraph only to sit back and level her favorite exasperated interdiction at herself and her page: "No. You can't say that. You'll bore them to death."

Ruth is one of ten UCLA undergraduates with whom I discussed writer's block, that frustrating, self-defeating inability to generate the next line, the right phrase, the sentence that will release the flow of words once again. These ten people represented a fair cross-section of the UCLA student community: lower-middle-class to upper-middle-class backgrounds and high schools, third-world and Caucasian origins, biology to fine arts majors, C+ to A− grade point averages, enthusiastic to blasé attitudes toward school. They were set off from the community by the twin facts that all ten could write competently, and all were currently enrolled in at least one course that required a significant amount of writing. They were set off among themselves by the fact that five of them wrote with relative to enviable ease while the other five experienced moderate to nearly immobilizing writer's block. This blocking usually resulted in rushed, often late papers and resultant grades that did not truly reflect these students' writing ability. And then, of course, there were other less measurable but probably more serious results: a growing distrust of their abilities and an aversion toward the composing process itself.

94

What separated the five students who blocked from those who didn't? It wasn't skill; that was held fairly constant. The answer could have rested in the emotional realm—anxiety, fear of evaluation, insecurity, etc. Or perhaps blocking in some way resulted from variation in cognitive style. Perhaps, too, blocking originated in and typified a melding of emotion and cognition not unlike the relationship posited by Shapiro between neurotic feeling and neurotic thinking.[1] Each of these was possible. Extended clinical interviews and testing could have teased out the answer. But there was one answer that surfaced readily in brief explorations of these students' writing processes. It was not profoundly emotional, nor was it embedded in that still unclear construct of cognitive style. It was constant, surprising, almost amusing if its results weren't so troublesome, and, in the final analysis, obvious: the five students who experienced blocking were all operating either with writing rules or with planning strategies that impeded rather than enhanced the composing process. The five students who were not hampered by writer's block also utilized rules, but they were less rigid ones, and thus more appropriate to a complex process like writing. Also, the plans these non-blockers brought to the writing process were more functional, more flexible, more open to information from the outside.

These observations are the result of one to three interviews with each student. I used recent notes, drafts, and finished compositions to direct and hone my questions. This procedure is admittedly non-experimental, certainly more clinical than scientific; still, it did lead to several inferences that lay the foundation for future, more rigorous investigation: (a) composing is a highly complex problem-solving process[2] and (b) certain disruptions of that process can be explained with cognitive psychology's problem-solving framework. Such investigation might include a study using "stimulated recall" techniques to validate or disconfirm these hunches. In such a study, blockers and non-blockers would write essays. Their activity would be videotaped and, immediately after writing, they would be shown their respective tapes and questioned about the rules, plans, and beliefs operating in their writing behavior. This procedure would bring us close to the composing process (the writers' recall is stimulated by their viewing the tape), yet would not interfere with actual composing.

In the next section I will introduce several key concepts in the problem-solving literature. In section three I will let the students speak for themselves. Fourth, I will offer a cognitivist analysis of blockers' and non-blockers' grace or torpor. I will close with a brief note on treatment.

Selected Concepts in Problem Solving: Rules and Plans

As diverse as theories of problem solving are, they share certain basic assumptions and characteristics. Each posits an *introductory period* during which a problem is presented, and all theorists, from Behaviorist to Gestalt to Information Processing, admit that certain aspects, stimuli, or "functions" of the problem must become or be made salient and attended to in certain ways if successful problem-solving processes are to be engaged. Theorists also believe that some conflict, some stress, some gap in information in these perceived "aspects" seems to trigger problem-solving behavior. Next comes a *processing period,* and for all the variance of opinion about this critical stage, theorists recognize the necessity of its existence—recognize that man, at the least, somehow "weighs" possible solutions as they are stumbled upon and, at the most, goes through an elaborate and sophisticated information-processing routine to achieve problem solution. Furthermore, theorists believe—to varying degrees—that past learning and the particular "set," direction, or orientation that the problem solver takes in dealing with past experience and present stimuli have critical bearing on the efficacy of solution. Finally, all theorists admit to a *solution period,* an end-state of the process where "stress" and "search" terminate, an answer is attained, and a sense of completion or "closure" is experienced.

These are the gross similarities, and the framework they offer will be useful in understanding the problem-solving behavior of the students discussed in this paper. But since this paper is primarily concerned with the second stage of problem-solving operations, it would be most useful to focus this introduction on two critical constructs in the processing period: rules and plans.

Rules

Robert M. Gagné defines "rule" as "an inferred capability that enables the individual to respond to a class of stimulus situations with a class of performances." [3] Rules can be learned directly [4] or by inference through experience. [5] But, in either case, most problem-solving theorists would affirm Gagné's dictum that "rules are probably the major organizing factor, and quite possibly the primary one, in intellectual functioning." [6] As Gagné implies, we wouldn't be able to function without rules; they guide response to the myriad stimuli that confront us daily, and might even be the central element in complex problem-solving behavior.

Dunker, Polya, and Miller, Galanter, and Pribram offer a very useful distinction between two general kinds of rules: algorithms and heuristics. [7] Algorithms are precise rules that will always result in a specific answer if applied to an appropriate problem. Most mathematical rules, for example, are algorithms. Functions are constant (e.g., pi), procedures are routine (squaring the radius), and outcomes are completely predictable. However, few day-to-day situations are mathematically circumscribed enough to warrant the application of algorithms. Most often we function with the aid of fairly general heuristics or "rules of thumb," guidelines that allow varying degrees of flexibility when approaching problems. Rather than operating with algorithmic precision and certainty, we search, critically, through alternatives, using our heuristic as a divining rod—"if a math problem stumps you, try working backwards to solution"; "if the car won't start, check x, y, or z," and so forth. Heuristics won't allow the precision or the certitude afforded by algorithmic operations; heuristics can even be so "loose" as to be vague. But in a world where tasks and problems are rarely mathematically precise, heuristic rules become the most appropriate, the most functional rules available to us: "a heuristic does not guarantee the optimal solution or, indeed, any solution at all; rather, heuristics offer solutions that are good enough most of the time."[8]

Plans

People don't proceed through problem situations, in or out of a laboratory, without some set of internalized instructions to the self, some program, some course of action that, even roughly, takes goals and possible paths to that goal into consideration. Miller, Galanter, and Pribram have referred to this course of action as a plan: "A plan is any hierarchical process in the organism that can control the order in which a sequence of operations is to be performed" (p. 16). They name the fundamental plan in human problem-solving behavior the TOTE, with the initial T representing a *test* that matches a possible solution against the perceived end-goal of problem completion. O represents the clearance to *operate* if the comparison between solution and goal indicates that the solution is a sensible one. The second T represents a further, post-operation, *test* or comparison of solution with goal, and if the two mesh and problem solution is at hand the person *exits* (E) from problem-solving behavior. If the second test presents further discordance between solution and goal, a further solution is attempted in TOTE-fashion. Such plans can be both long-term and global and, as problem solving is underway, short-term and immediate.[9] Though the mechanicality of this information-processing model renders it simplistic and, possibly, unreal, the central notion of a plan and an operating procedure is an important one in problem-solving theory; it at least attempts to metaphorically explain what earlier cognitive psychologists could not—the mental procedures (see pp. 390-391) underlying problem-solving behavior.

Before concluding this section, a distinction between heuristic rules and plans should be attempted; it is a distinction often blurred in the literature, blurred because, after all, we are very much in the area of gestating theory and preliminary models. Heuristic rules seem to function with the flexibility of plans. Is, for example, "If the car won't start, try x, y, or z" a heuristic or a plan? It could be either, though two qualifications will mark it as heuristic rather than plan. (A) Plans subsume and sequence heuristic and algorithmic rules. Rules are usually "smaller," more discrete cognitive capabilities; plans can become quite large and complex, composed of a series of ordered algorithms, heuristics, and further planning "sub-routines." (B) Plans, as was mentioned earlier, include criteria to determine successful goal-attainment and, as well, include "feedback" processes—ways to

text. Martha, therefore, will bend the logic of her analysis to reason ambiguity out of existence. When I asked her about a strained paragraph in her paper on Camus' "The Guest," she said, "I didn't want to admit that it [the story's conclusion] was just hanging. I tried to force it into meaning."

Martha uses another rule, one that is not only problematical in itself, but one that often clashes directly with the elaborate plan and obsessive rule above. She believes that humanities papers must scintillate with insight, must present an array of images, ideas, ironies gleaned from the literature under examination. A problem arises, of course, when Martha tries to incorporate her myriad "neat little things," often inherently unrelated, into a tightly structured, carefully sequenced essay. Plans and rules that govern the construction of impressionistic, associational prose would be appropriate to Martha's desire, but her composing process is heavily constrained by the non-impressionistic and non-associational. Put another way, the plans and rules that govern her exploration of text are not at all synchronous with the plans and rules she uses to discuss her exploration. It is interesting to note here, however, that as recently as three years ago Martha was absorbed in creative writing and was publishing poetry in high school magazines. Given what we know about the complex associational, often non-neatly-sequential nature of the poet's creative process, we can infer that Martha was either free of the plans and rules discussed earlier or they were not as intense. One wonders, as well, if the exposure to three years of university physical science either established or intensified Martha's concern with structure. Whatever the case, she now is hamstrung by conflicting rules when composing papers for the humanities.

Mike's difficulties, too, are rooted in a distortion of the problem-solving process. When the time of the week for the assignment of writing topics draws near, Mike begins to prepare material, strategies, and plans that he believes will be appropriate. If the assignment matches his expectations, he has done a good job of analyzing the professor's intentions. If the assignment *doesn't* match his expectations, however, he cannot easily shift approaches. He feels trapped inside his original plans, cannot generate alternatives, and blocks. As the deadline draws near, he will write something, forcing the assignment to fit his conceptual procrustian bed. Since Mike is a smart man, he will offer a good deal of information, but only some of it ends up being appropriate to the assignment. This entire situation is made all the worse when the time between assignment of topic and generation of product is attenuated further, as in an essay examination. Mike believes (correctly) that one must have a plan, a strategy of some sort in order to solve a problem. He further believes, however, that such a plan, once formulated, becomes an exact structural and substantive blueprint that cannot be violated. The plan offers no alternatives, no "sub-routines." So, whereas Ruth's, Laurel's, and some of Martha's difficulties seem to be rule-specific ("always catch your audience," "write grammatically"), Mike's troubles are more global. He may have strategies that are appropriate for various writing situations (e.g., "for this kind of political science assignment write a compare/contrast essay"), but his entire approach to formulating plans and carrying them through to problem solution is too mechanical. It is probable that Mike's behavior is governed by an explicitly learned or inferred rule: "Always try to 'psych out' a professor." But in this case this rule initiates a problem-solving procedure that is clearly dysfunctional.

While Ruth and Laurel use rules that impede their writing process and Mike utilizes a problem-solving procedure that hamstrings him, *Sylvia* has trouble deciding which of the many rules she possesses to use. Her problem can be characterized as cognitive perplexity: some of her rules are inappropriate, others are functional; some mesh nicely with her own definitions of good writing, others don't. She has multiple rules to invoke, multiple paths to follow, and that very complexity of choice virtually paralyzes her. More so than with the previous four students, there is probably a strong emotional dimension to Sylvia's blocking, but the cognitive difficulties are clear and perhaps modifiable.

Sylvia, somewhat like Ruth and Laurel, puts tremendous weight on the crafting of her first paragraph. If it is good, she believes the rest of the essay will be good. Therefore, she will spend up to five hours on the initial paragraph: "I won't go on until I get that first paragraph down." Clearly, this rule—or the strength of it— blocks Sylvia's production. This is one problem. Another is that Sylvia has other equally potent rules that she sees as separate, uncomplementary injunctions: one achieves "flow" in one's writing through the use of adquate transitions; one achieves substance to one's writing through the use of evidence. Sylvia perceives both rules to be "true," but several times followed one to the exclusion of the other. Furthermore, as I talked to Sylvia, many other rules, guidelines, definitions were offered, but none with conviction. While she *is* committed to one rule about initial paragraphs, and that rule is dysfunctional, she seems very uncertain about the weight and hierarchy of the remaining rules in her cognitive repertoire.

"If It Won't Fit My Work, I'll Change It"—The Non-blockers

Dale, Ellen, Debbie, Susan, and Miles all write with the aid of rules. But their rules differ from blockers' rules in significant ways. If similar in content, they are expressed less absolutely—e.g., "*Try* to keep audience in mind." If dissimilar, they are still expressed less absolutely, more heuristically—e.g., "I can use as many ideas in my thesis paragraph as I need and then develop paragraphs for each idea." Our non-blockers do express some rules with firm assurance, but these tend to be simple injunctions that free up rather than restrict the composing process, e.g., "When stuck, write!" or "I'll write what I can." And finally, at least three of the students openly shun the very textbook rules that some blockers adhere to: e.g., "Rules like 'write only what you know about just aren't true. I ignore those. These three, in effect, have formulated a further rule that expresses something like: "If a rule conflicts with what is sensible or with experience, reject it."

On the broader level of plans and strategies, these five students also differ from at least three of the five blockers in that they all possess problem-solving plans that are quite functional. Interestingly, on first exploration these plans seem to be too broad or fluid to be useful and, in some cases, can barely be expressed with any precision. Ellen, for example, admits that she has a general "outline in [her] head about how a topic paragraph should look" but could not describe much about its structure. Susan also has a general plan to follow, but, if stymied, will quickly attempt to conceptualize the assignment in different ways: "If my original idea won't work, then I need to proceed differently." Whether or not these plans operate in TOTE-fashion, I can't say. But they do operate with the operate-test fluidity of TOTEs.

True, our non-blockers have their religiously adhered-to rules: e.g., "When stuck, write," and plans, "I couldn't imagine writing without this pattern," but as noted above, these are few and functional. Otherwise, these non-blockers operate with fluid, easily modified, even easily discarded rules and plans (Ellen: "I can throw things out") that are sometimes expressed with a vagueness that could almost be interpreted as ignorance. There lies the irony. Students that offer the least precise rules and plans have the least trouble composing. Perhaps this very lack of precision characterizes the functional composing plan. But perhaps this lack of precision simply masks habitually enacted alternatives and sub-routines. This is clearly an area that needs the illumination of further research.

And then there is feedback. At least three of the five non-blockers are an Information-Processor's dream. They get to know their audience, ask professors and T.A.s specific questions about assignments, bring half-finished products in for evaluation, etc. Like Ruth, they realize the importance of audience, but unlike her, they have specific strategies for obtaining and utilizing feedback. And this penchant for testing writing plans against the needs of the audience can lead to modification of rules and plans. Listen to Debbie:

> In high school I was given a formula that stated that you must write a thesis paragraph with *only* three points in it, and then develop each of those points. When I hit college I was given longer assignments. That stuck me for a bit, but then I realized that I could use as many ideas in my thesis paragraph as I needed and then develop paragraphs for each one. I asked someone about this and then tried it. I didn't get any negative feedback, so I figured it was o.k.

Debbie's statement brings one last difference between our blockers and non-blockers into focus; it has been implied above, but needs specific formulation: the goals these people have, and the plans they generate to attain these goals, are quite mutable. Part of the mutability comes from the fluid way the goals and plans are conceived, and part of it arises from the effective impact of feedback on these goals and plans.

Analyzing Writer's Block

Algorithms Rather Than Heuristics

In most cases, the rules our blockers use are not "wrong" or "incorrect"—it is good practice, for example, to "grab your audience with a catchy opening" or "craft a solid first paragraph before going on." The problem is that these rules seem to be followed as though they were algorithms, absolute dicta, rather than the loose heuristics that they were intended to be. Either through instruction, or the power of the textbook, or the predilections of some of our blockers for absolutes, or all three, these useful rules of thumb have been transformed into near-algorithmic urgencies. The result, to paraphrase Karl Dunker, is that these rules do not allow a flexible penetration into the nature of the problem. It is this transformation of heuristic into algorithm that contributes to the writer's block of Ruth and Laurel.

Questionable Heuristics Made Algorithmic

Whereas "grab your audience" could be a useful heuristic, "always make three or more points in an essay" is a pretty questionable one. Any such rule, though probably taught to aid the writer who needs structure, ultimately transforms a highly fluid process like writing into a mechanical lockstep. As heuristics, such rules can be troublesome. As algorithms, they are simply incorrect.

Set

As with any problem-solving task, students approach writing assignments with a variety of orientations or sets. Some are functional, others are not. Martha and Jane (see footnote 14), coming out of the life sciences and social sciences respectively, bring certain methodological orientations with them—certain sets or "directions" that make composing for the humanities a difficult, sometimes confusing, task. In fact, this orientation may cause them to misperceive the task. Martha has formulated a planning strategy from her predisposition to see processes in terms of linear, interrelated steps in a system. Jane doesn't realize that she can revise the statement that "committed" her to the direction her essay has taken. Both of these students are stymied because of formative experiences associated with their majors—experiences, perhaps, that nicely reinforce our very strong tendency to organize experiences temporally.

The Plan that Is Not a Plan

If fluidity and multi-directionality are central to the nature of plans, then the plans that Mike formulates are not true plans at all but, rather, inflexible and static cognitive blueprints.[15] Put another way, Mike's "plans" represent a restricted "closed system" (vs. "open system") kind of thinking, where closed system thinking is defined as focusing on "a limited number of units or items, or members, and those properties of the members which are to be used are known to begin with and do not change as the thinking proceeds," and open system thinking is characterized by an "adventurous exploration of multiple alternatives with strategies that allow redirection once 'dead ends' are encountered."[16] Composing calls for open, even adventurous thinking, not for constrained, no-exit cognition.

Feedback

The above difficulties are made all the more problematic by the fact that they seem resistant to or isolated from corrective feedback. One of the most striking things about Dale, Debbie, and Miles is the ease with which they seek out, interpret, and apply feedback on their rules, plans, and productions. They "operate" and then they "test," and the testing is not only against some internalized goal, but against the requirements of external audience as well.

Too Many Rules—"Conceptual Conflict"

According to D. E. Berlyne, one of the primary forces that motivate problem-solving behavior is a curiosity that arises from conceptual conflict—the convergence of incompatible beliefs or ideas. In *Structure and Direction in Thinking*,[17] Berlyne presents six major types of conceptual conflict, the second of which he terms "perplexity":

> This kind of conflict occurs when there are factors inclining the subject toward each of a set of mutually exclusive beliefs. (p. 257)

If one substitutes "rules" for "beliefs" in the above definition, perplexity becomes a useful notion here. Because perplexity is unpleasant, people are motivated to reduce it by problem-solving behavior that can result in "disequalization":

> Degree of conflict will be reduced if either the number of competing...
> [rules] or their nearness to equality of strength is reduced. (p. 259)

But "disequalization" is not automatic. As I have suggested, Martha and Sylvia hold to rules that conflict, but their perplexity does *not* lead to curiosity and resultant problem-solving behavior. Their perplexity, contra Berlyne, leads to immobilization. Thus "disequalization" will have to be effected from without. The importance of each of, particularly, Sylvia's rules needs an evaluation that will aid her in rejecting some rules and balancing and sequencing others.

A Note on Treatment

Rather than get embroiled in a blocker's misery, the teacher or tutor might interview the student in order to build a writing history and profile: How much and what kind of writing was done in high school? What is the student's major? What kind of writing does it require? How does the student compose? Are there rough drafts or outlines available? By what rules does the student operate? How would he or she define "good" writing? etc. This sort of interview reveals an incredible amount of information about individual composing processes. Furthermore, it ofen reveals the rigid rule or the inflexible plan that may lie at the base of the student's writing problem. That was precisely what happened with the five blockers. And with Ruth, Laurel, and Martha (and Jane) what was revealed made virtually immediate remedy possible. Dysfunctional rules are easily replaced with or counter-balanced by functional ones if there is no emotional reason to hold onto that which simply doesn't work. Furthermore, students can be trained to select, to "know which rules are appropriate for which problems."[18] Mike's difficulties, perhaps because plans are more complex and pervasive than rules, took longer to correct. But inflexible plans, too, can be remedied by pointing out their dysfunctional qualities and by assisting the student in developing appropriate and flexible alternatives. Operating this way, I was successful with Mike. Sylvia's story, however, did not end as smoothly. Though I had three forty-five minute contacts with her, I was not able to appreciably alter her behavior. Berlyne's theory bore results with Martha but not with Sylvia. Her rules were in conflict, and perhaps that conflict was not exclusively cognitive. Her case keeps analyses like these honest; it reminds us that the cognitive often melds with, and can be overpowered by, the affective. So while Ruth, Laurel, Martha, and Mike could profit from tutorials that explore the rules and plans in their writing behavior, students like Sylvia may need more extended, more affectively oriented counseling sessions that blend the instructional with the psychodynamic.

Notes

1. David Shapiro, *Neurotic Styles* (New York: Basic Books, 1965).

2. Barbara Hayes-Ruth, a Rand cognitive psychologist, and I are currently developing an information-processing model of the composing process. A good deal of work has already been done by Linda Flower and John Hayes (see p. 393 of this article). I have just received—and recommend—their "Writing as Problem Solving" (paper presented at American Educational Research Association, April, 1979).

3. *The Conditions of Learning* (New York: Holt, Rinehart and Winston, 1970), p. 193.

4. E. James Archer, "The Psychological Nature of Concepts," in H. J. Klausmeier and C. W. Harris, eds., *Analysis of Concept Learning* (New York: Academic Press, 1966), pp. 37-44; David P. Ausubel, *The Psychology of Meaningful Verbal Behavior* (New York: Grune and Stratton, 1963); Robert M. Gagné, "Problem Solving," in Arthur W. Melton, ed., *Categories of Human Learning* (New York: Academic Press, 1964), pp. 293-317; George A. Miller, *Language and Communication* (New York: McGraw-Hill, 1951).

5. George Katona, *Organizing and Memorizing* (New York: Columbia Univ. Press, 1940); Roger N. Shepard, Carl I. Hovland, and Herbert M. Jenkins, "Learning and Memorization of Classifications," *Psychological Monographs*, 75, No. 13 (1961) (entire No. 517); Robert S. Wood-worth, *Dynamics of Behavior* (New York: Henry Holt, 1958), chs. 10-12.

6. *The Conditions of Learning*, pp. 190-91.

7. Karl Dunker, "On Problem Solving," *Psychological Monographs*, 58, No. 5 (1945) (entire No. 270); George A. Polya, *How to Solve It* (Princeton: Princeton University Press, 1945); George A. Miller, Eugene Galanter, and Karl H. Pribram, *Plans and the Structure of Behavior* (New York: Henry Holt, 1960).

8. Lyle E. Bourne, Jr., Bruce R. Ekstrand, and Roger L. Dominowski, *The Psychology of Thinking* (Englewood Cliffs, N.J.: Prentice-Hall, 1971).

9. John R. Hayes, "Problem Topology and the Solution Process," in Carl P. Duncan, ed., *Thinking: Current Experimental Studies* (Philadelphia: Lippincott, 1967), pp. 167-81.

10. Hulda J. Rees and Harold E. Israel, "An Investigation of the Establishment and Operation of Mental Sets." *Psychological Monographs*, 46 (1925) (entire No. 210).

11. Ibid.; Melvin H. Marx, Wilton W. Murphy, and Aaron J. Brownstein, "Recognition of Complex Visual Stimuli as a Function of Training with Abstracted Patterns," *Journal of Experimental Psychology*, 62 (1961), 456-60.

12. James L. Adams, *Conceptual Blockbusting* (San Francisco: W. H. Freeman, 1974); Edward DeBono, *New Think* (New York: Basic Books, 1958); Ronald H. Forgus, *Perception* (New York: McGraw-Hill, 1966), ch. 13; Abraham Luchins and Edith Hirsch Luchins, *Rigidity of Behavior* (Eugene: Univ. of Oregon Books, 1959); N. R. F. Maier, "Reasoning in Humans. I. On Direction," *Journal of Comparative Psychology*, 10 (1920), 115-43.

13. "Plans and the Cognitive Process of Writing," paper presented at the National Institute of Education Writing Conference, June 1977; "Problem Solving Strategies and the Writing Process," *College English*, 39 (1977), 449-61. See also footnote 2.

14. Jane, a student not discussed in this paper, was surprised to find out that a topic paragraph can be rewritten after a paper's conclusion to make that paragraph reflect what the essay truly contains. She had gotten so indoctrinated with Psychology's (her major) insistence that a hypothesis be formulated and then left untouched before an experiment begins that she thought revision of one's "major premise" was somehow illegal. She had formed a rule out of her exposure to social science methodology, and the rule was totally inappropriate for most writing situations.

15. Cf. "A plan is flexible if the order of execution of its parts can be easily interchanged without affecting the feasibility of the plan ... the flexible planner might tend to think of lists of things he had to do; the inflexible planner would have his time planned like a sequence of cause-effect relations. The former could rearrange his lists to suit his opportunities, but the latter would be unable to strike while the iron was hot and would generally require considerable 'lead-time' before he could incorporate any alternative sub-plans" (Miller, Galanter, and Pribram, p. 120).

16. Frederic Bartlett, *Thinking* (New York: Basic Books, 1958), pp. 74–76.

17. *Structure and Direction in Thinking* (New York: John Wiley, 1965), p. 255.

18. Flower and Hayes, "Plans and the Cognitive Process of Writing," p. 26.

3

Revision

Betty Bamberg

This chapter traces varying perspectives on what is involved in revision and discusses what research and theory has revealed about the ways that writers, especially student writers, revise. It suggests ways for teachers to encourage students to revise in ways that develop and shape the meaning of their texts.

How can I change the introduction to make it more interesting to my readers?

How can I construct a more valid and convincing argument?

What example could I add to make this point clearer?

What is the most logical way to organize my argument?

How can I reword this sentence so it will read more smoothly?

How can I make this sentence less wordy?

What might be a better word to use here?

Questions like these are just a few of those that writers might ask themselves when they are composing or that readers might ask writers after reading drafts of their writing. Such questions help writers rethink and reconsider their initial rhetorical choices about content, development, organization, sentence structure, and word choice so they can revise their work and improve it. Some writers, however, especially student writers, typically ask different questions: Is my grammar correct? Is this word spelled correctly? Do I need a comma here? This second set of questions reflects an older view of revision, which considered revision to be a mechanical process involving little more than correcting errors or making minor changes in sentence structure or word choice to improve style. The first set of questions, on the other hand, illustrates a perspective on revision that has emerged from composing process research and theory over the last 30 years. This perspective, which is concerned primarily with issues of audience, purpose, content, organization, and style, reconceptualizes revision as a primary means of developing, elaborating, and shaping the intended meaning of a text.

This chapter discusses "revision" as an important theoretical and pedagogical concept in composition, focusing on the following aspects of the topic:

1. Why "revision" was initially seen as a process of correcting errors;
2. How research and theory in cognitive development and the composing process have led to a new concept of revision;
3. What research tells us about the ways that writers, especially student writers, revise;
4. What factors tend to inhibit or encourage meaningful revision; and
5. What teachers can do to encourage students to revise in ways that develop and shape the meaning of their texts.

OLDER CONCEPTS OF REVISION

Unlike invention, which was a key concept in classical rhetoric, commentary that could be construed as revision was rare in classical rhetorical theory. For Aristotle, composing involved finding and structuring content, then polishing the sentences, and he "relegates [alterations] to the sentence level, to the editing of forms and their arrangement" (Hodges, 1982, p. 26). Although Quintilian also commented on the importance of sentence-level corrections, he recognized the possibility that new ideas could suddenly arise while delivering a speech or reviewing a written composition and advocated integrating these new insights into the discourse rather than rejecting them. However, the narrow definition of the revision process as surface editing and correction continued to prevail. Throughout the Middle Ages, imitation rather than invention was emphasized, and style was further separated from content. During the Renaissance, the idea that revision primarily involved changes at the sentence-level was further strengthened when Ramus reorganized Aristotle's rhetoric, moving invention, arrangement, and logic to philosophy. Although both Francis Bacon and Ben Jonson spoke out against the preoccupation with style and proposed a more holistic view that would allow for revisioning of content and arrangement, their ideas failed to gain acceptance (Hodges, 1982). As a result, rhetoric was limited to considering how language might be used to "dress thought," and rhetoricians became concerned with finding the most effective tropes—"figures of thought"—which included metaphor, personification, and synecdoche (the substitution of the part for the whole), or "schemes," which included structures such as parallelism, ellipsis, and anaphora (repeating the same words at the beginning of successive phrases or clauses to create emphasis) to express ideas (Covino & Jolliffe, 1995, p. 23). Although the 18th century rhetoricians Hugh Blair and George Campbell explicitly rejected the narrow emphasis on style that characterized Renaissance rhetoric and, instead, revived a concern for ideas and persuasion in rhetoric, nevertheless their treatises focused on correctness and sentence-level changes insofar as they considered revision (Hodges, 1982).

In the United States, error correction as a major emphasis in writing instruction initially arose more from social conditions in late-19th-century America than from the rhetorical tradition (Connors, 1997; Berlin, 1987). Robert Connors argues that the emphasis on error correction in composition instruction arose from a linguistic insecurity that resulted from changes in American society in the second half of the 19th century. As universities moved away from studying classical languages and moved toward educating the new professional classes, the place of rhetoric in the university curriculum changed dramatically from the advanced study of effective persuasion to a concern with the ability to write acceptable compositions in English. In 1874, Harvard established an entrance examination, soon copied by other universities, that required students "to write a short English composition, correct in spelling, punctuation, grammar, and expression" (Bizzell, Herzberg & Reynolds, 2000, p. 4). When more than half of Harvard's prospective students failed the exam, the university and the press condemned students' prior preparation and called for reform of the secondary curriculum to improve their writing ability. However, Adams Sherman Hill, who oversaw the Harvard entrance exam, thought that results from improved secondary instruction would not be rapid enough and proposed that Harvard require "a temporary course in remedial writing instruction ... of all incoming freshmen" (Connors, 1997, p. 11). In the instructional model instituted at Harvard, subsequently copied by many other universities, students wrote frequent short compositions, which their instructors then read and marked to indicate grammatical errors. After these essays were returned, students were often expected to rewrite them to correct the errors. This approach to revision became an integral part of the "current-traditional" approach to rhetoric that dominated both university and high school composition instruction until the 1960s, and it firmly established a concept of revision as rewriting to correct grammatical errors.

CONTEMPORARY CONCEPTS OF REVISION
IN THE COMPOSING PROCESS

Revival of classical rhetoric in the 1960s led to a renewed interest in Aristotle's rhetorical principles, particularly his concern for audience and purpose, adapted for written rather than oral discourse. Rhetorical theorists reclaimed invention as an essential component of composing and drew on research in cognitive and developmental psychology to argue that language created meaning. In this context, knowledge and meaning were, thus, viewed as "constructed," rather than observed and reported. In addition, scholarly and pedagogical interest in how writers compose focused attention on revision as an important stage in the composing process. Initially, composing was viewed as linear, with writers moving through discreet steps: first, prewriting or invention, then drafting, revision, and finally editing. Murray (1978), for example, divided the process into three stages: first, prevision, which includes everything that precedes the first draft; second, vision, the completion of a first or discovery draft in which the writer "stakes out a territory to explore" (p. 87); and third, revision, which consists of everything a writer does to the draft to develop a meaning that can be communicated to a reader. However, later theorists and researchers rejected the linear model in favor of a recursive one in which writers moved back and forth among the activities of invention, drafting, and revision throughout the composing process (Perl, 1979). During this ongoing, cyclical process, writers could revise at any point during composing and at any level—from the major units of discourse such as the thesis or the main arguments to individual words and sentence. However, their primary concern was always developing meaning in terms of purpose and audience.

Donald Murray (1978) characterized the new approach to revision, which included "everything writers do to discover and develop what they have to say, beginning with the reading of a completed first draft" (p. 87), as "internal revision." He identified four aspects of discovery in the process of internal revision. First, writers discover content and information, which leads them to the second aspect—the discovery of form and structure. Third, writers discover meaning through language itself. Fourth, writers find a voice or point of view pertaining to their subject. Murray described the old approach to revision, which consisted of editing; proofreading; and attending to conventions of form, style, language, and mechanics, as "external revision." Because the process paradigm made discovering and developing meaning central to the composing process, composition teachers became concerned with encouraging what Murray called "internal revision." Questions of correctness—once the primary focus of revision—were to be addressed at the end, only after questions regarding content, organization, and audience had been resolved. To clearly distinguish the older concept of revision from

the newer one, all changes involving correctness were increasingly referred
to as editing rather than as revision

FOR WRITING AND DISCUSSION

What kinds of questions do you ask yourself when you reread your writing
to revise it? How well do they help you revise your writing? Has past
instruction or experience in composition influenced the questions you
ask yourself?

REVISION STRATEGIES OF STUDENT WRITERS

Although this new concept of revision emphasized its role in discovering and
shaping meaning, early composing process research showed that student
writers typically viewed revision as error correction and made only superficial
changes in their texts. In Janet Emig's (1971) groundbreaking study of the
composing processes of 12th graders, Lynn, the student writer she described
most extensively, recalled that her teacher made her revise by recopying
essays to correct errors and described the process as "punishment work"
(p. 68).

Charles Stallard (1974) analyzed the writing behaviors of 12th-grade writers and observed a number of aspects of composing, including revision. He
found that the kind and amount of revision characteristic of good writers
differed from that of a group of randomly selected student writers. Even
though both groups were concerned about spelling and mechanics in general, good writers made almost three times more revisions than writers in
the random group. Their major emphasis involved word choice, but they
were more likely to make multiple word, syntactic, and paragraph revisions.
Even for the good writers, however, the number of syntactic and paragraph
changes was small.

In an exploratory study of upper-division college students, Beach (1976)
found that some students followed the approach to revision used by students
in Stallard's study. Identifying these students as nonrevisers, he found they
relied on textbook formulas, expressed less interest in the writing tasks, and
limited the time and effort they spend on writing. However, other students
revised extensively and saw revision as an opportunity to discover and shape
their meaning. These extensive revisers conceived of their paper in holistic
terms and used subsequent drafts to work out their arguments and to make
any necessary changes. Beach attributed these differences to the students'
ability to evaluate their writing critically, an ability present in the extensive
revisers but lacking in the nonrevisers.

Bridwell's (1980) research, which focused exclusively on revision strategies, compared more and less successful 12th-grade writers. To analyze her data, she developed a comprehensive classification system to describe the types of revisions that students made. Each revision was categorized according to one of six levels, beginning with surface-level changes in mechanics and moving up to progressively more complex changes—individual words, then phrases, clauses, sentences, multiple-sentences, and finally the whole text. She also counted the number of revisions made at three points during composing: in-process first-drafts, between drafts, and in-process second drafts. Bridwell found that both groups of students revised substantially more during the two in-process stages and made the greatest number of changes at all levels while writing the second draft. However, the more successful writers made more changes between drafts. Despite these differences, she found that surface- and word-level revision accounted for over half of all revisions made by *both* the more and less successful writers. None of the students made revisions that involved the whole text level, and very few revisions were made at the sentence or multiple-sentence level.

A key research study on revision, conducted by Nancy Sommers (1980), compared revisions made by college freshmen with those of experienced writers, including journalists, editors, and academics. Because of its important insights, this essay is included as one of the readings in this book.

FOR READING AND DISCUSSION

Read "Revision Strategies of Student Writers and Experienced Adult Writers," pp. 130–140. Be prepared to discuss the following questions in small groups:

1. What kind of revisions do experienced writers make? How are these different from the revisions of student writers?

2. What is the attitude of student writers toward revising? What are their main concerns? How do these differ from the attitudes and concerns of experienced writers?

3. How do the revising strategies of student and adult writers in Sommers' study relate to Donald Murray's conception of internal and external revision?

FOR WRITING AND DISCUSSION

How would you describe your revision process? Do you engage primarily in external revision, focusing on words and sentences, or do you also use revision as a way of discovering, shaping, and developing your meaning (internal revision)? How has past writing instruction influenced your approach to revision?

COMPUTERS AND REVISION

With the advent of computers and word processing programs, theorists and researchers anticipated that the new technology, which eliminated the need to retype or recopy entire texts when revising, would encourage students to revise more extensively. They also hoped that the greater ease of manipulating text (i.e., adding, deleting, or moving) would encourage more meaning-based revisions. However, research results regarding the effect of computers and word processing programs on revision has been mixed. An early study by Hawisher (1987) compared the amount of revision and quality of writing when advanced college freshmen used computers and when they used pen and paper. In addition to receiving specific instruction on revising their writing, students also received specific instruction on the mechanics of using a word processor to revise, completed self-assessment forms designed to prompt revision, and wrote out plans for revising their final drafts. Hawisher found that students not only revised more when using paper and pen than when using the computer but also that there seemed to be no relationship between frequency of revision and quality ratings received by the essays. In addition, there were no significant differences in quality rating between paper and pen essays and those done on the computer. A later study involving average and above average 8th graders also found that papers produced using word processors were not higher in quality than those written with pen and paper (Joram, Woodruff, Bryson, & Lindsay, 1992).

On the other hand, some research has shown word processing to have a positive effect on revision and writing quality. For example, Owston, Murphy, & Wideman (1992) compared revision strategies and writing quality when 8th-grade students, all experienced computer users, composed on a computer or by hand. They found that papers written on computer received significantly higher quality ratings than those written by hand. However, computer revisions were likely to be microstructural rather than macrostructural changes, and most revision took place at the initial drafting stage. In a study of basic college writers, McAllister & Louth (1988) found that those students who used computers produced higher quality revisions of assigned paragraphs than basic writers who did not use computers. Reynolds and Bonk (1996) investigated the use of computer prompts to encourage revision. In their study, half of the students in an intermediate college composition class had access to 24 generative and evaluative prompts that supported previous ideas and instruction in the course about revision. The prompts could be self-initiated by writers, but were also available through a keyboard template. Results showed that students using the prompting system made more meaning-related changes in their texts and produced higher-quality texts.

Despite some positive results, the effects of computers and word processing on composing remain problematic. Crafton (1996), who surveyed studies conducted after computer use had become common and students were routinely using word processing programs to write their papers, concluded that the computer introduces new problems and complexities into the writing process and may, in some cases, emphasize the written product rather than support the composing process. Eklund (1994) found that computers encouraged localized revision because the size of the screen limits the amount of text that can be reread and reviewed, whereas Sharples (1994) suggested that the ease of making low-level revisions might actually disrupt the composing process by encouraging students to engage in continuous editing throughout the composing process. Moreover, text-editing tools such as grammar and spelling checkers seem to reinforce a concept of revision as error correction and surface-level changes. Heilker (1992) observed that students often respond to suggestions from text-analysis programs as if they were directives from a person rather than a machine. As a result, he concluded that "the writer–computer relationship is displacing and replacing the writer–audience relationship in the rhetorical situation" (p. 65).

Today, many high school and most college students use word processing and computers when writing their papers. However, interest in researching the effect of computers on revision has waned, and only a few studies have been conducted since 1996, most with special student populations. Nonetheless, results from existing studies suggest useful guidelines for teachers. The research makes clear that computers and word processing do not automatically lead students to make substantive revisions. Instead, the kinds of revisions made reflect the writers' conception of revision and their goals in revising. In some cases, therefore, computers may tend to reinforce a focus on sentence-level revision. Computers and word processing will facilitate substantive revision only if students view revision as a process of shaping the text in terms of purpose and audience. Students must also be able to identify the types of larger changes that are needed and have a repertoire of rhetorical strategies at their command to make the needed changes. As a result, teachers need to provide classroom instruction and responses to drafts that will prepare students to take advantage of the computer's potential for facilitating substantive revision.

FOR WRITING AND DISCUSSION

Do you use a computer when writing essays? If so, do you compose your first draft on the computer or by hand? How does the computer affect the way you revise? Do most of your computer revisions involve sentence-level changes in words and incorrect forms rather than changes in content, development, or organization? How frequently do you revise when composing on a computer? Do you print out a draft and revise on paper at any point in the process? Share your response in small groups.

OBSTACLES TO REVISION

Why do students tend to regard revision as rewording and error correction rather than as an activity for discovering meaning and shaping their ideas for readers? One explanation blames the nature of school-sponsored writing and classroom instructional approaches for creating obstacles to revision: School writing assignments often don't give students an opportunity to write for real audiences or purposes, while teachers may reinforce a view of revision as error hunting. Monahan (1984), for example, found that seven of the nine teachers in his study taught revision by having students write second drafts using a grammar-based checklist. Moreover, an emphasis on editing and sentence-level revision can occur even in a class in which a teacher employs a process approach and strategies such as peer revision and multiple drafts to emphasize revision. Yagelski (1995) studied such a class and found that students still focused their revision on surface and stylistic concerns. Despite the writing workshop structure of the class, students revised in response to the teacher's conception of "good" writing, which emphasized grammatical correctness, tight organization, and a straightforward prose style. Most of the teacher's comments on drafts focused on lower-level concerns with virtually no attention given to ideas, and peer responses to drafts reflected similar concerns. As a result, students revised primarily to improve their grades and considered the teacher to be the primary audience.

In addition, when revision involves larger textual elements and focuses on meaning, it becomes a complex cognitive process. Flower, Hayes, Carey, Schriver, and Stratman (1986) studied this complexity by comparing the cognitive processes used by experts and novice student writers while revising. Basing their study on the Flower-Hayes cognitive model of composing, they attempted to model the basic thinking process underlying revision and looked for places where experts and novices made different decisions or handled the process itself differently. They identified three major obstacles for beginning writers: detecting problems in the text, diagnosing the problems, and choosing a strategy to remedy the problems. In their model, revision begins as writers review their text and evaluate it. To detect problems, writers must evaluate the draft in terms of their goals or intentions and criteria for effective writing. Detection, therefore, involves two complex constructive processes: first, representing the text through the act of reading and then representing one's intentions. Expert writers are able to represent both their text and their intentions clearly and also have extensive knowledge of criteria for effective writing. As a result, they are able to read their drafts for rhetorical problems related to content, organization, genre, and audience as well as for sentence-level problems of style and correct form. Novice writers, on the other hand, typically work with a vague representation of their texts. They may read meanings in their head into the text and fail to realize these meanings are not actually present for a reader. In addition, they have difficulty representing the overall structure of a draft and so have trouble reading a draft for rhetorical problems. Finally, because they are likely to have a very limited set of criteria for evaluating writing, they are able to detect only a few problems.

Once writers sense that something is wrong in their texts, they must be able to turn that detection into a diagnosis that suggests what needs to be done to correct the problem. However, diagnosis requires writers to recognize and categorize problems, an ability that novices don't have. Experts are able to see the problems they identify as fitting within meaningful, familiar categories and are then able to use their past experience and knowledge to select strategies for revision. Novices, however, are able to categorize only a small number of problems—usually at the word or sentence level—and possess a limited repertoire of revision strategies. Therefore, the complex cognitive processes involved in revising, particularly at the rhetorical level, explain why novice student writers consistently revise in more narrow and limited ways than experienced writers.

FOR WRITING AND DISCUSSION

What kinds of difficulties do you experience when you revise your drafts? Are you able to identify problems in content, development, or organization as well as those involving sentences and correct form? What techniques or strategies do you use when you revise?

HELPING STUDENTS REVISE EFFECTIVELY: INTERVENING IN THE COMPOSING PROCESS

Given the importance of revision in composing, students' consistent tendency to view revision as correcting errors or making small changes in wording or sentence structure has led rhetoricians and composition specialists to search for strategies that would encourage more meaning-based revision. Beach (1976) who concluded that his nonrevisers' concept of revision reflected the attitudes of teachers and textbooks, recommended that we "provide alternative, helpful models of the revision process"(p. 164). Sommers (1980) also concluded that students had been taught to revise in a "narrow and predictable way." She observed that students "have strategies for handling words and phrases, but don't know what to do when they sense something larger is wrong" (p. 383). Composition instruction, therefore, has focused on expanding students' understanding of revision to include developing and shaping meaning, finding ways to intervene during the composing process, and teaching students to revise at the rhetorical level.

Whole-Class Workshops and One-to-One Conferences as Intervention Strategies

Ken Macrorie and Donald Murray, early proponents of the process approach, were among the first to develop intervention strategies to help students revise drafts. Adapting a structure used in creative writing classes, Macrorie created an in-class workshop that engaged the whole class, guided by the teacher, in reading and responding to work in progress. Murray also focused on students' in-progress drafts, but he relied primarily on one-to-one conferences. Both strategies continue to be used today, either in their original form or modified for different settings and types of students.

In *Writing to Be Read*, Macrorie (1968) provided the rationale for his approach by explaining that beginning writers need to gain experience "through engaging in critical sessions with peers" (p. 85) if their writing is to improve. He later (1984) described the peer response group as a "helping circle," where students and the teacher give truthful responses to drafts that students read aloud to the group. Because writers are anxious about receiving criticism, Macrorie prohibited negative criticism at the beginning and allowed students to comment only about those parts of the drafts that they liked. Once students experienced success by hearing positive comments, then other students, assisted by the teacher, could begin to criticize the drafts. Although teachers lead the writing workshop, they gave up some of their authority in what Macrorie (1970) called his "Third Way" of teaching. Rather than controlling all aspects of the class, teachers must allow "students [to] operate with freedom and discipline," by giving them "real choices" and by encouraging them "to learn the way of experts" (p. 27). Although he acknowledged that students cannot criticize writing unless they have developed evaluation standards, Macrorie argued that students learn such standards primarily from the responses of other students, rather than by having them imposed by the teacher, and that a teacher "needs to encourage the writers to criticize upon their own two feet, and to evolve their own standards" (1968, p. 85). Teachers assisted in this process by stating their opinions and pointing out examples of what they consider to be good and bad writing by both student and professional writers.

Like Macrorie, Donald Murray also endorsed supportive criticism of in-progress drafts and diminished the authority of the teacher in order to increase students' responsibility for their writing. However, he relied primarily on teacher–student conferences, rather than on class workshops to encourage revision. Murray (1985) structured conferences with students according to a basic pattern: First, students commented on their drafts; next the teacher read or reviewed the drafts and responded to the students' comments. Finally, the students responded to the teacher's responses. Murray (1985) explained that the purpose of this structure is "to help students learn to read their own drafts with increasing effectiveness" (p. 148). He described the conference as a "co-reading" of students' texts, which helps them read their writing more intensively and see its features more clearly. The teacher focused on "what is working and what needs work," made comments that were designed to stimulate and encourage students to revise their drafts, and avoided offering evaluative generalizations. Over the course of several conferences, students began to develop criteria for evaluating their own work. After students had a grasp of evaluative criteria, Murray added in-class workshops in which student writers read their work either to a small group or the whole class. However, unlike Macrorie's students, who offered first-draft free writing for peer response, Murray's students revised their initial drafts before presenting them to a group.

Peer Response Groups as an Intervention Strategy

Peter Elbow's work popularized peer response groups as a strategy for encouraging revision. As the title of his book *Writing without Teachers* (1973) indicates, Elbow's approach further de-emphasized the role of the teacher by placing full responsibility for responding to drafts on writers themselves. Elbow's initial guidelines for listeners outlined a descriptive approach to giving feedback: pointing to words and phrases they find particularly striking and effective or weak and empty; summarizing what they consider to the main point, feelings, or center of gravity; telling the writer what they experience as they tried to read the writer's words carefully; and describing their perceptions through metaphors or analogies (e.g., talking about the writing by comparing it to voices, the weather, motion, clothing, terrain, color, shape, etc.). However, Elbow's later books and articles provided more structured guidelines for peer response groups and placed a greater emphasis on helping students learn criteria for good writing. In *Sharing and Responding*, Elbow and Belanoff (1989) expanded Elbow's earlier descriptive approach to responding and also added sections on analytic responding, reader-based responding, and criterion-based or judgment-based responding. For example, readers may ask for responses to specific features or dimensions of writing such as structure, point of view, attitude toward the reader, diction, or syntax. In analytic responding, readers ask for "skeleton feedback" about three main dimensions of a paper—reasons and support, assumptions, and audience. They may also play the "doubting and believing game," in which the reader is first asked to "believe (or pretend to believe) everything I have written" and give more facts to build the writer's case. Next, the reader is asked to "doubt everything" and give arguments against the writer's case (p. 66). In criterion-based or judgment-based responding, which Elbow identified as useful when writers want to know how their writing measures up to specific criteria, response groups respond in terms of traditional criteria for different types of writing. For example, criteria for expository or essay writing include such dimensions as focus on the task, content, clarity, organization, and mechanics. With these additions, Elbow not only provided more direction for peer response groups but also encouraged writers to respond to writing in terms of traditional evaluative criteria.

RESEARCH ON THE EFFECTIVENESS OF INTERVENTION STRATEGIES

What evidence do we have that intervening during the composing process prompts more extensive and meaningful revision? There is relatively little research that specifically investigates the effectiveness of peer group and teacher responses to drafts, as it is difficult to isolate these factors from other related instructional strategies. In addition, researchers have been more concerned about whether instructional strategies improve students' writing overall rather than in the effect on students' revision practices. For example, Clifford (1981) studied the effect of composing in stages where writing was taught as a process, and students wrote multiple drafts of their essays. In the experimental classes, students engaged in brainstorming, free writing, and peer response groups that used feedback sheets to guide group discussion about sentence structure and syntax, paragraph patterns and structure, and support for generalizations. Students also evaluated their peers' papers, using an evaluation sheet, based on criteria developed collaboratively by the class, that indicated the strongest and weakest parts of the paper, and made specific suggestions for revisions. At the end of the term, the writing of these students was compared to that of students who were taught by a traditional "product" approach, in which the teacher read and evaluated only finished essays. In these classes, revision was optional and occurred only after students had received comments and a grade from their teacher. Clifford found that students in the process writing classes wrote essays that were significantly better than those written by students in the traditional classes. Although he attributed much of the improvement in writing ability to the peer workshops that focused on revision, undoubtedly other aspects of the class also had an effect, so the total approach, rather than peer response alone, was responsible for students' improved writing. In another study, Hillocks (1982) studied the effect of brief or extended teacher comments, revision versus no revision, and prewriting instruction versus no prewriting instruction in various combinations on the quality of student writing. Hillocks found that teacher comments, revision, and prewriting instruction contributed to improved writing; however, the design of his study did not allow him to determine the separate contribution of each strategy.

Audience and purpose are central concerns of experienced writers when they revise, and two research studies examined the effect of directing students' attention to these aspects of composing. In a 1981 study, Hays asked basic and advanced writers to write an essay for high school students about the effects of using marijuana. Based on her analysis of composing protocols and interviews, Hays found that those students, whether basic or advanced writers, who had a strong sense of audience and of purpose wrote better papers than those who lacked a strong sense of purpose and focused on the teacher as the audience or had little awareness of the audience. Roen & Wylie (1988) conducted a study that asked students to focus on audience by considering the knowledge that their readers probably possessed. Students who considered their audience during revision received higher holistic scores than those who did not.

In a study specifically designed to investigate the effect of teacher comment and self-evaluation on revision, Beach (1979) compared students who used a self-evaluation guide to revise drafts, received teacher responses to drafts, or were told to revise on their own. After analyzing the amount and kind of revision that resulted with each of these instructional strategies, he found that students who received teacher evaluation showed a greater degree of change, higher fluency, and more support in their final drafts than students who received no evaluation or who used the self-evaluation forms. Moreover, students who used the self-evaluation guides engaged in no more revising than those who were asked to revise on their own without any assistance. Beach concluded the self-evaluation forms were ineffective because students had received little instruction in self-assessment and were not used to detaching themselves critically from their writing. As a result, he recommended that teachers "provide evaluation during the writing of drafts" (p. 119).

Although peer response groups have been a popular and highly recommended instructional strategy for encouraging students to revise, a number of studies have discovered that difficulties may arise when they are used. For example, Kraemer (1993) found that students were often uncomfortable being critical and, therefore, chose to be nice rather than helpful. When Styslinger (1998) investigated students' views on peer-revision, students reported that they generally focused on sentence-level problems and discussed ways to edit papers. Many of her students also expressed frustration with the peer-revision process. They complained about the comments made by peers, describing them as too limiting, general, or nice and not always based on a careful reading of the paper. Students also judged the value of peer comments in relation to their perceptions of a peer's ability and course grade. In general, they wanted teachers to play a larger role during the peer-revision process. Styslinger concluded that teachers could improve peer groups by teaching students how to comment, reinforcing careful readings and responses, and allowing enough time for the process.

Further insights into the difficulties of using peer response groups effectively can be found in studies that focus on the interaction and dynamics within these groups. Carol Berkenkotter (1984) studied the comments made by three students participating in a peer response group in her freshman composition class. After discovering that students responded to peer readers in "significantly different ways depending on the writer's personality, level of maturity, and ability to handle writing problems" (p. 313), she concluded that these differences made it difficult to make generalizations about the effect of peer response groups on revision and that using peer response groups effectively was neither simple nor straightforward. In another study, Thomas Newkirk (1984) investigated the differences between instructor and peer evaluation by comparing the responses that freshman English students and instructors gave to four papers, in which students were asked to use personal experience to support generalizations. Before the papers were evaluated, mechanical errors in spelling and punctuation were corrected so that these factors would not enter into the evaluations. When Newkirk compared students' and teachers' evaluations, he found that they often used different criteria in judging student work. For example, students consistently responded to papers in terms of whether they could "relate to" the topic, whereas teachers rarely expressed a concern for such personal identification. Given their use of different criteria, Newkirk concluded that peer groups might be limited in their ability to provide an adequate response to student papers without careful preparation and training.

Adapting Intervention Strategies for a Wide Range of Contemporary Students

Because of the difficulties encountered in intervening effectively during the composing process, the individual conferences, writing workshops, and peer response groups popularized by Macrorie, Murray, and Elbow, along with the classroom structures for implementing them, have been adapted by later rhetoricians and composition specialists to make them more workable and effective. Because these strategies were initially designed for students in regular first-year or advanced composition classes, they often did not work for younger or less able students. In addition, they initially relied primarily on an inductive approach to developing criteria for effective writing. Most adaptations are more structured and directive than the strategies originally proposed and, thus, are appropriate for a wider range of students and classroom settings.

Adapting the Whole-Class Workshop

The whole-class workshop is now often used as an instructional strategy to teach students criteria for evaluating writing and to model the peer review process. Most students, especially younger and less able writers, need direct instruction in evaluating writing and guidance in responding to the writing of peers. Connors and Glenn (1995) offer the following guidelines for conducting successful whole-class workshops: "(1) Use examples of strong writing so students can easily recognize a paper's strengths. (2) Hand out copies of a student's paper in advance and ask other students to read and write comments before the class workshop begins. (3) Have the writer read his/her paper aloud and then ask for guidance on specific concerns" (p. 45). Axelrod, Cooper, and Warriner (1994) suggest an alternative approach that uses an anonymous draft on the same or a similar assignment written by a student in another class. During the whole-class workshop, teachers explain the evaluative criteria to be used and consciously model the kinds of questions and responses that students should use in responding to each other's drafts.

Adapting Individual Conferences

Nancie Atwell (1987) has adapted Murray's conference approach for the secondary school curricula by conducting all conferences within the classroom. These conferences are at the center of an overall approach to writing instruction in which all class activities center on writing and responding. To increase student involvement, Atwell refers to students as "authors," and students write primarily for themselves and their peers. In the first edition of *In the Middle*, Atwell (1987) recommends scheduling large blocks of class time for writing, ideally every day, but at least three consecutive days a week. In her classroom, students choose the topics and forms for their writing projects, and also move through the writing process at their own pace. They revise their drafts in response to feedback received during short conferences with the teacher, with each conference focusing on only one aspect of writing at a time (i.e., content, organization, development, etc.). In addition, students may confer with a peer or use a list of questions that help them confer with themselves about possible revisions. They develop criteria for evaluating and revising their writing through various activities: participating in brief mini-lessons where the teacher presents writing strategies, by seeing what works in the writing of other students and professional writers, and participating in "share" sessions, where they read their own work and respond to the writing of other students. Finally, students learn grammar and mechanics in context, primarily through editing conferences with the teacher.

Adapting Peer Response Groups

Elbow's "teacherless" peer response groups have been widely adopted as a strategy for encouraging revision. However, these groups have often worked better in theory than in practice (typical problems were discussed earlier in the section that examined research on intervention strategies), and Elbow himself adapted peer response groups by providing the more structured and directive approaches found in *Sharing and Responding* (1989). When peer response groups work, however, they have many benefits. Anne Gere (1987) pointed out that they are particularly effective in addressing the problem of audience awareness and provide an opportunity for collaborative learning in which students come to understand how knowledge is socially constructed. Lindemann (1995) believes that the peer workshop is "one of the best ways to teach students to become independent critics" (p. 202).

Given their potential value in developing students' writing skills, many teachers and researchers have looked for ways to overcome the difficulties that can arise when using peer response groups. For example, Hacker (1996) focused on systematically training students in peer response techniques. For each of the first three writing assignments, he modeled examples of successful peer response episodes. In addition, some students had two individual conferences with him where they reviewed two drafts that they had read prior to the conference. In the conferences, he and the student discussed issues to be addressed in an upcoming peer evaluation workshop. Hacker found that those students who had conferences with him asked more questions of their peers when they were in the role of writer and made more responses when in the role of responder. He concluded that students generally don't know how to respond to drafts in "consistent, systematic ways" and "[t]he time and care taken by writers before peer response determines in large part the types and amount of commentary" that students give (p. 125). Although conferring with students before they participate in peer response groups is time-consuming and too labor-intensive to be practical in most settings, Hacker's success with his approach illustrates the importance of carefully preparing and guiding students before they respond to papers written by their peers.

Lindemann (1995) outlines procedures for improving the effectiveness of peer response workshops that can be used in many classroom settings. She observes that writing workshops need careful planning because "students aren't accustomed to working in groups" and "need explicit instructions for using their time in groups constructively" (p. 199). Teachers must also give students a language for discussing their work and assign concrete, manageable tasks. She recommends dividing the class into heterogeneous groups of five to seven students that remain together for the entire term and suggests beginning with brief tasks. At the beginning of a term, workshop groups might, for example, examine only the first paragraph of an essay or a single paragraph in detail for 10 or 15 minutes. As they become more experienced, they would gradually address larger and more difficult tasks that would require more time to complete. She also recommends that students, guided by the teacher, generate their own list of evaluative criteria stated in language they understand. Although teachers monitor the groups to ensure that they stay on task or to help them refocus the discussion, it is important for them to stay in the background if students are to become independent critics.

Virtually all adaptations recommend that students write as well as talk during the peer response workshops so that writers have a written record of critical comments that they can refer to when they revise. Sometimes students are asked to write comments on peer's draft or on a blank piece of paper that is stapled or clipped to the draft. However, structured peer response forms are a popular method for guiding students' responses and providing specific feedback. For these forms to work successfully, they must be carefully designed and linked to prior classroom instruction. According to the model developed by Flower and her colleagues (1986), the first steps in the revision process are detecting and diagnosing problems. Because novice student writers have difficulty with these steps, particularly in identifying rhetorical problems, a well-designed peer response form will help students focus on the relevant rhetorical issues.

The following is an example of a peer response form that could be used in conjunction with the draft essay on page 125. It focuses the readers' attention on argument strategies, audience, and development. If students were evaluating a different type of essay, a personal narrative for example, the form would need to be modified to focus students' attention on different aspects of writing (i.e., those that make for an effective narrative). The form assumes that students have had previous instruction regarding the rhetorical principles that it asks them to analyze. In addition, students need instruction on strategies that can be used to eliminate the problems that have been identified if they are to revise successfully.

English 1 Title of Essay: ————————————————————

Peer Suggestion Sheet

Your Name: ———————— Writer: ——————————————

1. Is there a clear thesis in the essay? If so, locate and write down the thesis statement. If not, what do you think that the thesis statement seems to be? What do you think about the writer's thesis?

2. What are two reasons that the writer gives to support his/her thesis? Are these effective? Why or why not?

3. Has the writer considered any objection(s) that a reader might make to the position he/she takes? If so, how does the writer deal with the objection(s)? If not, what objections can you think of that the writer should consider?

4. Where would you like to see more development, specifics, or details? In other words, where do you want to know more?

5. How well could you follow the general flow or arrangement of the essay? Were there places that confused you? If so, explain what they were and why they were confusing? Is the essay written in a five-paragraph form? If so, what suggestions can you make to the writer to change that structure?

6. Are the transitions between sentences and paragraphs easy to follow? Point to places where the transitions are unclear.

FIG. 3.1.   Peer Response Form.

FOR WRITING AND DISCUSSION

The essay below is a draft written in response to an assignment that asked the writer to take and support a position on an issue. If this writer were a student in your class, what would be the main rhetorical problems—audience, content, development, and organization—that you would point out as needing revision? Select two or three rhetorical problems and write comments that you might put on a paper to guide this writer's revision.

PC is Ridiculous!

A debate has scourged the United States for several decades regarding the issue of "PC." The abbreviation is often confused with several different means, such as Personal Computer, President's Choice, but instead I am addressing the coined term "Political Correctness." Everyday the debate about PC becomes a more prominent topic in the classroom, the newspapers, and casual conversation and people are getting sick of it.

The truth of the matter is actually simple. No matter what Stanley Fish might claim, political correctness stifles free speech and will ultimately lead to a completely repressive society. At this point, students are afraid to open their mouths and say

what they really think because they are afraid of being labeled "racist" or "sexist."
Is this what education is about? Is this what our society has come to? Isn't it time
we stopped being afraid of telling the truth?

Our country was founded on the Bill of Rights and the first amendment to
that document guarantees freedom of speech. If the PC people continue to make
policy in our colleges and universities, free speech will no longer be a guaranteed
right for students. Are students supposed to be considered second citizens? Isn't
the university a place where people can speak freely? The PC movement has gotten
completely out of hand and all policies concerned with it on campus ought to be
eliminated.

Helping Students Become Independent Revisers

If students are to write effectively for different audiences and purposes
throughout their academic and professional lives, they must become confident writers who can move through the composing process independently.
Classroom instruction along with feedback from teachers and peers all contribute to helping students become independent revisers. However, most
students will benefit from developing procedures and strategies for revising
without the support of teachers and peers.

In her text *Work in Progress,* Lisa Ede (1989) asks students to identify their
preferred composing style and to analyze and monitor their writing process.
Drawing on these insights, students then develop personal guidelines for revision that include reminders about typical problems, strategies successfully
used in the past to address these problems, and productive work habits that
will lead to successful revision. Ede provides students with a practical, three-
stage process for revising that begins with asking the "BIG" questions about
focus, content, and organization, next considers coherence, and finally examines stylistic options.

The St. Martin's Guide to Writing by Axelrod and Cooper (1997) offers a
comprehensive approach to revision that is linked to instruction on critical
features of different genres of writing and fits within the overall writing process. They advise students to begin their revisions by getting a critical reading
from a classmate, friend, or family member. Then, they outline a detailed
procedure for students to follow when revising. First, students reread their
draft straight through to get an objective overview and identify possible
problems. Next, they make a scratch outline of the essay's development and
a two-column chart of a revision plan. In the left column, the student lists
the basic features of the writing task assigned. For example, if the purpose of
the assignment was to explain a concept, the list would include such features
as concept focus, a logical plan, clear definitions, and careful use of sources.
However, if students were writing about a remembered event, they would
need to consider different features: a well-told story, vivid presentation of

significant scenes and people, and an indication of the event's significance. Students then analyze their drafts in terms of the basic features, identifying problems to be solved by referring to questions provided in a critical reading guide. Finally, using detailed suggestions from Axelrod and Cooper (1997), they consider ways to solve the problems identified. The revision process created by Axelrod and Cooper models the strategies characteristic of expert, experienced writers. If students repeat these procedures as they revise each assignment, they are likely to learn strategies and internalize an approach that will enable them to revise independently whenever they have a writing project.

FOR WRITING AND DISCUSSION

Do you usually find that teachers' oral or written comments on your writing, either drafts or final copies, are helpful? How do you make use of their comments? What has been your experience with peer response groups? Have you found them helpful? If so, in what ways? If not, why weren't they helpful? Do you have a specific plan or strategy for revising independently? If so, what is it? Share your answers in small groups.

CONCLUSION

Revision is now seen as crucial to shaping and discovering meaning during composing. However, helping students learn to make meaning-based revisions is a challenging task. To begin, students must develop a different concept of revision. Instead of viewing it as changing sentences and words or hunting for errors, they need to see it as a process of making changes in content and organization and of shaping the text in terms of their purpose and audience. Next, students must learn criteria for evaluating writing. Most students need direct instruction not only in gaining an understanding of these criteria but also in applying them. Teachers play a crucial role in providing this instruction, but, such instruction is often difficult. Not only is the writing process itself complex but also school-sponsored writing often lacks real purposes and audiences and most classroom structures constrain and limit the composing process. Despite these difficulties, knowledgeable teachers can create classroom environments that encourage and support substantive revision. If students learn how to evaluate their own writing and that of their peers and are able to draw on a repertoire of rhetorical strategies for revision, they will be able to use revision as a means of discovering meaning and shaping their texts for specific audiences and purposes.

FOR FURTHER EXPLORATION

Look at a composition textbook designed for high school students and a rhetoric used by first-year composition classes. Compare the concept of revision that each presents? What strategies does each book recommend to help students revise effectively? How would you evaluate these concepts and strategies based on what you have read in this chapter?

REFERENCES

Atwell, N. (1987). *In the middle: Writing, reading, and learning with adolescents*. Portsmouth, NH: Boynton/Cook Publishers.

Axelrod, R. B., & Cooper, C. R. (1997). *The St. Martin's guide to writing* (5th ed.) New York: St. Martin's Press.

Axelrod, R. B., Cooper, C. R., & Warriner, A. M. (1994). *Instructor's resource manual: The St. Martin's guide to writing*. New York: St. Martin's Press.

Beach, R. (1976). Self-evaluation strategies of extensive revisers and nonrevisers. *College Composition and Communication, 27* (2), 160–163.

Beach, R. (1979). The effects of between-draft teacher evaluation versus student self-evaluation on high school students' revising of rough drafts. *Research in the Teaching of English, 13* (2), 111–120.

Berlin, J. A. (1987). *Rhetoric and reality: Writing instruction in American colleges, 1900–1985*. Carbondale and Edwardsville, IL: Southern Illinois University Press.

Bizzell, P., Herzberg, B. & Reynolds, N. (2000). *Bedford bibliography of writing* (5th ed.) Boston and New York: Bedford/St. Martin's.

Bridwell, L. S. (1980). Revising strategies in twelfth grade students' transactional writing. *Research in the Teaching of English, 14* (3), 197–222.

Clifford, J. (1981). Composing in stages: The effects of a collaborative pedagogy. *Research in the Teaching of English, 15* (1), 37–53.

Connors, R. J. (1997). *Composition-rhetoric: Backgrounds, theory, and pedagogy*. Pittsburgh: University of Pittsburgh Press.

Connors, R. J., & Glenn, C. (1995). *The St. Martin's guide to teaching writing* (3rd ed.). New York: St. Martin's Press.

Covino, W. A., & Jolliffe, D. A. (1995). *Rhetoric: Concepts, definitions, boundaries*. Boston: Allyn and Bacon.

Crafton, R. E. (1996). Promises, promises: Computer-assisted revision and basic writers. *Computers and Composition, 13*, 317–326.

Ede, L. (1989). *Work in progress: A guide to writing and revising*. New York: St. Martin's Press.

Eklund, K. S. (1994). Linear and nonlinear strategies in computer-based writing. *Computers and Composition, II*, 227–235.

Elbow, P. (1973). *Writing without teachers*. New York: Oxford University Press.

Elbow, P., & Belanoff, P. (1989). *Sharing and responding*. New York: Random House.

Emig, J. (1971). *The composing process of twelfth graders*. Urbana, IL: NCTE.

Flower, L., Hayes, J. R., Carey, L., Schriver, K., & Stratman, J. (1986). Detection, diagnosis, and the strategies of revision. *College Composition and Communication, 37* (1), 16–55.

Gere, A. R. (1987). *Writing groups: History, theory, and implications*. Carbondale & Edwardsville, IL: Southern Illinois University Press.

Hacker, P. (1996). The effect of teacher conferences on peer response discourse. *Teaching English in the Two-Year College, 23* (2), 112–126.

Hawisher, G. (1987). The effects of word processing on the revision strategies of college freshmen. *Research in the Teaching of English, 21* (2), 145–159.

Hays, J. N. (1981). *The effect of audience considerations upon the revisions of a group of basic writers and more competent junior and senior writers.* Urbana, IL. (ERIC Document Reproduction Service No. ED 204 802)

Heilker, P. (1992). Revision worship and the computer as audience. *Computers and Composition, 9* (3), 59–69.

Hillocks, G., Jr. (1982). The interaction of instruction, teacher comment, and revision in teaching the composing process. *Research in the Teaching of English, 16* (3), 261–278.

Hodges, K. (1982). A history of revision: Theory versus practice. In R. A. Sudol (Ed.), *Revising: New essays for teachers of writing* (pp. 24–42). Urbana, IL: NCTE.

Joram, E., Woodruff, E., Bryson, M., & Lindsay, P. H. (1992). The effects of revising with a word processor on written composition. *Research in the Teaching of English, 26* (2), 167–193.

Kraemer, K. (1993). Revising responding. In K. Spear (Ed.), *Peer response groups in action* (pp. 133–150). Portsmouth, NH: Heinemann.

Lindemann, E. (1995). *A rhetoric for writing teachers* (3rd ed.). New York & Oxford: Oxford University Press.

Macrorie, K. (1968). *Writing to be read.* New York: Hayden Book Company.

Macrorie, K. (1970). *Uptaught.* New York: Hayden Book Company.

McAllister, C., & Louth, R. (1988). The effect of word processing on the quality of basic writers' revisions. *Research in the Teaching of English, 22* (4), 417–427.

Monahan, B. D. (1984). Revision strategies of basic and competent writers as they write for different audiences. *Research in the Teaching of English, 18* (3), 288–304.

Murray, D. M. (1978). Internal revision: A process of discovery (pp. 85–104). In C. R. Cooper & L. Odell (Eds.), *Research on composing: Points of departure.* Urbana, IL: NCTE.

Murray, D. M. (1985). *A writer teaches writing* (2nd ed.). Boston: Houghton Mifflin Company.

Newkirk, T. (1984). Direction and misdirection in peer response. *College Composition and Communication, 35* (3), 300–311.

Owston, R. D., Murphy, S., & Wideman, H. H. (1992). The effects of word processing on students' writing quality and revision strategies. *Research in the Teaching of English, 26* (3), 249–276.

Quintilian (1921). The Institutio oratoria. H. E. Butler, trans. Cambridge: Harvard UP.

Perl, S. (1979). The composing processes of unskilled college writers. *Research in the Teaching of English 13,* 317–336.

Reynolds, T. H., & Bonk, C. J. (1996). Facilitating college writers revisions within a generative evaluative computerized prompting framework. *Computers and Composition 13,* (1), 93–108.

Roen, D. H., & Wylie, R. J. (1998) The effects of audience awareness on drafting and revising. *Research in the Teaching of English, 22* (1), 75–88.

Sharples, M. (1994). Computer support for the rhythms of writing. *Computers and Compositon, II,* 237–250.

Sommers, N. (1980). Revision strategies of student writers and experienced adult writers. *College Composition and Communication, 31* (4), 378–388.

Stallard, C. (1974). An analysis of the writing behavior of good student writers. *Research in the Teaching of English, 8* (2), 206–218.

Styslinger, M. (1998). Some milk, a song, and a set of keys: Students respond to peer revision. *Teaching and Change, 5* (2), 116–138.

Yagelski, R. P. (1995). The role of classroom context in the revision strategies of student writers. *Research in the Teaching of English, 29* (2), 216–238.

Reading

REVISION STRATEGIES OF STUDENT WRITERS AND EXPERIENCED ADULT WRITERS

Nancy Sommers

Although various aspects of the writing process have been studied extensively of late, research on revision has been notably absent. The reason for this, I suspect, is that current models of the writing process have directed attention away from revision. With few exceptions, these models are linear; they separate the writing process into discrete stages. Two representative models are Gordon Rohman's suggestion that the composing process moves from prewriting to writing to rewriting and James Britton's model of the writing process as a series of stages described in metaphors of linear growth, conception—incubation—production.[1] What is striking about these theories of writing is that they model themselves on speech: Rohman defines the writer in a way that cannot distinguish him from a speaker ("A writer is a man who...puts [his] experience into words in his own mind"—p. 15); and Britton bases his theory of writing on what he calls (following Jakobson) the "expressiveness" of speech.[2] Moreover, Britton's study itself follows the "linear model" of the relation of thought and language in speech proposed by Vygotsky, a relationship embodied in the linear movement "from the motive which engenders a thought to the shaping of the thought, *first* in inner speech, *then* in meanings of words, and *finally* in words" (quoted in Britton, p. 40). What this movement fails to take into account in its linear structure—"first ...then...finally"—is the recursive shaping of thought by language; what it fails to take into account is *revision*. In these linear conceptions of the writing process revision is understood as a separate stage at the end of the process—a stage that comes after the completion of a first or second draft and one that is temporally distinct from the prewriting and writing stages of the process.[3]

The linear model bases itself on speech in two specific ways. First of all, it is based on traditional rhetorical models, models that were created to serve the spoken art of oratory. In whatever ways the parts of classical rhetoric are described, they offer "stages" of composition that are repeated in contemporary models of the writing process. Edward Corbett, for instance, describes the "five parts of a discourse"—*inventio, dispositio, elocutio, memoria, pronuntiatio*—and, disregarding the last two parts since "after rhetoric came to be concerned mainly with written discourse, there was no further need to deal with them,"[4] he produces a model very close to Britton's conception [*inventio*], incubation [*dispositio*], production [*elocutio*]. Other rhetorics also follow this procedure, and they do so not simply because of historical accident. Rather, the process represented in the linear model is based on the irreversibility of speech. Speech, Roland Barthes says, "is irreversible":

> "A word cannot be retracted, except precisely by saying that one retracts it. To cross out here is to add: if I want to erase what I have just said, I cannot do it without showing the eraser itself (I must say: 'or rather...' 'I expressed myself badly ...'); paradoxically, it is ephemeral speech which is indelible, not monumental writing. All that one can do in the case of a spoken utterance is to tack on another utterance."[5]

What is impossible in speech is *revision:* like the example Barthes gives, revision in speech is an afterthought. In the same way, each stage of the linear model must be exclusive (distinct from the other stages) or else it becomes trivial and counterproductive to refer to these junctures as "stages."

By staging revision after enunciation, the linear models reduce revision in writing, as in speech, to no more than an afterthought. In this way such models make the study of revision impossible. Revision, in Rohman's model, is simply the repetition of writing; or to pursue Britton's organic metaphor, revision is simply the further growth of what is already there, the "pre-conceived" product. The absence of research on revision, then, is a function of a theory of writing which makes revision both superfluous and redundant, a theory which does not distinguish between writing and speech.

What the linear models do produce is a parody of writing. Isolating revision and then disregarding it plays havoc with the experiences composition teachers have of the actual writing and rewriting of experienced writers. Why should the linear model be preferred? Why should revision be forgotten, superfluous? Why do teachers offer the linear model and students accept it? One reason, Barthes suggests, is that "there is a fundamental tie between teaching and speech," while "writing begins at the point where speech becomes *impossible*."[6] The spoken word cannot be revised. The possibility of revision distinguishes the written text from speech. In fact, according to Barthes, this is the essential difference between writing and speaking. When we must revise, when the very idea is subject to recursive shaping by language, then speech becomes inadequate. This is a matter to which I will return, but first we should examine, theoretically, a detailed exploration of what student writers as distinguished from experienced adult writers *do* when they write and rewrite their work. Dissatisfied with both the linear model of writing and the lack of attention to the process of revision, I conducted a series of studies over the past three years which examined the revision processes of student writers and experienced writers to see what role revision played in their writing processes. In the course of my work the revision process was redefined as *a sequence of changes in a composition—changes which are initiated by cues and occur continually throughout the writing of a work.*

Methodology

I used a case study approach. The student writers were twenty freshmen at Boston University and the University of Oklahoma with SAT verbal scores ranging from 450–600 in their first semester of composition. The twenty experienced adult writers from Boston and Oklahoma City included journalists, editors, and academics. To refer to the two groups, I use the terms *student writers* and *experienced writers* because the principal difference between these two groups is the amount of experience they have had in writing.

Each writer wrote three essays, expressive, explanatory, and persuasive, and rewrote each essay twice, producing nine written products in draft and final form. Each writer was interviewed three times after the final revision of each essay. And each writer suggested revisions for a composition written by an anonymous author. Thus extensive written and spoken documents were obtained from each writer.

The essays were analyzed by counting and categorizing the changes made. Four revision operations were identified: deletion, substitution, addition, and reordering. And four levels of changes were identified: word, phrase, sentence, theme (the extended statement of one idea). A coding system was developed for identifying the frequency of revision by level and operation. In addition, transcripts of the interviews in which the writers interpreted their revisions were used to develop what was called a *scale of concerns* for each writer. This scale enabled me to codify what were the writer's primary concerns, secondary concerns, tertiary concerns, and whether the writers used the same scale of concerns when revising the second or third drafts as they used in revising the first draft.

Revision Strategies of Student Writers

Most of the students I studied did not use the terms *revision* or *rewriting*. In fact, they did not seem comfortable using the word *revision* and explained that revision was not a word they used, but the word their teachers used. Instead, most of the students had developed various functional terms to describe the type of changes they made. The following are samples of these definitions:

Scratch Out and Do Over Again: "I say scratch out and do over, and that means what it says. Scratching out and cutting out. I read what I have written and I cross out a word and put another word in; a more decent word or a better word. Then if there is somewhere to use a sentence that I have crossed out, I will put it there."

Reviewing: "Reviewing means just using better words and eliminating words that are not needed. I go over and change words around."

Reviewing: "I just review every word and make sure that everything is worded right. I see if I am rambling; I see if I can put a better word in or leave one out. Usually when I read what I have written, I say to myself, 'that word is so bland or so trite,' and then I go and get my thesaurus."

Redoing: "Redoing means cleaning up the paper and crossing out. It is looking at something and saying, no that has to go, or no, that is not right."

Marking Out: "I don't use the word rewriting because I only write one draft and the changes that I make are made on top of the draft. The changes that I make are usually just marking out words and putting different ones in."

Slashing and Throwing Out: "I throw things out and say they are not good. I like to write like Fitzgerald did by inspiration, and if I feel inspired then I don't need to slash and throw much out."

The predominant concern in these definitions is vocabulary. The students understand the revision process as a rewording activity. They do so because they perceive words as the unit of written discourse. That is, they concentrate on particular words apart from their role in the text. Thus one student quoted above thinks in terms of dictionaries, and, following the eighteenth century theory of words parodied in *Gulliver's Travels,* he imagines a load of things carried about to be exchanged. Lexical changes are the major revision activities of the students because economy is their goal. They are governed, like the linear model itself, by the Law of Occam's razor that prohibits logically needless repetition: redundancy and superfluity. Nothing governs speech more than such superfluities; speech constantly repeats itself precisely because spoken words, as Barthes writes, are expendable in the cause of communication. The aim of revision according to the students' own description is therefore to clean up speech; the redundancy of speech is unnecessary in writing, their logic suggests, because writing, unlike speech, can be reread. Thus one student said, "Redoing means cleaning up the paper and crossing out." The remarkable contradiction of cleaning by marking might, indeed, stand for student revision as I have encountered it.

The students place a symbolic importance on their selection and rejection of words as the determiners of success or failure for their compositions. When revising, they primarily ask themselves: can I find a better word or phrase? A more impressive, not so cliched, or less hum-drum word? Am I repeating the same word or phrase too often? They approach the revision process with what could be labeled as a "thesaurus philosophy of writing"; the students consider the thesaurus a harvest of lexical substitutions and believe that most problems in their essays can be solved by rewording. What is revealed in the students' use of the thesaurus is a governing attitude toward their writing: that the meaning to be communicated is already there, already finished, already produced, ready to be communicated, and all that is necessary is a better word "rightly worded." One student defined revision as "redoing"; "redoing" meant "just using better words and eliminating words that are not needed." For the students, writing is translating: the thought to the page, the language of speech to the more formal language of prose, the word to its synonym. Whatever is translated, an original text already exists for students, one which need not be discovered or acted upon, but simply communicated.[7]

The students list repetition as one of the elements they most worry about. This cue signals to them that they need to eliminate the repetition either by substituting or deleting words or phrases. Repetition occurs, in large part, because student writing imitates—transcribes—speech: attention to repetitious words is a manner of cleaning speech. Without a sense of the developmental possibilities of revision (and writing in general) students seek, on the authority of many textbooks, simply to clean up their language and prepare to type. What is curious, however, is that students are aware of lexical repetition, but not conceptual repetition. They only notice the repetition if they can "hear" it: they do not diagnose lexical repetition as symptomatic of problems on a deeper level. By rewording their sentences to avoid the lexical repetition, the students solve the immediate problem, but blind themselves to problems on a textual level; although they are using different words, they are sometimes merely restating the same idea with different words. Such blindness, as I discovered with student writers, is the inability to "see" revision as a process: the inability to "re-view" their work again, as it were, with different eyes, and to start over.

The revision strategies described above are consistent with the students' understanding of the revision process as requiring lexical changes but not semantic changes. For the students, the extent to which they revise is a function of their level of inspiration. In fact, they use the word *inspiration* to describe the ease or difficulty with which their essay is written, and the extent to which the essay needs to be revised. If students feel inspired, if the writing comes easily, and if they don't get stuck on individual words or phrases, then they say that they cannot see any reason to revise. Because students do not see revision as an activity in which they modify and develop perspectives and ideas, they feel that if they know what they want to say, then there is little reason for making revisions.

The only modification of ideas in the students' essays occurred when they tried out two or three introductory paragraphs. This results, in part, because the students have been taught in another version of the linear model of composing to use a thesis statement as a controlling device in their introductory paragraphs.

Since they write their introductions and their thesis statements even before they have really discovered what they want to say, their early close attention to the thesis statement, and more generally the linear model, function to restrict and circumscribe not only the development of their ideas, but also their ability to change the direction of these ideas.

Too often as composition teachers we conclude that students do not willingly revise. The evidence from my research suggests that it is not that students are unwilling to revise, but rather that they do what they have been taught to do in a consistently narrow and predictable way. On every occasion when I asked students why they hadn't made any more changes, they essentially replied, "I knew something larger was wrong, but I didn't think it would help to move words around." The students have strategies for handling words and phrases and their strategies helped them on a word or sentence level. What they lack, however, is a set of strategies to help them identify the "something larger" that they sensed was wrong and work from there. The students do not have strategies for handling the whole essay. They lack procedures or heuristics to help them reorder lines of reasoning or ask questions about their purposes and readers. The students view their compositions in a linear way as a series of parts. Even such potentially useful concepts as "unity" or "form" are reduced to the rule that a composition, if it is to have form, must have an introduction, a body, and a conclusion, or the sum total of the necessary parts.

The students decide to stop revising when they decide that they have not violated any of the rules for revising. These rules, such as "Never begin a sentence with a conjunction" or "Never end a sentence with a preposition," are lexically cued and rigidly applied. In general, students will subordinate the demands of the specific problems of their text to the demands of the rules. Changes are made in compliance with abstract rules about the product, rules that quite often do not apply to the specific problems in the text. These revision strategies are teacher-based, directed towards a teacher-reader who expects compliance with rules—with pre-existing "conceptions"—and who will only examine parts of the composition (writing comments about those parts in the margins of their essays) and will cite any violations of rules in those parts. At best the students see their writing altogether passively through the eyes of former teachers or their surrogates, the textbooks, and are bound to the rules which they have been taught.

Revision Strategies of Experienced Writers

One aim of my research has been to contrast how student writers define revision with how a group of experienced writers define their revision processes. Here is a sampling of the definitions from the experienced writers:

> *Rewriting:* "It is a matter of looking at the kernel of what I have written, the content, and the thinking about it, responding to it, making decisions, and actually restructuring it."

Rewriting: "I rewrite as I write. It is hard to tell what is a first draft because it is not determined by time. In one draft, I might cross out three pages, write two, cross out a fourth, rewrite it, and call it a draft. I am constantly writing and rewriting. I can only conceptualize so much in my first draft—only so much information can be held in my head at one time; my rewriting efforts are a reflection of how much information I can encompass at one time. There are levels and agenda which I have to attend to in each draft."

Rewriting: "Rewriting means on one level, finding the argument, and on another level, language changes to make the argument more effective. Most of the time I feel as if I can go on rewriting forever. There is always one part of a piece that I could keep working on. It is always difficult to know at what point to abandon a piece of writing. I like this idea that a piece of writing is never finished, just abandoned."

Rewriting: "My first draft is usually very scattered. In rewriting, I find the line of argument. After the argument is resolved, I am much more interested in word choice and phrasing."

Revising: "My cardinal rule in revising is never to fall in love with what I have written in a first or second draft. An idea, sentence, or even a phrase that looks catchy, I don't trust. Part of this idea is to wait a while. I am much more in love with something after I have written it than I am a day or two later. It is much easier to change anything with time."

Revising: "It means taking apart what I have written and putting it back together again. I ask major theoretical questions of my ideas, respond to those questions, and think of proportion and structure, and try to find a controlling metaphor. I find out which ideas can be developed and which should be dropped. I am constantly chiseling and changing as I revise."

The experienced writers describe their primary objective when revising as finding the form or shape of their argument. Although the metaphors vary, the experienced writers often use structural expressions such as "finding a framework," "a pattern," or "a design" for their argument. When questioned about this emphasis, the experienced writers responded that since their first drafts are usually scattered attempts to define their territory, their objective in the second draft is to begin observing general patterns of development and deciding what should be included and what excluded. One writer explained, "I have learned from experience that I need to keep writing a first draft until I figure out what I want to say. Then in a second draft, I begin to see the structure of an argument and how all the various sub-arguments which are buried beneath the surface of all those sentences are related." What is described here is a process in which the writer is both agent and vehicle. "Writing," says Barthes, unlike speech, "develops like a seed, not a line,"[8] and like a seed it confuses beginning and end, conception and production. Thus, the experienced writers say their drafts are "not determined by time," that rewriting is a "constant process," that they feel as if (they) "can go on forever." Revising confuses the beginning and end, the agent and vehicle; it confuses, *in order to find,* the line of argument.

After a concern for form, the experienced writers have a second objective: a concern for their readership. In this way, "production" precedes "conception." The experienced writers imagine a reader (reading their product) whose existence and whose expectations influence their revision process. They have abstracted the standards of a reader and this reader seems to be partially a reflection of themselves and functions as a critical and productive collaborator—a collaborator who has yet to love their work. The anticipation of a reader's judgment causes a feeling of dissonance when the writer recognizes incongruities between intention and execution, and requires these writers to make revisions on all levels. Such a reader gives them just what the students lacked: new eyes to "re-view" their work. The experienced writers believe that they have learned the causes and conditions, the product, which will influence their reader, and their revision strategies are geared towards creating these causes and conditions. They demonstrate a complex understanding of which examples, sentences, or phrases should be included or excluded. For example, one experienced writer decided to delete public examples and add private examples when writing about the energy crisis because "private examples would be less controversial and thus more persuasive." Another writer revised his transitional sentences because "some kinds of transitions are more easily recognized as transitions than others." These examples represent the type of strategic attempts these experienced writers use to manipulate the conventions of discourse in order to communicate to their reader.

But these revision strategies are a process of more than communication; they are part of the process of *discovering meaning* altogether. Here we can see the importance of dissonance; at the heart of revision is the process by which writers recognize and resolve the dissonance they sense in their writing. Ferdinand de Saussure has argued that meaning is differential or "diacritical," based on differences between terms rather than "essential" or inherent qualities of terms. "Phonemes," he said, "are characterized not, as one might think, by their own positive quality but simply by the fact that they are distinct."[9] In fact, Saussure bases his entire *Course in General Linguistics* on these differences, and such differences are dissonant; like musical dissonances which gain their significance from their relationship to the "key" of the composition which itself is determined by the whole language, specific language (parole) gains its meaning from the system of language (langue) of which it is a manifestation and part. The musical composition—a "composition" of parts—creates its "key" as in an over-all structure which determines the value (meaning) of its parts. The analogy with music is readily seen in the compositions of experienced writers: both sorts of composition are based precisely on those structures experienced writers seek in their writing. It is this complicated relationship between the parts and the whole in the work of experienced writers which destroys the linear model; writing cannot develop "like a line" because each addition or deletion is a reordering of the whole. Explicating Saussure, Jonathan Culler asserts that "meaning depends on difference of meaning."[10] But student writers constantly struggle to bring their essays into congruence with a predefined meaning. The experienced writers do the opposite: they seek to discover (to create) meaning in the engagement with their writing, in revision. They seek to emphasize and exploit the lack of clarity, the differences of meaning, the dissonance, that writing as opposed to speech allows in the possibility of revision. Writing has spatial and temporal features not apparent in speech—words are recorded in space and fixed in time—which is why writing is susceptible to reordering and later addition. Such features make possible the dissonance that both provokes revision and promises, from itself, new meaning.

For the experienced writers the heaviest concentration of changes is on the sentence level, and the changes are predominantly by addition and deletion. But, unlike the students, experienced writers make changes on all levels and use all revision operations. Moreover, the operations the students fail to use—reordering and addition—seem to require a theory of the revision process as a totality—a theory which, in fact, encompasses the *whole* of the composition. Unlike the students, the experienced writers possess a non-linear theory in which a sense of the whole writing both precedes and grows out of an examination of the parts. As we saw, one writer said he needed "a first draft to figure out what to say," and "a second draft to see the structure of an argument buried beneath the surface." Such a "theory" is both theoretical and strategical; once again, strategy and theory are conflated in ways that are literally impossible for the linear model. Writing appears to be more like a seed than a line.

Two elements of the experienced writers' theory of the revision process are the adoption of a holistic perspective and the perception that revision is a recursive process. The writers ask: what does my essay as a *whole* need for form, balance, rhythm, or communication. Details are added, dropped, substituted, or reordered according to their sense of what the essay needs for emphasis and proportion. This sense, however, is constantly in flux as ideas are developed and modified; it is constantly "re-viewed" in relation to the parts. As their ideas change, revision becomes an attempt to make their writing consonant with that changing vision.

The experienced writers see their revision process as a recursive process—a process with significant recurring activities—with different levels of attention and different agenda for each cycle. During the first revision cycle their attention is primarily directed towards narrowing the topic and delimiting their ideas. At this point, they are not as concerned as they are later about vocabulary and style. The experienced writers explained that they get closer to their meaning by not limiting themselves too early to lexical concerns. As one writer commented to explain her revision process, a comment inspired by the summer 1997 New York power failure: "I feel like Con Edison cutting off certain states to keep the generators going. In first and second drafts, I try to cut off as much as I can of my editing generator, and in a third draft, I try to cut off some of my idea generators, so I can make sure that I will actually finish the essay." Although the experienced writers describe their revision process as a series of different levels or cycles, it is inaccurate to assume that they have only one objective for each cycle and that each cycle can be defined by a different objective. The same objectives and sub-processes are present in each cycle, but in different proportions. Even though these experienced writers place the predominant weight upon finding the form of their argument during the first cycle, other concerns exist as well. Conversely, during the later cycles, when the experienced writers' primary attention is focused upon stylistic concerns, they are still attuned, although in a reduced way, to the form of the argument. Since writers are limited in what they can attend to during each cycle (understandings are temporal), revision strategies help balance competing demands on attention. Thus, writers can concentrate on more than one objective at a time by developing strategies to sort out and organize their different concerns in successive cycles of revision.

It is a sense of writing as discovery—a repeated process of beginning over again, starting out new—that the students failed to have. I have used the notion of dissonance because such dissonance, the incongruities between intention and execution, governs both writing and meaning. Students do not see the incongruities. They need to rely on their own internalized sense of good writing and to see their writing with their "own" eyes. Seeing in revision—seeing beyond hearing—is at the root of the word *revision* and the process itself; current dicta on revising blind our students to what is actually involved in revision. In fact, they blind them to what constitutes good writing altogether. Good writing disturbs: it creates dissonance. Students need to seek the dissonance of discovery, utilizing in their writing, as the experienced writers do, the very difference between writing and speech—the possibility of revision.

Notes

1. D. Gordon Rohman and Albert O. Wlecke, "Pre-writing: The Construction and Application of Models for Concept Formation in Writing," Cooperative Research Project No. 2174, U.S. Office of Education, Department of Health, Education, and Welfare; James Britton, Anthony Burgess, Nancy Martin, Alex McLeod, Harold Rosen, *The Development of Writing Abilities (11–18)* (London: Macmillan Education, 1975).

2. Britton is following Roman Jakobson, "Linguistics and Poetics," in T. A. Sebeok, *Style in Language* (Cambridge, Mass: MIT Press, 1960).

3. For an extended discussion of this issue see Nancy Sommers, "The Need for Theory in Composition Research," *College Composition and Communication.* 30 (February, 1979), 46–69.

4. *Classical Rhetoric for the Modern Student* (New York: Oxford University Press, 1965), p. 27.

5. Roland Barthes, "Writers, Intellectuals, Teachers," in *Image-Music-Text.* trans. Stephen Heath (New York: Hill and Wang, 1977), pp. 190–191.

6. "Writers, Intellectuals, Teachers," p. 190.

7. Nancy Sommers and Ronald Schleifer, "Means and Ends: Some Assumptions of Student Writers," *Composition and Teaching,* II (in press).

8. *Writing Degree Zero* in *Writing Degree Zero and Elements of Semiology,* trans. Annette Lavers and Colin Smith (New York: Hill and Wang, 1968), p. 20.

9. *Course in General Linguistics,* trans. Wade Baskin (New York, 1966), p. 119.

10. Jonathan Culler, *Saussure* (Penguin Modern Masters Series; London: Penguin Books, 1976), p. 70.

Acknowledgment: The author wishes to express her gratitude to Professor William Smith, University of Pittsburgh, for his vital assistance with the research reported in this article and to Patrick Hays, her husband, for extensive discussions and critical editorial help.

4

Audience

Irene L. Clark

This chapter discusses varying perspectives and controversies associated with audience, examines the relationship between audience and discourse community, and suggests possibilities for addressing audience in the writing class:

> Who is going to read this?
> Who cares about this topic?
> How have you considered your audience?

Writing teachers ask students questions such as these to focus attention on "audience," a concept in composition that has generated considerable theoretical discussion over the past 25 years. Once equated simply with the reader or readers of a text, "audience" in scholarly journals has now become "audiences," and is accompanied by a set of complex terms such as "invoked," "evoked," "fictionalized," "intended," or "general." However, despite the flurry of attention to audience as a theoretical issue, the concept of audience has had less of an impact in the writing class, because most students, when they think about audience, assume that they are writing for their teacher and are unaware of how audience awareness affects other aspects of a text, such as purpose, form, style, and genre. To foster student understanding of the importance of audience, some composition teachers will remind students to "consider your audience"—good advice, certainly, but difficult for students to follow, unless the teacher helps them understand the complexity of the concept and demonstrates how audience awareness is manifested within a text.

This chapter discusses "audience" as a significant theoretical and pedagogical concept in composition, focusing on the following facets of the topic:

Varying perspectives on audience.

Controversies associated with the concept of audience.

The relationship between audience and discourse community.

How the concept of audience can be used in the writing class.

STUDENT PERSPECTIVES ON AUDIENCE

Student writers tend to think of audience in terms of an actual reader, in this case their own teacher. Indeed, teachers do read their students' essays, acting as a type of audience that exists in no other rhetorical context. School-based writing constructs a reader–writer relationship that is unlike any communication in the real world because as Reid and Kroll (1995) have noted, its purpose "is not to inform, persuade, or entertain the teacher—it is to demonstrate understanding of the assignment in ways that the teacher-reader already anticipates" (p. 18). The type of relationship that exists in a school setting, is thus unlike any other:

> Instead of an expert-to-expert relationship or a colleague-to-colleague relationship between the writer and the reader (as in "real" writing–reading events), the relationship is skewed: novice-to-expert (teacher-reader) assessing the novice (student-writer) in ways that have consequences for the writer's life. (p. 18)

Academic writing tasks are tests and students understand this. They ask themselves, "what does the teacher want?" and they view their audience as the person who wields the corrective pen and assigns the grade.

College writing assignments, however, are not intended to teach students to write directly to their teacher. Rather, their goal is to enable students to construct discourse for a wider academic audience and to master the text genres that such audiences expect. Therefore, although the teacher is a significant actual reader, college writing assignments require students to "pretend" that they are writing for a more encompassing, general audience and to orient their discourse toward that audience. If students think of audience solely in terms of their teacher, the nature of the discourse instantly changes. Sometimes, students may omit necessary explanations, definitions, or support, because they assume, quite reasonably, that the teacher is already familiar with the topic and, therefore, does not need such information. In fact, in some instances, students may actually address the teacher directly, almost as if they were writing personal letters instead of formal essays. One of my students, for example, began his paper as follows:

> My paper is about how the traditional family will not be a workable social
> entity in the twenty-first century. When we discussed Stephanie Coontz's book
> in class, it showed that the idea of the ideal traditional family is only a myth.

Other problems associated with students' obliviousness to audience are
the assumption of an inappropriate tone or, when students write about controversial topics, the presentation of only one side of an issue. Seemingly
insensible to the rhetorical goals of college writing, students may write blatantly opinionated, aggressive, or poorly reasoned diatribes on the topic,
rather than an appropriately thoughtful, reasoned response. They don't
seem to realize that an outrageous or insulting statement such as "Anyone
who believes this is just a racist," or "Women are naturally inferior to men,"
might have a negative, rather than a persuasive, effect on a reader. Nor do
they seem conscious of the potential role an audience might have in shaping
other facets of the text.

AUDIENCE AND THE WRITING PROCESS

How one addresses the concept of audience in the composition class depends, to a great extent, on one's concept of audience within the communicative act—that is, whether one believes that writers aim to communicate
with an actual, known reader or set of readers, or that writers create roles
for a broader, unfamiliar audience by providing audience-oriented textual
cues. For classical rhetoricians, this was not an important issue because they
conceived of audience in terms of an oral model for an audience that was
most likely known. Plato, in the *Phaedrus* (370 B.C.), asserted that the rhetorician should adapt a speech to characteristics of an audience, classifying "the
type of speech appropriate to each type of soul" (p. 147). Aristotle also conceived of audience in terms of actual "hearers" of persuasive discourse. In
Book II of the *Rhetoric,* Aristotle discussed the ways a speaker might adapt
his discourse to various audiences, categorizing audiences according to their
time in life (youth, age, the prime of life etc.) and discussing various appeals
by means of which a rhetor could be persuasive. This rhetorical model, as
Kirsch and Roen (1990) have pointed out, rests on several assumptions:
that the audience is known, the values and needs of the audience can be
identified, and the audience is separate from the discourse and its social
context. Although somewhat applicable to oral communication, the notion
that an audience is completely knowable does not transfer easily to written
discourse, in which an audience is often completely removed in both time
and space from the writer. More important, from the perspective of the composition class, this model characterizes a rhetorical interaction as moving in

only one direction, from the rhetor (the speaker or writer) to the audience or reader. The writer, according to this model, is conceived of as a sender and the audience as merely a receiver.

FOR WRITING AND DISCUSSION

1. How do you consider audience in your own writing?
2. Classical rhetoricians conceived of audience in terms of oral discourse, a model that has only limited applicability to the concept of audience in the composition class. List as many differences as you can think of between an audience that "hears" a speech and an audience that "reads" an essay.
3. How can the concept of audience help a writer explore a topic?

WRITER–AUDIENCE CONNECTIONS: RECENT PERSPECTIVES

This notion that audience is equivalent to an actual reader, a living flesh and blood person who will actually read the text, has been challenged and broadened by a number of 20th-century scholars who conceive of the communication act as interactive and more complex than the sender-to-receiver model would suggest. Recent scholarship conceives of writers and audiences as dynamically linked, working cooperatively to make meaning; the writer creates an audience within the text during composing and readers recreate that text when they read it. Peter Elbow, in *Writing with Power* (1981), suggested that we picture readers and writers as two riders on the same bicycle. As writers, we can steer, but the readers have to pedal. If we don't explain where we are going and why, and convince our readers that they should keep pedaling, the bicycle will stop and both will tumble off.

This interactive relationship between writers and readers was described by George Dillon (1981) through a metaphor of musical notation. He noted that:

> The written marks on the page more resemble a musical score than a computer program: they are marks cueing or prompting an enactment or realization by the reader, rather than a code requiring deciphering. (p. xi)

Other models of composing depicting this interactivity include one that was developed by James Kinneavy (1971), who, in *A Theory of Discourse*, constructed a dynamic model of communication between the writer, topic, and audience interacting dynamically with one another and Wayne Booth's concept of the rhetorical triangle. Booth (1983) maintained that audience exerts a formative influence on the text, because whether one emphasizes the writer, subject, or audience determines one's "rhetorical stance," which Booth defined as follows:

> What makes the differences between effective communication and mere wasted effort ... is something I shall call the rhetorical stance, a stance which depends on discovering and maintaining in any writing situation a proper balance among the three elements that are at work in any communicative effort, the available arguments about the subject itself, the interests and peculiarities of the audience, and the voice, the implied character, of the speaker. (pp. 139–145)

FOR WRITING AND DISCUSSION

Which metaphor depicting the relationship between writer and audience do you feel is most useful? Write a paragraph indicating which one you prefer, considering how this model can be helpful to novice writers.

The Work of James Moffett

James Moffett's *Teaching the Universe of Discourse* (1968) presents a view of audience based on an interrelationship between the writer, subject, and reader. According to Moffett, communication involves two relationships: how the writer views the subject, which he calls the "I–It" relation, and how the writer views the reader, which he calls the "I–you relation." Moffett characterizes the "I–It" relationship as a continuum between reporting an event at the time it occurs and generalizing about that event at a more distant time. This continuum between the concrete and the abstract "indicate when events occurred in relation to when the speaker is speaking about them" (p. 244) and the main points along this continuum are conceived of in terms of four levels of increasing abstraction:

What is happening?
What happened?
What happens?
What may happen?

To give an example, suppose you were standing in the post office with a friend, commenting on how long the lines were. As you observed the lines, you would not be very distant from your subject matter—that is, the experience of standing in the line. Later on, you might recall those lines in narrative form to another friend, a process that would require you to select and incorporate details of the experience from memory. Still later, recalling those lines, you might write a report in expository form about the line at the post office, a process that would involve further generalization and abstraction, and then, months or years later, you might use that experience of waiting in line and other experiences occurring since then to argue a position about those long lines, a process that would involve still greater abstraction and generalization.

In terms of the "I–you" relation, Moffett defines degrees of distance not between the writer and the subject, but, rather, between the writer and the audience. Students might begin by writing for themselves and then move beyond to write for increasingly abstract audiences, from the known to the unknown. Moffett maintains that an effective writing curriculum would enable students to write about "what is happening" for a variety of audiences, from recreating an experience for oneself, to narrating the experience to a close friend, to writing formally about the experience for a public audience whom the writer does not know. Moffett's curriculum, then, is based on a "universe of discourse," which moves the student from concrete experience to abstract idea, and from the self to the world. The teacher's role within this universe is to construct writing assignments that enable students to move in this progression and to gain consciousness of how different audiences require different conceptual and textual strategies.

THE FICTIONALIZED AUDIENCE

Another concept of how audience awareness affects writing is that an author *creates* an audience and provides cues within a text about who that audience might be. This idea is the basis of a widely anthologized essay, "The Writer's Audience is Always a Fiction" (1975) in which Walter Ong maintained that "the historian, the scholar or scientist, and the simple letter writer all fictionalize their audiences, casting them in a made-up role and calling on them to play the role assigned" (p. 17). Claiming that all writers, even student writers, must fictionalize their audience, Ong (1975) illustrated his point by citing the following passage from *A Farewell to Arms:*

> In the late summer of that year we lived in a house in a village that looked across the river and the plain to the mountains. (p. 15)

This passage, Ong pointed out, fictionalizes a reader who is close to the writer, close enough to know which year is meant by "that" year, which river, which plain, and which mountains, thereby fostering a "you and me" relationship between writer and reader that the writer develops and the reader reacts to when he or she "reads" the text. All authors, Ong claimed, fictionalize their audience, even Homer, who constructed his audience through a "once upon a time" framework. Ong's main position is that student writers will be more successful if they, too, can learn to fictionalize their audiences.

How can a student envision an audience when he or she is assigned to write an essay for a class? According to Ong, a student who understands the concept of fictionalizing an audience will adopt the voices that he or she knows from reading, for example, the voice of Samuel Clemens in Tom Sawyer, with which the student knows his teacher will be familiar. Ong suggested that to develop awareness of audience for a particular writing task, student writers should not begin with the traditional question, "Who *is* my audience?" but, rather, with the question, "Who do I *choose* as my audience?"

Ong's view of audience as being created by the writer has been supported by a number of scholars, among them, Douglas Park (1982), who noted in his essay "The Meanings of Audience" that even when an audience really exists outside of the text, the argumentative context or situation requires the writer to "invent" an audience that goes beyond a specific individual to encompass a set of attitudes toward or acquaintance with the subject. Park cited the example of an article concerned with how to plant asparagus root, which postulates an audience as an enthusiastic "home gardener, eager for hard work and fresh vegetables" (p. 249). Park also noted that even when the audience seems to be a particular person who really exists, the President of the United States, for example, the audience is not only the President as an individual that the text addresses but also the President in his presidential position, someone who represents a set of attitudes toward the subject. Writing a request to the President, thus, involves an act of imagination beyond that of simply knowing that particular President's attitudes and political position. The writer must also use the text to "create" a president that under the right circumstances will be receptive to the request, a president who is concerned about the subject, and a president who is open to new suggestions. Were the President not perceived as receptive, concerned, and open, there would be no rhetorical aim in writing to him. But once the writer conceives of these qualities, he or she must then address that conception of the president by indicating through cues in the text that the audience is perceived in this way. Thus, regardless of whether a real reader exists, most writing tasks, and particularly argumentative or persuasive writing, require the writer to create a fictionalized audience that embodies "a complex set of conventions, estimations, implied responses, and attitudes" (Park, 1982, p. 251).

Audience Addressed/Audience Invoked: Fictionalized and Real Audiences

The idea that audience can be both real and imagined was clarified and elaborated on in the award-winning article that appears at the end of this chapter, in which Lisa Ede and Andrea Lunsford distinguished between what they term the "audience addressed" and the "audience invoked." Ede and Lunsford (1984) maintained that writers must both analyze a possible real audience and invent a chosen one, that the two are not incompatible, and that the concept of audience encompasses a synthesis of both:

> The addressed audience, the actual or intended readers of a discourse, exists outside of the text. Writers may analyze these readers' needs, anticipate their biases, even defer to their wishes. But it is only through the text, through language, that writers embody or give life to their conception of the reader. In so doing, they do not so much create a role for the reader—a phrase which implies that the writer somehow creates a mold to which the reader adjusts—as invoke it. (p. 169)

Citing the example of a student who wishes to persuade her neighbors that a proposed home for mentally retarded adults would not be a disaster for the neighborhood, Ede and Lunsford pointed out that the student must not only analyze the real audience—that is, not only know demographic factors such as age, race, and class—but also assess how much the real audience actually knows about mental retardation, in particular, what fears the subject might raise and what values might be used in making an appeal to change the audience's belief or attitude. But beyond learning as much as possible about the real audience and tailoring the text to suit the needs of that real audience, the student might also invite that audience to see itself in an especially admirable light, that is, to *create* a role for that audience as enlightened and humanitarian; an audience who would be inclined to behave charitably once it was properly informed. Ede and Lunsford also pointed out that writers play the additionally creative roles as the readers of their own writing, testing the effectiveness of the cues within the text during rereading. They maintained that "it is the writer who, as writer and reader of his or her own text, one guided by a sense of purpose and by the particularities of a specific rhetorical situation, establishes the range of potential roles an audience may play" (Ede & Lunsford, 1984 p. 166).

This dual concept of real and created audience was further problematized by Barbara Tomlinson (1990), in "Ong May Be Wrong: Negotiating with Non-fictional Readers." Tomlinson agrees that writers must both address actual readers as well as invoke fuller representations of audiences, but she emphasizes that writers must first consider real readers on whom we depend for esteem and approval. "It is only because we have those idiosyncratic, individual readers that we can ever learn to generalize about readers, to fictionalize our audiences effectively," Tomlinson observed. "These are the readers we learn to generalize from" (p. 88). This idea that the fictionalized audience derives from one that a writer has had acquaintance with was supported by Jack Selzer (2000), who noted that "like the intended reader . . . and like other fictional characters, narratees and implied readers can be based on real people, can be idealizations of real people, or can be pure creations" (p. 78). More concrete is the term "informed reader," suggested by Stanley Fish (1980), denoting "neither an abstraction nor an actual living reader but a hybrid—a real reader (me) who does everything within his power to make himself informed" (p. 49). The informed reader is both the communal reader of the discourse community and an individual real reader who is actively engaged in understanding the text.

USING FICTIONAL CHARACTERS AND DIALOGUE TO FOCUS STUDENT ATTENTION ON THE CONCEPT OF AUDIENCE

A classroom strategy that is useful in helping students gain awareness of audience involves having students create a fictional character who is likely to have a strong position on the topic they are writing about. Students try to understand that character's opinion on the topic, and they then write a hypothetical dialogue between this character and themselves in which they discuss the issue for the paper. Having students create a fictional audience and engage in a dialogue with that audience not only makes the class interesting and lively as students share their creations but it also fosters several important insights associated with audience, in particular:

1. It helps students understand that the teacher is not the only audience for an assigned essay.
2. It serves as a heuristic to generate ideas.
3. Because it fosters respect for an audience's humanity and opinions, it helps students understand that an essay is not simply a vehicle for the writer to express his or her own ideas, but, rather, that its goal is for the writer to engage in a cooperative activity with the reader. In this context, rhetoric is conceived of as inherently social.
4. It enables students to distinguish when it is appropriate to confront an opponent directly and when it is appropriate to strive for change through mutual acceptance and understanding by each party of the other's views.
5. It helps students determine which cues in their own text are likely to be effective in addressing their created audience.

When students create their characters and attempt to imitate these characters' voices in writing, they gain a more immediate sense of their potential audience and a greater insight into the audience's beliefs, attitudes, and values. Such understanding enables students to become sensitive to when such an audience would experience a sense of threat and anticipate potential areas of conflict. It also helps students understand the complexity of the issues involved. Working with dialogue also has the advantage of tapping into students' skills at speaking and listening, which are often better developed than their writing skills. Students can, thus, use their knowledge of what is appropriate in oral discourse to detect what may be inappropriate in their writing. The inappropriateness of statements such as "this idea is just ridiculous" or "that idea is just crazy" or "anyone who believes that is just a racist" is more easily discerned if students imagine themselves actually saying them to real people; they are better able to gauge the effect of extreme statements on the persuasiveness of their papers. The term "audience," then, becomes something real for them, not just an abstract concept.

The following section includes an exercise based on the idea of fictionalizing an audience. I suggest that you work through this exercise yourself and also adapt it for your students.

Creating Characters

Creating characters in class allows you and your students to experiment with forms of writing usually associated with fiction or drama. To use this strategy, imagine that you are at a gathering (e.g., a party, dinner, or meeting) where the subject of your assignment is being discussed. You listen to the conversation for a while and then notice someone who has a particularly strong opinion about it. Study this character and pay close attention to what he or she is saying. Try to gain insight into his or her values and ideas and to understand the feelings behind the words. Then answer the following questions:

1. What is this person's name, age, and profession? Describe this person's physical appearance.
2. What is this person's current attitude toward this topic?
3. How much does this person know about the topic?
4. Describe this person's value system.
5. How does this person's value system influence his or her attitude toward the topic?
6. What aspect of the topic does this character find most important?
7. What aspect of the topic does this character find most disturbing?

Writing a Dialogue

To utilize dialogue in the exploration of a topic, recall the character you created through "Character Prompts." Then, assume that after listening to the character you have imagined, you decide to enter the discussion and engage in a dialogue with him or her. Script this exchange in a dialogue of one to two pages, remembering that both participants should be presented as polite and intelligent people. In this interchange, no one should make outrageous or insulting statements and no one should win. The aim is to generate an exchange of ideas, not to score points over an adversary.

FOR WRITING AND DISCUSSION

The following assignment will enable you to practice creating characters and writing dialogues as a means of focusing attention on audience.

The Controversy Over School Uniforms

At Madison High School, located in a large American city, Principal Martin Blair has drafted a memo to the Board of Education arguing in favor of requiring all students to wear school uniforms beginning next year. Principal Blair is concerned primarily with the issue of safety, and he feels that the uniform requirement will protect children from attacks by gang members. He also believes that requiring all students to dress alike will focus their attention on their studies, rather than on their clothes. The President of the Parent–Teachers Association, Beverly Woodson, however, opposes the uniform requirement and thinks that whether a child wears a uniform to a public school should be the parents' and even the children's choice. President Woodson feels that schools should not be allowed to dictate personal decisions regarding clothing and that the imposition of such a requirement would stifle children's creativity.

How do you (or your students) feel about the issue of school uniforms? Were you (or your students) required to wear a uniform in school? If so, how did you (or they) feel about it? Do you perhaps have children of your own who are required to wear a uniform to school? If so, are you in favor of such a policy? If not, do you wish they had such a requirement?

Choose a position in this controversy and write a dialogue between yourself and either Principal Blair or President Woodson discussing this issue.

MULTIPLE CONCEPTS OF AUDIENCE

Although recent scholarship concerned with audience generally agrees that writers and audiences interact with one another and that there is no such thing as a totally accurate decoding of a text (i.e., a text in which the receiver extracts exactly what the sender encoded in it), there has been little consensus over what the term "audience" means definitively. Peter Elbow (1987) has attributed this lack of agreement to the fact that "there are many different entities called audience" (p. 50), among them, actual readers of the text, the writer's conception of those readers (which may or may not be accurate), and the audience that the genre of the text implies, to name a few. Barry Kroll (1984), in "Writing for Readers: Three Perspectives on Audience," examined three types of audience: the rhetorical, the informational, and the social. The rhetorical, which Kroll maintained is the traditional view of many composition textbooks, is addressed to a speaker whom one wants to persuade; a process that means finding out as much as possible about this particular audience. Kroll noted a number of problems with this approach to audience: that students will then see all discourse as antagonistic, encouraging them to become overly strident and ultimately unpersuasive, that the belief in a completely knowable audience is simplistic, and that this model encompasses only a limited account of the relationship between writer and reader.

Kroll's second perspective conceived of audience "as a process of conveying information, a process in which the writer's goal is to transmit, as effectively as possible, a message to the reader" (p. 176). However, this perspective is also limited in that it doesn't acknowledge the role of the reader in constructing the text. As Kroll phrases it, "filling a reader's head with information is not nearly as simple as filling a glass of water" (p. 176). Writing is not simply encoding, nor is reading simply decoding.

Kroll's third perspective conceived of writing as social interaction, a view that emphasizes the importance of peer response and cooperative learning. The social perspective suggests that "novice writers need to experience the satisfactions and conflicts of reader response—both the satisfaction that comes from having successfully shaped the reader's understanding and experience, and the conflict that arises when a concept that seemed clear to the writer baffles the reader, when a phrase which held special meaning for the writer evokes no response, or when an omitted detail—clear enough in the writer's mind—causes the reader to stumble" (Kroll, p. 181). Theorists such as Ong, however, would question whether the process of writing for readers is social at all, because writers create or project an audience with particular attitudes toward the writer and the subject.

In terms of classroom pedagogy, a particularly useful means of categorizing different types of writer–audience relationships was presented by Ryder, Lei, and Roen (1999), who based their distinction on whether a writer is writing solely for oneself, for an actual person or persons, or for a third party. These distinctions were explained as follows:

> The student who writes to express herself might imagine that she is in a monadic writing situation. She is both the writer and the audience; no one else need be involved. A second writing/speaking situation is dyadic. Such cases, where the writer/speaker is addressing a particular person, are often seen as the most important kinds of persuasion because of the relationship

between the author/speaker and reader/listener.... A third option is a triadic situation. Here, the author/speaker is one of two opponents before an audience. We see this happen during public debates, when two candidates spar before a crowd. The two are not trying to persuade each other; rather, each is trying to persuade the audience, the third party. (p. 55)

Ryder, Lei, and Roen claimed that the triadic situation is the one that is most suited to college writing assignments, and that it is, therefore, important for teachers to articulate their expectations in their assignments, because students will otherwise assume a dyadic relationship between student and teacher. Persuasive topics, they suggest, forefront the importance of audience and lend themselves to audience analysis more effectively than other types of writing assignments.

AUDIENCE AND THE DISCOURSE COMMUNITY

Another perspective on how writers and audience interact with one another can be obtained through the concept of discourse community, which over the past 15 years has received considerable scholarly attention. Discourse communities consist of members who share language, values, generic conventions, and a set of expectations of the requirements for an effective text. Lawyers, English teachers, and doctors all belong to different discourse communities and each adheres to different ideas about how a text should be written. Thus, if a student wishes to become an attorney, he or she will have to learn how to write and "sound" like an attorney. Otherwise, that person will always be perceived as an outsider, and his or her opinion will not be considered credible. Bennet Rafoth (1988) suggested that the term "discourse community" may be more helpful for students because it is more encompassing than the term "audience." Rafoth noted that "discourse community" more effectively captures:

the language phenomena that relate writers, readers, and texts. Whereas the audience metaphor tends naturally to represent readers or listeners as primary, and to admit writers and texts only as derivatives, discourse communityadmits writers, readers and texts all together. Instead of forcing the question "Who is the audience for this writer or this text" ... discourse community directs attention to the contexts that give rise to a text, including the range of conventions that govern different kinds of writing. (p. 132)

Distinguishing Between New and Common Knowledge

Understanding the discourse community for which a text is intended can certainly provide additional insight into audience and extend that insight into an awareness of purpose, genre, language, and convention. However, what Rafoth does not acknowledge sufficiently is that when students write essays for college classes, especially when they are in their first year, they are unlikely to be actual members of the discourse communities for which they are writing, and, in fact, must *pretend* to be so, doing the best they can to imagine a discourse community and fictionalizing their own insider status within it. This problem becomes particularly apparent when students must decide what information they should include in an essay as "new" knowledge, as opposed to what can be omitted because it is assumed to be "common knowledge." Distinguishing between new and common knowledge is confusing not only because students are not true members of the academic discourse communities for which they are writing, and are therefore unfamiliar with what members of that community are likely to know or need to know, but also because they are frequently given ambiguous advice. They are told to omit what might be considered "shared" or "common" knowledge, yet the knowledge that students "share" is changing on a daily basis. Two weeks ago, for example, students may not have heard of the term "discourse community," but now they are supposed to write as if the subject is widely known and does not need explanation. Moreover, in terms of shared knowledge, students are often told "not to assume that the reader knows what the writer is talking about," but also "not to tell the reader what he or she already knows."

Students' inability to distinguish between shared and common knowledge within a discourse community may be manifested in an opening line such as "Shakespeare was a well-known English playwright" or "Abraham Lincoln was the President of the United States during the Civil War"— information that members of an English-speaking academic discourse community would be expected to know. But the question of new versus shared knowledge is difficult to address in terms of a fail-safe classroom strategy or maxim, because we learn to interact in any community by observing the conventions of discourse within that group over a long period of time. With my own students and those I have worked with in the Writing Center, I have found that it is best to address this concept during revision, working with individual students on individual texts.

FOSTERING AUDIENCE AWARENESS
IN THE WRITING CLASS

To help students develop greater audience awareness, composition instructors have used a variety of consciousness-raising approaches for the classroom, some, of course, more successful than others. One approach involves focusing student attention on the audience in assigned readings; the assumption being that when students examine how experienced writers consider their audience, they will then be able to apply their insights to their own writing. Usually, though, this hoped-for carryover rarely happens when students write their own essays. A slightly more successful approach has been to provide students with broad demographic characteristics of a specified audience; a strategy that has been criticized, not only because it encourages stereotypes but also because it is questionable whether students gain sufficient insight into a potential audience when information is simply fed to them in the form of lists or facts. Finally, some instructors require students to write to "real" audiences, people who actually exist—such as the school principle or the President of the United States, for example. This approach will sometimes result in writing that is, indeed, directed to a specific audience. Its limitation is that it does not foster student awareness of audience as a generic construct—that is, it does not enable students to understand that the projection of an audience pertains to all writing tasks, regardless of whether the writer can define a so-called "real" one. The other limit of this approach is that it gives students the impression that the "audience" always exists independently of the text, the "sender-to-recipient model." Students, therefore, gain little insight into the role that envisioned audiences play in generating text and in determining the role of the writer within that text.

In fact, given the multiplicity of audiences and the difficulty of finding useful strategies for addressing audience in the classroom, Peter Elbow (1987) suggested that student writers are more likely to generate good writing when they concentrate on what they, as writers, want to say and ignore audience entirely. According to Elbow, worrying about who will be reading or judging their work, especially during an initial draft, can be inhibiting, although awareness of audience can certainly be useful during revision.

The question of which stage in the writing process is best for considering audience is the focus of a study by Roen and Willey (1988), which indicated that it is during revision that attention to audience can most contribute to the quality of a text. In Roen and Willey's study, sixty students were randomly assigned to one of three treatment conditions: no attention to audience, attention to audience before and during drafting, and attention to audience before and during revision. The treatment consisted of four questions:

1. Make a list of things your readers most likely already know.
2. List what they don't know and most likely need to know.
3. Explain how you decided what the audience's prior knowledge or lack of prior knowledge was about the topic.
4. Consider responses to 1, 2, and 3. How will you adapt your essay to accommodate readers?

The results of this study indicated that the essays for which students addressed audience before and during revision were rated the highest, suggesting that an audience analysis guide sheet can be an effective intervention tool for student writers. The worksheet that follows can be used for this purpose.

| AUDIENCE ANALYSIS SHEET |

1 Who is my audience? What knowledge about the subject does my audience already have?

2 What does my audience think, believe, or understand about this topic before he or she reads my essay?

3 What do I want my audience to think, believe, or understand about this topic after he or she reads my essay?

4 How do I want my audience to think of me?

FIG. 4.1.   Audience Analysis Sheet.

INVOKING AUDIENCE CUES IN A TEXT

In the composition class, examining texts for audience-based cues can help students understand the concept more fully. Obviously, in a text written only for oneself, as in a diary or list, no audience cues need be provided. If the writer is writing for a specific person or organization, such as NOW or The Audubon Society, he or she can signal those readers directly about which position they are expected to take. Ryder, Lei, and Roen (1999) refer to these cues as "naming moves," which "involve particular pronouns, such as you/your or we/our" (p. 57). They also name those groups their readers belong to, using phrases such as "those of us at MADD," or refer to positions that their readers are likely to hold, such as "those of us who care about preserving wildlife." "Naming moves" specify an intended audience, enabling other audiences to realize that the text was not intended for them and to situate themselves in relation to the writer and the intended audience.

Another cueing device concerns how much background information or context to include or exclude. This is an aspect of writing with which students often have considerable difficulty if they are under the impression that they are writing solely for their teacher. For example, if students are writing about whether speech codes should be part of campus policy, and that topic has been assigned by their teacher, they may see no reason to explain the background of the controversy, under the impression that the teacher already is aware of it.

How much background information should be included in a college essay? When students ask me whether they should include contextual information in their essays, I tell them to pretend that they have left their essay on a table in the college library where it can be read by any student who happens to find it. If they have explained and supported their ideas adequately and have included sufficient background and context for the topic, any intelligent student who comes upon the essay would be able to understand its central point, even if he or she were not thoroughly familiar with the topic or the assignment.

Peer Feedback

Peer feedback is one of the most useful strategies I know of for helping students gain awareness of audience. My own practice is to have students bring in several copies of their *first* (not rough!) draft and devote class time for peer review, making myself available to answer specific questions and to ensure that the class remains focused on the task. In holding a peer review workshop, however, it is crucial to hand out a list of specific questions; otherwise, students are likely either to focus on stylistic or grammatical concerns or simply to offer praise (It flows. I can relate to it. It speaks to me). The questions you hand out can be tailored to the particular assignment or can be sufficiently general to apply to many different assignments. Ryder, Lei, and Roen (1999) offer the following set of questions to structure a peer response session:

1. I identify with _____ in your writing.
   This is a way for peer readers to tell the writer that they have had a common experience. It is a way of beginning the conversation.
2. I like _____ about your writing.
   A little praise is always reassuring.
3. I have these questions about what you have written.
   This enables the writer to understand what readers need to know that might not be included in the text. Additional information might include additional detail, definition of terms, narration of background, or establishing a context for a controversy.
4. I have these suggestions.
   Suggestions are likely to develop from the questions.

Using the Computer to Foster Audience Awareness

Increasingly, teachers are tapping the resources of the computer to help foster student awareness of audience. Setting up a class list-serve, requiring students to respond to one another about readings and assigned topics, and creating collaborative writing assignments are all useful in helping students understand how others are likely to react to their writing. Partnerships between different classes or schools who correspond by e-mail can expand students' perspective on how different audiences respond to a text, focusing attention on the necessity of envisioning multiple perspectives during drafting and revising.

Audience awareness is a crucial component of learning to write. Helping students understand multiple notions of audience, incorporating audience specifications into writing assignments, and spending time in class examining audience cues in texts will enable students to write for a broad range of readers in both their educational and professional lives.

FOR WRITING AND DISCUSSION

Read the student essay "PC is Ridiculous" in chapter 3. How would attention to audience have improved this essay? Construct a peer review sheet that would generate revision of this essay.

FOR WRITING AND DISCUSSION

1. Respond to Peter Elbow's (1987) essay "Closing My Eyes As I Speak: An Argument for Ignoring Audience." To what extent do you agree with Elbow's position on the role of audience during early stages in the composing process?
2. Summarize Ede and Lunsford's (1984) article "Audience Addressed/Audience Invoked: The Role of Audience in Composition Theory and Pedagogy." How can their ideas be used in the composition class?

FOR FURTHER EXPLORATION

Kirsch, G., & Roen, D. H. (1990). *A sense of audience in written communication.* Newbury Park, CA: Sage Publications.

This collection consists of 16 essays on the subject of audience, 10 concerned with the history and theory of audience as a rhetorical concern and six discussing empirical studies.

Kroll, B. M. (1984, May). Writing for readers: Three perspectives on audience. *College Composition and Communication, 35,* 172–185.

Kroll presents three conceptions of audience that have influenced composition teaching: the rhetorical, the informational, and the social. The article also raises issues about whether the effectiveness of a text is more fully connected to genre and convention than to social knowledge.

Long, R. C. (1980, May). Writer–audience relationships. *College Composition and Communication, 31,* 221–226.

Park advocates the importance of the created rather than real audience. The question to ask is not "Who is my audience?" but, rather, "Who do I want my audience to be?"

Park, D. B. (1982). The Meanings of Audience. *College English, 44,* 246–257.

Park distinguishes readers from audience, noting that audience exists within the text as well as external to it.

Porter, J. E. (1992). *Audience and rhetoric: An archeological composition of the discourse community.* Englewood Cliffs, NJ: Prentice Hall.

Porter surveys conceptions of audience from Aristotle through the New Rhetoric, discussing a number of theoretical positions that impact audience, such as reader-response criticism and social constructionism. His focus tends to be on social constructionist perspective in which the audience collaborates with the writer in composing a text.

Wilson, W. D. (1981). Readers in texts. *PMLA, 96,* 848–863.

Wilson isolates three distinct kinds of reading presences: the real reader, the implied reader, and the characterized reader.

REFERENCES

Aristotle. (1991). Aristotle on Rhetoric: A theory of civic discourse. ed & trans. George A. Kennedy. New York: Oxford University Press.

Booth, W. (1963). The rhetorical stance. *College Composition and Communication, 14,* 139–145.

Dillon, G. (1981). *Constructing texts: Elements of a theory of composition and style.* Bloomington, IN: Indiana University Press.

Ede, L. & Lunsford, A. (1984, May). Audience addressed/audience invoked: The role of audience in composition theory and pedagogy. *College Composition and Communication, 35,* 155–171.

Elbow, P. (1981). *Writing with power.* New York: Oxford University Press.

Elbow, P. (1987). Closing my eyes as I speak: An argument for ignoring audience. *College English, 49,* 50–69.

Fish, S. (1980). *Is there a text in this class?* Cambridge, MA: Harvard University Press.

Kinneavy. J. (1971). *A theory of discourse.* New York: Norton.

Kirsch, G., & Roen, D. H. (1990). *A sense of audience in written communication.* Newbury Park, CA: Sage.

Kroll, B. M. (1984, May). Writing for readers: Three perspectives on audience. *College Composition and Communication, 35,* 172–185.

Ong, W. (1975). The writer's audience is always a fiction. *PMLA, 90,* 9–21.

Moffett, J. (1968). *Teaching the universe of discourse.* New York: Boynton Cook.

Park, D. (1982). The meanings of audience. *College English, 44,* 247–257.

Plato. (1952). *Phaedrus.* (A. Hackforth, trans.). Indianapolis, IN: Bobs Merrill.

Rafoth, B. (1988). Discourse community: Where writers, readers, and texts come together. In B. Rafoth & D. Ruden (Eds.), *The social construction of written communication.* Norwood, New Jersey: Ablex.

Reid, J., & Kroll, B. (1995). Designing and assessing effective classroom writing assignments for NES and ESL students. *Journal of Second Language Writing, 4* (1), 17–41.

Roen, D. H., & Willey, R. J. (1988). The effects of audience awareness on drafting and revising. *Research in the Teaching of English, 22,* 75–88.

Roth. R. G. (1987). The evolving audience: Alternatives to audience accommodation. *College Composition and Communication, 38,* 47–55.

Ryder, P. M., Lei, V. M., & Roen, D. H. (1999). Audience considerations for evaluating writing. In C. R. Cooper & L. Odell (Eds.), *Evaluating writing* (pp. 53–71). Urbana: NCTE.

Selzer, J. (2000). More meanings of audience. In J. C. McDonald (Ed.), *The Allyn and Bacon sourcebook for college writing teachers.* Needham, MA: Pearson.

Tomlinson, B. (1990). Ong may be wrong: Negotiating with non-fictional readers. In G. Kirsch & D. H. Roen (Eds.), *A sense of audience in written communication* (pp. 85–93). Newbury Park, CA: Sage.

Readings

CLOSING MY EYES AS I SPEAK: AN ARGUMENT FOR IGNORING AUDIENCE

Peter Elbow

> Very often people don't listen to you when you speak to them. It's only when you
> talk to yourself that they prick up their ears.
>
> John Ashberry

When I am talking to a person or a group and struggling to find words or thoughts,
I often find myself involuntarily closing my eyes as I speak. I realize now that this
behavior is an instinctive attempt to blot out awareness of audience when I need
all my concentration for just trying to figure out or express what I want to say.
Because the audience is so imperiously *present* in a speaking situation, my instinct
reacts with this active attempt to avoid audience awareness. This behavior—in a
sense impolite or anti-social—is not so uncommon. Even when we write, alone
in a room to an absent audience, there are occasions when we are struggling to
figure something out and need to push aside awareness of those absent readers.
As Donald Murray puts it, "My sense of audience is so strong that I have to
suppress my conscious awareness of audience to hear what the text demands"
(Berkenkotter and Murray 171). In recognition of how pervasive the role of
audience is in writing, I write to celebrate the benefits of ignoring audience.[1]

Reprinted from *College English*, Volume 49, Number 1, January 1987. Used with permission.

[1] There are many different entities called audience: (a) The actual readers to whom the text
will be given; (b) the writer's conception of those readers—which may be mistaken (see Ong; Park;
Ede and Lunsford); (c) the audience that the text implies—which may be different still (see Booth);

It will be clear that my argument for writing without audience awareness is not meant to undermine the many good reasons for writing *with* audience awareness some of the time. (For example, that we are liable to neglect audience because we write in solitude; that young people often need more practice in taking into account points of view different from their own; and that students often have an impoverished sense of writing as communication because they have only written in a school setting to teachers.) Indeed I would claim some part in these arguments for audience awareness—which now seem to be getting out of hand.

I start with a limited claim: even though ignoring audience will usually lead to weak writing at first—to what Linda Flower calls "writer-based prose," this weak writing can help us in the end to better writing than we would have written if we'd kept readers in mind from the start. Then I will make a more ambitious claim: writer-based prose is sometimes better than reader-based prose. Finally I will explore some of the theory underlying these issues of audience.

A Limited Claim

It's not that writers should never think about their audience. It's a question of when. An audience is a field of force. The closer we come—the more we think about these readers—the stronger the pull they exert on the contents of our minds. The practical question, then, is always whether a particular audience functions as a helpful field of force or one that confuses or inhibits us.

Some audiences, for example, are *inviting* or *enabling*. When we think about them as we write, we think of more and better things to say—and what we think somehow arrives more coherently structured than usual. It's like talking to the perfect listener; we feel smart and come up with ideas we didn't know we had. Such audiences are helpful to keep in mind right from the start.

Other audiences, however, are powerfully *inhibiting*—so much so, in certain cases, that awareness of them as we write blocks writing altogether. There are certain people who always make us feel dumb when we try to speak to them: we can't find words or thoughts. As soon as we get out of their presence, all the

---

(d) the discourse community or even genre addressed or implied by the text (see Walzer); (e) ghost or phantom "readers in the head" that the writer may unconsciously address or try to please (see Elbow, *Writing with Power* 186ff. Classically, this is a powerful former teacher. Often such an audience is so ghostly as not to show up as actually "implied" by the text). For the essay I am writing here, these differences don't much matter: I'm celebrating the ability to put aside the needs or demands of *any* or all of these audiences. I recognize, however, that we sometimes cannot fight our way free of unconscious or tacit audiences (as in b or e above) unless we bring them to greater conscious awareness.

things we wanted to say pop back into our minds. Here is a student telling what happens when she tries to follow the traditional advice about audience:

> You know _____ [author of a text] tells us to pay attention to the audience that will be reading our papers, and I gave that a try. I ended up without putting a word on paper until I decided the hell with _____; I'm going to write to who I damn well want to; otherwise I can hardly write at all.

Admittedly, there are some occasions when we benefit from keeping a threatening audience in mind from the start. We've been putting off writing that letter to that person who intimidates us. When we finally sit down and write to them—walk right up to them, as it were, and look them in the eye—we may manage to stand up to the threat and grasp the nettle and thereby find just what we need to write.

Most commonly, however, the effect of audience awareness is somewhere between the two extremes: the awareness disturbs or disrupts our writing and thinking without completely blocking it. For example, when we have to write to someone we find intimidating (and of course students often perceive teachers as intimidating), we often start thinking wholly defensively. As we write down each thought or sentence, our mind fills with thoughts of how the intended reader will criticize or object to it. So we try to qualify or soften what we've just written—or write out some answer to a possible objection. Our writing becomes tangled. Sometimes we get so tied in knots that we cannot even figure out what we *think*. We may not realize how often audience awareness has this effect on our students when we don't see the writing processes behind their papers: we just see texts that are either tangled or empty.

Another example. When we have to write to readers with whom we have an awkward relationship, we often start beating around the bush and feeling shy or scared, or start to write in a stilted, overly careful style or voice. (Think about the cute, too-clever style of many memos we get in our departmental mailboxes—the awkward self-consciousness academics experience when writing to other academics.) When students are asked to write to readers they have not met or cannot imagine, such as "the general reader" or "the educated public," they often find nothing to say except cliches they know *they* don't even quite believe.

When we realize that an audience is somehow confusing or inhibiting us, the solution is fairly obvious. We can ignore that audience altogether during the *early* stages of writing and direct our words only to ourselves or to no one in particular—or even to the "wrong" audience, that is, to an *inviting* audience of trusted friends or allies. This strategy often dissipates the confusion; the clenched, defensive discourse starts to run clear. Putting audience out of mind is of course a traditional practice; serious writers have long used private journals for early explorations of feeling, thinking, or language. But many writing teachers seem to think that students can get along without the private writing serious writers find so crucial—or even that students will *benefit* from keeping their audience in mind for the whole time. Things often don't work out that way.

After we have figured out our thinking in copious exploratory or draft writing—perhaps finding the right voice or stance as well—*then* we can follow the traditional rhetorical advice: think about readers and revise carefully to adjust our words and thoughts to our intended audience. For a particular audience it may even turn out that we need to *disguise* our point of view. But it's hard to disguise something while engaged in trying to figure it out. As writers, then, we need to learn when to think about audience and when to put readers out of mind.

Many people are too quick to see Flower's "writer-based prose" as an analysis of what's wrong with this type of writing and miss the substantial degree to which she was celebrating a natural, and indeed developmentally enabling, response to cognitive overload. What she doesn't say, however, despite her emphasis on planning and conscious control in the writing process, is that we can *teach* students to notice when audience awareness is getting in their way—and when this happens, consciously to put aside the needs of readers for a while. She seems to assume that when an overload occurs, the writer-based gear will, as it were, automatically kick into action to relieve it. In truth, of course, writers often persist in using a malfunctioning *reader*-based gear despite the overload—thereby mangling their language or thinking. Though Flower likes to rap the knuckles of people who suggest a "correct" or "natural" order for steps in the writing process, she implies such an order here: when attention to audience causes an overload, start out by ignoring them while you attend to your thinking; after you work out your thinking, turn your attention to audience.

Thus if we ignore audience while writing on a topic about which we are not expert or about which our thinking is still evolving, we are likely to produce exploratory writing that is unclear to anyone else—perhaps even inconsistent or a complete mess. Yet by doing this exploratory "swamp work" in conditions of safety, we can often coax our thinking through a process of new discovery and development. In this way we can end up with something better than we could have produced if we'd tried to write to our audience all along. In short, ignoring audience can lead to worse drafts but better revisions. (Because we are professionals and adults, we often write in the role of expert: we may know what we think without new exploratory writing; we may even be able to speak confidently to critical readers. But students seldom experience this confident professional stance in their writing. And think how much richer *our* writing would be if we defined ourselves as *in*expert and allowed ourselves private writing for new explorations of those views we are allegedly sure of.)

Notice then that two pieties of composition theory are often in conflict:

1. Think about audience as you write (this stemming from the classical rhetorical tradition).

2. Use writing for *making new meaning,* not just transmitting old meanings already worked out (this stemming from the newer epistemic traditon I associate with Ann Berthoff's classic explorations).

It's often difficult to work out new meaning while thinking about readers.

A More Ambitious Claim

I go further now and argue that ignoring audience can lead to better writing—immediately. In effect, writer-based prose can be *better* than reader-based prose. This might seem a more controversial claim, but is there a teacher who has not had the experience of struggling and struggling to no avail to help a student untangle his writing, only to discover that the student's casual journal writing or freewriting is untangled and strong? Sometimes freewriting is stronger than the essays we get only because it is expressive, narrative, or descriptive writing and the student was not constrained by a topic. But teachers who collect drafts with completed assignments often see passages of freewriting that are strikingly stronger *even* when they are expository and constrained by the assigned topic. In some of these passages we can sense that the strength derives from the student's unawareness of readers.

It's not just unskilled, tangled writers, though, who sometimes write better by forgetting about readers. Many competent and even professional writers produce mediocre pieces *because* they are thinking too much about how their readers will receive their words. They are acting too much like a salesman trained to look the customer in the eye and to think at all times about the characteristics of the "target audience." There is something too staged or planned or self-aware about such writing. We see this quality in much second-rate newspaper or magazine or business writing: "good-student writing" in the awful sense of the term. Writing produced this way reminds us of the ineffective actor whose consciousness of self distracts us: he makes us too aware of his own awareness of us. When we read such prose, we wish the writer would stop thinking about us—would stop trying to "adjust" or "fit" what he is saying to our frame of reference. "Damn it, put all your attention on what you are saying," we want to say, "and forget about us and how we are reacting."

When we examine really good student or professional writing, we can often see that its goodness comes from the writer's having gotten sufficiently wrapped up in her meaning and her language as to forget all about audience needs: the writer manages to "break through." The Earl of Shaftesbury talked about writers needing to escape their audience in order to find their own ideas (Cooper 1:109; see also Griffin). It is characteristic of much truly good writing to be, as it were, on fire with its meaning. Consciousness of readers is burned away; involvement in subject determines all. Such writing is analogous to the performance of the actor who has managed to stop attracting attention to her awareness of the audience watching her.

The arresting power in some writing by small children comes from their obliviousness to audience. As readers, we are somehow sucked into a more-than-usual
connection with the meaning itself because of the child's gift for more-than-usual
concentration on what she is saying. In short, we can feel some pieces of children's
writing as being very writer-based. Yet it's precisely that quality which makes it
powerful for us as readers. After all, why should we settle for a writer's entering
our point of view, if we can have the more powerful experience of being sucked
out of our point of view and into her world? This is just the experience that
children are peculiarly capable of giving because they are so expert at total ab-
sorption in their world as they are writing. It's not just a matter of whether the
writer "decenters," but of whether the writer has a sufficiently strong focus of
attention to make the *reader* decenter. This quality of concentration is what D. H.
Lawrence so admires in Melville:

> [Melville] was a real American in that he always felt his audience in front of him. But
> when he ceases to be American, when he forgets all audience, and gives us his sheer
> apprehension of the world, then he is wonderful, his book *[Moby Dick]* commands
> a stillness in the soul, an awe. (158)

What most readers value in really excellent writing is not prose that is right
for readers but prose that is right for thinking, right for language, or right for the
subject being written about. If, in addition, it is clear and well suited to readers,
we appreciate that. Indeed we feel insulted if the writer did not somehow try to
make the writing *available* to us before delivering it. But if it succeeds at being
really true to language and thinking and "things," we are willing to put up with
much difficulty as readers:

> [G]ood writing is not always or necessarily an adaptation to communal norms (in
> the Fish/Bruffee sense) but may be an attempt to construct (and instruct) a reader
> capable of reading the text in question. The literary history of the "difficult" work—
> from Mallarme to Pound, Zukofsky, Olson, etc.—seems to say that much of what
> we value in writing we've had to learn to value by learning how to read it. (Trimbur)

The effect of audience awareness on *voice* is particularly striking—if paradoxical. Even though we often develop our voice by finally "speaking up" to an audience
or "speaking out" to others, and even though much dead student writing comes
from students' not really treating their writing as a communication with real
readers, nevertheless, the opposite effect is also common: we often do not really
develop a strong, authentic voice in our writing till we find important occasions
for *ignoring* audience—saying, in effect, "To hell with whether they like it or not.
I've got to say this the way *I* want to say it." Admittedly, the voice that emerges
when we ignore audience is sometimes odd or idiosyncratic in some way, but
usually it is stronger. Indeed, teachers sometimes complain that student writing is
"writer-based" when the problem is simply the idiosyncrasy—and sometimes in
fact the *power*—of the voice. They would value this odd but resonant voice if they

found it in a published writer (see "Real Voice," Elbow, *Writing with Power*). Usually we cannot *trust* a voice unless it is unaware of us and our needs and speaks out in its own terms (see the Ashberry epigraph). To celebrate writer-based prose is to risk the charge of *romanticism:* just warbling one's woodnotes wild. But my position also contains the austere *classic* view that we must nevertheless *revise* with conscious awareness of audience in order to figure out which pieces of writer-based prose are good as they are—and how to discard or revise the rest.

To point out that writer-based prose can be *better* for readers than reader-based prose is to reveal problems in these two terms. Does *writer-based* mean:

1. That the text doesn't work for readers because it is too much oriented to the writer's point of view?
2. Or that the writer was not thinking about readers as she wrote, although the text *may* work for readers?

Does *reader-based* mean:

3. That the text works for readers—meets their needs?
4. Or that the writer was attending to readers as she wrote although her text may *not* work for readers?

In order to do justice to the reality and complexity of what actually happens in both writers and readers, I was going to suggest four terms for the four conditions listed above, but I gradually realized that things are even too complex for that. We really need to ask about what's going on in three dimensions—in the *writer,* in the *reader,* and in the *text*—and realize that the answers can occur in virtually any combination:

— Was the *writer* thinking about readers or oblivious to them?
— Is the *text* oriented toward the writer's frame of reference or point of view, or oriented toward that of readers? (A writer may be thinking about readers and still write a text that is largely oriented towards her own frame of reference.)
— Are the readers' needs being met? (The text may meet the needs of readers whether the writer was thinking about them or not, and whether the text is oriented toward them or not.)

Two Models of Cognitive Development

Some of the current emphasis on audience awareness probably derives from a model of cognitive development that needs to be questioned. According to this model, if you keep your readers in mind as you write, you are operating at a higher level of psychological development than if you ignore readers. Directing words to readers is "more mature" than directing them to no one in particular or to yourself. Flower relates writer-based prose to the inability to "decenter" which is characteristic of Piaget's early stages of development, and she relates reader-based prose to later more mature stages of development.

On the one hand, of course this view must be right. Children do decenter as they develop. As they mature they get better at suiting their discourse to the needs of listeners, particularly to listeners very different from themselves. Especially, they get better at doing so *consciously*—thinking *awarely* about how things appear to people with different viewpoints. Thus much unskilled writing is unclear or awkward *because* the writer was doing what it is so easy to do— unthinkingly taking her own frame of reference for granted and not attending to the needs of readers who might have a different frame of reference. And of course this failure is more common in younger, immature, "egocentric" students (and also more common in writing than in speaking since we have no audience present when we write).

But on the other hand, we need the contrary model that affirms what is also obvious once we reflect on it, namely that the ability to *turn off* audience awareness—especially when it confuses thinking or blocks discourse—is also a "higher" skill. I am talking about an ability to use language in "the desert island mode," an ability that tends to require learning, growth, and psychological development. Children, and even adults who have not learned the art of quiet, thoughtful, inner reflection, are often unable to get much cognitive action going in their heads unless there are other people present to have action *with*. They are dependent on live audience and the social dimension to get their discourse rolling or to get their thinking off the ground.

For in contrast to a roughly Piagetian model of cognitive development that says we start out as private, egocentric little monads and grow up to be public and social, it is important to invoke the opposite model that derives variously from Vygotsky, Bakhtin, and Meade. According to this model, we *start out* social and plugged into others and only gradually, through learning and development, come to "unplug" to any significant degree so as to function in a more private, individual and differentiated fashion: "Development in thinking is not from the individual to the socialized, but from the social to the individual" (Vygotsky 20). The important general principle in this model is that we tend to *develop* our important cognitive capacities by means of social interaction with others, and having done so we gradually learn to perform them alone. We fold the "simple" back-and-forth of dialogue into the "complexity" (literally, "foldedness") of individual, private reflection.

Where the Piagetian (individual psychology) model calls our attention to the obvious need to learn to enter into viewpoints other than our own, the Vygotskian (social psychology) model calls our attention to the equally important need to learn to produce good thinking and discourse *while alone*. A rich and enfolded mental life is something that people achieve only gradually through growth, learning, and practice. We tend to associate this achievement with the fruits of higher education.

Thus we see plenty of students who lack this skill, who have nothing to say when asked to freewrite or to write in a journal. They can dutifully "reply" to a question or a topic, but they cannot seem to *initiate* or *sustain* a train of thought on their own. Because so many adolescent students have this difficulty, many teachers chime in: "Adolescents have nothing to write about. They are too young. They haven't had significant experience." In truth, adolescents don't lack experience or material, no matter how "sheltered" their lives. What they lack is practice and help. Desert island discourse is a learned cognitive process. It's a mistake to think of private writing (journal writing and freewriting) as merely "easy"—merely a relief from trying to write right. It's also hard. Some exercises and strategies that help are Ira Progoff's "Intensive Journal" process, Sondra Perl's "Composing Guidelines," or Elbow's "Loop Writing" and "Open Ended Writing" processes (*Writing with Power* 50–77).

The Piagetian and Vygotskian developmental models (language-begins-as-private vs. language-begins-as-social) give us two different lenses through which to look at a common weakness in student writing, a certain kind of "thin" writing where the thought is insufficiently developed or where the language doesn't really explain what the writing implies or gestures toward. Using the Piagetian model, as Flower does, one can specify the problem as a weakness in audience orientation. Perhaps the writer has immaturely taken too much for granted and unthinkingly assumed that her limited explanations carry as much meaning for readers as they do for herself. The cure or treatment is for the writer to think more about readers.

Through the Vygotskian lens, however, the problem and the "immaturity" look altogether different. Yes, the writing isn't particularly clear or satisfying for readers, but this alternative diagnosis suggests a failure of the private desert island dimension: the writer's explanation is too thin because she didn't work out her train of thought fully enough *for herself*. The suggested cure or treatment is *not* to think more about readers but to think more for herself, to practice exploratory writing in order to learn to engage in that reflective discourse so central to mastery of the writing process. How can she engage readers more till she has engaged herself more?

The current emphasis on audience awareness may be particularly strong now for being fueled by *both* psychological models. From one side, the Piagetians say, in effect, "The egocentric little critters, we've got to *socialize* 'em! Ergo, make them think about audience when they write!" From the other side, the Vygotskians say, in effect, "No wonder they're having trouble writing. They've been bamboozled by the Piagetian heresy. They think they're solitary individuals with private selves when really they're just congeries of voices that derive from their discourse community. Ergo, let's intensify the social context—use peer groups and publication: make them think about audience when they write! (And while we're at it, let's hook them up with a better class of discourse community.)" To advocate ignoring audience is to risk getting caught in the crossfire from two opposed camps.

Two Models of Discourse: Discourse as Communication and Discourse as Poesis or Play

We cannot talk about writing without at least implying a psychological or developmental model. But we'd better make sure it's a complex, paradoxical, or spiral model. Better yet, we should be deft enough to use two contrary models or lenses. (Bruner pictures the developmental process as a complex movement in an upward reiterative spiral—not a simple movement in one direction.)

According to one model, it is characteristic of the youngest children to direct their discourse to an audience. They learn discourse *because* they have an audience; without an audience they remain mute, like "the wild child." Language is social from the start. But we need the other model to show us what is also true, namely that it is characteristic of the youngest children to use language in a *non-social* way. They use language not only because people talk to them but also because they have such a strong propensity to play and to build—often in a *non-*social or non-audience-oriented fashion. Thus although one paradigm for discourse is social communication, another is private exploration or solitary play. Babies and toddlers tend to babble in an exploratory and reflective way—to themselves and not to an audience—often even with no one else near. This archetypally private use of discourse is strikingly illustrated when we see a pair of toddlers in "parallel play" alongside each other—each busily talking but not at all trying to communicate with the other.

Therefore, when we choose paradigms for discourse, we should think not only about children using language to communicate, but also about children building sandcastles or drawing pictures. Though children characteristically show their castles or pictures to others, they just as characteristically trample or crumple them before anyone else can see them. Of course sculptures and pictures are different from words. Yet discourse implies more media than words; and even if you restrict discourse to words, one of our most mature uses of language is for building verbal pictures and structures for their own sake—not just for communicating with others.

Consider this same kind of behavior at the other end of the life cycle: Brahms staggering from his deathbed to his study to rip up a dozen or more completed but unpublished and unheard string quartets that dissatisfied him. How was he relating to audience here—worrying too much about audience or not giving a damn? It's not easy to say. Consider Glenn Gould deciding to renounce performances before an audience. He used his private studio to produce recorded performances for an audience, but to produce ones that satisfied *himself* he clearly needed to suppress audience awareness. Consider the more extreme example of Kerouac typing page after page—burning each as soon as he completed it. The language behavior of humans is slippery. Surely we are well advised to avoid positions that say it is "always X" or "essentially Y."

James Britton makes a powerful argument that the "making" or poesis function of language grows out of the expressive function. Expressive language is often for the sake of communication with an audience, but just as often it is only for the sake of the speaker—working something out for herself (66–67, 74ff). Note also that "writing to learn," which writing-across-the-curriculum programs are discovering to be so important, tends to be writing for the self or even for no one at all rather than for an outside reader. You throw away the writing, often unread, and keep the mental changes it has engendered.

I hope this emphasis on the complexity of the developmental process—the limits of our models and of our understanding of it—will serve as a rebuke to the tendency to label students as being at a lower stage of cognitive development just because they don't yet write well. (Occasionally they *do* write well—in a way—but not in the way that the labeler finds appropriate.) Obviously the psychologistic labeling impulse started out charitably. Shaughnessy was fighting those who called basic writers *stupid* by saying they weren't dumb, just at an earlier developmental stage. Flower was arguing that writer-based prose is a natural response to a cognitive overload and indeed developmentally enabling. But this kind of talk can be dangerous since it labels students as literally "retarded" and makes teachers and administrators start to think of them as such. Instead of calling poor writers *either* dumb or slow (two forms of blaming the victim), why not simply call them poor writers? If years of schooling haven't yet made them good writers, perhaps they haven't gotten the kind of teaching and support they need. Poor students are often deprived of the very thing they need most to write well (which is given to good students): lots of extended and adventuresome writing for self and for audience. Poor students are often asked to write *only* answers to fill-in exercises.

As children get older, the developmental story remains complex or spiral. Though the first model makes us notice that babies start out with a natural gift for using language in a social and communicative fashion, the second model makes us notice that children and adolescents must continually learn to relate their discourse better to an audience—must struggle to decenter better. And though the second model makes us notice that babies also start out with a natural gift for using language in a *private,* exploratory and playful way, the first model makes us notice that children and adolescents must continually learn to master this solitary, desert island, poesis mode better. Thus we mustn't think of language only as communication—nor allow communication to claim dominance either as the earliest or as the most "mature" form of discourse. It's true that language is inherently communicative (and without communication we don't develop language), yet language is just as inherently the stringing together of exploratory discourse for the self—or for the creation of objects (play, poesis, making) for their own sake.

In considering this important poesis function of language, we need not discount (as Berkenkotter does) the striking testimony of so many witnesses who think and care most about language: professional poets, writers, and philosophers. Many of them maintain that their most serious work is *making*, not *communicating*, and that their commitment is to language, reality, logic, experience, not to readers. Only in their willingness to cut loose from the demands or needs of readers, they insist, can they do their best work. Here is William Stafford on this matter:

> I don't want to overstate this ... but ... my impulse is to say I don't think of an audience at all. When I'm writing, the satisfactions in the process of writing are my satisfactions in dealing with the language, in being surprised by phrasings that occur to me, in finding that this miraculous kind of convergent focus begins to happen. That's my satisfaction, and to think about an audience would be a distraction. I try to keep from thinking about an audience. (Cicotello 176)

And Chomsky:

> I can be using language in the strictest sense with no intention of communicating. ... As a graduate student, I spent two years writing a lengthy manuscript, assuming throughout that it would never be published or read by anyone. I meant everything I wrote, intending nothing as to what anyone would [understand], in fact taking it for granted that there would be no audience. ... [C]ommunication is only one function of language, and by no means an essential one. (Qtd. in Feldman 5–6.)

It's interesting to see how poets come together with philosophers on this point—and even with mathematicians. All are emphasizing the "poetic" function of language in its literal sense—"poesis" as "making." They describe their writing process as more like "getting something right" or even "solving a problem" for its own sake than as communicating with readers or addressing an audience. The task is not to satisfy readers but to satisfy the rules of the system: "[T]he writer is not thinking of a reader at all; he makes it 'clear' as a contract with *language*" (Goodman 164).

Shall we conclude, then, that solving an equation or working out a piece of symbolic logic is at the opposite end of the spectrum from communicating with readers or addressing an audience? No. To draw that conclusion would be to fall again into a one-sided position. Sometimes people write mathematics *for* an audience, sometimes not. The central point in this essay is that we cannot answer audience questions in an *a priori* fashion based on the "nature" of discourse or of language or of cognition—only in terms of the different *uses* or *purposes* to which humans put discourse, language, or cognition on different occasions. If most people have a restricted repertoire of uses for writing—if most people use writing only to send messages to readers, that's no argument for constricting the *definition* of writing. It's an argument for helping people expand their repertoire of uses.

The value of learning to ignore audience while writing, then, is the value of learning to cultivate the private dimension: the value of writing in order to make meaning to oneself, not just to others. This involves learning to free oneself (to some extent, anyway) from the enormous power exerted by society and others, to unhook oneself from external prompts and social stimuli. We've grown accustomed to theorists and writing teachers puritanically stressing the *problem* of writing: the tendency to neglect the needs of readers because we usually write in solitude. But let's also celebrate this same feature of writing as one of its glories: writing *invites* disengagement too, the inward turn of mind, and the dialogue with self. Though writing is deeply social and though we usually help things by enhancing its social dimension, writing is also the mode of discourse best suited to helping us develop the reflective and private dimension of our mental lives.

"But Wait a Minute, ALL Discourse Is Social"

Some readers who see *all* discourse as social will object to my opposition between public and private writing (the "trap of oppositional thinking") and insist that *there is no such thing as private discourse*. What looks like private, solitary mental work, they would say, is really social. Even on the desert island I am in a crowd.

> [B]y ignoring audience in the conventional sense, we return to it in another sense. What I get from Vygotsky and Bakhtin is the notion that audience is not really out there at all but is in fact "always already" (to use that poststructuralist mannerism . . .) inside, interiorized in the conflicting languages of others—parents, former teachers, peers, prospective readers, whomever—that writers have to negotiate to write, and that we do negotiate when we write whether we're aware of it or not. The audience we've got to satisfy in order to feel good about our writing is as much in the past as in the present or future. But we experience it (it's so internalized) as *ourselves*. (Trimbur)

(Ken Bruffee likes to quote from Frost: "'Men work together, . . . /Whether they work together or apart'" ["The Tuft of Flowers"]). Or—putting it slightly differently—when I engage in what seems like private non-audience-directed writing, I am really engaged in communication with the "audience of self." For the self is multiple, not single, and discourse to self is communication from one entity to another. As Feldman argues, "The self functions as audience in much the same way that others do" (290).

Suppose I accept this theory that all discourse is really social—including what I've been calling "private writing" or writing I don't intend to show to any reader. Suppose I agree that all language is essentially communication directed toward an audience—whether some past internalized voice or (what may be the same thing) some aspect of the self. What would this theory say to my interest in "private writing"?

The theory would seem to destroy my main argument. It would tell me that there's no such thing as "private writing"; it's impossible *not* to address audience; there are no vacations from audience. But the theory might try to console me by saying not to worry, because we don't *need* vacations from audience. Addressing audience is as easy, natural, and unaware as breathing—and we've been at it since the cradle. Even young, unskilled writers are already expert at addressing audiences.

But if we look closely we can see that in fact this theory doesn't touch my central practical argument. For even if all discourse is naturally addressed to *some* audience, it's not naturally addressed to the *right* audience—the living readers we are actually trying to reach. Indeed the pervasiveness of past audiences in our heads is one more reason for the difficulty of reaching present audiences with our texts. Thus even if I concede the theoretical point, there still remains an enormous practical and phenomenological difference between writing "public" words for others to read and writing "private" words for no one to read.

Even if "private writing" is "deep down" social, the fact remains that, as we engage in it, we don't have to worry about whether it works on readers or even makes sense. We can refrain from doing all the things that audience-awareness advocates advise us to do ("keeping our audience in mind as we write" and trying to "decenter"). Therefore this social-discourse theory doesn't undermine the benefits of "private writing" and thus provides no support at all for the traditional rhetorical advice that we should "always try to think about (intended) audience as we write."

In fact this social-discourse theory reinforces two subsidiary arguments I have been making. First, even if there is no getting away from *some* audience, we can get relief from an inhibiting audience by writing to a more inviting one. Second, audience problems don't come only from *actual* audiences but also from phantom "audiences in the head" (Elbow, *Writing with Power* 186ff). Once we learn how to be more aware of the effects of both external and internal readers and how to direct our words elsewhere, we can get out of the shadow even of a troublesome phantom reader.

And even if all our discourse is *directed to* or *shaped by* past audiences or voices, it doesn't follow that our discourse is *well directed to* or *successfully shaped for* those audiences or voices. Small children *direct* much talk to others, but that doesn't mean they always *suit* their talk to others. They often fail. When adults discover that a piece of their writing has been "heavily shaped" by some audience, this is bad news as much as good: often the writing is crippled by defensive moves that try to fend off criticism from this reader.

As teachers, particularly, we need to distinguish and emphasize "private writing" in order to teach it, to teach that crucial cognitive capacity to engage in extended and productive thinking that doesn't depend on audience prompts or social stimuli. It's sad to see so many students who can reply to live voices but cannot engage in productive dialogue with voices in their heads. Such students often lose interest in an issue that had intrigued them—just because they don't find other people who are interested in talking about it and haven't learned to talk reflectively to *themselves* about it.

For these reasons, then, I believe my main argument holds force even if I accept the theory that all discourse is social. But, perhaps more tentatively, I resist this theory. I don't know all the data from developmental linguistics, but I cannot help suspecting that babies engage in *some* private poesis—or "play-language"—some private babbling in addition to social babbling. Of course Vygotsky must be right when he points to so much social language in children, but can we really trust him when he denies *all* private or nonsocial language (which Piaget and Chomsky see)? I am always suspicious when someone argues for the total nonexistence of a certain kind of behavior or event. Such an argument is almost invariably an act of definitional aggrandizement, not empirical searching. To say that *all* language is social is to flop over into the opposite one-sidedness that we need Vygotsky's model to save us from.

And even if all language is *originally* social, Vygotsky himself emphasizes how "inner speech" becomes more individuated and private as the child matures. "[E]gocentric speech is relatively accessible in three-year-olds but quite in-scrutable in seven-year-olds: the older the child, the more thoroughly has his thought become inner speech" (Emerson 254; see also Vygotsky 134). "The in-ner speech of the adult represents his 'thinking for himself' rather than social adaptation.... Out of context, it would be incomprehensible to others because it omits to mention what is obvious to the 'speaker'" (Vygotsky 18).

I also resist the theory that all private writing is really communication with the "*audience of self.*" ("When we represent the objects of our thought in language, we intend to make use of these representations at a later time.... [T]he speaker-self must have audience directed intentions toward a listener-self" [Feldman 289].) Of course private language often *is* a communication with the audience of self:

— When we make a shopping list. (It's obvious when we can't decipher that third item that we're confronting *failed* communication with the self.)

— When we make a rough draft for ourselves but not for others' eyes. Here we are seeking to clarify our thinking with the leverage that comes from standing outside and reading our own utterance as audience— experiencing our discourse as receiver instead of as sender.

— When we experience ourselves as slightly split. Sometimes we experience ourselves as witness to ourselves and hear our own words from the outside—sometimes with great detachment, as on some occasions of pressure or stress.

But there are other times when private language is *not* communication with audience of self:

— Freewriting to no one: for the *sake* of self but not *to* the self. The goal is not to communicate but to follow a train of thinking or feeling to see where it leads. In doing this kind of freewriting (and many people have not learned it), you don't particularly plan to come back and read what you've written. You just write along and the written product falls away to be ignored, while only the "real product"—any new perceptions, thoughts, or feelings produced in the mind by the freewriting—is saved and looked at again. (It's not that you don't experience your words *at all* but you experience them only as speaker, sender, or emitter—not as receiver or audience. To say that's the same as being audience is denying the very distinction between 'speaker' and 'audience.')

As this kind of freewriting actually works, it often *leads* to writing we look at. That is, we freewrite along to no one, following discourse in hopes of getting somewhere, and then at a certain point we often sense that we have *gotten* somewhere: we can tell (but not because we stop and read) that what we are now writing seems new or intriguing or important. At this point we may stop writing; or we may keep on writing, but in a new audience-relationship, realizing that we *will* come back to this passage and read it as audience. Or we may take a new sheet (symbolizing the new audience-relationship) and try to write out for ourselves what's interesting.

— Writing as exorcism is a more extreme example of private writing *not* for the audience of self. Some people have learned to write in order to get rid of thoughts or feelings. By freewriting what's obsessively going round and round in our head we can finally let it go and move on.

I am suggesting that some people (and especially poets and freewriters) engage in a kind of discourse that Feldman, defending what she calls a "communication-intention" view, has never learned and thus has a hard time imagining and understanding. Instead of always using language in an audience-directed fashion for the sake of communication, these writers unleash language for its own sake and let *it* function a bit on its own, without much *intention* and without much need for *communication,* to see where it leads—and thereby end up with some intentions and potential communications they didn't have before.

It's hard to turn off the audience-of-self in writing—and thus hard to imagine writing to no one (just as it's hard to turn off the audience of *outside* readers when writing an audience-directed piece). Consider "invisible writing" as an intriguing technique that helps you become less of an audience-of-self for your writing. Invisible writing prevents you from seeing what you have written: you write on a computer with the screen turned down, or you write with a spent ball-point pen on paper with carbon paper and another sheet underneath. Invisible writing tends to get people not only to write faster than they normally do, but often better (see Blau). I mean to be tentative about this slippery issue of whether we can really stop being audience to our own discourse, but I cannot help drawing the following conclusion: just as in freewriting, suppressing the *other* as audience tends to enhance quantity and sometimes even quality of writing; so in invisible writing, suppressing the *self* as audience tends to enhance quantity and sometimes even quality.

Contraries in Teaching

So what does all this mean for teaching? It means that we are stuck with two contrary tasks. On the one hand, we need to help our students enhance the social dimension of writing: to learn to be *more* aware of audience, to decenter better and learn to fit their discourse better to the needs of readers. Yet it is every bit as important to help them learn the private dimension of writing: to learn to be *less* aware of audience, to put audience needs aside, to use discourse in the desert island mode. And if we are trying to advance contraries, we must be prepared for paradoxes.

For instance if we emphasize the social dimension in our teaching (for example, by getting students to write to each other, to read and comment on each others' writing in pairs and groups, and by staging public discussions and even debates on the topics they are to write about), we will obviously help the social, public, communicative dimension of writing—help students experience writing not just as jumping through hoops for a grade but rather as taking part in the life of a community of discourse. But "social discourse" can also help private writing by getting students sufficiently involved or invested in an issue so that they finally want to carry on producing discourse alone and in private—and for themselves.

Correlatively, if we emphasize the private dimension in our teaching (for example, by using lots of private exploratory writing, freewriting, and journal writing and by helping students realize that of course they may need practice with this "easy" mode of discourse before they can use it fruitfully), we will obviously help students learn to write better reflectively for themselves without the need for others to interact with. Yet this private discourse can also help public, social writing—help students finally feel full enough of their *own* thoughts to have some genuine desire to *tell* them to others. Students often feel they "don't have anything to say" until they finally succeed in engaging themselves in private desert island writing for themselves alone.

Another paradox: whether we want to teach greater audience awareness or the ability to ignore audience, we must help students learn not only to "try harder" but also to "just relax." That is, sometimes students fail to produce reader-based prose because they don't *try* hard enough to think about audience needs. But sometimes the problem is cured if they just relax and write *to* people—as though in a letter or in talking to a trusted adult. By unclenching, they effortlessly call on social discourse skills of immense sophistication. Sometimes, indeed, the problem is cured if the student simply writes in a more social *setting*—in a classroom where it is habitual to share lots of writing. Similarly, sometimes students can't produce sustained private discourse because they don't try hard enough to keep the pen moving and forget about readers. They must persist and doggedly push aside those feelings of, "My head is empty, I have run out of anything to say." But sometimes what they need to learn through all that persistence is how to relax and let go—to unclench.

As teachers, we need to think about what it means to *be an audience* rather than just be a teacher, critic, assessor, or editor. If our only response is to tell students what's strong, what's weak, and how to improve it (diagnosis, assessment, and advice), we actually *undermine* their sense of writing as a social act. We reinforce their sense that writing means doing school exercises, producing for authorities what they already know—*not* actually trying to say things to readers. To help students experience us as *audience* rather than as assessment machines, it helps to respond by "replying" (as in a letter) rather than always "giving feedback."

Paradoxically enough, one of the best ways teachers can help students learn to turn off audience awareness and write in the desert island mode—to turn off the babble of outside voices in the head and listen better to quiet inner voices—is to be a special kind of private audience to them, to be a reader who nurtures by trusting and believing in the writer. Britton has drawn attention to the importance of teacher as "trusted adult" for school children (67–68). No one can be good at private, reflective writing without some *confidence and trust in self*. A nurturing reader can give a writer a kind of permission to forget about other readers or to be one's own reader. I have benefitted from this special kind of audience and have seen it prove useful to others. When I had a teacher who believed in me, who was interested in me and interested in what I had to say, I wrote well. When I had a teacher who thought I was naive, dumb, silly, and in need of being "straightened out," I wrote badly and sometimes couldn't write at all. Here is an interestingly paradoxical instance of the social-to-private principle from Vygotsky and Meade: we learn to listen better and more trustingly to *ourselves* through interaction with trusting *others*.

Look for a moment at lyric poets as paradigm writers (instead of seing them as aberrant), and see how they heighten *both* the public and private dimensions of writing. Bakhtin says that lyric poetry implies "the absolute certainty of the listener's sympathy" (113). I think it's more helpful to say that lyric poets learn to create more than usual privacy in which to write *for themselves*—and then they turn around and let *others overhear*. Notice how poets tend to argue for the importance of no-audience writing, yet they are especially gifted at being public about what they produce in private. Poets are revealers—sometimes even grandstanders or showoffs. Poets illustrate the need for opposite or paradoxical or double audience skills: on the one hand, the ability to be private and solitary and tune out others—to write only for oneself and not give a damn about readers, yet on the other hand, the ability to be more than usually interested in audience and even to be a ham.

If writers really need these two audience skills, notice how bad most conventional schooling is on both counts. Schools offer virtually no privacy for writing: everything students write is collected and read by a teacher, a situation so ingrained students will tend to complain if you don't collect and read every word they write. Yet on the other hand, schools characteristically offer little or no social dimension for writing. It is *only* the teacher who reads, and students seldom feel that in giving their writing to a teacher they are actually communicating something they really want to say to a real person. Notice how often they are happy to turn in to teachers something perfunctory and fake that they would be embarrassed to show to classmates. Often they feel shocked and insulted if we want to distribute to classmates the assigned writing they hand in to us. (I think of Richard Wright's realization that the naked white prostitutes didn't bother to cover themselves when he brought them coffee as a black bellboy because they didn't really think of him as a man or even a person.) Thus the conventional school setting for writing tends to be the least private and the least public—when what students need, like all of us, is practice in writing that is the most private and also the most public.

Practical Guidelines about Audience

The theoretical relationships between discourse and audience are complex and paradoxical, but the practical morals are simple:

1. Seek ways to heighten both the *public* and *private* dimensions of writing. (For activities, see the previous section.)

2. When working on important audience-directed writing, we must try to emphasize audience awareness *sometimes*. A useful rule of thumb is to start by putting the readers in mind and carry on as long as things go well. If difficulties arise, try putting readers out of mind and write either to no audience, to self, or to an inviting audience. Finally, always *revise* with readers in mind. (Here's another occasion when orthodox advice about writing is wrong—but turns out right if applied to revising.)

3. Seek ways to heighten awareness of one's writing process (through process writing and discussion) to get better at taking control and deciding when to keep readers in mind and when to ignore them. Learn to discriminate factors like these:

   (a) The writing task. Is this piece of writing *really* for an audience? More often than we realize, it is not. It is a draft that only we will see, though the final version will be for an audience; or exploratory writing for figuring something out; or some kind of personal private writing meant only for ourselves.

   (b) Actual readers. When we put them in mind, are we helped or hindered?

   (c) One's own temperament. Am I the sort of person who tends to think of what to say and how to say it when I keep readers in mind? Or someone (as I am) who needs long stretches of forgetting all about readers?

(d) Has some powerful "audience-in-the-head" tricked me into talking to it when I'm really trying to talk to someone else—distorting new business into old business? (I may be an inviting teacher-audience to my students, but they may not be able to pick up a pen without falling under the spell of a former, intimidating teacher.)

(e) Is *double audience* getting in my way? When I write a memo or report, I probably have to suit it not only to my "target audience" but also to some colleagues or supervisor. When I write something for publication, it must be right for readers, but it won't be published unless it is also right for the editors—and if it's a book it won't be much read unless it's right for reviewers. Children's stories won't be bought unless they are right for editors and reviewers *and* parents. We often tell students to write to a particular "real-life" audience—or to peers in the class—but of course they are also writing for us as graders. (This problem is more common as more teachers get interested in audience and suggest "second" audiences.)

(f) Is *teacher-audience* getting in the way of my students' writing? As teachers we must often read in an odd fashion: in stacks of 25 or 50 pieces all on the same topic; on topics we know better than the writer; not for pleasure or learning but to grade or find problems (see Elbow, *Writing with Power* 216–36).

To list all these audience pitfalls is to show again the need for thinking about audience needs—yet also the need for vacations from readers to think in peace.

Works Cited

Bakhtin, Mikhail. "Discourse in Life and Discourse in Poetry." Appendix. *Freudianism: A Marxist Critique.* By V. N. Volosinov. Trans. I. R. Titunik. Ed. Neal H. Bruss. New York: Academic, 1976. (Holquist's attribution of this work to Bakhtin is generally accepted.)

Berkenkotter, Carol, and Donald Murray. "Decisions and Revisions: The Planning Strategies of a Publishing Writer and the Response of Being a Rat—or Being Protocoled." *College Composition and Communication* 34 (1983): 156–72.

Blau, Sheridan. "Invisible Writing." *College Composition and Communication* 34 (1983): 297–312.

Booth, Wayne. *The Rhetoric of Fiction.* Chicago: U of Chicago P, 1961.

Britton, James. *The Development of Writing Abilities, 11–18.* Urbana: NCTE, 1977.

Bruffee, Kenneth A. "Liberal Education and the Social Justification of Belief." *Liberal Education* 68 (1982): 95–114.

Bruner, Jerome. *Beyond the Information Given: Studies in the Psychology of Knowing.* Ed. Jeremy Anglin. New York: Norton, 1973.

———. *On Knowing: Essays for the Left Hand.* Expanded ed. Cambridge: Harvard UP, 1979.

Chomsky, Noam. *Reflections on Language.* New York: Random, 1975.

Cicotello, David M. "The Art of Writing: An Interview with William Stafford." *College Composition and Communication* 34 (1983): 173–77.

Clarke, Jennifer, and Peter Elbow. "Desert Island Discourse: On the Benefits of Ignoring Audience." *The Journal Book*. Ed. Toby Fulwiler. Montclair, NJ: Boynton, 1987.

Cooper, Anthony Ashley, 3rd Earl of Shaftesbury. *Characteristics of Men, Manners, Opinions, Times, Etc.* Ed. John M. Robertson. 2 vols. Gloucester, MA: Smith, 1963.

Ede, Lisa, and Andrea Lunsford. "Audience Addressed/Audience Invoked: The Role of Audience in Composition Theory and Pedagogy." *College Composition and Communication* 35 (1984): 140–54.

Elbow, Peter. *Writing with Power*. New York: Oxford UP, 1981.

———. *Writing Without Teachers*. New York: Oxford UP, 1973.

Emerson, Caryl. "The Outer Word and Inner Speech: Bakhtin, Vygotsky, and the Internalization of Language." *Critical Inquiry* 10 (1983): 245–64.

Feldman, Carol Fleisher. "Two Functions of Language." *Harvard Education Review* 47 (1977): 282–93.

Flower, Linda. "Writer-Based Prose: A Cognitive Basis for Problems in Writing." *College English* 41 (1979): 19–37.

Goodman, Paul. *Speaking and Language: Defense of Poetry*. New York: Random, 1972.

Griffin, Susan. "The Internal Voices of Invention: Shaftesbury's Soliloquy." Unpublished. 1986.

Lawrence, D. H. *Studies in Classic American Literature*. Garden City: Doubleday, 1951.

Ong, Walter. "The Writer's Audience Is Always a Fiction." *PMLA* 90 (1975): 9–21.

Park, Douglas B. "The Meanings of 'Audience.'" *College English* 44 (1982): 247–57.

Perl, Sondra. "Guidelines for Composing." Appendix A. *Through Teachers' Eyes: Portraits of Writing Teachers at Work*. By Sondra Perl and Nancy Wilson. Portsmouth, NH: Heinemann, 1986.

Progoff, Ira. *At A Journal Workshop*. New York: Dialogue, 1975.

Shaughnessy, Mina. *Errors and Expectations: A Guide for the Teacher of Basic Writing*. New York: Oxford UP, 1977.

Trimbur, John. Letter to the author. September 1985.

———. "Beyond Cognition: Voices in Inner Speech." Forthcoming in *Rhetoric Review*.

Vygotsky, L. S. *Thought and Language*. Trans. and ed. E. Hanfmann and G. Vakar. 1934. Cambridge: MIT P, 1962.

Walzer, Arthur E. "Articles from the 'California Divorce Project': A Case Study of the Concept of Audience." *College Composition and Communication* 36 (1985): 150–59.

Wright, Richard. *Black Boy*. New York: Harper, 1945.

I benefited from much help from audiences in writing various drafts of this piece. I am grateful to Jennifer Clarke, with whom I wrote a collaborative piece containing a case study on this subject. I am also grateful for extensive feedback from Pat Belanoff, Paul Connolly, Sheryl Fontaine, John Trimbur, and members of the Martha's Vineyard Summer Writing Seminar.

AUDIENCE ADDRESSED/AUDIENCE INVOKED

The Role of Audience in Composition Theory and Pedagogy

Lisa Ede and Andrea Lunsford

One important controversy currently engaging scholars and teachers of writing involves the role of audience in composition theory and pedagogy. How can we best define the audience of a written discourse? What does it mean to address an audience? To what degree should teachers stress audience in their assignments and discussions? What *is* the best way to help students recognize the significance of this critical element in any rhetorical situation?

Teachers of writing may find recent efforts to answer these questions more confusing than illuminating. Should they agree with Ruth Mitchell and Mary Taylor, who so emphasize the significance of the audience that they argue for abandoning conventional composition courses and instituting a "cooperative effort by writing and subject instructors in adjunct courses. The cooperation and courses take two main forms. Either writing instructors can be attached to subject courses where writing is required, an organization which disperses the instructors throughout the departments participating; or the composition courses can teach students how to write the papers assigned in other concurrent courses, thus centralizing instruction but diversifying topics."[1] Or should teachers side with Russell Long, who asserts that those advocating greater attention to audience overemphasize the role of "observable physical or occupational characteristics" while ignoring the fact that most writers actually create their audiences. Long argues against the usefulness of such methods as developing hypothetical rhetorical situations as writing assignments, urging instead a more traditional emphasis on "the analysis of texts in the classroom with a very detailed examination given to the signals provided by the writer for his audience."[2]

To many teachers, the choice seems limited to a single option—to be for or against an emphasis on audience in composition courses. In the following essay, we wish to expand our understanding of the role audience plays in composition theory and pedagogy by demonstrating that the arguments advocated by each side of the current debate oversimplify the act of making meaning through written discourse. Each side, we will argue, has failed adequately to recognize (1) the fluid, dynamic character of rhetorical situations; and (2) the integrated, interdependent nature of reading and writing. After discussing the strengths and weaknesses of the two central perspectives on audience in composition—which we group under the rubrics of *audience addressed* and *audience invoked*[3] — we will propose

Reprinted from *College Composition and Communication* 35.2 (May 1984): 155–71. Used with permission.

an alternative formulation, one which we believe more accurately reflects the richness of "audience" as a concept.*

Audience Addressed

Those who envision audience as addressed emphasize the concrete reality of the writer's audience; they also share the assumption that knowledge of this audience's attitudes, beliefs, and expectations is not only possible (via observation and analysis) but essential. Questions concerning the degree to which this audience is "real" or imagined, and the ways it differs from the speaker's audience, are generally either ignored or subordinated to a sense of the audience's powerfulness. In their discussion of "A Heuristic Model for Creating a Writer's Audience," for example, Fred Pfister and Joanne Petrik attempt to recognize the ontological complexity of the writer-audience relationship by noting that "students, like all writers, must fictionalize their audience."[4] Even so, by encouraging students to "construct in their imagination an audience that is as nearly a replica as is possible of *those many readers who actually exist in the world of reality*," Pfister and Petrik implicitly privilege the concept of audience as addressed.[5]

Many of those who envision audience as addressed have been influenced by the strong tradition of audience analysis in speech communication and by current research in cognitive psychology on the composing process.[6] They often see themselves as reacting against the current-traditional paradigm of composition, with its a-rhetorical, product-oriented emphasis.[7] And they also frequently encourage what is called "real-world" writing.[8]

Our purpose here is not to draw up a list of those who share this view of audience but to suggest the general outline of what most readers will recognize as a central tendency in the teaching of writing today. We would, however, like to focus on one particularly ambitious attempt to formulate a theory and pedagogy for composition based on the concept of audience as addressed: Ruth Mitchell and Mary Taylor's "The Integrating Perspective: An Audience-Response Model for Writing." We choose Mitchell and Taylor's work because of its theoretical richness and practical specificity. Despite these strengths, we wish to note several potentially significant limitations in their approach, limitations which obtain to varying degrees in much of the current work of those who envision audience as addressed.

---

*A number of terms might be used to characterize the two approaches to audience which dominate current theory and practice. Such pairs as identified/envisaged, "real"/fictional, or analyzed/created all point to the same general distinction as do our terms. We chose "addressed/invoked" because these terms most precisely represent our intended meaning. Our discussion will, we hope, clarify their significance; for the present, the following definitions must serve. The "addressed" audience refers to those actual or real-life people who read a discourse, while the "invoked" audience refers to the audience called up or imagined by the writer.

In their article, Mitchell and Taylor analyze what they consider to be the two major existing composition models: one focusing on the writer and the other on the written product. Their evaluation of these two models seems essentially accurate. The "writer" model is limited because it defines writing as either self-expression or "fidelity to fact" (p. 255)—epistemologically naive assumptions which result in troubling pedagogical inconsistencies. And the "written product" model, which is characterized by an emphasis on "certain intrinsic features [such as a] lack of comma splices and fragments" (p. 258), is challenged by the continued inability of teachers of writing (not to mention those in other professions) to agree upon the precise intrinsic features which characterize "good" writing.

Most interesting, however, is what Mitchell and Taylor *omit* in their criticism of these models. Neither the writer model nor the written product model pays serious attention to invention, the term used to describe those methods designed to aid in retrieving information, forming concepts, analyzing complex events, and solving certain kinds of problems.[9] Mitchell and Taylor's lapse in not noting this omission is understandable, however, for the same can be said of their own model. When these authors discuss the writing process, they stress that "our first priority for writing instruction at every level ought to be certain major tactics for structuring material because these structures are the most important in guiding the reader's comprehension and memory" (p. 271). They do not concern themselves with where "the material" comes from—its sophistication, complexity, accuracy, or rigor.

Mitchell and Taylor also fail to note another omission, one which might be best described in reference to their own model (Figure 1). This model has four components. Mitchell and Taylor use two of these, "writer" and "written product," as labels for the models they condemn. The third and fourth components, "audience" and "response," provide the title for their own "audience-response model for writing" (p. 249).

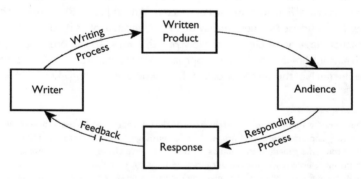

FIG. R4.1.   Mitchell and Taylor's "general model of writing" (p. 250).

Mitchell and Taylor stress that the components in their model interact. Yet, despite their emphasis on interaction, it never seems to occur to them to note that the two other models may fail in large part because they overemphasize and isolate one of the four elements—wrenching it too greatly from its context and thus inevitably distorting the composing process. Mitchell and Taylor do not consider this possibility, we suggest, because their own model has the same weakness.

Mitchell and Taylor argue that a major limitation of the "writer" model is its emphasis on the self, the person writing, as the only potential judge of effective discourse. Ironically, however, their own emphasis on audience leads to a similar distortion. In their model, the audience has the sole power of evaluating writing, the success of which "will be judged by the audience's reaction: 'good' translates into 'effective,' 'bad' into 'ineffective.'" Mitchell and Taylor go on to note that "the audience not only judges writing; it also motivates it" (p. 250),[10] thus suggesting that the writer has less control than the audience over both evaluation and motivation.

Despite the fact that Mitchell and Taylor describe writing as "an interaction, a dynamic relationship" (p. 250), their model puts far more emphasis on the role of the audience than on that of the writer. One way to pinpoint the source of imbalance in Mitchell and Taylor's formulation is to note that they are right in emphasizing the creative role of readers who, they observe, "actively contribute to the meaning of what they read and will respond according to a complex set of expectations, preconceptions, and provocations" (p. 251), but wrong in failing to recognize the equally essential role writers play throughout the composing process not only as creators but also as *readers* of their own writing.

As Susan Wall observes in "In the Writer's Eye: Learning to Teach the Rereading/Revising Process," when writers read their own writing, as they do continuously while they compose, "there are really not one but two contexts for rereading: there is the writer-as-reader's sense of what the established text is actually saying, as of this reading; and there is the reader-as-writer's judgment of what the text might say or should say...."[11] What is missing from Mitchell and Taylor's model, and from much work done from the perspective of audience as addressed, is a recognition of the crucial importance of this internal dialogue, through which writers analyze inventional problems and conceptualize patterns of discourse. Also missing is an adequate awareness that, no matter how much feedback writers may receive after they have written something (or in breaks while they write), as they compose writers must rely in large part upon their own vision of the reader, which they create, as readers do their vision of writers, according to their own experiences and expectations.

Another major problem with Mitchell and Taylor's analysis is their apparent lack of concern for the ethics of language use. At one point, the authors ask the following important question: "Have we painted ourselves into a corner, so that the audience-response model must defend sociologese and its related styles?" (p. 265). Note first the ambiguity of their answer, which seems to us to say no and yes at the same time, and the way they try to deflect its impact:

> No. We defend only the right of audiences to set their own standards and we repudiate the ambitions of English departments to monopolize that standard-setting. If bureaucrats and scientists are happy with the way they write, then no one should interfere.
>
> But evidence is accumulating that they are not happy. (p. 265)

Here Mitchell and Taylor surely underestimate the relationship between style and substance. As those concerned with Doublespeak can attest, for example, the problem with sociologese is not simply its (to our ears) awkward, convoluted, highly nominalized style, but the way writers have in certain instances used this style to make statements otherwise unacceptable to lay persons, to "gloss over" potentially controversial facts about programs and their consequences, and thus violate the ethics of language use. Hence, although we support Mitchell and Taylor when they insist that we must better understand and respect the linguistic traditions of other disciplines and professions, we object to their assumption that style is somehow value free.

As we noted earlier, an analysis of Mitchell and Taylor's discussion clarifies weaknesses inherent in much of the theoretical and pedagogical research based on the concept of audience as addressed. One major weakness of this research lies in its narrow focus on helping students learn how to "continually modify their work with reference to their audience" (p. 251). Such a focus, which in its extreme form becomes pandering to the crowd, tends to undervalue the responsibility a writer has to a subject and to what Wayne Booth in *Modern Dogma and the Rhetoric of Assent* calls "the art of discovering good reasons."[12] The resulting imbalance has clear ethical consequences, for rhetoric has traditionally been concerned not only with the effectiveness of a discourse, but with truthfulness as well. Much of our difficulty with the language of advertising, for example, arises out of the ad writer's powerful concept of audience as addressed divorced from a corollary ethical concept. The toothpaste ad that promises improved personality, for instance, knows too well how to address the audience. But such ads ignore ethical questions completely.

Another weakness in research done by those who envision audience as addressed suggests an oversimplified view of language. As Paul Kameen observes in "Rewording the Rhetoric of Composition," "discourse is not grounded in forms or experience or audience; it engages all of these elements simultaneously."[13] Ann Berthoff has persistently criticized our obsession with one or another of the elements of discourse, insisting that meaning arises out of their synthesis. Writing is more, then, than "a means of acting upon a receiver" (Mitchell and Taylor, p. 250); it is a means of making meaning for writer *and* reader.[14] Without such a unifying, balanced understanding of language use, it is easy to overemphasize one aspect of discourse, such as audience. It is also easy to forget, as Anthony Petrosky cautions us, that "reading, responding, and composing are aspects of understanding, and theories that attempt to account for them outside of their interaction with each other run the serious risk of building reductive models of human understanding."[15]

Audience Invoked

Those who envision audience as invoked stress that the audience of a written discourse is a construction of the writer, a "created fiction" (Long, p. 225). They do not, of course, deny the physical reality of readers, but they argue they writers simply cannot know this reality in the way that speakers can. The central task of the writer, then, is not to analyze an audience and adapt discourse to meet its needs. Rather, the writer uses the semantic and syntactic resources of language to provide cues for the reader—cues which help to define the role or roles the writer wishes the reader to adopt in responding to the text. Little scholarship in composition takes this perspective; only Russell Long's article and Walter Ong's "The Writer's Audience Is Always a Fiction" focus centrally on this issue.[16] If recent conferences are any indication, however, a growing number of teachers and scholars are becoming concerned with what they see as the possible distortions and oversimplifications of the approach typified by Mitchell and Taylor's model.[17]

Russell Long's response to current efforts to teach students analysis of audience and adaptation of text to audience is typical: "I have become increasingly disturbed not only about the superficiality of the advice itself, but about the philosophy which seems to lie beneath it" (p. 221). Rather than detailing Long's argument, we wish to turn to Walter Ong's well-known study. Published in *PMLA* in 1975, "The Writer's Audience Is Always a Fiction" has had a significant impact on composition studies, despite the fact that its major emphasis is on fictional narrative rather than expository writing. An analysis of Ong's argument suggests that teachers of writing may err if they uncritically accept Ong's statement that "what has been said about fictional narrative applies ceteris paribus to all writing" (p. 17).

Ong's thesis includes two central assertions: "What do we mean by saying the audience is a fiction? Two things at least. First, that the writer must construct in his imagination, clearly or vaguely, an audience cast in some sort of role.... Second, we mean that the audience must correspondingly fictionalize itself" (p. 12). Ong emphasizes the creative power of the adept writer, who can both project and alter audiences, as well as the complexity of the reader's role. Readers, Ong observes, must learn or "know how to play the game of being a member of an audience that 'really' does not exist" (p. 12).

On the most abstract and general level, Ong is accurate. For a writer, the audience is not *there* in the sense that the speaker's audience, whether a single person or a large group, is present. But Ong's representative situations—the orator addressing a mass audience versus a writer alone in a room—oversimplify the potential range and diversity of both oral and written communication situations.

Ong's model of the paradigmatic act of speech communication derives from traditional rhetoric. In distinguishing the terms audience and reader, he notes that "the orator has before him an audience which is a true audience, a collectivity.... Readers do not form a collectivity, acting here and now on one another and on the speaker as members of an audience do" (p. 11). As this quotation indicates, Ong also stresses the potential for interaction among members of an audience, and between an audience and a speaker.

But how many audiences are actually collectives, with ample opportunity for interaction? In *Persuasion: Understanding, Practice, and Analysis,* Herbert Simons establishes a continuum of audiences based on opportunities for interaction.[18] Simons contrasts commercial mass media publics, which "have littile or no contact with each other and certainly have no reciprocal awareness of each other as members of the same audience" with "face-to-face work groups that meet and interact continuously over an extended period of time." He goes on to note that: "Between these two extremes are such groups as the following: (1) the *pedestrian audience,* persons who happen to pass a soap box orator ... ; (2) the *passive, occasional audience,* persons who come to hear a noted lecturer in a large auditorium ... ; (3) the *active, occasional audience,* persons who meet only on pecific occasions but actively interact when they do meet" (pp. 97–98).

Simons' discussion, in effect, questions the rigidity of Ong's distinctions between a speaker's and a writer's audience. Indeed, when one surveys a broad range of situations inviting oral communication, Ong's paradigmatic situation, in which the speaker's audience constitutes a "collectivity, acting here and now on one another and on the speaker" (p. 11), seems somewhat atypical. It is certainly possible, at any rate, to think of a number of instances where speakers confront a problem very similar to that of writers: lacking intimate knowledge of their audience, which comprises not a collectivity but a disparate, and possibly even divided, group of individuals, speakers, like writers, must construct in their imaginations "an audience cast in some sort of role."[19] When President Carter announced to Americans during a speech broadcast on television, for instance, that his program against inflation was "the moral equivalent of warfare," he was doing more than merely characterizing his economic policies. He was providing an important cue to his audience concerning the role he wished them to adopt as listeners—that of a people braced for a painful but necessary and justifiable battle. Were we to examine his speech in detail, we would find other more subtle, but equally important, semantic and syntactic signals to the audience.

We do not wish here to collapse all distinctions between oral and written communication, but rather to emphasize that speaking and writing are, after all, both rhetorical acts. There are important differences between speech and writing. And the broad distinction between speech and writing that Ong makes is both commonsensical and particularly relevant to his subject, fictional narrative. As our illustration demonstrates, however, when one turns to precise, concrete situations, the relationship between speech and writing can become far more complex than even Ong represents.

Just as Ong's distinction between speech and writing is accurate on a highly general level but breaks down (or at least becomes less clear-cut) when examined closely, so too does his dictum about writers and their audiences. Every writer must indeed create a role for the reader, but the constraints on the writer and the potential sources of and possibilities for the reader's role are both more complex and diverse than Ong suggests. Ong stresses the importance of literary tradition in the creation of audience: "If the writer succeeds in writing, it is generally because he can fictionalize in his imagination an audience he has learned to know not from daily life but from earlier writers who were fictionalizing in their imagination audiences they had learned to know in still earlier writers, and so on back to the dawn of written narrative" (p. 11). And he cites a particularly (for us) germane example, a student "asked to write on the subject to which schoolteachers, jaded by summer, return compulsively every autumn: 'How I Spent My Summer Vacation'" (p. 11). In order to negotiate such an assignment successfully, the student must turn his real audience, the teacher, into someone else. He or she must, for instance, "make like Samuel Clemens and write for whomever Samuel Clemens was writing for" (p. 11).

Ong's example is, for his purposes, well-chosen. For such an assignment does indeed require the successful student to "fictionalize" his or her audience. But why is the student's decision to turn to a literary model in this instance particularly appropriate? Could one reason be that the student knows (consciously or unconsciously) that his English teacher, who is still the literal audience of his essay, appreciates literature and hence would be entertained (and here the student may intuit the assignment's actual aim as well) by such a strategy? In Ong's example the audience—the "jaded" school-teacher—is not only willing to accept another role but, perhaps, actually yearns for it. How else to escape the tedium of reading 25, 50, 75 student papers on the same topic? As Walter Minot notes, however, not all readers are so malleable:

> In reading a work of fiction or poetry, a reader is far more willing to suspend his beliefs and values than in a rhetorical work dealing with some current social, moral, or economic issue. The effectiveness of the created audience in a rhetorical situation is likely to depend on such constraints as the actual identity of the reader, the subject of the discourse, the identity and purpose of the writer, and many other factors in the real world.[20]

An example might help make Minot's point concrete.

Imagine another composition student faced, like Ong's, with an assignment. This student, who has been given considerably more latitude in her choice of a topic, has decided to write on an issue of concern to her at the moment, the possibility that a home for mentally-retarded adults will be built in her neighborhood.

She is alarmed by the strongly negative, highly emotional reaction of most of her neighbors and wishes in her essay to persuade them that such a residence might not be the disaster they anticipate.

This student faces a different task from that described by Ong. If she is to succeed, she must think seriously about her actual readers, the neighbors to whom she wishes to send her letter. She knows the obvious demographic factors—age, race, class—so well that she probably hardly needs to consider them consciously. But other issues are more complex. How much do her neighbors know about mental retardation, intellectually or experientially? What is their image of a retarded adult? What fears does this project raise in them? What civic and religious values do they most respect? Based on this analysis—and the process may be much less sequential than we describe here—she must, of course, define a role for her audience, one congruent with her persona, arguments, the facts as she knows them, etc. She must, as Minot argues, *both* analyze and invent an audience.[21] In this instance, after detailed analysis of her audience and her arguments, the student decided to begin her essay by emphasizing what she felt to be the genuinely admirable qualities of her neighbors, particularly their kindness, understanding, and concern for others. In so doing, she invited her audience to see themselves as *she* saw them: as thoughtful, intelligent people who, if they were adequately informed, would certainly not act in a harsh manner to those less fortunate than they. In accepting this role, her readers did not have to "play the game of being a member of an audience that 'really' does not exist" (Ong, "The Writer's Audience," p. 12). But they did have to recognize in themselves the strengths the student described and to accept her implicit linking of these strengths to what she hoped would be their response to the proposed "home."

When this student enters her history class to write an examination she faces a different set of constraints. Unlike the historian who does indeed have a broad range of options in establishing the reader's role, our student as much less freedom. This is because her reader's role has already been established and formalized in a series of related academic conventions. If she is a successful student, she has so effectively internalized these conventions that she can subordinate a concern for her complex and multiple audiences to focus on the material on which she is being tested and on the single audience, the teacher, who will respond to her performance on the test.[22]

We could multiply examples. In each instance the student writing—to friend, employer, neighbor, teacher, fellow readers of her daily newspaper—would need, as one of the many conscious and unconscious decisions required in composing, to envision and define a role for the reader. But *how* she defines that role—whether she relies mainly upon academic or technical writing conventions, literary models, intimate knowledge of friends or neighbors, analysis of a particular group, or some combination thereof—will vary tremendously. At times the reader may establish a role for the reader which indeed does not "coincide[s] with his role in the rest of actual life" (Ong, p. 12). At other times, however, one of the writer's primary tasks may be that of analyzing the "real life" audience and adapting the discourse to it. One of the factors that makes writing so difficult, as we know, is that we have no recipes: each rhetorical situation is unique and thus requires the writer, catalyzed and guided by a strong sense of purpose, to reanalyze and reinvent solutions.

Despite their helpful corrective approach, then, theories which assert that the audience of a written discourse is a construction of the writer present their own dangers.[23] One of these is the tendency to overemphasize the distinction between speech and writing while undervaluing the insights of discourse theorists, such as James Moffett and James Britton, who remind us of the importance of such additional factors as distance between speaker or writer and audience and levels of abstraction in the subject. In *Teaching the Universe of Discourse,* Moffett establishes the following spectrum of discourse: recording ("the drama of what is happening"), reporting ("the narrative of what happened"), generalizing ("the exposition of what happens") and theorizing ("the argumentation of what will, may happen").[24] In an extended example, Moffett demonstrates the important points of connection between communication acts at any one level of the spectrum, whether oral or written:

> Suppose next that I tell the cafeteria experience to a friend some time later in conversation. . . . Of course, instead of recounting the cafeteria scene to my friend in person I could write it in a letter to an audience more removed in time and space. Informal writing is usually still rather spontaneous, directed at an audience known to the writer, and reflects the transient mood and circumstances in which the writing occurs. Feedback and audience influence, however, are delayed and weakened. . . . *Compare in turn now the changes that must occur all down the line when I write about this cafeteria experience in a discourse destined for publication and distribution to a mass, anonymous audience of present and perhaps unborn people.* I cannot allude to things and ideas that only my friends know about. I must use a vocabulary, style, logic, and rhetoric that anybody in that mass audience can understand and respond to. I must name and organize what happened during those moments in the cafeteria that day in such a way that this mythical average reader can relate what I say to some primary moments of experience of his own. (pp. 37–38; our emphasis)

Though Moffett does not say so, many of these same constraints would obtain if he decided to describe his experience in a speech to a mass audience—the viewers of a television show, for example, or the members of a graduating class. As Moffett's example illustrates, the distinction between speech and writing is important; it is, however, only one of several constraints influencing any particular discourse.

Another weakness of research based on the concept of audience as invoked is that it distorts the processes of writing and reading by overemphasizing the power of the writer and undervaluing that of the reader. Unlike Mitchell and Taylor, Ong recognizes the creative role the writer plays as reader of his or her own writing, the way the writer uses language to provide cues for the reader and tests the effectiveness of these cues during his or her own rereading of the text. But Ong fails adequately to recognize the constraints placed on the writer, in certain situations, by the audience. He fails, in other words, to acknowledge that readers' own experiences, expectations, and beliefs do play a central role in their reading of a text, and that the writer who does not consider the needs and interests of his audience risks losing that audience. To argue that the audience is a "created fiction" (Long, p. 225), to stress that the reader's role "seldom coincides with his role in the rest of actual life" (Ong, p. 12), is just as much an oversimplification, then, as to insist, as Mitchell and Taylor do, that "the audience not only judges writing, it also motivates it" (p. 250). The former view overemphasizes the writer's independence and power; the latter, that of the reader.

Rhetoric and its Situations[25]

If the perspectives we have described as audience addressed and audience invoked represent incomplete conceptions of the role of audience in written discourse, do we have an alternative? How can we most accurately conceive of this essential rhetorical element? In what follows we will sketch a tentative model and present several defining or constraining statements about this apparently slippery concept, "audience." The result will, we hope, move us closer to a full understanding of the role audience plays in written discourse.

Figure 2 represents our attempt to indicate the complex series of obligations, resources, needs, and constraints embodied in the writer's concept of audience.

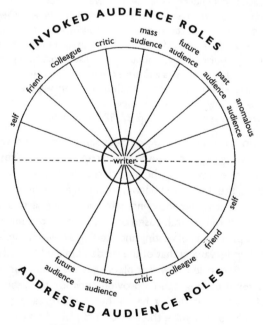

FIG. R4.2.   The concept of audience.

(We emphasize that our goal here is *not* to depict the writing process as a whole—a much more complex task—but to focus on the writer's relation to audience.) As our model indicates, we do not see the two perspectives on audience described earlier as necessarily dichotomous or contradictory. Except for past and anomalous audiences, special cases which we describe paragraphs hence, all of the audience roles we specify—self, friend, colleague, critic, mass audience, and future audience—may be invoked or addressed.[26] It is the writer who, as writer and reader of his or her own text, one guided by a sense of purpose and by the particularities of a specific rhetorical situation, establishes the range of potential roles an audience may play. (Readers may, of course, accept or reject the role or roles the writer wishes them to adopt in responding to a text.)

Writers who wish to be read must often adapt their discourse to meet the needs and expectations of an addressed audience. They may rely on past experience in addressing audiences to guide their writing, or they may engage a representative of that audience in the writing process. The latter occurs, for instance, when we ask a colleague to read an article intended for scholarly publication. Writers may also be required to respond to the intervention of others—a teacher's comments on an essay, a supervisor's suggestions for improving a report, or the insistent, catalyzing questions of an editor. Such intervention may in certain cases represent a powerful stimulus to the writer, but it is the writer who interprets the suggestions—or even commands—of others, choosing what to accept or reject. Even the conscious decision to accede to the expectations of a particular addressed audience may not always be carried out; unconscious psychological resistance, incomplete understanding, or inadequately developed ability may prevent the writer from following through with the decision—a reality confirmed by composition teachers with each new set of essays.

The addressed audience, the actual or intended readers of a discourse, exists outside of the text. Writers may analyze these readers' needs, anticipate their biases, even defer to their wishes. But it is only through the text, through language, that writers embody or give life to their conception of the reader. In so doing, they do not so much create a role for the reader—a phrase which implies that the writer somehow creates a mold to which the reader adapts—as invoke it. Rather than relying on incantations, however, writers conjure their vision—a vision which they hope readers will actively come to share as they read the text—by using all the resources of language available to them to establish a broad, and ideally coherent, range of cues for the reader. Technical writing conventions, for instance, quickly formalize any of several writer-reader relationships, such as colleague to colleague or expert to lay reader. But even comparatively local semantic decisions may play an equally essential role. In "The Writer's Audience Is Always a Fiction," Ong demonstrates how Hemingway's use of definite articles in *A farewell to Arms* subtly cues readers that their role is to be that of a "companion in arms...a confidant" (p. 13).

Any of the roles of the addressed audience cited in our model may be invoked via the text. Writers may also invoke a past audience, as did, for instance, Ong's student writing to those Mark Twain would have been writing for. And writers can also invoke anomalous audiences, such as a fictional character—Hercule Poirot perhaps. Our model, then, confirms Douglas Park's observation that the meanings of audience, though multiple and complex, "tend to diverge in two general directions: one toward actual people external to a text, the audience whom the writer must accommodate; the other toward the text itself and the audience implied there: a set of suggested or evoked attitudes, interests, reactions, conditions of knowledge which may or may not fit with the qualities of actual readers or listeners."[27] The most complete understanding of audience thus involves a synthesis of the perspectives we have termed audience addressed, with its focus on the reader, and audience invoked, with its focus on the writer.

One illustration of this constantly shifting complex of meanings for "audience" lies in our own experiences writing this essay. One of us became interested in the concept of audience during an NEH Seminar, and her first audience was a small, close-knit seminar group to whom she addressed her work. The other came to contemplate a multiplicity of audiences while working on a textbook; the first audience in this case was herself, as she debated the ideas she was struggling to present to a group of invoked students. Following a lengthy series of conversations, our interests began to merge; we shared notes and discussed articles written by others on audience, and eventually one of us began a draft. Our long distance telephone bills and the miles we travelled up and down I-5 from Oregon to British Columbia attest most concretely to the power of a co-author's expectations and criticisms and also illustrate that one person can take on the role of several different audiences: friend, colleague, and critic.

As we began to write and re-write the essay, now for a particular scholarly journal, the change in purpose and medium (no longer a seminar paper or a textbook) led us to new audiences. For us, the major "invoked audience" during this period was Richard Larson, editor of this journal, whose questions and criticisms we imagined and tried to anticipate. (Once this essay was accepted by CCC, Richard Larson became for us an addressed audience: he responded in writing with questions, criticisms, and suggestions, some of which we had, of course, failed to anticipate.) We also thought of the readers of CCC and those who attend the annual CCCC, most often picturing you as members of our own departments, a diverse group of individuals with widely varying degrees of interest in and knowledge of composition. Because of the generic constraints of academic writing, which limit the range of roles we may define for our readers, the audience represented by the readers of CCC seemed most vivid to us in two situations: (1) when we were concerned about the degree to which we needed to explain concepts or terms; and (2) when we considered central organizational decisions, such as the most effective way to introduce a discussion. Another, and for us extremely potent, audience was the authors—Mitchell and Taylor, Long, Ong, Park, and others—with whom we have seen ourselves in silent dialogue. As we read and reread their analyses and developed our responses to them, we

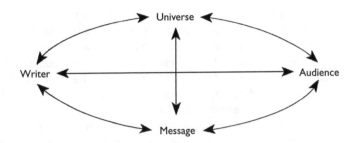

FIG. 3. Corbett's model of "The Rhetorical Interrelationships" (p. 5).

felt a responsibility to try to understand their formulations as fully as possible, to play fair with their ideas, to make our own efforts continue to meet their high standards.

Our experience provides just one example, and even it is far from complete. (Once we finished a rough draft, one particular colleague became a potent but demanding addressed audience, listening to revision upon revision and challenging us with harder and harder questions. And after this essay is published, we may revise our understanding of audiences we thought we knew or recognize the existence of an entirely new audience. The latter would happen, for instance, if teachers of speech communication or some reason found our discussion useful.) But even this single case demonstrates that the term *audience* refers not just to the intended, actual, or eventual readers of a discourse, but to *all* those whose image, ideas, or actions influence a writer during the process of composition. One way to conceive of "audience," then, is as an overdetermined or unusually rich concept, one which may perhaps be best specified through the analysis of precise, concrete situations.

We hope that this partial example of our own experience will illustrate how the elements represented in Figure 2 will shift and merge, depending on the particular rhetorical situation, the writer's aim, and the genre chosen. Such an understanding is critical: because of the complex reality to which the term audience refers and because of its fluid, shifting role in the composing process, any discussion of audience which isolates it from the rest of the rhetorical situation or which radically overemphasizes or underemphasizes its function in relation to other rhetorical constraints is likely to oversimplify. Note the unilateral direction of Mitchell and Taylor's model (p. 5), which is unable to represent the diverse and complex role(s) audience(s) can play in the actual writing process—in the creation of meaning. In contrast, consider the model used by Edward P. J. Corbett in his *Little Rhetoric and Handbook*.[28] This representation, which allows for interaction among all the elements of rhetoric, may at first appear less elegant and predictive than Mitchell and Taylor's. But it is finally more useful since it accurately represents the diverse range of potential interrelationships in any written discourse.

We hope that our model also suggests the integrated, interdependent nature of reading and writing. Two assertions emerge from this relationship. One involves the writer as reader of his or her own work. As Donald Murray notes in "Teaching the Other Self: The Writer's First Reader," this role is critical, for "the reading writer—the map-maker and map-reader—reads the word, the line, the sentence, the paragraph, the page, the entire text. This constant back-and-forth reading monitors the multiple complex relationships between all the elements in writing."[29] To ignore or devalue such a central function is to risk distorting the writing process as a whole. But unless the writer is composing a diary or journal entry, intended only for the writer's own eyes, the writing process is not complete unless another person, someone other than the writer, reads the text also. The second assertion thus emphasizes the creative, dynamic duality of the process of reading and writing, whereby writers create readers and readers create writers. In the meeting of these two lies meaning, lies communication.

A fully elaborated view of audience, then, must balance the creativity of the writer with the different, but equally important, creativity of the reader. It must account for a wide and shifting range of roles for both addressed and invoked audiences. And, finally, it must relate the matrix created by the intricate relationship of writer and audience to all elements in the rhetorical situation. Such an enriched conception of audience can help us better understand the complex act we call composing.

Notes

1. Ruth Mitchell and Mary Taylor, "The Integrating Perspective: An Audience-Response Model for Writing," *CE*, 41 (November, 1979), 267. Subsequent references to this article will be cited in the text.

2. Russell C. Long, "Writer-Audience Relationships: Analysis or Invention," *CCC*, 31 (May, 1980), 223 and 225. Subsequent references to this article will be cited in the text.

3. For these terms we are indebted to Henry W. Johnstone, Jr., who refers to them in his analysis of Chaim Perelman's universal audience in *Validity and Rhetoric in Philosophical Argument: An Outlook in Transition* (University Park, PA: The Dialogue Press of Man & World, 1978), p. 105.

4. Fred R. Pfister and Joanne F. Petrik, "A Heuristic Model for Creating a Writer's Audience," *CCC*, 31 (May, 1980), 213.

5. Pfister and Petrik. 214; our emphasis.

6. See, for example, Lisa S. Ede, "On Audience and Composition," *CCC*, 30 (October, 1979), 291–295.

7. See, for example, David Tedlock, "The Case Approach to Composition," *CCC*, 32 (October, 1981), 253–261.

8. See, for example, Linda Flower's *Problem-Solving Strategies for Writers* (New York: Harcourt Brace Jovanovich, 1981) and John P. Field and Robert H. Weiss' *Cases for Composition* (Boston: Little Brown, 1979).

9. Richard E. Young, "Paradigms and Problems: Needed Research in Rhetorical Invention," in *Research on Composing: Points of Departure*, ed. Charles R. Cooper and Lee Odell (Urbana, IL: National Council of Teachers of English, 1978), p. 32 (footnote #3).

10. Mitchell and Taylor do recognize that internal psychological needs ("unconscious challenges") may play a role in the writing process, but they cite such instances as an "extreme case (often that of the creative writer)" (p. 251). For a discussion of the importance of self-evaluation in the composing process see Susan Miller, "How Writers Evaluate Their Own Writing," *CCC*, 33 (May, 1982), 176–183.

11. Susan Wall, "In the Writer's Eye: Learning to Teach the Rereading/Revising process," *English Education*, 14 (February, 1982), 12.

12. Wayne Booth, *Modern Dogma and the Rhetoric of Assent* (Chicago: The University of Chicago Press, 1974), p. xiv.

13. Paul Kameen, "Rewording the Rhetoric of Composition," *Pre/Text*, 1 (Spring-Fall, 1980), 82.

14. Mitchell and Taylor's arguments in favor of adjunct classes seem to indicate that they see writing instruction, wherever it occurs, as a skills course, one instructing students in the proper use of a tool.

15. Anthony R. Petrosky, "From Story to Essay: Reading and Writing," *CCC*, 33 (February, 1982), 20.

16. Walter J. Ong, S. J., "The Writer's Audience Is Always a Fiction," *PMLA*, 90 (January, 1975), 9–21. Subsequent references to this article will be cited in the text.

17. See, for example, William Irmscher, "Sense of Audience: An Intuitive Concept," unpublished paper delivered at the CCCC in 1981; Douglas B. Park, "The Meanings of Audience: Pedagogical Implications," unpublished paper delivered at the CCCC in 1981; and Luke M. Reinsma, "Writing to an Audience: Scheme or Strategy?" unpublished paper delivered at the CCCC in 1982.

18. Herbert W. Simons, *Persuasion: Understanding, Practice, and Analysis* (Reading, MA: Addison-Wesley, 1976).

19. Ong, p. 12. Ong recognizes that oral communication also involves role-playing, but he stresses that it "has within it a momentum that works for the removal of masks" (p. 20). This may be true in certain instances, such as dialogue, but does not, we believe, obtain broadly.

20. Walter S. Minot, "Response to Russell C. Long," *CCC*, 32 (October, 1981), 337.

21. We are aware that the student actually has two audiences, her neighbors and her teacher, and that this situation poses an extra constraint for the writer. Not all students can manage such a complex series of audience constraints, but it is important to note that writers in a variety of situations often write for more than a single audience.

22. In their paper on "Student and Professional Syntax in Four Disciplines" (unpublished paper delivered at the CCCC in 1981), Ian Pringle and Aviva Freedman provide a good example of what can happen when a student creates an aberrant role for an academic reader. They cite an excerpt from a third year history assignment, the tone of which "is essentially the tone of the opening of a television travelogue commentary" and which thus asks the reader, a history professor, to assume the role of the viewer of such a show. The result is as might be expected: "Although the content of the paper does not seem significantly more abysmal than other papers in the same set, this one was awarded a disproportionately low grade" (p. 2).

23. One danger which should be noted is a tendency to foster a questionable image of classical rhetoric. The agonistic speaker-audience relationship which Long cites as an essential characteristic of classical rhetoric is actually a central point of debate among those involved in historical and theoretical research in rhetoric. For further discussion, see: Lisa Ede and Andrea Lunsford, "On Distinctions Between Classical and Modern Rhetoric," in *Classical Rhetoric and Modern Discourse: Essays in Honor of Edward P. J. Corbett*, ed. Robert Connors, Lisa Ede, and Andrea Lunsford (Carbondale, IL: Southern Illinois University Press, 1984).

24. James Moffett, *Teaching the Universe of Discourse* (Boston: Houghton Mifflin, 1968), p. 47. Subsequent references will be mentioned in the text.

25. We have taken the title of this section from Scott Consigny's article of the same title, *Philosophy and Rhetoric*, 7 (Summer, 1974), 175–186. Consigny's effort to mediate between two opposing views of rhetoric provided a stimulating model for our own efforts.

26. Although we believe that the range of audience roles cited in our model covers the general spectrum of options, we do not claim to have specified all possibilities. This is particularly the case since, in certain instances, these roles may merge and blend—shifting subtly in character. We might also note that other terms for the same roles might be used. In a business setting, for instance, colleague might be better termed co-worker; critic, supervisor.

27. Douglas B. Park, "The Meanings of 'Audience,'" *CE*, 44 (March, 1982), 249.

28. Edward P. J. Corbett, *The Little Rhetoric & Handbook*, 2nd edition (Glenview, IL: Scott, Foresman, 1982), p. 5.

29. Donald M. Murray, "Teaching the Other Self: The Writer's First Reader." *CCC*, 33 (May, 1982), 142.

5

Assessing Writing

Julie Neff Lippman

> This chapter discusses the issue of assessment, examining the topic in a political and programmatic context. It also provides strategies for helping teachers design effective assignments and respond to them.

Looking forward to reading his students' first essays, the new teacher of writing pours a cup of coffee and sits down at his desk to grade them. He picks up the first essay, which is printed elegantly on good quality paper. The paper has only one grammatical error, but little content. He moves it to the "later" pile and picks up the next. The second paper has many grammatical and usage errors, but it also has passages that seem to be insightful and poignant. He moves it to the "later" pile. The third is good, almost too good, as if it had been copied out of a book. "Maybe it was," he thinks. It, too, goes to the "later" pile. He has been at the task more than 2 hours, but he has not written a comment or put a grade on a single essay. In the subsequent papers, he marks spelling and punctuation errors. He rewrites whole sentences and refers the students to pages in the handbook. Time passes, and he still has not written a comment or put a grade on a paper. He pours another cup of coffee and opens a bag of M & Ms. He thinks back to courses he has taken and to what expert writers have said about writing: "What oft was thought but ne'er so well expressed." "Clear writing reflects clear thinking." "Easy writing makes for hard reading." All seem to be true in one way or another, but none are of any help when assessing this stack of essays.

Many teachers of writing have experienced this same frustration with assessing and responding to student writing. Whether assessment is occurring in the classroom or on a programmatic scale, evaluation of student writing continues to present teachers and administrators with a plethora of challenges. Assessment has become a complex and often political topic that has been debated at every level from the individual classroom to school boards and state legislatures. This chapter will discuss these challenges, putting them in historical and programmatic contexts, and it will provide strategies for helping teachers design effective assignments and respond to student essays.

WRITING ASSESSMENT: AN OVERVIEW

Historical Context

Originating in about 1950, writing assessment focused on objective testing and was used to determine who would take the pre-college writing courses and who would not, or who would be excused from a required composition class (Yancey, 1999, pp. 484–485). Since then assessment has changed dramatically, in many ways reflecting the changes in the field of composition (Yancey, 1999, p. 484). From approximately 1950–1970, assessment reflected ideas about composition that were current at the time—that is, that writing ability could be measured by having students answer questions about grammar, usage, and punctuation in a multiple choice test. The objective test was popular with teachers and administrators: It was easy and inexpensive to administer, and it was reliable. In other words, it was easy to "control" variables. But the problem became obvious; it was not valid; that is, it did not measure what it purported to measure. A student's score on an objective grammar test did not predict whether the student could actually write any more than the written drivers' test can predict whether a person can drive a car.

From about 1970–1986, assessment relied primarily on essay tests that had been written in a single session (Yancey, 1999, p. 484). Most compositionists considered these tests to be an improvement over the objective tests because they actually measured what they were intended to measure—writing—and, therefore, were more valid than objective tests. However, as the profession began to see composing as a process (Flower & Hayes, 1981) and writing as a rhetorical and social act (Bruffee, 1986), many questioned the efficacy of such tests. Were students who had been trained in invention and revision put at a disadvantage by a timed test that did not allow for process? The advantage to writing tests was that they measured "writing" proficiency rather than grammar proficiency, but they defined writing in a narrow, reductive way.

Until recently, assessment was achieved by evaluating a specific text written at a given time, but from 1986 to the present, it has increasingly been done through portfolios (Yancey, 1999, p. 485). Reflecting current thinking about process, portfolio assessment takes into account the need for the generation of ideas and thoughtful revision over time. Portfolios have been seen as valid because they measure what they say they will measure—students' ability to write and revise in a rhetorical setting. However, critics question the reliability of portfolio assessment. Pointing to the number of times a paper can be revised, some claim it is often impossible to determine how competent the student writer is or how much help a student has received during the revision process (Wolcott, 1998, p. 52). Others claim there are too many variables with portfolio assessment and that portfolios do not hold up well enough to statistical measures for them to be considered a reliable assessment instrument (Wolcott, 1998, p. 1). To address the problems with reliability, some schools have added a timed essay test to the portfolio assessment. Still, others believe that the validity of portfolio assessment outweighs the reliability problems associated with it and that portfolio assessment is the kind of evaluation most consistent with the values of compositionists.

Moreover, over the last 50 years, the focus of assessment has begun to shift to program assessment as a means of measuring how well a program as a whole is working. In programmatic assessment, the focus is taken off the individual learner and instead placed on the outcomes that the program can demonstrate. This kind of assessment attempts to measure how much students have grown or learned as the result of a particular program. While this kind of assessment is useful to programs, it does not provide much information about individual writers and learners. Kathleen Yancey (1999) has challenged compositionists to think about how programmatic assessment can be used to help the individual, a challenge that we are likely to read more about in the next several years.

Nevertheless, although writing assessment has changed over the years, it has also stayed the same depending on the geography and institution. Some universities continue to administer an objective grammar test as part of an institutional exit exam, whereas others use the holistically scored essay exam, portfolio assessment, programmatic assessment, or some combination of assessment techniques.

THE LANGUAGE OF ASSESSMENT

As we look at assessment, it is useful to understand the terms commonly associated with it. Assessment is often divided into indirect assessment and direct or performance assessment. Relying primarily on norm-referenced standardized tests, indirect assessment, a characteristic assessment in the 1950s and 1960s, has been widely criticized by groups such as the National

Council of Teachers of English (NCTE) and International Reading Association (IRA) because the tests decontextualize knowledge and meaning making. They also pay too much attention to lower-order skills and usurp classroom time that could be used for more relevant instruction. However, they have been popular with administrators because they are easy and inexpensive to administer, and they provide results that can be charted across schools and across districts (Wolcott, 1998). Some even see them as being a step toward national standards.

Characteristic of assessment in the 1970s and 1980s, "direct" or "performance assessment" measures students' writing ability by having students write. Students demonstrate their ability by writing an essay or solving a problem. In this kind of assessment, students must demonstrate writing competence rather than recognizing the correct answer; teachers exercise their judgment and this judgment replaces the scoring of the scantron (Wolcott, 1998, p. 5). While this kind of assessment is superior to indirect assessment, it does not grow out of recent thinking about composition as process (Flower & Hayes, 1981) or social constructivist theory (Bruffee, 1986). Lee Odell (1981) has argued that direct writing assessment defines competence too narrowly. Students should be able to demonstrate "the ability to discover what one wishes to say and to convey one's message through language, syntax and content that are appropriate for one's audience and purpose"(p. 103). Direct assessment does not give the writer the opportunity to demonstrate these rhetorical abilities.

Although there are numerous problems with direct assessment, many schools employ it to determine who takes certain courses, who may pass over a requirement, and who may receive a diploma. Because direct assessment is still widely used, it may be useful to take a few moments to reflect on the qualities of successful direct assessment. Students do their best writing when they care about their topics (Atwell, 1997; Graves 1993) and when they have a clearly defined audience and purpose. Therefore, topics for direct assessment should be (a) accessible, (b) stated clearly, (c) broadbased, (d) engaging, but not so emotional that students lose control of their writing, and (e) encouraging of the type of writing sought by the curriculum (Wolcott, pp. 24–25). The audience and purpose of the writing should also be clearly stated.

Another important characteristic of effective assessment is that it be "authentic"—that is, the assessment, as much as possible, should occur in a meaningful, real-life context. For example, portfolios that reveal the student's process over time are considered "authentic assessment." Developed as a way to look at students' work over time, valuing the writing process and the context, portfolio assessment allows the student to choose his or her best work, revise it, and put it in a portfolio. Then, just as they did in performance assessment through evaluating timed writing, teams of trained readers score the portfolios. Both performance and authentic assessment have been used by departments and whole universities to measure student success; most compositionists consider both of these methods to be superior to indirect assessment, which depends on norm-based standardized tests.

We can also divide assessment into internal and external assessment. Internal assessment, whether papers, tests, or portfolios, focuses on the individual's learning and will be tied to the curriculum for the class. Internal assessment has two main advantages. First, if an essay test is being given, the teacher will be able to give extra help to students who do not understand the test directions, and she can extend the time if students have not finished. Second, when the student has finished a paper or test, the evaluation is usually given to the student and in K-12, to the parents. With internal assessment, teachers have a great deal of control over the evaluation process; they can even throw out a whole set of results if they see a problem with the test or the testing situation (Wolcott, 1998).

External assessment, usually considered top down because it is initiated by those outside the classroom, is not tied to a particular class and the teacher has little discretion about giving extra explanations or extending the time. However, external assessment does have advantages. The directions and the prompts have usually been created with great care to improve the validity of the sample (Wolcott, 1998, p. 3). In addition, external assessment gives teachers and administrators a chance to compare student achievement between campuses and among districts. The reporting of the results is much more public, as they are sent to state legislatures and occasionally to newspapers. Students and parents may not even see the results of the tests (Wolcott, 1998, p. 3).

Formative/Summative

Assessment has many purposes, which determine when it is conducted and what is done with the results. *Summative assessment* aims to measure the success of a particular endeavor after it is over, when there is no opportunity for revision. SATs, GREs, and even the licensing exam for drivers provide summative assessment because they measure ability at a certain point. In assessing writing, the goal of summative assessment is not to shape students' thinking or learning, but rather to judge how well students have accomplished the writing task. The grade at the end of a course is an example of summative assessment, and, in this way, all instructors engage in it. External assessment is always summative. In contrast, *formative assessment,* which is generally internal, puts emphasis on shaping students' writing while they are still in the process of writing. The goal of most formative assessment is to help students improve their writing and writing ability.

"Outcomes" assessment, an increasingly popular term in educational circles, has also influenced how writing teachers think about assessment. William Spady (1994) defines outcomes assessment in the following way: "Outcomes are high-quality, culminating demonstrations of significant learning in context"(p. 18). Outcomes are based on clearly defined goals at the beginning of a course or an educational experience and a measure of students' achievement of those goals. The emphasis is on process, learning in depth, and problem solving within a context.

Closely related to outcomes assessment, programmatic assessment, likely to be the next wave of assessment (Yancey, 1999, p. 484), takes the emphasis off the individual learner and places it on the program. It asks the question: "Is the program successful in meeting its goals?" Although it may not provide specific information about how well Johnny or Maria can write, it will provide information about how students generally are doing as the result of a particular program. This type of assessment will not help decide whether a particular student may pass into the next grade or be excused from a remedial writing class, but will give information about how well a program is meeting its goals. If the goal is to assess a program, then individual learners who may already face issues of poverty or learning differences need not be put at risk.

Programmatic assessment may rely on random sampling and the collection of papers in a "folder." Unlike portfolios that involve students in the selection process, "folders" contain all of a student's writing over a period of time. All the papers may be judged or a random sample selected from papers in the folder. In any case, the scores are then analyzed statistically to discover gains between the beginning and end of the course or from the beginning of an academic career until the end. For instance, the University of Puget Sound has used statistical sampling and folders to demonstrate significant gains in student writing from matriculation until graduation. Relying on cross-curricular teams of faculty for blind holistic scoring, the university has been able to do "authentic" assessment while statistically demonstrating gain scores.

Assessment is often political and contentious because the stakeholders, those who have an interest in assessment, have agendas that are at odds. Generally, administrators want summative assessment that is inexpensive and easy to control with outcomes that can be reduced to tables and graphs. Teachers generally favor formative assessment that grows out of the curriculum and resides in the classroom where they can monitor the progress of individual students. Parents want assessment that holds schools accountable but emphasizes the growth of the individual child—especially their child.

School boards and legislators want to see that their investment in schools is paying off in terms of improved test scores. With so many people having sometimes competing agendas, as Willa Wolcott (1998) has pointed out, the real challenge with any kind of assessment is bringing together all of the stakeholders to develop a plan that they all can agree on—parents, teachers, school boards, community groups, and state legislators (Wolcott, 1998).

WORKING WITH STUDENT WRITING

Let's go back to our composition teacher, who, for now doesn't care about schoolwide writing assessment but, rather, about finishing this set of compositions before dawn. These first papers respond to the question: "What is good writing?" This is a question that the British essayist and novelist, George Orwell addressed in his essay "Politics and the English Language" (1949), in which he defined good and bad writing. This essay has been widely anthologized and has been influential in describing "good writing" in the latter half of the 20th century.

FOR WRITING AND DISCUSSION

1. How does Orwell define good writing? Is his definition adequate? What has he left out? In a position paper, develop your own definition of "good writing." Be sure to use specific examples to back up your points. The audience for this paper is the class; the purpose of the paper is for you to put forward a definition of good writing and to defend it. The paper should be 3–4 typed, double-spaced pages.

2. Write a page or two explaining what good writing is and what it is not. How would you define "good writing? Include specific examples from your own writing or the writing of others. How important are audience, purpose, and writer to the determination of what is "good"? Break into groups of three or four and share what you've written with your group members. The group should then make a master list of qualities of "good writing" to share with the whole class. Does the class's master list define good writing? Is there anything the class would add to the list?

The working definition of "good writing" is helping our teacher assess the strengths and weaknesses of the papers on his desk, but he is still puzzled about how to turn his thinking about good writing into grades on a paper. He is pondering the following questions: "How do I help my students become better writers? How much should I correct? How can I speed up my process? What is the difference between an A and a B and between a B− and a C+?" Because the ultimate goal of assessment is to improve student learning, let's think about the teacher, classroom, student, and the student's writing. At the heart of our inquiry lies this key question: "How do we use assignments and assessment to help students become better writers?"

FOR WRITING AND DISCUSSION

Imagine that you have been given the following topics for an essay. The department chair has told you that your success with these topics will determine whether you will retain your job. How difficult would it be to write with only this information? Develop a list of questions you would have before you started on these essays. Share them with a small group and present your findings to the rest of the class.

1. Winter doldrums
2. Define "education"
3. Write an assessment plan for the department
4. About Joe Kozminki—A LETTER TO A PARENT
5. Describe your classroom
6. Comment on the last image in *The Great Gatsby*

Designing Assignments

Most of your problems with these prompts probably grow out of the missing rhetorical context—the purpose of the paper, the audience for it, and the situation within which it would be produced. Because all writing is produced in a rhetorical context, it is important to let students know what that context or situation is. Although we might agree with Orwell about clarity and precision, we might wonder how we can decide what is really "good" without a rhetorical and cultural context. Furthermore, Charles Cooper in "What We Know about Genres" encourages teachers to give students explicit information about the genre the teacher is expecting the students to write. Broadening the concept beyond literary categories (novel, romance, epic), Cooper defines genre broadly as "types of writing produced every day in our culture, types of writing that make possible certain kinds of learning and social interaction" (p. 25).

Similarly, because each assignment offers students an "invitation" to write, the inadequate "invitation" may lead students astray. Therefore, weak papers may be the fault of the assignment or "invitation" rather than the fault of the student (Lindemann, 1995, p. 207). As you looked at the aforementioned writing prompts, you probably discovered how difficult it would be to write a paper that would fulfill the readers' "invitation" or expectations. Although there will always be variables in the directions for an assignment, the writer must have explicit information about some of them: (a) the purpose of the writing, (b) the audience, (c) the role the writer is to take in relation to the subject and the audience, (d) the form the writing should take, and (e) criteria for success (Lindemann, 1995, p. 212). In each of these previous examples, the prompt does not provide enough rhetorical context for the writer.

Ryder, Vander Lei, and Roen (1999), in "Audience Considerations of Evaluating Writing," claim that it is especially important that students know from the beginning who they are writing for. "Because writing is an interactive process, an audience has an impact on all parts of a text—the way a topic is developed, the organization, the diction, the tone, and so on. Clearly then, questions of audience cannot be left to the end of the writing process" (p. 59). Teachers might also consider taking the different kinds of relationships with audience into account when they design and sequence assignments: monadic relationship occurs when the writer writes for herself (personal journals or exploratory writing), dyadic relationship occurs when the writer writes with one other person in mind (an essay for a teacher or a letter to a friend), and triadic relationship occurs when the writer takes a side against an opponent before an audience (the argumentative paper or an academic article) (Ryder, Vander Lei, & Roen, 1995, p. 212).

In *Teaching and Assessing Writing,* Edward White has provided a list of questions that guide teachers as they make assignments. The following list is adapted from White's book (1994, pp. 22–23).

1. What do I want the writer to do? Is it worth doing? Why? Is it interesting and appropriate? What will it teach—specifically? What will the assignment tell me?

2. How do I want the writer to do the assignment? Will the writers collaborate or work alone?

3. Does the assignment give enough information about required length and the use of sources?

4. For whom are the writers writing? Who is the audience? What do they know about the topic? What are their predispositions toward it? Is the teacher the only audience or part of the audience?

5. How much time do the writers need for the assignment? How much class time is needed for the process? How much time outside of class is necessary?

FOR WRITING AND DISCUSSION

1. Rewrite the prompts on the previous page so that you or someone else could actually carry out the writing. Indicate what kind of relationship the writer should have with the audience. When you've finished, share your writing prompts with others in the class and use Ed White's list to evaluate and revise the prompts.

2. After you've revised the prompts, exchange one of them with another class member who will then write the paper. When the student has finished writing, he or she should write another paragraph evaluating the effectiveness of the prompt. Did the prompt provide enough information? What other information might have been useful?

Some teachers object to specificity in assignments, claiming that the students should have the freedom to approach the assignment as they see fit. But a rhetorical situation is inherent in most all of the writing we do. For instance, when I agreed to write this chapter, I knew the approximate length, the audience, the purpose of the book, and the purpose of my chapter. I also had an outline of the book so I could see how my chapter would complement the others. And I had a sample chapter that gave me ideas about voice, tone, stance, format, and level of detail. Shouldn't students have the benefit of similar details about audience, purpose, and reader expectations?

It would be impossible for the writing teacher to spell out every variable in every assignment. In fact, doing so would take away the students' agency and make writing a rote activity rather than a rhetorical one that allows the students to solve problems as they produce a text. On the other hand, vague assignments with mixed messages almost guarantee that only a few papers will actually meet the readers' or the teachers' expectations.

Although good assignments will help students with their writing tasks, teachers still need to assess and respond to student writing. Nancy Sommers, Sosland Director of Harvard's Expository Writing Program, has found that teachers' responses to student writing are often harsh and ineffective. Her essay "Responding to Student Writing" is included at the end of this chapter.

FOR WRITING AND DISCUSSION

1. Summarize *Responding to Student Writing*. What is Sommers' argument? Do your own experiences with teacherly comments mirror what Sommers has found? Explain in a few paragraphs. Be sure to be specific.

2. What flaws exist in Sommers' research? How would you design a study to solve these problems?
3. What should be the goals of feedback on student papers? Brainstorm a list of goals and share them with the class or in small groups.

Language for Feedback

In order for teachers to write meaningful responses, it is useful for them to have language to talk about the writing—about what is working as well as what needs improvement. These responses go beyond what appears in a grading rubric. Many teachers have found that dividing the feedback into two categories is useful: suggestions for global revision and suggestions for local revision.

Global issues include:

1. Thesis or point.
2. Structure or organization.
3. Development or evidence.
4. Appropriateness and consistency of tone.
5. Appropriateness for the audience and purpose.

Local issues include:

1. Diction.
2. Syntax.
3. Grammatical structure.
4. Punctuation.
5. Spelling.

It seems obvious that the global issues need attention first, because there is no use checking spelling when the whole sentence may be eliminated before the final copy is turned in. However, sometimes problems with transitions indicate a problem with structure rather than the need for a connecting adverb. Similarly, a sentence that lacks clarity because of syntactical problems may indicate problems with content. Although we know that words and ideas are inextricably linked, giving attention to the global issues first lets students know that the instructor values their thinking and ideas over their ability to use "spell check." And in the end, the instructor will help students become better writers if they pay attention to the students' ideas first.

Ultimately, though, teachers need to put grades on papers. The following analytical scale makes the teacher's expectations explicit for an argumentative paper. In fact, one of the advantages of an analytic scale is that it can be used with this same type of writing in the future. The disadvantage is that it is not sensitive to purpose, speaker role, and audience that occur within the same kind of paper (Cooper 1977, p. 14). Keep in mind, though, that assessment criteria will change, depending on the kind of writing the students are doing and the assignment's place in the term. Providing the students with a copy of the analytical scale makes it a useful instructional tool as well.

FOR WRITING AND DISCUSSION

1. Read the assignment, "An Invitation" (see next "Writing Assignment" section), and the following grading rubric. Do you feel the rubric needs changes in order for it to suit the assignment? If so, make these changes and share them with other students in the class. Then grade the paper "An Invitation" and share your grade and the reasons for it.

2. Write a paragraph or two to the student about the strengths and weaknesses of the paper. Be sure to be specific with your comments. Exchange the written comments with a class member. The other student should read the comments and answer the following questions: "What was especially useful? What was not? Did the evaluator omit the pitfalls that Sommers (1982) says are characteristic of teacherly comments? How could the comments be improved?"

Grading Scale

An "A" Paper

- Answers a question at issue. The answer to the question provides a thesis and a means for organizing the paper.
- Makes good use of sources for analysis, discussion, and clarity.
- Has a title that creates expectations.
- Has paragraphs that have a central idea and purpose related to the thesis.
- Has smooth transitions between paragraphs, which clarify reasoning.
- Is untroubled by numerous spelling, punctuation, and syntax errors.
- Correctly uses the MLA format for citation of sources.

A "B" Paper

- Has a clear thesis, which organizes the paper.
- Makes good use of sources for analysis, discussion, and clarity.
- Has a title that relates to the content of the paper.
- Has paragraphs that have a central idea and purpose.

- Has some sense of transition or development from paragraph to paragraph.
- Is untroubled by numerous spelling, punctuation, and syntax errors.
- Correctly uses the MLA format for citation of sources.

A "C" Paper

- Has a purpose but is not organized around a thesis or a question at issue.
- Has no title or uses the paper assignment as the title.
- Has paragraphs that have a discernible purpose.
- Is relatively untroubled by numerous spelling, punctuation, and syntax errors.
- Provides some consistent form of documentation of sources.

A "D" Paper

- Purpose is not clear and does not have a thesis or question.
- Has a significant number of paragraphs that are confused by lack of purpose, contradictory ideas, or lack of clarity.
- Has no title.
- Has a significant number of spelling, punctuation, and syntax errors.
- Has little or no documentation.

An "F" Paper

- Has no discernible purpose, question, or thesis.
- Discussion rambles from topic to topic and paragraphs are without purpose.
- Has no title.
- Is plagued with spelling, punctuation, and syntax errors.
- Has little or no documentation.

WRITING ASSIGNMENT

Write a personal narrative that tells us something about who you are. The audience for this paper is the class and the purpose is to introduce yourself to the class in a way that is both engaging and revealing. Your narrative should be 2–4 pages. Then read the student paper that grew out of the assignment and make a list of the strengths and weaknesses

In his poem, Black has many thoughts about love. I don't think he was talking about romantic love though. The clod is well cloddy but he is still happy. But the clod can not protect itself from the cattle who tromp along, sometimes tromping on the clod. Even so he has a bright out look on life and a warm heart. He is also innocent.

The pebble is the opposite of the cold. It is beautiful. It sits in the water, and sings. But the song doesn't sound like much it doesn't sound like the beautiful song of the clod because the pebble has a hard heart.

The pebble has had experience and that makes him unhappy.

This demonstrates that the clod is full of love and the pebble is not. The love idea relates to the Bible where it says that: "Love does not delight in evil but rejoices in the truth". The clod represents truth because it is happy. The pebble represents "sin" because it is unhappy.

William Blake does an excellent job of bring together the ideas of innocence and experience especially in this poem.

6 Range

AN EXCELLENT PAPER   It has substantial content and clear organization and focus. It presents ideas clearly and even gracefully.

5 Range

A VERY GOOD PAPER   The strengths outweigh its weaknesses. It has solid development and is clearly organized and focused, but it is not as strong as a 6.

4 Range

A GOOD PAPER   The strengths of the folder outweigh the weaknesses, but the development of ideas is not as complete, the organization and focus are not as clear, and the language is not as strong.

3 Range

A FAIR PAPER   The strengths and weakness are about equally balanced. The writer has tried to develop ideas, focus the paper, and use effective language. But parts are underdeveloped, disorganized, or confusing. The writing may also be too general or predictable.

2 Range

A WEAK PAPER   The weaknesses outweigh the strengths. The folder is weak, underdeveloped, poorly focused, and too general. However, it could be error-free.

1 Range

A POOR PAPER   Its weaknesses outweigh its strengths in most ways. It is unfocused, underdeveloped, and also plagued with grammatical errors that make it unintelligible.

FIG. 5.1.   Holistic Scoring Rubric.

The Clod & the Pebble:

The Summation of Blake's Innocence and Experience

All throughout his Songs of innocence and of Experience, *William Blake makes comparisons between the naivete_ and goodness of youth and the cynicism and pain of age. Many of his innocence poems have parallel lyrics of experience, showing the two sides of the same social or political coin. It is through these comparisons that Blake seeks to compare the harsh realities that come with age and with the clear, unsullied ideals of youth. Yet a few of his poems attempt to contain both aspects of life, exposing innocence and experience within the same context and effectively linking the two. In "The Clod & the Pebble," Blake discusses the Christian virtue love, first ideally and then pessimistically.*

The Clod of Clay represents all that is rough on the edges, still moldable, and unaffected by life and time. Not only does the Clod express its joy and love, it does so in song, with the happiness and melody of an unharmed innocence. At the same time, the Clod is not impressive to look at; one must truly look deep to find any beauty in a piece of clay. But appearance is not the goal of the Clod. Instead, its focus is upon pleasing those around it, making any attempt possible to create a "Heaven in Hell's despair" (ln 4). Although recognizing the sadness, pain, and death of hell, The Clod does not give up hope that, with enough love, the despair of hell can be changed into the hope of heaven. The Clod is idealistic, optimistic, and most of all selfless. It seeks to exemplify the principles of 1 Corinthians 13, specifically the phrases "It is not self-seeking" (vs 5). The Clod has not been hardened by sin, by pain, by experience of any kind. Yet the Clod is also easily moved—quickly "trodden with the cattle's feet" (ln 6). It has not yet built any sort of protective shell and is, therefore, quite susceptible to any outside force. The cattle of the world have every power to move the Clod because it does not suspect any interference and cannot protect itself.

The Pebble of the brook is clearly the opposite of the Clod. The Pebble, hard, smooth, and immutable, warbles out its tuneless words of woe. As the Clod looked rugged and ugly on the outside so the Pebble, refined by the constant stream of water, shines and glistens. It looks beautiful on the outside, but has nothing of softness or warmth on the inside. As the Clod sought to make a heaven out of hell, so the Pebble manages to create a hell despite the power and existence of heaven. Hurt and used by the experiences of coming of age, the Pebble is selfish and egocentric. It directly opposes 1 Corinthians 13, not just in seeking its own delight but also in taking joy in the pain of another (1 Cor. 13:6 says that "Love does not delight in evil but rejoices with the truth." The Pebble has become hard and cold by sin, pain, and experience, but it has also somewhat established itself. Constantly opposing the water of the brook the Pebble has learned to rely upon itself. It remains where it is, despite the continual pressure to submit to the power of the water. As time has pressed forward, the Pebble has learned to stand on its own, to be only mildly affected by the things of life, to look at life through tainted eyes.

Most of Blakes' poetry only focuses upon one aspect of existence—either the ideal or the reality. In "The Clod & the Pebble," Blake effectively sets the two extremes against each other to truly bring out their opposites. By doing so, he has in many ways summed up the who effect of the rest of his work on innocence and experience and, consequently, the futility of either perspective. To look at life as the Clod would, without defense or protection is just as meaningless as taking the Pebble's hardened and unloving perspective. It must be, then, that reality is a focus of the two extremes.

You may have found this assessment exercise both enlightening and frustrating. No one wants to do assessment (Yancey & Huot, 1997). Yet whether it is summative assessment conducted systemwide or formative assessment conducted in the classroom, assessment should be an integral part of teaching writing. When classroom teachers develop a clear approach, good assessment can improve student writing and learning. Specific goals for good writing clearly communicated to students will allow both teachers and students to be more successful in the writing classroom.

CONCLUSION

Since George Orwell wrote "Politics and the English Language," our notions about what good writing is and how to help students write well have changed dramatically. As Irene Clark points out in the first chapter of this book, process now influences how we think about writing. In this chapter, we see how our ideas about process shape how we think about designing assignments and evaluating students' written work. In addition, our increasing awareness of the importance of rhetorical and cultural situations shapes how we assess and respond to written texts. As Chris Anson writes in *Reflective Reading: Developing Thoughtful Ways to Respond to Students' Writing*, "Response to writing has become more complex taking into account the context"(p. 303). Because assessing writing is complex, contextual, and integrally tied to good teaching and learning, it is essential that we do it thoughtfully and well.

Teachers' Checklist for Writing Assessment

Is my assessment of writing tied to my goals for the course?

Have I used authentic assessment?

Have I made the goals and the criteria for assessment clear to students?

Have I engaged them in the assessment process?

Have I provided formative assessment during the writing process?

Have I used students' errors to correct problems with my teaching or assignments?

Are my comments on papers specific, useful, balanced, and encouraging?

Could I write this paper?

Have I provided enough context writing assignments?

Will the assignments and the evaluation of them be important to the students' learning?

FOR FURTHER EXPLORATION

Charles C., & Odell, L. (1999). *Evaluating writing: The role of teachers' knowledge about text, learning and culture.* Urbana, IL: NCTE.
> This book offers essays that put assessment into a contemporary context with essays on the role genre, audience, and cultural context.

Meyers, M. (1994). *A procedure for writing assessment and holistic scoring.* Urbana, IL: NCTE.
> Meyers provides the nuts and bolts guide for those who want to conduct large-scale holistic scoring.

White, E. (1994). *Teaching and assessing writing.* NY: Jossey-Bass.
> This book, arguably one of the most important books in the field, explores all aspects of assessment but focuses on portfolio assessment.

Wolcott, W. & Legg, S. (1998). *An overview of writing assessment: Theory, research, and practice.* Urbana, IL: NCTE.
> Willa Wolcott with Sue Legg provides a thick description of the controversies and theories that have shaped current assessment practices.

Yancey, K., & Huot, B. (1997). *Assessing writing across the curriculum.* Greenwich, CT: Ablex.
> The essays in this collection examine mainly qualitative assessment that has been done in college settings.

REFERENCES

Anson, C. (1999). Reflective reading: Developing thoughtful ways to respond to students' writing. In C. R. Cooper & S. L. Odell (Eds.), *Evaluating writing: The role of teachers' knowledge about text, learning and culture* (pp. 302–324). Urbana, IL: NCTE.

Atwell, N. (1987). *In the middle: Writing, reading and learning with adolescents.* Portsmouth, NH: Boynton/Cook, Heinemann.

Bruffee, K. A. (1986). Social construction, language and authority of knowledge: A bibliographic essay. *College English, 48,* 773–790.

Cooper, C. R. (1977). Holistic evaluation of writing. In C. R. Cooper & S. L. Odell (Eds.), *Evaluating writing: Describing, measuring, judging* (p. 10). Urbana, IL: NCTE.

(1999). What we know about genres. In C. R. Cooper & S. L. Odell (Eds.), *Evaluating writing: The role of teachers' knowledge about text, learning and culture* (p. 25). Urbana, IL: NCTE.

Flower, L., & Hayes, J. (1981). A cognitive process and theory of writing. *College Composition and Communication, 32,* 365–387.

Graves, D. H. (1983). *Writing: Teachers and children at work.* Exeter, NH: Heinemann Educational Books.

Lindemann, E. (1995). *A rhetoric for writing teachers.* NY: Oxford University Press.

Mellon, J. (1975). *National assessment of teaching of english.* Urbana, IL: NCTE.

Myers, M. (1980). *A procedure for writing assessment and holistic scoring.* Urbana, IL: NCTE.

Odell, L. (1981). Defining and assessing competence in writing. In C. Cooper (Ed.), *The nature and measurement of competency in English* (pp. 95–138). Urbana, IL: National Council of Teachers of English.

Orwell, G. (1950). "Politics & the English Language." *Shooting an Elephant.* London: Secker Warburg, 1950.

Ryder, P. M., Vander Lei, E., & Roen, D. H. (1999). Audience considerations for evaluating writing. In C. R. Cooper & S. L. Odell (Eds.), *Evaluating writing: The role of teachers' knowledge about text, learning and culture* (pp. 55–60). Urbana, IL: NCTE.

Sommers, Nancy. (1982 May). Responding to student writing. *College Composition and Communication* 33, 148–56.

Spady, W. G. (1994). Choosing outcomes of significance. *Educational leadership, 51* (6), pp. 18–22.

White, E. (1994). *Teaching and assessing writing.* NY: Jossey-Bass.

White, E. (2000, November). Bursting the bubble sheet: How to improve evaluations of teaching. *Chronicle of Higher Education.* p. B11.

Wolcott, W. (1998). *An overview of writing assessment theory, research, and practice.* Urbana, IL: NCTE.

Yancy, K. (1999, February). Looking back as we look forward: Historicizing writing assessment. *College Composition and Communication, 50,* 483–503.

Yancey, K., & Huot, B. (1997). *Assessing writing across the curriculum.* Greenwich, CT: Ablex.

Readings

POLITICS AND THE ENGLISH LANGUAGE

George Orwell

1 Most people who bother with the matter at all would admit that the English language is in a bad way, but it is generally assumed that we cannot by conscious action do anything about it. Our civilization is decadent and our language—so the argument runs—must inevitably share in the general collapse. It follows that any struggle against the abuse of language is a sentimental archaism, like preferring candles to electric light or hansom cabs to aeroplanes. Underneath this lies the half-conscious belief that language is a natural growth and not an instrument which we shape for our own purposes.

2 Now, it is clear that the decline of a language must ultimately have political and economic causes: it is not due simply to the bad influence of this or that individual writer. But an effect can become a cause, reinforcing the original cause and producing the same effect in an intensified form, and so on indefinitely. A man may take to drink because he feels himself to be a failure, and then fail all the more completely because he drinks. It is rather the same thing that is happening to the English language. It becomes ugly and inaccurate because our thoughts are foolish, but the slovenliness of our language makes it easier for us to have foolish thoughts. The point is that the process is reversible. Modern English, especially written English, is full of bad habits which spread by imitation and which can be avoided if one is willing to take the necessary trouble. If one gets rid of these habits one can think more clearly, and to think clearly is a necessary first step

From *Shooting an Elephant and Other Essays* by George Orwell (Copyright © George Orwell 1946) by permission of Bill Hamilton as the Literary Executor of the Estate of the Late Sonia Brownell Orwell and Secker & Warburg, Ltd.

were choosing his words for himself. If the speech he is making is one that he is accustomed to make over and over again, he may be almost unconscious of what he is saying, as one is when one utters the responses in church. And this reduced state of consciousness, if not indispensable, is at any rate favorable to political conformity.

14 In our time, political speech and writing are largely the defence of the indefensible. Things like the continuance of British rule in India, the Russian purges and deportations, the dropping of the atom bombs on Japan, can indeed be defended, but only by arguments which are too brutal for most people to face, and which do not square with the professed aims of political parties. Thus political language has to consist largely of euphemism, question-begging and sheer cloudy vagueness. Defenceless villages are bombarded from the air, the inhabitants driven out into the countryside, the cattle machine-gunned, the huts set on fire with incendiary bullets: this is called *pacification*. Missions of peasants are robbed of their farms and set trudging along the roads with no more than they can carry: this is called *transfer of population* or *rectification of frontiers*. People are imprisoned for years without trial, or shot in the back of the neck or sent to die of scurvy in Arctic lumber camps: this is called *elimination of unreliable elements*. Such phraseology is needed if one wants to name things without calling up mental pictures of them. Consider for instance some comfortable English professor defending Russian totalitarianism. He cannot say outright, "I believe in killing off your opponents when you can get good results by doing so." Probably, therefore, he will say something like this:

> While freely conceding that the Soviet régime exhibits certain features which the humanitarian may be inclined to deplore, we must, I think, agree that a certain curtailment of the right to political opposition is an unavoidable concomitant of transitional periods, and that the rigours which the Russian people have been called upon to undergo have been amply justified in the sphere of concrete achievement.

15 The inflated style is itself a kind of euphemism. A mass of Latin words falls upon the facts like soft snow, blurring the outlines and covering up all the details. The great enemy of clear language is insincerity. When there is a gap between one's real and one's declared aims, one turns as it were instinctively to long words and exhausted idioms, like a cuttlefish squirting out ink. In our age there is no such thing as "keeping out of politics." All issues are political issues, and politics itself is a mass of lies, evasions, folly, hatred and schizophrenia. When the general atmosphere is bad, language must suffer. I should expect to find—this is a guess which I have not sufficient knowledge to verify—that the German, Russian and Italian languages have all deteriorated in the last ten or fifteen years, as a result of dictatorship.

16 But if thought corrupts language, language can also corrupt thought. A bad usage can spread by tradition and imitation, even among people who should and do know better. The debased language that I have been discussing is in some

ways very convenient. Phrases like *a not unjustifiable assumption, leaves much to be desired, would serve no good purpose, a consideration which we should do well to bear in mind,* are a continuous temptation, a packet of aspirins always at one's elbow. Look back through this essay, and for certain you will find that I have again and again committed the very faults I am protesting against. By this morning's post I have received a pamphlet dealing with conditions in Germany. The author tells me that he "felt impelled" to write it. I open it at random, and here is almost the first sentence that I see: "[The Allies] have an opportunity not only of achieving a radical transformation of Germany's social and political structure in such a way as to avoid a nationalistic reaction in Germany itself, but at the same time of laying the foundations of a co-operative and unified Europe." You see, he "feels impelled" to write—feels, presumably, that he has something new to say—and yet his words, like cavalry horses answering the bugle, group themselves automatically into the familiar dreary pattern. This invasion of one's mind by ready-made phrases (*lay the foundations, achieve a radical transformation*) can only be prevented if one is constantly on guard against them, and every such phrase anaesthetizes a portion of one's brain.

17 I said earlier that the decadence of our language is probably curable. Those who deny this would argue, if they produced an argument at all, that language merely reflects existing social conditions, and that we cannot influence its development by any direct tinkering with words and constructions. So far as the general tone or spirit of a language goes, this may be true, but it is not true in detail. Silly words and expressions have often disappeared, not through any evolutionary process but owing to the conscious action of a minority. Two recent examples were *explore every avenue* and *leave no stone unturned,* which were killed by the jeers of a few journalists. There is a long list of flyblown metaphors which could similarly be got rid of if enough people would interest themselves in the job; and it should also be possible to laugh the *not un-* formation out of existence,[3] to reduce the amount of Latin and Greek in the average sentence, to drive out foreign phrases and strayed scientific words, and, in general, to make pretentiousness unfashionable. But all these are minor points. The defence of the English language implies more than this, and perhaps it is best to start by saying what it does *not* imply.

18 To begin with it has nothing to do with archaism, with the salvaging of obsolete words and turns of speech, or with the setting up of a "standard English" which must never be departed from. On the contrary, it is especially concerned with the scrapping of every word or idiom which has outworn its usefulness. It has nothing to do with correct grammar and syntax, which are of no importance so long as one makes one's meaning clear, or with the avoidance of Americanisms,

---

[3]One can cure oneself of the *not un-* formation by memorizing this sentence: *A not unblack dog was chasing a not unsmall rabbit across a not ungreen field.*

or with having what is called a "good prose style." On the other hand it is not concerned with fake simplicity and the attempt to make written English colloquial. Nor does it even imply in every case preferring the Saxon word to the Latin one, though it does imply using the fewest and shortest words that will cover one's meaning. What is above all needed is to let the meaning choose the word, and not the other way about. In prose, the worst thing one can do with words is to surrender to them. When you think of a concrete object, you think wordlessly, and then, if you want to describe the thing you have been visualizing you probably hunt about till you find the exact words that seem to fit it. When you think of something abstract you are more inclined to use words from the start, and unless you make a conscious effort to prevent it, the existing dialect will come rushing in and do the job for you, at the expense of blurring or even changing your meaning. Probably it is better to put off using words as long as possible and get one's meaning as clear as one can through pictures or sensations. Afterwards one can choose—not simply *accept*—the phrase that will best cover the meaning, and then switch round and decide what impression one's words are likely to make on another person. This last effort of the mind cuts out all stale or mixed images, all prefabricated phrases, needless repetitions, and humbug and vagueness generally. But one can often be in doubt about the effect of a word or a phrase, and one needs rules that one can rely on when instinct fails. I think the following rules will cover most cases:

(i) Never use a metaphor, simile or other figure of speech which you are used to seeing in print.

(ii) Never use a long word where a short one will do.

(iii) If it is possible to cut a word out, always cut it out.

(iv) Never use the passive when you can use the active.

(v) Never use a foreign phrase, a scientific word or a jargon word if you can think of an everyday English equivalent.

(vi) Break any of these rules sooner than say anything outright barbarous.

These rules sound elementary, and so they are, but they demand a deep change of attitude in anyone who has grown used to writing in the style now fashionable. One could keep all of them and still write bad English, but one could not write the kind of stuff that I quoted in those five specimens at the beginning of this article.

19 I have not here been considering the literary use of language, but merely language as an instrument for expressing and not for concealing or preventing thought. Stuart Chase and others have come near to claiming that all abstract words are meaningless, and have used this as a pretext for advocating a kind of political quietism. Since you don't know what Fascism is, how can you struggle against Fascism? One need not swallow such absurdities as this, but one ought to recognize that the present political chaos is connected with the decay of language, and that one can probably bring about some improvement by starting at the verbal

end. If you simplify your English, you are freed from the worst follies of orthodoxy. You cannot speak any of the necessary dialects, and when you make a stupid remark its stupidity will be obvious, even to yourself. Political language—and with variations this is true of all political parties, from Conservatives to Anarchists— is designed to make lies sound truthful and murder respectable, and to give an appearance of solidity to pure wind. One cannot change this all in a moment, but one can at least change one's own habits, and from time to time one can even, if one jeers loudly enough, send some worn-out and useless phrase—some *jackboot, Achilles' heel, hotbed, melting pot, acid test, veritable inferno* or other lump of verbal refuse—into the dustbin where it belongs.

RESPONDING TO STUDENT WRITING

Nancy Sommers

More than any other enterprise in the teaching of writing, responding to and commenting on student writing consumes the largest proportion of our time. Most teachers estimate that it takes them at least 20 to 40 minutes to comment on an individual student paper, and those 20 to 40 minutes times 20 students per class, times 8 papers, more or less, during the course of a semester add up to an enormous amount of time. With so much time and energy directed to a single activity, it is important for us to understand the nature of the enterprise. For it seems, paradoxically enough, that although commenting on student writing is the most widely used method for responding to student writing, it is the least understood. We do not know in any definitive way what constitutes thoughtful commentary or what effect, if any, our comments have on helping our students become more effective writers.

Theoretically, at least, we know that we comment on our students' writing for the same reasons professional editors comment on the work of professional writers or for the same reasons we ask our colleagues to read and respond to our own writing. As writers we need and want thoughtful commentary to show us when we have communicated our ideas and when not, raising questions from a reader's point of view that may not have occurred to us as writers. We want to know if our writing has communicated our intended meaning and, if not, what questions or discrepancies our reader sees that we, as writers, are blind to.

In commenting on our students' writing, however, we have an additional pedagogical purpose. As teachers, we know that most students find it difficult to imagine a reader's response in advance, and to use such responses as a guide in composing. Thus, we comment on student writing to dramatize the presence of a reader, to help our students to become that questioning reader themselves, because, ultimately, we believe that becoming such a reader will help them to evaluate what they have written and develop control over their writing.[1]

Even more specifically, however, we comment on student writing because we believe that it is necessary for us to offer assistance to student writers when they are in the process of composing a text, rather than after the text has been completed. Comments create the motive for doing something different in the next draft; thoughtful comments create the motive for revising. Without comments from their teachers or from their peers, student writers will revise in a consistently

---

Reprinted from *College Composition and Communication,* Vol. 33, No. 2, May 1982. Used with permission.

narrow and predictable way. Without comments from readers, students assume that their writing has communicated their meaning and perceive no need for revising the substance of their text.[2]

Yet as much as we as informed professionals believe in the soundness of this approach to responding to student writing, we also realize that we don't know how our theory squares with teachers' actual practice—do teachers comment and students revise as the theory predicts they should? For the past year my colleagues, Lil Brannon, Cyril Knoblauch, and I have been researching this problem, attempting to discover not only what messages teachers give their students through their comments, but also what determines which of these comments the students choose to use or to ignore when revising. Our research has been entirely focused on comments teachers write to motivate revisions. We have studied the commenting styles of thirty-five teachers at New York University and the University of Oklahoma, studying the comments these teachers wrote on first and second drafts, and interviewing a representative number of these teachers and their students. All teachers also commented on the same set of three student essays. As an additional reference point, one of the student essays was typed into the computer that had been programed with the "Writer's Workbench," a package of twenty-three programs developed by Bell Laboratories to help computers and writers work together to improve a text rapidly. Within a few minutes, the computer delivered editorial comments on the student's text, identifying all spelling and punctuation errors, isolating problems with wordy or misused phrases, and suggesting alternatives, offering a stylistic analysis of sentence types, sentence beginnings, and sentence lengths, and finally, giving our freshman essay a Kincaid readability score of 8th grade which, as the computer program informed us, "is a low score for this type of document." The sharp contrast between the teachers' comments and those of the computer highlighted how arbitrary and idiosyncratic most of our teachers' comments are. Besides, the calm, reasonable language of the computer provided quite a contrast to the hostility and mean-spiritedness of most of the teachers' comments.

The first finding from our research on styles of commenting is that *teachers' comments can take students' attention away from their own purposes in writing a particular text and focus that attention on the teachers' purpose in commenting.* The teacher appropriates the text from the student by confusing the student's purpose in writing the text with her own purpose in commenting. Students make the changes the teacher wants rather than those that the student perceives are necessary, since the teachers' concerns imposed on the text create the reasons for the subsequent changes. We have all heard our perplexed students say to us when confused by our comments: "I don't understand how you want me to change this" or "Tell me what you want me to do." In the beginning of the process there was the writer, her words, and her desire to communicate her ideas. But after the comments of the teacher are imposed on the first or second draft, the student's attention dramatically shifts from "This is what I want to say," to "This is what you the teacher are asking me to do."

This appropriation of the text by the teacher happens particularly when teachers identify errors in usage, diction, and style in a first draft and ask students to correct these errors when they revise; such comments give the student an impression of the importance of these errors that is all out of proportion to how they should view these errors at this point in the process. The comments create the concern that these "accidents of discourse" need to be attended to before the meaning of the text is attended to.

It would not be so bad if students were only commanded to correct errors, but, more often than not, students are given contradictory messages; they are commanded to edit a sentence to avoid an error or to condense a sentence to achieve greater brevity of style, and then told in the margins that the particular paragraph needs to be more specific or to be developed more. An example of this problem can be seen in the following student paragraph:

> *which*   *comma*
> *wordy—be precise*   *Sunday?*   ↓ *needed*
> Every year [on one Sunday in the middle of January] tens of mil-
>   *word choice*
> lions of people cancel all events, plans or work to watch the Super Bowl.
>   *wordy*
> This audience includes [little boys and girls, old people, and house-
>   *Be specific—what reasons?*
> wives and men.] Many reasons have been given to explain why the
>   *and why*   *what spots?)*
> Super Bowl has become so popular that commercial (spots cost up to
>   *awkward*
> $100,000.00. One explanation is that people like to take sides and root
>   *another what?*   ↓ *spelling*
> for a team. Another is that some people like the pagentry and excite-
>   *too colloquial*
> ment of the event. These reasons alone, however, do not explain a hap-
>
> pening as big as the Super Bowl.

You need to do more research

This paragraph needs to be expanded in order to be more interesting to a reader.

In commenting on this draft, the teacher has shown the student how to edit the sentences, but then commands the student to expand the paragraph in order to make it more interesting to a reader. The interlinear comments and the marginal comments represent two separate tasks for this student; the interlinear comments encourage the student to see the text as a fixed piece, frozen in time, that just needs some editing. The marginal comments, however, suggest that the meaning of the text is not fixed, but rather that the student still needs to develop the meaning by doing some more research. Students are commanded to edit and develop at the same time; the remarkable contradiction of developing a paragraph after editing the sentences in it represents the confusion we encountered in our teachers' commenting styles. These different signals given to students, to edit and develop, to condense and elaborate, represent also the failure of teachers' comments to direct genuine revision of the text as a whole.

Moreover, the comments are worded in such a way that it is difficult for students to know what is the most important problem in the text and what problems are of lesser importance. No scale of concerns is offered to a student, with the result that a comment about spelling or a comment about an awkward sentence is given weight equal to a comment about organization or logic. The comment that seemed to represent this problem best was one teacher's command to his student: "Check your commas and semi-colons and think more about what you are thinking about." The language of the comments makes it difficult for a student to sort out and decide what is most important and what is least important.

When the teacher appropriates the text for the student in this way, students are encouraged to see their writing as a series of parts—words, sentences, paragraphs—and not as a whole discourse. The comments encourage students to believe that their first drafts are finished drafts, not invention drafts, and that all they need to do is patch and polish their writing. That is, teachers' comments do not provide their students with an inherent reason for revising the structure and meaning of their texts, since the comments suggest to students that the meaning of their text is already there, finished, produced, and all that is necessary is a better word or phrase. The processes of revising, editing, and proofreading are collapsed and reduced to a single trivial activity, and the students' misunderstanding of the revision process as a rewording activity is reinforced by their teachers' comments.

It is possible, and it quite often happens, that students follow every comment and fix their texts appropriately as requested, but their texts are not improved substantially, or, even worse, their revised drafts are inferior to their previous drafts. Since the teachers' comments take the students' attention away from their own original purposes, students concentrate more, as I have noted, on what the teachers commanded them to do than on what they are trying to say. Sometimes students do not understand the purpose behind their teachers' comments and take these comments very literally. At other times students understand the comments, but the teacher has misread the text and the comments, unfortunately, are not applicable. For instance, we repeatedly saw comments in which teachers commanded students to reduce and condense what was written, when in fact what the text really needed at this stage was to be expanded in conception and scope.

The process of revising always involves a risk. But, too often revision becomes a balancing act for students in which they make the changes that are requested but do not take the risk of changing anything that was not commented on, even if the students sense that other changes are needed. A more effective text does not often evolve from such changes alone, yet the student does not want to take the chance of reducing a finished, albeit inadequate, paragraph to chaos—to fragments—in order to rebuild it, if such changes have not been requested by the teacher.

The second finding from our study is that *most teachers' comments are not text-specific and could be interchanged, rubber-stamped, from text to text.* The comments are not anchored in the particulars of the students' texts, but rather are a series of vague directives that are not text-specific. Students are commanded to "Think more about [their] audience, avoid colloquial language, avoid the passive, avoid prepositions at the end of sentences or conjunctions at the beginning of sentences, be clear, be specific, be precise, but above all, think more about what [they] are thinking about." The comments on the following student paragraph illustrate this problem:

> ↓ *Begin by telling your reader*
> *what you are going to write about.*
> In the sixties it was drugs, in the seventies it was rock and roll.
> *avoid—"one of the"*
> Now in the eighties, one of the most controversial subjects is nuclear
> *elaborate*
> power. The United States is in great need of its own source of power.
>
> Because of environmentalists, coal is not an acceptable source of energy.
> *be specific*
> [Solar and wind power have not yet received the technology necessary
> *avoid—"it seems"*
> to use them.] It seems that nuclear power is the only feasible means
>
> right now for obtaining self-sufficient power. However, too large a per-
>
> centage of the population are against nuclear power claiming it is un-
> *be precise*
> safe. With as many problems as the United States is having concerning
>
> energy, it seems a shame that the public is so quick to "can" avery fea-
>
> sible means of power. Nuclear energy should not be given up on, but
>
> rather, more nuclear plants should be built.

Think more about your reader.

needed

One could easily remove all the comments from this paragraph and rubber-stamp them on another student text, and they would make as much or as little sense on the second text as they do here.

We have observed an overwhelming similarity in the generalities and abstract commands given to students. There seems to be among teachers an accepted, albeit unwritten canon for commenting on student texts. This uniform code of commands, requests, and pleadings demonstrates that the teacher holds a license for vagueness while the student is commanded to be specific. The students we interviewed admitted to having great difficulty with these vague directives. The students stated that when a teacher writes in the margins or as an end comment, "choose precise language," or "think more about your audience," revising becomes a guessing game. In effect, the teacher is saying to the student, "Somewhere in this paper is imprecise language or lack of awareness of an audience and you must find it." The problem presented by these vague commands is compounded for the students when they are not offered any strategies for carrying out these commands. Students are told that they have done something wrong and that there is something in their text that needs to be fixed before the text is acceptable. But to tell students that they have done something wrong is not to tell them what to do about it. In order to offer a useful revision strategy to a student, the teacher must anchor that strategy in the specifics of the student's text. For instance, to tell our student, the author of the above paragraph, "to be specific," or "to elaborate," does not show our student what questions the reader has about the meaning of the text, or what breaks in logic exist, that could be resolved if the writer supplied specific information; nor is the student shown how to achieve the desired specificity.

Instead of offering strategies, the teachers offer what is interpreted by students as rules for composing; the comments suggest to students that writing is just a matter of following the rules. Indeed, the teachers seem to impose a series of abstract rules about written products even when some of them are not appropriate for the specific text the student is creating.[3] For instance, the student author of our sample paragraph presented above is commanded to follow the conventional rules for writing a five-paragraph essay—to begin the introductory paragraph by telling his reader what he is going to say and to end the paragraph with a thesis sentence. Somehow these abstract rules about what five-paragraph products should look like do not seem applicable to the problems this student must confront when revising, nor are the rules specific strategies he could use when revising. There are many inchoate ideas ready to be exploited in this paragraph, but the rules do not help the student to take stock of his (or her) ideas and use the opportunity he has, during revision, to develop those ideas.

The problem here is a confusion of process and product; what one has to say about the process is different from what one has to say about the product. Teachers who use this method of commenting are formulating their comments as if these drafts were finished drafts and were not going to be revised. Their commenting vocabularies have not been adapted to revision and they comment on first drafts as if they were justifying a grade or as if the first draft were the final draft.

Our summary finding, therefore, from this research on styles of commenting is that the news from the classroom is not good. For the most part, teachers do not respond to student writing with the kind of thoughtful commentary which will help students to engage with the issues they are writing about or which will help them think about their purposes and goals in writing a specific text. In defense of our teachers, however, they told us that responding to student writing was rarely stressed in their teacher-training or in writing workshops; they had been trained in various prewriting techniques, in constructing assignments, and in evaluating papers for grades, but rarely in the process of reading a student text for meaning or in offering commentary to motivate revision. The problem is that most of us as teachers of writing have been trained to read and interpret literary texts for meaning, but, unfortunately, we have not been trained to act upon the same set of assumptions in reading student texts as we follow in reading literary texts.[4] Thus, we read student texts with biases about what the writer should have said or about what he or she should have written, and our biases determine how we will comprehend the text. We read with our preconceptions and preoccupations, expecting to find errors, and the result is that we find errors and misread our students' texts.[5] We find what we look for; instead of reading and responding to the meaning of a text, we correct our students' writing. We need to reverse this approach. Instead of finding errors or showing students how to patch up parts of their texts, we need to sabotage our students' conviction that the drafts they have written are complete and coherent. Our comments need to offer students revision tasks of a different order of complexity and sophistication from the ones that they themselves identify, by forcing students back into the chaos, back to the point where they are shaping and restructuring their meaning.[6]

For if the content of a student text is lacking in substance and meaning, if the order of the parts must be rearranged significantly in the next draft, if paragraphs must be restructured for logic and clarity, then many sentences are likely to be changed or deleted anyway. There seems to be no point in having students correct usage errors or condense sentences that are likely to disappear before the next draft is completed. In fact, to identify such problems in a text at this early first draft stage, when such problems are likely to abound, can give a student a disproportionate sense of their importance at this stage in the writing process.[7] In responding to our students' writing, we should be guided by the recognition that it is not spelling or usage problems that we as writers first worry about when drafting and revising our texts.

We need to develop an appropriate level of response for commenting on a first draft, and to differentiate that from the level suitable to a second or third draft. Our comments need to be suited to the draft we are reading. In a first or second draft, we need to respond as any reader would, registering questions, reflecting befuddlement, and noting places where we are puzzled about the meaning of the text. Comments should point to breaks in logic, disruptions in meaning, or missing information. Our goal in commenting on early drafts should be to engage students with the issues they are considering and help them clarify their purposes and reasons in writing their specific text.

For instance, the major rhetorical problem of the essay written by the student who wrote the second paragraph (the paragraph on nuclear power) quoted above was that the student had two principal arguments running through his text, each of which brought the other into question. On the one hand, he argued that we must use nuclear power, unpleasant as it is, because we have nothing else to use; though nuclear energy is a problematic source of energy, it is the best of a bad lot. On the other hand, he also argued that nuclear energy is really quite safe and therefore should be our primary resource. Comments on this student's first draft need to point out this break in logic and show the student that if we accept his first argument, then his second argument sounds fishy. But if we accept his second argument, his first argument sounds contradictory. The teacher's comments need to engage this student writer with this basic rhetorical and conceptual problem in his first draft rather than impose a series of abstract commands and rules upon his text.

Written comments need to be viewed not as an end in themselves—a way for teachers to satisfy themselves that they have done their jobs—but rather as a means for helping students to become more effective writers. As a means for helping students, they have limitations; they are, in fact, disembodied remarks—one absent writer responding to another absent writer. The key to successful commenting is to have what is said in the comments and what is done in the classroom mutually reinforce and enrich each other. Commenting on papers assists the writing course in achieving its purpose; classroom activities and the comments we write to our students need to be connected. Written comments need to be an extension of the teacher's voice—an extension of the teacher as reader. Exercises in such activities as revising a whole text or individual paragraphs together in class, noting how the sense of the whole dictates the smaller changes, looking at options, evaluating actual choices, and then discussing the effect of these changes on revised drafts—such exercises need to be designed to take students through the cycles of revising and to help them overcome their anxiety about revising: that anxiety we all feel at reducing what looks like a finished draft into fragments and chaos.

The challenge we face as teachers is to develop comments which will provide an inherent reason for students to revise; it is a sense of revision as discovery, as a repeated process of beginning again, as starting out new, that our students have not learned. We need to show our students how to seek, in the possibility of revision, the dissonances of discovery—to show them through our comments why new choices would positively change their texts, and thus to show them the potential for development implicit in their own writing.

Notes

1. C. H. Knoblauch and Lil Brannon, "Teacher Commentary on Student writing. The State of the Art," *Freshman English News,* 10 (Fall 1981), 1–3.

2. For an extended discussion of revision strategies of student writers see Nancy Sommers, "Revision Strategies of Student Writers and Experienced Adult Writers." *College Composition and Communication,* 31 (December 1980), 378–388.

3. Nancy Sommers and Ronald Schleifer, "Means and Ends: Some Assumptions of Student Writers," *Composition and Teaching,* 2 (December 1980), 69–76.

4. Janet Emig and Robert P. Parker, Jr., "Responding to Student Writing: Building a Theory of the Evaluating Process," unpublished paper, Rutgers University.

5. For an extended discussion of this problem see Joseph Williams, "The Phenomenology of Error," *College Composition and Communication,* 32 (May 1981), 152–168.

6. Ann Berthoff, *The Making of Meaning* (Montclair, N.J.: Boynton/Cook Publishers, 1981).

7. W. U. McDonald, "The Revising Process and the Marking of Student Papers," *College Composition and Communication,* 24 (May 1978), 167–170.

6

Genre

Irene L. Clark

> This chapter addresses the concept of genre as it impacts the
> writing class, exploring the distinction between traditional and
> rhetorical notions of genre and examining the controversy about
> which text genres should be focused on in the writing class.

During the early days of the process movement, articles in composition
journals rarely addressed the concept of "genre." Because the movement
focused on self-expression and the discovery of personal voice as a means of
empowering marginalized populations, "genre" was viewed as an old fash-
ioned, traditional, and outmoded concept, associated with an emphasis on
rigidity and formalist conventions. Recently, however, the word "genre" has
been redefined in terms of *function* rather than form, appearing with increased frequency in scholarly journals and offering new possibilities for
the composition class. This chapter will discuss the recent reconceptualization of genre as a significant concept in composition, focusing on the
following aspects of the topic:

The distinction between traditional and rhetorical notions of genre.

The genre-based curriculum in Australia.

The controversy over which genres should be privileged in the writing
   class.

The relationship between genre knowledge and creativity.

The question of whether academic genres should or can be taught
   explicitly.

Connections between the new "rhetorical" concept of genre and recent
   reconceptions of literary genres.

TRADITIONAL NOTIONS OF GENRE

Genre has been a subject of scholarly interest at least since Aristotle, who defined literary genres in *The Poetics* and characterized various types of oratory in the *Rhetoric*. For Aristotle, genre was simply a way of classifying text types, and it is this concept of genre that has persisted until only fairly recently. As Freedman and Medway (1994) noted in their introduction to *Learning and Teaching Genre*, the traditional view was that genres were (a) primarily literary, (b) entirely defined by textual regularities in form and content, (c) fixed and immutable, and (d) classifiable into neat and mutually exclusive categories and subcategories (1994, p. 1). Defined in this way, the concept of genre was perceived as unrelated to, and even incompatible with, the new ideology of composition and the pedagogy that evolved from it. As represented in the work of Elbow, Emig, and Murray, process and expressivist pedagogy defined effective learning in terms of its relevance to the individual, rather than through the imposition of institutional goals, certainly not through learning particular genres. (see Chapter 1)

RECONCEIVING GENRE IN TERMS OF FUNCTION[1]

Over the past twenty years, the concept of genre has been broadened and redefined as *typified social action* that responds to a recurring situation, that is, "that people use genres to do things in the world (social action and purpose) and that these ways of acting become typified through occurring under what is perceived as recurring circumstances" (Devitt, 2000, p. 698). Carolyn Miller's seminal article titled "Genre as Social Action" (1984) redefined genre by building on earlier work in 20th-century rhetorical theory, first drawing on Kenneth Burke's (1969) discussion of rhetorical acts in terms of responding to particular situations and then referring to Lloyd Bitzer's definition of the rhetorical situation as a "complex of persons, events, objects, and relations" presenting an "exigence" or necessity (Miller, 1984, p. 152) that the rhetorical act addresses. Miller's article thus extended notions of genres beyond their association with a relatively stable set of discourse conventions, defining them in terms of purpose and action.

How can the concept of genre be viewed in terms of function? Consider a genre that many of us receive frequently in the mail—a fundraising letter for a charity. In analyzing this genre, one could note a number of relatively

---

[1]Some of this background material also appears in "Addressing Genre in the Writing Center," *The Writing Center Journal*, (Fall/Winter, 1999): 7–32.

stable and easily identifiable textual features: the heart-rending sketch of the situation or cause in need of additional funds (often presented in terms of an individual case selected for its potential in eliciting an emotional response), praise of the recipient's presumed charitable impulses and humanitarian concerns, a reference to other citizens who have contributed to this worthy cause, and a concluding section in which the request for a donation is made. From a traditional point of view, one might examine this genre in terms of its formal features—structure, tone, and style—whereas current conceptions of genre would view the letter as a typical rhetorical action (the request for money) in response to a recurring situation (the need of charitable organizations for contributions), in which the structure, tone, and style contribute to the genre's effectiveness and thereby become typical.

This new way of understanding a genre in terms of its social context provides a perspective that has potential for examining many different genres, real-world genres such as business letters or greeting cards as well as academic genres such as lab reports or school essays. This perspective views a text as a typical rhetorical interaction that is situated within a social context. Because genres develop through writers' effective responses to those situations, the new concept of genre views generic conventions as arising from suitability and appropriateness, rather than from arbitrary formal conventions. As Devitt (1993) explained the current view of genre:

> Genres develop ... because they respond appropriately to situations that writers encounter repeatedly. In principle, that is, writers first respond in fitting ways and hence similarly to recurring situations; then the similarities among those appropriate responses become established as generic conventions. (p. 576)

Devitt cited lab reports or letters to a friend as examples of genres that developed in response to recurring situations. However, the recent reconceptualization of genre goes beyond the development of appropriate text forms. As Anis Bawarshi (1997) pointed out in a thoughtful article titled "The Genre Function," genres also help shape and maintain the ways we act within particular situations—helping us as both readers and writers to function within those situations while also shaping the ways we come to know them. As an example, Bawarshi used the first State of the Union Address given by George Washington, who was confronted with a situation that had never been encountered before (an American president addressing Congress). Never having given a State of the Union Address, Washington based his speech on those given by British kings to Parliament, even though Washington and Congress were both opposed to the very notion of kings and the concept of inequality from which the notion derived. (In fact, Washington had led a successful rebellion against the British monarchy.) As a result, Washington's speech, reminiscent of the king's authority, elicited

in Congress a response characterized by homage and subservience, an example that illustrates the powerful role that genre plays in influencing not
only the text itself but also the roles played by both writers and readers as
they are constructed by that text within a social context.

FOR WRITING AND DISCUSSION

Writing Assignment

In the context of recent genre theory, text genres are viewed as typified
responses to recurring rhetorical situations, both reflecting and creating
the social contexts in which they occur. Lab reports or letters to a friend
are examples of genres that developed in response to recurring situations. Moreover, the concept of genre goes beyond the development of
appropriate text forms, revealing how we think about and react to particular situations, as well as telling us a great deal about a community's or
culture's attitudes and beliefs.

Select a genre (or two, if you wish to compare one with the other)
and analyze it for what it tells us about the people and/or culture or
community who use it and the situation to which it responds. *Your thesis
for this assignment, then, will be a claim about what a particular genre tells us
about how people respond to and experience a particular situation.*

You may select any written genre that interests you, although you
should not choose a broad topic about which many books have been written (such as novels or plays). Some examples might be greeting cards,
letters of recommendation, personal letters, postcards, billboards, and
the like. Whichever genre you use, you should make sure that you describe what the genre is, paying special attention to its features (physical
and textual), who uses it, and when and why it is used. Here are some
questions to consider:

1. What is the history of this genre?
2. What do the genre conventions reveal about the culture,
   community, and people?
3. What is its primary function?
4. What textual and formal features are associated with it?
5. What style is associated with it?

For examples of how other students have addressed this assignment,
please see the essays by Karin Woiwode, and Clifton Justice at the end
of this chapter.

GENRE THEORY AND OTHER
RHETORICAL PERSPECTIVES

Although the rhetorical view of genre can be considered a "new" approach, it has significant roots in other concepts of how texts interact with experience. In *Counterstatement,* philosopher Kenneth Burke (1968) observed that texts can be viewed as symbolic actions that have meaning only in terms of situation and motive. Burke noted that although there are "stock patterns of experience which seem to arise out of any system of living" (1968, p. 171), such as the return of youth as in Faust, or betrayal, as in Brutus conspiring against Caesar, the effect of these patterns as manifested in literature are strongly influenced by formal elements of the particular time and scene. "Elizabethan audiences, through expecting the bluster of the proscenium speech, found it readily acceptable—but a modern audience not schooled in this expectation will object to it as 'unreal,' " Burke stated, arguing that what is perceived as effective or eloquent is strongly influenced by audience expectation:

> The distinction between style and manner is also fluctuant, as a change in conventional form can make one aspect of a style very noticeable and thus give it the effect of manner. (p. 173)

Burke's perspective emphasized connections between genre expectations and situation—that is, as writing has been increasingly perceived as a way of responding to readers within a given context, the resulting texts have correspondingly been viewed as incorporating particular strategies and approaches that have proven effective under similar circumstances.

Genre theory, then, views texts in a social context, a perspective that parallels other socially oriented theories that emphasize the rhetorical goal of text. Because genre theory conceives of writing as a way of responding to a specific reader or readers within a specific context on a specific occasion (Freedman & Medway, 1994, p. 5), it is consistent with the social constructionist privileging of context, audience, and occasion as well as with speech act theory, which emphasizes the function of language as a way of acting in the world and the importance of context in creating meaning.

GENRE AND THE CRITIQUE OF PROCESS
PEDAGOGY: THE AUSTRALIAN PERSPECTIVE

The process movement resulted in important developments in the teaching of writing, notably a flowering of interest in composition pedagogy; the creation of an established research discipline concerned with writing and writing pedagogy; the realization that people learn to write by actually writing and revising, rather than by completing decontextualized exercises; and a renewed attention to individualized instruction. However, the recent reconsideration of how genre knowledge facilitates literacy acquisition has raised questions about whether process pedagogy, with its focus on individual expression and personal voice, has been helpful for all students. In fact, those associated with the genre-based curriculum in Sydney, Australia have voiced the concern that process pedagogy in its most rigid manifestations has resulted in only limited success for the groups that it was originally intended to help. Their position is that the process-oriented classroom, despite its original goal of validating culturally marginalized groups, has done nothing to empower those groups or break entrenched class divisions in western culture. Outlining what they refer to as an education experiment that has international significance, Cope and Kalantzis (1993) argued that:

> Many working-class, migrant and Aboriginal children have been systematically barred from competence with those texts, knowledges, and 'genres' that enable access to social and material resources. The culprits, they argue, are not limited to traditional pedagogies that disregard children's cultural and linguistic resources and set out to assimilate them into the fictions of mainstream culture. But the problem is also located in progressive 'process' and 'child-centered' approaches that appear to 'value differences but in so doing leave social relations of inequity fundamentally unquestioned. (p. vii)

Contributors to Cope and Kalantzis' book *The Powers of Literacy: A Genre Approach to Teaching Writing*, which is intended to explain the Australian genre approach to non-Australians, have maintained that the "progressivist" stress on text ownership and personal voice and the corresponding reluctance of teachers to intervene directly in changing students' texts has, ironically, promoted a situation in which only the brightest middle-class children, who are already familiar with the genres of privilege, will be able to learn what is needed for social, and, ultimately, economic success. Noting that "by the 1980's it was clear that . . . the new progressivist curriculum was not producing any noticeable improvement in patterns of educational attainment" (Cope & Kalantzis, p. 1), these critics also point out that such a curriculum "encourages students to produce texts in a limited range of written genres, mostly personalised recounts" (Cope & Kalantzis, p. 6).

A key point in the Australian perspective on genre is that school genres should be taught more explicitly, and that a more directive approach is not incompatible with helping students acquire a workable writing process. In fact, it may yield more fruitful results in terms of helping students master unfamiliar genres. The rationale is explained as follows:

> For those outside the discourses and cultures of certain realms of power and access, acquiring these discourses requires explicit explanation: the ways in

which the "hows" of text structure produce the "whys" of social effect. If you live with the "hows"—if you have a seventh sense of how the "hows" do their social job by virtue of having been brought up with those discourses—then they will come to you more or less "naturally." Students from historically marginalised groups, however, need explicit teaching more than students who seem destined for a comfortable ride into the genres and cultures of power. (Cope & Kalantzis, 1993, p. 8)

The Australian School of genre, explored in *The Powers of Literacy* edited by Bill Cope and Mary Kalantzis, advocates the following principles:

Genres of writing are identifiable and fixed and that boundaries can be drawn around them.

Genres ought to be consciously chosen by writers and their writing should conform to the particular genre's structure.

Structures of genres ought to be taught to pupils so that they will model their writing on the genre structure.

There is too much emphasis on narrative forms in primary school and this is poor preparation for working in expository modes in secondary school, especially because such modes are characterized by an impersonal, neutral tone not provided for in most primary school narrative.

Not surprisingly, a number of scholars disagree with these principles. An early work associated with the process movement, *The Development of Writing Abilities* (Britton, Burgess, Martin, McLead & Rosen, 1975), maintained that genre boundaries are fluid, not identifiable and fixed. Others argue strongly against the explicit teaching of genre because of its association with authoritarian "top-down" pedagogy and an emphasis on form. Critics such as Sawyer and Watson (1987) are suspicious of the use of modeling. Sawyer and Watson point out that there is little evidence to indicate that modeling is effective, question whether conscious knowledge of structure makes for more effective performance in writing, and argue that although students may be unfamiliar with a genre, it does not necessarily have to be directly explicated to become known (p. 48).

THE CONTROVERSY OVER EXPLICIT TEACHING

A major issue associated with the teaching of genre concerns whether the direct teaching of genre is useful in helping students acquire and apply genre knowledge. Aviva Freedman (1995) maintained that the explicit teaching of genre is not even possible because genre knowledge requires immersion into the discourse community, which will enable students to "ventriloquate the social language, to respond dialogically to the appropriate cues from this context" (p. 134). Freedman (1995) argued that:

> The accomplishment of school genres is achieved without either the writers or those eliciting the writing being able to articulate the sophisticated rules that underlie them. These rules are complex, nuanced, variable, context-specific, and as yet unamenable to complete reconstruction even by skilled researchers. (pp. 130–131)

Only in the disciplinary classroom, an environment that provides a rich context of reading, lecture, and discussion, does Freedman perceive that students can acquire the necessary "felt sense" of the genre that will yield successful writing.

The idea that explicit teaching is both desirable and possible, however, also has its advocates. Critics such as Williams and Colomb (1993) supported the explicit teaching of genre because "what you don't know won't help you." John Swales (1990), one of the most widely known of the genre theorists, applied genre theory to what he referred to as the characteristic "moves" within a scientific article. Working in the area of ESP (English for Special Purposes), Swales defined genre primarily by its common communicative purposes, arguing that a genre-centered approach to teaching would enable students to understand why a particular genre had acquired its characteristic features and ultimately help them to create that genre more successfully.

PERSONAL NARRATIVE
IN THE COMPOSITION CLASS

The fourth principle of the Australian school of genre—that there is too much emphasis on narrative forms in primary school and that narrative writing does not prepare students for working in expository modes—raises the question of whether personal narrative writing should be taught in the writing class, particularly in the college writing class. Victor Villanueva views personal writing as a means of generating student self-awareness. Villanueva associates this perspective with the work of Paulo Freire, who constructs the idea of "critical consciousness" as a means of bridging the gap between the private and the public. Freire (1968) stressed the importance of having students look at their individual histories and cultures, to compare them with what they have been led to believe are their social places in the world—that is, to distinguish myth from reality. For Freire, the more students are aware of how their personal environment has been affected by social, political, and economic factors, the more they will be able to institute necessary change, both in themselves and in their environment. From Freire's political perspective, the self-awareness generated through writing personal narratives becomes an important source of political empowerment.

The use of personal narrative has also been justified in terms of helping novice writers find their "voice," a position that is epitomized in the work of Peter Elbow. In his article "Being a Writer vs. Being an Academic: A Conflict in Goals," Elbow (1995) maintained that the goals of the "writer" conflict with the goals of the "academic," because academics "carry on an unending conversation, not just with colleagues, but with the dead and unborn—the Burkean Parlor metaphor." Elbow acknowledged that students, eventually, will need to enter that conversation as academics; however, in the composition class, students must first be *writers*. Toward this end, Elbow has his students write from a personal perspective, pretending that no one has written about their subject before:

> I invite them to write as though they are a central speaker at the center of the universe—rather than feeling, as they often do, that they must summarize what others have said and only make modest rejoinders from the edge of the conversation. (p. 80)

Elbow maintained that for students to be writers (rather than academics), they must write about something that they know better than the teacher, and that "something" is usually their own experience. Otherwise, they are writing as test-takers, not as writers. For Elbow, the writing of first-person narrative is empowering, celebrating a world approached from a private perspective.

Others, of course, disagree. In a published interchange with Peter Elbow, David Barthomae (1995) argued that academic writing, not narrative, is the real work of the university; if an important goal in the university is to help students understand how power, tradition, and authority are transmitted, then we must ask students to do what academics do—work with the past; work with key texts; work with other's terms; and struggle with the problems of quotation, citation, and paraphrase. Bartholomae maintained that although many students will not feel the pleasure of power of authorship unless we provide them with opportunities to write in the first person, they will ultimately need to engage in "critical writing," which, he maintained, is "at the heart of academic writing."

Robert Connors and Mike Rose assume a middle position between those of Elbow and Bartholomae. Connors (1987) traced the question of what students are supposed to know and write about from classical times until the present, showing that there have always been two positions on the subject. In the ancient world, lines of argument were all impersonal, "the idea being that until a speaker had established his own ethos, usually through community service or previous rhetorical success, his own experiences were not important to the discourse" (p. 167). "Ancient rhetoric was a public discipline," Connors (1987) pointed out, "devoted to examining and arguing questions that could be shared by all members of the polity (p. 167). He noted that proofs of argument were impersonal and that "to argue from personal opinion was both hubristic and stupid" (p. 167). A perspective on rhetoric that persisted up until the middle of the 19th century— when interest in impersonal abstract topics was replaced by a strong emphasis on personal experience, novelty, and the use of the senses. Connors noted that recent history of rhetoric has been characterized by a revival of the "romantic" notion of authorship, exemplified in the work of Peter Elbow, Ken Macrorie, and James Britton, and that the controversy over what sort of writing should be taught in school, "honest personal writing" or "writing that gets the world's work done" has yet to be resolved.

Addressing this question, Mike Rose, whose internationally known books, *Lives on the Boundary* and *Possible Lives,* focus on the needs of at-risk students, maintained in "Remedial Writing Courses: A Critique and a Proposal" that personal topics are not necessarily more relevant than academic ones and that some students, particularly those from minority cultures, "might not feel comfortable revealing highly personal experiences" (1983, p. 113). Rose also problematized the notion of "authenticity" that is often associated with expressivist writing, questioning whether personal genres are any more "authentic" than nonpersonal ones. Moreover, in the context of remedial writing courses—which frequently assign fairly simple topics to put students at ease and help them avoid error—Rose observed that such assignments do not prepare students for their "university lives" (p. 110). Rose advocated a remedial curriculum that "slowly but steadily and systematically introduce[s] remedial writers to transactional/expositional academic discourse" (p. 112), the genre that students will need to be familiar with as they proceed in their academic and professional careers.

FOR WRITING AND DISCUSSION

Read the following essays:

Rose, M. (1983). Remedial writing courses: A critique and a proposal. *College English, 45* (2), 109–122.
Elbow, P. (1995). Being a writer vs. being an academic: A conflict in goals. *College Composition and Communication, 46* (1), 72–83.
Bartholomae, D. (1995). Writing with teachers: A conversation with Peter Elbow. *College Composition and Communication, 46* (1), 62–71.

Compare the perspectives in each essay. Then write an essay that addresses the following question:

To what extent should the personal essay be included in the freshman writing class?

GENRE AND CREATIVITY

Resistance to the explicit teaching of genre is also associated with the issue of creativity and the extent to which attention to genre could produce formulaic, mechanical texts, all of them alike. This potential problem is exemplified in the importance given to the five-paragraph essay that many students have been taught in high school and continue to write, whatever the assignment happens to be. However, there is no evidence to suggest that helping students understand the purpose and conventions of academic discourse will necessarily result in dull, formulaic writing or preclude creative exploration of a topic.

In fact, a number of scholars have recently begun to acknowledge that genre awareness may actually contribute to creativity, fostering, rather than inhibiting, creative variation. Christie (1987) argued that genre enables choice and that "choice is enhanced by constraint, made possible by constraint" (p. 53). Devitt (1997) similarly maintained that "meaning is enhanced by both choice and constraint ... in genre no less than in words" (p. 53) and that "within any genre there is a great deal of free variation" (p. 52). A related connection between genre and creativity was presented by David Bleich in a 1997 presentation at the Conference of College Composition and Communication. Bleich argued that creativity can exist only within the context of genre, because genres become more effective and revitalized when their formal properties are altered by the incorporation of the personal. Characterizing genres as identifiable, but not fixed, and stable, but subject to cultural influences of the community, Bleich argued that contrary to what is currently believed, genre awareness is a prerequisite for creativity, and that students will be unable to engage in create adaptation of a genre if they are unaware of what the genre is.

This association between genre and creativity suggests that for any text to be considered "creative," it must push across the boundaries that define it, but that at least some of those boundaries must be present for creativity to occur. A work is designated "creative" when it incorporates both constraint and choice. Thus, Mozart's achievement in the sonata form had to occur within the context of that form, as did Picasso's visual juxtapositions within an established tradition of form and color. Because creativity rattles established certitudes, it cannot occur without some element of certitude. This association suggests that in order for any piece of writing to be considered "creative," it must be recognizable for what it is—a school essay, poem, short story, and the like—as opposed to some other genre.

If one assumes a connection between creativity and genre, then it is likely that the explicit teaching of genre will enable, rather than stifle, opportunities for creative variation. As Bakhtin (1986) pointed out:

> Where there is style, there is genre. The transfer of style from one genre to another not only alters the way a style sounds under conditions of a genre unnatural to it but also violates or renews the given genre. (p. 66)

This idea that genre awareness facilitates rather than constrains creativity is implicit in Wendy Bishop's criticism of how academic writing is presented in the writing classroom. Bishop (1997) noted that writing teachers tend to accept only one rigidly defined genre of writing from their students, even though their own scholarship utilizes "alternative styles, mixed genres, co-authored texts" (p. 5). Referring to teachers who do not encourage experimentation with genre as "discourse autocrats" (p. 5), Bishop argued that excellence in writing occurs when resources from one genre are superimposed on another and pointed out that scholars in composition have recently learned to broaden their writing and thinking so that "thesis and data driven work now thrives side by side with narrative and metaphor-rich investigations" (p. 4). Good writing is characterized by both "control and carnival," Bishop maintained; moreover, it is important for composition teachers to rethink "the ways we teach convention making and convention breaking in first-year writing classrooms" (p. 4). And such a rethinking, Bishop argued, requires understanding of genre.

FOR WRITING AND DISCUSSION

How do you define creativity? What do you think is the relationship between genre awareness and creativity?

Writing Assignment

Write an essay that explores the extent to which creativity should be considered important in the writing class. If you are teaching a class yourself, discuss the extent to which you reward creative papers with higher grades.

FOR WRITING AND DISCUSSION

Gunter Kress, in *Learning to Write* (London: Routledge & Kegan Paul, 1982), argued that "there is a small and fixed number of genres in any written tradition" and that "the individual can no more create a new genre type than he or she can create a new sentence type" (pp. 98–99). Kress went on to say that "the creativity which is permitted to the individual exists in deciding in which type or sentence or genre to encode the idea" (p. 99), thereby limiting the possibilities of creativity to those of form and the choice of form.

Discuss this perspective among fellow students. Then write an essay in which you respond to Kress's perspective.

ACADEMIC ARGUMENT IN THE WRITING CLASS

The question of which genres should be taught in the writing class continues to be debated, but over the past several years, the argument essay has assumed increasing importance, in many instances supplementing or supplanting the personal narrative. Mike Rose in 1983 referred to this type of essay as "academic argument," which he defined as an essay that requires the "calculated marshalling of information, a sort of exposition aimed at persuading" (p. 111). Rose's essay stressed the importance of preparing students to work with large bodies of information and to grapple with complex ideas. With its emphasis on reason, abstract thinking, and intertextuality, the argument essay frequently serves the gate-keeping function of delineating which students are intellectually equipped to participate in the conversations of the academy. Presumably, this is the sort of text that students are expected to be able to write in their college classes.

This privileging of the argument essay in the writing class is based on the notion that a number of its generic features are relevant to other academic and professional settings, although, once again, not everyone accepts that this is the case. Those who question whether the type of argument taught in the writing class pertains across disciplines point out that discourse communities differ in their construction of knowledge and rhetorical conventions, and that what Joseph Petraglia refers to as "general writing skills instruction" (GWSI) does not necessarily apply across disciplines. Petraglia (1995) defined GWSI as a set of rhetorical skills that can be mastered through formal instruction, skills that include the "general ability to develop and organize ideas, use techniques for inventing topics worthy of investigation, adapt one's purpose to an audience, and anticipate reader response" (p. xi). Petraglia felt that these skills are not "synonymous with all writing instruction," in that they do not "characterize writing instruction in the forms of basic writing, technical writing, writing-intensive content courses, or creative writing" (p. xii).

Another criticism of the importance given to the argument essay in college-level writing courses is based on political and cultural factors. Shirley Brice Heath (1993), in particular, not only has questioned the relevance of the argument essay to other academic and professional writing tasks but also has castigated it for what she perceives as its exclusion of "many of our current students from the educational process" (p. 106). In her discussion of the origins of the "school essay," Heath pointed out that originally "English Composition emerged as a gatekeeping mechanism for immigrants and the increasing portion of working-class students attempting to make their way into secondary and higher education at the end of the 19th century... The school essay stood as the external evidence of one's capacity to organize thought, to be logical, and to think in an orderly and predicable fashion" (p. 116).

Heath maintained that this genre of writing excludes a significant portion of the school population:

> Collaborative voices at leisure in the freedom to think and explore ideas; it excludes those whose habits of argument and uses of ideas as prompts to action depend on explorations of alternatives ... It excludes narratives, quick asides of witty observation, brief question-answer dyads that challenge but do not drive to a single truth. (p. 122)

Heath thus criticized the school essay as an example of what happens "when belief systems are taken up as institutional rules and practices." She maintained that we should "look at texts, not as autonomous artifacts but as open interwoven forms backed by belief systems and highly interdependent with both oral and written channels" (p. 124).

On the other side of the controversy, those who support the significance given to argumentation in the writing class have maintained that several modes of thought and conventions associated with academic argument do pertain in other contexts, both within and beyond the university, and, therefore, that students need to be familiar with it. Susan Peck MacDonald (1987) argued for the pervasiveness of "problem definition" in multiple academic venues, noting that "the subject of academic writing either already is or is soon turned into a problem before the writer proceeds. No matter how tentative the solutions are, it is problem-solving that generates all academic writing" (p. 316). Similarly, in a comparative study of two hundred essays, Ellen Barton (1993) discussed the importance of "evidentials" as a distinguishing mark between arguments written by experienced academic writers and those written by students. In the context of the academic argumentative essay, Barton's essay is noteworthy for two claims: that evidentials reveal underlying differences in epistemological stance and that although each field is defined by its own special patterns of rhetoric, "argument is more unified than is commonly understood and far more unified than the fragmentation of academic fields might imply. Every scientist or scholar, regardless of field, relies on common devices of rhetoric, on metaphors, invocations of authority, and appeals to audiences" (p. 4).

Even Peter Elbow, whose work is characterized by concern with enabling students to find a voice through personal writing, has acknowledged the existence of "academic writing in general," which he characterizes as the:

> Giving of reasons and evidence rather than just opinions, feelings, experiences: being clear about claims and assertions rather than just employing or insinuating; getting thinking to stand on its own two feet rather than leaning on the authority of who advances it or the fit with who hears it. In describing academic discourse in this general way, surely I am describing a major goal of literacy, broadly defined. Are we not engaged in schools and colleges in trying to teach students to produce reasons and evidence which hold up on their own rather than just in terms of the tastes or prejudices of readers or how attractively they are packaged? (1991, p. 140)

Elbow's definition implies that students are more likely to acquire academic literacy through exposure to argumentation. Yet, what is also generally recognized is that argumentation is difficult for a number of students to understand. In a study published in *Research in the Teaching of English,* George Kamberelis (1999) explored children's "working knowledge of narrative, scientific, and poetic genres" and concluded that "participants had significantly more experience with narrative genres than either scientific or poetic genres and that they possessed significantly more working knowledge of narrative genres than the other focal genres" (p. 403). My own experience in working with college students at various levels supports Kamberelis' conclusions about students' familiarity with narrative strategies, which, unfortunately, do not seem to transfer easily to argumentation. As Connors and Glenn (1987) pointed out, "students who are confident and even entertaining when narrating experiences and describing known quantities sometimes flounder when asked to generalize, organize, or argue for abstract concepts" (p. 61).

Another reason that students experience difficulty with argumentation is that what is regarded as a convincing argument depends a great deal on the audience or community to which the argument is addressed. As Freedman & Medway (1994) explained:

> Communities differ in the expectations they have of arguments expressed by their members and in the kind of argument they are prepared to recognize as persuasive and appropriate. We all know, for example, that in our everyday experience, a very small sample is enough to convince us. One spoiled jar of Brand X mayonnaise deters us (and likely our friends) from buying Brand X. A sociology paper, in contrast, is successful within its community only when it shows that the sample selected can be shown to be representative by complex statistical maneuvers. The grounds or the kinds of evidence required are very different in the two cases. (p. 7)

Students, thus, do not define "argument" the way it is defined in an academic context, and because teachers tend not to present writing assignments in terms of genre, students are frequently unclear about what sort of text they are supposed to produce.

FOR WRITING AND DISCUSSION

Consider the perspectives of McDonald, Bartholomae, and Heath on the importance of the argument essay in the writing class. Write an essay in which you explore the reasons for focusing or not focusing on this genre in college writing courses.

THE APPLICATION OF GENRE THEORY: A VARIETY OF GENRES

Creative Nonfiction

Recently, a number of teachers and scholars have embraced a new genre, which they are calling "creative nonfiction," a genre that combines the scholarly rigor and public concerns of academic writing with the energy and personal involvement of personal narrative. Because this genre often utilizes first-person perspectives as a means of developing a topic, creative nonfiction enables students to include relevant personal experience and opinion within an academic context. An advocate of introducing creative nonfiction to the composition class, Wendy Bishop (1997) noted that many of the journal articles in rhetoric and composition now include personal opinion and examples based on lived experience, allowing the writer to move back and forth between an informal, casual tone to the more formal, depersonalized tone associated with academic discourse. As rigid standards for academic writing are being examined, the text strategies associated with creative nonfiction are appearing with increasing frequency in the writing class.

Literary Genres

In a recent article, Amy Devitt (2000) called for rhetorical and literary genre theorists to recognize commonalities. Whereas literary genres tended to be regarded as a static categorization of textual features, recent concern with the "interactive nature of textual meaning" suggests that both rhetorical and literary genres "can be defined as a dynamic concept created through the interaction of writers, readers, past texts, and contexts" (p. 699). Devitt suggested that genre provides an important approach for examining all kinds of texts, because, as Derrida (1980) maintained, "every text participates in one or several genres, there is no genreless text; there is always a genre and genres, yet such participation never amounts to belonging" (p. 65). Similarly, Marjory Perloff (1989), addressing the question of whether genre is a necessary term in a post-modern world, observed that "even as we pronounce on the 'irrelevance' of genre in a time of postmodern openness, inclusiveness, and flexibility, we are all the while applying generic markers to the subjects of our discussion" (pp. 5–6).

ADDRESSING GENRE IN THE WRITING CLASS

Although critics have expressed concern about overly prescriptive applications of genre theory in the writing class, pragmatic approaches based on genre have increasingly become a feature of teaching academic or professional writing in courses focusing on English for specific purposes. Fostering awareness of genre appears to be most useful for genres that are characterized by consistent and stable sections or "moves" that occur in a more or less fixed order. Swales (1990), for example, models the "moves" in article introductions, Swales and Feak (1994) apply genre theory to academic writing for graduate students, and Swales and Lindemann (2002) discuss the literature review in terms of genre. For more flexible, less predictable genres with a number of optional moves, such as in the typical first-year essay, a genre approach is likely to be more limited. Nevertheless, the writing class can utilize a genre perspective in a number of ways, such as those suggested below:

1. The writing class can help students understand that genres have political and social implications that provide access to power. Thus, genres can be presented in terms of discourse community, as a form of rhetorical etiquette that, like language, enables group membership. Students can then be encouraged to discover genres with which they are familiar as well as those that push linguistic, intellectual, and social boundaries.

2. The writing class can help students understand that both speaking and writing are strongly influenced by generic conventions, even when the goal is to break them.

3. The writing class can present generic form as the product of particular social relations between writer and audience. Students need to understand that "what counts as an example of a genre is historically determined and affected by social expectations" (Bazerman, 1991, p. 21).

4. The writing class can foster awareness of various genres.

5. The writing class can encourage creative variation by providing opportunities for students to push generic boundaries and examine the extent to which features from one genre can be transposed to another.

Thus, a genre such as the argument essay can be presented in terms of more familiar ones, such as the advertisement.

6. The writing class can present the academic essay in terms of the writer's stance and definable features, "notably the use of an appropriate style in writing, the presentation and discusson of data, the use of hedging devices in the making of claims, and the use of sources" (Dudley-Evans, 2002).

7. Writing assignments can require students to define the rhetorical situation motivating the writing. The resulting essay can then be evaluated according to how well it achieved its purpose (Coe, 2002).

Whether the context is rhetorical or literary, genre is an important concept to introduce into the composition class because our students are already working in text genres that a short time ago did not exist—e-mail, Web pages, hypertext literature, and collaborative texts. Genre knowledge will enable students to examine texts in terms of their cultural function and to use their awareness of generic expectations to transcend generic boundaries, both within and beyond the writing class.

FOR FURTHER EXPLORATION

Essay Collections

Berkenkotter, C., & Huckin. T. N. (1995). *Genre knowledge in disciplinary communication.* Hillsdale, New Jersey: Lawrence Erlbaum.

Bishop, W., & Ostrom, H. (Eds). (1997). *Genre and writing: Issues, arguments, alternatives.* Portsmouth, New Hampshire: Boynton/Cook.

Freedman, A., & Medway, P. (Eds.). (1994). *Learning and teaching genre.* Portsmouth, New Hampshire: Boynton/Cook.

Freedman, A., & Medway, P. (Eds.). (1994).*Genre and the new rhetoric.* London: Taylor and Francis.

Johns, Ann M. (Ed). (2002). *Genre in the classroom: Multiple perspectives.* Mahwah, New Jersey, Lawrence Erlbaum.

The Explicit Teaching of Genre

Fahnestock, J. (1993). Genre and rhetorical craft. *Research in the teaching of English, 27* (3), 265–271.

Fahnestock responds to Aviva Freedman's article on explicit instruction of genre, which appears in the same issue of the journal. She questions Freedman's conclusions by asking how explicit instruction and genre should be defined and considers how craft, as opposed to a body of knowledge, can be learned.

Freedman, A. (1993). Show and tell? The role of explicit teaching in learning new genres. *Research in the Teaching of English, 27* (3), 222–251.

Freedman maintains that genre knowledge cannot be taught explicitly because it is only through immersion in a discourse community that students can develop a "felt sense" of a genre.

Mustaha, Z. (1995). Effect of genre awareness on linguistic transfer. *English for Specific Purposes, 14* (3), 247–256.

This article examines the effect of raising university students' awareness of term paper conventions through formal instruction in second language in producing this genre in the same language or another language. The results indicate that although formal instruction is important, that variation in professors' evaluation of these aspects are the main factor affecting whether this awareness is put into practice.

Williams, J., & Colomb, G. (1993). The case for explicit teaching: Why what you don't know won't help you. *Research in the Teaching of English, 27* (3), 252–264.

Academic Versus Personal Writing

Bawarshi, A. S. (1997). Beyond dichotomy: Toward a theory of divergence in composition studies. *JAC: Journal of Advanced Composition Theory, 17* (1), 69–82.

Bawarshi examines the dichotomy posited by Bartholomae and Elbow between institutional and personal writing, or, more generally, between social constructivism and expressivism. He attempts to propose a means of mediation between the two positions that goes beyond previous attempts.

Glasgow, J. (1995). Surface tension between two paradigms of writing instruction. *Teaching English in the Two-Year College, 22* (2), 102–109.

Glasgow reviews the tensions between discourse-centered writing instruction and expressivist approaches, considering the conflict that occurs when the writing instructor's approach differs from the writing tutor's approach. The article explores the possibilities of a reflective-response style of writing instruction and advocates that such an approach is a useful means of fostering writing development.

MacDonald, S. P. (1987). Problem definition in academic writing. *College English, 49* (3), 315–331.

MacDonald maintains that problem solving generates all academic writing and that, in this regard, writing about literature shares the same assumptions as other academic writing tasks. On the continuum of problem definition, the scientist is at one end and literary interpretation is at the other with its relatively undefined problems. Yet it is important for composition teachers to construct assignments that adequately define a problem.

Creativity in the Composition Class

Bawarshi, A. S. (1997). Beyond dichotomy: Toward a theory of divergence in composition studies. *JAC: Journal of Advanced Composition Theory, 17* (1), 69–82.

Bawarshi critiques the notion of creativity as unprecedented or passing, arguing instead that there can be no transcendence without derivation.

Bloom, L. Z. (1998). *Composition studies as a creative art.* Logan, Utah: Utah State University Press.

Bloom discusses the role of creativity in the composition class through narratives of her own history as a compositionist. Advocates that compositionists write in the genres they teach.

Christie, F. (1987). Genres as choice. In I. Reid (Ed.), *The place of genre in learning: current debates* (pp. 22–34). Australia: Deakin University Press.

Christie maintains that creativity and genre are not incompatible, and that genre awareness is a prerequisite for creative variation.

Dacey, J. S., & Lennon, K. H. (1998). *Understanding creativity.* San Francisco: Jossey-Bass.

Discusses various components of "creativity" as it has been defined, focusing on the interplay between biological, psychological, and social factors.

Weiner, R. P. (2000). *Creativity and beyond.* Albany, New York: State University of New York Press.

Discusses the importance given to creativity in western culture and traces the concept from medieval times until the present in several societies.

Examining Particular Genres

Bazerman, C. (1991). *Shaping written knowledge: The genre and activity of the experimental article in science.* Madison, Wisconsin: University of Wisconsin Press.

Berkenkotter, C., & Huckin, T. N. (1995). Gatekeeping at an academic convention. In C. Berkenkotter, & T. N. Huckin, (Eds.), *Genre knowledge in disciplinary communication.* Hillsdale, New Jersey: Lawrence Erlbaum.

Paley, K. S. (1996). The college application essay: A rhetorical paradox. *Assessing Writing, 3,* 85–105.

Soven, M., & Sullivan, W. M. (1990). Demystifying the academy: Can exploratory writing help? *Freshman English News, 19* (1), 13–16.

Swales, J. M. (1990). *Genre analysis.* Cambridge: New York.

Swales, J. M., & Feak, C. B. (1994). *Academic writing for graduate students: Essential tasks and skills.* Ann Arbor: University of Michigan Press.

REFERENCES

Bakhtin, M. (1986). The problem of speech genres. In C. Emerson, M. Holquist (Eds.), & V. W. McGee, (Trans.), *Speech genres and other late essays* (pp. 60–102). Austin, Texas: University of Austin Press.

Bartholomae, D. (1995, February). Writing with teachers: A conversation with Peter Elbow. *College Composition and Communication, 46* (1), 62–71.

Barton, E. (1993). Evidentials, argumentation, and epistemological stance. *College English, 55* (7), 745–769.

Bawarshi, A. S. (1997). Beyond dichotomy: Toward a theory of divergence in composition studies. *JAC: Journal of Advanced Composition Theory, 17* (1), 69–82.

Bazerman, C. (1991). *Shaping written knowledge: The genre and activity of the experimental article in science.* Madison, Wisconsin: University of Wisconsin Press.

Bishop, W. (1997). Preaching what we practice as professionals. In W. Bishop, & H. Ostrom (Eds), *Genre and writing: Issues, arguments, alternatives* (pp. 3–16). Portsmouth, New Hampshire: Boynton/Cook.

Bitzer, L. (1968). The rhetorical situation. *Philosophy and Rhetoric, 1,* 1–14.

Bleich, D. (1997). Genre theory and the teaching of writing. *Conference on College Composition and Communication.* Phoenix, Arizona.

Britton, J., Burgess, T., Martin, N., Mc Lead, A., & Rosen, H. (1975). *The development of writing abilities.* London: McMillan Education Ltd.

Burke, K. (1968). *Counterstatement.* Berkeley and Los Angeles: University of California Press.

Burke, K. (1969). *A rhetoric of motives.* Berkeley: University of California Press.

Christie, F. (1987). Genres as choice. In *The Place of Genre in Learning: Current Debates* I. Reid (ed). Deakin University: Centre for Studies in Literary Education.

Christie, F. (1987). Genres as choice. In I. Reid (Ed.), *The place of genre in learning: Current debates* (pp. 22–34). Geelong, Australia: Deakin University Press.

Coe, R. M. (2002). The new rhetoric of genre: Writing political briefs. In A. M. Johns (Ed). *Genre in the classroom: Multiple perspectives* (pp. 197–207). Mahwah, New Jersey, Lawrence Erlbaum.

Connors, R. J. (1987). Personal writing assignments. *College Composition and Communication, 38* (1), 166–183.

Connors, R., and Glenn, C. (1987). The St. Martin's Guide to Teaching Writing. New York: St. Martin's Press.

Cope, B., & Kalantzis, M. (Eds.). (1993). *The powers of literacy: A genre approach to teaching writing.* Pittsburgh, PA: University of Pittsburgh Press.

Derrida, J. (1980, Autumn). The law of genre. *Critical inquiry, 7,* 55–82.

Devitt, A. J. (1993). Generalizing about genre: New conceptions of an old concept. *College Composition and Communication, 44,* 573–586.

Devitt, A. J. (1997). Genre as language standard. In W. Bishop, & H. Ostrom (Eds.), *Genre and writing: Issues, arguments, alternatives* (pp. 45–55). Portsmouth, New Hampshire: Boynton/Cook.

Devitt, A. J. (2000). Integrating rhetorical and literary theories of genre. *College English, 62* (6), 697–718.

Dudley-Evans, T. (2002). The teaching of the academic essay: Is a genre approach possible? In Johns, Ann M. (Ed.). *Genre in the Classroom: Multiple Perspectives.* Mahwah, New Jersey, Lawrence Erlbaum.

Elbow, P. (1991). Reflections on academic discourse: How it relates to freshmen and colleagues. *College English, 53* (2), 135–155.

Elbow, P. (1995). Being a writer vs. being an academic: A conflict in goals. *College Composition and Communication, 46* (1), 72–83.

Freedman, A. (1993). Show and tell? The role of explicit teaching in learning new genres. *Research in the Teaching of English, 27,* 222–251.

Freedman, A. (1995). The what, where, when, why, and how of classroom genres. In *Reconceiving Writing, Rethinking Writing Instruction.* J. Petraglia (ed). Mahwah, New Jersey: Lawrence Erlbaum.

Freedman, A. (1997). Situating 'genre' and situated genres. In W. Bishop, & H. Ostrom (Eds.), *Genre and writing: Issues, arguments, alternatives* (pp. 179–189). Portsmouth, New Hampshire: Boynton/Cook.

Freedman, A., & Medway, P. (Eds.). (1994). *Learning and teaching genre.* Portsmouth, New Hampshire: Boynton/Cook.

Freire, P. (1968). *The pedagogy of the oppressed.* New York: Seabury.

Heath, S. B. (1993). Rethinking the sense of the past: The essay as legacy of the epigram. In L. Odell (Ed.), *Theory and practice in the teaching of writing: Rethinking the discipline* (pp. 105–131). Carbondale, Illinois: Southern Illinois University Press.

Kamberelis, G. (1999). Genre development and learning: Children writing stories, science reports and poems. *Research in the Teaching of English, 33* (4), 403–460.

Kress, G. (1982). *Learning to write.* London: Routledge and Kegan Paul.

MacDonald, S. P. (1987). Problem definition in academic writing. *College English, 49* (3), 315–331.

Miller, C. (1984). Genre as social action. *Quarterly Journal of Speech, 70,* 151–167.

Perloff, M. (Ed.). (1989). *Postmodern genres.* University of Oklahoma Press: Norman and London.

Petraglia, J. (1995). Introduction: General writing skills instruction and its discontents. In J. Petraglia (Ed), *Reconceiving writing, rethinking writing instruction* (pp. xi–xvii). Mahwah, New Jersey: Lawrence Erlbaum.

Rose, M. (1983). Remedial writing courses: A critique and a proposal. *College English, 45* (2), 109–122.

Sawyer, W., & Watson, K. (1987). Questions of genre. In I. Reid (Ed.), *The place of genre in learning: Current debates* (pp. 46–57). Deakin University, Centre for Studies in Literary Education, Geelong, Vic., Australia.

Swales, J. (1990). *Genre analysis.* Cambridge: Cambridge University Press.

Swales, J. M., & Feak, C. B. (1994). *Academic writing for graduate students: Essential tasks and skills.* Ann Arbor: University of Michigan Press.

Swales, J. M., & S. Lindemann, Teaching the literature review to international graduate students. In A. M. Johns (Ed.), *Genre in the classroom: Multiple perspectives* (pp. 105–119). Mahwah, New Jersey, Lawrence Erlbaum.

Williams, J., & Colomb, G. G. (1993). The case for explicit teaching: Why what you don't know won't help you. *Research in the Teaching of English, 27* (3), 252–264.

Villanueva, V. (ed). (1997). Cross-talk in Comp Theory: A Reader. Urbana, Illinois: NCTE.

Karin Woiwode
Dr. Irene L. Clark
English 406
31 October 2000

Women's Periodicals – How Genre Re-enforces Stereotypes

In her essay Generalizing about Genre: New Conceptions of an Old Concept, *Amy J. Devitt stipulates that it is no longer judicious to adhere to the Aristotelian concept of genre as a classification of literary form and text type. Inasmuch as genres change with society, it is necessary to redefine and expand Aristotle's static interpretation to a dynamic one, namely to see genre as a "patterning of human experience," to understand genre as a social action. This wider interpretation integrates form and text and allows the inclusion of function or purpose and the "making of meaning," resulting not only in the development of genres as a response to recurring situations, but also in their construction.*

This interrelationship between response to and construction of a recurring situation is exemplified by the proliferation of women's periodicals. As a genre, the publication of magazines strictly aimed at women re-enforces the cultural assumptions of a patriarchy, depicting women as subordinate to men, while women who support the production of periodicals by reading them, perpetuate these false assumptions. Thus, women periodicals both reflect and create the social context, which mirrors our cultural "values."

Henrik Ibsen once said: "It is essential to see, not to mirror—the latter is an indulgence." Perhaps indulgence best describes the aura surrounding the history of these publications. Women had to be indulged, humored; men had to be tolerant of women's inferior intellectual capacity. Men, indeed the publishers of these magazines were all men, assumed a condescending attitude toward the "little doves" and made millions in the process. It boggles the mind that legions of women for more than a hundred years were and still are unable to "see" their own gullibility, were incapable of realizing how those in control decided for them what their "proper" interests should be. Had women been able to clearly "see", this genre may have died an early death!

Instead, the genre shrived and grew out of all proportion, as it responded to the recurring situation of a woman's place in a society entrenched with masculine values. Inherent in this response is the genre's ability to construct and thus to further perpetuate a false image of women. It is truly a deadly embrace—one from which women have been hard pushed extricating themselves. Indeed, a quick perusal of current women's periodicals confirms that stereotyping women as airheads is not a thing of the past, again proving that genre is actively involved as a maker of meaning.

It does not come as a surprise then, that many of the women's magazines one sees in today's supermarkets and bookstores, are hardly new conceptions. Most of them have been in circulation for more than a hundred years, having been started by men, since women had no access to the business world. Godey's Lady's Book, *the first woman's magazine in the US, started in 1830 by L.A. Godey, no longer exists. However, fifty-three years later, Cyrus Curtis published the periodical that has consistently had the highest circulation in the world of the so-called "service" magazines,* Ladies' Home Journal. *In the same league are* Good Housekeeping, McCalls *and* Redbook. *Though* Family Circle, Woman's Day, Woman's World *and* American Woman *were started later, the entire "collection" was and is aimed at one single audience-women.*

Available monthly, these periodicals focus entirely on "women's issues", reinforcing the prevailing ideology that equates women with the domestic sphere. Articles on cooking and cleaning, home decoration and budgeting, childbirth and motherhood, leave no doubt as to the nature of women's roles and interests. An army of "experts"—dieticians, sociologists, marriage counselors, pediatricians and psychologists—stand ready to advise women on how to make casseroles, how to make their marriages work, how to raise sons who are not "sissies", etc., etc., (Walker, 10). The very premise of these magazines—to advise, enlighten and entertain women, but not men—diminishes women, as does the overt emphasis on domesticity to the exclusion of intellectual topics.

While domestic duties form a large part of the textual content of periodicals, another function of this genre, closely tied to a woman's place in society, is to drive home the importance of appearance. Women simply cannot be left to their own devices! The implicit assumption is, of course, that women, seen at best uncon- fident, at worst incompetent, need or want instructions "on the arts and skills of femininity" (Walker, 5). Such topics as "Slip into Silks," "Do you make these Beauty Blunders?" and "Are you a happily Married Woman?" (Walker, 9), send the message that women had better sharpen their "feminine skills" in order to please their "men."

It can certainly be argued that this particular genre—women's periodicals— clearly reflects or mirrors the attitudes and beliefs prevalent in our culture. But how does it create *them?*

The answer is that women themselves create the social context in which this genre flourishes. This phenomenon can be seen in the fact that editors do not operate in a vacuum; that they do not make choices about content vacuously. Indeed, the relationship between readers and the editorial department of a magazine is remarkably interactive, so that content is at least in part informed by reader preferences. Though the following quote appeared in McCalls *in 1942, it still expresses the mentality of many of today's home-makers: "We all want but one thing from our magazines: inspiration...something that helps us make our lives better and richer with the beauty of living" (Walker, 5). Echoing this sentiment is the "editor's memo" in the November 2000 issue of* Ladies' Home Journal: *"You'll notice there is a lot about being a mom today in this issue. That's no surprise, since we know how many of you are focused on raising your family." And..."What are the greatest joys and biggest challenges of mothering in our complex world?" (Blyth, page 8). With revolting condescension the editor ends by admonishing to "vote for the sake of the children."*

Language, of course, is the essence of a genre, uniting both text and context; its syntactic, semantic and pragmatic features are the "makers of meaning." It is therefore impossible to miss the condescending tone of the editor and the sentimental one of the homemaker. Thus, *genre is both the product and the process that creates it. It is the process of language then within this particular genre, that prevents, indeed forbids women to be seen as autonomous and intelligent.*

This point is further driven home when one examines the language typically used in magazines geared to men. Gone is admonishing condescension. Rather, language is rationale and logical, characteristics most often used to describe men.

One example from TIME, *April, 1998, will suffice: an article on America's most influential First Lady, Eleanor Roosevelt, is interwoven with such phrases as "social reform, post-suffrage feminism, civil rights, racism, discrimination, ideological argument, effective advocacy." Ironically, contained in the article is a question put to the president on Eleanor's outspokenness on political issues which sums up the prevailing attitude toward women: "Why can't she stay home and tend to her knitting?"*

The year, of course, was 1936, about forty years after the first and forty years before the second women's rights movements. While these feminist movements have raised women's collective consciousness and have brought about the sexual revolution of the 1970s, they have had very little effect on content and language of women's periodicals. Should an article appear today on the famous Eleanor in one of the women's magazines, it would most likely concern her relationship with her husband, rather than her political and social accomplishments, pointing out just how deep-seated cultural believes and attitudes are and how difficult it is to change them. Of course, women's magazines, reaching millions of women readers, could be a useful tool in re-directing these attitudes. However, one has to ask whether the people behind women's magazines would be interested to re-direct, whether millions of women would still buy if a more intellectually challenging content were offered? These questions then reflect a genre's power to influence and its ability to mirror patterns of human experience.

Often, these patterns are so deeply ingrained, that change comes about only very slowly. An example is our present society's apparent ease with the status quo. A case in point is this: the November, 2000 issue of the Journal *contains an interview with the two presidential candidates and their wives, focusing on the candidate's private lives', rather than on their public accomplishments. A sampling of the interviewers' questions follows: "What's his worst husband habit? Did he change diapers? Well, you couldn't complain about his kissing style. At the convention it looked like passion on the podium. Love at first sight? So, no bad habits?" (Blyth, Evans, pages 130–136).*

The interviewers does touch upon educational issues and the effects of popular music on children, but even these topics represent a woman's concern for children and family, rather than her ability to grabble with problems of national or international import. This particular interview is hailed as a "election report," but its content is as shallow as anything written under the rubric of "regular features" such as "Home, Beauty and Fashion, People, Relationships, Food." It is obvious that neither the feminist movement, nor WWII, as Walker points out, has had an impact; the content of the magazines was and still is much the same: "food, fashion, beauty, childcare, home decorations" (Walker, 33).

Adding injury to insult, the primary function of periodicals is not to advise, enlighten and entertain, but to sell products. I counted no less than ninety-five advertisements of beauty products, cleaners, washing machines, medications, clothing, fabrics, food, etc. in the earlier mentioned Journal. *This hidden dimension thrusts women into the role of consumers, with the magazines providing a "particular female world view of the desirable, the possible, and the purchasable" (Walker, 9). That this female worldview is imposed on women by the concealed but powerful hands of the patriarchy is hardly perceived.*

Women's periodicals, then, are purposely crafted to encourage women to become willing participants in consumerism. Women's periodicals function as tools of a society that continue to demean and diminish women. Women's periodicals, as a genre, reflect this diminished stature of women in our culture through their content. Yet, as long as women remain willing participators in this vicious cycle by purchasing the magazines, as long will the genre respond to a culture of conspicuous consumption, to a culture that stereotypes women as still not quite measuring up.

BIBLIOGRAPHY

Walker, N. A. ed. Women's Magazines 1940–1960 Gender Roles and the Popular Press. *Boston: Bedford/St. Martins, 1998.*

Amy J. Devitt. *"Generalizing about Genre: New Conceptions of an Old Concept."* College Composition and Communication *44 (December, 1993): 573–86*

Blyth, Myrna, Evans, Nancy. *"Election Report: Fighting for the Family."* Ladies' Home Journal *November 2000: 130–36*

Clifton Justice

How Do You Raise That Money?

Without ever intending to become one, I have become an expert on soliciting and receiving foundation support for charitable programs. Over a four-year period of time I raised from both public and private sources more than $100,000.00 each year for a small nonprofit performing arts group. Arts organizations often get short shrift by foundations because they are not able to substantiate their community impact, but with issues of literacy dominating the field in the 1990's, I was able to find a way of blending foundation concerns and arts programming. To be successful in this arena, it was necessary that I learn to write the two-page request for support letter. This letter is the instrument whereby a nonprofit organization solicits money from a charitable foundation. This mechanism brings together features from academic writing and business writing in order to make a compelling case for funding an organization's project. The genre reveals a system that favors structured management, clear outcomes for complex problems, and measured advances in changing people's lives. It is conservative, like the people who established the foundations.

In the early part of the 20th century the U.S. developed tax codes that placed federal taxes on each citizen or resident of the country. The federal tax was a progressive act that allowed the federal government to raise additional revenue. Since there were no government services for those who faced personal or economic catastrophe, the government used the increased funds from taxes to lead the way in providing a social safety net for its citizens who had fallen on hard times. But conservatives in the government did not want citizens to look just to the government for assistance. Private individuals were encouraged to participate in the enterprise and if they did, their taxes would be exempted or reduced. The most popular method used by the wealthy to assist those less fortunate than themselves was to establish foundations designed to fund worthy enterprises by nonprofit organizations. Nonprofit organizations provide services to the community through their programs, and since their programs are offered free or at a reduced cost to the community, outside funds must be solicited in order to continue operations. Because of the federal government's tax codes, wealthy individuals and their foundations have financial as well as humanitarian reasons to give money to nonprofit organizations.

Now the two entities, foundation and nonprofit, have a reason to talk with one another, but how will they communicate? The last thing a wealthy individual wants is every director of a charity banging on his door with a personal appeal. In the beginning of a foundation, the man (sometimes a woman) with the money has pet projects, such as Carnegie and his libraries, and as long as the philanthropist is alive, giving his money away is a relatively simple task. The foundation donates to whatever organizations the gentleman (sometimes gentlewoman) prefers. But after that individual's passing, a professional staff and board of directors must decide each year how to give away a percentage of the founder's lifetime accumulation of wealth as mandated by the tax code. The staff and the board of foundations are usually well-educated, often holding advanced degrees, so asking nonprofits to put their requests in writing made sense and it was an easy solution to a pressing problem. From the 1960's forward, nonprofit growth skyrocketed and pleas to foundations increased each year. Foundations wanted an orderly way of communicating with nonprofits to be imposed. Personal visits and telephone calls could take up too much of the staff's day. Comfortable with academic writing, the grantsmakers borrowed the concept of "thesis" and "support" and merged it into "problem to be addressed" and "community impact," then imposed that all requests must be in writing. To assist fundraisers in conforming to the requirements, pamphlets, such as the PP & PG (Program Planning and Proposal Guide), were printed and widely distributed.

Another prominent reason for demanding that requests be in writing is to avoid personal involvement in projects. With the internal structure based in academic writing, the two-page request for support letter serves the foundation's need of creating a space between themselves and the nonprofit. Since a substantial percentage of the proposals, well over 50%, will be rejected, foundations want to maintain distance from the organizations. Distance allows them a more careful and objective examination. It also forces both sides to take a "cool" approach to the problem, viewing it with a dispassionate nature.

Of course, this style of discourse has its vagaries that favor college-educated, economically advantaged grant writers. These individuals, particularly those who

come from a composition background, are able to communicate in a manner so-
ciety has determined superior. Thus, their programs are deemed superior and re-
ceive funding. Rarely do you see awards given to organizations run by individ-
uals without a strong writing background. At the time, I was one of those few
exceptions.

The components of the two-page request for support letter are: 1) mission of the
organization or the purpose of the group, 2) history of the organization focusing
on recent accomplishments by the organization, 3) the community problem to be
addressed—and you never say the problem is lack of money (even though it often
is), 4) the actions your organization will take to address the problem, 5) the long
term impact of your program and their money on the community to be addressed,
and 6) how much money you want from the foundation along with who else is
supporting the project. Funders rarely go it alone.

While the genre's internal structure is derived from academia, its appearance
is similar to that of a business letter. It is most often single-spaced, printed on
organization letterhead, and has a clean, no-fuss appearance. This appearance
somehow conveys to the foundation strong management, fiscal responsibility, and
community involvement. It does this through paragraphs borrowed from the busi-
ness world that are ten to twelve lines long, often with a space between them and no
indentation. On the page, the paragraphs form powerful-looking blocks meant to
inspire trust in the organization. Letterhead, in and of itself, indicates the serious
intent of the organization. It is printed, not photocopied, on heavy stock, and may
include wood pulp mixed with cotton or linen. Generally, letterhead includes a
listing of the board of directors, which indicates a system of hierarchy similar to the
foundation's own structure. Familiarity, in this instance, breeds confidence rather
than contempt.

Certainly the limit of two pages is derived from the genre's attachment to the
business letter. In that form the writer needs to get to the point quickly and move
on. Two pages are a limited amount of space to describe the project; great care must
be taken with each word and phrase. Confusion is disastrous. If the foundation
looks favorably on the request letter then the next step is usually to require a more
formal proposal that can run many pages. The essence of that well-thought out
proposal must be synthesized within the two-page appeal. This is challenging since
the project is almost always over two years away from starting. Foundation's move
at such a slow pace that even an affirmative response to a funding request can
take over a year and a half. Negative responses to the request for support letter come
quicker, usually within a few weeks or months, so no news can be good news to the
grantwriter.

The organization I wrote grants for presented programs that were based on classic
*stories or poems—*The Walrus and the Carpenter, Jabberwocky*—and folk*
tales from Mexico, Africa, and Asia. I partnered with larger organizations, such
as the Los Angeles City Library, to bring further attention to the company's work
by local foundations. With support from the Parsons Foundation, the Weingart

Foundation and the Norris Foundation, the company twice visited all 89-library sites in Los Angeles providing them with family programs designed to encourage reading. I believe much of my success came from knowing how to tailor my program to the foundation's goals of literacy, particularly for children. The more the nonprofit advances the goals of the foundation in their request, the more likely the organization will receive funding. This can have a detrimental aspect; organizations can lose their own sense of mission when they are chasing funds from a foundation. I believe, for the most part, I was able to avoid this error.

The skill I learned in writing two-page requests for support letters has served me well in college. First, it provided me a way to earn a living. By working part time out of my home, I have been able to pursue a career in teaching. My reputation as a grantwriter is such that I have numerous organizations desiring my services and I can choose for whom I want to write. Second, I find that determining what a professor wants and then giving it to them is remarkably similar to structuring a program that a foundation will fund. The ability to mold your idea to the vision of another without losing your way is central to success, not only in college, but also in life.

Reading

GENERALIZING ABOUT GENRE: NEW CONCEPTIONS OF AN OLD CONCEPT

Amy J. Devitt

Our field has become riddled with dichotomies that threaten to undermine our holistic understanding of writing. Form and content (and the related form and function, text and context), product and process, individual and society—these dichotomies too often define our research affiliations, our pedagogies, and our theories. If we are to understand writing as a unified act, as a complex whole, we must find ways to overcome these dichotomies. Recent conceptions of genre as a dynamic and semiotic construct illustrate how to unify form and content, place text within context, balance process and product, and acknowledge the role of both the individual and the social. This reconception of genre may even lead us to a unified theory of writing.

The most recent understandings of genre derive from the work of several significant theorists working with different agendas and from different fields: from literature (M. M. Bakhtin, Tzvetan Todorov, Jacques Derrida), linguistics (M. A. K. Halliday, John Swales), and rhetoric (Carolyn Miller, Kathleen Jamieson). However, this work has not yet widely influenced how most scholars and teachers of writing view genre. Our reconception will require releasing old notions of genre as form and text type and embracing new notions of genre as dynamic patterning of human experience, as one of the concepts that enable us to construct our writing world. Basically, the new conception of genre shifts the focus from effects

Reprinted from *College Composition and Communication,* Vol. 44, No. 4, December 1993. Used with permission.

(formal features, text classifications) to sources of those effects. To accommodate our desires for a reunified view of writing, we must shift our thinking about genre from a formal classification system to a rhetorical and essentially semiotic social construct. This article will explain the new conception of genre that is developing and will suggest some effects of this new conception on our thinking about writing.[1]

The Conventional Conception of Genre

The common understanding of genre among too many composition scholars and teachers today is that genre is a relatively trivial concept, a classification system deriving from literary criticism that names types of texts according to their forms. Viewed in this way, genre is not only a rather trivial concept but also a potentially destructive one, one that conflicts with our best understandings of how writing, writers, and readers work, one that encourages the dichotomies in our field.

Treating genre as form requires dividing form from content, with genre as the form into which content is put; but we have largely rejected this container model of meaning in favor of a more integrated notion of how meaning is made: "Form and content in discourse are one," as Bakhtin writes ("Discourse" 259). Similarly, treating genre as form and text type requires binding genre to a product perspective, without effect on writing processes or, worse yet, inhibiting those processes. As a product-based concept, in fact, this view of genre seems to have more to do with reading than with writing (as attested to by the frequency of genre interpretations among literary critics). Finally, a formal view of genre exaggerates one of the most troubling current dichotomies, that between the individual and the group or society. It makes genre a normalizing and static concept, a set of forms that constrain the individual; genuine writers can distinguish themselves only by breaking out of those generic constraints, by substituting an individual genius for society's bonds.

Though this conventional conception of genre contradicts our best knowledge of how writing works, it has a long history and is not so easily discarded. Formalisms in general have sustained much of the work in linguistics, rhetoric, and literature in the past, the fields out of which genre theories have developed. Not surprisingly, then, most genre theories in the past have been concerned with classification and form, with describing the formal features of a particular genre, describing the embodiment of a genre in a particular work, or delineating a genre system, a set of classifications of (primarily literary) texts. The emphasis on classification can be traced back to the followers of Aristotle, who turned his initial treatment in the *Poetics* of the epic, tragedy, and comedy into an infinitely modifiable classification scheme. The rhetorical division of discourse into epideictic, judicial, and deliberative can be seen as a similar classification system, one still in use by some today. Other writers propose broader or narrower schemes of text types: literature and nonliterature; narrative and nonnarrative; narrative, exposition, argument, description; the lyric, the sonnet; the Petrarchan sonnet. Whether called genres, subgenres, or modes, whether comprehensive or selective, whether generally accepted or disputed, these systems for classifying texts focus attention on static products.

The efforts spent on devising a classification scheme may be time well spent for some purposes: for supporting or elaborating an interpretation of literature (that literature's import is its effect on readers, for example, or that all literature tells stories), or, to use Anne Freadman's examples (106), for developing a filing system, a library classification system, or disciplinary divisions within a university. For our purposes, perhaps it is enough to agree with Todorov that "We do not know just how many types of discourse there are, but we shall readily agree that there are more than one" (9). Or, along with Miller, perhaps we can accept that "the number of genres current in any society is indeterminate and depends upon the complexity and diversity of the society" (163). Understanding genre requires understanding more than just classification schemes; it requires understanding the origins of the patterns on which those classifications are based. As I. R. Titunik comments in summarizing P. M. Medvedev's ideas about genre, "Genre is not that which is determined and defined by the components of a literary work or by sets of literary works, but that which, in effect, determines and defines them" (175).

Once our attention shifts to the origins of genres, it also shifts away from their formal features. Traditional genre study has meant study of the textual features that mark a genre: the meter, the layout, the organization, the level of diction, and so on. Where literary criticism has delineated its invocation to the muse and its fourteen-line sonnet, composition has delineated its five-paragraph theme, the inverted-triangle introductory paragraph, the division into purpose, methods, results, and discussion of the lab report, and the you-attitude in the business letter. Certainly, such formal features are the physical markings of a genre, its traces, and hence may be quite revealing. In merging form and content, we do not wish to discard the significance of form in genre (see Coe, "Apology"). But those formal traces do not *define* or *constitute* the genre (see Freadman 114). Historical changes in generic forms argue against equating genre with form; note the formal changes in what we call a poem, for example, or in the familiar letter. The forms may change but the generic label stays the same. Distinguishing definitive from insignificant forms has proven troublesome, perhaps possible only after the fact. More importantly, equating genre with form is tenable only within the container model of meaning. By integrating form and content within situation and context, recent work in genre theory makes genre an essential player in the making of meaning.

To begin seeing how much more than classification or textual form genre comprehends, consider what we know when, *as readers,* we recognize the genre of a text. Based on our identification of genre, we make assumptions not only about the form but also about the text's purposes, its subject matter, its writer, and its expected reader. If I open an envelope and recognize a sales letter in my hand, I understand that a company will make a pitch for its product and want me to buy it. Once I recognize that genre, I will throw the letter away or scan it for the product it is selling. If, in a different scenario, I open an envelope and find a letter from a friend, I understand immediately a different set of purposes and a different relationship between writer and reader, and I respond/read accordingly. What I understand about each of these letters and what I reflect in my response to them is much more than a set of formal features or textual conventions. Our theory of genre, therefore, must allow us to see behind particular classifications (which change as our purposes change) and forms (which trace but do not constitute genre). Genre entails purposes, participants, and themes, so understanding genre entails understanding a rhetorical and semiotic situation and a social context.

New Conceptions of Genre

To develop our new genre theory, we begin with rhetorical situation and expand it to encompass a semiotic situation and social context. One major strain of recent genre theory which connects genre to purposes, participants, and themes derives from the notion of genre as response to recurring rhetorical situation. In particular, Miller defines genres as "typified rhetorical actions based in recurrent situations" (159). Although potentially deriving from Aristotle or Burke, the connection of genre to rhetorical situation has been most frequently drawn from the 1968 work of Lloyd Bitzer. In his elaborate exploration of rhetorical situation, Bitzer refers to what happens when situations recur:

> Due to either the nature of things or convention, or both, some situations recur. . . . From day to day, year to year, comparable situations occur, prompting comparable responses; hence rhetorical forms are born and a special vocabulary, grammar, and style are established. . . . The situation recurs and, because we experience situations and the rhetorical response to them, a form of discourse is not only established but comes to have a power of its own—the tradition itself tends to function as a constraint upon any new response in the form. (13)

Genres develop, then, because they respond appropriately to situations that writers encounter repeatedly. In principle, that is, writers first respond in fitting ways and hence similarly to recurring situations; then, the similarities among those appropriate responses become established as generic conventions. In practice, of course, genres already exist and hence already constrain responses to situations. Genre's efficiency and appropriateness appear clearly in a relatively fixed genre like the lab report: its particular purposes and reader's needs can best be met by its formal features—such as a quick statement of purpose or separate methods and results sections. If all writers of lab reports use these forms, then all lab reports will respond in some appropriate ways to the needs of their situation. Even a more loosely defined genre reveals the appropriateness of generic conventions to situation. The opening of a letter to a friend, for example, just like all our everyday greetings, signals affection and maintains contact, whether the standard "Hi! How are you?" or a more original nod to the relationship. The features that genres develop respond appropriately to their situations.

If each writing problem were to require a completely new assessment of how to respond, writing would be slowed considerably. But once we recognize a recurring situation, a situation that we or others have responded to in the past, our response to that situation can be guided by past responses. Genre, thus, depends heavily on the intertextuality of discourse. As Bakhtin points out in his important essay on speech genres, a speaker "is not, after all, the first speaker, the one who disturbs the eternal silence of the universe" (69). The fact that others have responded to similar situations in the past in similar ways—the fact that genres exist—enables us to respond more easily and more appropriately ourselves. Knowing the genre, therefore, means knowing such things as appropriate subject matter, level of detail, tone, and approach as well as the usual layout and organization. Knowing the genre means knowing not only, or even most of all, how to conform to generic conventions but also how to respond appropriately to a given situation.

This straightforward connection of genre to recurring situation begins but does not complete our understanding of genre's origins, for recent theory has expanded the notion of situation. Bitzer's definition of the rhetorical situation has come under attack (see, for example, Vatz; Consigny), and his requirement of a narrowly defined rhetorical exigence as a main component of situation has been troublesome for more wide-ranging composition theory. Based on a fuller range of language behavior, B. Malinowski's concepts of context of situation and context of culture have been developed by M. A. K. Halliday and others (see, especially, Halliday and Hasan), and this conception offers perhaps the best contemporary understanding of situation. Specifically, as Halliday defines it, situation consists of a field (roughly, what is happening), a tenor (who is involved), and a mode (what role language is playing) (31–35). Those components of situation determine what Halliday calls "register," essentially the linguistic equivalent to what I and many of his followers, including Hasan, have called "genre." Like so many other important concepts in Halliday's system, register/genre is a semantic as well as functional concept. He defines it as "the configuration of semantic resources that the member of a culture typically associates with a situation type. It is the meaning potential that is accessible in a given social context" (111). Halliday's definition associates genre/register with situation type and the making of meaning, the most important elements of our reconception of genre so far. It keeps genre as a semantic and functional concept.

Even with a more comprehensive definition of situation, one problem remains with our treatment of genre as response to recurring situation: where does the "situation" come from? In light of recent nonfoundational philosophy and social construction, I would suggest that our construction of genre is what helps us to construct a situation. Genre not only responds to but also constructs recurring situation.

Context, often seen as the larger frame of situation, has long been a troubling concept for linguists and rhetoricians because, among other reasons, it is difficult to specify what context includes. Not everything about the surrounding environment (the temperature, what is happening in the next block) is relevant for the language use being considered, and some things outside the surrounding environment (potential readers, previous texts) are relevant. The concepts of context of situation and context of culture were devised in part to deal with this problem of framing. Yet, if the context of situation is not a physical fact of the surrounding environment, as it clearly is not, where does it come from? Today's answer would be that writers and readers construct it. Halliday and Hasan come close to this perspective when they write, "Any piece of text, long or short, spoken or written, will carry with it indications of its context.... This means that we reconstruct from the text certain aspects of the situation, certain features of the field, the tenor, and the mode. Given the text, we construct the situation from it" (38). In fact, the situation may exist only as writers and readers construct it. As Miller writes, "Situations are social constructs that are the result, not of 'perception,' but of 'definition'" (156), or what Halliday would call semiotic structures. Even more clearly, the recurrence of situation cannot be a material fact but rather what Miller calls "an intersubjective phenomenon, a social occurrence" (156).

We do not construct the situation directly through the text, however; rather, we reach the situation through the genre. Since genre responds to recurring situation, a text's reflection of genre indirectly reflects situation. Thus the act of constructing the genre—of creating or perceiving the formal traces of a genre—is also the act of constructing the situation. As discussed earlier, when we as readers recognize the genre of a particular text, we recognize, through the genre, its situation. Like readers, writers also construct situation by constructing genre. A writer faced with a writing task confronts multiple contexts and must define a specific context in relation to that task (teachers tells writers to "figure out who your audience is" or "state your purpose"). By selecting a genre to write in, or by beginning to write within a genre, the writer has selected the situation entailed in that genre. The assignment may ask for a letter to the editor, but the writer who begins with an inverted-triangle introduction is still writing for the teacher.

Writers and readers may, of course, mix genres and situations and may use genres badly. Consider, for example, what happens when writers or readers match genre and situation differently. A writer may try to vary the *situation*—say by treating the audience as a friend in a formal scholarly article—but the readers will likely note a change in the *genre* (either noting a flawed text that violates the genre or concluding that the writer is changing the genre). Similarly, a writer who shifts *genre* in the middle of a text causes confusion for the reader, not because the reader cannot label the genre but because the reader cannot be sure of the writer's purpose or the reader's role—cannot be sure of the *situation*. For a final example, a reader who "misreads" a text's genre—who reads "A Modest Proposal" as a serious proposal, say—most significantly misreads the situation as well. Genre and situation are so linked as to be inseparable, but it is genre that determines situation as well as situation that determines genre.

If genre not only responds to but also constructs recurring situation, then genre must be a dynamic rather than static concept. Genres *construct* and *respond* to situation; they are *actions* (see Miller). As our constructions of situations change and new situations begin to recur, genres change and new genres develop. Since situation is inherently a social as well as rhetorical concept, genres change with society, as Gunther Kress explains:

> If genre is entirely imbricated in other social processes, it follows that unless we view society itself as static, then neither social structures, social processes, nor therefore genres are static. Genres are dynamic, responding to the dynamics of other parts of social systems. Hence genres change historically; hence new genres emerge over time, and hence, too, what appears as 'the same' generic form at one level has recognizably distinct forms in differing social groups. (42)

Dynamic genres are also fluid rather than rigid, are possible responses that writers choose and even combine to suit their situations. "The wealth and diversity of speech genres are boundless," Bakhtin writes, "because the various possibilities of human activity are inexhaustible, and because each sphere of activity contains an entire repertoire of speech genres that differentiate and grow as the particular sphere develops and becomes more complex" ("Problem" 60). The connection to social spheres and groups has led some to tie genre to the constructions of a discourse community, a promising connection developed most fruitfully by John Swales in his 1990 book on genre. Whether through discourse communities or some other social frame, genre must respond dynamically to human behavior and social changes.

One concern that has been raised in the past is that genre can become deterministic. Especially for such a social view of genre as this, some worry that the individual writer no longer matters. The split between the individual and society, however, is another false dichotomy that our new conception of genre can help to resolve. Denigrating genre became popular with the glorification of the individual, a romantic strain in literary criticism that considers genre and previous texts as constraints, as something that great writers must transcend, as producing anxiety for the writer. Yet an opposing trend has seen the inherent intertextuality of all writing, has discerned that T. S. Eliot's "historical sense" enriches rather than constrains the individual writer. Writers work creatively within the frame of past texts and given genres just as they work within the frame of a given language.

It is indeed true that "the single utterance, with all its individuality and creativity, can in no way be regarded as a *completely free combination* of forms of language" (Bakhtin, "Problem" 81). Genres are existing and somewhat normative constructs, some more rigid than others, but so too are all language forms. All language constrains the individual to the extent that language is an existing set of forms; however, as Bakhtin points out, "Speech genres are much more changeable, flexible, and plastic than language forms are" ("Problems" 80). Language and genre constrain but do not eliminate the individual writer. As constituents of society, individuals create language and create genre. Being part of society enables individuals to change society, and hence to change genres, for genres, as Volosinov/Bakhtin writes, "exhibit an extraordinary sensitivity to all fluctuations in the social atmosphere" (20). Individuals may, of course, combine different genres or may "violate" the norms of an existing genre, thereby confirming that genre's existence and potentially changing it. (See discussions in Todorov, Derrida, and Freadman.) Working within existing genres as well, individuals choose and create: even the most rigid genre requires some choices, and the more common genres contain substantial flexibility within their bounds. Ultimately, as Frances Christie writes in her article "Genres as Choice," "Capacity to recognise, interpret and write genres is capacity to exercise choice" (32). Individuals choose within linguistic and generic conventions, and they create and recreate the society that those conventions reflect. Although genre thus is a social concept and construct, it also clarifies the nature of individual choices. Again, genre proves the dichotomy false.

In sum, genre is a dynamic response to and construction of recurring situation, one that changes historically and in different social groups, that adapts and grows as the social context changes. This new conception of genre has managed to overcome several dichotomies in our understanding of language use and writing. In reuniting genre and situation, it reunites text and context, each constructing and responding to the other in a semiotic interchange. Form and function are both inherent in genre, as are form and content. Miller explains that genre semiotically fuses the syntactic, semantic, and pragmatic. Sigmund Ongstad has genre fusing the form, content, and function. Genre is both the product and the process that creates it. Genre is what Bakhtin calls "the *whole* of the utterance" ("Problem" 60), a unity and a unifier.

This new conception of genre helps us to see how individual writers and individual texts work, then, by removing us one level from the individual and particular. Genre is an abstraction or generality once removed from the concrete or particular. Not as abstract as Saussurian notions of *langue* or language system, genre mediates between *langue* and *parole*, between the language and the utterance. Not as removed as situation, genre mediates between text and context. Not as general as meaning, genre mediates between form and content. Genre is patterns and relationships, essentially semiotic ones, that are constructed when writers and groups of writers identify different writing tasks as being similar. Genre constructs and responds to recurring situation, becoming visible through perceived patterns in the syntactic, semantic, and pragmatic features of particular texts. Genre is truly, therefore, a maker of meaning.

Implications

So what does such a reconception of genre do for us as composition scholars and teachers? For our scholarship, a new conception of genre might fill some significant gaps in our existing theories of writing.[2] We have already seen how genre can help us to reintegrate several dichotomies in our view of writing. Most particular to genre theory might be the better reintegration of form with content and of text with context, the former a longstanding marriage we still struggle to explain to others, the latter a more recent split whose divorce we are just beginning to contest. Can we speak of context apart from text? Contexts are always textualized. Through genre we can speak of both, as do many scholars who study particular genres in particular communities (such as Bazerman and Myers, in their studies of the experimental article in science and articles in biology, respectively). Studies of particular genres and of particular genre sets (as, for example, the research-process genres in Swales, or the genre sets of tax accountants in Devitt, "Intertextuality") can reveal a great deal about the communities which construct and use those genres, and studies of particular texts within those genres can reveal a great deal about the choices writers make.

The reintegration of product and process that this new genre theory enables can clarify the value of studying products or texts, but it also can contribute to our understanding of process and text-making. Some of the longstanding (and often unspoken) questions about writing processes can be addressed through considering genre's role. Two such questions will illustrate: Where do writers goals come from? How do writers know what to change when they are revising?

One of the classic articles on writing processes, Linda Flower and John Hayes's 1981 article "A Cognitive Process Theory of Writing," might have had a different emphasis had a better understanding of genre been well shared when it was written. Flower and Hayes concentrated in part on how writers generate and regenerate goals. In one paragraph, they acknowledge a small role for genre:

> but we should not forget that many writing goals are well-learned, standard ones stored in memory. For example, we would expect many writers to draw automatically on those goals associated with writing in general, such as, "interest the reader," or "start with an introduction," or on goals associated with a given genre, such as making a jingle rhyme. These goals will often be so basic that they won't even be consciously considered or expressed. And the more experienced the writer the greater this repertory of semi-automatic plans and goals will be. (381)

With our new conception of genre, we would agree that "well-learned, standard" goals are "so basic that they won't even be consciously considered or expressed," and that more experienced writers will be well-stocked with "semiautomatic plans and goals." However, rather than being uninteresting because unconscious and rather than being trivial ("such as making a jingle rhyme"), these "basic" and "well-learned" generic goals may be the stuff of which all writing goals (at least partly) are made. Bakhtin ("Problem"), for example describes "primary" speech genres, which are the culturally established building blocks of more complex "secondary" genres, most written genres being secondary genres. To understand the situational and social constructs behind such primary and secondary genres may be to understand more deeply the goals that writers have and the forces at work in their generation and regeneration. Understanding writing processes, then, must include understanding generic goals: what they are—the historical, community, and rhetorical forces that shape them—how writers learn them, and how writers use them.

Similarly, a better understanding of genre may help us understand better how writers know when and what to revise. As an important part of revision, scholars have described the perception of dissonance, between intention and text or between intention and execution (see, for example, Sommers; and Flower and Hayes). But James Reither asserts that "Composition studies does not seriously attend. . . to the knowing without which cognitive dissonance is impossible" (142). A large part of that "knowing" must be knowing genres. How, Flower and her coauthors ask, "can we say that a writer detects a dissonance or a failed comparison between text and intention when the second side of the equation, an 'ideal' or 'correct' or intended text doesn't exist—when there is no template to 'match' the current text against?" (27). Genre might provide at least part of that template, might provide at least part of the writer's notion of the ideal text. If a writer has chosen to write a particular genre, then the writer has chosen a template, a situation and an appropriate reflection of that situation in sets of forms.[3] In revising, a writer may check the situation and forms of the evolving text against those of the chosen genre: where there is a mismatch, there is dissonance. Genre by no means solves the problem of determining why writers revise what they do; but without genre a complete solution to the problem is impossible.

As these brief discussions of goals and dissonance illustrate, studies of writing processes and cognitive perspectives on writing must take genre into account. In fact, researchers most interested in the cognition of individual writers can make essential contributions to genre theory by studying how writers learn and use a variety of genres. The creation, transmission, and modification of genres can be studied further by those most interested in social and rhetorical perspectives on writing.

As mentioned earlier, many scholars studying nonacademic discourse have used genre as a variable, even as a controlling concept for understanding the community. In my study of tax accountants' writing ("Intertextuality"), for example, understanding the group's values, assumptions, and beliefs is enhanced by understanding the set of genres they use, their appropriate situations and formal traits, and what those genres mean to them. Swales develops the fullest and most complex treatment of genre's relationship to discourse communities in his important book *Genre Analysis*. His significant work embedding genre in discourse communities can be extended and developed by others, if we can resolve such discourse-community issues as the nature of the community, overlapping communities, and writers participating in multiple communities. In fact, the same kind of semiotic interchange that is so useful for understanding genre may help us to understand discourse community. Just as genres construct situations and situations construct genres, discourse may construct communities and communities construct discourse. Thus, rather than looking at human membership to define community, perhaps discourse membership—that is, genre sets—can better define the nature and constitution of a discourse community, just as the community, better defines the nature of the discourse.

As someone who has been working on understanding genre for many years, I, of course, see the potential benefits of genre in virtually every article or book I read on composition theory and teaching. Studies of the relationship between reading and writing need to acknowledge that genre connects readers and writers, both their products and their processes, and need to investigate how their interpretations of genre vary (or do not). Research on assessment and on assignments needs to consider the power of differing generic demands to influence results. Judith A. Langer, for example, found that "genre distinctions were stronger than grade distinctions in their effects on student writing" (167). Researchers of basic writing need to go beyond the forms of academic genres to see their situational constructs, with ideologies and roles that may pose conflicts for some basic writers. A study of Athabaskans, a group of Alaskan Indians, discussed by Michael B. Prince, found that learning to write a new genre "implied cultural and personal values that conflicted with pre-existing patterns of thought and behavior" (741). Christie goes so far as to assert that "Those who fail in schools are those who fail to master the genres of schooling: the ways of structuring and of dealing with experience which schools value in varying ways" ("Language" 24).

Although it may be premature to outline full programs, many powerful revolutions in our teaching might develop from a better understanding of genre. Teachers of writing need to discover how to teach novices the situations and forms of the genres they will need without undermining the wholeness of a genre. Aviva Freedman's research suggests that some novices may learn to write particular genres without explicit instruction, even ignoring explicit feedback. Richard M. Coe, on the other hand, argues for making all such models conscious "so that we may use them critically instead of habitually" ("Rhetoric" 11). Research needs to be done to discover the most effective techniques of translating our better genre theory into better writing instruction and thence into practice.

Even as we await more substantial knowledge of how novices can best learn and use genres, we can use the new conception of genre to improve our teaching, especially our diagnosis and treatment of students' problems. Since the genre constructs the situation, students will not be able to respond appropriately to assigned situations unless they know the appropriate genre. What we often diagnose as ignorance of a situation or inability to imagine themselves in another situation may in fact be ignorance of a genre or inability to write a genre they have not sufficiently read: they may feel great love but be unable to write a love sonnet. Conversely, since genre and situation are mutually constructive, what we diagnose as inability to write a particular genre may in fact be unfamiliarity with the genre's situation: students may know the genre of letters to the editor in a superficial way, but if they have never felt the need to write such a letter—if they have never experienced the situation—they may be incapable of writing one that appropriately responds to that situation. When we create assignments and as we evaluate responses to them we must consider both their situational and generic demands.

Once we acknowledge genre as more than a formal constraint on writers but rather an essential component of making meaning, we might find it influencing other notions that we teach. Prewriting and revising processes probably differ for different genres, since those genres represent different situations, including constraints. Certainly, teaching students how to define their audiences and purposes would change under a new notion of genre since it would be clear that selecting a genre would automatically narrow the possibilities for audience and purpose; conversely, wanting to address a particular audience and purpose constrains one's choice of genre. Newly conceived genres should, of course, serve the final death notice to the modes as a classification system. Even usage standards might be most clearly explained through genre, as sets of language forms that are a small part of the larger conventions of some genres deriving from particular situations. Depending on our individual theories of writing and teaching, we may still value originality above all, or self-expression, or clarity, or correctness; but we may no longer ignore the fact that genre operates as a force on our students as they try to meet our expectations.

In spite of what my genre-colored glasses show me, genre may not be the answer to all of our dilemmas in composition theory and teaching. But only by ignoring what writers themselves recognize can we ignore the significance of genre. This new theory of genre reveals and explains the centrality of genre to writing, its importance to understanding how writers and writing work. It also suggests how we might develop an integrated, unified theory of writing. With a unified theory of genre, we can reintegrate text and context, form and content, process and product, reading and writing, individual and social. In the end, genre's ability to capture both form and situation, both constraint and choice, may capture the essence of writing as well.

Notes

1. This article was supported in part by the University of Kansas general research allocation #3629-0038. I would like to thank those who gave me many helpful comments on an earlier draft of this article: Richard Coe, Aviva Freedman, James Hartman, Michael Johnson, Pat McQueeney, and the anonymous readers for *CCC*.

2. See Devitt, "Genre" for a discussion of the implications of a new genre theory for the study of language.

3. The notion of genre as template might be indebted to schemata theory and script theory. These theories, as rich as they are for understanding the complexities of human conventions, may have been a necessary precursor to this understanding of generic conventions.

Works Cited

Bakhtin, M. M. "Discourse in the Novel." *The Dialogic Imagination: Four Essays by M. M. Bakhtin*. Ed. Michael Holquist. Trans. Caryl Emerson and Michael Holquist. Austin and London: U of Texas P, 1981. 259–422.

———. "The Problem of Speech Genres." *Speech Genres and Other Late Essays*. Ed. Caryl Emerson and Michael Holquist. Trans. Vern W. McGee. Austin: U of Texas P, 1986. 60–102.

Bazerman, Charles. *Shaping Written Knowledge: The Genre and Activity of the Experimental Article in Science*. Madison: U of Wisconsin P, 1988.

Bitzer, Lloyd F. "The Rhetorical Situation." *Philosophy and Rhetoric* 1 (Winter 1968): 1–14.

Campbell, Karlyn Kohrs, and Kathleen Hall Jamieson, eds. *Form and Genre: Shaping Rhetorical Action*. Falls Church: Speech Communication Association, 1978.

Christie, Frances. "Genres as Choice." Reid 22–34.

———. "Language and Schooling." *Language, Schooling, and Society*. Ed. Stephen N. Tchudi. Upper Montclair: Boynton/Cook, 1984. 21–40.

Coe, Richard M. "An Apology for Form; or, Who Took the Form Out of the Process?" *College English* 49 (Jan. 1987): 13–28.

———. "Rhetoric 2001." *Freshman English News* 3.1 (Spring 1974): 1–13.

Consigny, Scott. "Rhetoric and Its Situations." *Philosophy and Rhetoric* 7 (Summer 1974): 175–86.

Derrida, Jacques. "The Law of Genre." Trans. Avital Ronell. *Critical Inquiry* 7 (Autumn 1980): 55–82.

Devitt, Amy J. "Genre as Textual Variable: Some Historical Evidence from Scots and American English." *American Speech* 64 (Winter 1989): 291–303.

———. "Intertextuality in Tax Accounting: Generic, Referential, and Functional." *Textual Dynamics of the Professions: Historical and Contemporary Studies of Writing in Professional Communities*. Ed. Charles Bazerman and James Paradis. Madison: U of Wisconsin P, 1991. 336–57.

Flower, Linda, and John R. Hayes. "A Cognitive Process Theory of Writing." *College Composition and Communication* 32 (Dec. 1981): 365–87.

Flower, Linda, et al. "Detection, Diagnosis, and the Strategies of Revision." *College Composition and Communication* 37 (Feb. 1986): 16–55.

Freadman, Anne. "Anyone for Tennis?" Reid 91–124.

Freedman, Aviva. "Learning to Write Again: Discipline-Specific Writing at University." *Carleton Papers in Applied Language Studies* 4 (1987): 95–115.

Halliday, M. A. K. *Language as Social Semiotic: The Social Interpretation of Language and Meaning*. London: Edward Arnold, 1978.

Halliday, M. A. K., and Ruqaiya Hasan. *Language, Context, and Text: Aspects of Language in a Social-Semiotic Perspective*. 2nd ed. Oxford: Oxford UP, 1989.

Jamieson, Kathleen "Antecedent Genre as Rhetorical Constraint." *Quarterly Journal of Speech* 61 (Dec. 1975): 406–15.

Kress, Gunther. "Genre in a Social Theory of Language: A Reply to John Dixon." Reid 35–45.

Langer, Judith A. "Children's Sense of Genre: A Study of Performance on Parallel Reading and Writing Tasks." *Written Communication* 2 (Apr. 1985): 157–87.

Malinowski, B. "The Problem of Meaning in Primitive Languages." Supplement I. *The Meaning of Meaning: A Study of the Influence of Language upon Thought and of the Science of Symbolism*. C. K. Ogden and I. A. Richards. 10th ed. New York: Harcourt and London: Routledge, 1952. 296–336.

Miller, Carolyn R. "Genre As Social Action." *Quarterly Journal of Speech* 70 (May 1984): 151–67.

Myers, Greg. *Writing Biology: Texts in the Social Construction of Scientific Knowledge*. Madison: U of Wisconsin P, 1990.

Ongstad, Sigmund. "The Definition of Genre and the Didactics of Genre." Rethinking Genre Colloquium. Ottawa, April 1992.

Prince, Michael B. "Literacy and Genre: Toward a Pedagogy of Mediation." *College English* 51 (Nov. 1989): 730–49.

Reid, Ian, ed. *The Place of Genre in Learning: Current Debates*. Deakin University: Centre for Studies in Literary Education, 1987.

Reither, James A. "Writing and Knowing: Toward Redefining the Writing Process." *College English* 47 (Oct. 1985): 620–28. Rpt. in *The Writing Teachers' Sourcebook*. Ed. Gary Tate and Edward P. J. Corbett. 2nd ed. New York: Oxford UP, 1988. 140–48.

Sommers, Nancy. "Revision Strategies of Student Writers and Experienced Adult Writers." *College Composition and Communication* 31 (Dec. 1980): 378–88.

Swales, John M. *Genre Analysis: English in Academic and Research Settings*. Cambridge: Cambridge UP, 1990.

Titunik, I. R. "The Formal Method and the Sociological Method (M. M. Baxtin, P. N. Medvedev, V. N. Volosinov) in Russian Theory and Study of Literature." Volosinov [Bakhtin] 175–200.

Todorov, Tzvetan. *Genres in Discourse*. Trans. Catherine Porter. Cambridge: Cambridge UP, 1990.

Vatz, Richard. "The Myth of the Rhetorical Situation." *Philosophy and Rhetoric* 6 (Summer 1973): 154–61.

Volosinov, V. N. [M. M. Bakhtin]. *Marxism and the Philosophy of Language*. Trans. Ladislav Matejka and I. R. Titunik. Cambridge and London: Harvard UP, 1986.

7

Voice

Darsie Bowden

> This chapter discusses the perplexing concept of "voice," exam-
> ining what we mean when we talk about voice in writing and the
> relationship between voice and style.

One is hard pressed to avoid the mention of the term *voice* in talk about the
teaching and learning of writing. Teachers of writing, professional writers,
and students use it, generally to describe a feature or set of features of style
in writing. Sometimes *stance* or *persona* can be substituted for voice; other
times, it is *style* or *tone*. A longtime critic of voice, I rail against its use in my
courses. Despite this, the term invariably emerges, often sheepishly from
one of my students and, more frequently than I'd like to admit, from me
as I stumble over my own inability to describe what I mean. What *do* we
mean when we talk about voice in writing? What is understood by finding
your own voice when you write? What relationship does voice have with *style?*
Perhaps most important, why might voice be valuable and why might it be
problematic?

Voice is a metaphor—a very powerful one. Metaphors, by their very nature, enable us to talk about abstract concepts (such as *love, war, time,* or
argument) that are difficult if not impossible to talk about in any other way.
When we talk about argument, for example, battle metaphors often seem
to creep in: "She challenged John and trounced him in the debate," or "I
attacked him in open court and was victorious," or "The two sides could
never agree and remain in an uneasy truce." *Writing* is no different. Despite
the concreteness of production—you take a pen or computer and produce
tangible text—composing text is as abstract and mysterious as love, war, or
argument.

But as valuable and necessary as metaphors are in enabling us to understand phenomena, they also lead us down certain conceptual pathways that severely limit our perceptions. For example, framing argument in battle- or war-like terms suggests that when we argue we are in a contest, the goal of which is to win; the objective is conquest. But we could also consider argument as a method to engage in an exchange of differing points of view or the bringing together and sorting through of opinions that can help both parties come to new understandings. Here, argument is not a battleground, but, rather, a meeting place where the players are partners—not opponents.

So what avenues of perception does the use of voice open up when we refer to "voice in writing" and what does it foreclose? It helps to know where the concept of "voice" comes from.

A LITTLE HISTORY

Despite the frequency and effortlessness with which voice is used today, it hasn't always been part of our lexicon about writing. T. S. Eliot used it in his 1943 in his essay, "The Three Voices of Poetry. On Poetry and Poets" where he asserts that:

> [I]n writing [nondramatic] verse, I think that one is writing, so to speak, in terms of one's own voice: the way it sounds when you read it to yourself is the test. For it is yourself speaking. The question of communication, of what the reader will get from it, is not paramount... (p. 100)

But its first chronicled use in composition studies occurred, according to Walker Gibson, at the Dartmouth Conference in 1966 (See chapter 1) and became very popular in articles and essays about composition and composition classrooms in the 1970s, in which teachers were exhorted to help students find their own voices in their writing.

As Irene Clark points out in chapter 1, the voice movement paralleled the process movement; some of the strongest supporters of process were also leading advocates of voice (Peter Elbow, Donald Stewart, Walker Gibson, and Ken Macrorie). And as with the process movement, voice was often associated with the so-called "expressionist school," which wasn't really a school at all, but rather a groundswell of sentiment reacting against traditional ways of teaching writing and toward self-expression. Traditional ways of teaching that most dismayed voice promoters included a primary focus on grammar and mechanics, the compartmentalizing of style into discrete categories (word, sentence, and paragraph), and the emphasis on style at the expense of self-expression and other aspects of discourse. (See Berlin's 1987) definition of *current-traditional rhetoric* in *Rhetoric and Reality: Writing Instruction in American Colleges, 1900–1985*.) Voicists argued that this kind of focus on form created a teaching and learning environment that stifled students' interest and left them with no option but to write boring, tedious, and listless prose. As a result, students emerged from their writing classes able to produce writing that was flawless mechanically, but which also seemed to indicate that they clearly had nothing to say.

Trends in composition tend to follow trends in politics. The 1960s and early 1970s were particularly volatile years in American history. There was trouble on college campuses in response to the unpopular and ultimately unsuccessful Vietnam War. The inner cities became much more explosive and dangerous then in previous decades as minorities and lower socioeconomic groups felt increasingly disenfranchised and excluded from the American ideal of prosperity and justice for all. Racism and poverty exacerbated conditions in a number of schools, which were already wretched and ineffective places to learn. The institutionalized government, business, and the university bureaucracies not only invited little confidence but also were presumed to be destructive to social values of individualism, personal expression, equality, and freedom. Hence, outlets for self-expression in writing were suddenly highly valued. It is small wonder that both the process movement (which paid attention to how writing was produced) and voice (which privileged the expression of emotions, passions, ideals, and a writer's inner character) not only took hold but also became quickly entrenched.

Certainly, individualism and self-expression were not new phenomena; they have been part of American identity since pre-Revolutionary War days. But trends both in education and in politics tended to force those values to a back burner. In 1957, the Soviet launched the Sputnik rocket, making the Soviet Union the first country to enter outer space. As a consequence, the United States decided it needed to dramatically improve its educational system—particularly the sciences—to catch up. There ensued an infusion of funding for the sciences from which the other liberal arts, including English, were initially excluded. To compete with the sciences, English quickly redefined itself in more scientific terms. What emerged were programs that led students through a clearly and strictly specified sequence of literary works, designed primarily to promote a thorough knowledge of the power of American heritage. The progressive movement in education— which gained popularity in the 1920s and focused on individual interests, skills, and adjustment—was reviled and abandoned in favor of this new curriculum, which Applebee called the "academic" approach, an approach that was not unlike the "back to basics" lobbying that seems to be a familiar part of educational rhetoric today.

Thus, as historical trends most often are, the move to expressivism was essentially a reaction against what had existed previously, both politically and in the writing classroom. The strong connections between political trends and what is going on in composition is of critical important in understanding the shifts and permutations in public and theoretical perceptions of writing and literacy, and the move to expressivism is no exception.

SELF-EXPRESSION IN THE WRITING CLASSROOM

What were the early explanations of voice in writing? In 1969, Robert Zoellner laid out his "Talk-Write" pedagogy in a well-known essay in *College English* where he attempted to explain the writer's voice:

> A striking characteristic of many students' verbal behavior is that they 'sound' one way when talking, and quite another way when writing. If they have a consistent 'voice' at all, it is in the speech area. In contrast, their writing is simply congeries of words, entirely lacking in any distinguishing 'voice.' One of the objectives of the talk-write pedagogy is to overcome this modal distinction: on the one hand, the rapid alternation between vocal and scribal activity should lead to a reshaping and vitalizing of the scribal modes, so that the students' written 'voice' begins to take on some of the characteristics of the speaking 'voice.' (p. 301)

Peter Elbow, one of most vocal and persuasive proponents of voice in the 1970s and 1980s, portrayed his concept of voice as "what most people have in their speech but lack in their writing—namely, a sound or texture—the sound of 'them'" (*Writing With Power: Techniques for Mastering the Writing Process,* 1981, p. 288). A reader knows that she has encountered the writer's real voice, Elbow continued, when she feels a "resonance" not necessarily with the writer, but with "the words and themselves" (p. 300). With Zoellner and Elbow, we have some of key components of early voice pedagogy, that of lending to writing the kind of identifiable imprint that the spoken voice has. In so doing, the writer's voice can be "heard" in the reading of her work; that voice is unique and consequently more compelling.

This perspective maintained that writers could find their own voice writing if they trusted themselves and did the appropriate exercises. Among the activities that Elbow suggested to facilitate the discerning of one's voice was "freewriting," usually a timed writing done *without* the reader in mind, in other words, before presentation. Because writing for an audience can potentially change a writer's voice and undermine a writer's power, it's advisable to begin without imagining a reader. Freewriting is intended to be truly free. There are no rules because there is no reader; it doesn't even necessarily need to make sense. It is a way for the writer to get at what he truly feels, to generate ideas that are his alone, to explore—or to find—his own words (his voice) on paper without risk.

Ken Macrorie's complaint about "Engfish" (see chaper 1) raised another aspect of the voice movement. "Engfish," Macrorie explained in *Telling*

Writing (1985) lacks life, spontaneity, dynamism, and authenticity. The typical example of Engfish is standard academic writing in which students attempt to replicate the style and form of their professors. By contrast, writing with voice has life because it's ostensibly connected to a real speaker—the student writer herself. Here's what Macrorie said about a particular student paper that has voice:

> In that paper, a truthtelling voice speaks, and its rhythms rush and build like the human mind travelling at high speed. Rhythm, rhythm, the best writing depends so much upon it. But as in dancing, you can't get rhythm by giving yourself directions. You must feel the music and let your body take its instructions. Classrooms aren't usually rhythmic places. (p. 160)

The "truthtelling voice" is the authentic one. Good writers are authentic because they tap into their inner selves. Here is how Donald Stewart described that authenticity in *The Authentic Voice: A Pre-Writing Approach to Student Writing* (1972):

> Your authentic voice is that authorial voice which sets you apart from every living human being despite the number of common or shared experiences you have with many others: it is not a copy of someone else's way of speaking or of perceiving the world. It is your way. Because you were born at a certain time, in a certain place, to certain parents, with a particular position in the family structure, you have a unique perception of your experience. All the factors of your environment plus your native intelligence and particular response to that environment differentiate you from every other person in the world. Now the closer you come to rendering your particular perception of your world in your words, the closer you will come to finding your authentic voice. (pp. 2–3)

The valuing of the individual, both her experience and what she feels and thinks is still intoxicating, but in the volatile period of the 60s and 70s, it struck just the right chord with students learning to write. No longer would they be forced to replicate the stilted prose of status quo writing on topics that might have been "good for them" but about which they had no interest and could see no relevance. Instead, their own lives and words were validated. The classrooms were to become their own.

VOICE AS ROLE PLAYING

Another permutation of the authentic voice emerged during this period as well, one that emphasized the representation of emotion and feeling in the classroom through drama and role playing. The concept can be traced to a new pedagogical model of the classroom imported from Great Britain in the late 1960s; it is an important one because it is the precursor of how voice evolved in the latter part of the last century (1980s & 1990s). This concept, defined below, conferred less value on the authentic individual voice than on the taking on of a voice for particular occasions (Gibson, 1969):

> [I]t is as if the author, as he "puts on his act" for a reader, wore a kind of disguise, taking on, for a particular purpose, a character who speaks to the reader. This persona may or may not bear considerable resemblance to the real author, sitting there at his typewriter; in any case, the created speaker is certainly less complex than his human inventor. He is inferred entirely out of the language; everything we know about him comes from the words before us on the page. In this respect he is a made man, he is artificial. (pp. 3–4)

Thus, in the service of conveying a message to an audience, voice—or persona—is created for specific rhetorical occasions, a concept stemming from the notion of *ethos* in classical rhetoric. Gibson's voice is constructed by "design" to change a reader's mind. Contrast this with Elbow's conception in *Writing Without Teachers* (1973):

> In your natural way of producing words there is a sound, a texture, a rhythm—a voice—which is the main source of power in your writing. I don't know how it works, but this voice is the force that will make a reader listen to you, the energy that drives the meanings through his thick skull. Maybe you don't *like* your voice; maybe people have made fun of it. But it's the only voice you've got. It's your only source of power.... If you keep writing in it, it may change into something you like better. But if you abandon it, you'll likely never have a voice and never be heard. (pp. 6–7)

Just as the spoken voice has the rhythm, tone, and intonations of the individual speaker, so can writing—and this, for Elbow, represents rhetorical power. Creating or designing a speaking voice does not seem to have a place here; it seems antithetical to the concept of one's "natural" voice.

More recently, the use of voice has tended to echo Walker Gibson rather than Peter Elbow. Here is a fairly typical presentation of voice in a writing textbook (*Work in Progress: A Guide to Writing and Revising*) by Lisa Ede (1989):

> Just as you dress differently on different occasions, as a writer you assume different voices in different situations. If you're writing an essay about a personal experience, you may work hard to create a strong personal voice in your essay.... If you're writing a report or essay exam, you adopt a more formal, public tone. Whatever the situation, the choices you make as you write and revise... will determine how readers interpret and respond to your presence in the text. (p. 158)

Note the absence of any reference to authentic voice. For Ede, voice is created for specific rhetorical occasions and is not necessarily a phenomena stemming from the author's character or inner being. Even so, authentic voice proponents are certainly not extinct, and there are, I would argue, important reasons why this is true, which I will cover in the next section.

CRITIQUE OF VOICE

Major developments emerged with the voice movement that have dramatically changed the composition classroom for the better. These include the emphasis on the writing process (see chapter 1) and on collaborative work where students learn to rely on readers other than the teacher, creating for themselves environments that are less oppressive and threatening. Concomitant with this is the reduction of the teacher's authority in controlling every aspect of the writing classroom, resulting (to some degree) in the relegation of more responsibility to the student.

Up through 1960, personal writing was primarily considered the means to an end; that end was expository writing—critical, analytical, and argumentative writing that was both formal and academic (see Robert Connors, 1987). Personal writing served as invention or prewriting for the more valued type of texts, and was intended to help students write more fluidly in formal exposition. By contrast, the voice period helped us to conceive of personal writing as a legitimate endproduct and its value was reinforced by other studies, including Janet Emig's *The Composing Process of Twelfth Graders* (1971) where she argued for the value of reflexive (or personal) writing in the classroom, not only to get writers to write but also as a necessary component of the writer's development. Ultimately, the voice pedagogy introduced into the composition classroom the kinds of changes that were going on in politics and society: mistrust of the status quo; attention to the individual writer, especially those traditionally in marginalized social groups; and, in some sense, a politicization of the composition classroom.

Since the 1970s, voice has been appropriated to refer to a variety of textual phenomena including register, style, persona, and tone. It has been used by activists from a range of marginalized groups, including women, African Americans, Native Americans, and other minorities to talk about power—both political and discursive.

But voice has also come under attack, particularly the notion of authentic voice, for a variety of reasons. In his 1987 article in *College Composition and Communication,* Hashimoto argued that the "evangelical" approach taken by some voice enthusiasts, notably Peter Elbow, promoted a kind of anti-intellectualism, particularly in the way voice proponents urged students to tap into their emotional selves for their writing, often consciously ignoring— even if temporarily—the intellectual and discursive values of the community within which they were writing. Others have questioned whether it is even possible to have one "true" voice and if this, indeed, leads to power in writing, as voice proponents have claimed.

As a metaphor, voice locates the source of its explanatory power in the human voice, which is audible, measurable, and identifiable. In the history of Western tradition beginning with Plato, the spoken voice was often understood as being closer to thought and an authentic self. However, although a writer himself, Plato dismissed writing as inferior to speech (see the *Phaedrus* dialogue) because, he argued, without the give and take of conversation, we cannot get at "truth"; we cannot truly understand the world. Writing, according to Plato, only gives us the semblance of permanence or objective truth and, consequently, is misleading and ultimately dangerous.

Furthermore, our spoken voice is one of the key features that identifies us and distinguishes us from others. Voice has often been considered to have presence, the presence of the speaker. It is in that presence that listeners can sense (or not sense) authenticity, genuineness, and passion. For many people, it follows then, that for writing to have presence, it must also have voice. Writing with presence is powerful writing; it resonates with the reader.

The idea that spoken language more accurately reflects thought than writing, has been, since the late 1970s, a source of controversy. French philosopher Jacques Derrida (1976) argued that Western thought (including Platonic thought) presumes an ultimate point of reference, a transcendent truth that language—the spoken word or *phoné*—can express:

> Within ... logos [voice, speech, reason], the original and essential link to the *phoné* has never been broken .... As has been more or less implicitly determined, the essence of the *phoné* would be immediately proximate to that which within "thought" as logos relates to "meaning," produces it, receives it, speaks it, "composes" it. If, for Aristotle, for example, "spoken words are the symbols of mental experience and written words are the symbols of spoken words," (*De interpretatione, 1,* 16a3) it is because the voice, producer of the first symbols, has a relationship of essential and immediate proximity with the mind. (Derrida, 1976, p. 11)

For many Western thinkers, voice has interiority—that is, "proximity" to the self; voice is the closest thing to being. Derrida maintains, however, that the spoken language is merely a set of symbols or signs that only vaguely (and inadequately) represent reality. Writing, as symbols representing spoken language, is even further removed, and the relationship between language and thought or meaning is not stable, as Western philosophers would have us believe. Both speech and writing give us the illusion of presence, but it is illusion only.

Derrida goes even further to argue that language (spoken or written) cannot express consciousness. In fact, it works the other way around: Language makes consciousness possible. This reversal in thinking "deconstructs" Western assumptions about the function and primacy of consciousness and language. This movement, called *deconstruction,* is a fundamental component of postmodernism, which has been a major influence on the teaching of writing and the consideration of texts since the 1980s. It serves, among other things, to shift the emphasis from the author as the purveyor of meaning (and owner of the voice) and from text (as meaningful) to the rhetorical situation in which text, author, context, audience, and purpose all influence meaning, making language much more unstable. Voice is definable and recognizable where deconstruction tends to move us the other direction, toward plurality, instability, and disintegration that comes from understanding writing from perspectives other than the author's. The implications for teaching writing are important. In the postmodern classroom—influenced by the project of deconstruction—writing does not originate and end with the author, but is subject to multiple forces that motivate the act of writing. Hence, writers must consider the context, purpose, and reader for their writing, and must also assume that texts cannot be simply conduits for the writer's intentions ... or voice. (For an excellent discussion of deconstruction, see Sharon Crowley's *A Teacher's Introduction to Deconstruction* (1989).)

Nonetheless, the notion of voice remains very popular. In much of the recent work on voice, concerted efforts—particularly in Kathleen Yancey's volume on voice, *Voices on Voice: Perspectives, Definitions, Inquiry* (1994)—have been made to reconfigure voice to make it fit in a postmodern (which embodies deconstruction), technological, and multicultural era. Drawing in part on M. M. Bakhtin's use of multiple voices (*The Dialogic Imagination,* 1981)—and his notion of heteroglossia in discourse—theorists, teachers, and textbooks now generally acknowledge that writers may not have one true voice, but, rather, many voices, each used for particular occasions and with particular audiences. Still, a writer's voice should be consistent, unified, and stable, if only for that rhetorical instance. And in a remarkable essay in the Yancey volume, Randall Freisinger argues for working toward a synthesis of expressionist and postmodern attitudes toward voice.

Even so, the continued use of voice in writing pedagogy seens to be an attempt to fit a square peg into a round hole. Efforts to reconfigure the voice metaphor into an environment that has significantly changed since the 1960s patches together important conflicts that are not so easily conflated. Among these conflicts are the nature of speaking and writing, differing individual and social perspectives on rhetoric, and even differences between literary and expository writing. (For more on this, see Bowden, *The Mythology of Voice,* 1999). To explore the problem of voice in the theoretical and pedagogical climate of the new century, two examples are given here, one from women's studies and the other from electronic technology, to suggest just how perplexing voice has become in the face of some potentially much more powerful metaphors.

OTHER METAPHORS: WOMEN'S STUDIES

It is not uncommon in women's studies and feminist studies to assert that women have long been deprived of having a voice in politics and society. Well-known books such as Belenky, Clinchy, Goldberger, and Tarule's *Women's Ways of Knowing* (1986) and Carol Gilligan's *In a Different Voice: Psychological Theory and Women's Development* (1993) make much of women's voices. Gilligan, in particular, uses voice to mean a kind of communicative energy that emanates from deep inside a person, from the heart of a person's being. Voice, she explained is "something like what people mean when they speak of the core of the self ... [it is] a powerful psychological instrument and channel, connecting inner and outer worlds" (Gilligan, 1993, p. 178).

In *Women's Ways of Knowing,* many of the women interviewed by the authors talk about their desire to find their voice, a voice that will be heard, presumably in a world that is populated with other, often male voices that tend to drown out theirs. These uses of voice have considerable resonance with the way voice was used in the 1970s. Perhaps it is true that finding one's voice and using that voice leads to power in a male-dominated society where having a voice is seen to be the source of that power. However, in using voice, two different discourse behaviors are conflated, each having a different underlying assumption. The discourse of power seems to be one in which a person uses his voice to promote himself and his ideas and win over or dominate other voices. For one voice to speak, another must be silenced or somehow incorporated. For good or ill, this discourse style most often leads to acquisition of social goods in our society, that is, money, status, and power. By contrast, women's discourse—and this is a theory that Gilligan's book promotes so persuasively—tends to view the repair and maintenance of social networks as a priority. Here, voice may not come into play at all; in fact, silence has a value, because it assumes listening, hearing, thinking, caring, and embracing. These are two different definitions of power in which the discourse of self-assertion tends to be valued more than the other.

It might be argued, then, that those who use voice to refer to the source of their rhetorical power, are subscribing to the patriarchal discourse from which they are trying to break free. In other words, using voice plays into the hands of dominant voices because it configures power in terms that insist on silence and then devalue it. And, of course, women have commonly been accorded the devalued, silent voice.

Another metaphor suggested in *Woman's Ways of Knowing*—one that seems far more in keeping with what many women's discourses seem to value—is the *web* or *network* because both focus more attention on interdependency, celebrating rather than debasing it. The idea of a network assumes that there is not necessarily one individual holding sway over another or others, but a web of interconnected strands—wherein much of the power lies in the connectedness and wherein the integrity of the individual is, although not irrelevant, certainly secondary.

Network has a strong affinity with text as texture, the weaving together of signs. One way of looking at this is to consider that in writing we must attend to the weave of interrelationships between authorial stance, impact or effect on listeners and readers, the text itself, and the context within which the act takes place. Networks and textures lead to the second example, electronic technology.

FROM ANOTHER ANGLE: ELECTRONIC TECHNOLOGY

In *Writing Space: The Computer, Hypertext, and the History of Writing,* Jay Bolter (1991) wrote that "it is somehow uncanny how well the post-modern theorists seem to be anticipating electronic writing" (p. 156). Regardless of whether this is true, voice—however you define it (as persona, tone, style, etc.)—is unquestionably problematic in electronic writing for a number of reasons.

First, electronic technology diffuses, in fact, often ravages the integrity of the authorial voice. Electronic texts have multiple users; some log-on as readers, some as writers; users are often both, constantly and sometimes exuberantly blurring the boundary between writer and reader, as they add to texts, collaborate on texts, and follow links from one text to another as their interest dictates, making the act of reading truly an example of textual construction. The electronic text rarely remains static; it can potentially be rewritten each time some new user encounters it. Even though writers might plan for the reading of texts in certain ways, by programming links and connections, the reading/writing movement is often spontaneous and often haphazard.

One of the hallmarks of voice is that it helps identify, if not an author, at least a tone. In electronic texts, the lack of stability and integrity militates against the creation of a consistent persona or a consistent tone. In fact, although it frequently remains possible to find a voice, persona, or tone, it is just as frequently impossible. In fact, the technology often seems to defy that impulse to find unity and integrity by its nature: A user can disrupt entire textual configurations—and stable meaning—with a single keystroke or click of a mouse.

Furthermore, the strong visual component of electronic writing, through the use of font styles, font sizes, colors, screen movement, hypertexts, screen configurations, audio-visual tools, and layering—all of which convey meaning—don't necessarily translate into an oral function, which is what gives voice its explanatory power. In addition, texts can exist literally, virtually, or as a combination of the two.

If there is a voice, it is disrupted and disrupting. Responsibility is diffused; authority is scattered into cyberspace. It is hard to have power over someone who refuses to play. Thus voice, although it still might be possible to use it as a metaphor, is in some ways antithetical to the medium.

WHAT ABOUT STYLE?

Despite misgivings about the voice metaphor, the consideration of style remains a crucial aspect of writing and writing instruction. What difference does it make to refer to certain aspects of style as "voice" or as "networks"? I believe it does make a difference, and a significant one. If one conceives of the work of writers as participating in a network, then stylistic choices (vocabulary, sentencing, structure, & other aspects of form) stem from the interaction between writer, audience, context, and purpose—in other words, from a consideration of how the piece fits, frames, and adjusts the network.

Voice, by contrast, encourages writers to simplify the rhetorical situation and to focus first (if not primarily) on the expression of a self—whether it be an authentic self or a self-constructed self for the rhetorical occasion. Here's an example. A student, John, is assigned to write an editorial about an issue on campus. For a topic, he selects the food in the cafeteria because he feels strongly (often a good place to start) that it lacks variety and is both unappetizing and unhealthy. In his first draft, he taps into what could easily be construed as his own voice. He's angry that he is put into a position where he has to eat the food or go hungry, and he wants to express that anger. The resulting essay is a sarcastic diatribe explaining why he hates the university's cafeteria food. The essay is informal, personal, and passionate. One could argue that it is possible to hear his voice as one reads the essay. And if it is believed, as it is believed by the voice proponents, that hearing that voice is powerful, then the essay should be powerful.

John's essay is not, however, powerful writing. His stylistic choices are based on whether the wording, sentencing, and structure conveyed his feelings accurately, on whether he clearly expressed himself. But the essay is not as effective rhetorically, unless the reader is purely interested in John and in understanding John's feelings. Even then, an accurate understanding of the complexity of John's feelings (if he even cares that much about this assignment) is impossible. Powerful discourse is discourse that makes a difference; has a rhetorical purpose; and informs, persuades, or moves an audience from their present state of mind to a new one. To do that, one needs to enter the game, to participate in the discursive network. Another approach John might have taken, then, is to determine what he wanted to *do* with his essay, given the context and purpose of the assignment. If he wants a change in the cafeteria policies, then he needs to determine who might be able to effect those changes. Assuming the school food services is his target audience, he'd need to make stylistic choices that would be most effective in getting that audience to buy into his argument (i.e., a formal, even dispassionate tone so he sounds objective; the use of rhetorical strategies designed to get the audience on his side rather that antagonize them; and the introduction of concrete evidence [detailed language] that would make the audience believe his claims). This shift involves a *network* of choices in which he wants to demonstrate his authority, appeal to his readers, and adjust what he says to do both.

What is that dynamic, powerful quality that we're referring to when we refer to voice? It's often hard to tell and, as a consequence, most likely more difficult to teach. Rather than personal passions and identifiable— and sometimes idiosyncratic—twists and turns of phrase that put a personal stamp on prose (or poetry) passages, the powerful style is style that is shaped for specific purposes. And this may be a much more democratic way of approaching the teaching of writing. Although the ability to write well in one's own voice is quite often the result of innate talent, style is not. Its features can be identified, explored, and demystified. Although voice remains a powerful and compelling tool in our writing and teaching, style and craft can be taught and learned. For the classroom teacher, awareness of how style contributes to effectiveness in writing is an important consideration.

FOR WRITING AND DISCUSSION

Becoming Familiar With Voice

Writing Before Reading: If you have a voice in writing, how would you characterize it? Do you feel you have your own, identifiable voice? If not, is having a voice in writing something you aspire to have?

Readings

Elbow, P. (1994) What do we mean when we talk about voice in texts? In K. B. Yancey (Ed.), *Voices on voice: Perspectives, definitions, inquiry*. Urbana, Illinois NCTE, 1–35.

Fulwiler, T. (1990). Looking and listening for my voice. *College Composition and Communication*. 41.2 (October) 214–20.

Hashimoto, I. (1987). Voice as juice: Some reservations about evangelic composition. *College Composition and Communication*, 38, 70–80.

Follow-Up Questions and Activities

1. Do you adjust your voice for different speaking or writing occasions? Some definitions of voice assume that your voice can be adjusted for different rhetorical situations. Imagine that despite the warnings and misgivings of your parents who are currently living in Mexico City, you were skiing in some

backcountry in Colorado—as you do every weekend—and were caught in an avalanche. This has happened before, only this time, you couldn't just ski out of it. The impact of the avalanche broke your leg and buried you under 8 feet of snow. Through pure dint of willpower, you were able to shovel a tunnel with your ski pole and drag yourself out, making it to safety. Rescuers found you shortly thereafter. Now that you are recovering, you find you need to do some writing about the event. This first is an e-mail to your best friend (also a skiier) who lives in Washington State; the second is a letter to your parents, explaining what happened, and the third is an opinion piece to a local newspaper who is interested in your story. Each should be about a page long.

2. If you can, determine and describe your voice for each passage in the previous exercise. Then write a stylistic assessment of how each piece of writing differs from the next. Here are some features to consider as you construct your response.

- Diction (philosophical, polysyllabic, Latinate, formal, abstract, informal, monosyllabic, concrete nouns, slang, idiomatic expressions, etc.). What kinds of word choices are most effective? Why?

- Sentencing (short, simple sentences; long sentences; complex sentences; fragments; imperatives; questions; etc.). What kinds of sentences would work best? Why?

- Tone (ironic, sarcastic, humorous, serious, casual, objective, personal, etc.).

- Paragraphing (short, long, meandering, direct, etc.).

- Structure/organization (chronological, comparison/contrast, problem/solution, deductive/inductive, etc.).

- Figures of speech (metaphors, similes, analogies, personification, etc.).

3. Is it easier to teach voice or style? What are the differences?

Reading for Voice

The following passages are taken from student papers. Which one has "voice"? Identify as many features as you can that contribute to this voice.

The following are two first-year students' responses to a "reflective essay" assignment, which asked student writers to introduce their final writing portfolios and comment on (a) what the writer now understands to be good writing, (b) how their portfolios reflect this understanding, and (c) what they might still want to work on. Designated audience:

first-year writing instructors. Note that these papers are used with little or no editing.

Student A (Eli Britt)

I have never done this before. I have never had to make something as utterly boring as the five-paragraph format seem interesting and appealing. My teacher gave me the final edits on the paper. Now suppose it all lies on my shoulders.

I kind of feel like a super hero, my grades are my Metropolis and I am Superman. O.K. Playtime is over please focus now Eli. Put on the headphones, bump the euro-trash techno and pump out a masterpiece you can be proud of.

Jen (My English 101 teacher) is right about this first sentence. "Five-paragraph essays suck serious a**." It needs to go. I have this sick compulsion to swear now that I don't have high school teachers salivating at the chance to slap a red mark on it. I'll go with a more intellectual form of shock value. Evil is such a good word, so vague, but you just know it's bad.

Audience. Oh man, how am I going write to two difference audiences. I just wanted write for people that didn't really know too much about five-paragraph essays. That way I so much easier, they are putty in my hands (cue menacing laugh) . . . delusional hands, you cocky little punk. I have to stop getting caught in this whole power of writing thing. Focus. So I have to focus on two audiences, those that know and those that don't. That means more evidence, stronger claims and an over-all wholesome feeling. I am going to have to give a lot of credit to Jen on this paper. Most of her ideas are really good. Moving the paragraph about our conversation is a good cure for a rather boring intro, I never would have thought about it that way. I need to elaborate on the conversation with Jen. People aren't going to know what made me think differently. It's difficult to articulate the process of my thought to others and yet I have had to do it so much in this class. I like it though, it is definitely something I want to get better at, maybe make it not so difficult.

Now I have to "go into more detail on my high school paper" says Jen. All right, I'll buy that and see where it goes. I can't really see the point but I'll trust her. Oh . . . evidence.

Always with the evidence it's like I have to prove everything. I know it's good. It's just difficult.

That clock had better not say 2:00 am, it is Saturday night I should be at a party. Yeah, the TA's grading this will be crying in their fourth lukewarm cup of Maxwell House for me. Focus. . . .

Student B (Lisa Cooper)

To begin with, defining the characteristics of audience impacted my style as a writer. I have come to understand that an audience consists of those who agree with you, those who disagree with you, and those who are undecided. For the most part, it's the undecided crowd that your writing needs to be directed to. The group that agrees with you will support what you say no matter how you say it to some degree. Those who disagree will tear your writing apart. The undecided will tear it apart but with an open mind. Understanding the audience plays a big part in informing or persuading diverse members. Read All About It (But Don't Believe It) by Caryl Rivers is a perfect example of the latter. She proclaims, "The American press greatly exaggerates the problems of women—especially working women." Although her arguments are strong and her support is sturdy, she is one-sided, judgmental, and close-minded. Even though I agree with her line of reasoning, the manner in which she presented the facts is clouded with a harsh and condescending tone of voice. She did not take the audience into account nor did she seem to care. Rivers gave me, as the reader, the sense that she was just an angry person venting to anyone willing to listen long enough. The piece by Kurt Vonnegut Jr., entitled "How to Write with Style" was similarly belittling to the reader. His use of imaginative language and word play captivated me, a word choice fanatic; however, it detracted from the actual point of the writing. Furthermore, he did not follow his own tips on "how to write with style." In my persuasive essay about night classes, I attempted to tailor the tone of my paper toward the undecided by focusing on my point while acknowledging arguments of the opposing side as well. I made it clear how I felt, that night classes are bothersome without becoming overly emotional. I had sound arguments supported by common sense and fact rather than judgment justified by opinion. Realizing that the audience will not always agree with what you are writing is a considerable step on the path to effective writing. . . .

Here is an excerpt from different paper by the same student, Lisa Cooper. This time, the assignment was to "enter the conversation" about a controversial issue, do her own study of the data, and come up with a claim supported by evidence that in some way makes a contribution to the issue.

It has been stated that a picture is worth a thousand words, and in the case of describing events it is often true. Neil Postman and Steve Powers, authors of "The Bias of Language, the Bias of Pictures" state, "The words people use to describe [an] event are not the event itself and are only abstracts through re-presentations of the event." Each individual interprets an event using personal attitudes and points of view, which, when relaying that information to another, are injected into the event. This is where television comes into play. With the addition of pictures, the art of recounting worldwide happenings has attained a new level. But how much do the pictures really say? By examining one television newscast and comparing it to the newspaper version of the same story, it is possible to identify the differences. In contrast to conventional wisdom, the addition of moving pictures detracts from the accuracy and content of the story, thus causing the newspaper article to be more informative than the newscast.

Which of the three passages is "effective"? Note that you'll need to define "effective." Examine the success of each passage in terms of what you think might be intended by "voice."

1. In a Washington State testing rubric for essays written at the secondary level, voice is one of six components that are scored. In addition to voice, the other elements are: *ideas* and *content, organization, word choice, sentence fluency,* and *conventions.* Voice is defined as "the heart and soul of a piece, the magic, the wit. It is the writer's unique and personal expression emerging through words" (Testing Rubric Washington State). Write an essay in which you explore what you think voice means in this context, and what you might be looking for in students' writing. What are the advantages in considering student writing in these terms? What are the liabilities? Develop an argument where you defend or disagree with the use of voice in this rubric.

2. If you believe that focusing on voice is an effective way to teach writing, develop a definition of voice and sketch out some activities that would help students develop their own voices. If, on the other hand, you believe in an alternative approach to understanding style, sketch this out with appropriate activities.

Read the excerpt at the end of this chapter, "How to Get Power Through Voice" by Peter Elbow (1981), from chapter 26 of *Writing with Power: Techniques for Mastering the Writing Process* (pp. 304–313). New York: Oxford UP. Then respond to the following questions:

1. Draw up a list of features that you believe would exist in a text that has "real voice" as Elbow defines it. Are these features that you believe constitute good writing? Or powerful writing? If you can think of other features that might contribute to powerful writing, what are these? In other words, in what ways do you and Elbow see eye-to-eye and to what extent do you disagree? How do you account for this?

2. Find a piece of writing that you believe has "real voice" as described by this article. Justify your selection.

3. How would you teach students to use the kind of voice that Elbow talks about in this chapter?

4. What kinds of writing do you see yourself or your students doing in the next 10 years? How might Elbow's techniques help? Where would they be of no help? Where would they be a problem?

5. Note that this excerpt is from a book designed to help writers "master the writing process." In other words, it's from a textbook of sorts. Describe how Elbow's style in this excerpt differs from that of other textbooks on writing that you are familiar with. How does this seem to support his argument about finding voice in writing? What do you think of his style? Does it seem to have "voice"? Why or why not?

FOR WRITING AND DISCUSSION

Theories about writing always emerge from specific historical and political contexts. What was going on in 1981—in the field of teaching writing as well as in the political climate—that might have influenced the way Elbow conceptualized voice and treated voice in writing? Discuss the specific influences that you see.

Note that Peter Elbow's book from which this excerpt is taken was published in 1981. Since then he has somewhat revised his stance on voice. Locate some of Elbow's more recent articles or books in which he discusses voice and see if you can trace shifts in his thinking. Do you believe these changes are more or less productive in helping students learn to write?

FOR FURTHER EXPLORATION

Bowden, D. (1999). *The mythology of voice*. Portsmouth, N.H. Heinemann-Boynton/Cook.

A critique of the voice metaphor.

Elbow, P. (Ed.). (1994). *Landmark essays on voice and writing*. Davis, CA: Hermagorus Press.

Includes many of the essential readings on voice, including essays that lay out some of the important theoretical underpinnings.

Yancey, K. B. (Ed.). (1994). *Voices on voice: Perspectives, definitions, inquiry*. Urbana, IL: NCTE.

Contains newer essays on voice and on the use of voice in different genres of writing. Also includes a good annotated bibliography of work done on voice.

REFERENCES

Applebee, A. N. (1974). *Tradition and reform in the teaching of English: A history.* Urbana, IL: NCTE.

Bakhtin, M. (1981). *The dialogic imagination.* (M. Holquist, Ed. & C. Emerson, Trans.). Austin: University of Texas Press.

Belenky, M. F., Clinchy B., Goldberger N., & Tarule, J. (1986). *Women's ways of knowing: The development of self, voice, and mind.* New York: Basic Books.

Berlin, J. (1987). *Rhetoric and reality: Writing instruction in American colleges, 1900–1985.* Carbondale: Southern Illinois University Press.

Bolter, J. D. (1991). *Writing space: The computer, hypertext, and the history of writing.* Hillsdale, NJ: Lawrence Erlbaum.

Bowden, D. (1999). *The mythology of voice.* Portsmouth, NH: Boynton/Cook Heinemann.

Connors, R. (1987). Personal Writing Assignments. *College Composition and Communication, 38* (2), 166–183.

Crowley, S. (1989). *A teacher's introduction to deconstruction.* Urbana, IL: NCTE.

Derrida, J. (1976). *Of grammatology.* (G. C. Spivak, Trans.). Baltimore and London: The Johns Hopkins University Press.

Ede, L. (1989). *Work in progress: A guide to writing and revising.* New York: St. Martin's Press.

Elbow, P. (1973). *Writing without teachers.* Oxford, UK: Oxford UP.

Elbow, P. (1981). *Writing with power:* Techniques for Mastering the writing process. New York: Oxford UP.

Elbow, P. (Ed.). (1994). *Landmark essays on voice and writing.* Davis, CA: Hermagorus Press.

Eliot, T. S. (1943). The three voices of poetry. *On poetry and poets* (pp. 96–112). New York: Farrar.

Emig, J. (1971). *The composing process of twelfth graders.* Urbana, IL: NCTE.

Gibson, W. (1969). *Persona: A style study for readers and writers.* New York: Random.

Gilligan, C. (1993). *In a different voice: Psychological theory and women's development.* Cambridge: Harvard UP.

Hashimoto, I. (1987). Voice as juice: Some reservations about evangelic composition. *College Composition and Communication, 38,* 70–80.

Macrorie, K. (1985). *Telling writing* (4th ed.). Upper Montclair, NJ: Boynton/Cook.

Plato. (1961). *The collected dialogues of Plato.* (E. Hamilton & H. Cairns, Eds.). Princeton: NJ: Bollingen Series LXXI, Princeton UP.

Stewart, D. (1972). *The authentic voice: A pre-writing approach to student writing.* Dubuque, IA: Wm. C. Brown.

Yancey, K. B. (Ed.). (1994). *Voices on voice: Perspectives, definitions, inquiry.* Urbana, IL: NCTE.

Zoellner, R. (1969). Talk-write: A behavioral pedagogy for composition. *College English, 30* (4), 267–320.

Reading

HOW TO GET POWER THROUGH VOICE

Peter Elbow

What if this hypothesis about voice is correct? One thing follows from it that's more important than anything else: everyone, however inexperienced or unskilled, has real voice available; everyone can write with power. Even though it may take some people a long time before they can write well about certain complicated topics or write in certain formal styles, and even though it will take some people a long time before they can write without mistakes in spelling and usage, nevertheless, nothing stops anyone from writing words that will make readers listen and be affected. Nothing stops you from writing right now, today, words that people will want to read and even want to publish. Nothing stops you, that is, but your fear or unwillingness or lack of familiarity with what I am calling your real voice.

But this clarion call—for that's what I intend it to be despite my careful qualifiers—immediately raises a simple question: Why doesn't everyone use power if it is sitting there available and why does most writing lack power? There are lots of good reasons. In this section I will give advice about how to get real voice into your writing, but I will present it in terms of an analysis of why people so seldom use that power.

· · ·

People often lack any voice at all in their writing, even fake voice, because they stop so often in the act of writing a sentence and worry and change their minds about which words to use. They have none of the natural breath in their writing that they have in the conditions for speaking. The list of conditions is awesome: we have so little practice in writing, but so much more time to stop and fiddle as we write each sentence; we have additional rules of spelling and usage to follow in writing that we don't have in speaking; we feel more culpable for our written foolishness than for what we say; we have been so fully graded, corrected, and given feedback on our mistakes in writing; and we are usually trying to get our words to conform to some (ill-understood) model of "good writing" as we write.

Frequent and regular freewriting exercises are the best way to overcome these conditions of writing and get voice into your words. These exercises should perhaps be called compulsory writing exercises since they are really a way to *compel* yourself to keep putting words down on paper no matter how lost or frustrated you feel. To get voice into your words you need to learn to get each word chosen, as it were, not by you but by the preceding word. Freewriting exercises help you learn to stand out of the way.

In addition to actual exercises in nonstop writing—since it's hard to keep writing *no matter what* for more than fifteen minutes—force yourself simply to write enormous quantities. Try to make up for all the writing you haven't done. Use writing for as many different tasks as you can. Keep a notebook or journal, explore thoughts for yourself, write to yourself when you feel frustrated or want to figure something out. (See Chapter 10 for more ways to use writing.)

Practice revising for voice. A powerful exercise is to write short pieces of prose or poetry that work without any punctuation at all. Get the words so well ordered that punctuation is never missed. The reader must never stumble or have to reread a phrase, not even on first reading—and all without benefit of punctuation. This is really an exercise in adjusting the breath in the words till it guides the reader's voice naturally to each pause and full stop.

Read out loud. This is a good way to exercise the muscle involved in voice and even in real voice. Good reading out loud is not necessarily dramatic. I'm struck with how some good poets or readers get real voice into a monotone or chant. They are trying to let the words' inner resonance come through, not trying to "perform" the words. (Dylan Thomas reads so splendidly that we may make the mistake of calling his technique "dramatic." Really it is a kind of chant or incantation he uses.) But there is no right way. It's a question of steering a path between being too timid and being falsely dramatic. The presence of listeners can sharpen your ear and help you hear when you chicken out or overdramatize.

. . .

Real voice. People often avoid it and drift into fake voices because of the need to face an audience. I have to go to work, I have to make a presentation, I have to teach, I have to go to a party, I have to have dinner with friends. Perhaps I feel lost, uncertain, baffled—or else angry—or else uncaring—or else hysterical. I can't sound that way with all these people. They won't understand, they won't know how to deal with me, and I won't accomplish what I need to accomplish.

done this, I can turn to my official evaluation and find it much easier to write something fair in a suitable tone of voice (for a document that becomes part of the student's transcript). I finish these two pieces of writing much more quickly than if I just tried to write the official document and pick my way gingerly through my feelings.

. . .

Another reason people don't use real voice is that it makes them feel exposed and vulnerable. I don't so much mind if someone dislikes my writing when I am merely using an acceptable voice, but if I use my real voice and they don't like it—which of course is very possible—that hurts. The more criticism people get on their writing, the more they tend to use fake voices. To use real voice feels like bringing yourself into contact with the reader. It's the same kind of phenomenon that happens when there is real eye contact and each person experiences the presence of the other; or when two or more people stop talking and wait in silence while something in the air gets itself clear. Writing of almost any kind is exhibitionistic; writing with real voice is more so. Many professional writers feel a special need for privacy. It will help you, then, to get together with one or more others who are interested in recovering their power. Feeling vulnerable or exposed with them is not so difficult.

Another reason people don't use their real voice is that it means having feelings and memories they would rather not have. When you write in your real voice, it often brings tears or shaking—though laughter too. Using real voice may even mean finding you *believe* things you don't wish to believe. For all these reasons, you need to write for no audience and to write for an audience that's safe. And you need faith in yourself that you will gradually sort things out and that it doesn't matter if it takes time.

Most children have real voice but then lose it. It is often just plain loud: like screeching or banging a drum. It can be annoying or wearing for others. "Shhh" is the response we often get to the power of our real voice. But, in addition, much of what we say with real voice is difficult for those around us to deal with: anger, grief, self-pity, even love for the wrong people. When we are hushed up from those expressions, we lose real voice.

In addition, we lose real voice when we are persuaded to give up some of our natural responses to inauthenticity and injustice. Almost any child can feel inauthenticity in the voices of many TV figures or politicians. Many grown-ups can't hear it so well—or drown out their distrust. It is difficult to get along in the world if you hear all the inauthenticity: it makes you feel alone, depressed, hopeless. We need to belong, and society offers us membership if we stop hearing inauthenticity.

Children can usually feel when things are unfair, but they are often persuaded to go along because they need to belong and to be loved. To get back to those feelings in later life leads to rage, grief, aloneness and—since one has gone along—guilt. Real voice is often buried in all of that. If you want to recover it, you do well to build in special support from people you can trust so you don't feel so alone or threatened by all these feelings.

Another reason people don't use real voice is that they run away from their power. There's something scary about being as strong as you are, about wielding the force you actually have. It means taking a lot more responsibility and credit than you are used to. If you write with real voice, people will say "You did this to me" and try to make you feel responsible for some of their actions. Besides, the effect of your power is liable to be different from what you intended. Especially at first. You cause explosions when you thought you were just asking for the salt or saying hello. In effect I'm saying, "Why don't you shoot that gun you have? Oh yes, by the way, I can't tell you how to aim it." The standard approach in writing is to say you mustn't pull the trigger until you can aim it well. But how can you learn to aim well till you start pulling the trigger? If you start letting your writing lead you to real voice, you'll discover some thoughts and feelings you didn't know you had.

Therefore, practice shooting the gun off in safe places. First with no one around. Then with people you know and trust deeply. Find people who are willing to be in the same room with you while you pull the trigger. Try using the power in ways where the results don't matter. Write letters to people that don't matter to you. You'll discover that the gun doesn't kill but that you have more power than you are comfortable with.

Of course you may accept your power but still want to disguise it. That is, you may find it convenient, if you are in a large organization, to be able to write about an event in a fuzzy, passive "It has come to our attention that..." kind of language, so you disguise not only the fact that it was an action performed by a human being with a free will but indeed that *you did it*. But it would be incorrect to conclude, as some people do, that all bureaucratic, organizational, and governmental writing needs to lack the resonance of real voice. Most often it could do its work perfectly well even if it were strong and clear. It is the *personal, individualistic,* or *personality-filled* voice that is inappropriate in much organizational writing, but you can write with power in the impersonal, public, and corporate voice. You can avoid "I" and its flavor, and talk entirely in terms of "we" and "they" and even "it," and still achieve the resonance of real voice. Real voice is not the sound of an *individual personality* redolent with vibes, it is the sound of a *meaning* resonating because the individual consciousness of the writer is somehow fully behind or in tune with or in participation with that meaning.

I have stressed the importance of sharing writing without any feedback at all. What about asking people to give you feedback specifically on real voice? I think that such feedback can be useful, but I am leery of it. It's so hard to know whether someone's perception of real voice is accurate. If you want this feedback, don't get it early in your writing development, make sure you get it from very different kinds of people, and make sure not to put too much trust in it. The safest method is to get them to read a piece and then ask them a week later what they remember. Passages they *dislike* often have the most real voice.

But here is a specific exercise for getting feedback on real voice. It grows out of one of the first experiences that made me think consciously about this matter. As an applicant for conscientious objector status, and then later as a draft counselor, I discovered that the writing task set by Selective Service was very interesting and perplexing. An applicant had to write why he was opposed to fighting in wars, but there was no right or wrong answer. The draft board would accept any reasons (within certain broad limits); they would accept any style, any level of skill. Their only criterion was whether *they* believed that the *writer* believed his own words. (I am describing how it worked when board members were in good faith.)

Applicants, especially college students, often started with writing that didn't work. I could infer from all the arguments and commotion and from conversations with them that they were sincere but as they wrote they got so preoccupied with theories, argument, and reasoning that in the end there was no conviction on paper. When I gave someone this feedback and he was willing to try and try again till at last the words began to ring true, all of a sudden the writing got powerful and even skillful in other ways.

The exercise I suggest to anybody, then, is simply to write about some belief you have—or even some experience or perception—but to get readers to give you this limited, peculiar, draft-board-like feedback: where do they really believe that you believe it, and where do they have doubts? The useful thing about this exercise is discovering how often words that ring true are not especially full of feeling, not heavy with conviction. Too much "sincerity" and quivering often sounds fake and makes readers doubt that you really believe what you are saying. I stress this because I fear I have made real voice sound as though it is always full of loud emotion. It is often quiet.

. . .

In the end, what may be as important as these specific exercises is adopting the right frame of mind.

Look for real voice and realize it is there in everyone waiting to be used. Yet remember, too, that you are looking for something mysterious and hidden. There are no outward linguistic characteristics to point to in writing with real voice. Resonance or impact on readers is all there is. But you can't count on readers to notice it or to agree about whether it is there because of all the other criteria they use in evaluating writing (e.g., polished style, correct reasoning, good insights, truth-to-life, deep feelings), and because of the negative qualities that sometimes accompany real voice as it is emerging. And you, as writer, may be wrong about the presence or absence of real voice in your writing—at least until you finally develop a trustworthy sense of it. You have to be willing to work in the dark, not be in a hurry, and have faith. The best clue I know is that as you begin to develop real voice, your writing will probably cause more comment from readers than before (though not necessarily more favorable comment).

If you seek real voice you should realize that you probably face a dilemma. You probably have only one real voice—at first anyway—and it is likely to feel childish or distasteful or ugly to you. But you are stuck. You can either use voices you like or you can be heard. For a while, you can't have it both ways.

But if you do have the courage to use and inhabit that real voice, you will get the knack of resonance, you will learn to expand its range and eventually make more voices real. This of course is the skill of great literary artists: the ability to give resonance to many voices.

It's important to stress, at the end, this fact of many voices. Partly to reassure you that you are not ultimately stuck with just one voice forever. But also because it highlights the mystery. Real voice is not necessarily personal or sincere. Writing about your own personal concerns is only one way and not necessarily the best. Such writing can lead to gushy or analytical words about how angry you are today: useful to write, an expression of strong feelings, a possible *source* of future powerful writing, but not resonant of powerful for readers as it stands. Real voice is whatever yields resonance, whatever makes the words bore through. Some writers get real voice through pure fantasy, lies, imitation of utterly different writers, or trance-writing. It may be possible to get real voice by merging in your mind with another personality, pretending to be someone else. *Shedding* the self's concerns and point of view can be a good way to get real voice—thus writing fiction and playing roles are powerful tools. Many good literary artists sound least convincing when they speak for themselves. The important thing is simply to know that power is available and to figure out through experimentation the best way for you to attain it.

8

Grammar and Usage

James D. Williams

> This chapter presents an overview of the "problem" of gram-
> mar, exploring what has been learned from research on the rela-
> tionship between grammar and writing improvement. It distin-
> guishes between grammar and usage, and suggests strategies for
> working with grammar in the writing class.

The biggest myth about writing is that it is linked somehow to grammar.
Whenever politicians take notice of writing skills in our schools, they blame
poor writing on the failure to teach kids grammar, and they nearly always
propose a "back to basics" program that will force schools to teach even
more grammar. Ironically, most English textbooks for elementary, middle,
and high school students already focus on grammar. For example, a popular
text for middle school students, *Houghton-Mifflin English,* has little in it that
isn't related to grammar in one way or another. And, as a result, most teachers
in elementary, middle, and high schools already teach grammar when they
work on writing. Nevertheless, ask students what they need to do to improve
their writing, and inevitably the answer is "Work on my grammar." When parents see the low test scores in language arts at their children's schools, they
demand more emphasis be placed on grammar. When politicians turn their
attention to writing, their cry is "More grammar." Not surprisingly, students
spend more time on grammar than just about any other unit of study.

This chapter discusses the "problem" of grammar, focusing on the following questions:

What has been learned from research on the relationship between
grammar and writing improvement?

How has the history of grammar instruction contributed to the "problem" of grammar in the writing class?

What is the distinction between grammar and usage?

How can grammar best be addressed in the writing class?

THE PROBLEM OF GRAMMAR

Despite all the concern and attention devoted to it, grammar has not had any positive effect on writing performance. Even a quick glance at standardized test scores in districts across the country shows that writing skills have plummeted over the last decade or so. The 1998 report of the National Assessment of Educational Progress (NAEP) indicated that writing skills nationwide are extremely low, with only about 25% of 12th graders capable of producing a coherent, well-developed essay. Perhaps more revealing is that the writing of the 75% who are not capable of producing such an essay is, among other things, riddled with the sort of errors that grammar instruction is supposed to eliminate. Meanwhile, university writing programs wrestle with the annual influx of freshmen who, although usually graduating with high grades in English, don't have a clue about how to produce any kind of writing other than an account of what they did over their summer vacations or their "feelings" about a given topic—neither of which is worth anything at all at the university level or beyond.

The conclusion that grammar instruction fails to improve writing is not new. A large amount of research, going back many years, has examined the question, and the results are uniform and consistent. In 1963, for example, Braddock, Lloyd-Jones, and Schoer summarized contemporary research and reported the following:

> In view of the widespread agreement of research studies based upon many types of students and teachers, the conclusion can be stated in strong and unqualified terms that the teaching of formal [traditional] grammar has a negligible or, because it usually displaces some instruction and practice in actual composition, even a harmful effect on the improvement of writing. (pp. 37–38)

In spite of this assessment, other researchers continued to investigate the role of grammar instruction and writing performance because so many people assume that there is a strong connection. White (1965), for example, studied three seventh-grade classes: One class studied traditional grammar, one transformational grammar, and the third used the time to read popular novels. White found no significant differences in the students' writing skills at the end of the study. A year later, Whitehead (1966) compared two groups of high school students: One received grammar instruction; the other did not. At the end of the study, there were no measurable differences in writing performance. Then Gale (1968) studied fifth graders divided into four groups. Three of these groups received instruction in grammar, with each group studying a different type of grammar. The fourth group did not receive any grammar instruction. Although Gale reported that students who studied transformational-generative and phrase-structure grammars could write more complex sentences than the students in the other groups, there were no overall differences in writing quality across groups.

One of the more important studies on the question of grammar and writing was conducted by Bateman and Zidonis (1966)—important because it spanned 2 years. Starting with ninth-grade students, Bateman and Zidonis provided grammar instruction to half of the students; the other half received no grammar instruction. Like those who came before them, Bateman and Zidonis found, at the end of the study, that students who studied grammar could write slightly more complex sentences than those who could not, but, again, there were no measurable differences in writing ability across the groups.

The strength of these findings, however, did not convince skeptics who believed that the lack of any positive findings in the research had to be the result of methodological flaws. Some claimed, for example, that the studies failed to account for different teaching styles and that the lack of any measurable influence was related to poor teaching. Elley, Barham, Lamb, and Wyllie (1976) responded to this issue by designing a 3-year study that controlled, to the extent possible, for the effect of different teaching styles. They divided students into three groups. The first group of three classes of students studied transformational-generative grammar; organizational modes, such as narration, analysis, comparison and contrast, and argument; and literature. The second group, also a group of three classes, studied the same topics as the first group, with one exception: They did not study grammar. The final group, composed of two classes, studied traditional grammar and read a large amount of popular fiction.

At the end of each year of the study, students were evaluated on a range of factors to assess their growth in vocabulary, reading comprehension, sentence complexity, usage, spelling, and punctuation. The results were compared across groups each year. In addition, students wrote four essays at the end of the first year and three at the end of the second and third years. The essays were scored on the basis of content, style, organization, and mechanics. Finally, students completed questionnaires periodically to assess their attitudes toward the content of their English classes.

The results were again consistent. The writing of students who studied grammar, whether traditional or transformational, was not judged to be any better along any dimension than the writing of students who did not study grammar. In addition, the attitude questionnaires showed that, at the end of the second year, students who had studied transformational grammar not only disliked writing more than their counterparts did but also felt that English was quite difficult—understandable, perhaps, given the complexity of transformational grammar.

At the end of the third year, the researchers evaluated specific features of the students' writing—such as spelling, punctuation, sentence structure, and usage—using a variety of measures. A standardized test showed that the students who had studied grammar performed better on usage questions than did those students who had not studied grammar. However, no significant differences in any other area were found. The two groups who studied grammar also reported on their attitude surveys that they found English "repetitive" and that their English classes were boring and useless. The group that did not study grammar had a much more positive attitude toward English. More significant, however, is that after 3 years of instruction, the actual writing of the students showed no significant differences in overall quality across groups.

Such unequivocal findings dampened significantly the voices claiming some positive effect of grammar instruction on writing performance, but it did not silence them entirely. Kolln (1981), Holt (1982), and Davis (1984) argued that the studies showing no effect were flawed and that grammar did, in fact, lead to improved writing, but they were not able to provide any meaningful data to support their claim. Then, in 1986, Hillocks published his milestone *Research on Written Composition: New Directions for Teaching* a meta-analysis of thousands of studies on composition. His methodology included eliminating studies with flawed or inadequate designs, which made his conclusions more substantial and difficult to dismiss. On the question of grammar and writing, Hillocks' conclusion was blunt:

> The study of traditional school grammar (i.e., the definition of parts of speech, the parsing of sentences, etc.) has no effect on raising the quality of student writing. Every other focus of instruction examined in this review is stronger. Taught in certain ways, grammar and mechanics instruction has a deleterious effect on student writing. In some studies a heavy emphasis on mechanics and usage (e.g., marking every error) resulted in significant losses in overall quality. School boards, administrators, and teachers who impose the systematic study of traditional school grammar on their students over lengthy periods of time in the name of teaching writing do them a gross disservice which should not be tolerated by anyone concerned with the effective teaching of good writing. We need to learn how to teach standard usage and mechanics after careful task analysis and with minimal grammar. (1986, pp. 248–249)

Hillocks' work, a true *force majeure*, was compelling, at least among scholars in composition. A review of the major journals in composition studies—specifically, *College Composition and Communication, Research in the Teaching of*

English, Written Communication, and *College English*—from 1986 to the present does not produce even a single article addressing the question of grammar's effect on writing performance. The works that do emerge in this review are not empirical and do not focus on the question of grammar instruction and writing. Williams (1993), for example, examined the influence of grammar, as a rule-governed model of language, on composition studies. Parker and Campbell (1993) argued that the theoretical framework of linguistics would fill a significant theoretical vacuum in composition. Other scholars, such as Crowley (1989) and Noguchi (1991) reiterate the conclusion that grammar instruction does not raise writing performance.

FOR WRITING AND DISCUSSION

In a short paper, discuss your attitude toward grammar, tracing your experience with it in a school setting. Do you feel that learning grammar has been important for you? Indicate the extent to which you "believe" that students "should" learn grammar, despite the results of studies demonstrating that it has no effect on writing improvement.

GRAMMAR AND USAGE

Given the overwhelming weight of the research, why is it that politicians, teachers, administrators, and parents believe that the answer to student writing problems is an even stronger dose of grammar? One reason is that they simply don't know the research. Teachers might reasonably be expected to know something about the studies mentioned in the previous section, but can we honestly expect politicians and parents to have this knowledge? And even teachers fall short of expectations. We must consider that education courses focusing on the connection between grammar and composition are relatively new, having emerged at universities nationwide in the late 1970s and early 1980s, and that teacher training in this country is not standardized by any means. Thus, many teachers, especially those at the elementary level, can obtain a teaching credential without ever having taken a course on grammar and writing. Even most English teachers are not required to study grammar or composition, although they are primarily responsible for teaching grammar and writing in our schools. In fact, the majority of people who become English teachers are not even asked to take freshman composition because they have verbal SAT scores that allow them to exempt the requirement under the incorrect assumption that students who read well and have large vocabularies—and thus perform well on this test—are able to write well.

Another factor is that most people confuse grammar with usage and the conventions that govern academic writing. This confusion has several causes. The most significant, obviously, is ignorance. Without any courses in college on grammar and writing, newly credentialed teachers, faced with the reality of having to teach these subjects, rush to the nearest bookstore and buy a handbook. Even under ideal conditions, this autodidactic approach would not give many people an adequate understanding of grammar. Matters are made quite hopeless, however, by the fact that most authors of handbooks have little if any training in linguistics. Consequently, the grammar that these handbooks teach is a few hundred years old and has about as much to do with how people actually use language and writing as does a book on Sanskrit.

Traditional Grammar

The grammar that most teachers know, the grammar of most handbooks, the grammar that gets taught in our schools, is known as *traditional grammar*. We recognize traditional grammar—which is often called *school grammar*—by its emphasis on grammatical terminology, such as the eight parts of speech, and its emphasis on correcting errors. Traditional grammar is based on Latin for the simple reason that from the Middle Ages through the early 19th century Latin was the language of scholars and was deemed superior to the so-called "vulgar" tongues, such as English, French, Spanish, and Italian. Not many scholars were writing grammar books for these vulgar tongues, so the grammar of Latin was essentially imposed on them. In addition, up until the 20th century, language scholars suffered from a fundamental confusion. They noted that well-educated people wrote and spoke correct Latin, whereas people who weren't well educated did not but made numerous mistakes. They then applied their observation to modern languages and concluded that the purity of a language is preserved by the well-educated. People without a good education, on the other hand, corrupt the language by deviating from the norm recorded in the grammar. In this view, which seems widely accepted even today, grammar plays a major role in distinguishing between what people do with language and what they *ought* to do with it.

Thus, the idea of superiority is naturally associated with notions of correctness, so when, in the late Middle Ages, grammatical treatises became manuals on how to write, constructions that are natural in English but ungrammatical in Latin were labeled violations of the grammar. The problem was, is, and forever will be that English is based on German, not Latin. As a result, numerous features of traditional grammar that have been and continue to be taught to generations of students are just plain wrong.

Consider the split infinitive:

I'm going *to slowly open* the door.

In this sentence, the infinitive verb form, *to open,* is "split" by the adverb *slowly.* Most English teachers in our nation's schools, as well as many handbooks, view the split infinitive as a major error in grammar. From the perspective of Latin or one of the Latin-based languages, such as Spanish, this makes sense because the infinitive form in these languages is one word. In Spanish, for example, the infinitive form of *to open* is *abrir*—one word. Note that it is impossible to split *abrir* in any way. We simply cannot have **Voy a ab- despacio -ir la puerta*[1] ("I'm going to slowly open the door"); we can only have something like *Voy a abrir la puerta despacio.*

Or consider the issue of tense. *Tense* is a technical term in linguistics that describes how verbs change to signify when an action occurred. Anyone who thinks about the possibilities will quickly determine that there is a maximum of three times for any action: past, present, and future. The concept is fairly easy to illustrate. If we take the untensed form of a verb such as *speak,* we see that the past-tense form for the third-person singular is *spoke,* as in *She spoke softly.* By the same token, the present-tense form for the third-person singular is *speaks,* as in *She speaks softly.* The change is even more noticeable in Spanish, where the untensed form is *hablar.* The equivalent past-tense form is *habló,* and the equivalent present-tense form is *habla.* But what about the future tense? In Spanish, the future form is *hablaré.* But in English there is no equivalent change that we can make to the verb to signify the future. In other words, *English does not have a future tense.* Consequently, we have to use alternative means of signifying the future. English does so in a couple of different ways, one being the use of the auxiliary verb *will,* as in *She will speak,* and another being the use of an adverbial of time in conjunction with the present tense, as in *She speaks tomorrow.* Thus, English, unlike Latin and Latin-based languages, has only two tenses, not three.

Nevertheless, virtually all major handbooks claim that English has at least three tenses. *The St. Martin's Handbook,* by Lunsford and Connors (1989), for example, states that English has "the present tense, the past tense, and the future tense" (p. 198). Actually, the issue is more complex because these handbooks confuse other verb forms with tense. English uses progressive and perfect verb forms to signify when an action is ongoing and when it has been completed in the past, respectively. These verb forms are not tenses, yet nearly all handbooks describe them as such, with the result being in such accounts that English somehow is supposed to have as many as 12 tenses.

Given these problems, we should not be surprised to find that most teachers have a poor understanding of grammar and an even poorer understanding of the relation between grammar and writing. It should be noted that apologists for school grammar argue that not everything in the handbooks

---

[1]Linguists mark ungrammatical sentences with an asterisk.

is wrong and that some features of traditional grammar do, indeed, describe English. They are right, of course, but such arguments ignore the fact that the majority of the problems we find in student writing have little if anything to do with grammar. Instead, the problems, as Hillocks (1986) noted, are rooted in usage.

Bad Grammar or Bad Usage?

Usage can best be understood as conventions associated with language that govern how we use it in different contexts. On this account, we can recognize that a formal context will expect usage that is different from what is expected in an informal context. Also, linguists commonly differentiate English along the lines of acceptability. These two factors together explain why the language we use when talking with friends and family is inherently unlike the language we use in, say, a job interview. These differences are due to different conventions that govern the language we use in these two contexts. The most widely accepted English is called *Standard English,* whereas the least accepted is *nonstandard English.* With good reason, then, TV anchors for the national news use standard English rather than Black English, Southern English, or some other dialect. Academic writing is at an even higher level of formality and is governed by even stricter conventions; thus, academic writing represents what we call *formal Standard English.*

In addition, it must be understood that issues of usage generally do not have any connection with issues of grammar. Some of the more egregious problems we find in student writing are spelling errors, word errors (when students use the wrong word, such as *impact* for *affect*), subject–verb agreement errors, and sentence errors (such as fragments, run-ons, and what are deemed to be ungrammatical constructions). Asking students to study the parts of speech cannot have any effect on their ability to spell or use words correctly. These skills are developed through reading and writing. By reading widely, students internalize English spelling conventions, and they enlarge their vocabularies so that they are more inclined not only to use the right word but also to use precise words.

The other problems in student writing are equally unaffected by grammar instruction because they are unrelated to grammar. This point will become clearer if we consider a type of sentence that teachers often hold up as being an example of bad grammar:

I ain't got no money.

This sentence supposedly has two problems. First, many argue that *ain't* is not a word, although it is listed in most dictionaries as a word and looks, sounds, and feels like a word. Those who accede that it is a word argue that, as a contraction of *am not,* as well as *are not, is not, has not,* and *have not,* it is ungrammatical in this instance. The second problem is the double negative created by *ain't* and *no,* for as every self-respecting English teacher knows from basic math (and their handbooks), two negatives make a positive.

Let's address the second problem first. Although it is the case in math that two negatives make a positive, language is different, and the idea that what holds in math holds in English is fundamentally flawed. There isn't a single native speaker of English anywhere who would read or hear *I ain't got no money* and understand it to mean that the subject in fact *has* money. Moreover, the double negative has existed in English for centuries; we find it in Chaucer and Shakespeare, obviously well-established writers. The double negative also exists in other languages, such as French and Spanish. Therefore, rejecting our example sentence on the grounds that it fails to communicate the speaker/writer's intention—that its meaning is positive rather than negative—is simply silly.

Is *I ain't got not money* grammatical? Answering this question requires an understanding of what *grammatical* actually means. A sentence is grammatical when native speakers of a language accept a given utterance or written statement as meaningful. In English, grammaticality is also linked very closely to word order—in fact, to a specific word order that follows the pattern of subject (S)–verb (V)–object (O), or SVO.[2] An ungrammatical sentence would be one that does not follow the SVO word order, such as the sentences below:

*Cat my rat a chased.

*The into wind over blew hills the valley and.

Although, as an exercise, we can rearrange the words, putting them in their proper order, and understand what the utterances mean, they have no meaning as they stand and they violate the SVO word order of English. They, therefore, are ungrammatical. It is important to note that a native speaker of English will never and can never spontaneously produce sentences such as these previous examples. In fact, native speakers have a difficult time producing truly ungrammatical sentences.[3]

---

[2]The link between word order and grammaticality is so strong that Noam Chomsky (1957, 1965) argued that grammaticality is independent of semantics. On this account, Chomsky proposed that the sentence *Colorless green ideas sleep furiously* is grammatical, even though it is meaningless. More recently, a group of scholars advocating what is called *cognitive grammar,* argued that Chomsky's proposal is flawed and that we cannot separate syntax from semantics.

[3]There are certain exceptions that emerge in spoken English as a result of widespread distribution of nonstandard forms. One of the more egregious examples involves the response to why-questions. Consider the following: (A) "Why did you fail the exam?" (B) "The reason is because I didn't study." B's response is quite ungrammatical, even though most people do not recognize it as ungrammatical. Note that *is* in B's response is a linking verb. Linking verbs can only be followed by predicate adjectives, predicate nominatives, or prepositional phrases. Yet *because I didn't study* is a subordinate clause. Hence, the response is a clear violation of the grammar and, thus, is ungrammatical.

With this information in mind, let's return to our problem sentence, *I ain't got no money,* and consider its structure:

subject: *I*
verb phrase: *ain't got*
object: *no money*

This analysis shows clearly that the sentence structure follows the standard SVO pattern, with *ain't* functioning as an auxiliary to the verb *got.* Every native speaker of English understands the intended meaning of the sentence (the speaker/writer really is broke), and the sentence follows the standard SVO pattern of English. It therefore meets all the requirements of a grammatical sentence and, indeed, is grammatical.

Nevertheless, we would not want students to produce such a sentence in a typical writing assignment. Such sentences are unacceptable because they violate the usage conventions that govern academic writing, not because they are ungrammatical. They are the equivalent of wearing cutoff jeans, a tank top, and sandals to an elegant wedding service—simply unacceptable.

We can analyze in a similar fashion nearly all of the difficulties in student writing that usually are described as grammatical errors. For example, faulty punctuation, which can sometimes produce run-on sentences, fused sentences, and sentence fragments, may appear on the surface to be the result of students' failure to understand the grammatical structure of a sentence, but closer examination reveals something very different. Let's consider the following example:

> Plato had a great influence on Western civilization and his student
> Aristotle may have had an even greater influence.

Anyone who heard rather than read this sentence would find nothing unusual about it. The sentence has meaning, and it follows English word order, so it is grammatical. However, a person reading the sentence who happens to know something about punctuation would immediately recognize that the comma is missing before the conjunction *and.* Punctuation, however, is almost entirely a visual aid for readers and has little to do with grammar. In fact, punctuation is governed by convention, not rule. A simple example illustrates this point. Currently, there are two different conventions governing the use of the comma in lists. One convention, advocated by the Modern Language Association in its *MLA Guide,* specifies that a comma should separate each item in a list, including the last item, as illustrated below:

> Hobbes wrote that the life of man in his natural state is *dirty, nasty,*
> *brutish,* and *short.*

The second convention, advocated by journalists in the *Associated Press Guide*, specifies that a comma should *not* be used for the last item in a list, which gives us:

> Hobbes wrote that the life of man in his natural state is *dirty, nasty, brutish* and *short.*

Another example of a punctuation convention involves introductory phrases, usually prepositional phrases, similar to the following example:

> *In every instance,* we can show that the courts discriminate against men in general and men of color in particular.

Once again, we are faced with two different conventions. The first specifies that the length of the prepositional phrase determines whether it is set off with a comma in this position. The second, on the other hand, specifies that all introductory prepositional phrases should be set off with a comma, regardless of length.

In the anaerobic environs of the English class, the sentence fragment is deemed to be an even more egregious error than the run-on, but here again close examination reveals that what underlies the fragment is not an ignorance of grammar. The passage below comes from a paper written by a fifth grader who was asked to report on a field trip to a museum. The sentence fragments are in italics:

> We arrived at the Field Museum almost an hour late. *Because there was an accident on the highway.* We went first to the dinosaur exhibit on the second floor. The exhibit was about the life of the dinosaurs. They lived a long time ago. *Long before humans.* The exhibit showed us what the earth was like during the time of the dinosaurs. *Hot and humid.* I liked the exhibit very much and want to go back again soon.

What we notice is that in each instance the problem is one of punctuation, not grammar. If we put the proper punctuation in, there is nothing structurally wrong with this paragraph. Providing this student opportunities to see how other writers handled similar constructions, as well as some help understanding punctuation conventions through examining his own writing, would go a long way toward giving him better control over his sentences. Professional writers have such control, and we are not surprised or dismayed when we encounter fragments in their work. Yet we shine a harsh spotlight on students because we know that, in most cases, they do not yet have this control. In addition, it is worth noting that speech allows for such fragmented constructions. For example, if my wife asks me why I was late arriving home, I might well (and correctly) respond with, *Because of an accident on the highway.* No one would label this response as ungrammatical; instead, they would recognize that English allows for reduction of responses through ellipsis. In other words, I do not need to respond with, *I am late arriving home because of an accident on the highway.* In fact, if I were to offer that response rather than the elliptical one, *Because of an accident on the highway,* my utterance would be judged stilted at best, unnatural at worst.

The writing of the fifth above grader—and the writing of students who produce sentence fragments—manifests conventions of speech that have been transferred to writing. There are several reasons why students use conventions of speech when they write, perhaps the most obvious being lack of experience with the written word. To a significant degree, writing is an artificial representation of language, governed by conventions that are much more rigorous than anything we find in speech, and it takes people many years to master these conventions fully. Students are at a disadvantage because the majority get little instruction in usage conventions, so they may never become aware that what works in spoken discourse will not necessarily work in written discourse. In addition, people acquire the conventions of written discourse primarily through reading and most effectively through guided reading that provides opportunities to identify, discuss, and then practice the various conventions of written discourse. Yet reading skill among students has plummeted along with writing skill, and today our high school graduates have, on average, an eighth-grade reading level. Poor reading skill reinforces a pervasive aversion to reading, leading the majority of our students, when it comes to reading, to adopt the philosophy of Homer Simpson: "Anything that doesn't come easy isn't worth doing." More and more people are reading less and less. For several years, when I first started teaching at the university, I asked entering freshmen how many books they had read for pleasure during the past year. The response was discouraging, for class after class gave me the same average—zero. Such students simply have few, if any, chances to internalize the usage conventions that govern writing, and grammar instruction cannot serve as a substitute for reading.

WHY ISN'T GRAMMAR INSTRUCTION TRANSPORTABLE TO WRITING?

Many people resist the conclusion that grammar instruction fails to improve writing because it seems to fly in the face of common sense. After all, before we teach children how to read, we first teach them the alphabet. Letters form words, words form sentences, and so on. Common sense, therefore, tells us that writing instruction should follow a similar bottom-up approach, with grammar being the building block for sentences and paragraphs, just as the alphabet is the building block for words and reading. Experience shows, however, that common sense fails us here. Foreign students, especially those from Asia, illustrate the problem. English language instruction in Asia follows what is known as the *grammar-translation* method.[4] This method was originally designed to teach people how to read a language that they would never have to speak or write. It is grammar intensive. Students from places such as Japan come to the United States with a solid knowledge of grammar; indeed, many of them know more about English grammar than their American teachers. Nevertheless, they are poor writers. In many respects, such students are in the same situation as their American counterparts, for both have studied grammar but cannot write well.

The building-block approach fails with writing because it is inconsistent with the nature of grammar and how the mind processes language. It all begins at birth, when children are immersed immediately in a language environment (Kelso, 1995) and begin what is known as *language acquisition*. As Williams (1993) noted, parents naturally provide their children with the names of things. The ability to name the world, to assign labels, is fundamental to language acquisition; it creates order out of chaos. When a child sees a ball for the first time, for example, the parent always introduces the object along with the word *ball*. As a result, the child develops a mental model related to "ball-ness" that includes not only the physical attributes of the object but also the phonemic representation of the word *ball*. Currently, it appears that a similar process operates at the sentence level. Although we seem to have the ability to create an endless variety of sentences, we know that there actually is a limited number of sentence patterns. We've already encountered a basic sentence pattern—SVO. Another is SVC (subject–verb–complement). Perhaps an additional half dozen or so basic patterns exist, but most of the other patterns we find in English are permutations of SVO and SVC. Language acquisition on this account consists of internalizing not only the names of things, a lexicon, but also the basic sentence patterns and the means to modify them in various ways. Thus, acquisition of sentence patterns involves internalizing entire structures separate from the lexicon. It is not based on building these structures from smaller units, whatever they might be.

The process of language acquisition is extremely powerful. Williams (1999) noted that, "on a neurophysiological level ... [mental models of

---

[4]As of this writing, the only country in Asia that has moved beyond grammar-translation is Korea, where the Ministry of Education declared in 1998 that English as a foreign language instruction must follow a balanced communicative approach.

language consist] of modifications to the cerebral structure" (p. 232). In other words, the brain literally changes in response to linguistic input, developing new cells and a network of neural pathways to connect these cells into a communicative system. The word *ball*, on this account, literally resides as a physical structure in the brain. As language develops over many years, the neural network expands, grows more dense, and becomes richer.

The linguistic input children receive comes primarily from adults, who provide models of the language. Parents and other adults unconsciously invoke a matching procedure whenever they speak with children. A 3-year-old, for example, may utter the sound "mey-mey" the first time he or she tries to articulate "watermelon." All available data indicate that parents immediately correct the child, providing the correct pronunciation for the home dialect. Typically, without urging, the child makes another attempt, which may be a closer approximation of the target pronunciation. The parent and child will repeat this process up to three times before stopping. The process will occur again the next time the child utters the word, until at some point, often a year or more later, the parent determines that the match is a close enough fit to pass without correction.

Although children go through a period of development in which their language is characterized as "baby talk," this period is short-lived; they fairly quickly begin using the grammatical structures of those around them. What is fascinating is that parents generally correct their children's grammar during the "baby talk" period, with absolutely no effect. In other words, the sort of matching procedure that works so well with pronunciation of individual words does not work at all with grammar. In fact, we do not even observe children participating in the matching procedure when grammar is concerned. We don't know why. Once children are through the "baby talk" phase, the majority of parents stop trying to correct sentence structure, no doubt largely because children at this point begin producing sentences that follow standard syntax. But the connection between the home/community environment and a child's emerging language is important and accounts for the fact that children reared in the South grow up speaking a Southern dialect, that children reared in Boston grow up speaking a New England dialect, and so on. Children acquire not only the accents but also the grammar of these dialects, simply by being immersed in the language community. Although the language that children acquire seldom is congruent with standard English (and almost never with formal standard English), it, nevertheless, is grammatical, based on the linguistic input children receive from those around them. Anything else is not possible because children cannot process ungrammatical utterances. They cannot because ungrammatical utterances are not meaningful and because children's brains have been developing since birth to recognize and process only utterances that are congruent with the basic patterns of English.[5] As a result, after children pass through the "baby-talk" phase, they cannot naturally produce ungrammatical sentences.[6]

For teachers, the phenomenon of language acquisition means that students come to school with grammar already embedded in their brains. Grammar instruction is not transportable to writing, ultimately, because students already have the grammar. The writing is already grammatical, with the exception of those constructions that have become widespread throughout society, such as "The reason is because...."

NONSTANDARD DIALECTS

Although some teachers are willing to grant that the problems of their Anglo students are due to usage rather than grammar, the majority refuse to do so when it comes to black and Chicano students. When faced with sentences such as the following, many people naturally resist the suggestion that the structures are grammatical:

I is hungry.

I'm is thirsty.

They goes to da mall.

He like da woman has blonde hair.

She don' never goin' call.

Nevertheless, both Black English Vernacular (BEV) and Chicano English are grammatical—but their grammatical structures are different from Standard English. Whereas Standard English requires verbs to be tensed, for example, BEV does not. Likewise, whereas Standard English does not require

---

[5]Some scholars propose that all children are born with what is known as a "universal grammar" that allows for very early parameter setting (VEPS) with regard to language in general (Rice, 1996; Wexler, 1996). When we examine the known languages, we find that they all fall predominantly into three characteristic patterns: SVO, SOV, and VSO, with the majority of the world's languages characterized by the first two patterns. Three other possible patterns exist (VOS, OVS, & OSV), but only the first two are attested, and these are found among isolated traditional people in Australia, Indonesia, and South America (Comrie, 1981). Some who accept the notion of universal grammar and VEPS argue that the human brain is predisposed, some might even say genetically programmed, to accept and process linguistic input that follows certain patterns (Rice, 1996). Any input that does not match the set parameters is not recognized as language.

[6]Even "baby talk" seems to have its own grammar, characterized as a pivotal grammar, which orders actions around nouns and lacks function words.

verbs to indicate the duration or frequency of an action (a feature called *aspect*), BEV does.

Now we are in more complex territory. Few children grow up immersed in a language environment that consists of formal Standard English. In fact, if we think of language acquisition as existing on a continuum, with formal standard on one end and extremely nonstandard on the other, most children's home language is probably located somewhere south of the midpoint. For children of color, the home language can be very far south, indeed. The result is a gap between the language of the home and the language of the school, a gap that students are expected to bridge fairly quickly. They face a major difficulty, however, because their home language/dialect is already established firmly in the neural network. It is not readily malleable, and it is quite resistant to direct instruction. An easy way to grasp this reality is to consider the process of learning a second language. Like legions of others, I spent two years studying Spanish at the university but learned to speak it well only after living in Mexico for a while. While studying Spanish in class, the language seemed artificial, and I had no compelling reason to master it; after all, everyone around me spoke English. In Mexico, however, I had to use Spanish to communicate even my most basic needs (*¿Donde esta el baño?*), so my motivation to learn was high. Unfortunately, many black and Hispanic students have little motivation to master Standard English, for a wide variety of social reasons rooted in lack of socioeconomic opportunity, discrimination, and injustice.

In theory, school provides all students the opportunity to master standard, if not formal Standard English. Working-class children, upper-class children, black, white, brown, and yellow all come together under the great umbrella of compulsory education where they are immersed in a Standard English environment. This immersion, like my sojourn in Mexico, serves to move students forward along the continuum so that their language more closely resembles the language of the school.

In practice, this does not work. Grammar instruction is not only arcane but also simply incomprehensible to a large number of students. Moreover, the concept of the school as a great melting pot is obsolete, proven false by the failure of bussing and forced integration, the subsequent self-segregation of students, and the dramatic influx of illegal immigrants that has resulted in schools that are 80 or 90% limited English proficient. The situation has become more problematic over the last decade, as the language skills of teachers have declined. On college and university campuses where teachers are trained, it has become commonplace to hear students—and increasingly, faculty—using a whole range of nonstandard expressions and speech. The consequences are self-evident. Local newspapers periodically print copies of notes teachers send home with children that are riddled with errors, such as the following note that a third-grade boy brought home from his teacher:

> Bobby was not allowed to go out for recess today becuz he had to re-do his paper on dinosors, becuz I do not allow students to type there papers only to hand write them and Bobby's paper was typed or printed. Pleeze make sure that Bobby don't type his papers in the future.

This note is grammatical, but should we accept it from a teacher? Also, doesn't it raise an important empirical question? Can we reasonably expect students to apply conventions of formal Standard English when an increasing number of their teachers cannot? In the end, the idea that schools are places where students can master formal Standard English fails because our schools cannot adequately provide our children with the necessary models. Grammar instruction under these circumstances becomes even more divorced from the realities of everyday language. It can give students a vocabulary with which they can discuss language, but it will not give the majority any actual tools that they can use to improve their writing.

We need to bring into this analysis the fact that school grammar does an even worse job of describing nonstandard dialects than it does of describing Standard English. The child who speaks BEV or Chicano English will find it remarkably difficult to make a connection between his or her language and the grammar in his textbook. Such students must be immersed in a formal Standard English environment if their language is to improve, but for a society of nonreaders, where does this environment exist?

Some grammar advocates point to the fact that a few students develop, after intensive grammar study, what is called an internal *monitor,* which they can use to differentiate between the language of home and the language of school. This is a valid claim, for we see the monitor at work among some students who, for instance, typically use objective case pronouns in subject positions, as illustrated here:

> ?Macarena and *me* went to the movies last weekend.[7]

> ?Fred and *him* drove all the way to Port Orchard without stopping.

During an editing phase, students who apply their monitors will correct these sentences. But they usually do so not because they feel that the sentences are somehow unacceptable but because they have learned that objective-case pronouns in these positions are not acceptable to teachers. More often

---

[7]The question mark here indicates that these sentences, although deemed grammatical, violate standard usage conventions.

than not, we see these same students fail to apply the monitor to their speech, unless they are in a very formal situation. We can conclude from these observations that the grammar is not internalized even though it can be applied via the monitor.

The existence of the internal monitor may seem, initially, to be ample justification for spending many years teaching students traditional grammar. Unfortunately, this perception is flawed. One major problem is that not all students develop a monitor. In addition, definitive research by O'Hare (1973), as well as several studies reviewed by Hillocks (1986), showed that students could more easily learn even complex grammatical patterns without reliance on terminology. They simply had to study the patterns. On this account, the rather modest editing skills that grammar instruction provides hardly seem worth the massive effort involved, particularly considering that an alternative methodology is probably more effective and efficient. Even worse, many students develop internal monitors that produce incorrect results. Case, (changes in the form of a noun to indicate its function as either a subject or an object) once again, offers an example. Large numbers of people, having been drilled on nominative case, apply it uniformly, thereby producing sentences that are no better than those produced by people who have no monitor at all. Consider the following examples, taken from student writing:

The grades the teacher gave to my roommate and *I* were unfair.

The subjects met with the principal investigator and *I* to receive their instructions.

The differences between *he* and *I* are greater than I can explain in a short message.

During conferences, these writers stated that they thought the nominative-case pronouns were correct here, even though they would not use them in their speech. Their monitors had provided them with the incorrect case through what is called *hyper-correction.*

It is easy to assume that only students are guilty of such errors, but actually they riddle the language of huge numbers of people, even the highly educated. The blunders people make with language and grammar could fill a book. For example, English has a class of verbs known as *linking verbs,* words such as *taste, feel, seem, smell,* and forms of *be.* Linking verbs can only be followed, grammatically, by adjectives, nouns, and prepositional phrases, as shown in the sample sentences below:

Macarena is the winner. (linking verb + noun)

The bread tasted funny. (linking verb + adjective)

The room smelled like fish. (linking verb + prepositional phrase)

Few people have any trouble at all with linking verbs, with one notable exception involving the linking verb *feel* when used to describe remorse over some unpleasant situation. There are two possibilities, and one is incorrect. What is interesting is that the more education a person has, the more likely he or she is to use the incorrect form:[8]

I feel *bad*.

*I feel *badly*.

"I feel badly" is incorrect because *badly* is an adverb, not an adjective. And remember, linking verbs cannot be followed by adverbs. Once again, the monitor fails through hyper-correction.

FOR WRITING AND DISCUSSION

Write a brief essay discussing your feelings about people who do not speak English correctly. Do you have friends whose first language is English who do not speak "correctly?" If so, does their poor usage bother you in any way? Do you feel compelled to correct them?

TEACHING USAGE

If grammar instruction doesn't help students become better writers, if it doesn't even help them with simple issues such as case, does it have any value? Yes. Grammar can be one of the more interesting subjects a person can study—when it is taught the right way. The right way does not link it with writing but instead treats grammar as a way of studying the intricacies of language. But this grammar is not traditional grammar, which does a poor job of describing how English operates. In addition, there is value in knowing how to talk about language. Teachers and students benefit when they have a common vocabulary for analysis and when they share concepts of English structure.

The first step toward solving the problem of grammar instruction is to recognize that direct instruction is not particularly effective in the early grades and not particularly effective in the later grades when it relies on textbooks

---

[8]In a landmark study, Labov (1970) tabulated grammatical and ungrammatical sentences in a variety of social settings for several social classes. Although most sentences were technically grammatical, Labov found that working-class subjects had a higher percentage of grammatical utterances than middle-class subjects. More interesting still, academics had the *highest* percentage of ungrammatical sentences.

and exercises. More effective are approaches that immerse students in language itself, approaches that give students opportunities to analyze not only their own language but also the language of everyone around them. Students learn a great deal from observing and recording the language people use, and they find much delight in doing so. Most are fascinated to discover, when they listen carefully and apply their knowledge of grammar and usage, that highly paid and well-educated people frequently produce language that has some horrible errors in it.

Such approaches also need to be linked to other activities, reading in particular. Discussions of reading inevitably involve questions of meaning as students and teacher explore what a given author means in a text. And questions of "what" lead naturally to questions of "how," which is where issues of structure and usage come in. This strategy can be enhanced, at any grade level, when teachers read aloud to their students and make comments that focus student attention on a particular word or phrase. This indirect approach to grammar and usage reinforces concepts in ways that direct instruction cannot. Remarking, for example, that a certain word is an "interesting adjective" draws students to the word, and it also models the important idea that some words are more interesting than others, while simultaneously reinforcing the concept of "adjective."

A vital part of such teaching involves accepting the fact that most of the surface problems we find in student writing involve errors in usage, not errors in grammar. It also is important to understand that grammar is related to the structure of language, not its production. We also need to recognize that usage problems are pervasive; they permeate the language of all people. Even the writing of highly educated people is often plagued with errors in spite of the fact that this writing is always reviewed and copyedited numerous times by professionals. We also need to recognize that, in oral discourse, the message is the focus of attention, so mistakes tend to be less distracting. The situation is different for writing because readers have more time to attend to form. Some of the usage problems that we see in student writing are the result of their transporting informal conventions of speech to the more formal arena of writing. Perhaps the majority, however, are rooted in a pervasive lack of reading experience among students and an even greater lack of reflection on the fundamentals of textual form.

The greatest challenge teachers face, therefore, is helping students read more and motivating them to be more reflective. No doubt the hardest part of this challenge for the public school teacher is finding ways to individualize writing instruction, making it one-on-one. We know that this kind of instruction works best for writing; we know that pointing out and then showing students how to correct their usage blunders again and again, day after day, results in a substantial improvement. What we don't know how to do is to fit this kind of instruction into a teacher's schedule. Until we do, it is likely that grammar instruction will be viewed as a shortcut panacea for the usage problems we find in our students' writing.

FOR WRITING AND DISCUSSION

How would you describe your experience with grammar as a student in public school? For example, did you study traditional grammar? How many years did you study grammar? Was the instruction based on the idea that knowledge of grammar would improve your writing? Did your teacher ever comment that some feature of your writing was "ungrammatical"?

How would you describe your perception of the relation between grammar and writing prior to reading this chapter? Has this chapter changed your view? Why or why not? Consider some ways that you might use grammar and usage instruction to improve student writing. What approach would you advocate?

CLASSROOM ACTIVITY

In *The Teacher's Grammar Book,* Williams (1999) provides the following "make-believe" grammar. This grammar is designed to illustrate how learning grammar rules and applying them to writing tasks require significantly different abilities. Complete the activity and then write about what you learned from it.

A Make-Believe Grammar

Directions: Study the following grammar rules.

Rule 1:	All adjectives must follow the nouns they modify.
Example:	The car *old* stopped at the light *red.*
Exception:	Any adjective that modifies a noun signifying or related to the body of a person will come before the noun, but the noun will take the suffix -o.
Example:	The old *man-o* gave the flower to the young *woman-o* because he liked her pretty *face-o.*
Rule 2:	The indefinite article is *zot.* (Indefinite articles are *a* and *an.*)

Example: At the circus, the clown tooted *zot* horn.

Exception: Indefinite articles that come before an adjective are *zots*.

Example: We saw *zots* old policeman riding *zots* brown horse.

Rule 3:   The progressive verb form consists of *be* + *verb* + *ing*, but
                 tense is marked as follows—*x* for past, *y* for present, and *z*
                 for future.

Example: The man *be-y* washing his car.

Exception: All actions involving nonhumans form the progressive
                 with *be* + *verb* + *ing*, but tense in all instances is marked
                 with *k*.

Example: My dog *be-k* running in the yard.

Part 1

Directions: *Use these rules to correct the following "ungrammatical"*
                 sentences:

1. The wind blew in over the dark mountains and chilled the young
   boys.
2. There was a strange look on the woman's face, as though she was
   thinking deep thoughts.
3. The waves were crashing against the beach, but the hardy surfers
   were waiting until the foamy crests were higher.
4. Several people strolled down the boardwalk and tossed a handful
   of bread crumbs at the screeching gulls that were flying
   overhead.
5. Macarena was getting cold because she had forgotten to bring
   even a light jacket.
6. Fritz was bundled up snug and warm in a down parka, but he was
   not going to offer his warm coat to Macarena.
7. Macarena began walking to her old Ford as the noisy gulls were
   swooping down at her.
8. Fritz was following slowly behind when one of the gulls stole a
   piece of a derelict's soggy Big Mac.
9. A few more birds distracted the derelict until he dropped the
   burger, and then a huge gull grabbed it in his yellow beak.
10. Meanwhile, a sullen Macarena slid into the driver's seat and
    drove off, leaving Fritz standing in the lot with a silly look on his
    silly face.

Part 2

In about 10 minutes, write a description of the things you did before going to campus today. Be sure to use our make-believe grammar in your writing.

FOR FURTHER EXPLORATION

Amastae, J. (1984). The writing needs of Hispanic students. In B. Cronnell (Ed.), *The writing needs of linguistically different students.* Washington, DC: SWRL Educational Research and Development.

Although the focus of this work is on broad social and pedagogical issues, the author notes that too often writing instruction for Hispanic students has been rooted in bottom-up, grammar-based approaches that do little to teach the skills students need to succeed.

Christensen, F. (1967). *Notes toward a new rhetoric: Six essays for teachers.* New York: Harper & Row.

This slim volume broke new ground in the area of sentence combining. The author explains how to teach sentence combining without requiring students to know much at all about grammar.

Connors, R. (2000). The erasure of the sentence. *College Composition and Communication, 52,* 96–128.

An important review of the efficacy of sentence combining, a technique that builds syntactic maturity without reliance on grammar instruction.

Coulson, A. (1996). Schooling and literacy over time: The rising cost of stagnation and decline. *Research in the Teaching of English, 30,* 311–327.

The article examines the decline in SAT scores since 1967, focusing on the precipitous decline in verbal scores. A leading cause of this decline is the failure of schools to teach reading and writing effectively.

Crowhurst, M., & Piche, G. (1979). Audience and mode of discourse effects on syntactic complexity in writing at two grade levels. *Research in the Teaching of English, 13,* 101–109.

Although many people assume that grammar instruction results in syntactic complexity, there is no evidence to support this assumption. In fact, the authors show that this important factor in good writing is significantly influenced by audience and genre.

Gundlach, R. (1983). *How children learn to write: Perspectives on children's writing for educators and parents.* Washington, DC: National Institute of Education.

Grammar instruction is predicated on a bottom-up model of language learning. The author examines how top-down processes, related to desire to communicate and use of symbols to convey information, underlie how children learn to write.

Parker, R. (1979). From Sputnik to Dartmouth: Trends in the teaching of composition. *English Journal, 68* (6), 32–37.

This article analyzes some of the major trends in teaching composition from the 1950s through the 1960s. It addresses the role grammar played in composition instruction.

REFERENCES

Bateman, D., & Zidonis, F. (1966). *The effect of a study of transformational grammar on the writing of ninth and tenth graders.* Champaign, IL: National Council of Teachers of English.

Braddock, R., Lloyd-Jones, R, & Schoer, L. (1963). *Research in written composition.* Champaign, IL: National Council of Teachers of English.

Chomsky, N. (1957). *Syntactic structures.* The Hague, The Netherlands: Mouton.

Chomsky, N. (1965). *Aspects of the theory of syntax.* Cambridge, MA: MIT Press.

Comrie, B. (1981). *Language universals and linguistic typology.* Chicago, IL: University of Chicago Press.

Crowley, S. (1989). Linguistics and composition instruction: 1950–1980. *Written Communication, 6,* 480–505.

Davis, F. (1984). In defense of grammar. *English Education, 16,* 151–164.

Elley, W., Barham, L., Lamb, H., & Wyllie, M. (1976). The role of grammar in a secondary school English curriculum. *New Zealand Journal of Educational Studies, 10,* 26–42. Reprinted in *Research in the Teaching of English, 10,* 5–21.

Gale, I. (1968). An experimental study of two fifth-grade language-arts programs: An analysis of the writing of children taught linguistic grammar compared to those taught traditional grammar. *Dissertation Abstracts, 28,* 4156A.

Greenwald, E. A., Persky, H. R., Campbell, J. R., & Mazzed, J. (1994). *NAEP 1998 writing: Report card for the nation and the states.* Washington DC: The National Assessment of Educational Progress. (Publication No. NCES 1999462).

Hillocks, G. (1986). *Research on written composition: New directions for teaching.* Urbana, IL: National Conference on Research in English.

Holt, J. R. (1982). In defence of formal grammar. *Curriculum Review, 21,* 173–78.

Kelso, J. (1995). *Dynamic patterns: The self-organization of brain and behavior.* Cambridge, MA: MIT Press.

Kolln, M. (1981). Closing the books on alchemy. *College Composition and Communication, 32,* 139–151.

Labov, W. (1970). *The study of nonstandard English.* Urbana, IL: National Council of Teachers of English.

Lunsford, A., & Connors, R. (1989). *The St. Martin's handbook.* New York, NY: St. Martin's.

Noguchi, R. (1991). *Grammar and the teaching of writing: Limits and possibilities.* Urbana, IL: NCTE.

O'Hare, F. (1973). Sentence combining: Improving student writing without formal grammar instruction. *NCTE Committee on Research Report Series, Number 15*. Urbana, IL: National Council of Teachers of English.

Parker, F., & Campbell, K. (1993). Linguistics and writing: A reassessment. *College Composition and Communication, 44*, 295–314.

U.S. Department of Education. (1999). 1998 Writing report card on the nation and the states. Washington, DC: U.S. Printing Office.

Wexler, K. (1996). The development of inflection in a biologically based theory of language acquisition. In M. L. Rice (Ed.), *Toward a genetics of language* (pp. 113–144). Mahwah, NJ: Lawrence Erlbaum.

White, R. (1965). The effect of structural linguistics on improving English composition compared to that of prescriptive grammar or the absence of grammar instruction. *Dissertation Abstracts, 25*, 5032.

Whitehead, C. (1966). The effect of grammar diagramming on student writing skills. *Dissertation Abstracts, 26*, 3710.

Williams, J. (1993). Rule-governed approaches to language and composition. *Written Communication, 10*, 542–568.

Williams, J. (1999). *The teacher's grammar book*. Mahwah, NJ: Lawrence Erlbaum.

Reading

GRAMMAR, GRAMMARS, AND THE TEACHING OF GRAMMAR

Patrick Hartwell

For me the grammar issue was settled at least twenty years ago with the conclusion offered by Richard Braddock, Richard Lloyd-Jones and Lowell Schoer in 1963.

> In view of the widespread agreement of research studies based upon many types of students and teachers, the conclusion can be stated in strong and unqualified terms: the teaching of formal grammar has a negligible or, because it usually displaces some instruction and practice in composition, even a harmful effect on improvement in writing.[1]

Indeed, I would agree with Janet Emig that the grammar issue is a prime example of "magical thinking": the assumption that students will learn only what we teach and only because we teach.[2]

But the grammar issue, as we will see, is a complicated one. And, perhaps surprisingly, it remains controversial, with the regular appearance of papers defending the teaching of formal grammar or attacking it.[3] Thus Janice Neuleib, writing on "The Relation of Formal Grammar to composition" in *College Composition and Communication* (23 [1977], 247–50), is tempted "to sputter on paper" at reading the quotation above (p. 248), and Martha Kolln, writing in the same journal three years later ("Closing the Books on Alchemy," *CCC* 32 [1981], 139–51), labels people like me "alchemists" for our perverse beliefs. Neuleib reviews five experimental studies, most of them concluding that formal grammar instruction has no

---

Reprinted from *College English* 47.2 (February 1985): 105–27. This text was scanned directly from Victor Villanueava's anthology, "Crosstalk in Comp Theory." Used with permission.

effect on the quality of students' writing nor on their ability to avoid error. Yet she renders in effect a Scots verdict of "Not proven" and calls for more research on the issue. Similarly, Kolln reviews six experimental studies that arrive at similar conclusions, only one of them overlapping with the studies cited by Neuleib. She calls for more careful definition of the word grammar—her definition being "the internalized system that native speakers of a language share" (p. 140)—and she concludes with a stirring call to place grammar instruction at the center of the composition curriculum: "our goal should be to help students understand the system they know unconsciously as native speakers, to teach them the necessary categories and labels that will enable them to think about and talk about their language" (p. 150). Certainly our textbooks and our pedagogies—though they vary widely in what they see as "necessary categories and labels"—continue to emphasize mastery of formal grammar, and popular discussions of a presumed literacy crisis are almost unanimous in their call for a renewed emphasis on the teaching of formal grammar, seen as basic for success in writing.[4]

An Instructive Example

It is worth noting at the outset that both sides in this dispute—the grammarians and the antigrammarians—articulate the issue in the same positivistic terms: what does experimental research tell us about the value of teaching formal grammar? But seventy-five years of experimental research has for all practical purposes told us nothing. The two sides are unable to agree on how to interpret such research. Studies are interpreted in terms of one's prior assumptions about the value of teaching grammar: their results seem not to change those assumptions. Thus the basis of the discussion, a basis shared by Kolln and Neuleib and by Braddock and his colleagues—"what does educational research tell us?"—seems designed to perpetuate, not to resolve, the issue. A single example will be instructive. In 1976 and then at greater length in 1979, W. B. Elley, I. H. Barham, H. Lamb, and M. Wyllie reported on a three-year experiment in New Zealand, comparing the relative effectiveness at the high school level of instruction in transformational grammar, instruction in traditional grammar, and no grammar instruction.[5] They concluded that the formal study of grammar, whether transformational or traditional, improved neither writing quality nor control over surface correctness.

> After two years, no differences were detected in writing performance or language competence; after three years small differences appeared in some minor conventions favoring the TG [transformational grammar] group, but these were more than offset by the less positive attitudes they showed towards their English studies. (p. 18)

Anthony Petrosky, in a review of research ("Grammar Instruction: What We Know," *English Journal*, 66, No. 9 [1977], 86–88), agreed with this conclusion, finding the study to be carefully designed, "representative of the best kind of educational research" (p. 86), its validity "unquestionable" (p. 88). Yet Janice

Neuleib in her essay found the same conclusions to be "startling" and questioned whether the findings could be generalized beyond the target population, New Zealand high school students. Martha Kolln, when her attention is drawn to the study ("Reply to Ron Shook," *CCC*, 32 L1981], 139–151), thinks the whole experiment "suspicious." And John Mellon has been willing to use the study to defend the teaching of grammar; the study of Elley and his colleagues, he has argued, shows that teaching grammar does no harm.[6]

It would seem unlikely, therefore, that further experimental research, in and of itself, will resolve the grammar issue. Any experimental design can be nit-picked, any experimental population can be criticized, and any experimental conclusion can be questioned or, more often, ignored. In fact, it may well be that the grammar question is not open to resolution by experimental research, that, as Noam Chomsky has argued in *Reflections on Language* (New York: Pantheon, 1975), criticizing the trivialization of human learning by behavioral psychologists, the issue is simply misdefined.

> There will be "good experiments" only in domains that lie outside the organism's cognitive capacity. For example, there will be no "good experiments" in the study of human learning.
>
> This discipline... will, of necessity, avoid those domains in which an organism is specially designed to acquire rich cognitive structures that enter into its life in an intimate fashion. The discipline will be of virtually no intellectual interest, it seems to me, since it is restricting itself in principle to those questions that are guaranteed to tell us little about the nature of organisms. (p. 36)

Asking The Right Questions

As a result, though I will look briefly at the tradition of experimental research, my primary goal in this essay is to articulate the grammar issue in different and, I would hope, more productive terms. Specifically, I want to ask four questions:

1. Why is the grammar issue so important? Why has it been the dominant focus of composition research for the last seventy-five years?
2. What definitions of the word *grammar* are needed to articulate the grammar issue intelligibly?
3. What do findings in cognate disciplines suggest about the value of formal grammar instruction?
4. What is our theory of language, and what does it predict about the value of formal grammar instruction? (This question—"what does our theory of language predict?"—seems a much more powerful question than "what does educational research tell us?")

In exploring these questions I will attempt to be fully explicit about issues, terms, and assumptions. I hope that both proponents and opponents of formal grammar instruction would agree that these are useful as shared points of reference: care in definition, full examination of the evidence, reference to relevant work in cognate disciplines, and explicit analysis of the theoretical bases of the issue.

But even with that gesture of harmony it will be difficult to articulate the issue in a balanced way, one that will be acceptable to both sides. After all, we are dealing with a professional dispute in which one side accuses the other of "magical thinking," and in turn that side responds by charging the other as "alchemists." Thus we might suspect that the grammar issue is itself embedded in larger models of the transmission of literacy, part of quite different assumptions about the teaching of composition.

Those of us who dismiss the teaching of formal grammar have a model of composition instruction that makes the grammar issue "uninteresting" in a scientific sense. Our model predicts a rich and complex interaction of learner and environment in mastering literacy, an interaction that has little to do with sequences of skills instruction as such. Those who defend the teaching of grammar tend to have a model of composition instruction that is rigidly skills-centered and rigidly sequential: the formal teaching of grammar, as the first step in that sequence, is the cornerstone or linchpin. Grammar teaching is thus supremely interesting, naturally a dominant focus for educational research. The controversy over the value of grammar instruction, then, is inseparable from two other issues: the issues of sequence in the teaching of composition and of the role of the composition teacher. Consider, for example, the force of these two issues in Janice Neuleib's conclusion: after calling for yet more experimental research on the value of teaching grammar, she ends with an absolute (and unsupported) claim about sequences and teacher roles in composition.

> We do know, however, that some things must be taught at different levels. Insistence on adherence to usage norms by composition teachers does improve usage. Students can learn to organize their papers if teachers do not accept papers that are disorganized. Perhaps composition teachers can teach those two abilities before they begin the more difficult tasks of developing syntactic sophistication and a winning style. ("The Relation of Formal Grammar to Composition," p. 250)

(One might want to ask, in passing, whether "usage norms" exist in the monolithic fashion the phrase suggests and whether refusing to accept disorganized papers is our best available pedagogy for teaching arrangement.)[7]

But I want to focus on the notion of sequence that makes the grammar issue so important: first grammar, then usage, then some absolute model of organization, all controlled by the teacher at the center of the learning process with other matters, those of rhetorical weight—"syntactic sophistication and a winning style"—pushed off to the future. It is not surprising that we call each other names: those of us who question the value of teaching grammar are in fact shaking the whole elaborate edifice of traditional composition instruction.

an active language task, they show productive control over the rule they have denied knowing. I ask them to arrange the following words in a natural order:

French   the   young   girls   four

I have never seen a native speaker of English who did not immediately produce the natural order, "the four young French girls." The rule is that in English the order of adjectives is first, number, second, age, and third, nationality. Native speakers can create analogous phrases using the rule—"the seventy-three aged Scandinavian lechers"; and the drive for meaning is so great that they will create contexts to make sense out of violations of the rule, as in foregrounding for emphasis: "I want to talk to the French four young girls." (I immediately envision a large room, perhaps a banquet hall, filled with tables at which are seated groups of four young girls, each group of a different nationality.) So Grammar 1 is eminently usable knowledge—the way we make our life through language—but it is not accessible knowledge; in a profound sense, we do not know that we have it. Thus neurolinguist Z. N. Pylyshvn speaks of Grammar 1 as "autonomous," separate from common-sense reasoning, and as "cognitively impenetrable," not available for direct examination.[10] In philosophy and linguistics, the distinction is made between formal, conscious, "knowing about" knowledge (like Grammar 2 knowledge) and tacit, unconscious, "knowing how" knowledge (like Grammar 1 knowledge). The importance of this distinction for the teaching of composition—it provides a powerful theoretical justification for mistrusting the ability of Grammar 2 (or Grammar 4) knowledge to affect Grammar 1 performance—was pointed out in this journal by Martin Steinmann, Jr., in 1966 ("Rhetorical Research," *CE*, 27 [1966], 278–285).

Further, the more we learn about Grammar 1—and most linguists would agree that we know surprisingly little about it—the more abstract and implicit it seems. This abstractness can be illustrated with an experiment devised by Lise Menn and reported by Morris Halle,[11] about our rule for forming plurals in speech. It is obvious that we do indeed have a "rule" for forming plurals, for we do not memorize the plural of each noun separately. You will demonstrate productive control over that rule by forming the spoken plurals of the nonsense words below:

thole   flitch   plast

Halle offers two ways of formalizing a Grammar 2 equivalent of this Grammar 1 ability. One form of the rule is the following, stated in terms of speech sounds:

a. If the noun ends in /s z š ž č ǰ/, add /ɪz/;
b. otherwise, if the noun ends in /p t k f Ø/, add /s/;
c. otherwise, add /z/.[11]

This rule comes close to what we literate adults consider to be an adequate rule for plurals in writing, like the rules, for example, taken from a recent "common school grammar," Eric Gould's *Reading into Writing: A Rhetoric, Reader, and Handbook* (Boston: Houghton Mifflin, 1983):

> *Plurals* can be tricky. If you are unsure of a plural, then check it in the dictionary. The general rules are
>
> Add *s* to the singular: *girls, tables*
>
> Add *es* to nouns ending in *ch, sh, x* or *s*: *churches, boxes, wishes*
>
> Add *es* to nouns ending in *y* and preceded by a vowel once you have changed *y* to *i*: *monies, companies*. (p. 666)

(But note the persistent inadequacy of such Grammar 4 rules: here, as I read it, the rule is inadequate to explain the plurals of *ray* and *tray*, even to explain the collective noun *monies,* not a plural at all, formed from the mass noun *money* and offered as an example.) A second form of the rule would make use of much more abstract entities, sound features:

    a. If the noun ends with a sound that is [coronal, strident], add /ɨz/;

    b. otherwise, if the noun ends with a sound that is [non-voiced], add /s/;

    c. otherwise, add /z/.

(The notion of "sound features" is itself rather abstract, perhaps new to readers not trained in linguistics. But such readers should be able to recognize that the spoken plurals of *lip* and *duck,* the sound [s], differ from the spoken plurals of *sea* and *gnu,* the sound [z], only in that the sounds of the latter are "voiced"—one's vocal cords vibrate—while the sounds of the former are "non-voiced.")

To test the psychologically operative rule, the Grammar I rule, native speakers of English were asked to form the plural of the last name of the composer Johann Sebastian *Bach,* a sound [x], unique in American (though not in Scottish) English. If speakers follow the first rule above, using word endings, they would reject a) and b), then apply c), producing the plural as /baxz/, with word-final /z/. (If writers were to follow the rule of the common school grammar, they would produce the written plural *Baches,* apparently, given the form of the rule, on analogy with *churches.*) If speakers follow the second rule, they would have to analyze the sound [x] as [non-labial, noncoronal, dorsal, non-voiced, and non-strident], producing the plural as /baxs/, with word-final /s/. Native speakers of American English overwhelmingly produce the plural as /baxs/. They use knowledge that Halle characterizes as "unlearned and untaught" (p. 140).

Now such a conclusion is counterintuitive—certainly it departs maximally from Grammar 4 rules for forming plurals. It seems that native speakers of English behave as if they have productive control, as Grammar I knowledge, of abstract sound features (± coronal, ± strident, and so on) which are available as conscious, Grammar 2 knowledge only to trained linguists—and, indeed, formally available only within the last hundred years or so. ("Behave as if," in that last sentence, is a necessary hedge, to underscore the difficulty of "knowing about" Grammar I.)

Moreover, as the example of plural rules suggests, the form of the Grammar 1 in the heads of literate adults seems profoundly affected by the acquisition of literacy. Obviously, literate adults have access to different morphological codes: the abstract print -s underlying the predictable /s/ and /z/ plurals, the abstract print -ed underlying the spoken past tense markers /t/, as in "walked," /əd/, as in "surrounded," /d/, as in "scored," and the symbol /θ/ for no surface realization, as in the relaxed standard pronunciation of "I walked to the store." Literate adults also have access to distinctions preserved only in the code of print (for example, the distinction between "a good sailer" and "a good sailor" that Mark Aranoff points out in "An English Spelling Convention," *Linguistic Inquiry,* 9 [1978], 299–303). More significantly, Irene Moscowitz speculates that the ability of third graders to form abstract nouns on analogy with pairs like *divine::divinity* and *serene::serenity,* where the spoken vowel changes but the spelling preserves meaning, is a factor of knowing how to read. Carol Chomsky finds a three-stage developmental sequence in the grammatical performance of seven-year-olds, related to measures of kind and variety of reading; and Rita S. Brause finds a nine-stage developmental sequence in the ability to understand semantic ambiguity, extending from fourth graders to graduate students.[12] John Mills and Gordon Hemsley find that level of education, and presumably level of literacy, influence judgments of grammaticality, concluding that literacy changes the deep structure of one's internal grammar; Jean Whyte finds that oral language functions develop differently in readers and non-readers; José Morais, Jésus Alegria, and Paul Bertelson find that illiterate adults are unable to add or delete sounds at the beginning of nonsense words, suggesting that awareness of speech as a series of phones is provided by learning to read an alphabetic code. Two experiments—one conducted by Charles A. Ferguson, the other by Lary E. Hamilton and David Barton—find that adults' ability to recognize segmentation in speech is related to degree of literacy, not to amount of schooling or general ability.[13]

It is worth noting that none of these investigators would suggest that the developmental sequences they have uncovered be isolated and taught as discrete skills. They are natural concomitants of literacy, and they seem best characterized not as isolated rules but as developing schemata, broad strategies for approaching written language.

Grammar 2

We can, of course, attempt to approximate the rules or schemata of Grammar 1 by writing fully explicit descriptions that model the competence of a native speaker. Such rules, like the rules for pluralizing nouns or ordering adjectives discussed above, are the goal of the science of linguistics, that is, Grammar 2. There are a number of scientific grammars—an older structuralist model and several versions within a generative-transformational paradigm, not to mention isolated schools like tagmemic grammar, Montague grammar, and the like. In fact, we cannot think of Grammar 2 as a stable entity, for its form changes with each new issue of each linguistics journal, as new "rules of grammar" are proposed and debated. Thus Grammar 2, though of great theoretical interest to the composition teacher, is of little practical use in the classroom, as Constance Weaver has pointed out (*Grammar for Teachers* [Urbana, Ill.: NCTE, 1979], pp. 3–6). Indeed Grammar 2 is a scientific model of Grammar 1, not a description of it, so that questions of psychological reality, while important, are less important than other, more theoretical factors, such as the elegance of formulation or the global power of rules. We might, for example, wish to replace the rule for ordering adjectives of age, number, and nationality cited above with a more general rule— what linguists call a "fuzzy" rule—that adjectives in English are ordered by their abstract quality of "nouniness": adjectives that are very much like nouns, like *French* or *Scandinavian*, come physically closer to nouns than do adjectives that are less "nouny," like *four* or *aged*. But our motivation for accepting the broader rule would be its global power, not its psychological reality.[14]

I try to consider a hostile reader, one committed to the teaching of grammar, and I try to think of ways to hammer in the central point of this distinction, that the rules of Grammar 2 are simply unconnected to productive control over Grammar 1. I can argue from authority: Noam Chomsky has touched on this point whenever he has concerned himself with the implications of linguistics for language teaching, and years ago transformationalist Mark Lester stated unequivocally, "there simply appears to be no correlation between a writer's study of language and his ability to write."[15] I can cite analogies offered by others: Francis Christensen's analogy in an essay originally published in 1962 that formal grammar study would be "to invite a centipede to attend to the sequence of his legs in motion,"[16] or James Britton's analogy, offered informally after a conference presentation, that grammar study would be like forcing starving people to master the use of a knife and fork before allowing them to eat. I can offer analogies of my own, contemplating the wisdom of asking a pool player to master the physics of momentum before taking up a cue or of making a prospective driver get a degree in automotive engineering before engaging the clutch. I consider a hypothetical argument, that if Grammar 2 knowledge affected Grammar 1 performance, then linguists would be our best writers. (I can certify that they are, on the whole, not.) Such a position, after all, is only in accord with other domains of science: the formula for catching a fly ball in baseball ("Playing It by Ear," *Scientific American*, 248, No. 4 [1983], 76) is of such complexity that it is beyond my understanding and, I would suspect, that of many workaday centerfielders. But perhaps I can best hammer in this claim—that Grammar 2 knowledge has no effect on Grammar 1 performance—by offering a demonstration.

The diagram below is an attempt by Thomas N. Huckin and Leslie A. Olsen (*English for Science and Technology* [New York: McGraw-Hill, 1983]) to offer, for students of English as a second language, a fully explicit formution of what is, for native speakers, a trivial rule of the language—the choice of definite article, indefinite article, or no definite article.

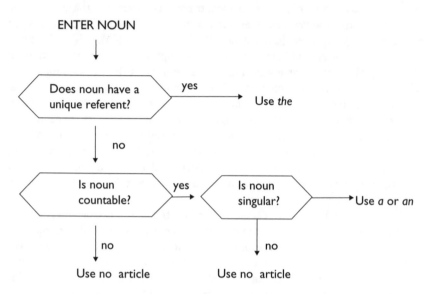

There are obvious limits to such a formulation, for article choice in English is less a matter of rule than of idiom ("I went to college" versus "I went to a university" versus British "I went to university"), real-world knowledge (using indefinite "I went into a house" instantiates definite "I looked at the ceiling," and indefinite "I visited a university" instantiates definite "I talked with the professors) and stylistic choice (the last sentence above might alternatively end with "the choice of the definite article, the indefinite article, or no article") Huckin and Olsen invite non-native speakers to use the rule consciously to justify article choice in technical prose, such as the passage below from P. F. Brandwein (*Matter: An Earth Science* [New York: Harcourt Brace Jovanovich, 1975]). I invite you to spend a couple of minutes doing the same thing, with the understanding that this exercise is a test case: you are using a very explicit rule to justify a fairly straightforward issue of grammatical choice.

Imagine a cannon on top of _____ highest mountain on earth. It is firing _____ cannonballs horizontally. _____ first cannonball fired follows its path. As _____ cannonball moves, _____ gravity pulls it down, and it soon hits _____ ground. Now _____ velocity with which each succeeding cannonball is fired is increased. Thus, _____ cannonball goes farther each time. Cannonball 2 goes farther than _____ cannonball 1 although each is being pulled by _____ gravity toward the earth all _____ time. _____ last cannonball is fired with such tremendous velocity that it goes completely around _____ earth. It returns to _____ mountaintop and continues around the earth again and again. _____ cannonball's inertia causes it to continue in motion indefinitely in _____ orbit around earth. In such a situation, we could consider _____ cannonball to be artificial satellite, just like _____ weather satellites launched by _____ U.S. Weather Service. (p. 209)

Most native speakers of English who have attempted this exercise report a great deal of frustration, a curious sense of working against, rather than with, the rule. The rule, however valuable it may be for non-native speakers, is, for the most part, simply unusable for native speakers of the language.

Cognate Areas of Research

We can corroborate this demonstration by turning to research in two cognate areas, studies of the induction of rules of artificial languages and studies of the role of formal rules in second language acquisition. Psychologists have studied the ability of subjects to learn artificial languages, usually constructed of nonsense syllables or letter strings. Such languages can be described by phrase structure rules:

$$S \Rightarrow VX$$
$$X \Rightarrow MX$$

More clearly, they can be presented as flow diagrams, as below:

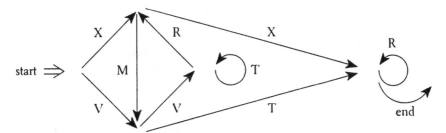

This diagram produces "sentences" like the following:

VVTRXRR.	XMVTTRX.	XXRR.
XMVRMT.	VVTTRMT.	XMTRRR.

The following "sentences" would be "ungrammatical" in this language:

*VMXTT.	*RTXVVT.	*TRVXXVVM.

Arthur S. Reber, in a classic 1967 experiment, demonstrated that mere exposure to grammatical sentences produced tacit learning: subjects who copied several grammatical sentences performed far above chance in judging the grammaticality of other letter strings. Further experiments have shown that providing subjects with formal rules remarkably degrades performance: subjects given the "rules of the language" do much less well in acquiring the rules than do subjects not given the rules. Indeed, even telling subjects that they are to induce the rules of an artificial language degrades performance. Such laboratory experiments are admittedly contrived, but they confirm predictions that our theory of language would make about the value of formal rules in language learning.[17]

The thrust of recent research in second language learning similarly works to constrain the value of formal grammar rules. The most explicit statement of the value of formal rules is that of Stephen D. Krashen's monitor model.[18] Krashen divides second language mastery into *acquisition*— tacit, informal mastery, akin to first language acquisition—and formal learning—conscious application of Grammar 2 rules, which he calls "monitoring" output. In another essay Krashen uses his model to predict a highly individual use of the monitor and a highly constrained role for formal rules:

> Some adults (and very few children) are able to use conscious rules to increase
> the grammatical accuracy of their output, and even for these people, very strict
> conditions need to be met before the conscious grammar can be applied.[19]

In *Principles and Practice in Second Language Acquisition* (New York: Pergamon, 1982) Krashen outlines these conditions by means of a series of concentric circles, beginning with a large circle denoting the rules of English and a smaller circle denoting the subset of those rules described by formal linguists (adding that most linguists would protest that the size of this circle is much too large):

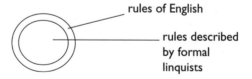

rules of English

rules described
by formal
linquists

(p. 92)

Krashen then adds smaller circles, as shown below—a subset of the rules described by formal linguists that would be known to applied linguists, a subset of those rules that would be available to the best teachers, and then a subset of those rules that teachers might choose to present to second language learners:

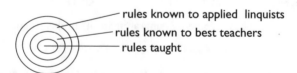

rules known to applied linquists

rules known to best teachers

rules taught

(P 93)

Of course, as Krashen notes, not all the rules taught will be learned, and not all those learned will be available, as what he calls "mental baggage" (p. 94), for conscious use.

An experiment by Ellen Bialystock, asking English speakers learning French to judge the grammaticality of taped sentences, complicates this issue, for reaction time data suggest that learners first make an intuitive judgment of grammaticality, using implicit or Grammar 1 knowledge, and only then search for formal explanations, using explicit or Grammar 2 knowledge.[20] This distinction would suggest that Grammar 2 knowledge is of use to second language learners only after the principle has already been mastered as tacit Grammar 1 knowledge. In the terms of Krashen's model, learning never becomes acquisition (*Principles*, p. 86).

An ingenious experiment by Herbert W. Seliger complicates the issue yet further ("On the Nature and Function of Language Rules in Language Learning," *TESOL Quarterly*, 13 [1979], 359–369). Seliger asked native and non-native speakers of English to orally identify pictures of objects (e.g., "an apple," "a pear," "a book," "an umbrella"), noting whether they used the correct form of the indefinite articles *a* and *an*. He then asked each speaker to state the rule for choosing between *a* and *an*. He found no correlation between the ability to state the rule and the ability to apply it correctly, either with native or non-native speakers. Indeed, three of four adult non-native speakers in his sample produced a correct form of the rule, but they did not apply it in speaking. A strong conclusion from this experiment would be that formal rules of grammar seem to have no value whatsoever. Seliger, however, suggests a more paradoxical interpretation. Rules are of no use, he agrees, but some people think they are, and for these people, assuming that they have internalized the rules, even inadequate rules are of heuristic value, for they allow them to access the internal rules they actually use.

The Incantations of The "Common School Grammars"

Such a paradox may explain the fascination we have as teachers with "rules of grammar" of the Grammar 4 variety, the "rules" of the "common school grammars." Again and again such rules are inadequate to the facts of written language; you will recall that we have known this since Francis' 1927 study. R. Scott Baldwin and James M. Coady, studying how readers respond to punctuation signals ("Psycholinguistic Approaches to a Theory of Punctuation," *Journal of Reading Behavior*, 10 [1978], 363–83), conclude that conventional rules of punctuation are "a complete sham" (p. 375). My own favorite is the Grammar 4 rule for showing possession, always expressed in terms of adding -'s or -s' to nouns, while our internal grammar, if you think about it, adds possession to noun phrases, albeit under severe stylistic constraints: "the horses of the Queen of England" are "the Queen of England's horses" and "the feathers of the duck over there" are "the duck over there's feathers." Suzette Haden Elgin refers to the "rules" of Grammar 4 as "incantations" (*Never Mind the Trees*, p. 9: see footnote 3).

It may simply be that as hyperliterate adults we are conscious of "using rules" when we are in fact doing something else, something far more complex, accessing tacit heuristics honed by print literacy itself. We can clarify this notion by reaching for an acronym coined by technical writers to explain the readability of complex prose—COIK: "clear only if known." The rules of Grammar 4—no, we can at this point be more honest—the incantations of Grammar 4 are COIK. If you know how to signal possession in the code of print, then the advice to add -'s to nouns makes perfect sense, just as the collective noun *monies is* a fine example of changing -*y* to -*i* and adding es to form the plural. But if you have not grasped, tacitly, the abstract representation of possession in print, such incantations can only be opaque.

Worse yet, the advice given in "the common school grammars" is unconnected with anything remotely resembling literate adult behavior. Consider, as an example, the rule for not writing a sentence fragment as the rule is described in the best-selling college grammar text, John C. Hodges and Mary S. Whitten's *Harbrace College Handbook,* 9th ed. (New York: Harcourt Brace Jovanovich, 1982). In order to get to the advice, "as a rule, do not write a sentence fragment" (p. 25), the student must master the following learning tasks:

Recognizing verbs.

Recognizing subjects and verbs.

Recognizing all parts of speech. (*Harbrace* lists eight.)

Recognizing phrases and subordinate clauses. (*Harbrace* lists six types of phrases, and it offers incomplete lists of eight relative pronouns and eighteen subordinating conjunctions.)

Recognizing main clauses and types of sentences.

These learning tasks completed, the student is given the rule above, offered a page of exceptions, and then given the following advice (or is it an incantation?):

Before handing in a composition, . . . proofread each word group written as a sentence. Test each one for completeness. First, be sure that it has at least one subject and one predicate. Next, be sure that the word group is not a dependent clause beginning with a subordinating conjunction or a relative clause. (p. 27)

The school grammar approach defines a sentence fragment as a conceptual error—as not having conscious knowledge of the school grammar definition of *sentence.* It demands heavy emphasis on rote memory, and it asks students to behave in ways patently removed from the behaviors of mature writers. (I have never in my life tested a sentence for completeness, and I am a better writer—and probably a better person—as a consequence.) It may be, of course, that some developing writers, at some points in their development, may benefit from such advice—or, more to the point, may think that they benefit—but, as Thomas Friedman points out in "Teaching Error, Nurturing Confusion" (*CE,* 45 [1983], 390–399), our theory of language tells us that such advice is, at the best, COIK. As the Maine joke has it, about a tourist asking directions from a farmer, "you can't get there from here."

Redefining Error

In the specific case of sentence fragments, Mina P. Shaughnessy (*Errors and Expectations* [New York: Oxford University Press, 1977]) argues that such errors are not conceptual failures at all, but performance errors—mistakes in punctuation. Muriel Harris' error counts support this view ("Mending the Fragmented Free Modifier," *CCC*, 32 [1981], 175–182). Case studies show example after example of errors that occur *because of* instruction—one thinks, for example, of David Bartholmae's student explaining that he added an *-s* to *children* "because it's a plural" ("The Study of Error," *CCC*, 31 [1980], 262). Surveys, such as that by Muriel Harris ("Contradictory Perceptions of the Rules of Writing," *CCC*, 30 [1979], 218–220), and our own observations suggest that students consistently misunderstand such Grammar 4 explanations (COIK, you will recall). For example, from Patrick Hartwell and Robert H. Bentley and from Mike Rose, we have two separate anecdotal accounts of students, cited for punctuating a *because*-clause as a sentence, who have decided to avoid using *because*. More generally, Collette A. Daiute's analysis of errors made by college students shows that errors tend to appear at clause boundaries, suggesting short-term memory load and not conceptual deficiency as a cause of error.[21]

Thus, if we think seriously about error and its relationship to the worship of formal grammar study, we need to attempt some massive dislocation of our traditional thinking, to shuck off our hyperliterate perception of the value of formal rules, and to regain the confidence in the tacit power of unconscious knowledge that our theory of language gives us. Most students, reading their writing aloud, will correct in essence all errors of spelling, grammar, and, by intonation, punctuation, but usually without noticing that what they read departs from what they wrote.[22] And Richard H. Haswell ("Minimal Marking," *CE*, 45 1983], 600–604) notes that his students correct 61.1% of their errors when they are identified with a simple mark in the margin rather than by error type. Such findings suggest that we need to redefine error, to see it not as a cognitive or linguistic problem, a problem of not knowing a "rule of grammar" (whatever that may mean), but rather, following the insight of Robert J. Bracewell ("Writing as a Cognitive Activity," *Visible Language*, 14 [1980], 400–422), as a problem of metacognition and metalinguistic awareness, a matter of accessing knowledges that, to be of any use, learners must have already internalized by means of exposure to the code. (Usage issues—Grammar 3— probably represent a different order of problem. Both Joseph Emonds and Jeffrey Jochnowitz establish that the usage issues we worry most about are linguistically unnatural, departures from the grammar in our heads.)[23]

The notion of metalinguistic awareness seems crucial. The sentence below, created by Douglas R. Hofstadter ("Metamagical Themes," *Scientific American*, 235, No. 1 [1981], 22–32), is offered to clarify that notion; you are invited to examine it for a moment or two before continuing.

Their is four errors in this sentence. Can you find them?

Three errors announce themselves plainly enough, the misspellings of *there* and *sentence* and the use of *is* instead of *are*. (And, just to illustrate the perils of hyperliteracy, let it be noted that, through three years of drafts, I referred to the choice of *is* and *are* as a matter of "subject-verb agreement.") The fourth error resists detection, until one assesses the truth value of the sentence itself—the fourth error is that there are not four errors, only three. Such a sentence (Hofstadter calls it a "self-referencing sentence") asks you to look at it in two ways, simultaneously as statement and as linguistic artifact—in other words, to exercise metalinguistic awareness.

A broad range of cross-cultural studies suggest that metalinguistic awareness is a defining feature of print literacy. Thus Sylvia Scribner and Michael Cole, working with the triliterate Vai of Liberia (variously literate in English, through schooling; in Arabic, for religious purposes; and in an indigenous Vai script, used for personal affairs), find that metalinguistic awareness, broadly conceived, is the only cognitive skill underlying each of the three literacies. The one statistically significant skill shared by literate Vai was the recognition of word boundaries. Moreover, literate Vai tended to answer "yes" when asked (in Vai), "Can you call the sun the moon and the moon the sun?" while illiterate Vai tended to have grave doubts about such metalinguistic play. And in the United States Henry and Lila R. Gleitman report quite different responses by clerical workers and PhD candidates asked to interpret nonsense compounds like "house-bird glass": clerical workers focused on meaning and plausibility (for example, "a house-bird made of glass"), while PhD candidates focused on syntax (for example, "a very small drinking cup for canaries" or "a glass that protects house-birds").[24] More general research findings suggest a clear relationship between measures of metalinguistic awareness and measures of literacy level.[25] William Labov, speculating on literacy acquisition in inner-city ghettoes, contrasts "stimulus-bound" and "language-bound" individuals, suggesting that the latter seem to master literacy more easily.[26] The analysis here suggests that the causal relationship works the other way, that it is the mastery of written language that increases one's awareness of language as language.

This analysis has two implications. First, it makes the question of socially non-standard dialects, always implicit in discussions of teaching formal grammar, into a non-issue.[27] Native speakers of English, regardless of dialect, show tacit mastery of the conventions of Standard English, and that mastery seems to transfer into abstract orthographic knowledge through interaction with print.[28] Developing writers show the same patterning of errors, regardless of dialect.[29] Studies of reading and of writing suggest that surface features of spoken dialect are simply irrelevant to mastering print literacy.[30] Print is a complex cultural code—or better yet, a system of codes—and my bet is that, regardless of instruction, one masters those codes from the top down, from pragmatic questions of voice, tone, audience, register, and rhetorical strategy, not from the bottom up, from grammar to usage to fixed forms of organization.

Second, this analysis forces us to posit multiple literacies, used for multiple purposes, rather than a single static literacy, engraved in "rules of grammar." These multiple literacies are evident in cross-cultural studies.[31] They are equally evident when we inquire into the uses of literacy in American communities.[32] Further, given that students, at all levels, show widely variant interactions with print literacy, there would seem to be little to do with grammar—with Grammar 2 or with Grammar 4—that we could isolate as a basis for formal instruction.[33]

Grammar 5: Stylistic Grammar

Similarly, when we turn to Grammar 5, "grammatical terms used in the interest of teaching prose style," so central to Martha Kolln's argument for teaching formal grammar, we find that the grammar issue is simply beside the point. There are two fully-articulated positions about "stylistic grammar," which I will label "romantic" and "classic," following Richard Lloyd-Jones and Richard E. Young.[34] The romantic position is that stylistic grammars, though perhaps useful for teachers, have little place in the teaching of composition, for students must struggle with and through language toward meaning. This position rests on a theory of language ultimately philosophical rather than linguistic (witness, for example, the contempt for linguists in Ann Berthoff's *The Making of Meaning: Metaphors, Models, and Maxims for Writing Teachers* [Montclair, N.J.: Boynton/Cook, 1981]); it is articulated as a theory of style by Donald A. Murray and, on somewhat different grounds (that stylistic grammars encourage overuse of the monitor), by Ian Pringle. The classic position, on the other hand, is that we can find ways to offer developing writers helpful suggestions about prose style, suggestions such as Francis Christensen's emphasis on the cumulative sentence, developed by observing the practice of skilled writers, and Joseph Williams' advice about predication, developed by psycholinguistic studies of comprehension.[35] James A. Berlin's recent survey of composition theory (*CE*, 45 [1982], 765–777) probably understates the gulf between these two positions and the radically different conceptions of language that underlie them, but it does establish that they share an overriding assumption in common: that one learns to control the language of print by manipulating language in meaningful contexts, not by learning about language in isolation, as by the study of formal grammar. Thus even classic theorists, who choose to present a vocabulary of style to students, do so only as a vehicle for encouraging productive control of communicative structures.

We might put the matter in the following terms. Writers need to develop skills at two levels. One, broadly rhetorical, involves communication in meaningful contexts (the strategies, registers, and procedures of discourse across a range of modes, audiences, contexts, and purposes). The other, broadly metalinguistic rather than linguistic, involves active manipulation of language with conscious attention to surface form. This second level may be developed tacitly, as a natural adjunct to developing rhetorical competencies—I take this to be the position of romantic theorists. It may be developed formally, by manipulating language for stylistic effect, and such manipulation may involve, for pedagogical continuity, a vocabulary of style. But it is primarily developed by any kind of language activity that enhances the awareness of language as language.[36] David T. Hakes, summarizing the research on metalinguistic awareness, notes how far we are from understanding this process: [the optimal conditions for becoming metalinguistically competent involve growing up in a literate environment with adult models who are themselves metalinguistically competent and who foster the growth of that competence in a variety of ways as yet little understood. ("The Development of Metalinguistic Abilities," p. 205: see footnote 25)]

Such a model places language, at all levels, at the center of the curriculum, but not as "necessary categories and labels" (Kolln, "Closing the Books on Alchemy," p. 150), but as literal stuff, verbal clay, to be molded and probed, shaped and reshaped, and, above all, enjoyed.

The Tradition of Experimental Research

Thus, when we turn back to experimental research on the value of formal grammar instruction, we do so with firm predictions given us by our theory of language. Our theory would predict that formal grammar instruction, whether instruction in scientific grammar or instruction in "the common school grammar," would have little to do with control over surface correctness nor with quality of writing. It would predict that any form of active involvement with language would be preferable to instruction in rules or definitions (or incantations). In essence, this is what the research tells us. In 1893, the Committee of Ten (*Report of the Committee of Ten on Secondary School Studies* [Washington, D.C.: U.S. Government Printing Office, 1893]) put grammar at the center of the English curriculum, and its report established the rigidly sequential mode of instruction common for the last century. But the committee explicitly noted that grammar instruction did not aid correctness, arguing instead that it improved the ability to think logically (an argument developed from the role of the "grammarian" in the classical rhetorical tradition, essentially a teacher of literature—see, for example, the etymology of *grammar* in the *Oxford English Dictionary*).

But Franklin S. Hoyt, in a 1906 experiment, found no relationship between the study of grammar and the ability to think logically; his research led him to conclude what I am constrained to argue more than seventy-five years later, that there is no "relationship between a knowledge of technical grammar and the ability to use English and to interpret language" ("The Place of Grammar in the Elementary Curriculum," *Teachers College Record,* 7 [1906], 483–484). Later studies, through the 1920s, focused on the relationship of knowledge of grammar and ability to recognize error; experiments reported by James Boraas in 1917 and by William Asker in 1923 are typical of those that reported no correlation.

In the 1930s, with the development of the functional grammar movement, it was common to compare the study of formal grammar with one form or another of active manipulation of language; experiments by I. 0. Ash in 1935 and Ellen Frogner in 1939 are typical of studies showing the superiority of active involvement with language.[37] In a 1959 article, "Grammar in Language Teaching" (*Elementary English*, 36 [1959], 412–421), John J. DeBoer noted the consistency of these findings.

> The impressive fact is ... that in all these studies, carried out in places and at times far removed from each other, often by highly experienced and disinterested investigators, the results have been consistently negative so far as the value of grammar in the improvement of language expression is concerned. (p. 417)

In 1960 Ingrid M. Strom, reviewing more than fifty experimental studies, came to a similarly strong and unqualified conclusion:

> direct methods of instruction, focusing on writing activities and the structuring of ideas, are more efficient in teaching sentence structure, usage, punctuation, and other related factors than are such methods as nomenclature drill, diagramming, and rote memorization of grammatical rules.[38]

In 1963 two research reviews appeared, one by Braddock, Lloyd-Jones, and Schorer, cited at the beginning of this paper, and one by Henry C. Meckel, whose conclusions, though more guarded, are in essential agreement.[39] In 1969 J. Stephen Sherwin devoted one-fourth of his *Four Problems in Teaching English: A Critique of Research* (Scranton, Penn.: International Textbook, 1969) to the grammar issue, concluding that "instruction in formal grammar is an ineffective way to help students achieve proficiency in writing" (p. 135). Some early experiments in sentence combining, such as those by Donald R. Bateman and Frank J. Zidonnis and by John C. Mellon, showed improvement in measures of syntactic complexity with instruction in transformational grammar keyed to sentence combining practice. But a later study by Frank O'Hare achieved the same gains with no grammar instruction, suggesting to Sandra L. Stotsky and to Richard Van de Veghe that active manipulation of language, not the grammar unit, explained the earlier results.[40] More recent summaries of research—by Elizabeth I. Haynes, Hillary Taylor Holbrook, and Marcia Farr Whiteman—support similar conclusions. Indirect evidence for this position is provided by surveys reported by Betty Bamberg in 1978 and 1981, showing that time spent in grammar instruction in high school is the least important factor, of eight factors examined, in separating regular from remedial writers at the college level.[41] More generally, Patrick Scott and Bruce Castner, in "Reference Sources for Composition Research: A Practical Survey" (*CE*, 45 [1983], 756–768), note that much current research is not informed by an awareness of the past. Put simply, we are constrained to reinvent the wheel. My concern here has been with a far more serious problem: that too often the wheel we reinvent is square.

It is, after all, a question of power. Janet Emig, developing a consensus from composition research, and Aaron S. Carton and Lawrence V. Castiglione, developing the implications of language theory for education, come to the same conclusion: that the thrust of current research and theory is to take power from the teacher and to give that power to the learner.[42] At no point in the English curriculum is the question of power more blatantly posed than in the issue of formal grammar instruction. It is time that we, as teachers, formulate theories of language and literacy and let those theories guide our teaching, and it is time that we, as researchers, move on to more interesting areas of inquiry.

Notes

1. *Research in Written Composition* (Urbana, Ill.: National Council of Teachers of English, 1963), pp. 37–38.

2. "Non-magical Thinking: Presenting Writing Developmentally in Schools," in *Writing Process, Development and Communication,* Vol. II of *Writing: The Nature, Development and Teaching of Written Communication,* ed. Charles H. Frederiksen and Joseph F. Dominic (Hillsdale, N.J.: Lawrence Erlbaum, 1980), pp. 21–30.

3. For arguments in favor of formal grammar teaching, see Patrick F. Basset, "Grammar—Can We Afford Not to Teach It?" *NASSP Bulletin,* 64, No. 10 (1980), 55–63; Mary Epes, et al., "The COMP-LAB Project: Assessing the Effectiveness of a Laboratory-Centered Basic Writing Course on the College Level" (Jamaica, N.Y.: York College, CUNY, 1979) ERIC 194 908; June B. Evans, "The Analogous Ounce: The Analgesic for Relief," *English Journal,* 70, No. 2 (1981), 38–39; Sydney Greenbaum, "What Is Grammar and Why Teach It?" (a paper presented at the meeting of the National Council of Teachers of English, Boston, Nov. 1982) ERIC 222 917; Marjorie Smelstor, *A Guide to the Role of Grammar in Teaching Writing* (Madison: University of Wisconsin School of Education, 1978) ERIC 176 323; and A.M. Tibbetts, *Working Papers: A Teacher's Observations on Composition* (Glenview, Ill.: Scott, Foresman, 1982).

For attacks on formal grammar teaching, see Harvey A. Daniels, *Famous Last Words: The American Language Crisis Reconsidered* (Carbondale: Southern Illinois University Press, 1983); Suzette Haden Elgin, *Never Mind the Trees: What the English Teacher Really Needs to Know about Linguistics* (Berkeley: University of California College of Education, Bay Area Writing Project Occasional Paper No. 2, 1980) ERIC 198 536; Mike Rose, "Remedial Writing Courses: A Critique and a Proposal." *College English,* 45 (1983), 109–128; and Ron Shook, "Response to Martha Kolln," *College Composition and Communication,* 34 (1983), 491–495.

4. See, for example, Clifton Fadiman and James Howard, *Empty Pages: A Search for Writing Competence in School and Society* (Belmont, Cal.: Fearon Pitman, 1979); Edwin Newman, *A Civil Tongue* (Indianapolis, Ind.: Bobbs-Merrill, 1976); and *Strictly Speaking* (New York: Warner Books, 1974); John Simons, *Paradigms Lost* (New York: Clarkson N. Potter, 1980); A. M. Tibbetts and Charlene Tibbetts, *What's Happening to American English?* (New York: Scribner's, 1978); and "Why Johnny Can't Write," *Newsweek,* 8 Dec. 1975, pp. 58–63.

5. "The Role of Grammar in a Secondary School English Curriculum." *Research in the Teaching of English,* 10 (1976), 5–21; *The Role of Grammar in a Secondary School Curriculum* (Wellington: New Zealand Council of Teachers of English, 1979).

6. "A Taxonomy of Compositional Competencies," in *Perspectives on Literacy,* ed. Richard Beach and P. David Pearson (Minneapolis: University of Minnesota College of Education, 1979), pp. 247–272.

7. On usage norms, see Edward Finegan, *Attitudes toward English Usage: The History of a War of Words* (New York: Teachers College Press, 1980), and Jim Quinn, *American Tongue in Cheek: A Populist*

Guide to Language (New York: Pantheon, 1980); on arrangement, see Patrick Hartwell, "Teaching Arrangement: A Pedagogy," *CE*, 40 (1979), 548–554.

8. "Revolution in Grammar," *Quarterly Journal of Speech*, 40 (1954), 299–312.

9. Richard A. Lanham, *Revising Prose* (New York: Scribner's, 1979); William Strunk and E. B. White, *The Elements of Style*, 3rd ed. (New York: Macmillan, 1979); Joseph Williams, *Style: Ten Lessons in Clarity and Grace* (Glenview, Ill.: Scott, Foresman, 1981); Christensen, "A Generative Rhetoric of the Sentence," *CCC*, 14 (1963), 155–161; Donald A. Daiker, Andrew Kerek, and Max Morenberg, *The Writer's Options: Combining to Composing*, 2nd ed. (New York: Harper & Row, 1982).

10. "A Psychological Approach," in *Psychobiology of Language*, ed. M. Studdert-Kennedy (Cambridge, Mass.: MIT Press, 1983), pp. 16–19. See also Noam Chomsky, "Language and Unconscious Knowledge," in *Psychoanalysis and Language: Psychiatry and the Humanities*, Vol. III, ed. Joseph H. Smith (New Haven, Conn.: Yale University Press, 1978), pp. 3–44.

11. Morris Halle, "Knowledge Unlearned and Untaught: What Speakers Know about the Sounds of Their Language," in *Linguistic Theory and Psychological Reality*, ed. Halle, Joan Bresnan, and George A. Miller (Cambridge, Mass.: MIT Press, 1978), pp. 135–140.

12. Moscowitz, "On the Status of Vowel Shift in English," in *Cognitive Development and the Acquisition of Language*, ed. T. E. Moore (New York: Academic Press, 1973), pp. 223–60; Chomsky, "Stages in Language Development and Reading Exposure," *Harvard Educational Review*, 42 (1972), 1–33; and Brause, "Developmental Aspects of the Ability to Understand Semantic Ambiguity, with Implications for Teachers," *RTE*, 11 (1977), 39–48.

13. Mills and Hemsley, "The Effect of Levels of Education on Judgments of Grammatical Acceptability," *Language and Speech*, 19 (1976), 324–342; Whyte, "Levels of Language Competence and Reading Ability: An Exploratory Investigation," *Journal of Research in Reading*, 5 (1982, 123–132; Morais, et al., "Does Awareness of Speech as a Series of Phones Arise Spontaneously," *Cognition*, 7 (1979), 323–331; Ferguson, *Cognitive Effects of Literacy: Linguistic Awareness in Adult Non-readers* (Washington, D.C.: National Institute of Education Final Report, 1981) ERIC 222 85; Hamilton and Barton, "A Word Is a Word: Metalinguistic Skills in Adults of Varying Literacy Levels" (Stanford, Cal.: Stanford University Department of Linguistics, 1980) ERIC 222 859.

14. On the question of the psychological reality of Grammar 2 descriptions, see Maria Black and Shulamith Chiat, "Psycholinguistics without 'Psychological Reality'," *Linguistics*, 19 (1981), 37–61; Joan Bresnan, ed., *The Mental Representation of Grammatical Relations* (Cambridge, Mass.: MIT Press, 1982); and Michael H. Long, "Inside the 'Black Box': Methodological Issues in Classroom Research on Language Learning," *Language Learning*, 30 (1980), 1–42.

15. Chomsky, "The Current Scene in Linguistics," *College English*, 27 (1966), 587–595; and "Linguistic Theory," in *Language Teaching: Broader Contexts*, ed. Robert C. Meade, Jr. (New York: Modern Language Association, 1966), pp. 43–49; Mark Lester, "The Value of Transformational Grammar in Teaching Composition," *CCC*, 16 (1967), 228.

16. Christensen, "Between Two Worlds," in *Notes toward a New Rhetoric: Nine Essays for Teachers*, rev. ed., ed. Bonniejean Christensen (New York: Harper & Row, 1978), pp. 1–22.

17. Reber, "Implicit Learning of Artificial Grammars," *Journal of Verbal Learning and Verbal Behavior*, 6 (1967), 855–863; "Implicit Learning of Synthetic Languages: The Role of Instructional Set," *Journal of Experimental Psychology: Human Learning and Memory*, 2 (1976), 889–894; and Reber, Saul M. Kassin, Selma Lewis, and Gary Cantor, "On the Relationship Between Implicit and Explicit Modes in the Learning of a Complex Rule Structure," *Journal of Experimental Psychology: Human Learning and Memory*, 6 (1980), 492–502.

18. "Individual Variation in the Use of the Monitor," in *Principles of Second Language Learning*, ed. W. Richie (New York: Academic Press, 1978), pp. 175–185.

19. "Applications of Psycholinguistic Research to the Classroom," in *Practical Applications of Research in Foreign Language Teaching*, ed. D. J. James (Lincolnwood, Ill.: National Textbook, 1983), p. 61.

20. "Some Evidence for the Integrity and Interaction of Two Knowledge Sources," in *New Dimensions in Second Language Acquisition Research,* ed. Roger W. Anderson (Rowley, Mass.: Newbury House, 1981), pp. 62–74.

21. Hartwell and Bentley, *Some Suggestions for Using Open to Language* (New York: Oxford University Press, 1982), p. 73; Rose, *Writer's Block: The Cognitive Dimension* (Carbondale: Southern Illinois University Press, 1983), p. 99; Daiute, "Psycholinguistic Foundations of the Writing Process," *RTE,* 15 (1981), 5–22.

22. See Bartholomae, "The Study of Error"; Patrick Hartwell, "The Writing Center and the Paradoxes of Written-Down Speech," in *Writing Centers: Theory and Administration,* ed. Gary Olson (Urbana, Ill.: NCTE, 1984), pp. 48–61; and Sondra Perl, "A Look at Basic Writers in the Process of Composing," in *Basic Writing: A Collection of Essays for Teachers, Researchers, and Administrators* (Urbana, Ill.: NCTE, 1980), pp. 13–32.

23. Emonds, *Adjacency in Grammar: The Theory of Language-Particular Rules* (New York: Academic, 1983); and Jochnowitz, "Everybody Likes Pizza, Doesn't He or She?" *American Speech,* 57 (1982), 198–203.

24. Scribner and Cole, *Psychology of Literacy* (Cambridge, Mass.: Harvard University Press, 1981); Gleitman and Gleitman, "Language Use and Language Judgment," in *Individual Differences in Language Ability and Language Behavior,* ed. Charles J. Fillmore, Daniel Kempler, and William S.-Y. Wang (New York: Academic Press, 1979), pp. 103–126.

25. There are several recent reviews of this developing body of research in psychology and child development: Irene Athey, "Language Development Factors Related to Reading Development," *Journal of Educational Research,* 76 (1983), 197–203; James Flood and Paula Menyuk, "Metalinguistic Development and Reading/Writing Achievement," *Claremont Reading Conference Yearbook,* 46 (1982), 122–132; and the following four essays: David T. Hakes, "The Development of Metalinguistic Abilities: What Develops?," pp. 162–210; Stan A. Kuczaj, II, and Brooke Harbaugh, "What Children Think about the Speaking Capabilities of Other Persons and Things," pp. 211–227; Karen Saywitz and Louise Cherry Wilkinson, "Age-Related Differences in Metalinguistic Awareness," pp. 229–250; and Harriet Salatas Waters and Virginia S. Tinsley, "The Development of Verbal Self-Regulation: Relationships between Language, Cognition, and Behavior," pp. 251–277; all in *Language, Thought, and Culture,* Vol. II of *Language Development,* ed. Stan Kuczaj, Jr. (Hillsdale, N.J.: Lawrence Erlbaum, 1982). See also Joanne R. Nurss, "Research in Review: Linguistic Awareness and Learning to Read," *Young Children,* 35, No. 3 [1980], 57–66.

26. "Competing Value Systems in Inner City Schools," in *Children In and Out of School: Ethnography and Education,* ed. Perry Gilmore and Allan A. Glatthorn (Washington, D.C.: Center for Applied Linguistics, 1982), pp. 148–171; and "Locating the Frontier between Social and Psychological Factors in Linguistic Structure," in *Individual Differences in Language Ability and Language Behavior,* ed. Fillmore, Kempler, and Wang, pp. 327–340.

27. See, for example, Thomas Farrell, "IQ and Standard English," *CCC,* 34 (1983), 470–84; and the responses by Karen L. Greenberg and Patrick Hartwell, *CCC,* in press.

28. Jane W. Torrey, "Teaching Standard English to Speakers of Other Dialects," in *Applications of Linguistics: Selected Papers of the Second International Conference of Applied Linguistics,* ed. G. E. Perren and J. L. M. Trim (Cambridge, Mass.: Cambridge University Press, 1971), pp. 423–428; James W. Beers and Edmund H. Henderson, "A Study of the Developing Orthographic Concepts among First Graders," *RTE,* 11 (1977), 133–148.

29. See the error counts of Samuel A. Kirschner and G. Howard Poteet, "Non-Standard English Usage in the Writing of Black, White, and Hispanic Remedial English Students in an Urban Community College," *RTE,* 7 (1973), 351–355; and Marilyn Sternglass, "Close Similarities in Dialect Features of Black and White College Students in Remedial Composition Classes," *TESOL Quarterly,* 8 (1974), 271–283.

30. For reading, see the massive study by Kenneth S. Goodman and Yetta M. Goodman, *Reading of American Children whose Language Is a Stable Rural Dialect of English or a Language other than English* (Washington, D.C.: National Institute of Education Final Report, 1978) ERIC 175 754; and

the overview by Rudine Sims, "Dialect and Reading: Toward Redefining the Issues," in *Reader Meets Author/ Bridging the Gap: A Psycholinguistic and Sociolinguistic Approach,* ed. Judith A. Langer and M. Tricia Smith-Burke (Newark, Del.: International Reading Association, 1982), pp. 222–232. For writing, see Patrick Hartwell, "Dialect Interference in Writing: A Critical View," *RTE,* 14 (1980), 101–118; and the anthology edited by Barry M. Kroll and Roberta J. Vann, *Exploring Speaking-Writing Relationships: Connections and Contrasts* (Urbana, Ill.: NCTE, 1981).

31. See, for example, Eric A. Havelock, *The Literary Revolution in Greece and its Cultural Conse-quences* (Princeton, N.J.: Princeton University Press, 1982); Lesley Milroy on literacy in Dublin, *Language and Social Networks* (Oxford: Basil Blackwell, 1980); Ron Scollon and Suzanne B. K. Scollon on literacy in central Alaska, *Interethnic Communication: An Athabascan Case* (Austin, Tex.: Southwest Educational Development Laboratory Working Papers in Sociolinguistics, No. 59, 1979) ERIC 175 276; and Scribner and Cole on literacy in Liberia, *Psychology of Literacy* (see footnote 24).

32. See, for example, the anthology edited by Deborah Tannen, *Spoken and Written Language: Exploring Orality and Literacy* (Norwood, N.J.: Ablex, 1982); and Shirley Brice Heath's continuing work: "Protean Shapes in Literacy Events: Ever-Shifting Oral and Literate Traditions," in *Spoken and Written Language,* pp. 91–117; *Ways with Words: Language, Life and Work in Communities and Classrooms* (New York: Cambridge University Press, 1983); and "What No Bedtime Story Means," *Language in Society,* 11 (1982), 49–76.

33. For studies at the elementary level, see Dell H. Hymes, et al., eds., *Ethnographic Monitoring of Children's Acquisition of Reading/Language Arts Skills In and Out of the Classroom* (Washington, D.C.: National Institute of Education Final Report, 1981) ERIC 208 096. For studies at the secondary level, see James L. Collins and Michael M. Williamson, "Spoken Language and Semantic Abbreviation in Writing," *RTE,* 15 (1981), 23–36. And for studies at the college level, see Patrick Hartwell and Gene LoPresti, "Sentence Combining as Kid-Watching," in *Sentence Combining: Toward a Rhetorical Perspective,* ed. Donald A. Daiker, Andrew Kerek, and Max Morenberg (Carbondale: Southern Illinois University Press, in press).

34. Lloyd-Jones, "Romantic Revels—I Am Not You," *CCC,* 23 (1972), 251–271; and Young, "Con-cepts of Art and the Teaching of Writing," in *The Rhetorical Tradition and Modern Writing,* ed. James J. Murphy (New York: Modern Language Association, 1982), pp. 130–141.

35. For the romantic position, see Ann E. Berthoff, "Tolstoy, Vygotsky, and the Making of Meaning," *CCC,* 29 (1978), 249–255; Kenneth Dowst, "The Epistemic Approach," in *Eight Approaches to Teaching Composition,* ed. Timothy Donovan and Ben G. McClellan (Urbana, Ill.: NCTE, 1980), pp. 65–85; Peter Elbow, "The Challenge for Sentence Combining"; and Donald Murray, "Following Language toward Meaning," both in *Sentence Combining: Toward a Rhetorical Perspective* (in press; see footnote 33); and Ian Pringle, "Why Teach Style? A Review-Essay," *CCC,* 34 (1983), 91–98.

For the classic position, see Christensen's "A Generative Rhetoric of the Sentence"; and Joseph Williams' "Defining Complexity," *CE,* 41 (1979), 595–609; and his *Style: Ten Lessons in Clarity and Grace* (see footnote 9).

36. Courtney B. Cazden and David K. Dickinson, "Language and Education: Standardization versus Cultural Pluralism," in *Language in the USA,* ed. Charles A. Ferguson and Shirley Brice Health (New York: Cambridge University Press, 1981), pp. 446–468; and Carol Chomsky, "Developing Facility with Language Structure," in *Discovering Language with Children,* ed. Gay Su Pinnell (Urbana, Ill.: NCTE, 1980), pp. 56–59.

37. Boraas, "Formal English Grammar and the Practical Mastery of English." Diss. University of Illinois, 1917; Asker, "Does Knowledge of Grammar Function?" *School and Society,* 17 (27 January 1923), 109–111; Ash, "An Experimental Evaluation of the Stylistic Approach in Teaching Composition in the Junior High School," *Journal of Experimental Education,* 4 (1935), 54–62; and Frogner, "A Study of the Relative Efficacy of a Grammatical and a Thought Approach to the Improvement of Sentence Structure in Grades Nine and Eleven," *School Review,* 47 (1939), 663–675.

38. "Research on Grammar and Usage and Its Implications for Teaching Writing," *Bulletin of the School of Education,* Indiana University, 36 (1960), pp. 13–14.

39. Meckel, "Research on Teaching Composition and Literature," in *Handbook of Research on Teaching*, ed. N. L. Gage (Chicago: Rand McNally, 1963), pp. 966–1006.

40. Bateman and Zidonis, *The Effect of a Study of Transformational Grammar on the Writing of Ninth and Tenth Graders* (Urbana, Ill.: NCTE, 1966); Mellon, *Transformational Sentence Combining: A Method for Enhancing the Development of Fluency in English Composition* (Urbana, Ill.: NCTE, 1969); O'Hare, *Sentence-Combining: Improving Student Writing without Formal Grammar Instruction* (Urbana, Ill.: NCTE, 1971); Stotsky, "Sentence-Combining as a Curricular Activity: Its Effect on Written Language Development," *RTE*, 9 (1975), 30–72; and Van de Veghe, "Research in Written Composition: Fifteen Years of Investigation," ERIC 157 095.

41. Haynes, "Using Research in Preparing to Teach Writing," *English Journal*, 69, No. 1 (1978), 82–88; Holbrook, "ERIC/RCS Report: Whither (Wither) Grammar," *Language Arts*, 60 (1983), 259–263; Whiteman, "What We Can Learn from Writing Research," *Theory into Practice*, 19 (1980), 150–156; Bamberg, "Composition in the Secondary English Curriculum: Some Current Trends and Directions for the Eighties," *RTE*, 15 (1981), 257–266; and "Composition Instruction Does Make a Difference: A Comparison of the High School Preparation of College Freshmen in Regular and Remedial English Classes," *RTE*, 12 (1978), 47–59.

42. Emig, "Inquiry Paradigms and Writing," *CCC*, 33 (1982), 64–75; Carton and Castiglione, "Educational Linguistics: Defining the Domain," in *Psycholinguistic Research: Implications and Applications*, ed. Doris Aaronson and Robert W. Rieber (Hillsdale, N.J.: Lawrence Erlbaum, 1979), pp. 497–520.

9

Non-Native Speakers of English

John R. Edlund

This chapter addresses several ideas associated with the field of second language acquisition that can help composition teachers work effectively with ESL students. These include theories of language acquisition, insights from contrastive rhetoric, and the role of grammar and error correction.

A recent post on the writing program administrator's e-mail list (WPA-L) asked if most composition programs "segregate ESL students into separate sections or mainstream them into existing sections of composition?" The responses indicated that both models are common across the country, but many other issues also arose that are appropriate for composition teachers to consider. Who is an ESL student? What are the advantages and disadvantages of segregating and mainstreaming? At what level is a student ready for mainstream composition, and how is this determined? Should students choose which program suits them best? How is an ESL composition course different from a mainstream one?

These are interesting and important questions, but whatever ideas emerge from them, the fact is that in many parts of the country, non-native speakers of English are likely to be a part of the population in every course. At California State University, Los Angeles, where I used to teach, the basic writing program was designed to include non-native speakers, non-standard dialect speakers, English-dominant bilinguals, and anybody else who scored below 151 on the English Placement Test. About 75% of the students in the university were non-native speakers of English. At Cal Poly Pomona, my current campus, there is a separate ESL track for developmental writing and freshman composition. Even so, in a recent survey, the most common complaint among the instructors in the mainstream composition courses was that there were too many ESL students in their classes.

In "Broadening the Perspective of Mainstream Composition Studies: Some Thoughts from the Disciplinary Margins" (1997), Tony Silva, Ilona Leki, and Joan Carson note that "English as a Second Language (ESL) writing, or, more generally, second language writing, is uniquely situated at the intersection of second language studies and composition studies," but they lament the fact that "the transfer of knowledge between the fields has primarily been a one way affair, from composition studies to second language studies" (p. 399). In their essay, they argue that there is much that mainstream composition could learn from second language writing research, and that without such influence, mainstream composition is too narrow, reduced to making "universalist claims about the phenomenon of writing almost exclusively on the basis of Western (Greco-Roman and Anglo-American) rhetorical traditions and/or on the findings of empirical research conducted primarily on undergraduate college students in North American colleges and universities" (p. 399).

Thus, there are two strong reasons why mainstream composition teachers should be interested in second language writing research: First, ESL students are already in mainstream classes. And second, without theory, research, and experience from the field of second language acquisition, mainstream composition is too provincial, basing grand claims on monolingual, monocultural evidence. This chapter addresses several ideas associated with the field of second language acquisition that can help composition teachers work effectively with ESL students. These include:

Theories of language acquisition.

The role of culture and rhetoric.

Insights from contrastive rhetoric.

Characteristics of Generation 1.5.

The role of grammar and error correction.

LANGUAGE ACQUISITION THEORY

In making the case that second language writing research has something to offer the mainstream composition tradition, Silva, Leki, and Carson provide a good overview of second language writing as a field. The overall thesis of their article, "Broadening the Perspective of Mainstream Composition Studies: Some Thoughts from the Disciplinary Margins" (1997) is that composition needs a "broader and more inclusive view of writing," and that it "could profit from the perspectives and insights of second language studies" (p. 402). However, there is always danger in importing theories from

outside disciplines, even closely related ones, if they are not clearly understood. Silva et al. open their discussion of SLA research with a critique of
Horning's *Teaching Writing as a Second Language,* apparently one of the few
books in mainstream composition that refers to SLA research, but they do
so to problematize her idea that the acquisition of written language, or academic language, is similar to second language acquisition (1987). They say
specifically that Horning relies too much on Stephen Krashen's distinction
between conscious learning and unconscious acquisition as unrelated processing mechanisms. They claim that this distinction has been "frequently
and convincingly challenged in second language acquisition research" (Silva
et al., 1997, p. 403). The authors do not, however, cite any anti-Krashen studies at this point.

Krashen's language acquisition theory is important to the connection between second language studies and mainstream composition for a number
of reasons. Composition has struggled with the role of grammar teaching for
decades. Although the research indicates that teaching grammar has either
no effect, or a negative effect, on writing skills, there is still considerable
pressure from administrators, parents, and even the students themselves,
to teach it. The often-cited article by Patrick Hartwell "Grammar, Grammars, and the Teaching of Grammar," (included in this book at the end
of chapter 7) actually cites Krashen in making the argument against grammar teaching (1985). Krashen has also gotten involved in other educational
issues such as bilingual education and the whole language versus phonics
controversy. Because Krashen's language acquisition theory has had both a
great deal of influence and caused a great deal of controversy, some further
information about Krashen's particular theory is useful.

Krashen's Theory

The acquisition/learning distinction is the first of five hypotheses that make
up Krashen's language acquisition theory. For Krashen, second language
acquisition is a natural unconscious process very similar to first language acquisition. Babies, after all, do not study grammar books or dictionaries, but
acquire language naturally from the surrounding linguistic environment.
Language *learning,* on the other hand, involves the conscious study of grammatical rules, vocabulary lists, practice exercises, memorized dialogues, and
other such strategies. Some researchers have assumed that children acquire
language, but that adults must learn it through an entirely different process.
Krashen argues that these processes are, indeed, separate, but that adults
are not merely *capable* of acquiring language naturally, it is, in fact, the most
powerful method (Krashen, 1982).

Krashen arrives at this position through morpheme studies, which show
that students acquire grammatical morphemes in a "natural" order that is

not influenced by instruction. (A *morpheme* could be a word, suffix, prefix, or any other bit of meaningful language.) This is the natural order hypothesis, the second of the five hypotheses. John Truscott (1996) notes that "Researchers investigating naturalistic L2 learning have found clear and consistent orders in which learners acquire certain grammatical structures; other research has found these same sequences in formal classroom learning situations, in spite of instructional sequences that run counter to them" (p. 337). Similarly, studies designed to show that a particular method of instruction was superior to another have produced mixed results at best. As Silva et al. state, "One of the surprising findings of second language acquisition theory is that there has been no convincing evidence for method superiority" (1997, p. 414).

Third is the "monitor" hypothesis. Krashen argues that acquisition initiates our utterances in a second language, but that learning functions only as a monitor or editor. Conscious learning can only function under the following conditions: (a) when there is sufficient *time* to employ a conscious rule, (b) when the speaker has a *focus on form,* and (c) when the speaker *knows the rule.* The monitor hypothesis is designed to explain why a student can pass a grammar test with flying colors but still make errors in speech or writing. So far, Krashen's theory appears to be quite intuitive and reasonable, although his position that conscious learning has no influence on unconscious acquisition, a position known as the *non-interface position,* may seem extreme.

Silva et al.'s second organizing question in their SLA research section is "How do learners acquire a second language?" Krashen's short answer is that they do it through receiving "comprehensible input." In a bit more detail, he says, "We acquire by understanding language that contains structure a bit beyond our current level of competence." (Krashen, 1982, p. 21). Thus, according to this fourth hypothesis, the input hypothesis, the job of the language teacher is not to provide a carefully sequenced and well-explained series of grammatical rules and exercises. Rather, it is to create an environment in which comprehensible input is present, making the input comprehensible by controlling the content and structures to some extent and by providing contextual and other extra-linguistic cues. In Krashen's view, simplified codes—caretaker speech, foreigner talk, and teacher talk— facilitate acquisition by making input more comprehensible. For Krashen, because direct teaching of rules and forms is not useful, the main task of a language teacher is to facilitate language acquisition by creating the proper linguistic environment.

The fifth and final part of Krashen's theory is the "affective filter" hypothesis. This part of the theory explains why language acquisition sometimes does not occur even when comprehensible input is present. There are three categories of affect: motivation, self-confidence, and anxiety. According to this theory, students with low motivation, low self-confidence, and high anxiety may not acquire the target language in spite of the presence of comprehensible input.

In one sense, the classroom implied by Krashen's theory is radically different from that of any traditional language course. Krashen himself says:

> The input hypothesis runs counter to our usual pedagogical approach in second and foreign language teaching. . . . our assumption has been that we first learn structures, then practice using them in communication, and this is how fluency develops. The input hypothesis says the opposite. It says we acquire by "going for meaning" first, and as a result, we acquire structure! (1982, p. 21)

From this perspective, the ideal classroom is a comfortable, nonthreatening place with rich opportunities for communicative interaction, lots of comprehensible input, and no grammar drills. For some teachers, this might be a scenario of liberation. For many ESL teachers, however, this is a profoundly counterintuitive approach. What is the role of the teacher? How can a teacher teach? How is the syllabus organized? What about grammatical error? Does the teacher even need to know grammatical rules?

In another sense, almost any class in any subject, including a grammar class, might meet the basic conditions for language acquisition to occur, a factor that may explain the mixed and ambiguous results in studies that attempt to assess the relative merits of different teaching methods. These conclusions have troubled a number of teachers and researchers and have led to numerous challenges to Krashen's theory.

Challenges to Krashen's Theory: Ellis and Rutherford

These challenges have mostly focused on the "non-interface" position, the claim that conscious learning cannot turn into acquisition. Rod Ellis provides a useful summary of the issues in his book *Understanding Second Language Acquisition* (1985, p. 264). First, the theory has been challenged because it is defined in terms of "subconscious" and "conscious" processes that are not open to empirical investigation. In other words, it is a "black box" theory that discusses inputs and outputs but does not describe or investigate the mental processes involved. This is especially true of the diagram in Krashen and Terrell (1983), which shows "input" flowing through the "affective filter" into the "language acquisition device" (represented by a box) and resulting in "acquired competence." When I took Krashen's language acquisition course in the mid-eighties, he admitted the truth of this criticism, but claimed to be uninterested in what was inside the box, which would have to be investigated through brain studies and neuro-linguistics.

To be fair, this critique should also be leveled at cognitive research in mainstream composition. The Flower and Hayes writing process model, for example, consists of three large boxes, one containing long-term memory, a second containing the three main processes that Flower and Hayes consider to be the essential components of the writing process itself ("planning," "translating," & "reviewing"), and a third box that represents the "task environment." According to Kim Sterelny in *The Representational Theory of Mind: An Introduction,* a number of different cognitive theorists have argued that there are three theoretical domains in psychology, and that each individual psychological mechanism and process exists and can be described in each of these domains:

> These domains are the subject matter of three *levels* of psychological theory. The top level is the level at which we specify the function a psychological device performs. It is the level at which we say what a system does. One down is the level at which we specify the information processing means by which the system performs its function or functions. At the base level we specify the physical realization of that information processing device. (Sterelny, 1990, p. 43)

Clearly, both Krashen and Flower and Hayes offer models that are descriptions at the functional level. Their focus is on *what* the mind is doing rather than on *how* it is doing it. They do not concern themselves with the physical realization of the processes they study, a concern that involves the study of neurology and the structures of the brain. In cognitive science, those who begin their study of the mind with the physical brain are often inclined to doubt the validity of approaches that begin with functions, but in linguistic research, the functional approach is common. Dismissal of Krashen's theory on these grounds is like saying that one can have no knowledge of the functions of Microsoft *Word* without a print-out of the software code and a good understanding of the Pentium III chip architecture.

Other researchers have articulated softer versions of the "non-interface" position. Ellis (1985) notes that a number of researchers have argued that learned knowledge can become "automatized" through practice and so become "acquired" and available for spontaneous conversation. However, without a clear distinction between the cognitive processes that lead to conscious learning, and those that lead to acquisition, or how these types of knowledge are different, it is impossible to distinguish between conscious knowledge of grammatical forms that has been "automatized," and subsequent acquisition of the same forms.

A different sort of critique is made by William Rutherford, a colleague of Krashen's at the University of Southern California. Rutherford notes that Krashen's language acquisition theory is based on morpheme studies of the natural order of acquisition, but that most of these studies involve the same limited set of morphemes. He also questions whether this same natural order hypothesis could say anything at all about the acquisition of the syntax of the language. In general, Rutherford questions the view that language acquisition consists of the steady mastery of a list of linguistic items.

Rutherford argues that when an adult language learner begins the process of acquiring a second language, that person is not a *tabula rasa*. The new learner already knows a lot about how language works and how people communicate, based on experiences with the first language. To begin to learn a new language is to embark on a journey across the *interlanguage continuum*, which we can imagine as a line that stretches from the L1 grammar (first language) to the L2 grammar (second language). Progress is made across the continuum by making and testing hypotheses about how the L2 grammar works. At first, the interlanguage system is based almost entirely on the L1 grammar, but as the learner acquires more of the L2 and makes further hypotheses about how it works, the interlanguage system becomes more and more like the "standard" grammar of the L2 (Rutherford, 1987).

Rutherford also argues that this hypothesis-testing process can be facilitated by what he calls "grammatical consciousness-raising" (C-R). Consciousness-raising is a process in which "data that are crucial for the learner's testing of hypotheses, and for his forming generalizations, are made available to him in somewhat controlled and principled fashion" (p.18). Rutherford notes that traditional grammar teaching can be a form of C-R, but that C-R is typically "a *means* to attainment of grammatical competence in another language (i.e., necessary but not sufficient, and the learner contributes), whereas 'grammar teaching' typically represents an attempt to *instil* that competence directly (i.e., necessary *and* sufficient, and the learner is a *tabula rasa*)" (p. 24).

In Rutherford's consciousness-raising theory, language acquisition is still more powerful than conscious learning, but there is the potential that pointing out a nonstandard form or teaching a grammatical rule might facilitate acquisition of that particular grammatical concept. In other words, there *is* an interface between conscious learning and unconscious acquisition. The nice thing about this theory is that it justifies what is common practice in both mainstream and second language composition classes: selectively marking errors.

Silva et al. discuss language acquisition largely in terms of a dichotomy between external or social factors, and internal factors related to cognition and psychology. The line between external and internal is a difficult one to maintain when talking about linguistic issues. The authors quickly blur the distinction when they begin to discuss the role of "sociopsychological" attitudes in language acquisition. Clearly, such concepts as "integrative" and "instrumental" motivation have both external and internal poles. However, Silva et al. (1997) maintain that this dichotomy serves to emphasize the overwhelming importance of social factors:

> Social factors play a major but indirect role in second language acquisition, insofar as acquisition is mediated by learner attitudes as well as by the nature and extent of input.... Learner attitudes are both cognitive and affective,

and they tend to be learned and persistent, but modifiable. Learner attitudes toward the acquisition of the target language are related to learner attitudes toward target language speakers, the target language culture, the social value of learning the target language, the particular uses that the target language might serve, and the learners' perceptions of their own culture. (p. 408)

The characterization of learner attitudes as "learned and persistent, but modifiable," is important for both the classroom and research. One of the goals of classroom instruction might be to facilitate language acquisition through changing learner attitudes toward the target language and target language speakers. Learner attitudes may also be an uncontrolled variable in many SLA studies, in part explaining the lack of convincing results for one pedagogical method over another. Age, gender, social class, cultural background, personal history, goals, motivation, and temperament all have the potential to influence language acquisition.

FOR WRITING AND DISCUSSION

1. Think about your own experiences learning a foreign language, including grammar study, opportunities for comprehensible input, attitudes toward the new language and its speakers, and communicative success. How well does Stephen Krashen's language acquisition theory account for your own experiences?

2. Take a popular writing handbook that includes information for ESL writers and look up the rules for using perfect tenses, the rules for articles, and the rules for using commas. Write a paragraph about your experience as a writing teacher or tutor, paying close attention to the rules in the handbook, so that nothing you write will deviate in any way from these rules. In class, discuss how the focus on rules affected your writing process.

CULTURE AND RHETORIC

Because affective and motivational issues are such important factors in language learning, and because the students *native* language and culture may have a strong influence on his or her writing, it is important to know basic information about the backgrounds of your ESL students. As Silva et al. (1997) note, cultural background influences everything from conceptions of audience to organizational patterns. Your strategies for working with a particular student, even what you say to that student, may be influenced by what you know about the student's background. The questions below could be put into a survey administered on the first day of class, but in many cases a few questions of this sort asked as part of an early writing conference are enough to clarify the situation:

- What is the student's native language?
- What other languages does the student speak?
- Is the student able to read and write in his or her native language?
- How much does the student read in English?
- How much does the student read in his or her native language?
- Is English the student's most comfortable language of literacy?
- What language(s) does the student speak at home?
- Is the student an "international" student? (Is the student studying in the United States on an F-1 student visa and returning home on completion of study?)
- If the student is an immigrant, how long has he or she been in this country?
- Why did the student come to this country?
- How does the student feel about being here?
- Where was the student educated, and what was the language of instruction?
- What is the student's major? What are the student's career goals?

These questions can be rather personal, and should be asked tactfully. Unless you are doing this in survey form, it would be best to ask these questions informally, and to ask only the ones that seem relevant to the student's situation at the time.

ESL Students/International Students

If the student was educated primarily outside of the U.S. in a language other than English, second language acquisition is probably in process, and the student's writing is likely to be strongly influenced by the attitudes and rhetorical patterns of his or her home culture. For example, Silva et al. (1997) note that cultural attitudes toward knowledge range from valuing the conservation of knowledge to valuing the extension of knowledge. Asian cultures tend to value the former, and, thus, emphasize the reproduction of information and strategies such as memorizing and imitating. Thus, although Scardamalia and Bereiter characterize knowledge telling in writing as "immature" writing, and knowledge transforming as characteristic of "mature" writing this distinction does not pertain in the context of working with students from Asian cultures. "What would appear to be a developmental continuum, then, from immature to mature writing in a knowledge extending culture, is recast as an issue of social context when viewed from the larger cross-cultural perspective" (p. 416).

CONTRASTIVE RHETORIC

The field of study known as "contrastive rhetoric" was essentially invented by Robert Kaplan in a 1966 article titled "Cultural Thought Patterns in Intercultural Education." He later expanded the concept in a 1972 book titled *The Anatomy of Rhetoric: Prolegomena to a Functional Theory of Rhetoric: Essays for Teachers*. In both works, Kaplan analyzes numerous examples of foreign student writing in English, and represents his findings as a series of five simple diagrams. These diagrams are not reproduced here, because although these "squiggles" have provoked both interest and controversy, I have found that once people see them they tend to remember the squiggles and forget the caveats. It is enough to say that "Semitic" writing is represented by a series of parallel lines with dotted connections, "Oriental" by a spiral, "Romance" by a crooked single line, and "Slavic" by a similar crooked, but dotted, line. The English pattern is represented as a single, direct, and vertical line. The squiggles have been criticized as simplistic, both in the patterns they represent and in breadth of their categories. Even Kaplan, responding to this criticism, acknowledged, "It is probably true that, in the first blush of discovery, I overstated both the difference and my case" (Conner & Kaplan, 1987, p. 9).

Contrastive rhetoric deals with organizational patterns, stylistic preferences (especially in terms of subordination and coordination), and other conventional aspects of specific genres, viewed across cultures. In general, this research contrasts American English rhetorical patterns with those of a second culture. This research is complex and difficult to do, because to be credible, the researcher must be fluent in both languages and cultures, or have access to bilingual, bicultural informants, and any insights gained by research into the patterns of one culture are unlikely to be applicable to another. In most cases, it would be unreasonable to expect composition teachers to be familiar with the rhetorical patterns of every culture they might deal with. Why then, is contrastive rhetoric important to composition teachers?

Contrastive rhetoric can help explain the following situation, described by a Chinese-speaking student in her Writing Proficiency Exam:

> *My friend and I read an article. Although my English-speaking friend thought it was very good convincing article, I, on the other hand, did not agree with him. What I thought was that it was very pushing one way argument . . . . Most of native-speaker agreed with him. Some foreigner agreed with him, some agreed with me . . . all Asian who have strong Asian background agreed with me.*

This writer has conducted her own survey research on an important issue in contrastive rhetoric, and found American patterns to be one-sided and narrow from an Asian point of view. Many non-native speakers would agree with her.

Kaplan says in his original article, "One should not judge the construction of a composition merely by the standards of a rhetoric which one takes for granted" (1966, p. 34). In other words, an essay that appears to be illogical or incoherent by American standards may be well crafted by the standards of another culture. This is not to say that the foreign pattern should simply be accepted as a cultural difference, but it is also clear that calling the paper "illogical" or "incoherent" probably won't help the student improve. A student is not a blank slate or an empty vessel, and a writing teacher must be prepared to help integrate new learning with what has been learned before. In the case of a foreign student, what has been learned previously may be very different from what American teachers expect.

Kaplan (2001) notes that "genres are nothing more nor less than conventional solutions to recurring communication problems" (p. xi). The problem for students and teachers arises when two cultures have conflicting solutions. In discussing the pedagogical issues raised by contrastive rhetoric, this chapter will focus first on Japanese patterns. Again, the most important concept for the composition teacher is the idea that there *are* different patterns, and that they may be influencing the writing of your students.

An Example From Japanese Composition

Shinshu Kokugo Soran (New Japanese Conspectus), a textbook or reference book commonly used in Japanese secondary education, contains an article titled "How to Construct a Sentence/Composition." Ema (1981) writes, "There are two main formats in the design of Japanese compositions: (1) a three-step construction called *jo ha kyu* (literally opening—breaking—rushing) and (2) a four-step construction *ki-shô-ten-ketsu* (introduction—development—turn—conclusion)" (p. 294–295). The author continues:

> The term *jo ha kyu* was originally used to name the three movements of music accompanying traditional Japanese Court dances, *bugaku.* Later, this idea was adapted for the method of dramatizing *nô* drama (creating dynamic movement, expression, or emphasis). Applied to the design of a written composition, it is considered as follows:
>
> <*jo*> Beginning. An introductory part or opening section.
>
> <*ha*> The portion which makes the center of a composition. A development part on a main subject.
>
> <*kyu*> Ending of a composition. The conclusion. (Ema, 1981, p. 294–295, [translated by Miri Park from the Japanese original])

On the surface, this sounds similar to the introduction—body—conclusion pattern that Americans are taught. However, the character that is here represented by *jo* can also be translated as "overture," and this section is seen as establishing a mood or a context for the rest of the communication. It would be unlikely for this section to contain a thesis statement. For example, once I was helping a Japanese professor draft a letter to a distinguished British colleague who was receiving an award, but who was gravely ill. In Japan, it is conventional to begin a business letter with a reference to the weather, using specific words appropriate to the season. This is felt to establish a personal connection before the business at hand is broached. To my American sensibility, the information about the weather seemed to be trivial and unimportant, especially in this serious context. I suggested that we leave it out, and get to the point more directly. Ultimately we did, but my colleague was uncomfortable about it.

Examining *jo ha kyu* also reveals differences in reader/writer roles that affect the extent to which topics are expected to be developed or explained. The character *ha* literally means "breaking" as in "daybreak" or even in the sense of breaking something open, such as a nut. It signifies new development and the introduction of new themes. However, in Japanese texts, topics may be "opened" without real development, in a mode that reminds the English reader of an encyclopedia, or even a laundry list, requiring more involvement from the reader than is expected from texts written in English and highlighting differences in the Japanese sense of the roles of writer and reader. Linguist John Hinds proposed a typology of language based on relative reader/writer responsibility. Hinds classifies Japanese as a reader-responsible language, English as writer-responsible, and Mandarin as a language in transition from reader-responsibility to writer-responsibility (Kaplan, 1988). This means that in Japanese the reader is expected to read between the lines, to supply missing connections and information, and in general to tolerate far more ambiguity than an American reader would be comfortable with. Thus, Kaplan argues "the fact that a student understands audience in one language does not mean the student understands audience in any other language system" (1988, p. 296).

Kyu carries the sense of "rushing" as water rushes into a drain. It means "processing with force." In this section, the writer gets to the point, and brings all the themes and topics together.

Shinshu Kokugo Soran notes that the alternative four-part construction *ki-shô-ten-ketsu* is adapted from the poetic form of a Chinese quatrain, *zekku:*

<ki> Beginning. A problem is shown.

<shô> In response to *ki,* it describes further detail.

<ten> A example which contrasts or is opposed to the idea presented in the former two steps is given to enhance the development of the subject.

<*ketsu*> Integrating the contents discussed in *ten* section, the whole comes to a conclusion with one theme. (Ema, 1981, p. 295, [trans. Miri Park])

K. Takemata defines the *ten* section in a slightly different way: "At the point where this development is finished, turn the idea to a subtheme where there is a connection, but not a directly connected association [to the major theme]" (1982, p. 80). Takemata also points out that a Japanese *ketsu* "need not be decisive [*danteiteki*]. All it needs to do is to indicate a doubt or ask a question" (Hinds, 1976, p. 26–27).

The *ki-shô-ten-ketsu* pattern can be seen as roughly analogous to the five-paragraph essay formula in English, and is often used for short essays and academic paper writing. Once, when I was browsing through some English materials in a Japanese bookstore, I found an article in a magazine that directly compared this pattern to the American five-paragraph essay. However, the *ten* and *ketsu* sections are especially problematic for English readers. Linguist John Hinds points out that:

> In *ten,* an abrupt shift takes place in which information only indirectly relevant to the major point is brought up with minimal syntactic marking. This obviously causes problems for English readers who do not expect "digressions" and "unrelated information" to come up suddenly.... In *ketsu,* the major difficulty involves the Japanese definition of this term and the difference between that and the English definition of "conclusion." (1982, p. 80)

Intermediate Japanese ESL students who are new to writing in English tend to produce four-paragraph essays in which the third paragraph seems to be entirely off topic. Japanese readers who know this pattern expect the third section to make some kind of turn away from the topic; American readers are confused; and American instructors are likely to ask, "How does this relate to your topic?" or "What's your point?"

For example, a Japanese graduate student recently came to see me because he was having trouble passing the university's writing proficiency test. He said that the writing center tutors told him that his problem was not grammatical errors, but, rather, that he kept going off the topic. We talked about this *ki-shô-ten-ketsu* pattern, and I explained that American readers have trouble following the *ten* section. I asked if he could simply leave that section out. He understood what I was saying, but he did not seem to think he could leave one section out. However, reflecting on this problem in this way may lead to adoption of more American patterns.

Japanese rhetorical patterns are influenced by earlier Chinese patterns. Kaplan found that some Korean and Chinese writing is marked by what may be called an "approach by indirection." In this kind of writing, the development of the paragraph may be said to be turning in circles around the subject, showing it from a variety of tangential views, but never looking at the subject directly. Things are developed in terms of what they are not, rather than in terms of what they are (Kaplan, 1966).

Kaplan also found that Chinese students writing in English were influenced by the Chinese eight-legged essay, the required form for the civil service exam from the middle of the 15th century to the early 20th. This form consists of the following sections:

1. "The breaking open"
2. "Accepting the title"
3. "Embarking" (introductory discourse)
4. "Introductory Corollary"
5. "First Middle Leg"
6. "Second Middle Leg"
7. "First Final Leg"
8. "Tying the Knot"

Cai (1993) says that the eight-legged essay is still a powerful organizing principle for many Chinese students and that a newer, four-part model, *qi-cheng-jun-he,* is commonly used to organize paragraphs. *Qi* prepares the reader for the topic, *cheng* introduces and develops the topic, *jun* turns to a seemingly unrelated subject, and *he* sums up the paragraph. An example:

> [*qi*] We are dependent, for understanding and for consolation and hope, upon what we learn of ourselves from songs and stories. [*cheng*] From this statement, we can know that through songs and stories, people realize themselves, humanity and their societies. The literacy—mastery of language and knowledge of books—is the essential factor that enlarges people's knowledge, and improves mutual realization of people, and then creates the smooth society. [*jun*] From kindergartens to colleges, from homes to offices, we learn how to interact with someone and how to realize ourselves and our societies. [*he*] Hence, "literacy is not an ornament, but a necessity." (Cai, 1996, p. 39)

The *qi* section states that we learn about ourselves from songs and stories. The *cheng* section notes that we "realize" or understand ourselves and mutually understand people through books. The *jun* section names places where we learn and use literacy, and also interact with others, but does not directly mention literacy or books. What an English reader might call the "topic sentence" appears at the end of the paragraph.

Hinds (1996) demonstrates that writing in Japanese, Chinese, Thai, and Korean follows an organizational pattern he calls "quasi-inductive." Generally, writing in English is deductive, with the thesis at the beginning. If the thesis is not at the beginning, readers expect an inductive pattern, with the thesis at the end. Instead, in this pattern, the thesis is implied or buried in the passage, involving what Hinds calls "a delayed introduction of purpose." Hinds (1990) says:

> Seen in this light, we must recognize that the traditional distinction that English-speaking readers make between deductive and inductive writing styles is inappropriate to the writing of some nonnative authors. We may more appropriately characterize this writing as quasi-inductive, recognizing that this technique has as its purpose the task of getting readers to think for themselves, to consider the observations made, and to draw their own conclusions. The task of the writer, then, is not necessarily to convince, although it is clear that such authors have their own opinions. Rather, the task is to stimulate the reader into contemplating an issue or issues that might not have been previously considered. (p. 42)

Additional Cultural Influences

Literature, culture, and education have rhetorical influences beyond organizational patterns. The Asian writer's tendency toward an approach through indirection may also result in a preference for the passive voice, which allows actors and agents to remain unspecified. Kaplan found that native speakers of Arabic tend to favor coordination over subordination, because of the stylistic influence of the Koran. "While the literary traditions of the Judeo-Greco literary influence do not penetrate in English much beyond the 17th century, the literary influences of the Koran in Arabic extend into the present day" (Kaplan, 1966, p. 35). Since the 17th century, the fashion in English prose has been to favor subordination over coordination. However, in Arabic, the stylistic preference is for elaborate coordination. Kaplan shows that when Arabic-speaking students revise compositions in English, they create *more* coordinated structures. (To get an idea of what such elaborate coordination sounds like, look at the beginning of Genesis, in the King James version.)

An Example From Mexican Spanish Composition

In "Discourse Features of Written Mexican Spanish: Current Research in Contrastive Rhetoric and Its Implications," Maria Montaño-Harmon describes a study of four groups of student writers: Mexican students in Mexico, who are native-speakers of Spanish, writing in Spanish; ESL students, who are native speakers of Mexican Spanish, writing in English; Mexican-American/Chicano students, who are English-dominant, writing in English; and Anglo-American students writing in English. She found that the compositions written in Mexican Spanish were longer overall than those written in English, but contained fewer sentences. Sentences in the Spanish compositions were longer and tended to be what English readers would characterize as run-ons, connected by conjunctions, commas, or no separation at all. On occasion, one sentence would occupy an entire paragraph. Anglo-American writers used simple subject-verb complement constructions or short complex sentences subordinated with "because" (Montaño-Harmon 1991).

Montaño-Harmon also found that students in Mexico:

> ...relied heavily on synonyms to unify their compositions, a skill that is emphasized and taught explicitly in the schools in Mexico. Their basic strategy was to state an idea, place a comma, and then repeat the same idea using a synonym, the same word, or a semantically related word (collocation) to create a build-up effect. This building on an idea was emphasized many times via the use of hyperbole. Thus, the result was a repetition of the same idea several times within a run-on sentence, each repetition becoming more fancy or formal. (p. 421)

Note that this pattern was explicitly taught by the Mexican teachers.

The compositions also differed in the representation of logical relationships. Anglo-American students most often used enumeration of ideas, represented by such connectors as *first, second, then,* and *finally.* On the other hand, the Spanish compositions were organized via additive or explicative relationships, in which the writer states an idea and adds restatements and explanations for why he or she believes it.

Perhaps the most important feature of the Spanish compositions was that they had many more deviations in their logical development, in some cases complete breaks in the connection between one idea and the next. As Montaño-Harmon explained:

> These deviations were *conscious deviations,* which are part of the discourse pattern of Mexican Spanish, for the writer was aware that he/she had gone off the topic and would often use transitional words or phrases to return to the previous idea before the deviation. (p. 422)

The Anglo-American students, if they deviated from the topic, did so unconsciously, without transitional phrases.

On the other hand, the writing of Mexican-American, or Chicano, students was unlike that of any of the other groups. These students "exhibited composition problems due to a clash between a non-standard dialect of English, Chicano English—used for oral, informal interaction with peers—and the standard/academic English."(p. 419) They did not exhibit Spanish language interference problems. These students are, in many cases, members of what has come to be called "Generation 1.5."

GENERATION 1.5

In the past, most writing programs divided developmental writing students into two categories: native speakers of English (or basic writers) and non-native speakers (or ESL students). In many programs, the non-native speakers were generally assumed to be international students, quite unfamiliar with American language and culture, or first-generation immigrants who had been in the United States for a short time. Time in the United States was seen as a major factor in determining who belonged in the ESL course. Second-generation students, born in the United States, were assumed to be assimilated and fluent. These categories have now become inadequate to describe current student populations, if indeed they ever were adequate. Now researchers are talking about "Generation 1.5."

Some researchers have defined Generation 1.5 students as immigrants who arrive in the United States as children or adolescents, and obtain a large part of their K-12 education in U.S. schools, thus sharing characteristics of both the first and second generations. However, there are also students who were born in the United States who speak a foreign language at home. For this latter group, English is an academic language, and the language of literacy, but the home environment does not support the development of English-language skills. Another possibility is a home environment in which English is spoken by parents or siblings who are in the midst of language acquisition themselves. In this case, some children may acquire someone else's interlanguage as a native language. *Generation 1.5 Meets College Composition: Issues in the Teaching of Writing to U.S.-Educated Learners of ESL* (1999), edited by Linda Harklau, Kay M. Losey, and Meryl Siegal, is an excellent introductory resource for issues related to this population.

In a study of students at U.C. Berkeley, Yuet-Sim D. Chiang and Mary Schmida found that:

> Of the students surveyed, 60% of the Asian American students reported that they were nonnative English speakers (NNES), and 91% reported they were bilingual according to their responses on the survey. Interestingly, although 91% of the students designated themselves as bilingual, only 37% reported they spoke both their ethnic (heritage) language and English at home. And among the 40% of the Asian American students who labeled themselves as native speakers of English, only 28% of those same students reported learning English as a first language. (1999, p. 84)

Chiang and Schmida also found that these students used language as a synonym for culture. They noted that "this double-edged consciousness—culture as language—operates at a very complex level, often forcing students to position themselves as in between worlds in spite of the publicly self-proclaimed bilingual identity" (1999, p. 85). Interviews with the students in the survey revealed very complex cultural and linguistic affiliations. One student said:

> I don't know if I am really bilingual because I don't really bond with—I don't really connect with the English culture. American Culture. I'm kind of in between, I guess. I don't really speak [Chinese] that well, therefore I'm non-native Chinese. But the language and culture are kind of connected, I think.... But I think more English 'cause I don't use Chinese on a regular basis. (Chiang & Schmida, 1999, p. 86)

Another student said:

> For abstract thinking, I would think in English most of the time, and in Chinese for concepts that are not readily expressed by English. Therefore, when I "flip-flop" between Chinese and English, I am relying on both at the same time in order to express my ideas. (Chiang & Schmida, 1999, p. 92)

One girl said that when she speaks English at home, her mother yells, "Speak Korean! Speak Korean!" (Chiang & Schmida, 1999, p. 94). The article contained many similar statements from students from a variety of Asian backgrounds. Chiang and Schmida also noted that although these students waver in their cultural identifications, and do not generally have native-speaker fluency in English, they are good students. To be accepted at U.C. Berkeley, students must be in the top 12% of graduates from California schools.

It is important for composition teachers to keep in mind, then, that International students and recent immigrants tend to have strong influences from the rhetorical patterns and epistemological attitudes of their home cultures, with which they strongly identify. In this group, language acquisition is ongoing, and the instructor's job is to negotiate an understanding between the rhetorical patterns and stylistic preferences of the student's home culture and those of the English-speaking world, as well as facilitating progress along the interlanguage continuum toward grammatical proficiency in standard written English. As language acquisition progresses, the goal is for nonstandard grammatical forms to be discarded in favor of standard ones. Generation 1.5 students, on the other hand, are likely to be familiar with American rhetorical patterns, especially the more formulaic ones, but may speak a nonstandard dialect of English. This dialect may be an essential part of home life, or communication with peers, and, thus, it is questionable whether the nonstandard forms—which are a feature of this dialect—can or should be discarded. In this case, standard written English must be considered as a new dialect to be acquired.

FOR WRITING AND DISCUSSION

1. Develop a survey based on the types of questions at the beginning of this section. Administer the survey to a writing class, and write a paper discussing the results.

2. Choose a topic related to language pedagogy or language policy, perhaps "grammar teaching" or "English-only" policies. Write an essay using an unfamiliar form of organization such as inductive or quasi-inductive. When finished, write a postscript about your experience of writing this essay.

GRAMMAR AND ERROR CORRECTION

Silva et al. (1997) characterize errors as "windows on the acquisition process," but note that it is hard to know if a particular error is a feature of the writer's interlanguage or simply a mistake. Language acquisition theory implies that teaching grammar directly will not be effective except perhaps in special cases. However, it is common practice in both ESL classes and mainstream composition classes to correct errors in written texts. Is this an effective practice?

In "The Case Against Grammar Correction in L2 Writing Classes," John Truscott describes a comprehensive survey of research he conducted on this question, both in mainstream and ESL composition. His conclusion is as follows:

> Grammar correction has no place in writing courses and should be abandoned. The reasons are (a) research evidence shows that grammar correction is ineffective; (b) this lack of effectiveness is exactly what should be expected, given the nature of language learning; (c) grammar correction has significant harmful effects; and (d) the various arguments offered for continuing it all lack merit. (Truscott, 1996, p. 328)

Truscott reached these conclusions after carefully evaluating many different kinds of studies covering many different kinds of grammar correction, including explicit correction, correction codes, and highlighting errors without explanation. Of selective correction, he says:

> One might think that at least some of these problems could be greatly reduced if teachers selected a few important errors and consistently corrected them over a long period, ignoring other, less important errors. ... Not surprisingly then, selective correction seems to be the generally accepted approach these

days .... However, the evidence is not encouraging on this matter. (1996, p. 352)

Truscott noted that various studies of L1 writing found that it makes no difference whether corrections are comprehensive or selective. "For L2, Hendrikson (1981) failed to find any difference between comprehensive correction and correction restricted to communicative errors. Thus, the evidence suggests that limiting the number of corrections is not a solution" (Truscott, 1996, pp. 352–353). Silva et al. (1997) noted that according to the "Teachabilty Hypothesis" (Pienemann, 1984) learners will learn what they are taught only if they are developmentally ready, but agreed with Truscott that "although many second language learners believe in the importance of correction, there is little evidence that correction has much effect on developing proficiency" (Silva et al., p. 414). Truscott left open the possibility that selective correction carefully timed in accordance with a developmental sequence might be effective, but he is not sanguine about the possibility.

In a response to Truscott's article published in the *Journal of Second Language Writing,* Dana Ferris characterized Truscott's position in the following way: "Based on limited, dated, incomplete, and inconclusive evidence, he argues for eliminating a pedagogical practice that is not only highly valued by students, but on which many thoughtful teachers spend a great deal of time and mental energy because they feel that helping students to improve the accuracy of their writing is vitally important" (Ferris, 1999, p. 9). Ferris calls for more research with better control of student, teacher, and contextual variables. She wonders whether the error correction was accurate, whether some types of errors might be more amenable to correction than others, whether some students might respond to correction better than others, and whether different modes of error correction might be more or less effective. In fact, however, most of these issues have been addressed in some way in the studies Truscott reviewed. Truscott's list of references contains 122 items over a period of about 25 years. No study is without flaw, but it would seem that if a case were to be made for error correction, some of these studies would show at least a small positive result.

Truscott responded to Ferris's article in the following issue of the same journal. He concluded:

> The first criticism is that there is research evidence for the effectiveness of correction, contrary to my conclusions. But no meaningful support is provided for this claim, and later discussion appears to contradict it at several points. Another criticism is that the evidence I reviewed cannot support any generalizations because of the variability among the studies. But this objection is based on an argument that mixes relevant and irrelevant work, includes wrong details about the studies I used and, as I have argued, misrepresents the logic of generalization. A third criticism is that I overstated the evidence

against correction. But only one unconvincing example is offered in support of this strong and general accusation. The final objection to my case against correction is that I illicitly dismissed evidence against my thesis. But this claim is left entirely unsubstantiated, and the supporting arguments I did provide in my paper are not addressed by Ferris. (Truscott, 1999, pp. 118–119)

Faced with this evidence, what is the poor writing instructor to do? As Truscott and Ferris both note, error correction is expected by students, and generally valued by teachers and programs.

Truscott's second reason for questioning the effectiveness of grammar correction is "this lack of effectiveness is exactly what should be expected, given the nature of language learning." Here he is referring to language acquisition theory. He notes that "Second language editing actually depends far more on intuitions of well-formedness, coming from the unconscious language system, than on metalinguistic knowledge of points of grammar." He points to studies "showing a disassociation between the ability to correct an error and the ability to state a rule that could guide the correction" (Truscott, 1996, p. 347). He continues:

> Probably the most interesting of these studies is Green and Hecht's (1992), in which they showed 300 German EFL students nine English grammar errors commonly committed by German students. They asked the students to correct the errors and to give a rule in each case. They found that learners who could not state a rule or who stated a wrong rule were nonetheless able to make a proper correction in most cases. In addition, relatively advanced students were far better than native speakers of English when it came to stating valid rules, although not in making corrections. (1996, pp. 347–398)

This is exactly as language acquisition theory predicts, and we know that as native speakers of English we can often find and correct errors without knowing any grammatical rule that covers the situation. Grammatical knowledge is clearly not a substitute for acquisition.

However, as noted in the previous section on language acquisition theory, consciousness-raising, the process of focusing heightened attention and awareness on particular grammatical forms that deviate from standard English, can theoretically facilitate acquisition of those forms. It is true that Truscott rejects the process of selective marking, because none of the studies he surveys support it. Rutherford's practice, however, requires no correction or grammatical teaching, but simply a focusing of attention, and is an attempt to guide the natural acquisition process, not to supplant it or substitute for it with explicit grammatical concepts. Until further research has been done and we know more, marking a small set of errors that the student appears to be almost ready to acquire is probably the best practice. In this way, the instructor works with the natural processes of language acquisition.

CONCLUSIONS

The theories outlined in this chapter have strong implications for what an ESL writing course should look like. The course should provide ample opportunities for comprehensible input, via both reading and listening. The atmosphere in the classroom should be positive and comfortable, so that anxiety is diminished, and there should be numerous opportunities for real communication. As Silva et al. noted, "It is thought that interactive input focused on communicating comprehensible messages of importance to both partners in a communicative event (rather than corrective feedback) is what helps learners most to progress in their second language" (p. 412).

The rhetorical expectations of English speakers, and the organizational patterns of academic genres such as the college essay, research essays, reports, memos, and letters, may have to be explicitly taught, especially to international students. John Swales, in *Genre Analysis: English in Academic and Research Settings* (1990), noted that case studies indicate that "there may be value in sensitizing students to rhetorical effects, and to the rhetorical structures that tend to recur in genre-specific texts," and that "formal schemata . . . need to be activated and developed, not so much as rigid templates against which all texts are forced to fit, but more as *caricatures* which self-evidently simplify and distort certain features in an attempt to capture general identity" (Swales, 1990, p. 213). However, instructors should use care when presenting formulaic approaches such as the five-paragraph essay, because students may overgeneralize the formula to inappropriate genres, and may become so reliant on the formula that they are unable to grow as writers.

Feedback on the writing should include selective attention to nonstandard forms, so that acquisition of standard forms can be facilitated. As Rod Ellis said, "formal instruction is best seen as facilitating natural language development rather than offering an alternative mode of learning." Ellis noted that formal instruction seems to work best when combined with opportunities to experience the structures taught in real communication, and recommended approaches that focus both on forms and the meanings they create (Ellis, 1994, p. 659).

I think it is clear that Tony Silva, Ilona Leki, and Joan Carson (1997) are correct in arguing that research in ESL composition has much to teach mainstream composition, especially regarding language acquisition theory, which connects easily with reading theory, vocabulary acquisition, and other matters of concern to all writing teachers. Contrastive rhetoric and the study of cross-cultural communication also offer important insights into the rhetorical patterns of English. In the matter of error correction, there is still research to be done and many questions to answer, but these questions are also relevant to mainstream composition.

FOR FURTHER EXPLORATION

Ferris, D., & Hedgcock, J. S. (1998). *Teaching ESL composition: Purpose, process, and practice.* Mahwah, NJ: Lawrence Erlbaum.

This work by Dana Ferris and John S. Hedgecock is a very thorough presentation of almost every aspect of teaching ESL writing, including theoretical issues, reading–writing connections, syllabus design, lesson planning, text selection, oral and written feedback, and improving grammatical accuracy.

Silva, T., & Matsuda, P. K. (Eds.). (2001). *Landmark essays on ESL writing.* Mahwah, NJ: Hermagoras Press.

Landmark Essays on ESL Writing, edited by Tony Silva and Paul Kei Matsuda, reprints 16 articles that have been influential in the field, including Kaplan's original 1966 contrastive rhetoric article "Cultural Thought Patterns in Inter-cultural Education."

Silva, T., & Matsuda, P. K. (Eds.). (2001). *On second language writing.* Mahwah, NJ: Lawrence Erlbaum Associates.

On Second Language Writing (2001), also edited by Silva and Matsuda, presents 15 new articles.

Swales, S. M. (1990). *Genre analysis: English in academic and research settings.* Cambridge: Cambridge University Press.

This work is an insightful and interesting analysis of the problems of genres and discourse communities, very applicable to the problems of ESL composition and contrastive rhetoric.

Ellis, R. (1994). *The study of second language acquisition.* Oxford: Oxford University Press.

This work is an authoritative compendium of research and theory concerning the problems of language acquisition.

FOR WRITING AND DISCUSSION

1. Look up the aforementioned articles by John Truscott and Dana Ferris. Write a paper analyzing their arguments and presenting your own case for or against grammar correction.
2. Do a Web search on "learn hiragana," "learn Chinese characters, learn Greek alphabet, or learn Arabic alphabet," or try a search on another writing system. Using the materials you find, try to learn to write five or six letters or characters from an unfamiliar writing

system. Write a description of your experiences, noting your
successes and problems. Discuss your experiences with the class.

REFERENCES

Cai, G. (1993, March). Beyond Bad Writing: Teaching English composition to Chinese ESL
    students. Paper presented at the Conference of College Composition and Communication.
    San Diego, CA.
Chiang, Y. D., & Schmida, M. (1999). Language identity and language ownership: Linguistic
    conflicts of first-year university writing students. In L. Harklau, K. M. Losey, & M. Siegal.
    *Generation 1.5 meets college composition: Issues in the teaching of writing to U.S.-educated learners
    of ESL*. Mahwah, NJ: Lawrence Erlbaum.
Connor, U. (1996). *Contrastive rhetoric: Cross-cultural aspects of second-language writing*. New York:
    Cambridge University Press.
Connor, U., & Kaplan, R. (Eds.). (1987). *Writing across languages: Analysis of L2 text*. Reading,
    MA: Addison Wesley.
Ellis, R. (1985). *Understanding second language acquisition*. New York: Oxford University
    Press.
Ellis, R. (1994). *The study of second language acquisition*. Oxford: Oxford University Press.
Ema, T, Taniyama, S. & Ino, K. (Eds.). (1981). Bunshô no kakikata [How to construct a sen-
    tence/ composition]. In *Shinshu kokugo soran* [New Japanese conspectus] (rev. ed., pp.
    294–295). Kyoto: Kyoto Shobô.
Ferris, D. (1999). The case for grammar correction in L2 writing classes: A response to Truscott
    (1996) *Journal of Second Language Writing, 8* (1), 1–11.
Ferris, D., & Hedgcock, J. S. (1998). *Teaching ESL composition: Purpose, process, and practice*.
    Mahwah, NJ: Lawrence Erlbaum.
Flower, L., & Hayes, J. (1980). Identifying the organization of writing processes. In L. W. Gregg
    & E. R. Steinberg (Eds.), *Cognitive processes in writing* (pp. 3–50). Hillsdale, NJ: Lawrence
    Erlbaum.
Green, P. S., & Hecht, K. (1992). Implicit and explicit grammar: An empirical study. *Applied
    Linguistics, 13*, 168–184.
Harklau, L., Losey, K. M., & Siegal M. (Eds.). (1999). *Generation 1.5 meets college composi-
    tion: Issues in the teaching of writing to U.S.-educated learners of ESL*. Mahwah, NJ: Lawrence
    Erlbaum.
Hartwell, P. (1985). Grammar, grammars, and the teaching of grammar. *College English 47*,
    105–127.
Henrikson, J. M. (1981). *Error analysis and error correction in language teaching*. Singapore:
    SEAMEO Regional Language Centre.
Hinds, J. (1976). *Aspects of Japanese discourse structure*. Tokyo: Kaitakusha.
Hinds, J. (1983). Linguistics and written discourse in English and Japanese: A contrastive
    study. In R. B. Kaplan (Ed.), *Annual Review of Applied Linguistics 1982* (pp.78–84). Rowley,
    MA: Newbury House.
Hinds, J. (1990). Inductive, deductive: Expository writing in Japanese, Korean, Chinese and
    Thai. In U. Connor & A. M. Johns (Eds.), Coherence in writing: Research & pedagogical
    perspectives (pp. 87–110). Alexandria, VA: TESOL.
Horning, A. S. (1987). *Teaching writing as a second language*. Carbondale: Southern Illinois
    University Press.
Kaplan, R. B. (1966). Cultural thought patterns in intercultural education. *Language Learning,
    16*, 1–20.

Kaplan, R. B. (1972). The anatomy of rhetoric: Prolegomena to a functional theory of rhetoric: Essays for teachers. *Language and the teacher: A series in applied linguistics* (Vol. 8). Philadelphia, PA: The Center for Curriculum Development.

Kaplan, R. B. (1988). Contrastive rhetoric and second language learning: Notes toward a theory of contrastive rhetoric. In A. C. Purves (Ed.), *Writing across languages and cultures: Issues in contrastive rhetoric* (pp. 275–304). Written Communication Annual Vol 2. Newbury Park: Sage.

Kaplan, R. B. (2001). Forward: What in the world is contrastive rhetoric? In C. G. Panetta (Ed.), *Contrastive rhetoric revisited and redefined* (pp. vii–xx). Mahwah, NJ: Lawrence Erlbaum.

Krashen, S. (1982). *Principles and practice in second language acquisition*. Oxford: Pergamon Press.

Krashen, S. (1984). *Writing: Research, theory and application*. Oxford: Pergamon Press.

Krashen, S., & Terrell, T. D. (1983). *The natural approach: Language acquisition in the classroom*. New York: Pergamon Press.

Montaño-Harmon, M. (1991). Discourse features of written Mexican Spanish: Current research in contrastive rhetoric and its implications. *Hispania, 74*, 417–425.

Pienemann, M. (1984). Psychological constraints on the teachability of languages. *Studies in Second Language Acquisition, 6*, 186–214.

Rutherford, W. E. (1987). *Second language grammar: Learning and teaching*. New York: Longman.

Scardamalia, M., & Bereiter, C. (1987). Knowledge telling and knowledge transforming in written composition. In S. Rosenberg (Ed). *Advances in applied psycholinguistics. Volume 2: Reading, writing and language learning* (pp. 142–175). Cambridge, UK: Cambridge University Press.

Silva, T., Leki, I., & Carson, J. (1997, July). Broadening the perspective of mainstream composition studies: Some thoughts from the disciplinary margins. *Written Communication, 14* (3), 398–428.

Silva, T., & Matsuda, P. K. (Eds.). (2001a). *On second language writing*. Mahwah, NJ: Lawrence Erlbaum.

Silva, T., & Matsuda, P. K. (Eds.). (2001b). *Landmark essays on ESL writing*. Mahwah, NJ: Hermagoras Press.

Sterelny, K. (1990). *The representational theory of mind: An introduction*. Cambridge, MA: Basil Blackwell.

Swales, J. M. (1990). *Genre analysis: English in academic and research settings*. Cambridge: Cambridge University Press.

Takamata, K. (1976). *Genkoo shippitsu nyuumon* {An introduction to writing manuscripts}. Tokyo: Natsumesha.

Truscott, J. (1996). The case against grammar correction in L2 writing classes. *Language Learning, 46* (2), 327–369.

Truscott, J. (1999). The case for "the case against grammar correction in L2 writing classes": A response to Ferris. *Journal of Second Language Writing, 8* (2), 111–122.

Reading

BROADENING THE PERSPECTIVE OF MAINSTREAM COMPOSITION STUDIES

Some Thoughts from the Disciplinary Margins

Tony Silva
Purdue University

Ilona Leki
University of Tennessee

Joan Carson
Georgia State University

In this article we (a) argue that mainstream composition studies is at present too narrow in its scope and limited in its perspective and (b) offer some thoughts, from our unique interdisciplinary position, that we feel could help mainstream composition professionals improve this situation. In our article, we first provide evidence that we feel suggests an unfortunate pattern of neglect in mainstream composition studies of writing in English as a second language (ESL) and writing in languages other than English. We then introduce a number of concepts from second language studies (primarily from second language acquisition and second language writing instruction) that we believe could help mainstream composition studies address its limitations; develop a more global and inclusive understanding of writing; and thus avoid being seen as a monolinguistic, monocultural, and ethnocentric enterprise.

Native language teachers have much to learn from ESL research and pedagogy.
—Smith, 1992

Reprinted from *Written Communication*, Vol. 14 No. 3, July 1997 398–428 © 1997 Sage Publications, Inc. Used with permission.

388

We agree.

English as a Second Language (ESL) writing, or more generally, second language writing is uniquely situated at the intersection of second language studies and composition studies. This position requires us as second language writing researchers and teachers to keep up on scholarship in two fairly distinct disciplines and invites us to compare developments in each and to observe how each influences the other. In our view, both disciplines have a lot to offer each other. A number of ideas and insights from composition studies have proved quite valuable for second language studies and have both broadened its perspectives and added depth to its discussions. Unfortunately, the transfer of knowledge between the fields has primarily been a one way affair, from composition studies to second language studies.[1]

There is no disputing that in recent years mainstream composition studies has been at great pains to articulate and promote a multicultural perspective that honors diversity. Composition studies has gained a great deal from attention to feminist, critical, postcolonial, and postmodernist perspectives imported from literary and cultural studies.[2] Yet from our vantage point, mainstream composition studies remains troublingly narrow in its scope. Mainstream composition scholars make what seem to us to be universalist claims about the phenomenon of writing almost exclusively on the basis of Western (Greco-Roman and Anglo-American) rhetorical traditions and/or on the findings of empirical research conducted primarily on undergraduate college students in North American colleges and universities. Muchiri, Mulamba, Myers, and Ndoloi (1995) propose a similar argument supported by compelling examples from the perspective of African writing researchers. They urge composition researchers to

> see how much of [their] work is tied to the particular context of the U.S. When composition researchers make larger claims about academic knowledge and language, it [sic] needs to acknowledge these ties. The very diversity rightly celebrated in the composition literature may lead a teacher to forget that it is diversity joined in a peculiarly American way, within American institutions, in an American space. The teacher in New York or Los Angeles may look out over a classroom and think, "the whole world is here." It isn't. (p. 195)

Canagarajah (1996) likewise provides a glimpse into the material conditions of scholars in third world countries, conditions so unlike those taken for granted, for example, in North America. But in mainstream composition studies little consideration has been given to writing in languages other than English—for example, there seems to be negligible concern for Asian, African, or Middle Eastern writing or rhetorics—or to writing done by individuals in a language that is not their mother tongue. This limited perspective is troubling to us in that we feel it could lead to inadequate theories of composition and consequently to instructional practices that are ineffective or even counter productive. We believe that the attention to issues raised by the examination of writers learning and composing in a second language can result in a broadening of perspectives that may enrich mainstream composition studies in the same way as feminist, critical, postcolonial, and postmodernist considerations have done.

Our discussion is in two parts. First, we offer evidence to support our claim about the limitations of mainstream composition studies. Second, we introduce and discuss some concepts from second language studies that we believe could help mainstream composition studies address these limitations.[3]

A Pattern of Neglect

The neglect of second and other language writing in mainstream composition studies becomes evident when some of the field's basic documents are examined. For example, a perusal of the program books for the Conference on College Composition and Communication (CCCC) conferences will reveal a very small number of sessions devoted to second and other language concerns, and a substantial percentage of the sessions labeled as such actually relate only marginally to second or other language matters. The CCCC Bibliography of Composition and Rhetoric, though it includes a subsection on ESL (placed under the heading of curriculum and thus implicitly put on a par with areas like research and study skills), devotes only a tiny percentage of its entries to second and other language matters. Furthermore, many of the relevant entries do not deal with writing issues, thus providing a partial and distorted picture of scholarship in second and other language writing.

A look at almost any of the monographs of the most widely known mainstream composition scholars (for example, those of Berlin, Berthoff, Elbow, Emig, Kinneavy, Flower) will turn up little if anything regarding second or other language writing. This also holds true for important collections and reviews of research in the field. For example, in Bizzell and Herzberg's (1990), The Rhetorical Tradition: Readings from Classical Times to the Present (our bold), all of the selections are from the Western (Greco-Roman and Anglo-American) rhetorical tradition; we found no focus on Asian, African, Middle Eastern, or other rhetorical traditions and no mention of this exclusion in the book's preface or elsewhere. Given the contents of this collection, its title is problematic; it is at best misleading and at worst exclusionary in its ethnocentricity.

With regard to reviews of empirical research, Braddock, Lloyd-Jones, and Schoer (1963) note as "unexplored territory" (p. 53) the effectiveness of "...procedures of teaching and learning composition ...for pupils learning to write English as a second language" (p. 54). Although none of the studies considered for this report focused on second or other language writing, the authors' recognition of the need to look at ESL writing is promising. Thus, it is disappointing and ironic to find in the introduction to Hillocks' (1986) follow up volume, Research on Written Composition: New Directions for Teaching, that " ... research dealing with spelling, vocabulary, initial teaching alphabet, or English as a second language was excluded" (p. xvii). Hillocks goes on to say that "Research written in languages other than English was not examined" (p. xviii)—with the exception of one review of research in Dutch—an exclusion that would certainly seem to work against globalization of the research base on writing.

An examination of scholarly journals in mainstream composition over the last 10 years would reveal a similar pattern. Although a few of these journals (*Journal of Basic Writing, Writing Center Journal,* and *Written Communication*) give what we would consider a meaningful amount of space to second and other language writing issues, in the majority of mainstream composition journals the treatment of second and other language writing concerns seems to us to be largely absent or negligible.

An examination of mainstream composition textbooks, handbooks, and readers reveals a more encouraging but not wholly satisfactory situation. Though many of the newest composition textbooks and handbooks include notes or sections to address ESL writers, these treatments are often limited to morphosyntactic considerations (for example, verb use, articles, adjective/adverb position, present and past participles). Although this is a step in the direction of inclusion, it implies a simplistic view of ESL writers, that is, that their differences from native English speaking writers are merely a matter of a few morphosyntactic oddities and that no consideration of discoursal, rhetorical, or cultural differences is necessary. The case with mainstream composition readers is similar. Although many focus on cross-cultural or multicultural issues, these issues are typically addressed in the North American context, thus making them somewhat culture bound and difficult to use with those ESL writers who are new to this context. That is, many of these readers assume knowledge or experience that many ESL writers do not possess.

On the basis of the foregoing, it is fair to suggest that, overall, mainstream composition studies' perspective on second and other language writing is indeed limited. We believe that such a limited perspective is problematic on both theoretical and practical levels. A theory of writing based only on one rhetorical tradition and one language can at best be extremely tentative and at worst totally invalid. Such a theory could easily become hegemonic and exclusionary; that is, English/Western writing behaviors could be privileged as somehow being "standard," thus stigmatizing other writing behaviors as "substandard" or "deviant." Such a theory could be seen as monolingual, monocultural, and ethnocentric. Pedagogical insights so based would seem inadequate even for those whose concerns are limited to North America because the population here is increasingly diverse and multicultural. For those with more global concerns, such narrowness of scope is untenable and unacceptable.

Clearly composition studies needs a broader and more inclusive view of writing, one that we feel could profit from the perspectives and insights of second language studies. Therefore, we will introduce and discuss insights from two wide domains of second language studies: second language acquisition (SLA) and ESL writing pedagogy. We believe these insights could help mainstream composition studies develop a more global and inclusive view of writing. Here it is not our intention to show explicitly how each issue we raise would play out in mainstream composition classrooms or research. We leave that to mainstream composition instructors and researchers. Rather we seek primarily to point to directions of potentially fruitful inquiry and reflection. Though we recognize that some mainstream composition professionals may find some of these concepts familiar, we expect that the second language spin provided here will be less familiar. We also believe that the examination of the large area of studies of writing in languages other than English, though regretfully beyond the scope of this article, would repay consideration by adding a needed depth to theories of rhetoric and writing.

Insights from Second Language Studies

Second Language Acquisition Research

The idea that inexperienced first language writers are like learners of a second language, most often the language of the academy, has been suggested by Horning (1987) whose central hypothesis is that "basic writers develop writing skills and achieve proficiency in the same way that other adults develop second language skills, principally because, for basic writers, academic, formal, written English is a new and distinct linguistic system" (p. 2). Although this hypothesis makes intuitive sense, Horning's account of SLA falls short in several crucial respects. We mention Horning's work here because reviewers' comments on previous drafts of this article indicate that it is one of the few sources of information about second language writing known by mainstream compositionists, and yet Horning's account is at best incomplete. Horning relies heavily on Krashen's learning-acquisition distinction in which conscious (learned) and unconscious (acquired) acquisition are said to result in distinct and unrelated processing mechanisms (see, for example, Krashen, 1981, 1982), a distinction that has been frequently and convincingly challenged in second language acquisition research. Furthermore, Horning's work presents, at best, an uneven explanation of concepts in second language acquisition and, at worst, explanations of complex phenomena (errors, for example) that do not accord with the findings of relevant research. Finally, she does not address some of the crucial aspects of second language acquisition theory that would be most relevant to an understanding of first language writing development (explanations of variability, for example). Thus, whereas Horning's initial analogy may be appealing, we hope to supplement and modify this account through a closer look at what second language acquisition theory has to offer first language composition studies.

Those who are developing expertise in writing already command a first—oral—language and through exposure to and practice with writing are expected to move progressively closer to the language norms of those in the community of writers they seek to join. However, this perspective describes developing writers primarily in terms of proficiency, or lack thereof. For example, in his review of 1,557 composition studies from 1984–1989, Durst (1990) notes that the most influential composition research has been with English speaking high school students (Emig, 1971); high school, college, and more experienced writers (Bridwell, 1980; Faigley & Witte, 1981; Sommers, 1980); expert and novice writers (Flower & Hayes, 1981); basic college writers (Perl, 1979); and early elementary students (Graves, 1978). This literature on composing processes provides a picture of writers arrayed on a developmental continuum from less to more proficient. Proficiency has been portrayed in mainstream composition research as an issue of development and as the primary factor distinguishing among first language writers. Research in second language studies, on the other hand, has been more concerned with *explaining* differential proficiency. In general, second language acquisition research seeks to answer four fundamental questions:

1. What does learner language look like? (This description needs to account for both synchronic and diachronic aspects of learner language.)
2. How do learners acquire a second language? (This explanation needs to include both internal and external factors.)
3. What accounts for the differences in learners' achievements? (This explanation attends to the fact that second language learners as a rule experience differential success.)
4. What are the effects of formal instruction? (This question investigates the extent to which instruction plays a role in the acquisition process.)

In the following section, we will review some of the major findings in each of these areas.

Question #1. What does learner language look like? In general, learner language can be characterized as having three dimensions: (a) it has errors; (b) it exhibits developmental patterns; and (c) it is variable.

Perspectives on error in second language acquisition are similar to those of Shaughnessy (1977) in that they are seen as windows on the acquisition process. Errors, however, are difficult to define and identify for several reasons. First, it is not always clear whether a learner is producing an error (generated by the learner's linguistic competence) or a mistake (generated by the learner's linguistic performance). Second, the variety of language that the learner has chosen to acquire is an intervening factor: what might be an error in one variety is not necessarily so in another. Finally, because learners' intended utterances are not always clear to native speakers, what constitutes the specific error in an utterance is not always immediately obvious. These issues of error definition and identification are undoubtedly applicable, as well, to the development of written language proficiency by providing different ways of interpreting possible errors in students' work.

Because error analysis does not provide a complete picture of learner language (a focus on errors fails to provide information about what learners are doing correctly, for example), errors are only a preliminary source of information about learner language. The recognition of developmental patterns allows a clearer picture of the general regularities that characterize second language acquisition. Typically, in the early stages of acquisition, learners use formulaic speech that consists of memorized language formulas or routines. This strategy allows learners to produce whole "chunks" of language, reducing the learning burden while maximizing communicative ability. These chunks are available later for analysis as learners figure out the items and rules used in creative speech. Do we see similar processes among inexperienced writers who try on the written language forms of the academy, for example, in chunks of overly academic phrasings? Borrowing unanalyzed chunks of such written language can be seen not negatively as indicating a lack of proficiency but rather positively as moving the learner forward toward target and flexible use of written forms.

The development of second language proficiency is understood as occurring on what Selinker (1972) calls the interlanguage continuum, in which the learner moves successively toward closer and closer approximations of the target language. This continuum is characterized by the acquisition of general patterns of language in a relatively predictable order, and this order does not vary regardless of the learner's first language background. In other words, all learners will develop linguistically along the same general route of acquisition. But a learner's interlanguage rules are not necessarily the rules of the target language; rather, they represent the learner's hypotheses at a single point in time about the target language.

Although the interlanguage continuum provides a perspective on the regularities in second language learners' acquisition patterns, there is an apparent contradiction between this systematicity and the variation that is evident in, and characteristic of, learner language. Variation is exhibited when learners apply a rule in one context but not in another. For example, a learner who writes "You depend on other people and they depend of you" has produced the target language rule in the first clause but not in the second.

What accounts for this variability? Variability of this type is described as occurring in three contexts: linguistic, situational, and psycholinguistic. Linguistic context refers to the language elements that precede and/or follow the variable in question. For example, a second language learner might easily produce subject-verb agreement in simple sentences (My sister lives in Washington), but might not in complex sentences (My sister, who live in Washington, is older than me.)

Situational context refers to many factors including speech styles (style shifting in socially appropriate ways), social factors (such as age, gender, class, ethnicity), and stylistic factors (situation and topic, for example). Each of these factors can result in the differential application of interlanguage rules. For example, producing an essay on a topic related to the learner's experiences in their native country might result in more first language interference (see discussion of Friedlander,

1990, below) than would an essay based on experiences in the learner's second language. This might be the case, too, with writers who speak a non-standard dialect, where certain topics might elicit more non-standard forms. Social Accommodation Theory (Beebe, 1988) can help explain some of the variability as well, to the extent that writers seek to converge with, diverge from, or maintain a social connection to the reader. (See issues of motivation and social distance below.)

Psycholinguistic context refers to the cognitive processing constraints imposed by the task in question. Learners must balance the demands of language production with the cognitive demands inherent in producing the text (oral or written). Speaking on a complex or abstract topic or under time constraints means that the language learner must focus not only on the difficulty of what s/he is trying to say, but also on the language that is needed to express her/his ideas. When attention is divided in this way, the speaker often attends primarily to the content of the utterance rather than to its form, resulting in language that is less native-like than would be the case if the speaker were talking about familiar, more concrete topics. With less complex tasks, in terms of topic or lack of time constraints or as the result of a process approach in which the writer focuses on language issues only in later drafts, a writer is likely to have time to employ a careful style, which is the most attended form. However, the attended style does not necessarily result in the most correct form. Monitoring in the careful style allows the learner/writer the time to consider competing hypotheses about language forms. Because writing eventually requires the selection of a single form—even when more than one possibility exists for the writer—the text may not only exhibit variability (when the writer in one place chooses one form and in another place the competing form) but may also give the reader an inaccurate perspective on the writer's developing competence.

Most adult second language learners never reach target language proficiency (this is commonly seen in the persistence of non-native pronunciation—foreign accents), and this failure to move toward native speaker norms is called "fossilization" (Selinker, 1972). Cognitive and social forces appear to intersect in the phenomenon of fossilization, in which a second language learner stops progressing toward proficiency in the second language despite continuing access to target or "correct" forms. Second language learners reach a level of competence in the target language that allows them to accomplish their communication tasks to their own satisfaction, and though they may assert that they want to continue to move toward target forms, they do not move farther. In fact, they may no longer even perceive the difference between their own production and target forms.

The construct of fossilization might apply to novices writing in their first language and help explain lack of progress toward target goals of institutionally accepted writing. It is possible that, despite conscious belief that they want to produce a change in their writing, novice writers considered unsuccessful are in fact satisfied with the communicativeness of what they produce and have no profound motivation to unfossilize. In the complex interaction between social and cognitive factors, an exploration of the implications of fossilization for mainstream composition studies might yield new insights.

Given this complex picture of learner language, it become clear that writers' errors are a window on the acquisition process. Errors exhibit the variability inherent in the acquisition process, and as such can be interpreted as evidence of the writer's potential (not unlike Vygotsky's (1978) zone of proximal development), rather than as a lack of proficiency.

Question #2. How do learners acquire a second language? Explaining second language acquisition requires a consideration of both external and internal factors. (Although linguistic universals are an important part of second language acquisition theory, they are probably not of relevance to composition studies and will not be discussed here.) Significant external factors are primarily social in nature; internal factors involve issues of language transfer and cognition.

External factors. Social factors play a major but indirect role in second language acquisition, insofar as acquisition is mediated by learner attitudes as well as by the nature and extent of input (as determined by learning opportunities related to such things as ethnic background and socioeconomic class). Learner attitudes are both cognitive and affective, and they tend to be learned and persistent, but modifiable. Learner attitudes toward the acquisition of the target language are related to learner attitudes toward target language speakers, the target language culture, the social value of learning the target language, the particular uses that the target language might serve, and the learners' perceptions of themselves as members of their own culture.

Social factors related to second language acquisition include sociolinguistic aspects of age (younger learners between the ages of 10 and 19 are more influenced by their peer group whereas middle aged learners from 30 to 60 are more influenced by mainstream social values, including standard language norms), sex (women tend to have more positive attitudes and to use more standard forms than men), and social class. In particular, social class is related to the role of sociopsychological attitudes, to the extent that second language acquisition implies the loss of the first language (referred to as subtractive bilingualism) or the maintenance of the first language as the second language is acquired (referred to as additive bilingualism). Subtractive bilingualism is typical of what happens in this country to immigrants and refugees who are expected to become "Americanized" linguistically by giving up their first language and adopting English. In this perspective, the first language is perceived as a problem that language learners must overcome. Additive bilingualism, on the other hand, is typical of middle- and upper-class bilinguals for whom knowing more than one language is seen as an advantage. In this view, bilingualism is seen as a resource that can be used for social, political, and economic gain.

The social context of subtractive bilingualism influences learners' attitudes and language acquisition in subtle but profound ways, having to do with the learner's identification with the first language social group. A parallel can be drawn here for middle- and upper-class writers who typically control a more or less standard variety of English (given regional variation). These writers are given the opportunity in school to develop the type of writing proficiency used in academic contexts, with no expectation that they will need to abandon/"correct" their oral language or their written language in nonacademic contexts. In other words, their writing development is more nearly like additive bilingualism. However, students who speak a nonstandard variety of English, typically associated with working-class writers, are most often taught that their oral and written language is "incorrect" and they are put in the position of subtractive bilinguals who feel that they must give up their first language to acquire the standard forms.

Related to this notion of ethnolinguistic vitality, Schumann's (1977) Acculturation Model of second language acquisition sees language as one aspect of becoming acculturated to the second language cultural context. According to Schumann, successful language acquisition depends on the learner's perceived social and psychological distance from the target language group. When the learner maintains this distance, pidginization is likely to occur in which the learner fossilizes on a relatively nonproficient point on the interlanguage continuum, resulting in the ability to produce limited language functions. (See Peirce, 1995 for a cogent critique of Schumann and others who appear to make language acquisition contingent on giving up first language social identities.)

This perspective on fossilization evokes issues of learner motivation, central to studies of second language acquisition. A widely used distinction in second language acquisition work that might be useful to mainstream writing research is the distinction between integrative motivation and instrumental motivation, originally proposed by Gardner and Lambert (1972). A learner who shows integrative motivation wants to become like the people who speak the target language. (See Alice Kaplan's [1993] autobiography of a French major for a striking example of this concept.) The target culture is admired and its representatives are sought out and imitated. A learner who shows instrumental motivation, on the other hand, is less interested in the target language, culture, and people for their inherent qualities, but more interested in developing skilled use of the target language for particular purposes. This might be the type of motivation of, for example, Chinese graduate students in physics studying in the United States for an advanced degree making some English speaking friends, but primarily interested in English to participate in, perhaps, the international dialogue in professional journals in physics.

Neither type of motivation is necessarily superior to the other; both have been shown to correlate with success in language learning. But the discussion in mainstream writing literature has implicitly focused almost exclusively on integrative motivation, urging an integrative desire on writing students. If we think of, for instance, the teachers of writing as the "native speakers" of the target culture, first language students with integrative motivation would want to become like those native speakers, to imitate their behavior and attitudes. Bartholomae

(1985) speaks of students having to invent the university; more dramatically, students are required to re-invent themselves, ideally to see themselves as indistinguishable from the people already there, already a part of the university culture. Although there has been recognition in the mainstream writing literature of the fact that students may not want to bring their image of themselves in line with the image projected by the "natives" of the university culture, second language writing research explicitly acknowledges the legitimacy and efficacy of instrumental, not just integrative, motivation in the pursuit of the second language, including writing.

The issue of social context for learning a second language that predominates in Schumann's work focuses on the importance of the social distance between the native and the target culture. A few of the conditions favorable to the acquisition of the second language that might be considered in thinking about mainstream writing instruction include the following: The learner's culture and the target culture admire each other and see each other as equals; both the learner's culture and the target culture expect the learner to succeed; the learner and the target culture share social environments; the learner plans to spend a great deal of time in the target culture. If we look at the first language learners' task in developing into proficient writers, we must question whether the optimal conditions laid out here for second language acquisition are met for first language writing students. When viewed from this perspective, we might feel humbled by the enormity of the social barriers faced especially by writing students from minority cultures not admired by the target culture, not seen as equal, not expected to succeed, and not socialized with. These barriers may be insurmountable for first language students from poor, rural, or minority cultures or backgrounds whose relationship to the majority culture is not optimal for acquisition of majority norms, even when such acquisition is desired.

Internal factors. The question of how the learner's first language knowledge influences the acquisition of the second language has long been an issue for second language theory. Second language acquisition researchers see a complex role for the first language in the acquisition of the second: sometimes negative, when reliance on first language intuitions causes errors in the second language; sometimes positive, when taking a chance using a first language form succeeds and results in appropriate use of the second language. This work has implications for mainstream writing research if extended to include attempts to understand, for example, the relationship between a student's oral language and that student's acquisition of written language. What features of the target language are difficult for writing students to acquire and which come easily? Which features of a student's oral language help in the acquisition of the written language and which do not? With a better sense of the answers to these questions, teachers might be more sensitive to the efforts students are required to make in order to function in written language and might have more realistic expectations of individual students and of writing curriculums.

The role of consciousness is also of interest to second language theorists. Bialystok (1978) claims that conscious and unconscious knowledge interact in second language acquisition.

Explicit knowledge arises when there is a focus on the language code, and the acquisition of explicit knowledge is facilitated by formal practice. Implicit knowledge is developed through exposure to communicative language use that is facilitated by functional practice. Bialystok's perspective is one that is relevant to composition theory to the extent that it can account for the fact that techniques such as explicit grammar teaching have been shown to be ineffective in improving writing proficiency. Functional practice, resulting in implicit knowledge, highlights the importance of audience and purpose in writing and suggests why a focus on these aspects of the writing process is more likely to lead to the development of writing ability.

Such internal factors interact with the external linguistic environment, a feature of the acquisition context stressed in second language research but perhaps underplayed in first language contexts. Target language input is presumed to be data that the learner must use to develop and adjust an internal picture (the interlanguage system) of how the target language is constructed. It is thought that interactive input focused on communicating comprehensible messages of importance to both partners in a communicative event (rather than corrective feedback) is what helps learners most to progress in their second language.

In terms of mainstream writing instruction, the question then would be: What kind of input are the learners getting? Are they aware of what the target language looks like? Do they get repeated samples of what they are expected to produce? Research in Canada shows high school writers able to adapt their writing for sixth graders but not for adult newspaper readers (Lusignan & Fortier, 1992). Is this perhaps because these young writers know from personal experience what sixth grade texts look like, but have no real internalized sense of what the other target language, here, the written language of newspaper readers, looks like? If this is the case, how can they be expected to produce similar language or rhetorical forms? Do first language writing students read material that they can realistically be expected to produce, or is it far too complicated, too far beyond their reach for them to be able to produce similar types of writing within the short amount of time designated as appropriate for learning to write, for example, during a first-year composition class? Clearly the role of input is as significant in composition studies as it is in second language acquisition research.

Question #3. What accounts for the differences in learners' achievements? It is a fact that few adult second language learners (perhaps only 5%) will acquire native-like proficiency in the target language, although many if not most learners will attain the ability to communicate relative to their needs. This fact of differential success requires explanation in second language acquisition theory and has resulted in many studies of learner differences.

In the context of writing, the recognition of learner differences and of differential success can lead to a deeper institutional acceptance of the idea that different students have differing goals and agendas in their study of writing. Second language research explicitly recognizes that because of differing motivations or differing amounts of contact with speakers of the target language some learners will become more proficient than others. Teachers and researchers in second language writing also acknowledge that those who are learning to write in a second language in an institutional setting may be doing so only to satisfy the requirements of the institutional setting and may never again need to write, or perhaps even to read, a single word in their second language in the rest of their lifetimes, particularly if these learners return to their native countries. These acknowledgments help to discourage an inappropriately inflated view of the importance of learning to write and a concomitant inappropriate negative evaluation of those who do not become particularly proficient. Although little attention is given in mainstream composition studies to gaining a sense of native English speaking students' goals and agendas in learning to write, such a focus might be revealing and might lead to a reconsideration of why students should necessarily learn to write for higher educational settings at all. (See discussion below on functions of writing.) Or, perhaps such a focus might lead to a refinement of notions of "proficiency" to include the recognition of student goals and agendas—that is, that students may be proficient when they have achieved what they want to achieve and not when they achieve what the academy wants them to. Proficiency might be seen as an individual concept rather than an institutional one.

Characterizations of good language learners parallel those of proficient writers: These learners are typically said to show a concern for form, concern for meaning/communication, an active task approach, an awareness of the learning process, and the capacity to use strategies flexibly vis-à-vis task requirements. Second language acquisition researchers distinguish between learning styles, understood as a consistent way of functioning, and learning strategies, assumed to be modifiable. (In mainstream composition studies, much of the work leading to the process paradigm in composition focuses on writer's strategies, e.g., Emig, 1971.) However, although open to modification and conscious manipulation, according to research by Bialystok (1985), learning strategies must be internally governed. That is, teaching the strategies of good learners to poor learners and urging the struggling learners to adopt them will not result in improvement. Such a claim has clear implications for composition instruction that is based on the notion that struggling writers are best served by being taught the composing strategies of successful writers. SLA research suggests that requisite internal government may not develop through instruction on composing processes.

Recognition in mainstream composition studies of differences in learner styles and strategies has not seemed to move far beyond noting that certain minority students are more orally or visually oriented than traditional, majority-culture students. Mainstream composition research may need to examine these preference among individuals (in either the majority or minority cultures) and propose alternative teaching methods to accommodate them. (See Carson & Nelson, 1996 for a second language perspective on culture-related problems of peer review in an ESL composition class, for example.) Such a focus seems particularly desirable in light of recent challenges to progressive and expressivist forms of writing instruction that assert that expressivist forms of instruction are effective primarily for White middle-class students and not for less advantaged writers (Cope & Kalantzis, 1993; Graff, 1996; Gore, 1993; Stotsky, 1995).

Question #4. What are the effects of formal instruction?   One of the surprising findings of second language acquisition research is that there has been no convincing evidence for method superiority. Several explanations have been offered for this finding. First, lessons of any type often result in relatively little progress in language acquisition. Second, individual learners benefit from different types of instruction. Finally, language classes tend to offer similar opportunities for learning irrespective of method. The most important question about formal classroom instruction, though, is whether learners learn what they are taught. The answer to this question may lie with what is referred to as the Teachability Hypothesis (Pienemann, 1984). According to this hypothesis, learners will learn what they are taught only if they are developmentally ready.

This perspective calls into question the role of error correction. Although many second language learners believe in the importance of correction, there is little evidence that correction has much effect on developing proficiency, although it may lead to undesirable types of communication. Chaudron's (1988) review of research on teachers' error correction behaviors concludes that many errors are not treated and that the more often an error is made, the less likely a teacher is to correct it. This may be due to teachers' tacit understanding that error treatment should be conducted in a manner compatible with general interlanguage development; that is, teachers may correct only errors that learners are ready to eliminate. In mainstream composition pedagogy, errors appear to be regarded somewhat monolithically (either we should pay attention to them or not), with seemingly little attention given to the relationship between error production/correction and learner development.

One hypothesis about the effects of formal instruction is that negotiation may be the most crucial aspect of classroom interaction. In this respect, closed task tend to produce more negotiation and more useful negotiation work than open tasks (where there is no predetermined solution). This would be analogous to the difference between (a) writing an essay exam in a history class (a closed tasks in which content is either correct or not and, thus, discussable/explainable/negotiable) and (b) writing an expressive essay in a composition class (an open task in which there is no one predetermined correct response). Furthermore, teachers play a central role in formal acquisition because language learners need grammatical input that is unavailable in sufficient quantity from peers. This may explain recent findings (e.g., Zhang, 1995) in second language composition research that nonnative English speaking writers much prefer teacher feedback to peer response group input.

Second Language Writing Instruction

Second language writing research takes place against a background of insights developed from second language acquisition research. Taking into consideration what is known about second language acquisition and about composition theory and pedagogy, second language writing instruction has developed perspectives that are in some respects different from first language writing instruction but that may provide insights for mainstream composition studies.

Epistemological Issues In second language writing instruction, cultural context is understood as a significant determinant of writers' purposes. Ballard and Clanchy (1991) argue that cultural attitudes toward knowledge range on a continuum from valuing the conservation of knowledge to valuing the extension of knowledge. "These different epistemologies are the bedrock of different cultures, yet they are so taken for granted, each so assumed to be 'universal,' that neither the teachers nor the students can recognize that they are standing on different ground" (p. 21). Ballard and Clanchy suggest that many Asian cultures favor conserving knowledge, with an emphasis on reproduction of information, and strategies such as memorizing and imitating. This is quite a different approach from the mainstream composition perspective of Scardamalia and Bereiter (1987), which highlights Western values of extending knowledge. Scardamalia and Bereiter characterize knowledge telling in writing as "immature" writing, and knowledge transforming as characteristic of "mature" writers. "What we see in the performance of expert writers is the execution of powerful procedures that enable them to draw on, elaborate, and refine available knowledge. For novices, however, writing serves more to reproduce than to refine knowledge" (p. 171). Asian writers who value the conservation of knowledge might be classified as "immature" knowledge tellers in the dichotomy Scardamalia and Bereiter present, although within their own cultural framework they would be "mature" writers. What would appear to be a developmental continuum, then, from immature to mature writing in a knowledge extending culture, is recast as an issue of social context when viewed from the larger crosscultural perspective.

Function of Writing Mainstream composition research, beginning with Emig's (1971) groundbreaking study, turned away from a conventional focus on the message or text toward an investigation of the writer or encoder, highlighting writers' composing processes. This perspective emphasizes the importance of writing as a way of knowing, as well as the place of writing in the writer's mental development. For example, Freedman, Pringle, and Yalden (1979) note that Britton and the British educationists talk about the value of writing in acquiring knowledge and in allowing writers to come to terms with their lives. In this view, "writing is seen ultimately as the great humanizing force; it is not the practical, mundane, communicative advantages of writing that are celebrated but rather its power to give form and significance to our lives" (p. 9).

The mainstream composition literature very much gives the sense that writing experiences have the potential for producing thoughtful, critical-thinking citizens, and the development of such citizens has appeared an important goal in main-stream writing instruction. Also, the idea of using writing to learn has been a strong theme, particularly in the Writing Across the Curriculum Movement. But these views seem to assume that all writers will have the same priorities—an assumption that is not validated by the experience of second language writers. For many second language writers, for example, writing in a nonnative language will never have a function beyond the "practical, mundane, and communicative," as may well be the case for some first language writers. Clearly an adequate theory must acknowledge more pointedly that in a multicultural society, as in the world, the role of writing in writers' lives has varying functions and even for first language writers may legitimately remain limited, never becoming an instrument for life changing experiences.

Writing Topics   Teachers of second language writing try to be sensitive to a given writing topic's potential for being culture bound and not addressable by or appropriate for all cultural groups. Although some groups have no problem with writing on personal topics that require a great deal of personal disclosure, other groups find topics like these invasive and are not comfortable writing on them. Some groups may be reluctant to take issue with what they read; others may take an automatically contestatory stance in relation to what they read.

The point is that none of these preferences is beyond the range of possibilities for individual writers in any culture, including native English speaking writers. Although a given topic may be inappropriate for some native English speaking writers, they may nevertheless feel compelled to address some topics without protest when assigned because they find no cultural support for rejecting them. In thinking about what is appropriate for a native English speaking population, mainstream writing professionals might consider taking into account the kinds of differences in preference and comfort levels that are displayed in an international population.

Knowledge Storage   The issue of appropriateness arises from another angle in research (Friedlander, 1990) that suggests that experiences committed to memory in one language and written about in another are more difficult to write about than experiences committed to memory and written about in the same language. It is then also possible that native English speaking students may have particular difficulty using written (or academic) language to relate an experience stored in oral language. They not only need to access the memory but also, in effect, translate the experience from one language (oral) to another (written). Yet assignments that ask for this very translation are not unusual and in fact are considered especially easy because they only call upon writers to recount what they have experienced, with perhaps a "what I learned from this experience" tacked on. Friedlander's research suggests that such assignments may be more difficult than teachers realize.

Writing from Reading   Although writing from reading is common in mainstream composition studies, what is less typical is recognition of the difficulty first language student writers have reading. For second language readers it is assumed that texts may be opaque and that, therefore, learners may need help with reading, but it is not clear that such consideration is granted to native English speaking readers who appear to be expected to understand college level reading without help. The mainstream composition literature has carefully and repeatedly considered the reciprocity of reading and writing, and many mainstream writing classes use readings to stimulate writing, yet there is little evidence that actual instruction in reading has played much of a role in writing instruction in mainstream classrooms. Discussions of how to teach first language reading at the college level appear to be limited to teaching students how to read literary texts. Might native English speaking students perhaps also benefit from help in constructing meaning not only from literary texts, but also from texts from other genres?

Audience Awareness   Another dimension of composition studies that seems somewhat limited is that of the writer's awareness of the reader or audience and the role that such awareness plays in composing. Flower's (1979) distinction between reader- and writer-based prose, for example, has been extremely influential in mainstream composition studies. In this view, writer-based prose is the result of the writer's lack of cognitive awareness of the reader; the resultant text is insufficient for readers who lack the writer's ability to "fill in the gaps" with necessary information that the writer has in her or his mind but that does not appear in the text. Mature writers are able to move beyond writer-based prose and can develop a text that is reader-sensitive.

This "cognitive problem," as Flower described it, receives a different interpretation when we consider Japanese writers, who, according to Hinds (1987), are socialized in their literacy development (a) to read between the lines to interpret a writer's intention, and (b) to assume that readers will be able to "fill in the gaps" of the texts writers produce. It is asserted that Japanese writers believe that readers have a significant responsibility for understanding text, and comprehensible texts are more the result of "reader responsible" prose than they are of typical Western "writer responsible" texts wherein the writer's obligation is to clarify for the reader's understanding. Thus, what the prevailing paradigm sees as an issue of cognitive development is understood from a larger multicultural perspective as an issue of social context. It is not always clear in developmental studies which aspects of development should be attributed to cognition and which to social forces, but unqualified valuing of reader-based over writer-based prose points to a culture-specific view of this distinction. A broader perspective would look for common features in cognitive processes, recognizing that cognitive performance is inevitably shaped by social forces.

Textual Issues One area of study completely indigenous to second language research has emerged in the large body of work examining cross-cultural discourse patterns, or contrastive rhetoric. Although initial findings (Kaplan, 1966) have been criticized (see Connor, 1996, for a thorough discussion of contrastive rhetoric), there is general recognition that rhetorical form is a product of a culture's world view and social conventions, and that the degree to which texts are logical, well-formed, and successful depends on their sociocultural context.

The findings of contrastive rhetoric research are unique within second language research because they are the only elements of second language research that have piqued the interest of mainstream writing studies to any noticeable degree. Unfortunately, that interest has been limited primarily to a focus on the varying patterns of organization that have been said to prevail in different cultures (e.g., English is direct; Romance languages, digressive; Asian languages, indirect). Other contrastive rhetoric areas of potential interest to mainstream composition studies might include the exploration of varieties of text-types written within and across cultures; in genre studies, for example, culture-based expectations for such genres as grant writing; types of appeals that are persuasive across cultures; citation patterns that point to different ways of belonging to a scholarly tradition; appropriate tone to adopt in writing that will signal one's right to speak; cross-cultural perspectives on various rhetorical devices (for example, the importance and value placed on ornateness, beauty of language, or moral exhortations); the role of literacy and the methods of literacy training across cultures. Even as brief a listing as this indicates something of the enormous variety and richness available in studies of writing that go beyond concerns with writing in English by North American college students.

Within second language composition studies contrastive rhetoric research has helped us to view variations from the text structure expected in the culture of the U.S. university not as examples of failure to think logically or failure to learn to write. Instead they are viewed from the broader perspective contrastive rhetoric provides as examples of alternative rhetorics. The idea is not to eliminate their traces and replace them with the correct rhetoric, but rather to add English rhetoric to the second language student's repertoire of possible rhetorical solutions. Difference, then, is regarded as explanation, not as deficit.

Mainstream composition studies might consider pursuing answers to the question contrastive rhetoric poses: What assumptions do native English speaking learners already have about writing that might not match those of their academic audience? In terms of pedagogy, mainstream writing classes might do as second language writing classes do and make part of the instructional strategy to discuss with students in class and individually their assumptions about writing and the assumptions of the academy. Addressing differences in assumptions explicitly validates the students' background and acknowledges that college students do not come to first-year writing classes as blank slates but with a culturally developed image of what good writing is and of how to go about producing it. The study of contrastive rhetoric suggests that these images have a place in writing classrooms. It is clear, in any case, that text cannot be defined from a monocultural perspective and that the influence of culturally-preferred text structures must be considered as one of the factors that affect writers' composing processes.

Plagiarism   Mainstream views of plagiarism provide a further example of the limitations of conceptions that grow out of monocultural models of writing. The issue of plagiarism becomes more complex than the standard view allows for with a look at other cultures that view intellectual heritage differently. In cultures beyond the borders of North America the use of another's words or ideas can have the function of demonstrating the writer's familiarity with those words and ideas and of honoring historically important writers by finding them pertinent again. It is a mark of intellectual accomplishment to be able to select and use these words and ideas, an attitude that we have vestigially as well when we quote Shakespeare or Plato. If we cite a line from, say, Emma Goldman, and give its source, we interpret that as intellectual honesty. Another culture interprets the lack of need to cite Lao Tzu as the source of a quotation as a sign of respect for the reader of the line, an acknowledgment of the reader's scholarly achievement, the ability to recognize the line without the need for a gloss. (See Pennycook, 1996, for an extensive discussion of plagiarism and cross-cultural contexts.)

Memorization, Imitation, Quotation   Another angle to consider in thinking about plagiarism is from the point of view of the learner of any new language, including the language of the academy. In effect, all the language that the second language student uses is a borrowing without credit. Imitation, necessary in all language learning, is a way of trying on the target language and gradually transforming the internal representation of that language until the target language and the learner's internal representation of it, or the learner's interlanguage, coincide. This imitation may take the form of memorization of poems, facts, or chunks of language, a form of learning valued in many cultures. Western culture's argument for dismissing both memorization and extensive direct quotation rest on the opinion that when a learner does this, the learner is not learning, only repeating mindlessly what someone else has said. Yet other cultures view these as valid forms of learning. How can they reasonably be simply dismissed as mindless in this culture? In what sense can Western culture make the claim that those trained by its methods are better educated than those trained using other methods? (See also Sampson, 1984, who questions the importance of "superior" North American teaching methods in China.) Thus, other cultural practices call into question our confidence that learning is *not* accomplished by having the exact phrasings rolling around in the learner's head in all their complexity instead of in simplified versions translated into teenage language and understanding. The experiences of other cultures complexify our own understandings and must be accounted for in any legitimate theory of writing or learning. These examples clearly demonstrate the importance of broadening the dimensions of context-specific categories.

Students' Right to Their Own Language   The notion of students having a right to their own languages has been an issue of concern to first language writing researchers. The issue has usually been examined essentially as a question of additive or subtractive bidialectalism, similar to additive or subtractive bilingualism, with discussion nearly always centered around the status of the students' home, usually oral, dialect and the role this home dialect can take in academic writing instruction. The Conference of College Composition and Communication long ago moved to officially support the idea of students' right to their own language, although critics like Delpit (1988) have wondered whether this "right" in fact denies access to powerful academic languages to the students whose home dialects are most dissimilar from academic language.

For years, the picture in second language writing instruction was different. Students' right to their own language was, in one sense, a non-issue. It seemed obvious that Chinese international students had a right to Chinese and, perhaps more pertinently, French students a right to French.[4] These languages and cultures are admired. Speakers of these languages are proud of their languages and cultures, and their pride is supported by our admiration of their ability to speak, read, and write in another language. But the picture has become more complicated as second language writing researchers have begun questioning the role of English, particularly internationally, as the gatekeeper to power and wealth. Those with access to English could expect to accrue to themselves that power and wealth; those without, often could not. And those who could not afford English lessons that would allow them to obtain a high enough score on the TOEFL to be admitted to, for example, a North American university would perhaps never study abroad.

Further complicating the picture is the question: Whose English? That is, ESL professionals have come to recognize the importance of the many varieties of world English, such as those spoken in India, Singapore, Nigeria—Englishes whose structures and vocabulary vary from those of speakers from the monolingual English speaking countries like the United States, Great Britain, and Australia. Indeed, scholars from multilingual Third World countries have helped those from monolingual English speaking countries to see the anomaly of our monolingualism in a world where *most* humans negotiate in more than one language.

With the many challenges to the status of English coming from second language researchers, particularly from the "outer circle" (Kachru, 1985), those teaching ESL are thus being required to develop a more humble conception of the place of "our" English in the world. Can this more humble view also challenge the hegemony of academic English as taught, for example, in first-year composition classes? And for those who disdain the supposed stodginess of academic English and look instead for authenticity and voice, can this more humble sense of ourselves, combined with a more sophisticated knowledge of conditions in which English is used world wide, shake our faith in the notion that finding one's voice is a preeminent concern in learning to write? Ramanathan and Kaplan (1996) raise these very questions for ESL writing instruction. Should they also be considered in mainstream composition?

Conclusion

As ESL researchers, in reading and listening to the discourse of mainstream composition research, we often find ourselves in the same kind of awkward position as women sometimes experience when someone refers to "mankind" or uses "he" to refer to mixed genders. We want to add the equivalent of "or she"; we want to say "look at our research." Our voices here come from the margins of U.S. academic life but we nevertheless have something to contribute. First language writing researchers and practitioners lose by remaining unaware of findings and thinking in second language research.

Limited perspectives are likely to cause problems not only for writing teachers with ESL students in their classes but also for teachers of other ethnic minorities, including African, Asian, Hispanic, and Native Americans who might have native English proficiency but different sociocultural and sociocognitive contexts for writing. The attitudes and practices of second language writing classrooms challenge assumptions underlying first language writing pedagogy by taking for granted such notions as: Writers are heterogeneous; they have differing agendas in learning the second language and learning to write in that language; they are all developmental in that their tackling of academic writing will be a new experience; they will achieve differing ultimate success in their second language; they bring to the classroom specific culturally determined educational, social, and linguistic characteristics to which they claim an undisputed right and to which academic English is merely one addition. When second language writing classrooms refuse to regard ESL writers as simply writers who are deficient in English language, this perspective specifically acknowledges the importance of their contexts for writing, including writers' goals (conserving or extending knowledge), their perceptions of audience (text as reader-responsible or writer-responsible), and the influence of culturally-specified rhetorical forms on their writing processes and products. These views of the second language writer are supported by instructional practices that regard difference as an explanation rather than as a deficit;

that acknowledge and openly address different learning (and teaching) styles and strategies; that assume and often openly address students' previous writing experiences and the way they contrast with rhetorical expectations in English; and that recognize that instruction is only one of many variables in writing development. These are all areas that might be considered in an attempt to broaden perspectives on teaching writing to native English speakers as well. Beyond classroom practices, a theory of composition that looks only at English writers, readers, texts, and contexts is an extremely narrow one. What can we know from a perspective limited to monolingual, monocultural writers and writing? Is the question really how a monolingual community learns culture-specific forms? Or is it the wider question of how different writers learn to deal with variable demands in various situations? Second language writers present the clearest picture of linguistic and cultural differences, yet they tend to be ignored by mainstream composition studies. Multilingualism and multiculturalism cannot be explored only from within the political borders of North America. Mainstream composition studies has given a great deal to second language writing research and teaching; it is time to take something in return. We feel that this something should be a larger, more inclusive, more global perspective on writers and writing, a perspective that can only enhance the validity and viability of mainstream composition theory.

Notes

1. In this article, we would like to begin to make this transfer a bit more balanced, and in doing so we will say some things about mainstream composition studies that may strike the reader as negative or uncomplimentary. However, we would like to make it clear up front that our purpose is not to chastise or impugn the motives of mainstream composition scholars or denigrate their work in any way. We respect these individuals and greatly value their efforts, which, we feel, are typically of the highest quality. Rather, our aim is to draw attention to what we see as a pattern of neglect of second and other language writing issues in the discipline today and to explore the potential consequences of that neglect.

2. We are also forced to recognize that second language composition studies has only just begun similar self-examinations, having for many years operated under an applied linguistics paradigm that viewed research into language learning, and by extension second language writing, as a question of science somehow free of ideological, social, and political constraints (see Santos, 1992). Given the highly charged nature of English teaching both in North America and around the world, such a parochial perspective seems quite astonishing. For discussions of the political, social, and ideological dimensions of teaching English, particularly worldwide, see work by, among others, Pennycook (1994, 1995, 1996), Phillipson (1988, 1991, 1992), and Tollefson (1989, 1995).

3. Second language studies in general and second language acquisition theory in particular have been accused of having a monolingual, ethnocentric bias (Kachru, 1994; Sridhar, 1994). The validity of this position is being discussed by second language researchers and theorists in professional forums and our goal in this article is to initiate the same type of discussion among mainstream composition researchers and theorists.

4. The picture has obviously never been as rosy for immigrants to this country who have always experienced strong pressure to assimilate and to suppress their connections to their native languages.

References

Ballard, B., & Clanchy, J. (1991). Assessment by misconception: Cultural influences and intellectual traditions. In L. Hamp-Lyons (Ed.), *Assessing second language writing in academic contexts* (pp. 19–36). Norwood, NJ: Ablex.

Bartholomae, D. (1985). Inventing the university. In M. Rose (Ed.), *When a writer can't write* (pp. 134–165). New York: Guilford.

Beebe, L. (1988). Five sociolinguistic approaches to second language acquisition. In L. Beebe (Ed.), *Issues in second language acquisition: Multiple perspectives* (pp. 43–77). New York: Newbury House.

Bialystock, E. (1978). A theoretical model of language learning. *Language Learning, 28*, 69–84.

Bialystock, E. (1985). The compatibility of teaching and learning strategies. *Applied Linguistics, 6*, 255–262.

Bizzell, P., & Herzberg, B. (1990). *The rhetorical tradition: Readings from classical times to the present.* Boston: Bedford.

Braddock, R., Lloyd-Jones, R., & Schoer, L. (1963). *Research in written composition.* Urbana, IL: National Council of Teachers of English.

Bridwell, L. (1980). Revising strategies in twelfth grade students' transactional writing. *Research in the Teaching of English, 14*, 197–222.

Canagarajah, A. S. (1996). "Nondiscursive" requirements in academic publishing, material resources of periphery scholars, and the politics of knowledge production. *Written Communication, 13*, 435–472.

Carson, J. G., & Nelson, G. L. (1996). Chinese students' perceptions of ESL peer response group interaction. *Journal of Second Language Writing, 5*, 1–19.

Chaudron, C. (1988). *Second language classrooms: Research on teaching and learning.* Cambridge, UK: Cambridge University Press.

Connor, U. (1996). *Contrastive rhetoric: Cross-cultural aspects of second language writing.* New York: Cambridge University Press.

Cope, B., & Kalantzis, M. (Eds.). (1993). *The powers of literacy: A genre approach to teaching writing.* London: Falmer.

Delpit, L. (1988). The silent dialogue: Power and ideology in education of other people's children. *Harvard Educational Review, 58*, 280–298.

Durst, R. K. (1990). The mongoose and the rat in composition research: Insights from the RTE annotated bibliography. *College Composition and Communication, 41*, 393–408.

Emig, J. (1971). *The composing process of twelfth graders.* Urbana, IL: National Council of Teachers of English.

Faigley, L., & Witte, S. (1981). Analyzing revision. *College Composition and Communication, 32*, 411–414.

Flower, L. (1979). Writer-based prose: A cognitive basis for problems in writing. *College English, 41*, 19–37.

Flower, L., & Hayes, J. R. (1981) A cognitive process theory of writing. *College Composition and Communication, 32*, 365–387.

Friedlander, A. (1990). Composing in English: Effects of first language on writing in English as a second language. In B. Kroll (Ed.), *Second language writing: Research Insights for the classroom* (pp. 109–125). New York: Cambridge University Press.

Friedman, A., Pringle, I., & Yalden, J. (1979). *Learning to write: First language/second language.* London: Longman.

Gardner, R. C., & Lambert, W. (1972). *Attitudes and motivation in second language learning.* Rowley, MA: Newbury House.

Gore, J. (1993). *The struggle for pedagogies: Critical and feminist discourses as regimes of truth.* London: Routledge.

Graff, G. (1996, May 27). Is progressive education growing up? *In These Times, 20*, 30–31.

Graves, D. (1978). *Balance the basics: Let them write.* New York: Ford Foundation.

Hillocks, G. (1986). *Research on written composition.* Urbana, IL: National Council of Teachers of English.

Hinds, J. (1987). Reader versus writer responsibility: A new typology. In U. Connor & R. B. Kaplan (Eds.), *Writing across languages: Analysis of L2 text* (pp. 141–152). Reading, MA: Addison Wesley.

Horning, A. (1987). *Teaching writing as a second language.* Carbondale: Southern Illinois University Press.

Kachru, B. (1985). Standards, codification and sociolinguistic realism: The English language in the outer circle. In R. Quirk & H. G. Widdowson (Eds.), *English in the world* (pp. 11–30). New York: Cambridge University Press.

Kachru, Y. (1994). Monolingual bias in SLA research. *TESOL Quarterly, 28*(4), 795–800.

Kaplan, A. (1993). *French lessons.* Chicago: University of Chicago Press.

Kaplan, R. B. (1966). Cultural thought patterns in inter-cultural education. *Language Learning, 16,* 1–20.

Krashen, S. (1981). *Second language acquisition and second language learning.* Oxford, UK: Pergamon.

Krashen, S. (1982). *Principles and practice in second language acquisition.* Oxford, UK: Pergamon.

Lusignan, G., & Fortier, G. (1992). Revision de textes et changement d'audience. *Canadian Journal of Education, 17,* 405–421.

Muchiri, M., Mulamba, N., Myers, G., & Ndoloi, D. (1995). Importing composition: Teaching and researching academic writing beyond North America. *College Composition and Communication, 46,* 175–198.

Peirce, B. (1995). Social identity, investment, and language learning. *TESOL Quarterly, 29,* 9–31.

Pennycook, A. (1994). *The cultural politics of English as an international language.* New York: Longman.

Pennycook, A. (1995). English in the world/the world in English. In J. Tollefson (Ed.), *Power and inequality in language education* (pp. 34–58). New York: Cambridge University Press.

Pennycook, A. (1996). Borrowing others' words: Text, ownership, memory, and plagiarism. *TESOL Quarterly, 30,* 201–230.

Perl, S. (1979). The composing process of unskilled college writers. *Research in the Teaching of English, 13,* 317–336.

Phillipson, R. (1988). Linguicism: Structures and ideologies in linguistic imperialism. In J. Cummins & T. Skutnabb-Kangas (Eds.), *Minority education: From shame to struggle* (pp. 339–378). Clevedon: Multilingual Matters.

Phillipson, R. (1991). Some items on the hidden agenda of second/foreign language acquisition. In R. Phillipson, E. Kellerman, L. Selinker, M. Sharwood-Smith, and M. Swain (Eds.). *Foreign/second language pedagogy research* (pp. 38–51). Bristol, PA: Multilingual Matters.

Phillipson, R. (1992). *Linguistic imperialism.* New York: Oxford University Press.

Pienemann, M. (1984). Psychological constraints on the teachability of languages. *Studies in Second Language Acquisition, 6,* 186–214.

Ramanathan, V., & Kaplan, R. B. (1996). Audience and voice in current L1 composition texts: Some implications for ESL student writers. *Journal of Second Language Writing, 5*(1), 21–24.

Sampson, G. P. (1984). Exporting language teaching methods from Canada to China. *TESL Canada, 1,* 19–31.

Santos, T. (1992). Ideology in composition: L1 and ESL. *Journal of Second Language Writing, 1,* 1–15.

Scardamalia, M., & Bereiter, C. (1987). Knowledge telling and knowledge transforming in written composition. In S. Rosenberg (Ed.), *Advances in applied psycholinguistics, Volume 2: Reading, writing, and language learning* (pp. 142–175). Cambridge, UK: Cambridge University Press.

Schumann, J. (1977). Second language acquisition: The pidginization hypothesis. *Language Learning, 26,* 391–408.

Selinker, L. (1972). Interlanguage. *International Review of Applied Linguistics, 10,* 209–231.

Shaugnessy, M. P. (1977). *Errors and expectations: A guide for the teacher of basic writing.* New York: Oxford University Press.

Smith, L. Z. (1992). Profession and vocation: Trends in publication. *Focuses, 6,* 75–86.

Sommers, N. (1980). Revision strategies of student writers and experienced adult writers. *College Composition and Communication, 31,* 378–388.

Sridhar, S. N. (1994). A reality check for SLA theories. *TESOL Quarterly, 28*(4), 800–805.

Stotsky, S. (1995). The uses and limitations of personal or personalized writing in writing theory, research, and instruction. *Reading Research Quarterly, 30,* 758–776.

Tollefson, J. (1989). *Alien winds: The re-education of America's IndoChinese refugees.* New York: Praeger.

Tollefson, J. (Ed.). (1995). *Power and inequality in language education.* New York: Cambridge University Press.

Vygotsky, L. (1978). *Mind in society.* Cambridge, MA: Harvard University Press.

Zhang, S. (1995). Reexamining the affective advantage of peer feedback in the ESL writing class. *Journal of Second Language Writing, 4,* 209–222.

10

Language and Diversity

Sharon Klein

> This chapter discusses the issue of linguistic diversity and explores possibilities for working with nonstandard dialect speakers in the writing class.

Composition teachers regularly encounter sentences, paragraphs, and essays, which, to varying degrees, are not consistent with the expectations of college writing. These teachers must respond both to the contents of such pieces, and to the lexical and syntactic choices made by the student writer. These responses are inevitably informed by what writing teachers believe about language: Its nature and ability to represent what its users think (if perhaps not how they think), as well as how it is being, or should be, used. These beliefs may be explicit, implicit, or even inchoate, and, thus, difficult to specify. But they are there, and one of this chapter's goals is to give shape to some them. A corollary goal of the chapter is to guide readers through a survey of the area of linguistic diversity and the questions about language that it addresses. Its ultimate goal is to contribute to the ways in which teachers can assist students in taking control of their writing. Along the way, readers may encounter some of the sources of the friction that occurs when diversity and institutional expectations meet. But an awareness of these sources (and of the friction), as much as a developing knowledge about linguistic diversity and its relationship to writing, should contribute to writing teachers' success in responding to their students.

Toward these goals, readers will find the following in this chapter:

- Ways of thinking and talking about language and linguistic variation.
- Discussion of a sampling of the actual forms found in some of the varieties.
- Attitudes toward the varieties.
- The connections between all of these strands and issues of composition.

SOME PRELIMINARIES AND TERMS

Any discussion about the connections between language and composition must at least acknowledge the complex relationship between *writing* and *speaking*. Writing and speaking (and signing, as we should recognize the existence of roughly 120 languages whose perceptual and delivery systems exclusively involve hand, arm, and facial movements and positions, and eye contact) are generally agreed to be the primary communicative outlets for language. But the two are distinct, and the distinction itself raises many issues, not the least of which is the question of what comes "first." The term *written language* hints at one position; the unmodified—unmarked—system, *language* is "first." Nonetheless, many do not agree about the relative primacy of these two outlets, arguing on both sides that one, more than the other, provides a better lens through which one can examine the nature of language (or communication, as we should keep the referents of these two words distinct). It is enough for us to recognize that the relationship is complex, having tantalized thinkers from Plato, Rousseau, Condillac, Saussure, and Husserl to Derrida, who himself challenges any attempt to establish either as exclusively fundamental to the other.

On the one hand, it is the case that although all written representations—or otherwise inscribed forms—of language may be traced to a spoken (or signed) system, the reverse is not true. Many of the world's six thousand or so languages do not have writing systems. And although every human develops at least one language without explicit instruction, very few are able to acquire the ability to write (or read) without fairly involved instruction. Conversely, the sort of inscribing that writing provides for (both literally and metaphorically) changes our mental maps of language—almost irretrievably—once we become writers (and readers). The general focus of the text in which this chapter is embedded is the nature of these reading and writing abilities and how to teach them at relatively advanced levels. Nonetheless, it is reasonable to keep these observations about "language" and "writing" in mind.

FOR WRITING AND DISCUSSION

Four terms here, *language* and *communication* and *language* and *writing* have been distinguished. What are your thoughts about *language* and *communication*? How do they overlap? In what ways are they distinct? How might both this overlap and distinction be reflected in the context of composition? What, in turn, are some of the differences between *language* and *writing* that require attention when thinking about how to talk with student writers?

When we teach writing, of course, we are working with students to develop a facility in using a system of structural conventions to represent and communicate a range of thoughts, some of which they may already be representing in spoken or signed languages. So, despite our careful separation of the written and nonwritten forms of expression, the two are related, albeit complexly. For that reason, we need to look at nonwritten linguistic systems, their workings, and the ways in which they are viewed, because this is where students' thoughts are initially represented.

But there is also a wrinkle. When we speak of written forms, we can be fairly confident that we are referring to a relatively established set of conventional structures, discourse patterns, and expected genres; many of them are represented and duplicated in handbooks, for example. This set, however, is assuredly different from virtually any of the nonwritten forms of expression that students bring to writing classes. No student's language corresponds completely to "the language" of writing. But all students ultimately will be asked to align the language(s) they know and to use the set of written conventions established, as that is, in somewhat oversimplified terms, what "learning to write" entails. The wrinkle is that we will not be engaged in a mapping of one system on to another. Rather, perhaps, we are talking of a many-to-one mapping. In other words, we are engaged in mapping any number of languages onto the relatively small set of forms of written discourse that are recognized and valued in American college classrooms.

In his chapter on non-native English speakers included in this volume, John Edlund acknowledges this situation, providing good reasons for developing stronger connections between the fields of second language acquisition studies and composition studies. He also talks about a group of student writers who are currently often referred to as "Generation 1.5". These are young people who immigrated to the United States as children, and who grew up primarily in the American educational system, but whose home and community languages may be Spanish, Tagalog, Bikol, Hmong, Korean, Mandarin, Armenian, or any other language distinct from some targeted form of American English.

The discussion in this chapter moves one step beyond, looking at linguistic systems that are part of the worlds of students who are sometimes also included in the Generation 1.5 category, but whose experiences also diverge from immigrant students. These are students who were born in the United States, but who, for any number of reasons, speak another language or dialect. As these linguistic systems rub up against the linguistic systems used for work in American writing courses (and the expectations of courses and faculty who ask students to write), students and their instructors find themselves amidst the aforementioned friction. Success in these classes requires students to develop and maintain a facility in this written system. But developing this facility has long challenged both students and their instructors. To understand a bit about why and how the process is challenging, and how the coexisting systems affect each other, it is crucial to understand something about the nature of language diversity and the relative positions of the varieties. The next section considers these questions

LANGUAGE AND VARIATION: SOME FUNDAMENTAL NOTIONS

Acknowledging that students arrive with fully developed linguistic systems, and that these languages are likely to be quite different from the language associated with writing, we turn briefly to a distinction that may be helpful in identifying some of the difficulties that arise in moving between the two.

I-Language and E-Language

There is a pair of language terms, introduced by Noam Chomsky (Chomsky, 1986) that focus conversations and treatments of linguistic phenomena in some helfpful ways. The pair is *I-language* and *E-language*. *I-language* (roughly, "internalized language") refers to the *internal* system of tacit knowledge that grows in every human being as he or she develops a language from infancy.[1] The language developed is just that: I-language. It is a system that assigns structure to sequences of seeable (in sign languages) or hearable (in spoken languages) elements and allows for them to be connected to meanings systematically associated with them. There are a number of assumptions about the first language embedded here: that it develops—virtually "grows" in every human child—and is not taught; that it develops as a result of an intricate

---

[1]If you look up the word *infancy* in a dictionary with etymological information (the text mentions the fourth edition of the *American Heritage Dictionary of the English Language*), you will find that it refers directly to language itself.

interaction between the child's environment and her biology; and that, in this way, language shares a number of important developmental features with lots of other human systems, including digestive or visual systems, for example. We will not pursue the evidence for these claims in this chater, but do acknowledge them, and provide references for further reading and study.

E-language refers to everything else. The irony is that even though its reference—everything else—makes it virtually impossible to define, it is what all of us typically use the word *language* for. We talk about the *English language*, or *writing in English* (or French, Armenian, or Korean, for that matter), or we say "*Julia speaks Hungarian and Hebrew*". But exactly what are our references in these expressions? Whenever we talk about speakers of Bikol, or of Swedish Sign Language, or when we're talking about "global English," AAVE, or Spanglish, we are using E-language terms. The terms don't really refer to anything tangible; they refer to our *ideas* of what the languages are, tacitly including social and political components. And typically it is these *ideas* of language—rather than the realities of the linguistic systems in the heads of the individuals—that guide teachers in their work with student writers.

FOR WRITING AND DISCUSSION

Do two small experiments. First, do a survey. Find out what the language backgrounds of your classmates or students are (perhaps anonymously; language, as this chapter will continue to note, is a club, and as students begin to talk about their language and their own language profiles, it may be more comfortable to do so anonymously, at least at first). Ask them about differences they notice in the languages they use outside of the classroom—on campus or off—and what they find in textbooks, lectures, and what they do in discussions. Ask them to jot down what they mean when they specify the language they speak. What, in other words, do they mean when they say " 'I' or 'we' speak Spanish," for example? Consider the answers you get, and how people talk about such issues. Next, do some observations of your own language use and of language around you. Listen to talk radio, interviews with public figures, or your friends and family and note (preserving anonymity) how people use various forms of language. How many "complete sentences" do you hear? Record pronunciations, or words and expressions that you find interesting, and save them to use later in the chapter.

Language and Dialect

The distinction between *I-language* and *E-language*, although only roughly drawn here, also helps us in understanding the terms *language* and *dialect,* critical terms in this chapter. A distinction that has been part of our language consciousness for so long, and that is perpetuated in many of the texts that teachers of writing consult, it is, nonetheless, not a linguistically motivated one. The following epigrammatic statement about the distinction summarizes the point best. "A language," it says, "is a dialect with an army and a navy."[2] That definition suggests that we are, as we use the terms *dialect* and *language*, making, at best, an E-language distinction, but in fact, more precisely, merely a political one.

Examples of how the term *language* and its companion *dialect* range over the world's linguistic systems and our perceptions of them abound. There are at least nine identifiable linguistic systems—many that are mutually unintelligible—in Chinese. But they are referred to as dialects, a reference that corresponds to the writing system and national identity. And what was known for much of the 20th century as the Serbo-Croatian language was, in fact an attempt to interweave two related, but distinct languages into a unified and, presumably, a unifying language. But the two have always used different writing systems, and have distinct vocabularies. Languages more similar than these two have remained separate for converse political reasons: Flemish and Dutch, or Norwegian and Danish, for example. And now, for the very same reasons, Serbian and Croatian are recognized as distinct languages (McAdams, 1989). We even have named something a language—Spanglish—that is an artifact. The term *Spanglish* grows out of our need to categorize and label a set of very real, recognizable, but complexly changing language patterns, perhaps thinking that the label will suffice for understanding and describing the patterns.[3]

If trying to understand *language* and *dialect* takes us this far in the realm of E-language, readers might imagine what the phrase *Standard English* could mean.

FOR WRITING AND DISCUSSION

The Klingon Dictionary, Marc Okrand, 1985.

As part of the Star Trek enterprise, a non-Terran language identified with the Klingon beings was developed for Paramount Pictures by Marc Okrand, a linguist. The introduction to the dictionary providing a detailed description of the language is quite instructive for us in a number

---

[2] This epigram is traceable to a coterie of scholars—Max Weinreich, his son Uriel Weinreich, and Joshua Fishman, all grandparents of the field of sociolinguistics, whose complex object of study is the intersection of language structure with the forces of social structure.

[3] Spanglish receives more attention in the general discussion of language varieties.

of ways, working as a mirror of sorts for the ways we think about linguistic variation and privileged forms. Consider some of the assertions in this excerpt. What comments does the piece make about the roles of dialect and language in society? What parallels can you draw in universes with which you are more familiar? What is *Standard Klingon*, for example? How is it defined?

> *Although Klingons are proud of their language and frequently engage in long discussions about its expressiveness and beauty, they have found it impractical for communication outside the Klingon Empire. For intra- and intergalactic communication, the Klingon government, along with most other governments, has accepted English as the lingua franca. In general, only those Klingons of the upper classes (which include higher-level governmental and military officials) learn English. As a result, English has taken on two additional functions in Klingon society. First, it is used as a symbol of rank or status. Those Klingons who know English will use it among themselves to show off their erudition and make their place in society known to all who happen to be listening. Second, English is used when it is thought best to keep servants, soldiers, or even the general populace uninformed. Thus, on a Klingon vessel, the commanding officer will often speak Klingon when giving orders to his crew, but choose English when having discussions with his officers. On the other hand, a Klingon officer may use Klingon in the presence of non-Klingons to prevent them from knowing what is going on. This use of Klingon seems to be quite effective.*
>
> *There are a number of dialects of Klingon. Only one of the dialects, that of the current Klingon emperor, is represented in this dictionary. When a Klingon emperor is replaced, for whatever reason, it has historically been the case that the next emperor speaks a different dialect. As a result, the new emperor's dialect becomes the official dialect. Those Klingons who do not speak the official dialect are considered either stupid or subversive, and are usually forced to undertake tasks that speakers of the official dialect find distasteful. Most Klingons try to be fluent in several dialects.*
>
> *Some dialects differ only slightly from the dialect of this dictionary. Differences tend to be in vocabulary (the word for forehead, for example is different in almost every dialect) and in the pronunciation of a few sounds. On the other hand, some dialects differ significantly from the current official dialect, so much so that speakers have a great deal of difficulty communicating with current Klingon officialdom. The student of Klingon is warned to check into the political situation of the Klingon Empire before trying to talk. (pp. 10–11)*

So, specifying what one means in the assertion "Students should write in Standard English" requires that we understand what *English* refers to even before we try to lay out the territory of *Standard English*. No mean feat. This is another distinction related to our general *idea* of language, again, influenced by all the forces that we've seen can contribute to it.

One more preliminary term requires attention before the discussion turns directly to language varieties and what understanding them can contribute to the ultimate goal: writing teachers' success with their students. That term is *grammar,* and it will be discussed briefly, as it is treated in some detail in the chapter by James Williams.

GRAMMAR

When most people think of the word *grammar,* they tend to associate it with what they were taught in high school—parts of speech, rules of punctuation, and the marking of error. Linguists, however, conceive of the term as more complex, using the word to refer at once to the linguistic description of internalized systems and some sort of representation that could correspond to the I-language we have described. Teachers inhabit a sort of odd conceptual territory along the boundaries of these two definitions, a territory that has been recognized and, consequently, has been labeled the area of *pedagogical grammar.* The goal of a pedagogical grammar is to provide a description of a particular linguistic system (the term used here to avoid the danger of using either the terms *dialect* or *language* arbitrarily) that would allow someone to understand the system well enough to learn to use it. Of course the phrase *learn to use the system* raises the questions of what happens when learners go through this process consciously (usually learning a new system in addition to the one they have developed as children) and what they come out with. Another way to ask this question is to ask what the connection between I-language, E-language and pedagogical grammar is (or what the connections are). And this is why we say that pedagogical grammars inhabit the borderlands between them.

As discussion turns to language varieties, readers should keep in mind two points about the notions under the umbrella of the term *grammar.* First, presentations of descriptions in specific varieties straddle that very fence; they are not representations of any single individual's I-language, but, rather, a rough characterization of some of the features, and they border on E-language type descriptions. Second, as the chapter moves into the nature of language diversity and the general structure of the linguistic systems themselves, the referent of *grammar* more closely parallels its use in linguistic work. So, we move back and forth across the borders.

LINGUISTIC VARIATION AND DIVERSITY

Because terms such as *language* and *dialect* (as well as the problems with what they mean) are now familiar, we now move onto the observation that there are multiple linguistic forms across groups of people. The organization of these varieties and their sources have kept linguists working for some time now, and offer multiple challenges for attempts to develop descriptions that would lead to an understanding of how the systems work. Fundamental to the work is the understanding that at their most elemental level, all linguistic systems must correspond to the universal principles and conditions that define human language, and that make up the grammatical system linguists refer to as "Universal Grammar". *Human language* has been proposed as describing the epiphenomenon that an extraterrestrial scientist might observe when she first arrived to study Earthlings. They all would seem to be speaking variants of some common language. As she moved on to understanding the nature of this common language—what linguistically unites the Earthlings, the scientist would move into constructing hypotheses about the nature of Universal Grammar—its defining principles and conditions.

These principles range over *phonology* (the features of sounds that structure themselves into recognizable sound patterns in spoken languages, and the features of hand shape and movement that structure themselves into parallel systems in sign languages), *morphology* (the patterns structured from minimal-meaning-bearing units in a linguistic system), syntax (the patterns of phrases, clauses, and sentences), and *semantics* (the ways in which words, phrases, and sentences constitute meanings). There is no linguistic system that does not correspond precisely to the possibilities these principles provide for. Additionally, human beings make use of their knowledge of the world, their respective cultural identities, and of how these interact with communicative expectations in particular situations. The range of generalizations here are referred to collectively as *pragmatics,* and are a significant component of human communicative competence in any linguistic system.

These constants provide for a range of variation, which develops across a number of boundaries: actual geographical boundaries (including the political boundaries that define *language*), gender boundaries, boundaries of income (translating into boundaries of "class"), and ethnic boundaries. In turn, these boundaries interact, as one might imagine, complicating the picture somewhat, but also providing a way to understand the interplay that contributes to attitudes toward divergent linguistic forms. The boundaries and contacts between and among speakers with different linguistic systems interact in complex ways, providing for the crucibles of language.

The Blending of Language: Pidgin, Creole, and Interlanguage

These meetings of languages and the linguistic products of prolonged contact of various kinds have become an important focus of study. Over the years, they have been labeled in various ways, and these names are likely to come up in any discussion about language that readers might have with their students. An overview of the labels, and an introduction to some of the results of current, closer scrutiny appear here. One set of contact products, *pidgins,* may be loosely defined as varieties of language that develop out of contact between some nonstandard (i.e., already stigmatized. These varieties of language were likely to have been spoken by people already marginalized for reasons never fully clear) forms of colonial European languages (including English) and clusters of non-European languages spoken around the Atlantic Ocean and in sites in the Indian and Pacific Oceans between the 16th and 19th centuries. Often there would be one European language and multiple non-European ones. The European languages are referred to as the *lexifiers,* because it is from them that most of the vocabulary in pidgins comes, and the non-European languages are known as the *substrate* languages.[4] These contact languages developed primarily in the context of trade and initial stages of colonization, and would have identifiable features, varying with respect to how close the created language was to the forms of the lexifier language—or even more educated forms of it, or how much like itself (and different from either the lexifier or any one of the substrate languages) the pidgin became. The forms closest to the lexifier are what linguists call the *acrolects,* and the forms most different from the lexifier are referred to as *basilets.*

The companion term, *creole,* has an interesting history, as it was first used to describe a people: that is, nonindigenous, but clearly not European people, born in the colonies of the Americas in the 1500s (Mufwene, 2001). Gradually, the term came to refer to other such transplants and mixes involving plants and animals, until it came to refer to the languages that grew out of the experiences.

Linguists have used the term *creole,* along with *pidgin* to define not only a language type but also a process of language formation, with *pidgins* first, then *creoles* developing as children learn a pidgin as their first language. Linguists embraced this continuum enthusiastically, because the connections between the creation of languages out of the crucible of contact (however difficult the surrounding social conditions may be) and the recreation of language by children provided a compelling set of questions, and the opportunity to delve further into a developing understanding of the universal nature of language and the development of I-language. But many argue that the picture is not so clear, and that there may be creoles without pidgins; pidgins without creoles; and contact-language situations with features of both.

---

[4]In the context of our discussion about linguistic variation and the sources of attitudes about the varieties, it seems appropriate to note the language of terms here. *Lexifier* has an *-er* agentive suffix: Lexifier languages provide words; they have an active role. Compare the term *substrate,* which translates roughly to "bottom layer."

Of particular relevance to writing teachers in this vein, is that the set of language-creation processes share a number of features with the contact-language situation we call second (or subsequent) language acquisition. Second language acquisition occurs when one speaker of some language is encountering a new (presumably *target*) language. The intermediate result, often called *interlanguage* (a term with a history as well, related to all of these contact-language situations[5]) bears some resemblance both to pidgin and creole situations. Thus, the ESL students that Edlund discusses are themselves involved in the process of language creation. And speakers of a number of varieties of English that garner attention mostly in the context of the classroom are also involved in various processes of language creation.

One such process that may be familiar to readers, and that the chapter has already mentioned briefly, is *Spanglish.* Ilan Stavans (2000) traces the historical underpinnings of the language back to the beginnings of Spanish colonialization of the Americas in the 1500s (which brought an already heterogeneous language into contact with multiple indigenous ones—the crucible) and the subsequent Anglo colonization, introducing English into the mix, the two interacting most dramatically with the treaty of Guadalupe Hidalgo in 1848, signing over almost one third of what had been Mexican territory to the United States. But most importantly, he notes that the history of this contact between two languages—neither homogeneous—has resulted in a multiple of linguistic forms. One might say "many Spanglishes." Cuban Americans have different vocabulary and sound patterns from the "Nuyorican" ones, and both differ from the various forms that are found in the Los Angeles area—from East Los Angeles (with roots in Pachuco and Caló) to the San Fernando Valley. And other parts of the Southwest have varying forms as well, traceable to the interaction of indigenous languages, English, and Spanish. Linguists are involved in trying to understand the extent to which Spanglish could be considered a linguistic system in and of itself—a type of interlanguage of the sort previously defined—or whether the name Spanglish is a label for the complex *code switching* that speakers who are relatively competent in more than one language do. Speakers take words and phrases from one language and reanalyze them using forms from the other: *parkear,* "to park" uses an English word with Spanish verb suffixes; *el maus,* the label for a computer "mouse," which already involves a lexical appropriation, uses spelling that obeys Spanish conventions, and *llamar pa'tras,* "to call back" borrows syntax, keeping the Spanish

---

[5]In, *An Introduction to Second Language Acquisition Research* (1991), Diane Larsen-Freeman and Michael Long, note that the term was first used by a pidgin/creole scholar, John Reinecke, in 1935, when he talked of the plantation contact language that developed in Hawaii, and gained use as a *lingua franca* (a common language, used by speakers of different languages to speak to one another, accorded some prestige by its very commonality and function).

words. And such examples illustrate code switching, which entails moving back and forth between (at least) two languages, in conversation, sentences, phrases, and words. The smaller the switching moves (the selection of systematically chosen forms even smaller below than the level of "word", for example), and the more frequently the moves occur (a frequency whose nature and design are also the objects of linguistic study), the more the process begins to resemble what we think of as a "new" language... out of the crucible.

Because speakers of all these varieties are living in the midst of another, dominant language culture, they are all also involved in moving back and forth—in situations that call for such moving—between these systems and other forms of English, which are collectively referred to as mainstream U.S. English,[6] or MUSE (Lippi-Green, 1997), the term we will use here. In a writing classroom, speakers, who are also students, are directing their attention to learning yet another set of codes related to the conventions of written exposition. Writing teachers should have as clear a picture as can be drawn of the linguistic systems from which their students work, the processes underlying their travels along and across the linguistic borders they must navigate, and the various distances involved in such journeys.

The issues around the classification and nature of pidgins, creoles, and interlanguages, and questions of code switching are relevant for trying to understand a range of issues. Some linguists are currently enthusiastic about what seems a fruitful perspective. Mufwene (2001) uses the notion of an ecology of language evolution, that sifts all of the pieces together and notes that differing situations will inescapably result in slightly different outcomes for developing (and endangered) languages. Some of the pieces are linguistic, and others are a mix of social, cultural, and political factors. Careful observation of what has happened in a number of language contact situations has allowed Mufwene to suggest this framework; it seems helpful in the context of the questions about the next variety: African American Vernacular English, AAVE. AAVE is a linguistic system available to most African Americans, as well as to any speakers who are part of and identify with the African American community, but is not necessarily spoken by everyone who is African American.

For some time, much has been at stake in establishing the connections between AAVE and the African languages brought (predominately from the languages of the Niger-Congo family spoken in West Africa) by the imported slaves who were likely to have been among the agents of language creation.

---

[6]We say **perceived** of" because it is in a chapter entitled "The **Myth** of Standard English" that Rosina Lippi-Green introduces the term *MUSE*.

There is little controversy over that connection. What is disputed is whether contemporary AAVE derives from a creole that formed out of the extended contact between the slaves and their captors, traders, and owners. Gullah, a language of the South Sea Islands off the coast of South Carolina, and Jamaican Creole, along with a number of other related linguistic systems, are thought to reflect such a process. But the AAVE generally spoken elsewhere in the United States not only has a strong core of specific characteristics, which the discussion here will look at, but also has a number of features that are not unlike other vernacular Englishes, notably those spoken in lower-income areas of some southern states and of northern cities, as well as in some identifiable vernacular areas in Britain. Such findings about common features have led some linguists to lean in the direction of claiming that AAVE has stronger roots in English. It may not be possible to categorize the origins of AAVE as creole or argue that it has other, noncreole origins; this chapter certainly will not. What is important is that AAVE has features that make it noticeably and systematically different from other forms of English and that its speakers are generally required to learn and be prepared to use MUSE in appropriate situations.

FOR WRITING AND DISCUSSION

Issues of income, ethnicity, and hierarchy are inevitably part of any conversation about the linguistic systems that are not part of MUSE. Knowing how our perceptions about these issues affect our attitudes toward forms of language and their speakers is crucial for teachers. Hence, this small exercise. Look up the words *churlish, villain,* and *vulgar.* What sort of etymologies do you find? What might the semantic changes observable in these words tell us about the perspectives used to categorize people into desirable and less desirable groups, and thus, how we come to think about the characteristics—such as their language forms, for example—that identify them?

Moving back to language, one might also say that *language is a club.* What are the relevant meanings of such an assertion in the context of discussing these linguistic varieties? Consult a good dictionary with etymological information (*The American Heritage Dictionary of the English Language,* 4th Edition, has such information) and consider both the current definitions and the respective histories of the words *shibboleth* and *barbarian.* How do these meanings contribute to your developing view of how people come to make judgments about others, and what such judgments reflect? Of what relevance are such findings to working with students' writing?

FOR WRITING AND DISCUSSION

Note that MUSE is the language of this chapter, and other forms, predominately AAVE, are also discussed. Imagine the reverse. You have additional opportunities to imagine this reverse in James Williams' chapter.

THE OAKLAND DECISION

This divergence between AAVE and MUSE—and the requirement that students develop reading and writing skills in MUSE—brought AAVE to the attention of the courts in the context of education for the first time in 1978–1979. Based on the testimony of a number of linguists, Judge Joiner in Ann Arbor, Michigan found for the plaintiffs, a group of 15 school children, in a decision about language barriers and discrimination. He ruled, essentially, that the school district in question take appropriate action to overcome a clear language barrier impeding the children's access to equal educational opportunity. And the language barrier, he had been convinced, was largely a function of teachers' lack of knowledge about AAVE in sufficient detail to permit them to understand what the children were saying. Teachers had not been given the opportunity to learn about this language system.

The differences, stigma, and absence of understanding about AAVE is symptomatic. Despite subsequent attempts to introduce teachers at all levels to forms of the language, topics related to language variation, and interwoven pedagogical issues, a fair level of institutionalized misunderstanding continues to prevail. In December of 1996, the Oakland School District in California tried to respond (again) to a similar situation. The discussion here focuses on the educational goals of the District's decision. But their position also had the effect of popularizing the label *Ebonics,* which had not been previously used widely. The label was coined, from *ebony* and *phonics,* by Robert Williams, an African American psychologist, in the 1970s, but in those 20 years had not gained the usage accorded it almost overnight after the Oakland proposal became public.

Observation by Oakland educators and others had revealed that the longer African American children stayed in school, the worse became their performances on tests, as reported by the National Assessment of Educational Progress. The School Board was primarily interested in building students' English language proficiency, and sought to use their primary language as a vehicle for instruction. Note the clause in the proposal:

> Be it further resolved that the Superintendent in conjunction with her staff shall immediately devise and implement the best possible academic program for *imparting instruction to African-American students in their primary language* for

the combined purposes of *maintaining the legitimacy and richness of such language* **[facilitating the acquisition and mastery of English language skills, while respecting and embracing the legitimacy and richness of the language patterns]** whether it is **[they are]** known as "Ebonics," "African Language Systems," Pan African Communication Behaviors," or other description, *and to facilitate their acquisition and mastery of English language skills* (Rickford & Rickford, 2000, p. 168)

Italicized language was in the original, December, 1996 document, but was deleted from the January, 1997 document; boldfaced print in brackets includes language substituted in January.)

The board was interested in "transitioning students from the language patterns they bring to school to English." Again, it was a matter of educating students in MUSE. But the middle step, which involved recognizing AAVE long enough to instruct teachers and empower them (and to understand them), to use it to acknowledge and maintain the identity it affords their students, set off wildfires among whose smoldering coals we continue to walk. Because language does play such a central role in constructing and maintaining one's identity, as well as in representing one's world, it seems reasonable to understand and use students' languages to support their acquisition and use of MUSE.

GRAMMATICAL PROPERTIES OF AAVE

The chapter now turns to a somewhat detailed discussion of some *grammatical* properties of AAVE, where *grammar* here refers to a somewhat pedagogical description. Being aware of these properties has two potential applications for writing teachers. Some of what are generally called "surface errors" in exposition are structures that parallel but diverge from those in MUSE. In composition classes, there are occasions to see through such surface errors and focus on other features of the writing—treatments of topics, persuasiveness of an argument, or the quality of a narrative, for example. Outside of writing classes, however, such differences in sentence structure are what readers and evaluators may emphasize. Students should be able to choose whether to translate; writing teachers are in the best positions to help them be able to have the choice. The second and corollary application has to do with standardized testing of writing proficiency. These tests often use just such differences in questions about sentence structures. In other words, such tests are asking questions about fluency in MUSE. Again, writing teachers are in positions to provide students with insight about the two language systems and, with sufficient fluency in MUSE, to be able to call on it in these situations.

The description begins with an overview, summarizing a number of the syntactic structures that characterize sentences in the system, and explaining some of the terminology. Examples and descriptions come from Green (1998); Pullum (1999); Wolfram, Temple-Adger, and Christian (1999); Smitherman (1977; 1994) and Rickford and Rickford (2000), where readers can find much more information.

Copula Sentences

It is generally possible to isolate about five sentence patterns in languages, based on what sorts of meanings a verb has and what structures that meaning provides for. One of those patterns involves a subject coupled to a predicate whose basic function is to provide more information about the subject. In the following examples, the subject and additional information are in bold, and the connecting verb form is underlined.

> *Her comment <u>was</u> mysterious.*
> *Writing instruction <u>is</u> a complicated process.*
> *My friends <u>will be</u> at the beach.*

Many languages do not use a verb form in positions with the underlined forms from MUSE. Or they'll put the verb form in only to mark a past or future as in the first and third examples, respectively. Russian is such a language. When systems have patterns of omission, the patterns are referred to as *zero copula* patterns.[7] AAVE has such patterns, and these patterns, along with the tense/aspect structures explained in the next section, may have attracted the most attention from scholars and non-AAVE speakers alike.

Tense/Aspect

Although readers may not be aware of making the distinction, human language has two ways of talking about events. They can be aligned in a chronological relation to one another from the perspective of the speaker, or they can be described as ongoing, habitual, or continuous, on the one hand, or punctual, momentary, or complete, on the other. The systems of chronological alignment are generally referred to as *tense,* whereas those that provide for these other features of events are called *aspect systems.* The two can—and

---

[7]In some texts, readers may find the expression *be deletion* instead of *zero copula.* The term *be deletion* suggests that the copula verb *be* was there and was then taken out. Because they do not wish to make that claim with the term, many linguists have taken to using *zero copula* as the label.

regularly do—co-occur and intermingle, and they are not always indicated by what we consider to be markers. The MUSE sentence *He does windows,* for example, has a present-tense marking, but is making a general statement about a habitual activity. AAVE has borrowed forms from MUSE (remember, MUSE is the *lexifier* language) and put them to work in a different system. This borrowing/reanalysis process is very common in the language contact situations out of which AAVE has evolved; reanalysis itself is part of what any human language does over time and space. When the two systems (AAVE and MUSE, in this case) are in constant contact, however, the combination of common vocabulary and the different uses can cause difficulties. Unraveling the respective systems is important for writing teachers, as well as for anyone seeking to understand the two systems.

Another strand to keep track of in the unraveling is the actual form *be.* In both AAVE and MUSE, *be* has two functions. And the two interact. It is, as previously noted, the copula. In other words, it functions as what is called a *main* verb. Alternatively, the *be* is what texts refer to as an *auxiliary* verb. It can signal either the progressive, with a (*main*) verb ending in the *-ing* suffix (*Students are writing in a range of forms*), or the passive, with a (main) verb carrying the perfective marking, which may take a range of forms (e.g., *eaten, rung,* or *walked* [*Most of his comments were refuted quite easily*]). Sometimes the copula connects the subject with an adjective phrase that is constructed by making use of what started out its life as an *-ing* verb (e.g., *writing, going, leaving,* or *sweeping*) or a perfective one (*written, gone, left,* or *swept*). Speakers of all forms of MUSE or AAVE must rely on context to distinguish between these progressives and passives and the distinct adjectival meanings. The patterns for marking them in the two systems differ. Consider, for example, what happens when the string in parentheses is removed from either of these two sentences: *The toddlers were charming (the pants off their grandparents)./ The ship was painted blue (by a crew of teenagers).* Knowing which meaning writers intend is critical for writing teachers, as is the ability to make certain that the writers are in control of what they intend for their readers.

Be is a complicated form, marking a number of meanings in AAVE, with both its presence and absence, and its different forms (*am, is, were, was*) alternating with its infinitive form (*be*) indicating these meanings. For example, *be* used in its infinitive form marks habitual aspect. This *be* is always translated as "typically" or "generally" in contrast to "now," which is the interpretation of sentences with no form of 'be' at all:

He be singing translates as "*He sings.*"

He singing translates as "*He is singing.*"

She be testy translates as "*She is typically testy.*"

She testy translates as "*She is testy now.*"

In its participle form, *been,* this verb has a specific aspectual meaning in AAVE, and it is pronounced with special stress, which we indicate here with uppercase letters. First, note these two MUSE sentences and their meanings (uppercase letters here indicate increased loudness, what linguists call greater "stress"):

> *She's BEEN married* means *She was married for a while, but certainly is not now.*

> *She's been married (for a while, since yesterday, for five minutes)* means *She got married and still is.*

In AAVE, the BEEN (stressed *been*) means specifically that the event or condition not only still exists but also began in the distant past, never 5 minutes ago, or yesterday, for example. So, in AAVE, the sentence *She BEEN married* must be interpreted as meaning that the person in question got married in the distant past and remains married now. That meaning is different from either of the two MUSE meanings with *been.*

Another example will lead us to a third aspectual form. Consider this sentence and its meaning:

> *I BEEN finish(ed) my homework* translates as *I have COMPLETELY finished my homework (a while back).*

This example provides a form of *perfective,* the aspect associated with completeness and related senses.

The third aspectual form (distinct from invariant *be,* and stressed *BEEN*) is the use of *done,* which also provides a sense of completedness. Used without stress, *done* with a past-tense-marked verb indicates the perfective—as in the following examples:

> *The mirror done broke* translates as *The mirror has (just) broken.*

> *The chef done cooked the food* translates as *The chef has (just/already) cooked the food.*

> *The students done went/gone to class* translates as *The students have (just/already) gone to class.* (Green 1998, pp. 51–52)

The *done* combines with other verb forms, including the *be,* and BEEN (here BIN) to form a range of constructions with related meanings (Green, 1998):

I/you/s/he shoulda done ate/run.	I/you/s/he should have already eaten/run.
I/you/s/he BIN done ate/run.	I/you/s/he (had) already ate (eaten)/ran(run).
I/you/s/he ain't BIN done ate/run.	I/you/s/he hadn't (yet) eaten/run.
I/you/s/he be done ate/run.	I/you/s/he usually have already eaten/run.

I/you/s/he don't be done ate/run.	I/you/s/he usually won't have already eaten/run.
I/you/s/he'uh be done ate/run.	I/you/s/he will have already eaten/run.

A fairly striking application of knowledge about the uses of unstressed *done* and the fact that it must be used with a marked form of the verb (e.g., *ate* or *run*) comes from the sort of worksheet one might find in the context of SAT II preparation materials. As it turns out, the portions of the test that ask students to look for sentence errors, and to identify and correct them are quite explicitly in pursuit of identifying dialect knowledge (Wolfram, Temple-Adger, & Christian, 1999, pp. 138–144). A speaker of AAVE would be stopped if he or she were confronted with a test question such as the following: "Select the best word form to complete the sentence: *He_____ what he had to. [done/did]*" A well-formed, meaningful AAVE sentence would require both *done* and *did*, in that order, in the remote perfective, and some speakers might use the form *done*, with stress, for a simple past. Without context, the student would be at a clear disadvantage without carefully designed preparation including strategic work for maneuvering around such questions.

Negation

This term is fairly self-explanatory, and refers to how linguistic systems negate expressions. Primary forms of AAVE negation include *don't* and *ain't*. *Ain't* is the most frequent, but *don't* must occur in negative forms of habitual *be* sentences (sentences with the unchanged—the invariant *be*):

> *I been here three days, the boy ain't move a muscle.* (from a Richard Pryor monologue, 1975, from Rickford & Rickford, 2000, p. 59)
>
> *Ain't nobody gonna spend no time going to no doctor.* (translation: Nobody is gonna spend any time going to a/any doctor; Martin & Wolfram, 1948, p. 18)
>
> *An she don't be listenin'.* (translation: 'And, she doesn't listen.'; Rickford & Rickford, 2000, p. 114)
>
> *An she ain't listening.* (translation: 'And, she is not listening.')

So, *don't* and *ain't* are not interchangeable; each has a specific sense.

MUSE has an interesting pattern referred to as *negative polarity*, which requires speakers to use forms such as *any* or *ever* in the structural vicinity of a negative (e.g., *no, not,* or *none*). AAVE uses *negative concord*, putting a second negative element in places where a negative *polarity* one would appear in MUSE: *Ain't **nobody** gonna spend **no** time going to **no** doctor. Ain't* is the primary negative marker here, and the boldfaced elements are concord markers. A MUSE translation might be something like (with optional elements in parentheses, indicating that either, both, or neither might be in the sentence. The second 'any' would alternate with 'a' *'Nobody is going to spend (any) time going to (any) doctor.'*

Often, AAVE negation will be at the beginning of the sentence:

Ain't nobody done nothing.

Couldn't nobody in the place do more than they did.

Wouldn't nobody help the poor man?

Ain't no car in that lot got a speck of rust on it.

Can't no man round here get enough money to buy their own farm.

FOR WRITING AND DISCUSSION

How would these sentences be expressed in MUSE? Compare these and your translations to MUSE forms such as the following: *Never would I consider reading that book. Seldom did he utter even a greeting.* What differences and similarities do you find? What sort of "diction" is involved in the MUSE examples here? And what is "diction"?

Existential Sentences

This term refers to a construction that speakers of many forms of English are familiar with. Sentences with indefinite subjects and linking (copula) verbs such as *be, seem,* or *appear* may take one of two forms:

No shelf is **without books.**	There is **no shelf without books.**
Two women are **in the administration.**	There are **two women in the administration.**
We want **clean dishes** to be **in the cupboard.**	We want there to be **clean dishes in the cupboard.**

The sentences in the right-hand column are referred to as *existential sentences.*

FOR WRITING AND DISCUSSION

What do you think the pattern of existential sentences might be? Try to provide a general statement of the pattern, and construct additional examples to test your hypothesis. If a speaker or writer may be said to put the information s/he wants readers or speakers to attend to most at the ends of sentences, rather at the beginnings, what sorts of communicative functions might you see for these so-called "existential sentences" sentences with *there* as the stand-in subject?[8]

Another type of sentence also uses a stand-in subject. Here are some examples:

It seemed that **the students were a bit overwhelmed.**

The students seemed (to be) **a bit overwhelmed.**

It bothers me **that not everyone can study language.**

That not everyone can study language bothers me.

We will not discuss this second set of sentences in any detail, but they, too, are quite common in a number of forms of English, and have interesting communicative functions. What is important here is that although non-AAVE forms of English alternate between *there* and *it* as stand-in subjects, using the *it* in these sentences and the *there* in the existential ones, the *it* typically appears in both these sorts of sentences and the existential ones in AAVE.

It a big closet filled with junk. (translation: There's a big closet filled with junk).[9]

Some Other Structures

Pronouns

Rickford and Rickford (2000) note two places where AAVE uses pronouns in ways that non-AAVE forms of English do not. Both are interesting and may appear in the writing of AAVE speakers. But because both can also be found in some non-AAVE forms of English, they may not appear only as part of AAVE systems. The first has to do with using a pronoun as a subject even after the sort of logical subject has already been introduced. Some grammarians refer to this construction as a "topic" structure, noting that the *that man* and the *my mother,* respectively act as topics, setting the stage

---

[8]Your pattern description should have the subject "moved" from its sentence-initial position to the position directly adjacent to the predicate. The "vacated" sentence-initial subject position is filled with **there**. You might notice sentences such as *There's three guys out on the porch.* Why do you think the copula might change from the plural, matching *three guys* to the singular?

[9]In AAVE, this sentence could also mean that the speaker is referring to some big closet, and describing it. The sentence here could translate into *It is a big closet, filled with junk,* depending on how it is uttered when spoken or on the context in which it appears in written form. But a teacher would want to ask before making any suggestions for changes or translations.

for what the sentence tells, and the pronouns *he* and *she* do the work of subjects:

> *That man **he** walks to the store.*   [That man walks to the store.]
>
> *My mother **she** told me, "There's a song I want you to learn."* [My mother told me....]

The second involves the introduction of pronouns in the indirect object position when they are also identical to the subject. MUSE typically omits the indirect object in this context.

> *Ahma git **me** a gig.* (translation: I'm going to get (me/myself) a job/gig.)

Relative Clauses

As readers may know, relative clauses are clauses that modify a noun in a noun phrase; they have a missing piece corresponding to that noun. The following examples include relative clauses (in boldfaced type) with a parenthesized line indicating the missing piece. The noun they modify is also underlined, corresponding to the missing piece.

> *The <u>children</u> **who(m) we saw** (___) **in the library** are working on a project.*
>
> *We saw the <u>people</u> **who** (___) **were trying to get on the airplane** wandering around the airport.*
>
> *We noticed the <u>book</u> **that you wanted** (___).*
>
> *No one knows the <u>person</u> **from whom this letter came** (___).*

Sometimes in MUSE, it is possible to replace the *who(m)* with *that,* or to omit the marker completely. (Here, parentheses indicate that the *that* is optional) giving us a zero marker):

> The children (that) we saw in the library are working on a project.
>
> We noticed the book (that) you wanted.

Yet when the missing element is the subject in MUSE, the *who* or *that* must appear. In AAVE (e.g., as in a number of languages, including Japanese), it is also possible to have a zero marker setting off relative clauses with missing subjects. You can see this structure at work in the next example:

He the man got all the old records. (translation: He is the man who/that got all the old records. (Martin & Wolfram, 1998, p. 32)

Embedded Questions

In AAVE, when questions are embedded in sentences themselves, the order of the subject (boldfaced) and the auxiliary (italicized) may be inverted unless the embedded question begins with *if*:

> They asked *could* **she** go to the show.
>
> I asked Alvin whether *did* **he** know how to play basketball.
>
> *I asked Alvin if *did* **he** know how to play basketball.

These are the syntactic features of AAVE you are most likely to encounter, either in exchanges with students or in readings. These features also constitute the subset that plays a central role for researchers who are asking questions about the beginnings of AAVE and its relationship to other linguistic systems—whose origins have to do with the interaction their speakers have had with multiple languages. Sustained study and analysis continue to uncover explanatory patterns and raise new questions.

We turn now to the sound patterns that contribute to the system of AAVE.

SOUNDS AND SOUND PATTERNS[10]

The furor surrounding the Oakland decision highlights the necessity for teachers at all levels to understand how the linguistic system of human language is structured, including the relevance of sounds and sound patterns to spoken languages. Why are these important? We talk about "accents" all the time. They define people as being "from somewhere else," and they define "us" as well—as we remember that the reference of "us" changes with the sets of readers turning these pages, as the forms of language used may also change. Opera singers who know nothing of the languages in which they may be singing an aria may study the sounds and sound patterns of the language with a coach so that their pronunciation makes them sound like native speakers. Actors may similarly study the speech patterns of people who are from the same communities as characters they are portraying to

---

[10]It is perilously difficult to talk about sounds with recourse only to the representations that letters of the alphabet provide for us. We are all readers (evident from the fact that you are here), and the very process of learning to read does change our awareness of sound and the patterning of sound in the language. I will try to describe the sounds without engaging in a phonetics and phonology course, but show how they are distinct from the letters that we typically use to represent them, and how this distinction, along with different systems in AAVE and non-AAVE phonologies may affect students' writing. A particular danger in using letters to represent the sounds is that there is a long tradition of what is called "eye-dialect," where such forms as *wuhz* for 'was', or *kumbine* for 'combine' are used in written forms of dialogue in narratives, and are frequently used to derogate the characters who utter them, although they represent not any particularly stigmatized pronunciations of the words at all, but the typical ones. Readers should take care to avoid making any such connections when they look through the letter representations in the chart provided here. No symbol (especially letter) can make a sound, of course. Symbols may only represent sounds, more or less precisely.

learn such "accents." The nature and distribution of these accents may also contribute to the way speakers spell words. Finally, researchers have found that even recorded babbling in babies as young as 8 months old from French, Arab, and Cantonese language communities is recognizable by adults as being in or out of their own language communities. And experimentation with the babies of similar ages have yielded long acknowledged evidence that by ten months of age, children have organized their mental systems related to phonology. They recognize the sounds that are part of the language and distinguish between sound differences that affect meaning and those whose distributions are patterned and do not affect meaning consistently (de Boysson-Bardies, 1999). The sound patterns of language are learned early and stay with us in ways that linguists are still trying to understand.[11]

Therefore, sound—both the patterning of consonants and vowels into syllables, and the relative volume and pitch of these syllables as they group into larger structures (what linguists refer to as prosodic units)—is a critical part of the linguistic system of every spoken language. When humans who have developed a spoken language go on to learn to use the alphabet, read, and write, a number of events occur that make dialect study, the role of sounds and sound patterns, and the role of syntax and word structure important. For example, the interaction of the way -*'ve'* (as in *I'd've* or *she'd've*) is pronounced and the insight that many pieces of inflection in a language (including English) use the same sounds (think about the range of meanings that the sound represented by the letter '*s*' makes: plural, so-called possessive, and the third-person-singular present tense marking on regular verbs) results in many writing students spelling -*ve* as 'of' without "confusing" it with the meaning of the preposition.

Thus, if writing teachers study at least one system, and have some developing ideas about how linguists believe that system works, they should be in a stronger position to analyze what their students are doing, whatever system it is that students may be using.[12]

---

[11] Importantly, the parallel features related to hand shapes, positions, and movements work in precisely the same ways for sign languages. Deaf babies born amidst speakers of a signed language show babbling behaviors using their hands that are linguistically identical to the oral babbling of hearing infants. There are "accents" in signed languages, and the same issues about variation and its effects are raised. There are also important questions that must be considered when deaf students are required to write in MUSE. We cannot consider such questions in this chapter, but encourage readers to consult relevant materials that do treat them (Emmorey, 1998; Meier, 1991; Hickok, Bellugi, & Klima 2001; Supalla, Wix, & McKee, 2001; and Weisel, 1998, among others).

[12] In the writing of a sixth-grade English learner whose first language is Spanish, for example, a teacher discovered the spelled form "verer" in the phrase "a verer day." Working with context and the insights of understanding the sound-letter correspondences in Spanish, the teacher was able to discover that the student's intended word was "better," and that his spelling was very

To facilitate discussion, a table is provided and adapted, with annotations and some changes from Bailey and Thomas (1998; who attribute the observations there to Wolfram [1994] and Stockman [1996]). In this table, readers will find selected forms and descriptions of the observed sounds and sound patterns. It is difficult to represent pronunciations using alphabet letters, an observation that should, by itself, initiate some thought and discussion about the nature of alphabets in general. There are, as well, some other points to make, and terms to explain. The terms *voicing* and *stops* (or "obstruents") need some definition. The smallest pieces of spoken language are features of sounds. Readers can hear themselves using the features, but you have probably rarely, if ever, talked about the internal structure of sounds, and how they combine. Voicing is such a feature, and although every speaker of English uses it to know how to pronounce the past tense on a verb such as *walk* or on a verb such as *cry* or *sob,* most are quite unaware of what knowledge they're appealing to to do this. It is possible to perceive voicing at work, nonetheless. Consider the two phrases *'a dune'* and *'a tune.'* By placing the palm of your hand gently over the front of your neck, where your larynx is (this is our 'voicebox'—where our vocal cords are), and saying these two phrases slowly, but without stopping between the article *'a'* and the following words, you should be able to feel a continuous vibrating in the *'a dune'* phrase, yet feel a short cessation of vibration in the *'a tune'* phrase. That cessation reflects the "voicelessness" of the /t/ in the pronunciation of the word *tune.*

Obstruent is a term that refers to whether or not the air coming up from our lungs and passing between the vocal cords (they're really folds of tissue, but calling them cords allows us to think of stringed instruments, and may help understand how their vibration works) moves unobstructed through the mouth or nose. The unobstructed sounds include roughly four sets: first, the vowels; second, what some books call "liquids"—the sounds we think of as 'l' or 'r' (although there are at least two pronunciations of 'l', if you think about the words *let* and *tell,* and there are many sorts of 'r', which you'll notice if you stop to think about it); third, the glides—what some people call 'y' (the first sound in *yes,* the sound after 'p' in *computer,* and also the sound that makes *ah* into what rhymes with *eye* in words such as *sigh,* or even *I*), and 'w' (the first sound in *wither* and the sound after the 'k' sound in *quick,* as well as the sound that makes *ah* into what rhymes with *Ow!* in *sound,* or *crowd*); and fourth, nasals, the sounds whose noise comes through our noses. (Try to say *mom, nose,* or *thing* while you hold your nose tightly closed and see what happens.) All four of these unobstructed categories, although each is different, as we can see, are also categorized as sonorants; they resonate. Not only can some start syllables but some can also be almost

---

systematic, involving hypotheses based on how Spanish orthography could represent English words.

entire syllables (taking on some of the work of the vowel), which we can hear in the unstressed (less loud, roughly) syllables of words such as *paper*, *table*, *bottom*, or *common*, for example.

The obstructed sounds—which interfere with what comes out of the mouth (we leave the air coming through our noses alone) can be categorized into three groups: stops the sounds typically represented by the letters *p, t, k* and *b, d, g*, (until we say them, our vocal area is pretty much shut, and air is stopped, literally); fricatives (relatively noisy sounds) including the sounds typically represented by *f*, and *v*, the two pronunciations of *th* (in **thigh** and **thy**, for example, where voicing is at work, distinguishing meaning), the sounds in *s*eal and li*ce* or in *z*eal and lie*s* (often represented by the letters *s* and *z*) *s* and *z*, the sounds in **shield** or **crush,** and the sounds in the beginning of the second syllables of *pleasure*, or *treasure;* and finally, a set called affricates, that begin with a stop and finish with a fricative. We hear both affricates in the word *change*, and hear one each in *lurch* and *lunge.* A way to distinguish the sounds, and to see, again, how the feature voicing works in the language to make meaning distinctions, is to contrast the word *lunge* with the word *lunch*. It is this feature that is at work in final position of those two words, creating the meaning distinction, signaled by the distirict affricates.

Now you have made a working acquaintance with terms, sounds; and some sound features that are at work in all varieties of language; they are part of the human language faculty. These sound features work to define sounds and sound patterns, resulting in identifiable linguistic systems; they interact in systematic (if complex) ways with the writing systems that provide ways to represent, preserve, and sometimes even change the original systems.

Figure 10.1 indicates whether each feature is specifically an AAVE feature or is also found in the other vernacular Englishes that AAVE has had the most contact with. Many of the forms may be familiar, but readers should take care to pronounce and consider them.

FOR WRITING AND DISCUSSION

Some of these patterns may, indeed, sound familiar. Listen carefully to speakers that you interact with, and that you hear on the radio or on television. Do you notice some of the features described here? Do any of them contribute to making people sound a certain way? What sound patterns, for example, would you think of in saying that someone "sounds French," "Spanish," "Southern," "Texan," or "Latina"? Listen again to the speakers you recorded earlier, too.

A number of the characteristic regularities described in (figure 10.1), as well as a number of the syntactic characteristics previously described, have

Feature	Example	Linguistic systems where observed
final consonant cluster reduction	'cold' *col* 'hand' *han* 'desk' *des*	most Engl. varieties, more frequent in AAVE
unstressed syllable deletion (at the beginnings in the middles of words)	'about' *'bout* 'government' *go(v)'* *mint*	most Engl. varieties, more frequent in AAVE
haplogogy (deletion of reduplicated syllable)	'mississippi' *misipi* 'general' *genrl*(with the 'l' representing its own syllable)	most AAVE and non-AAVE forms
making the syllable-final l more like a vowel	'bell' *beuw* 'pool' *poow* 'will' -> 'll-> *uw*	most AAVE and non-AAVE forms
loss of 'r' after 'th' and in initial clusters of unstressed syllables	'throw' *thow* 'professor' *puhfessor*	general vernacular feature
word final 'th' sounds become 'f' and 'v' sounds depending on voicing.	'bath' *baff*; 'baths' *bavz*	AAVE and southern vernaculars (also found in some British dialects)
word initial 'th' sounds become stops	'those' *doze* 'these' *deeze* 'thing' *ting*	vernacular forms
word-final voiceless 'th' becomes a stop, especially after a nasal	'tenth' *tint* 'with' *wit*	vernacular forms
metathasis (inversion) of 's' and a voiceless stop consonant at the ends of words	'ask' *aks*	older general Southern speech and AAVE
vocalization or deletion of end of syllable 'are'	'bird' *buhd,* 'father' *fathuh* 'four' *fahw*	older white Southern speech and AAVE
deletion of 'are' before an unstressed syllable	'carol' *ca(r)uhl* 'hurry' *huh(r) y*	older white Southern speech and AAV

FIG. 10.1.

Feature	Example	Linguistic systems where observed
change of the diphthong sound 'eye' to 'ah' before b,d,g, v, and z, and at word ends	'tied' *tahd* 'wise' *wahz* 'pie' *pah*	older general Southern speech and AAVE
change of the diphthong 'oy' to 'awh' before l	'boil' *bawhl* 'soil' *sawhl*	older general Southern speech and AAVE
merger of short 'e' and short 'i' sounds before n and m at the ends of syllables	'pin' *pin* 'pen' *pin* 'Wednesday' *winsday*	older general Southern speech and AAVE
changing of z, v and th to d,b,and d, respectively, before nasals	'wasn't' *wahdn't* 'seven' *seb'm* 'heathen' *heed'n*	southern midland and AAVE
stressing of first syllables in two syllable words	'police' *POlice* 'supper' *SUHpuh* 'Detroit' *DEtroit* 'hotel' *HOtel*	AAVE (Rickford and Rickford 2000)
changing of 'd' at the ends of words to 't' (This sometimes happens also to 'b' and 'g', which change to 'p' and 'k', respectively)	'bad' *bat*	AAVE
making word final 't' a glottal t or a glottal stop (a glottal stop is the sound between the 'uh' and 'oh' in 'uh-oh' and the most speakers' of the sound–spelled by 'tt'–in 'kitten,' or 'mitten')	'bat' *bat?*	a number of non-AAVE forms and AAVE

FIG. 10.1. (*continued*)

developed the status of shibboleth, the meaning of which readers have discovered in "For Writing and Discussion number four. This status seems to provide these particular linguistic features with two functions. They flag speakers as part of the African American community and they are used as foci for discussions about the nature and origins of AAVE. Probably the most "notorious" of features is the pronunciation *aks*. Consider the following:

> One of the most salient points of phonological variation which is strongly stigmatized from outside the [B]lack community might be called the great *ask-aks* controversy. . . . The Oxford English Dictionary establishes this variation. . .as very old, a result of the Old English metathesis *asc- acs-*. From this followed Middle English variation with many possible forms: *ox, ax, ex, ask, esk, ash, esh, ass, ess*. Finally, *ax* (aks) survived to almost 1600 as the regular literary form, when *ask* became the literary preference. Most people know nothing of the history of this form, and believe the *aks* variant to be an innovation of the AAVE community. In fact, it is found in Appalachian speech, in some urban dialects in the New York metropolitan area, and outside the US in some regional varieties of British English.
>
> Non-AAVE speakers are eager and willing to point out this usage, which is characterized as the most horrendous of errors. (Lippi-Green, 1997, pp. 179–180)

The "most horrendous of errors," speakers are told. In fact, the difference merely reflects an arbitrary victory of one form over another. There is no logical superiority of one pronunciation over another. But "aks" is a shibboleth. And this particular form eclipses other similar processes, resulting in pronunciation differences that may affect written forms. Listening to popular pronunciations of the words "jewelry," "realtor," or "nuclear," for example, should reveal some interesting changes, none as marked (and thus not as well-noticed or well-studied) as the ask/aks example.

Some other examples of more or less shibbolethed regularities in AAVE are found in the changes of the *th* interdental voiceless and voiced sounds to *f* or *v* respectively at the ends of words, and to *t* or *d* at the beginnings of words, the stressing of the first syllables, and the influences of the *r* and *l* sounds in syllable ending or word-ending positions. Equally noteworthy is the observation that non-AAVE forms—quite standard ones—make use of a number of the same or parallel processes. The absence of the *d* in *hand*, for example, is much like the absence of *g* in *long* and the absence of *b* in *bomb*. All three reappear in other contexts, viz., *handy, longest*, and *bombast*, for example.[13]

---

[13]The nasals and the stops in each of the words match as to where they're pronounced (place of articulation, more precisely), and there is often either a predilection for such matching, or there are processes centered around it.

Some of the changes interact with other patterns. The absence of /t/ after /p/ or /k/ and the absence of /d/ after /n/ can affect the marking of past tense in verbs such as *wipe, walk,* or *loan,* for example. So, a MUSE speaker might imagine that an AAVE speaker has "failed" to acknowledge that a verb is in the past tense in a sentence, such as the following (Where the ' indicates the absence of a pronounced /d/) *Yesterday I loan' her a table.* In reality, the sound pattern has hidden the marker. These changes may also have consequences in writing, and the response to a spelling that seems to indicate a misuse of tense should take into consideration the possibility that it reflects a sound pattern. Thus, intervention would recognize a student's understanding of tense, and might begin with a conversation about sound and spelling, rather than one about tense marking. An analogous example in MUSE is the increasingly frequent menu entry "ice tea." Once, it read "iced tea," but the juxtaposition of the two identical sounds, at the end of "iced" and at the beginning of "tea." led to the loss of one, and this new spelling—and expression—evolved.

The inflectional forms, syntactic markers, and these sound patterns make up the structure of clauses and sentences in AAVE. But as important as these characteristics are for writing, features beyond—discourse and narrative styles—are also important. These patterns beyond the sentence have been described in the context of oral traditions as well as written ones. We turn now to them, looking briefly at each, as they are mutually dependent.

DISCOURSE, NARRATIVE STRUCTURE, AND BEYOND

We have seen that there are differences in the forms of the language that student writers are expected to access as they construct college essays. But there are also differences in the presentation, flow, and organization of ideas. A natural question arises: What can teachers do to ensure that all students have an opportunity to learn multiple languages and multiple discourses? An obvious beginning to an answer is to have teachers develop the linguistic, composition, and cultural savvy requisite to describing the languages and discourses. The chapters in this text, including this one, along with the readings, have as their collective goal to lead readers in that direction.

That step itself is important, and involves at least two preliminary steps. For a discourse to be described, it must be visible. Very often the dominant discourse is invisible because it is dominant; certainly its speakers are often as unaware of it as Earth dwellers are unaware of the multiple effects of gravity or the presence of the atmosphere. Learning explicitly about the dominant language and discourse, as well as the myths (e.g., the describable existence of MUSE), is critical. The next step is to learn about the structure and nature of the nondominant languages and discourses.

When there is no question about the national status of a language or a discourse, scholars and students are enthusiastic and willing to consider it as one among many. When, however, there is some question—whatever the sources or the validity of the questions may be—about the status of the language, its rhetorical patterns, its speakers and their discourses, the situation is more complex. People question the need to look at different styles or discourses, and deny the very existence of any framework or different system, as in the case of the Oakland School Board crisis. However, as the discussion here has indicated, it is important for teachers to acknowledge and work with the language variations students bring to the classroom. The following suggestions for doing so are offered by Lisa Delpit (2001):

First, Delpit argues, "teachers must acknowledge and validate students' home language without using it to limit students' potential. Students' home discourses are vital to their perception of self and sense of community connectedness. Second, teachers must recognize the conflict...between students' home discourses and the discourse of school. They must understand that students who appear to be unable to learn are in many instances choosing to 'not-learn,' as Kohl puts it [a response which, as Claude Steele (1999) has shown, is influenced by school culture itself], choosing to maintain their sense of identity in the face of what they perceive as a painful choice between allegiance to 'them' [an often unaccepting or critical 'other'] or 'us' [themselves].

Bridging this chasm in the context of sometimes hostile environments is complex. Delpit notes effective use of Afrocentric curriculum, providing students with some rediscovery and ownership of areas whose content otherwise seems more central to what are taken as Eurocentric values. She reminds her readers of the *Stand and Deliver* story of Jaime Escalante's admonishing of his Latino students from poor neighborhoods, as he taught them calculus and the dialogue that his film persona is given: 'You have to learn math. The Mayans discovered zero. Math is in your blood.' (Delpit, 2001, p. 554). Finally, she argues that teachers "can acknowledge the unfair 'discourse-stacking' that our society engages in. They can discuss openly the injustices of allowing certain people to succeed, based not on merit, but on which family they were born into, and on which discourse they had access to as children [given that some discourses are privileged and some are not]. The students, of course, already know this, but the open acknowledgement of it in the very institution that facilitates the sorting process is liberating in itself" (Delpit, 2001, p. 554).

A next step is to provide descriptions of the discourses, both those that students know and the ones they are being asked to develop proficiency in, insofar as comprehensive and objective description is possible. For that reason, it is crucial to look carefully at descriptions of distinct modes of discourse, and to put them in context. References to what has come to be called "contrastive rhetoric," the study of varying styles of presentation, organization, and infusion of voice are particularly helpful in this context, as they provide descriptions of such styles (e.g., the work of Kaplan [1996] & Connor [1996]). Readers have already encountered this spectrum in the ESL chapter, where Edlund discusses the range of rhetorical styles and their resulting organizational features in some detail. The writing differences across languages are not unlike those that distinguish AAVE and MUSE writing.

Furthermore, it is often the case that different organizational modes match up differently with particular contexts to create genres. So, for example, a topic-centered approach, laying out the thesis and circling around it, may alternate with a topic-associated approach, which more or less concatenates a set of related topics, leading "up" to the one central to the thesis of the essay, depending on the goal or the discipline of the writing. The two may not just exist as mutually exclusive approaches in different linguistic/cultural systems. Thus, students writing in MUSE, whatever their first language, must also learn all of these patterns and their perceived matchings to genres or other contexts.

Understanding how writers may vary not only across discourse cultures, but also across genres and contexts, offers new possibilities for writing instruction. It may not be a particular narrative style that is "different" and that must be supplanted for student writing to meet expectations. Instead, the "difference" may be due to a matching of a particular framework to a context, which must be observed, demonstrated, and practiced. The goal becomes learning alignment skills: learning to align style and contexts. This goal entails access to, and developing proficiency in more than one style.

With this understanding, writing teachers can develop a greater range of expectations and understandings, as well as an increased awareness of their own modes of discourse, their own assumptions about their uses, and the assumptions about them that prevail in academic communities. This triangle—descriptions of multiple rhetorical frameworks, clear understanding of the structures of target frameworks and their preferred matchings (those privileged in university classrooms and academic disciplines, for example, that create genres), and a well-developed awareness of one's own writing patterns in relation to these frameworks—is a critical piece of geometry. It outlines the context for understanding what is said about variation in discourse strategies.

For example, consider the following description: "traditional African American discourse characteristics [incorporate] the quality of a performance in [texts]"; techniques that create a performance may vary across different communities, and "within the African American tradition those techniques include such musical phenomena as the rhythmic use of language, patterns of repetition and variation, expressive sounds, and phenomena encouraging participatory sense making, like using dialogue, tropes, hyperbole, and call and response patterns within the text." (Ball, 1996, p. 30, with indicated changes). On the surface, such performance seems different from (orderly) presentation, involving aspects of author presence, and even orality—another feature often attributed to the discourses of many students categorized as nonmainstream. Although these features do exist, and certainly play a role in affecting how readers of student essays respond to them, they are all features of writing that can appear in various genres across discourse cultures as well.[14] They should not, in other words, become stereotypes or be seen as obstacles to overcome in pursuit of a particular approach to exposition. The chapters that treat audience and genre in this text provide more detailed explanations that can, in turn, be woven in with the topics discussed here.

Recognizing the sorts of structures that their own exchanges involve—another leg of the triangle—requires instructors to learn something about discourse, including some study of what seem the most quotidian conversational or written experiences. Asking questions about how requests are made; how one is convinced of a position by a colleague, friend, or adversary; what it means to "be polite"; where to look for the point, or the new information in a sentence or a paragraph; or about how simple conversations are structured (how one knows when to take a turn speaking, for example, or how one might flout such principles) provide first (but not uncomplicated) steps.[15] As instructors learn about their own patterns, and how they may be described, they are also learning about some of the more "dominant" patterns, and how these come to be accepted as mainstream, thus structuring our expectations.

---

[14]Having taken these descriptions from Ball (1996) I do not wish to suggest that she is herself categorizing or stereotyping. In fact, in her discussion, Ball invokes the work and views of Bakhtin, noting the dialogic and multi-voiced nature of writing itself.

[15]Introductory linguistics textbooks can be helpful here, as they provide entry-level information about such areas as ethnographies of communication and components for describing them, as well as how communicative structures are understood. Two such resource texts are Nancy Bonvillain, 2000, *Language, Culture, and Communication*, 3rd edition, Upper Saddle River, NJ: Prentice-Hall (particularly chapters 4 and 5, which address how speakers address one another, forms of politeness, conversational expectations, etc.) and E. Finegan, 1999, *Language: Its Structure and Use*. Fort Worth, TX: Harcourt Brace (particularly chapters 8, 9, and 10, which deal with the ways in which information is organized, the structures of conversations, and the interaction of situational conditions and linguistic forms). All of these topics are relevant to writing classrooms. Another resource is *An Introduction to Functional Grammar*, 2nd edition (1994) by M. A. K. Halliday (New York: Arnold), whose work connecting structure to communicative function is often cited. But this text is more involved than the first two, which also make mention of Halliday's contributions.

Writing teachers and their students are in complex positions, juggling multiple objects—including conceptual triangles of the sort we've been constructing. Collectively, students are seeking admission to and recognition from institutional systems—universities—that both present and challenge prevailing values. Admission and recognition require some level of control over the means of exchange—language. We have seen further that there is significant variation in language—some of which we notice more, and some less, for complex reasons—and that admission and recognition seem to require attention to the variation, demanding that students make some choices.

University (writing) instructors are asked both to staff the admission booth and to provide students with the means of achieving recognition—or at least to point them to the most promising paths in that direction. But we're not just guides and gatekeepers. As our students navigate the paths, juggling their own and institutional values (their baggage), we must help them learn to develop their own sense of a sort of map—to become language savvy themselves. Such savvy, then, informs their choices, making the choices part of a navigational strategy. Knowledge of this sort of metaphoric geography, of course, requires at least an understanding of how forms and the meanings we make of them interact, not only with each other but also with the cultural/communicative contexts in which we use them. This knowledge provides the sorts of legends and labels that such maps require. It has been the goal of this chapter to introduce readers to some small foundational parts of that knowledge.

FOR WRITING AND DISCUSSION

A. Attached here is an editorial, "Racial Ventriloquism," by the lawyer-writer, Patricia Williams. After reading it, consider watching the film it discusses. What do you find? What sorts of dialect are used in other films, animated and acted? What other instances of dialect can you observe. Consider seeing "The Sound of Music," or one of the following Disney animted features: "Lion King," the "Aristocats," "Dumbo," or "Lady and the Tramp" (You may think of others, as well). What do you notice about forms of language used by the actors doing the voiceovers? (cf., Lippi-Green "Teaching children how to discriminate," in *English with an accent* [1997])

B. (1) Consult the Conference on College Composition and Communication Web site. (Note that Web sites do change, so some hunting may be required.) One of the conference's early position statements about language variation is available (www.ncte.org/ccc/12/sub/) on the Website. Compare the positions taken there to some of what is written currently about the relationship between individual languages and the expectations of college composition classrooms. Visit the Web site of the Linguistic Society of America (www.lsadc.org) and look there for the LSA statements about language rights and Ebonics. You can find these by selecting the virtual button labeled *Resolutions.*

(2) Read both the O'Neil essay "Dealing With Bad Ideas: Twice is Less" from the *English Journal* and the Coleman essay, "Our Students Write With Accents," from the *College Composition and Communication.* Both essays refer to work by Eleanor Orr, investigating the connection between language (more precisely, the way someone uses vocabulary and syntax) and thought. Compare the two sorts of references and the positions that Coleman and O'Neil take, respectively. Consider the implications for interpreting student writing, and for understanding the student performance each position has.

FOR FURTHER EXPLORATION

Language Variation, Pidgins, Creoles, and Related Issues

Bonvillain, N. (2000). *Language, culture and communication* (3rd ed.). Upper Saddle River, NJ: Prentice Hall.

Finegan, E. (1999). *Language: Its structure and use* (3rd ed.). Fort Worth, TX. Harcourt Brace.

Fromkin, V., Rodman, R, and Hyams, N. (2003). *An Introduction to Language* (7th ed) Heinle. Fort Worth, Texas.

Steven Pinker. (1994). *The language instinct.* New York: Harper Collins.

Linguistic Ideas

Anderson, S. R., & Lightfoot, D. W. (in press). *The language organ: Linguistics as cognitive physiology.* Cambridge: Cambridge University Press.

Baker, M. C. (2001). *The atoms of language.* New York: Basic Books.

Jackendoff, R. (1994). *Patterns in the mind.* New York: Basic Books.

Dialects, Attitudes, and Classrooms

Gilyard, K. (1996). *Let's Flip the Script.* Detroit, MI. Wayne State University Press.

Lippi-Green, R. (1997). *English with an accent.* London: Routledge.

Wolfram, W. Temple-Adger, C., & Christian, D. (1999). *Dialects in schools and communities.* Mahwah, NJ: Lawrence Erlbaum.

AAVE

Smitherman, G. (1977). *Talkin and testifyin.* Detroit: Houghton Mifflin. New York: Republished by Wayne State University Press. 1986

Rickford, J., & Rickford, R. (2000). *Spoken soul.* New York: John Wiley and Sons.

REFERENCES

Aarons, A. C., Barbara Y. Gordon, William A. Stewart (Eds.). (1969, Spring/Summer). Linguistic-cultural differences and American education. Special Anthology Issue of *The Florida FL Reporter,* 7 (1).

Bailey, G., & Thomas, E. (1998). Some aspects of AAVE phonology. In S. Mufwene, J. R. Rickford, G. Bailey, and J. Baugh (Eds). *African-American English.* London and New York: Routledge.

Baldwin, J. (1979, July). If Black English isn't a language, then tell me, what is? *New York Times* editorial.

Ball, A. (1996, January). Expository writing patterns of African American students. *English Journal, 85* (1): 27–36.

Ball, A., & Lardner, T. (1997, December). Dispositions toward language: Teacher constructs of knowledge and the Ann Arbor Black English case. *College Composition and Communication, 48,* 469–485.

Baugh, J. (1983). *Black street speech: Its history, structure and survival.* Austin: University of Texas Press.

de Boysson-Bardies, B. (1999). *How language comes to children.* (M. DeBevoise, Trans.). Cambridge, MA: MIT Press.

Cameron, D. (1995). *Verbal hygiene.* New York and London: Routledge.

Chomsky, N. (1986). *Knowledge of language: Its nature, origin, and use.* New York: Praeger.

Chomsky, N. (2000). *New horizons in the study of language and mind.* Cambridge: Cambridge University Press.

Coleman, C. F. (1997, December). Our students write with accents—oral paradigms for ESD students. *College Composition and Communication, 48* (4), 486–500.

Connor, U. (1996). *Contrastive rhetoric: Cross-cultural aspects of second-language writing.* Cambridge: Cambridge University Press.

Culler, J. *On deconstruction.* Ithaca, New York: Cornell University Press.

Cushman, E., Kintgent, E. R., Kroll, B, & Rose, M. (Eds.). (2001). *Literacy: A critical source book.* Boston: Bedford/St. Martin's.

Daniell, B. (1996). Deena's Story: The discourse of the other. *JAC: A Journal of Composition Theory, 16* (2), 253–264.

Delpit, L. (2001). The Politics of teaching literate discourse. In E. Cushman, (Eds.), *Literacy: A critical sourcebook* (pp. 545–554). Boston: Bedford/St. Martin's.

Dillard, J. L. (1973). *Black English.* New York: Vintage Books.

Dillard, J. L. (1992). *A history of American English.* New York: Longman.

Emmorey, K. (1998). Sign language. In V. Clark, P. Escholholz, & E. Rosa (Eds.), *Language* (6th ed.), pp. 78–95). New York: St. Martins.

Field, F. (forthcoming). *Linguistic borrowing in bilingual contexts.* Amsterdam: John Benjamins.

Gilyard, K. (1991). *Voice of the Self.* Detroit: Wayne State University Press.

Green, L. (1998). Aspect and predicate phrases in African American vernacular English. In S. Mufwene, J. R. Rickford, G. Bailey, and J. Baugh, (Eds), *African-American English*: New York: Routledge.

Haake, K. (2000). *What our speech disrupts: Feminism and creative writing studies.* Urbana, IL: NCTE.

Hartwell, P. (1985). Grammar, grammars, and the teaching of grammar. *College English, 47,* 105–127.

Hickok, G., Bellugi, U., & Klima, E. S. (2002, June). Sign language in the brain. *Scientific American,* Special Edition, *The Hidden Mind* Vol 12, No. 1 (updated from *Scientific American,* June 2001.

Honda, M., & O'Neil, W. (1996). On making linguistics useful for teachers: What can you learn from plural nouns and R? In D. L. Lillian (Ed.), *Papers of the Annual Meeting of the Atlantic Provinces Lingustic Association/Actes du Colloque Annuel de l'Association de Linguistique de Provinces Atlantiques,* 81–92. Ontario, Canada: York University Press.

hooks, b. (1994). Language. In *Teaching to transgress* (pp. 167–175). London and New York: Routledge.

Howard, R. M. (1996, January). The great wall of African American Vernacular English in the American college classroom. *JAC, 16* (2), 265–283. *Special Issue: Who's Doing the Teaching?*

Hudson, G. (2000). *Essential introductory linguistics.* Malden, MA: Blackwell.

Jackendoff, R. (1994). *Patterns in the mind.* New York: Basic Books.

Jordan, J. (1972). White English/Black English: The politics of translation. *Civil Wars* appeared in Jardan, J. (1981) (pp. 59–73). Beacon Press Boston, MA (republished 1995). New York: Touchstone Press.

Kaplan, R. B. (1966). Cultural thought patterns in intercultural education. *Language Learning, 16,* 1–20.

Kochman, T. (1981). *Black and white styles in conflict.* Chicago: University of Chicago Press.

Kohl, H. (1991). *I won't learn from you! The role of assent in education.* Minneapolis, MN: Milkweed Editions.

Kozol, J. (1975, December). The politics of syntax. *English Journal,* Vol 64, No. 9, 22–27.

Krapp, G. P. (1925). *The English language in America.* New York: Modern Language Association.

Labov, W. (1972). *Language in the inner city: Studies in the Black English vernacular.* Philadelphia: University of Pennsylvania Press.

Labov, W. (1995). The case of the missing copula: The interpretation of zeroes in African-American English. In L. R. Gleitman & M. Liberman (Eds.), *Language, An Invitation to Cognitive Science,* (2nd ed., Vol. 1) Cambridge, MA: MIT Press.

Lanehart, S. (1998). African American vernacular English and education: The dynamics of pedagogy, ideology, and identity. *Journal of English Linguistics: Special Issue: Ebonics,* Vol. 26. No 2, June 1998. Thousand Oaks, CA. Sage Publications, 122–136.

LePage, R. (1986). Acts of identity. *English Today, 8,* 21–24.

Lippi-Green, R. (1997). *English with an Accent.* London and New York: Routledge.

Maher, J., & Groves, J. (1996). *Introducing Chomsky.* New York: Totem Books.

Marback, R. (2001). Ebonics: Theorizing in public our attitudes toward literacy. *The Journal of the Conference on College Composition and Communication.* Vol 53, No 1, pp. 11–32

Martin, S., & Wolfram, W. (1998). The sentence in AAVE. In S. Mufwene, J. R. Rickford, G. Bailey, & I. Baugh (Eds), *African-American English* (pp. 11–36). London and New York: Routledge.

McAdams, C. M. (1989). Croatia: Myth and reality. www.hrvatska.org/mcadams/myth

McIntosh, P. (1989, July/August). White Privilege: Unpacking the invisible knapsack. Excerpt from Working Paper 189. *Peace and freedom.* Philadelphia: Women's International League for Peace and Freedom.

Meier, R. P. (1991). Language acquisition by deaf children. *American Scientist, 79,* 60–70. January-February.

Mufwene, S. North American Varieties of English. In R. Wheeler, (1999). *The workings of language.* New York: Praeger Press.

Mufwene, S. (1998, October). *The ecology of language: New imperatives in linguistics curriculua* (pp. 30–31). Paper presented at the Symposium on *The Linguistic Sciences in a Changing Context,* University of Illinois, Urbana-Champagne. [available at www.uchicago.edu/linguistics/faculty/mufw_ecol.html]

Mufwene, S. (2001). Pidgins and Creoles. www.uchicago.edu/linguistics/faculty /mufw_pdgcreo.html

Mufwene, S., Bailey, R. G., & Baugh, J. (Eds.) (1998). *African-American English.* London and New York: Routledge.

Okrand, M. (1985). *The Klingon dictionary.* New York: Pocket Books.

Olson, D. R. (1994). *The world on paper.* Cambridge: Cambridge University Press.

O'Neil, W. (1972). The politics of bidialectalism. *College English, 33,* 433–438.

O'Neil, W. (1990, April). Dealing with bad ideas: Twice is less. English Journal, *79* (4), 80–88.

O'Neil, W. (1991). Ebonics in the media. Radical Teacher, *54,* 13–17.

Palacas, A. L. (2001, January). Liberating American Ebonics from Euro-English. College English, *63* (3), 326–352.

Perry, T., & Delpit, L (Eds.). (1999). *The real ebonics debate: Power, language and the education of African American children.* Boston: Beacon Press.

Peñalosa, F. (1980). *Chicano sociolinguistics: A brief introduction.* Rowley, MA: Newbury House.

Pullum, G. (1999). African American English is not standard English with mistakes. In R. Wheeler (Ed.), *The workings of language.* New York: Praeger Press.

Read, C. (1975). *Children's categorization of speech sounds in English.* Urbana, IL: NCTE.

Rickford, J. (1998). *African American vernacular English.* London: Blackwell.

Rickford, J. R., & Rickford, R. J. (2000). *Spoken soul.* New York: John Wiley and Sons.

Sebba, M. (1997). *Contact languages.* New York: St. Martin's Press.

Sledd, J. (1969). Bi-dialectalism: The linguistics of white supremacy. *English Journal, 58,* 1307–1315.

Smith, N. (1999). *Chomsky: Ideas and ideals.* Cambridge: Cambridge University Press.

Smitherman, G. (1977). *Talkin and testifyin.* New York: Houghton Mifflin. [republished by Wayne State University Press, 1986]

Smitherman, G. (1994). *Black talk.* New York: Houghton Mifflin.

Stavans, I. (2000, October 13). The gravitas of Spanglish. *The Chronicle of Higher Education, 10.*

Steele, C. (1999). Thin ice. *The Atlantic Monthly, 284* (2), 44–54.

Stockman, I. J. (1996). Phonological development and disorders in African American children. In A. G. Kamhi, K. E. Pollock, & J. L. Harris (Eds.), *Communication development and disorders in African American children* (pp. 117–153). Baltimore: H. Brookes.

Supalla, S. J., Wix, T. R., & McKee, C. (2001). Print as a primary source of English for deaf learners. In J. Nicol (Ed.), *One mind, two languages: Bilingual language processing.* Malden, MA: Blackwell

Turner, L. (1949). *Africanisms in the Gullah dialect.* Chicago: University of Chicago Press.

Wallace, D. F. (2001, April). Tense present: Democracy, English, and the wars over usage. *Harper's,* 39–58.

Wardaugh, R. (1999). *Proper English.* Malden, MA: Blackwell.

Weisel, A. (Ed). (1998). *Issues unresolved: New perspectives on deaf education.* Washington, DC: Gallaudet University Press.

Wheeler, R. (1999). *The workings of language.* New York: Praeger Press.

Williams, J. (1998). *Preparing to teach writing: Research, theory, and practice* (2nd ed.) Mahwah, NJ: Lawrence Earlbaum.

Wolfram, W. (1994). The phonology of a sociocultural variety: The case of African American vernacular English. In J. Bernthal & N. Bankston (Eds.), *Child phonology: Characteristics, assessment, and intervention with special populations.* New York: Thieme.

Wolfram, W., & Whiteman, M. (1971, Spring/Fall). The role of dialect interference in composition. *Florida FL Reporter, 9,* 34–48.

Wolfram, W., & Schilling-Estes, N. (1998). *American English.* New York: Blackwell.

Wolfram, W., Temple-Adger, C., & Christian, D. (1999). *Dialects in schools and communites.* Mahwah, NJ. Lawrence Earlbaum.

Readings

OUR STUDENTS WRITE WITH ACCENTS—ORAL PARADIGMS FOR ESD STUDENTS

Charles F. Coleman

The oral configurations and practices of the language of some of our students are often in conflict with those of school-based English. Because we fail to address differences between speech and writing, some of the problems we encounter in literacy instruction are the result of trying to correct and explain oral language patterns and practices by using the rules and practices of the academic written language. More specifically, some traditional explanations involving terms such as dangling participle, comma splice, diction error, possessive and plural markers, and even subject-verb agreement are often neither helpful nor relevant in dealing with some of the language configurations our students produce in writing.

Academic English is just another language variety. Structurally, its surface features are not significantly more complex than those of other language varieties such as African American Vernacular English (AAVE). No language variety is inherently inferior or superior to another, but no language variety can be separated from the assumptions and practices which drive interactions between people. We make assumptions about people's intelligence, their likelihood of academic success, and even their worth based in part on our perceptions of how they manage or fail to manage a particular language variety. We learn the rules of our family-community-based spoken language varieties orally, in broad social contexts. In contrast, educators then attempt to teach academic English based on rules taken from its written forms, in the relatively narrower context of the classroom. The centrality of schooling for literacy acquisition is, however, contradicted in studies by Bernstein (1971), Heath (1983) and Gilyard's self-study (1991). Though methodologically different, these studies suggest that the home and community play a much larger role in academic literacy acquisition than does schooling. In practical terms, the centrality of schooling for literacy acquisition is further contradicted by the many high school graduates who are in college developmental reading and writing classes.

In my title, I use the word *accent* as a reference point. When we talk of accent, we most often mean *how* sounds and words are pronounced. But accent also includes prosodic features such as intonation, pauses, and stress patterns. These features are in turn part of the larger language practices of particular communities. One does not have to speak a foreign language to have an accent. Indeed, all speakers of American English have accents that mark them as members of various age, ethnic, gender, geographical, occupational, or social groups. Furthermore, just as all native speakers of American English speak with accents, the various genres and forms of academic writing involve prosodic features that I am loosely calling accent manifestations. These features include variations in spelling, punctuation, and word use as well as ways of highlighting texts such as bolds, capitals, icons, italics, and font manipulations. These prosodic features combine with metaphor and discourse practices to give texture and voice to written texts.

Academic English is not the home-community language variety for AAVE speakers born in this country and for many English speaking Caribbean students. The language features and practices of AAVE speakers diverge from those of academic English. The areas of divergence and related assumptions and practices contribute to AAVE speakers' difficulties in learning academic English. The English-Creole influenced language varieties and practices of some Caribbean students have likewise conflicted with mastery of academic British English, further complicating their mastery of academic American English. These AAVE and Creole-based English-speaking students are English as a Second Dialect (ESD) learners. I propose to broaden the context of our literacy instruction to take into account oral language paradigms and practices that shape the writing of some ESD students.

First, I will look at phonological transfer in developmental student writing, that is spellings or word configurations that represent what the writer hears. Next, I will examine two discourse features, *by strings* and *topic/comment* sentence structures, that appear to be influenced by the tension between oral and written language practices. An example of a *by string* is "By making English the official language of the United States will discriminate against speakers of other languages." It appears that a prepositional phrase beginning with *by* fills the subject position. An example of a *topic/comment* sentence structure is "There was this guy that came into the bank he was the banks mail man." Traditionally, this would simply be called a run-on sentence. Such traditional explanations, I believe, are incomplete. Finally, I analyze an essay by an African American student in a developmental writing class. The essay is instructive in demonstrating both the power and tension in the writing of students who are struggling with mastery of academic writing. Though I separate the samples into three parts for analysis and discussion, the points illustrated by each, as well as other language dynamics, are always at work simultaneously.

Oral/Aural Word Configurations

In the samples listed below, words and phrases are contextualized in sentences. This is helpful in demonstrating how students work toward a sense of what academic writing should feel like. These configurations are labeled aural/oral because they are the written representations of what listeners hear speakers say. All the samples are from the writing of African American students, some of whom are second generation Caribbean-Americans. The aural/oral configurations are in parentheses; words added by me help the reader make sense of the texts are bracketed.

(1) Not every successful person has worked day in and day out to get to (were) they are.

Most native speakers of American English do not aspirate the *h* in *where*. For some student writers then *were* and *where* or even *wear* become homographs.

(2) Most 15 year old drop-outs have very little job training. Without a job most of them will (result) to stealing.

There are several possibilities for *will result*. Some AAVE speakers tend to reduce final consonant clusters. Since *l* is a liquid consonant, pronounced without friction or a stop, it is natural to reduce toward the pronunciation of the *t*, which is a stop. Additionally, the spelling of the word *resort* may be influenced by the fact that resort *to* and result *from/in* can follow or be part of causative constructions, as in "Because there were no alternatives, we resorted to violence" or "Violence resulted from the lack of alternatives."

(3) I remember it so clearly, as if it were yesterday. I guess what makes it so vivid is the way my father looked when I asked him what sex was and the way he (use) to (figit) and clear his throat. My mother would just turn red as a cherry and tell me the (stalk) delivers babies to our door step.

Assimilation accounts for *use to* instead of *used to*. The articulation points in the mouth for *d* and *t* are so close that when *d* precedes *t*, the two sounds are assimilated to *t*. For the word *fidget*, the medial *d* is omitted; medial consonants are often omitted or softened. Like the *will resort* in sample 2, the word *stalk*, in *the stalk delivers babies*, results from consonant cluster reduction.

(4) (*Do*) to his (curiousness) Richard [Wright] wants to take books from the library but is not able to because no blacks (*was allow*) in the library.

Do is a homophone of *due* in many American English dialects. *Curiousness,* similar to occurrences of words like *conversate* or *supposably* in some student writing, makes sense as a word. The *was allow* is much less due to a failure to produce correct grammar as it is to the absence of the kind of obligatory redundancy features Labov reports in "The Logic of Non-Standard English" (74). Academic dialect requires a past participle marker on verbs following *was* and *were.* In the speaker/writer's dialect, the word *was* places the action of the sentence in past time; it is therefore not necessary to mark the participle following *was* with a redundancy feature. The prevalence of *was* in places where Academic English requires *were* is also a strong AVVE marker which Mary Epes attributes to what she calls "inner speech patterns," (28), that is language in which the mind speaks to itself.

(5) It's a (*doggy dog* world) [dog eat dog world].

In language varieties such as AAVE, final consonants are often softened and sometimes omitted (Smitherman 7). In this case both the final *g* in *dog* and the final *t* in *eat* are softened; this and the process of assimilation may produce *doggy dog.*

Word configurations like *doggy dog world* are of course not always the result of an individual speaker's production. These configurations may have been reshaped and passed along as part of the practices of a particular language community. When I was a child, for example, the expression *pop a wheelie* described pulling up on the handlebars of a bicycle so that one could ride with the front wheel off the ground. Today, I hear children saying, "I'm gonna do a *papa wheelie,*" which I assume to be a reduction that has replaced to pop a wheelie.

By Strings

The *by strings* that follow contain samples of word configurations discussed in the previous section, e.g. *wear* for *where* (10) and *do to* for *due to* (7). Word and language configurations crossing more than one of the areas covered in this paper are characteristic of the writing of many ESD students. A typical *by string* appears to consist of a *by* prepositional phrase functioning as a nominal cluster in the subject position. Again, all the samples are taken from the writing of African American students.

(6) (By making English the official language would take away one's constitutional rights). One would not have freedom of speech, choice, writing or the press if this was to happen.

(7) The decline in language is (do) to political and economic causes. The influence of the changes can be a cause. (By reinforcing the original cause can produce the same influence in a more intensified form), which can go on indefinitely.

(8) Anywhere one goes around [the] US one will find signs and posters written in English, Spanish or in some languages. These different languages are useful to those who can't read English. (By eliminating these languages from signs and posters will cause a lot of problems for foreigners to understand what these signs mean).

(9) I agree with this totally for the younger generation bursting with energy need outlets to let themselves go: (By providing centers for them where they could get together with other young people, playing different kinds of sports and games etc. could provide something for them to become involved in; thus keeping them out of trouble).

(10) (By Richard begin [being] accidently sent to a school wear [where] many of the children parents was doctors, lawyers, and business executives). Richard had to face language barrier and socially disadvantages.

With the exception of (10), it's very tempting in these cases to tell students to eliminate the preposition by and point out that the sentences often make their point without it. The by string in number (10) would be identified as a sentence fragment; note, however, the presence of a verb, *was*, which, for the student, might make this appear to be an academically acceptable sentence. Also, note the complex sentence structure in (9)—a by-string, followed by a locative adverbial clause, followed by a gerund phrase. The prevalence of these by strings among ESD students and the complexity of some of the structures make them worth further examination.

Most of the by strings in the examples above are all produced in the context of students doing response writing to reading assignments. Their response writing is not graded for organization or grammar, but I believe the assignments lead students to attempt to produce academic-sounding written texts.

The by string seems to be used to set up an agent-action or a causative relationship. The use of *by* as an agent-action or causative marker is characteristic of some versions of AAVE. In *Twice as Less,* Eleanor Wilson Orr, writing about what she believes is AAVE interference in learning mathematics and science, cites a paper by Elizabeth Sommers on differences in the use of prepositions of African American and European American fifth-graders in Atlanta, Georgia, and a chart developed by Francisca Sanchez based on lists of differences she collected from interviews in California and from several books. Sommers offers the example. "Then she had a telephone call by one of her friends," and Sanchez offers, "I got a black eye by this boy" (131). The first example seems to use *by* to mark an agent-action relationship. Sanchez's example indicates that for some of the youngsters studied a by-unit characterizes an agent-action or causative relationship.

Prepositions often mark locative and spatial constructions. Because different language communities see location and space in different ways, it is expectable

TABLE R1

In-Tandem Imagery	Face to Face Imagery
The card IN FRONT	The card BEHIND
The card BEHIND	The card IN FRONT
↑	↑
Observers	Observers

(a word not in my unabridged *American Heritage Dictionary,* but it makes a sense as a word) that this would be reflected in writing configurations. Clifford Hill conducted research on the concepts of *in front of* and *in back of* for some African American and European American children. McKenna used Hill's conceptual framework to devise a card game to investigate differences in orientation among 500 secondary students, of whom half were African American and half European American. McKenna found that three-quarters of the African Americans used what Hill calls in-tandem imagery for identifying *in front of* and *in back of,* and a nearly equal percentage of European Americans used what he calls face-to-face imagery. These contrasting patterns of imagery are illustrated in Table 1.

These anomalous uses of prepositions do not directly explain students' use of by strings, but they do contribute to the notion that language features such as prepositions connect to deeper language practices. These by strings, I believe, represent an area of tension between speech and writing.

Topic/Comment Structures

American English dialects typically have a subject/predicate sentence structure; a stated subject is followed by a predication. Some speakers, however, seem to alternate between subject/predicate and what Li and Thompson call *topic/comment* structures. In the topic/comment structure, a topic is stated; then a comment is made about the topic. Examples of the two structures follow.

Subject/predicate:
(subject) (predicate)
I / am not impressed with the Republican Revolution.

Topic/comment:
(topic) (comment)
As far as the Republican revolution is concerned/ I am not impressed.

Or the more typically oral

(topic) (comment)
The Republican Revolution/ I am not impressed.

The following topic/comment examples were collected from the writing of some African American students.

(11) There was this guy that came into the bank/he was the banks mail man.

(12) To work hard and become successful is great. Letting it take away your time with your friends and families/it's not worth it.

(13) There are too many negative influences causing our children to go the wrong way/which we seem to be losing the battle.

Examples (11) and (12) contain what we would commonly call run-on sentences, but the traditional explanation that these result from running two or more independent clauses together assumes that students are working from a subject/predicate orientation. The topic/comment orientation is helpful for understanding all three examples.

In topic/comment structures, which Li and Thompson have studied for Mandarin, and Yom for Korean, the topic is not determined by the verb but rather by "temporal or individual framework[s] within the main predication" (Li and Thompson 464). In other words, in languages and language varieties where tense is less reliant on verb position and form, topic/comment structures establish the situational context for tense as well as for the sentence topic. Most of the sentences in the essays of the students with whom I work follow the subject/predicate structure, but, like by strings, topic/comment structures occur regularly. I believe they are another area of tension between speaking and writing. There is the possibility that by strings and topic/comment structures may be motivated by students' attempts to sound academic in response to writing about academic texts in an academic setting. A kind of left branching seems to lend itself to academic-like text.

I was punished

The following essay was written by a 19-year-old African American male student in a developmental writing class. I will call the student Jamal. The essay prompt was, "Have you ever been punished for something you didn't do?" The class had read a chapter from Maya Angelou's *I Know Why the Caged Bird Sings* in which Maya, who had been raped by her mother's boyfriend, is punished for the first words she speaks to an adult in several years.

I was Punished. But It Was Not My Fault

I get along well with all my friends, except one particular friend; named Fatima, Fatima swears I don't call her. I can't remember, but I call her at least fifteen or twenty times in one day? I have spoking to her mother, her mother's fiance and her sister at different times. In every request for her, each of the three in her family says, "Fatima is not home." Can I take a message." I would respond, yes, "Tell Fatima, that her friend Jamal called." It seemed like the message did not get to Fatima. I saw her in __College. She said, "why you never call me?" I replied, "You never be home." Fatima have a attitude now, because she thinks I don't be trying to contact her.

Furthermore, over the summer, after calling her home every three or four days out of a week with no response, I sent her an "I miss you" card.

Unfortunately, she acts like she couldn't get card's message. But she wrote back telling me where she is going to be for me to contact her. So, I called her aunt's house. She wasn't there. She stepped out. We finally had a little conversation about our lack of communications. She said she comes in late, when everybody is asleep. All of this time, I'm trying to contact her. Nobody is able to leave the message, because she comes home when everybody is asleep in my house. I also see she didn't take it into consideration that I be trying to contact her. She gets mad at me because she believe I never call.

I just can't see why she's mad at me. It's not fair to me. I can't point out no mistakes on my behalf. If she can't believe I haven't been calling. She should have at least get the card messages. "Friends like you are few and Much to far between."

Jamal's essay succeeds very well in conveying his sense of frustration about the "lack of communications" between Fatima and him. The essay topic lends itself to narrative writing. Narrative style and Jamal's very personal topic in turn lend themselves to the presence of AAVE features: use of habitual be; AAVE subject-verb agreement patterns; negative concord. These AAVE features and practices contribute to Jamal's voice and ownership of the text.

Jamal's essay also evidences conventions and features of school-based essay writing. The essay's introduction builds to a statement of the problem, "Fatima (have) a attitude now, because she thinks I don't (be trying) to contact her." He appropriately uses the transition "Furthermore" to lead to further illustration of the problem, and his conclusion has emotional appeal. For the most part, his subject-verb agreement and punctuation are appropriate for school-based writing, and there is variety in his sentence structure.

There are, of course, ample opportunities for teachers to use our red pens (or green for us progressives): misuse of the semi-colon; run-on sentence; misuse and absence of question marks; sentence fragment; verb tense error; it is not clear what Jamal's quote "Friends like you..." should mean to Fatima, and of course the AAVE features would be marked as incorrect.

The texture of the essay comes then from a combination of school-based and AAVE-based features and conventions. For many teachers the AAVE features create a dissonance, and the power of the text may be lost. Jamal, and students like him, are aware of this. While they seem to succeed better in maintaining voice and ownership of their writing when doing narrative writing (Ball 1990, 1992), they are nevertheless aware that narrative writing sometimes situates them in oral language paradigms conducive to producing surface features that are unacceptable in academic essay writing. Jamal later wrote the following essay. The writing assignment followed a reading and discussion of an excerpt from Tillie Olsen's *Silences*. The essay topic was "Girls and women should be encouraged to become whatever they want. If men feel threatened by this, that's their problem."

Feminist hare correct. Women are discriminated against, and little girls and women should be encouraged to become whatever they want. If men feel threatened by this that's their problem.

Feminist have many different beliefs about men and women. Many people regarded women as lower in quality and less essential than men. Many men believed that women should attend to their duties at home. Feminist believe that women should have political, economic, and social equality with men. Unfortunately, by law women did not have the right to vote in elections. Majority of professional careers were closed to women.

Women should be granted the same priviledges as men.

In this essay Jamal moves away from personal narrative objective writing, a strategy he has no doubt internalized as a style shift toward academic writing. Beliefs and comments are attributed to "Feminist" "Many people" and "Many men". But, while I am convinced that Jamal has serious communication problems with Fatima, I am not convinced that he believes that feminists are correct. His opening paragraph is a restatement of the topic. His middle paragraph lists a series of assertions and statements taken from our class discussion; none of them is supported or developed. He concludes with a one-sentence statement that women should be granted the same privileges as men.

A strategy some students develop, consciously or not, in order to pass exit writing examinations is to avoid extensive narrative as a way of maintaining what they perceive to be an academic voice. In my experience, they often succeed in avoiding many of the errors triggered by oral language paradigms and practices. Unfortunately, this strategy often results in flat, voiceless writing.

Jamal's writing, like that of other ESD students, reflects tension between speech and writing. As reflected in the above two essays, however, this tension is deeper than what appears as surface features. Jamal, without ever having developed a sense of belonging to an academic language community, is struggling to shape his writing toward academic-sounding language.

Pedagogical Considerations

Teachers' and students' preoccupation with surface features is understandable. We must resist, however, traditional grammar instruction aimed only at correcting surface features. This kind of instruction invariably lends itself to a repair model, which fails in at least two areas. First, it assumes that something is wrong or incomplete about the way students use language. And when students don't transfer instruction in grammar to their speaking and writing, there is then an assumption that something is wrong or incomplete in the students' cognitive development. Second, traditional grammar instruction tends to treat language learning as a series of isolable occurrences rather than as dynamic developmental sociocultural interactions. It does not take into account work in the areas of language acquisition, literacy studies, and speech and writing differences. Following are three suggestions in these areas.

We Should Re-examine Assumptions Underlying the Grammar We Teach

From medicine, we borrow the term *iatrogenic*. When a doctor prescribes a drug or a health regimen, sometimes the new drug or regime triggers other health problems; these are called iatrogenic effects. In explaining subject-verb agreement, traditional grammar texts say that a plural subject takes a plural verb. In fact, given our concept of plurality, there is no such thing as a plural verb. Plural essentially means countable, and words that function in the verb position of sentences are not countable.

Imagine the iatrogenic problems we encourage with students whose dialects do not require an -s marker on verbs to establish agreement between them and their subjects in the third-person present tense. This -s marker in academic grammar is a redundancy feature; it has nothing to do with making the verb plural. Furthermore, since the -s marker in school-based grammar is most often associated with plurality, we are adding to the confusion of some students. In the grammar of some AAVE speakers, -s or -es as plural markers are not always required. If an AAVE speaker states "I have *four* sister," the logic of the grammar says that once plurality is established by the word four, there is no need for a redundant -s marker on sister.

Possession is another area where ESD students and school language configurations and markers are sometimes in conflict. Basic writing and literacy instructors will recognize that some students who are taught to use -s as a possessive marker then begin to use it as a plural marker. This confusion, I believe, is related to at least two things. First, some students may be grappling with the seeming contradiction of -s as a plural maker for most nouns and a singular-agreement marker with present third-person verbs. Plural and possessive confusion is further confounded by the fact the apostrophe as possessive marker moves to the right side of a plural verb [my sister's diary; my sisters' diaries] and that the pronunciation of a word that ends in -s determines whether an apostrophe or an apostrophe s is added [the Smiths' dog; the Jones's dog]. Part of the problem is inherent in the way we describe possessive markers; we say that they indicate ownership or possession. In the phrase, "today's date," does the date really belong to today? Also, why don't we use the -'s with phrases such as "car door," "teacher talk," or "student empowerment?"

Some AAVE speakers use genitive positioning to indicate possession. In "my mother car," for example, the juxtaposition of *mother* with *car* indicates ownership by position. This kind of genitive juxtaposition can be expanded to constructions such as "my mother brother daughter car." Again academic grammar calls for the marker -'s while AAVE does this with juxtaposition of lexical items. We should first see the apostrophe errors our students make as interdialect and therefore growth errors. Equally important, however, we should find less confusing ways to talk about possession. For constructions such as "my mother's car," it might be helpful to point out that determiners such as *my, his, her, their* often signal the beginning of this kind of structure.

We Should Continue to Research Differences Between Speech and Writing

Halliday argues against what he calls the myth that written text is highly structured while speech is essentially structureless (69–71). He believes this myth comes from our failure to develop an appropriate grammar for spoken language and from a failure to understand the contexts in which we compare speech and writing. Speech, he says—spontaneous discourse marked by hesitations, false starts, and slips of the tongue—is compared to edited drafts of written language. Halliday concludes:

> Looked at from the point of view of the sentence structure, it is the spoken text that appears more complex than the written one. The spoken text has a lower degree of lexical density, but a higher degree of grammatical intricacy. (64)

Halliday offers the following examples.

A. More typical of writing

Every previous [visit] had left me with a [sense] of the [risk] to others in further [attempts] at action on my [part].

B. More typical of speech

Whenever I'd [visited] there before I'd end up [feeling] that other [people] might get [hurt] if I [tried] to do any thing more. (62)

Both versions have five lexical items (the bracketed words), but B is more complex than A, since A consists of only one clause while B consists of the following four clauses.

> Whenever I'd visited there before
> I'd end up feeling
> that other people might get hurt
> if I tried to do anything more (64)

Mary Schleppegrell, argues for the need to study linguistic structures at the discourse rather than only the sentence level. "[W]hat traditional grammar marks as subordinate may carry the ideational weight of the sentence" (119). A sentence such as, "Because it was raining, the game was called," seems to exemplify hierarchical embedding of the because clause. Schleppegrell argues that there is also a nonembedded because-type clause (120–21). In speech, the nonembedded because-type clause does not function as a subordinate in a hierarchical relation-ship with a main clause.

Both the nonembedded because-clause and the hierarchically embedded one appear in the following excerpt from Amy Tan's *Joy Luck Club*. The main character is fretting over her mother's reaction to her European American fiancé, Rich.

> But I worried for Rich. Because I knew my feelings for him were vulnerable to being felled by my mother's suspicions, passing remarks, and innuendoes. And I was afraid of what I would lose, because Rich Scheilds adored me in the same way I adored Shoshana. (175)

We Should Consider the Applicability of Interlanguage and Interdialect Research

Selinker, theorizes that *interlanguage* forms develop as a middle ground among some speakers going from a native language to a target language— forms develop that are neither characteristic of the native speaker's language nor of the target language. Trudgill uses the term *interdialect* to describe incomplete accommoda-tion in dialect interaction. Trudgill cites Cheshire's 1982 study of working-class adolescents in Reading, England. Chesire found that "I does" and "he do," as well as "I dos" and "he dos" occur in the speech of the youngsters. "He do," she be-lieves, which occurs neither in the original Reading dialect nor in Standard English, is an interdialect form (63–65). Trudgill believes "we must be alert to interaction among dialects, rather than straightforward influence, as being instrumental in the development of interdialect" (65). Interlanguage/interdialect theory may be helpful because it allows us to see a class of student errors as growth. As Eleanor Kutz argues:

> Interlanguage provides a conceptual framework for seeing student writing as a stage in the developmental process, for seeing what is there as opposed to what isn't . . . 'Interlanguage analysis' allows another perspective from which to view stu-dent texts, in order to elicit and build on these in future assignments. (393)

Students should be encouraged to develop strategies for having something to say in writing in a variety of genres. To encourage their participation in academic discourse communities, students should read practiced writers in a variety of genres, who, like them, are sometimes successful and sometimes not. In this broader context of participation, we can better assist them in mastering the features, forms and practices of academic communities.

I end this paper with the voices of two students. The first is a young African American woman in a developmental writing class; her topic is "How I learned to read and write." Students were asked to write about their earliest memories of reading and writing and about times when they were made to feel good or bad about the way they read, speak, or write. The non-school-based features of her writing give strength to her text; they are also part of her recognition that she is not a member of an academic language community.

> I plan to write short novels some day, about my battles with school and the english language. When I was in high school I didn't think that the english language was very important, until I took the entrence test for college. My english wasn't straightened, so it was difficult for me to write a proper paper. I thought I was going to become a writer when I was finished with high school, but I guessed I was only fooling myself. I didn't know that I still had to struggled to improved the way I talked and write.

Attention to language must also move beyond the developmental English, reading, and speech classrooms. Writing in the disciplines and writing across the curriculum initiatives should actively involve all instructors in finding ways of examining our own discourses and recognizing student discourses. The following is the first paragraph from an assignment by a young African American male student in a junior-level African American literature course. He has good mastery of academic discourse. The assignment was to write a letter in the voice of a character from one story to a character in another. The student chose to write in the voice of Janie, from Zora Neale Hurston's *Their Eyes Were Watching God,* to Roselily, a character in an Alice Walker short story of the same name. Hurston's Janie is an AAVE speaker.

> Dear Roselily (my sister in spirit),

> My name is Janie. I ain't too up on correct english an' 'spellin' and such, but I expect you know what I'm tryin' to say, You about to enter a union with somebody, an' if ever'thin was as it should be then you s'pose to be happier than a pear tree at the first kiss of spring. You should be floatin' without so much as a drop' a water settlin' 'tween your toes. But you sound like youse about to be marched oll to work in the fields pickin' cotton again. Girl, you ain't even close enough to happy to smell it. You sound scared an' sad, an' ain't no man s'pose to make you sorrier with him at your side. If you is, then you better off on your own. The world is cold enough without no man tryin' to steal more o'your warmth.

Works Cited

Ball, Arnetha. "A study of the Oral and Written Descriptive Patterns of Black Adolescents in Vernacular and Academic Discourse Settings." American Educational Research Association. New Orleans, LA, April, 1990.

———. "Cultural Preferences and the Expository Writing of African-American Adolescents." *Written Communication* 9 (1992): 501–532.

Bernstein, Basil. *Class, Codes and Control: Vol 1.* London: Routledge, 1971.

Cheshire, Jenny. *Variation in an English Dialect.* New York: Cambridge UP, 1982.

Epes, Mary. "Tracing Errors to Their Source." *Journal of Basic Writing* 4.4 (1985): 4–33.

Gilyard, Keith. *Voices of the Self: A Study of Language Competence* Detroit: Wayne State UP, 1991.

Halliday, M. A. K. "Spoken and Written Modes of Meaning." *Comprehending Oral and Written Language.* Eds. R. Horowitz and J. Samuels. New York: Academic P, 1987. 51–83.

Heath, Shirley Brice. *Ways With Words: Language, Life, and Work in Communities and Classrooms.* Cambridge, New York: Cambridge UP, 1983.

Hill, Clifford. A Research Proposal on Socio-cultural Transmission and Interaction: Variant Modes of Constructing Spatial and Temporal Fields. New York: Teachers College, Columbia University, Institute for Urban and Minority Education, 1984.

Kutz, Eleanor. "Between Students, Language and Academic Discourse: Interlanguage as a Middle Ground." *CCC* 48 (December 1986): 387–96.

Labov, William. "The Logic of Non-Standard English." *The Florida FL Reporter* 7 (Summer/Fall 1969): 60–74, 169.

Li, Charles and S. A. Thompson. "Subject and Topic: A New Typology of Language." *Subject and Topic.* Ed. Charles Li. (457–490). New York: Academic, 1976. 451–90.

McKenna, S. C. Cross-Cultural Variation in the Use of Locative Constructs: A Case Study in Metropolitan New York. Diss. Teachers College, Columbia University, 1985.

Orr, Eleanor Wilson. *Twice as Less: Black English and the Performance of Black Students in Mathematics and Science.* New York: Norton, 1987.

Schleppegrell, Mary L. "Subordination and Linguistic Complexity." *Discourse Processes* 15 (1992): 117–31.

Selinker, Larry. "Interlanguage." *New Frontiers in Second Language Learning.* Ed. Schuman and Stenson. New York: Newbury, 1974.

Smitherman, Geneva. *Talkin' and Testifyin': The Language of Black America.* Detroit: Wayne State UP, 1977.

Tan, Amy. *The Joy Luck Club.* New York: Putnam, 1989.

Trudgill, Peter. "Dialects in Context," *Language in Society.* Oxford: Basil Blackwell, 1986. 62–78.

Yom, Haeng-Il. Topic-Comment Structures: A Contrastive Study of Simultaneous Interpretation from Korean into English. Diss. Teachers College, Columbia University, 1993.

RACIAL VENTRILOQUISM

Patricia J. Williams

I know I'm not supposed to read too much into a movie like *Episode I: The Phantom Menace,* but when you're living with a 6-year-old whose entire generation role-plays and reiterates each and every line, you tend to sit up and take exception when what comes out of those innocent little mouths suggests some not-very-subtle ethnic stereotypes of simpletons and shysters. Let's just take the movie's chief comic relief, the popeyed, brainless Jar Jar Binks, who is, apparently, a black man in frog face. Nothing wrong with that, says Lucasfilm; this is science fiction. Except he's a froggy alien who talks, yet says nothing. And who "lopes" (as per George Lucas's specifications, according to Ahmed Best, who plays Jar Jar) in a prancing, high-stepping cakewalk. He is a "Gungan Chuba Thief," as a *Star Wars* card in my son's little trading collection proclaims.

Whether intentionally or not, Jar Jar's pratfalls and high jinks borrow heavily from the genre of minstrelsy. Despite the amphibian get-up, his relentless, panicky, manchild-like idiocy is imported directly from the days of Amos 'N' Andy. And whether it were a white man, a black woman or Al Jolson himself beneath the mask, what would still make all the clowning so particularly insulting is the fact that Jar Jar's speech is a weird pidgin mush of West African, Caribbean and African-American linguistic styles.

Jar Jar bubbles with soundbites: "You-sa Jedi not all you-sa cracked up to be." "Me berry berry scay-yud." "We-sa goin in da wah-tah, okeyday?" Or, every time he does something so buffoonish as to require outright sanction: "Why me-sa always da one?" None of the Gungans have mastered much in the way of oratory. Indeed, *Star Wars Episode I: The Visual Dictionary,* now peddled in bookstores everywhere, assures us that "few Gungans speak the pure Gungan language." Yet English (or "Galactic Basic," as the dictionary calls it) is also beyond their command. The fat-faced, toadlike ruler of the Gungan race, who is called Boss Nass and who seems to be wearing the distinctive West African robe known as a *boubou,* expresses his resentment of his grammatically coherent planetary neighbors, the Naboo, in the following terms: "Dey tink dey so smartee, dey tink dey brains so big."

The Phantom Menace is filled with the hierarchies of accent and class status. The Jedi knights speak in full paragraphs, resonant baritones and crisp British accents. White slaves (like Anakin Skywalker and his mother) and the graceful conquered women of the Naboo speak with the brusque, determined innocence of middle-class Americans. The "status-obsessed," hivedwelling Neimoidians, on the other hand—who are "known for their exceptional organizing abilities," and who lead "a labyrinthine organization of bureaucrats and trade officials from many worlds that has insinuated itself throughout the galaxy"—speak like Charlie Chan. (In the dictionary, pictures of the Neimoidians are embellished with explanatory captions like: "underhanded gesture," "wheedling expression" and "insincere gesture of innocence.")

And then there's Watto, the "shrewd and possessive" junk dealer with a "sharp eye for a bargain" and a "dubious squint" who owns the tow-headed Anakin Skywalker. Watto sports a "three-day stubble," has a hooked nose that curves to his chin, cheats at games and doesn't give credit. He speaks in a gravelly Middle Eastern accent. Although a number of groups have protested that Watto is an insulting Arab stereotype, he struck me as more comprehensively anti-Semitic—both anti-Arab and anti-Jew. Indeed, Watto bears a striking similarity to a caricature of a Jewish journalist published in a Viennese magazine called *Kikeriki* at the turn of the last century. Reproduced in Sander Gilman's insightful book *The Jew's Body,* the cartoon shows a large-nosed, round-bellied man with spindly arms, bandy little legs and flat feet. An enormous fat chain, perhaps a giant watch fob, hangs across his waist. Wings sprout from his shoulders, and in his left hand he carries a scroll that says "anything for money."

Watto has a similar set of wings. He has an almost identically distended belly (the dictionary says it is "mostly composed of gas"). Watto's arms are spindly, his legs are bandy, and his feet are large and webbed. He has a pocket welder with a long, spiraling power cord that loops across his belly with almost the same degree of conspicuousness. And in the dictionary portrait, Watto's left hand grasps a data pad in which he is "careful to maintain accounting records."

As this movie is distributed worldwide and dubbed into a variety of languages, it will be interesting to see just how the accents are translated. If, as the studio maintains, the voices were assigned without thought to the stereotypes against which they play, the translation process provides an opportunity to rethink all that. If, on the other hand, they are merely reiterated in a multitude of tongues, then I fear this signals a determination to perpetuate some pretty poisonous prejudices on a global scale.

It's depressing. Given all the money spent on special effects, what would it have taken to have used computer-generated voices, let's say—to create comic effects or menace or innocence by a mixture of accents and tones and inflections and images that were not at the expense of historically demonized groups? It is the fervent hope of many of us of the post–civil rights generation to launch our children into a social galaxy far, far away from all the old prejudices. Yet for all such efforts, the phantom menace of popular culture seeps in through the cracks in the windows, the attitudes in the movies, the games children play with their friends, bearing prejudices at least as complex and pervasive as those of generations past, if somewhat more subtle.

At a moment when the media are being held accountable for all sorts of farfetched conspiratorial causes and violent effects, let's not let them off the hook for what they accomplish most directly. Films provide an expressive lexicon and romanticized reinforcement of cultural attitudes. They endow with mythic status the sight and sound of those whom the camera makes larger than life: they seduce us with, if not instruct us about, whom to love or hate or mock—and how.

DEALING WITH BAD IDEAS: TWICE IS LESS

Wayne O'Neil

It is an unfortunate fact about intellectual life in the United States, and certainly in other places as well, that bad and discredited ideas from the past keep reappearing. Particularly vulnerable to their reappearance are the "softer" areas of inquiry and work: the study of mind and of education and teaching. For there seems always to be the hope that human nature is less interesting and complex than it is; that there is somewhere to be found a quick educational fix for the overwhelming social problems of the day; that there is a science and technology that will solve all. From my particular vantage point, nowhere do these bad ideas roll so badly back, penny-like, than in discussions that link language with this or that aspect of education. These general remarks and the detailed ones that follow are largely motivated by the recent reappearance of many such bad ideas in the form of Eleanor Wilson Orr's *Twice as Less: Black English and the Performance of Black Students in Mathematics and Science* (1987).

Whatever her concerns, Orr's *Twice as Less* falls exactly into this category of research and band-aiding, with its attendant simplistic and wishful thinking. For her work sustains the fantasy of the intellectual that the basic injustices of society are subject to relatively simple technical correction. Thus—in education, for example—armed with the proper science and a derivative technology, the "experts" lead teachers to expect to find solutions to their problems close and easily at hand. In Orr's case, her goal is to explain the failure of urban, poor African American students to survive educationally in school, in particular in mathematics and science. Linguistics is then brought to bear on these problems. This brings Orr to an Ann Arbor-type solution (for more about this matter, see below, "Some Further Points"), according to which educators are enjoined to "seek out the knowledge of linguists" so that they can understand what their African American students are saying–thinking as well as what they are not saying–thinking (Orr 215: all page references are to Orr's book unless otherwise noted). (The wavering mark [–] between *saying* and *thinking* is to indicate that Orr does not distinguish between language and thought very carefully, if at all: see the following section for further discussion.) African American students then need only get "in the habit of . . . using the conventions of standard [= international] English" (48) and "to gain control over the construction of complex sentences that depend on relative pronouns and conjunctions and contain many prepositional phrases" (212) in order to get on with an understanding of science and mathematics.

Author's note: These comments constitute an extensively revised and expanded version of remarks presented at a 1988 Harvard Graduate School of Education panel discussion with Orr about her research. Thanks to Carol Chomsky, Morris Halle, Maya Honda, Ben Nelms, and to Don M. Lance for reading earlier drafts of these comments and for their own helpful comments.

The nature of the educator's task is then clear enough—though the job is not an easy or pleasant one, as it never seems to be in these "hard" cases: some basic concepts supposedly have to be drummed or built into the minds of African American students. Allegedly great difficulty is experienced due to the underlap between two varieties of a language. For by proclamation it is supposed to be easier for a speaker of a foreign language to get international English down perfectly than it is for a speaker of a nonstandard form of the language (125–26, citing several such unsupported assertions). This is a familiar enough truth about language learning, and thus, like all such "truths" held to be true without examination, should be considered suspect.

Scientific Critique: Language and Thought

However, as with any scientific-technical solution to a problem, we need to evaluate its intellectual foundations. In this case, an evaluation requires that we look not only at linguistic theory but at the cognitive sciences more generally. To her credit, Orr has a sense that she is treading on some pretty unsteady ground: Harvard's Roger Brown has warned her about the Sapir-Whorf hypothesis (11), that rather vague notion that "one's cognitive structure is largely determined by the structure (including the vocabulary) of the language one speaks" (Fodor, Bever, and Garrett 1974, 384). Unfortunately, however, Brown has misinformed Orr about the status of this hypothesis (which, indeed, we dignify by so labeling it). For the Sapir-Whorf hypothesis has just the standing and just the persistency as, for example, the notion that the earth is flat: it conforms to our common-sense view of things in nature, but it is dead wrong and is not a serious candidate for the explanation of the things in nature.

Thus misinformed and misled, Orr is encouraged to march into the swamp, with predictable and disastrous results. For, like a lot of people, Whorf included, Orr has great difficulty distinguishing concepts from their labels in language (words, more or less). Thus, she (half-)believes that in giving her students the words, she is giving them the concepts involved. In her discussion of location and distance, for example, Orr concludes that the fundamental question is,

> Does Jane think in terms of two distinct entities—location and distance—even though she uses the same symbol for both? Or does she think in terms of only one entity, which she accordingly represents by a single symbol? And if she does think in terms of only one entity, is it some kind of hybrid of the conventional notions of location and distance? (25)

Moreover, Orr adds a curious wrinkle of her own to Sapir-Whorf by expressing the nonstandard belief that "in the case of the three modes of expressing comparisons [the noun mode, the *than* mode, and the *as* mode], the grammar of Standard English has been shaped by what is true mathematically" (158), a remarkable observation, if true. For her observation here is rather like assuming that in language as in logic, two negatives make a positive. But we know that, in fact, two negatives in *natural* language make an emphatic negative, as distinct from their canceling effect in the *artificial* language of logic.

Indeed, my co-worker Morris Halle (1988, personal communication) has carried out a small and contrary experiment on this point with fluent MIT graduate-student speakers of international English in connection with Orr's statement (192) that the synonymy of "John does not have as much money as Sam" with "John has less money than Sam" is paralleled by the synonymy of "John does not have as little money as Sam" and "John has more money than Sam." All of the students agreed that the members of the first pair were clearly synonymous but disagreed widely about the second pair. One person said that "only logical consistency" convinced him that the second set of sentences contained synonymous members. Thus, it seems obvious that it is the requirements of scientific discourse that ensure synonymity in the second pair, not the language of everyday use.

In thinking this way, Orr fails to notice that the mathematical and scientific education of us all involves our learning narrow and fixed definitions of the words of ordinary language. These new definitions correspond only partially, if at all, to those of ordinary language. Take the word *hypothesis,* for example, or nearly any word from among those that Orr finds her students having difficulty with. Each of them has a meaning, indeed several meanings in the language of everyday speech, different from its narrower technical or scientific one(s). The word *distance,* for example, has several abstract nominal meanings ("the fact or condition of being apart in space or time"; "the interval separating any two specified instants in time"; "a point removed in space or time"; "chilliness of manner, aloofness"; and the like.) In addition, the word *distance* has three meanings special to geometry— not to mention the fact that it functions as a verb as well with its particular, nontechnical definitions. Moreover, some terms of science (*quantum potential,* for example) and of even quite ordinary discourse have no sense outside of scientific or technical discourse. The label *live oak,* for example, refers to a tree of the sort that an expert tells me is a live oak; indeed I may always need an expert to tell me or point out to me which are the live oaks as distinct from the other trees in the world.

Moving beyond mere matters of vocabulary, we know that great numbers of students, both younger and older than Orr's, as well as at the same age, have difficulty with mathematical and arithmetical problems. The extent of this difficulty in the United States is urgently reported to us from time to time, recently, for example, in "The Mathematics Report Card: Are We Measuring Up," from the National Assessment of Educational Progress (NAEP, see Fiske 1988), in which it is revealed that only 6.4% of the tested seventeen-year-olds (down from 7.4% in 1978) could handle multistep problems and algebra, problems far simpler than those administered by Orr. Given the general scope of the difficulties reported, clearly something here runs far deeper than the specifics of the grammar of Black English. What is it?

Language and Thought: An Alternative View

However, more reasonable assumptions about human nature exist than the ones Orr unquestioningly adopts: namely, that on the basis of their species-specific genetic endowment, human beings are equipped as a matter of course with all the natural concepts there are. The maturation of a child in this respect is then simply the child's learning which labels (words, crudely speaking) go with the concepts that receive expression in its language and world. (For some discussion, see Noam Chomsky 1988 passim.) Among languages and among varieties of what we loosely call a language, differences as to how the concepts are labeled will occur. There will also be minor variation over which concepts are labeled and about whether the mapping between concepts and labels is many-to-one, one-to-many, one-to-one, and the like.

Most obvious and trivial is the fact that different languages will label the same concept in phonologically very different ways: thus, the notion "reflexive" is generally (but not only) labeled with some form of -*self* in English, with a form of -*ziji* (including the "plain" form, without a personal pronoun attached) in Chinese, and the like. More interestingly, for example, many languages label the number concepts beyond "two" with only two additional terms roughly equivalent to "few" and "many." Moreover, in some varieties of English (in the Creole English of Nicaragua, for example), the concepts that many of us separate with the labels *learn* and *teach* are covered with the single label *learn*—a concept-to-label mapping that is common in the languages of the world. This offers no difficulties of communication apart from those that arise from the sort of elitism recently exhibited by the English Prince Charles.

Closer to Orr's concerns are the many varieties of English marked by subtle differences in the way the prepositional labels are tied up with the relational concepts involved. In Appalachian speech, for example, *at* labels the directional concept *to;* in other varieties *at* labels the locational *in,* and the like. The varieties of American English exhibit fine differences in the exact forms that comparative constructions take, with the label *as* doing the work of the standard *than* in some varieties, for example. (See Cassidy 1985 for details.)

In this view, we do not expect to find that a person or a group of people will lack certain concepts. Nor are we surprised to find languages that lack labels for particular concepts. (See Hale 1975 for discussion.) Presumably, if nothing in the culture focuses attention on particular concepts, then there is no reason to label them. For example, in English (as distinct from many other languages of the world) a rudimentary set of labels for kinship relations exists. From this observation, we conclude nothing about the human mind, however much we may want to conclude about the culture to which the language gives partial expression. For under the normal notions of translatability, where there is a mind and time there is a way to go from one language to another, in principle. That is, all the mind's concepts are hypothesized to be available for labeling in language—any

12 The distance from Washington, DC, to New York City is equal to the distance from Washington to Cleveland. Ohio Johnstown, Ohio, is fifty miles further from Washington than Cleveland is Springsville. New York, is fifty miles further from Washington than New York City is.

a) In the space below draw a labeled diagram that depicts the distance from Washington to New York City and the distance from Washington to Cleveland

(E. g. 0_____x_____0_____y_____0
           DC   NYC   Springsville NY
        0_____x_____0_____y_____0
           DC   Cleveland   Johnstown OH)

b) To the diagram you drew for 12a, add whatever is necessary in order to also show the locations of Springsville. New York, and Johnstown, Ohio. Label these locations.

FIG. R10.1.

language. Thus, when it became crucial for the Walpiri (an aboriginal people of Australia) to have mathematics, words for the number concepts involved became easily available to their language, which had previously lacked labels for the distinct number concepts beyond "two" (having cover terms roughly equivalent to "few" and "many" for larger sets). Indeed, it is an interesting fact about human beings that they continue to learn new labels (i.e., words) throughout their lives, whether in their native language or in a second, third, or nth language, this being a major insight of work on second language acquisition about the difference between the acquisition of grammar and of the lexicon (or mental dictionary).

Orr's Problem

In this light, consider again Orr's concern with the notions "location" and "distance," which the African American students she works with seem to confuse so badly as to lead her to wonder whether they have the two distinct concepts at all. Yet these particular concepts are so fundamental to human nature as to be necessarily labeled in all languages. Indeed, in one widely respected view, they are at the foundation of the interplay between language and conceptual structure. (See Jackendoff 1983.)

If this view is accepted, then how are we to explain the behavior typical of Orr's students with respect to such problems as those in Figure 1? Instead of a standard diagram of the sort shown in square brackets, the students drew diagrams in which the various cities were expressed as lines and in which the lines were connected in various relational ways reflecting the notion "distance" in the statement of the problem.

How, then, do we explain their behavior? As I read Orr's distance and location problems, I was struck by how much their proper expression, which absolutely requires that cities be represented by points and the distances between them by connecting lines, depends on a familiarity with the conventions of maps. In fact, if you are too familiar with maps and with the geography of the United States, you will be astounded by some of the assertions made in the problems—the relative location of Cleveland and New York City with respect to Washington, DC, for example. Thus, without an acceptance of or familiarity with the abstraction from reality that mapping conventions demand—not to mention the suspension of beliefs that is required by the problems themselves—it is difficult to see why anyone should imagine Washington, DC, Cleveland, and New York City to be points: that is, to have no extension—especially if one travels each day from some *point* in DC to another and back again. Now since it is unbelievable that the students lack the concepts or the language required to solve these problems, it is quite likely that Orr's problems simply lack any semblance of reality or interest for the students. Indeed, from the NAEP report cited above, we learn that "most students see mathematics as having little use in their future work life" (Fiske A28), that is that they find it irrelevant. Thus, from this behavior, it is wrong to conclude that the students lack the relevant concepts, however much we might want to conclude about the limited imagination of those who would try to delve into their minds.

Science Education

In fact, the problems cited throughout Orr's book bear little relation to anything in the real world, and they often involve so many unknowns that they are unsolvable, emphasizing the form of a solution rather than the satisfaction of a solution itself. In this connection, it is worth examining Orr's notion that it was "more effective to have these students not take any science until they had successfully completed algebra and geometry" (211). The misconception here is to believe that science is principally formalism, when, in fact, modern science arose out of the realization that it was the simplest things in the physical world that defied our understanding, and that our common-sense misunderstanding of them (that the earth is flat, for example) could give way to widely appreciated explanations through the careful exercise of the human science-forming capacity (Noam Chomsky 156–59). As Randolph Bourne somewhere wrote. "Scientific method is simply a sublimely well-ordered copy of our own best and most fruitful habits of thought." And as we go about trying to understand "our own best and most fruitful habits of thought," formalism will play little role, as it plays only a small role in science itself except at its most advanced and technical levels.

Orr's book, however, is subtitled in such a way as to make the reader think that Orr is going to deal with science education in some serious way as well as with mathematics (severely limited in her case to algebra and geometry), but in fact, what little attention she does pay to science is disappointingly devoted to following one of her students through a logical maze of someone else's making (211–14), working out a rather sophisticated problem little different in structure from her usual type that involves "two people start[ing] from the same place at the same time and travel[ing] in opposite directions. One of these travels twenty mph faster . . ." (67).

Our own work in science education, at the middle- and high-school levels, derives from a view of science as cooperative intellectual interplay between the human, science-forming capacity and things in nature. From this point of view, we have developed an introduction to the style and activity of modern scientific thinking based on very simple things: on the careful observation and explanation of simple linguistic phenomena, the behavior of floating and sinking objects, and the properties of dry yeast, for example. (See Carol Chomsky et al.; Carey et al. 1986, *A Progress Report;* Carey et al. 1988, *A Technical Report;* Bemis et al. 1988.)

Setting these important considerations about the general nature of scientific inquiry and science education aside, we conclude that Orr is naive about the relationships between language and thought. And it is this naiveté that simply cuts the scientific ground out from under her technical solution to the problems of education on which she fixes her attention.

Linguistic Critique: Black English

I turn now to other, increasingly more serious matters that Orr has gotten wrong: On the dust jacket of Orr's book, Roger Brown is quoted as saying that "this book is not naive about the Black English Vernacular and it is untainted by racism"—basic prerequisites, one would hope, given the topics that Orr addresses. However, neither of these judgments is true.

First about Black English. Although Orr writes as if there is little controversy over the origins and development of Black English and of the so-called creole languages generally, she has come to this conclusion by walking lightly past the incompatible views that she cites of Derek Bickerton and Joe Dillard (in Newmeyer 1988, 268–84), among others. The former claims that creoles are what they are because of the human bioprogram; the latter, that creolized European languages have become what they are through the intermixture of the lexicon of the European language and the syntax of African languages. (See Newmeyer 268–84; 285–301; 302–06; Holm 1988.)

A third view, one that I share, is that the so-called creole languages are largely varieties of the European languages from which they principally derive—on a par with the Englishes, the Spanishes, and the like found many places in the world (O'Neil, Joiner, and Taylor 1987; O'Neil and Honda 1987). It should be clear, then, that a great deal of controversy about these matters is now the basis of much lively and interesting linguistic research. Thus, what is known about creoles and about the creole basis for Black English cannot be assumed to be fixed. The answers to these interesting questions are, indeed, wide open, as is the formulation of the questions themselves. Thus, some of the conclusions that Orr reaches about, say, the differences between the ways prepositions work in Black English and in international English are easily challenged.

Moreover, Orr's discussion of several aspects of the grammar and the history of Black English is quite misleading. For example, she misunderstands the double-negative construction in Black English as somehow a hybrid of the international English "I don't know / anything about it" plus "I know / nothing about it" equaling "I don't know nothing about it" (148) and thoroughly neglects the thousand-year history of the double-negative construction in the English language. She also fails to see that an African American child's repetition of the sentence "he's not as smart as he thinks he is" as "he ain't as ... he not so smart as what he thinks he be" (186) shows a perfect perception of the international English sentence through an exact translation of it into Black English. The translation even contains the relative pronoun *what*, clearly indicating the relative-clause structure of the comparative construction characteristic of all varieties of English at a sufficient level of abstraction.

As this last observation suggests, the linguistic goals for the study of Black English ought to be the same as for any language or language variety: linguists are concerned to understand the variety of human linguistic expression as well as its underlying and universal sameness. They pursue their studies in order to try to understand one aspect of human knowledge.

It is then intriguing to ask why so much emphasis has been put on the study of Black English in the recent history of dialect studies in the United States and not on its other varieties? In part, the answer to this question goes back to my opening (and what will be part of my closing) remarks: intellectuals want narrow, technical solutions to broad, nontechnical social problems. So funds get directed toward research on and dissection of the perceived sources of the problems, in this case the African American community. Whether such research is done in Vietnam, in Central America, or in the cities of the United States, the underlying goal of this sort of anthropological and sociological research, though not necessarily of the researchers themselves, is for the ruling class to seek to understand potential enemies in all ways so as to try to control and contain them. On the domestic side, such work serves to convince people that something important is being done for them, but in the end, the work is directed against them, toward preventing redistribution of the present imbalance of economic and cultural capital. It is for this reason that we know as much as we do about urban African American society and its varieties of English but so little about the Englishes and other languages of the many economically impoverished people of the United States: the urban rebellions of twenty or so years ago, which threaten always to recur, were rebellions of African American people, not rural rebellions of the farmers of Iowa, say, about whose language and social structure we know very little, consequently. It is in this way that the social sciences in general have served (since their birth in the United States) and continue to serve the interests of the state. In China, the government keeps its people down by shooting them: in the United States, the people are kept down by social science and propaganda, with shooting reserved for special occasions only.

Political Critique: Racism and Other Issues

Racism

As far as the question of racism is concerned, it is a matter of considerable insensitivity and extremely condescending—to say the least—for Orr to deny "these students" fundamental concepts of human mind: to suggest, for example, that they do not have the perceptions and the language to distinguish between where they are and where they would like to be and what it takes to get from here to there. In the literature of racism as well as that of sexism and classism, typically the racists (and other -ists) dehumanize the object of their attacks. (For discussion, see among many others, Gould 1981; Lewontin et al. 1984.) Orr's approach here may be gentler, superficially more understanding, and more nicely packaged than those discussed by Stephen J. Gould and R. C. Lewontin, Steven Rose, and Leon J. Kamin, but it is no less dehumanizing.

Some Further Points

Turning to other large political issues, which Orr neglects almost entirely, I began by saying that whatever her intentions, Orr's book falls into a category of research that comforts and sustains certain fantasies of the intelligentsia—two very favorable reviews in the New York Times (1 and 19 November 1987) exhibiting this perception of her work. Her study presents the calming view that there is a more or less simple answer to one of the many trying problems of our time—that in this case the answer lies in education, the last refuge of the intellectual being an unwarranted faith in education, a retreat from the political center and struggles of society into one of its marginal institutions.

Finally, by her silence, Orr appears to show no understanding of or concern for what I will refer to (in paraphrase of Jesse Jackson) as the social and economic violence of poverty and, in this case, its educational consequences.

Return for a moment to the Ann Arbor case: the central legal question there was whether Black English was a separate language or "just a dialect," a variety of English—an unanswerable question from a scientific point of view, although clearly answerable from, say, a political point of view. (See, for example, James Baldwin's "If Black English Isn't a Language, Then Tell Me, What Is?" 1985.) If the former, then its speakers were protected under the body of law supporting bilingual education. Not so if Black English was "merely" a variety of English. With the help of a battery of expert linguistic witnesses, the judge decided that Black English was not a separate language, but since the educators at the King school were not sufficiently sensitive to the language variety and culture of their African American students, he sentenced the teachers to inservice instruction about these matters.

However, few people remember, or even know, that the Ann Arbor case was originally more than a legal action about language, that it was a broad-based suit against the Ann Arbor school system, a suit demanding social and economic justice. It was the court that narrowed the case to a trial about the sociolinguistic status of Black English because, in the United States, the poor are not legally protected from the social and economic violence which they must endure, however marginally protected they may be by the various languages they speak. (See Perry 1980; Perry 1982.)

Conclusion

As far as I can see, technical answers of the type that Orr, the Ann Arbor judge, and others give us offer no way out of the present situation in which the gap between the educational achievements of the African American poor and other poor minority groups and those of the white majority correlates so strongly with other gaps: IQ and SAT scores, dropout rates, illiteracy rates, wage and salary ratios, unemployment rates, malnutrition rates, infant mortality rates, serious illness and longevity rates, violent-death rates, and so on. An understanding of the grammar of Black English will explain none of this. Perhaps the recent work that sees these differences to be the result of the caste-liké structure of our society will lead to an explanation of its present disgraceful state. But still better explanations will not eliminate the Third World conditions that characterize much of urban existence in the United States: for to change the world in a nonviolent way requires that those with social, political, and economic privilege and power give up much of what they have and work together with those without privilege and power in order to eliminate the economic and social violence of poverty and to participate in the building of a just society in which human differences are celebrated, human dignity restored, one in which material and cultural resources are shared equally and not hoarded through privilege.

Massachusetts Institute of Technology
Cambridge, Massachusetts 02139

Works Cited

Baldwin, James. 1979. "If Black English Isn't a Language, Then Tell Me, What Is?" *New York Times* 29 July: Op Ed Page. (Rpt. in James Baldwin. 1985. *The Price of the Ticket: Collected Nonfiction 1948–1985.* New York: St. Martin's. 649–52.)

Bemis, Diane, et al. 1988. *Nature of Science: Lesson Plans.* Cambridge, MA: Educational Technology Center.

Carey, Susan, et al. 1986. *What Junior High School Students Do, Can, and Should Know about the Nature of Science: A Progress Report.* Cambridge, MA: Educational Technology Center.

————. 1988. *What Junior High School Students Do, Can, and Should Know about the Nature of Science and Scientific Inquiry: A Technical Report.* Cambridge, MA: Educational Technology Center.

Cassidy, Frederic G., chief ed. 1985. *Dictionary of American Regional English. Vol. 1: Introduction and A-C.* Cambridge: Harvard UP.

Chomsky, Carol, et al. 1985. *Doing Science: Constructing Scientific Theories as an Introduction to Scientific Method: A Technical Report.* Cambridge, MA: Educational Technology Center.

Chomsky, Noam. 1988. *Language and Problems of Knowledge: The Managua Lectures.* Cambridge: MITP.

Fiske, Edward B. 1988. "Back-to-Basics in Education Produces Gains in Arithmetic." *New York Times* 8 June: A1, A28.

Fodor, Jerry A., Thomas G. Bever, and Merrill F. Garrett. 1974. *The Psychology of Language: An Introduction to Psycholinguistics and Generative Grammar.* New York: McGraw.

Gould, Stephen J. 1981. *The Mismeasure of Man.* New York: Norton.

Hale, Ken. 1975. "Gaps in Grammars and Cultures." *Linguistics and Anthropology: In Honor of C. F. Voegelin.* Ed. M. Dale Kinkade, Ken Hale, and O. Werner. Lisse: Peter de Ridder, 295–315.

Holm, John. 1988–89. *Pidgins and Creoles.* 2 vols. Cambridge: Cambridge UP.

Jackendoff, Rav. 1983. *Semantics and Cognition.* Cambridge: MIT P.

Lewontin, R. C., Steven Rose, and Leon J. Kamin. 1984. *Not in Our Genes: Biology, Ideology, and Human Nature.* New York: Pantheon.

Newmeyer, Frederick J., ed. 1988. *Linguistics: The Cambridge Survey: Volume II. Linguistic Theory: Extensions and Implications.* Cambridge: Cambridge UP.

O'Neil, Wayne, Dora Joiner, and Shirley Taylor. 1987. "Notes on NP Pluralization in Nicaraguan English." *Historical Studies in Honour of Taizo Hirose.* Tokyo: Kenkyusha. 81–91.

O'Neil, Wayne, and Maya Honda. 1987. "Nicaraguan English/El Inglés Nicaraguense." *Wani: Revista sobre la Costa Atlántica* 6: 49–60.

Orr, Eleanor Wilson. 1987. *Twice as Less: Black English and the Performance of Black Students in Mathematics and Science.* New York: Norton.

Perry, Theresa. 1980. "Towards an Interpretative Analysis of the Martin Luther King Jr., v. Ann Arbor School District Board Case." Harvard Graduate School of Education Qualifying Paper.

————. 1982. *An Interpretative Analysis of the Martin Luther King Jr. v. Ann Arbor School District Board Case.* Diss., Harvard.

11

Electronic Writing Spaces

Lisa Gerrard

> This chapter discusses the role of computers in the teaching of writing. It includes a historical overview of how computers were conceived of in the context of composition pedagogy, a discussion of issues concerned with computer literacy, and suggestions for working with computers in the writing class.

Many writing instructors teach their classes in a computer lab one day a week or more; for some, the computer lab replaces the traditional classroom entirely. Whereas these instructors embrace electronic technology as an engaging, powerful resource, others see the computer as unnecessary, distracting, and stressful. Teaching composition is a difficult enough job, they argue; why introduce a complex, and sometimes unreliable, technology that will require instructors and students to adapt to new software, upgrade their skills from year to year, and seek technical support when their equipment goes awry? Administrators also have their concerns: Computer labs are expensive, require maintenance and security measures, and need to be upgraded every few years. But anyone who uses a word processor to write, e-mail to converse with friends and colleagues, or the Web to find information will understand the attraction of this technology: Computers make research, writing, revising, and collaborating easier. Or more simply, nowadays, people write with computers; our teaching is enhanced when we acknowledge and build on this fact.

However, composition can be taught well with traditional technologies. In fact, almost any class activity that requires a computer could take place with a blackboard, pen, and paper, face-to-face conversation, or a bound and typeset book. I teach with all these devices, alongside a variety of electronic tools, because each offers something unique and worthwhile. But since I began teaching with computers (in 1980), I've found that electronic technology can enrich a course in ways that traditional technologies cannot. This chapter explains some of the ways this enrichment takes place.

THE BEGINNING

Computers were first used in composition in the 1960s—before process-based pedagogy took hold—in an effort to automate the teaching of grammar, spelling, and punctuation, and the evaluation of student compositions (Daigon, 1966; Engstrom & Whittaker, 1963; Fisher, & Kaess 1968; Page & Paulus, 1968). These computer systems were principally the experiments of a few English teachers, linguists, and educational psychologists, rather than commercial products designed for a wide audience. Nevertheless, they illustrated an emerging interest in combining computers with writing instruction. In the late 1970s, commercial systems such as PLATO (Control Data Corporation) were developed as multisubject teaching tools, which included electronic grammar drills, where students encountered grammar rules and corrected flawed sentences. These systems found a limited audience, largely because few English departments were interested in computers, even fewer could afford the equipment (the hardware and software had to be purchased as one expensive package), and, not incidentally, grammar-based writing instruction was beginning to lose favor around that time, the late 1970s–early 1980s.

WORD PROCESSING

The development of word processing software in the late 1970s marked the first and most pervasive influence of computers on composition. In the mid-1970s, I was writing my doctoral dissertation on a yellow pad, typing up my notes each night on an electric typewriter, and laying the typed pages across a table, where I revised them with scissors and tape—literally cutting my text apart and taping it back together. When I finished my dissertation in 1979, word processors had started to appear in offices, allowing typists, and later, writers, to edit with unprecedented ease—moving, deleting, and otherwise manipulating text before printing it.

If word processing arrived too late for my dissertation (Alas! It would have shaved a year off graduate school), it coincided neatly with the development of process-based writing instruction. Several writing instructors surmised that if students were to write on a word processor, they would be far more likely to revise—and to make wholesale changes in concept and organization rather than limit themselves to local editing (Daiute, 1983, Gerrard, 1982)[1]. As we shifted from product-based composition, where instructors commented only on the completed essay and never required a rewrite—to process pedagogy, which required multiple drafts of our students, taught them to view these drafts as malleable works in progress, and guided them toward a successful writing strategy—word processing, which invited repeated revision, became an invaluable tool. In addition to encouraging students to view writing as a process, word processing made writing less intimidating for novice writers (Bean, 1983), invited them to take risks (Feldman, 1984), gave them more control over their composing strategies (Gerrard, 1989), and led them to create more complex sentences and longer (if not necessarily better) papers (Collier, 1983).

Word processing is still the most versatile and readily available writing tool, with a variety of classroom uses. If you are fortunate to have a classroom outfitted with computers, you can use this room as your everyday classroom (as I do) or bring your students to the computer room occasionally. The advantage of having the computers available is that they make it easy to construct a class as a hands-on writers workshop, where students spend much of the class time writing. In preparation for discussing a reading, for example, students might write their reactions to it—then read each other's responses and comment on them, as in the following assignment.

FOR WRITING AND DISCUSSION

1. Go with your class to a computer lab. Using a word processor, open a new file, and type a response to one or more of the following assertions about computers and composition:
   - "To prepare for the future, our educators must pioneer our understanding of the workplace in which students will operate when they enter careers. To be effective, educators of electronically literate students need to become proficient in

---

[1]Technically, the software I used for my earliest computer-based classes (1980–1982) was a text editor (ours was called *Wylbur*), not a word processor. Although word processors were originally written for secretaries and writers, text editors were meant for programmers—for typing computer code—and were far more cumbersome than word processors, which came later. For example, to format a paper, my students had to run a separate program (called *Script*) and learn a few programming commands. Desktop computers were not yet widely available, so we worked on remote terminals, connected to mainframe computers hidden away in the math/sciences building. Print-outs took hours to appear, and when they did, students had to walk across campus to retrieve them. Still, even this awkward experience was an improvement over the pad/typewriter method.

handling text editors, in the use of personal microprocessors, in the ability to search data bases, in skills to address . . . complex networks. . . ." (Strassmann, 1983)

- "If the plasticity of the electronic text is a great liberation for the author, it can also license the forger, the plagiarist, the swindler, the impostor." (Hayes, 1993)

- "[M]ost teachers have to rely on prepackaged sets of material, existing software, and especially purchased material from any of the scores of software manufacturing firms that are springing up in a largely unregulated way . . . . Rather than teachers having the time and skill to do their own curriculum planning and deliberation, they become isolated executors of someone else's plans, procedures, and evaluative mechanisms." (Apple, 1991)

- "In composition classrooms, students and teachers may share files and documents, collaborating both in composing and in deriving standards for student writing. . . . The techniques of collaboration with students, and the revolutionary stance toward the teacher's authority allow students to witness pedagogical strategies, to catch the magician putting the rabbit into the hat . . . [and] to display the writing process in ways not previously available." (Barker, 1990)

2. When you finish writing, move to another computer, and read someone else's commentary. Write a response to it; for example, add a new idea, give an example to illustrate the idea, disagree with the commentary, explain your point of view.

3. Do the second step two more times.

Another advantage of having word processing software in the classroom is that students can bring their drafts to class on a disk, and apply what they're studying in class that day directly—immediately—to their paper-in-progress. After introducing a rhetorical device (e.g., the thesis statement), discussing it with students, and looking at examples, you can set students to work, applying the principles just discussed to their drafts. While my students revise their thesis statements (or whatever the day's curriculum is), I walk around the room, offering help as requested. Colleagues who have never taught with computers often worry that I'll have nothing to do, that after 10 or 15 minutes of lecture/discussion, I'll sit back and stare at the ceiling while students revise their papers. This has never happened; instead, there is rarely enough of me to go around. Students are eager for the instructor's reactions to their writing, and by responding to their sentence or paragraph or outline immediately after they compose it, the instructor can provide guidance not only when they are most receptive but also when they can go back to their work—right then and there—and implement the suggestion.

Although critics of computer-based composition often imagine a cold, mechanistic environment—students staring at machinery and ignoring one another—the opposite is true. Computers socialize the classroom. At the outset of the term, computers break down the initial reticence students have finding themselves among strangers: Students notice a classmate looking for the "on" switch and offer to help; they peek at the Web site their neighbor is reading and comment on its contents; and so on. Regardless of whether students are novices or computer whizzes, they have one thing in common: They're working with the same technology; this fact helps build community. This socializing phenomenon was one of the most obvious results of the early experiments in computer-based composition (Gerrard, 1983; Sommers; 1985), and it continues today. It is also one of the most powerful benefits of teaching in a classroom outfitted with computers— and an especially pertinent one, given the current emphasis on collective knowledge-building in the classroom and a composition pedagogy in which students often work in groups.

Word processing makes it easy for students to respond to one another's writing. The monitor displays text clearly enough for small groups of students (gathering around one computer) to see, so that groups of three students coauthoring a project (perhaps doing stylistic revision of a passage or preparing an oral presentation) can work together, with one "scribe" doing the typing. Peer editing—of an entire paper, a paragraph, or a sentence— also works well on the computer. The display provides unlimited room to insert comments; these comments can be highlighted with colors, fonts, or other graphic features. Although simply typing comments into a text file works quite well, some instructors take advantage of the special features found on many word processors. Microsoft *Word* has a "track changes" feature (under the "Tools" menu) that allows an editor to insert comments, draw a line through deleted text, and color-code different kinds of changes. It also allows students to set up a "shared documents" folder, so that students can leave documents for their classmates to read. Many word processing programs (such as Microsoft *Word*) also have an "Outline View," which allows writers to look at their (or their classmate's) paper in outline form, and isolate the headings, among other possibilities—a view that shows how the draft is organized.

FOR WRITING AND DISCUSSION

Consider your own use of computers—for e-mail, Web surfing, word processing, and so on. What difference has computer technology made in your life? How has it affected your research, writing, teaching, or relationship with colleagues?

INVENTION SOFTWARE

By treating invention as a separate stage of writing, writers can explore what they want to say before striving to find the right style or form for their ideas. Composition researchers have found invention exercises, or heuristics, useful for helping writers discover what they know about a subject (Flower & Hayes, 1977), generate new information (Murray, 1978), and relieve writer's block (Rose, 1980). Many kinds of invention assignments are possible using word processing alone. For example, students can do a form of freewriting called "invisible writing" by simply turning down the brightness of the monitor so that they cannot see what they're writing. Freewriting, promoted by Peter Elbow (1973), is intended to break down blocks to getting started; the writer writes continuously for a period of time, writing anything that pops into her head. The object is to produce words and ideas without prematurely censoring them. "Invisible writing" on the computer serves this purpose because it is impossible to edit—the writer cannot see her writing until she turns the brightness back up. In their early experiments with invisible writing, Stephen Marcus and Sheridan Blau found that, unlike freewriting on paper, the computer-based version "encouraged a quality of attention to the topic at hand" (1983) that didn't take place with pen and paper.

Invention software, meant to stimulate students' ideas, was among the earliest to be developed. Hugh Burns' doctoral dissertation described a computer program he developed with George Culp, which prompted students to think about their topics according to three different rhetorical schemes: Aristotle's topics, Kenneth Burke's pentad, and the tagmemic matrix of Pike, Becker, and Young (1979). After the writer typed in his name, the program engaged in a dialogue with him, asking questions about his topic, and using the terms he typed to generate additional questions:

> Now I need to find out what you are writing about, so would you please type in your subject. I am looking for one to three words.
>
> Protest against materialism.
>
> Hey, that's neat, Wally! . . .
>
> What special experiences made you select protest against materialism as your topic?
>
> The study of medieval man, the way in which he was led to believe at the time, the influence of the church.
>
> That's the idea, Wally. Give me some more information now. (Burns, 1984)

This invention exercise had some drawbacks; it easily invited parody, making it susceptible to the programmers' adage "Garbage In, Garbage Out": The dialogue was only as valuable as the ideas the students poured into it. Still, by prompting students step-by-step through their ideas, it allowed them to think through a topic in stages, a strategy that was exploited in software that came later.

WANDAH (Von Blum & Cohen, 1984) and shortly thereafter, *Writer's Helper* (Wresch, 1984), offered an array of prewriting exercises that were independent of one another and could be saved and edited in a word processor, thus allowing the writer to shape the invention exercise into a draft. Rather than react to what students typed, these programs provided a framework in which students could explore their ideas. In the "Planning an Argument" section of the *Prewriting Stacks* (Gerrard & Cohen, 1991), for example, students complete the prompt "In this paper I wish to prove that....," and, thus, create a sentence—a tentative thesis—that appears on the subsequent screens. The program then asks students to complete a series of prompts, each of which appears on its own screen, so that they can concentrate on one idea at a time: "I believe my thesis is true because...." or "Someone who disagrees with me might argue...." The program then presents these supporting and opposing points as a list and gives students an opportunity to revise and organize them. The object here is to give students a separate visual space for each idea and, later, to view the list against the thesis it's meant to support.

Not all prewriting strategies produce the same results with all people or work equally well for all tasks, so different invention routines stimulate thinking in a different ways. For example, in the *Prewriting Stacks,* the "Freewriting" and "Brainstorming" routines prompt quick, associative thinking and save reflection on these thoughts for later, whereas "Planning an Argument" is meant for a linear presentation of supporting and opposing ideas. I find invention aids most useful for novice writers—or for any writer who is having trouble getting started. By separating idea generation from the rest of the composing process, invention aids help writers who may get overwhelmed by the complexity of the writing task, especially those who try to decide what to say, and attempt to organize and correct sentences at the same time. Of course, the quality of the ideas is entirely up to the writer: garbage in, garbage out.

GRAMMAR TUTORIALS

Some of the earliest writing-software designers hoped that computers would identify grammar errors and teach students to write correctly. IBM worked throughout the late 1970s and 1980s on a program (first called *Epistle*, later *Critique*) that would do this kind of identification. Although it made impressive use of artificial intelligence principles, this program never identified errors with more than 80% accuracy. In the 1980s, writing instructors experimented with online workbooks, drill and practice programs, such as Little,

Brown, and Co.'s *Grammarlab* and Houghton Mifflin Co.'s *Microwriter,* which contained modules on noun and verb forms, sentence structure, punctuation, and similar mechanics.

The advantages of these programs were that they could present a sentence one frame at a time and, thus, keep a student's attention focused; they would automatically tell students when their corrections were right or wrong and allow students to repeat an exercise or a rule as often as they wanted to see it, thus avoiding the embarrassment of failure in front of a human; they kept track of a student's successes and failures and accordingly increased or decreased the difficulty of the exercises. Some instructors also praised these autotutorial programs for allocating responsibility for learning to the learner (Southwell, 1984). Over time, the popularity of these programs waned along with that of traditional workbooks and for the same reason: Teachers found that however skillful students became at locating and correcting flaws in the workbook's sentences, this ability did not carry over into their own writing.

GRAMMAR AND STYLE CHECKERS

These programs highlight common grammar errors (e.g., noun/verb disagreement, missing apostrophes, run-on sentences) as well as stylistic lapses (e.g., clichés, redundancy, vagueness) and often offer quantifiable information on the text, such as a bar graph showing sentence lengths or statistics on the number of "to be" verbs, prepositional phrases, or abstract nouns. Some, modeled on the earliest of these, Bell Laboratories' *Writer's Workbench* (which was adapted for college students by Colorado State University in 1982), also score the text according to any of several readability formulas.[2] These programs (e.g., *Homer* [Scribner's], *HBJ Writer* [Harcourt, Brace Jovanovich], *Grammatik* [Reference Software], *Editor* [MLA]) provide extensive information about a text's surface features; some of them offer alternatives to constructions the program recognizes as ungrammatical or undesirable:

Its. Wrong pronoun. Replace with "it's." (*Correct Grammar*)

First of all. Longwinded, wordy. Try "First." (*Grammatik III*)

Has past. Possible common phrase misspelled; "passed"? (*Editor*)

However, because computers cannot understand the content of a sentence, none of the programs that evaluate style and grammar are consistently accurate nor do they always offer appropriate alternatives. As their critics

---

[2]Readability formulas (e.g., *Kincaid, Flesch,* and *Coleman-Liau*) measure the difficulty of a text according to such features as sentence length and concreteness, and predict the level of schooling required for a reader to understand the text.

have long complained, they may flag effective constructions and ignore problems:

> ... these programs can numb your writing judgment by fussing over problems that don't even exist. Take, for example, an article I wrote for a business magazine. "My wife is a successful pharmacist, but she is a failure as a writer," the article began. *Grammatik,* when reviewing the sentence, paused to point out that "'she' is a gender-specific term." Thank heaven, because my wife is a gender-specific person. Oddly the program doesn't point out "wife," a term that has greater capability of sexist implications. ... (Brohaugh, 1984)

As Alex Vernon has pointed out (2000), more recent style checkers are more functional than their predecessors, but they have gained little in accuracy or reliability.

Although most of the early grammar/style checkers were used in campus computer labs (students rarely bought them for personal use), today, students are most likely to encounter the checkers that come with the most popular word processing programs, Microsoft *Word* and Corel *WordPerfect,* and to use them on their own rather than in a lab or classroom. This practice can be problematic for novice writers, many of whom have more confidence in the computer's judgment than in their own writing (Gerrard, 1989; Kiefer, 1987). Students rarely know what to make of statistical information such as this, calculated by *Word's* "Spelling and Grammar" feature on a student's sentence, "The only thing that will tell is time":

Readability Statistics

Counts	
Words	8
Characters	31
Paragraphs	1
Sentences	1
Averages	
Sentences per paragraph	1
Words per sentence	8
Characters per word	8
Readability	
Passive sentences	0
Flesch Reading Ease	100
Flesch-Kincaid Grade Level	0

For a technical writer, or under different circumstances, this might be useful information. But the only thing the student needed to know about the sentence, the computer didn't tell him: It's a cliché.

Having seen students ruin perfectly good sentences on advice from their computer's style checker, I make a point of warning them not to rely on this feature. However, used with an instructor's guidance, these programs can be excellent teaching tools. They can be used with poor writing as well as text by Hemingway or Woolf to show how much usage depends on context—how a sentence structure, such as a fragment or a very long sentence, that disrupts meaning in one instance, creates a strategic effect in another. By running the grammar checker on different texts, including student writing, and deciding how to interpret the computer's analysis, the class has an opportunity to discuss the relationship between sentence structure and meaning. This kind of software can also be used to initiate thought on how grammatical and stylistic norms come about. Who decides what practices are regarded as good writing? How might widely used programs such as *Word* or *WordPerfect* institutionalize certain language conventions? Why does *Word* label some usages matters of grammar and others matters of style? Why does *WordPerfect* allow writers to opt for a "Student Composition" style or other (business or professional) styles? What is the distinction between them? What other linguistic features might these checkers look for? (Vernon, 2000)

OWLs

For computerized help with grammar and style, students working alone or with assistance might do well consulting On-Line Writing Labs (OWLs), Web sites that offer help on sentence structure, grammar, organization, audience, and other rhetorical concerns. Most OWLs have been designed for a particular writing center at a university and offer tutorial help—comments from a live person—only to students enrolled at that school. But the generic advice is generally well written, up to date, and visually appealing and can supplement or replace a rhetoric text or grammar handbook. Most OWLs have a wide range of other resources and links to other sites, so that a student who consulted an OWL for help with apostrophes could easily discover something else he needed. OWLs typically offer information on specialized writing (e.g., for literature, science, journalism), the research process, and formatting conventions, along with links to such resources as dictionaries, thesauruses, and the MLA style manual. Purdue University's Online Writing Lab (http://owl.english.purdue.edu) is one of the most comprehensive and highly regarded, but there are many others; the OWL at the University of Maine (http://www.ume.maine.edu/~wcenter/others.html) offers links to a large number of other OWLs.

FOR WRITING AND DISCUSSION

1. Choose 2-5 pages of either your own, a student's, or a piece of published writing available to you online. Copy it into a word processor that has a grammar/style checker.

2. Run the checker on this piece of writing and analyze the results.

3. What was most and least informative in the output? What features of the text did the checker assess accurately? What was inaccurate?

4. Consider what the checker's responses reveal about the dependence of style on content. Does the checker seem to validate or criticize any particular kind of writing? Do you see social or political implications in these responses?

HYPERTEXT/HYPERMEDIA

Before the World Wide Web was generally available, many instructors took advantage of webbed technology—the ability to branch from one document to another without leaving the original text—made possible by hypertext. Hypertext, which became popular in 1987 when Apple Corporation introduced *HyperCard,* is a type of software now familiar to anyone who has surfed the Web: It allows the user to click on a "hot link" (a word or image) and go to a new space that offers additional information. Many of the earliest instructional hypertexts in English were created to teach literature; a hypertext on *Paradise Lost* might have hot links to biographical information on Milton, a discussion of the role of Satan in Puritan thought, or a list of the attributes of classical epic. My colleague, Douglas Lanier, constructed a hypertext to illustrate the cumulative sentence for a writing class. He broke down a complex sentence from Martin Luther King, Junior's "Letter from Birmingham Jail" to its core statement, "Let us hope that racial prejudice will pass away." When the student clicked on an individual word in this sentence, the original qualifiers would appear (e.g., after clicking on "racial prejudice," the student would see a new version of the sentence, with "racial prejudice" extended to "*clouds* of racial prejudice") "Clouds" was, in turn, glossed and expanded to "*dark* clouds of racial prejudice." This process continued through 35 glosses until the sentence grew to the form King had given it.[3] By unfolding this sentence bit by bit, the computer provided a visual illustration of how a cumulative sentence is constructed.

This was one way of taking advantage of the branching capabilities of hypertext for instruction, in this case, to teach students about style. Through branching, hypertext provides a different way of presenting relationships between pieces of information than is allowable with a block of linear text.

---

[3]King's original sentence was "Let us all hope that the dark clouds of racial prejudice will soon pass away and the deep fog of misunderstanding will be lifted from our fear-drenched communities and in some not too distant tomorrow the radiant stars of love and brotherhood will shine over our great nation with all of their scintillating beauty."

Hypermedia does the same thing, but expands this capability to include graphics, sound, color, and animation. Hypertext has had multiple classroom uses. Many teachers have exploited the possibilities it offers to challenge the traditional roles of reader and writer: Although the writer of a hypertext creates all the branches of the text, the reader chooses the pathway, the organization to follow in reading it. Thus, some have argued that hypertext supports acts of resistant reading and multiple interpretations of text (Bolter, 1991), making it a useful tool for instructors who work with reader-response theories of composition and want students to explore the boundaries between writer and reader or to challenge the notion that anyone owns a text (McDaid, 1991).

In addition to exploring other writers' hypertexts, some instructors have had students construct their own hypertext essays or stories, often using interactive fiction programs, such as *Storyspace* (Eastgate Systems). These programs allow students to interlink multiple documents, including pictures, video, and sound, creating fiction or research papers—projects that many instructors have favored partly because they allow for considerable creativity; require students to think about standard rhetorical concerns such as organization and audience in new ways; often necessitate innovative research; and lend themselves well to collaboration among groups of students, thus promoting socially based learning. As with all writing technologies, the use of hypertext as an instructional tool in composition has had its critics: Not everyone has been convinced that exploring hypertexts has any effect on students' understanding of the relationship between reader and writer. Critics also claim that constructing hypertexts does not necessarily improve a writer's ability to organize, because the concept of coherence becomes much more complex in a document made up of interlocked branches (Slatin, 1990).

Regardless of whether navigating or creating hypertext has had a salutary effect on student writing, hypertext programs, such as Apple's *HyperCard* or OWL International's *GUIDE,* have allowed writing instructors who are not computer programmers to create their own computer-based teaching materials, tailored to their particular curriculum.[4] Today, however, instructors inclined to construct their own online materials are likely to produce them as Web pages, using a simple word processor. And with the range and versatility of materials available on the World Wide Web, many instructors feel they no longer need any specialized software; they can do everything they need with a browser and access to the Internet.

---

[4]A few of the dozens of these hypertext writing aids are *Writing about Literature* (Mary Hocks & Rex Clark, University of Illinois, Urbana-Campaign), *HyperShelf* (Stephen Marcus, University of California, Santa Barbara), and *MacJournalism* (M. E. Abrams, Florida A & M University).

FOR WRITING AND DISCUSSION

If your campus has computing facilities for students, visit them. Talk to the lab manager or assistant and find out whether the lab is a walk-in facility or if anyone teaches there. If the lab functions partly or exclusively as a classroom, what courses are taught there? What software is available? How is the lab set up? What would encourage you to teach there—or inhibit you from doing so? If you can, observe a class being taught in the lab.

LOCAL AREA NETWORKS (LANs) AND THE INTERNET

E-mail, chat, and other forms of networked communication allow students to share their work with their peers during scheduled class time—over a local area network, which connects computers located in the same building— as well as outside of class—over the Internet, which connects computers around the world. Synchronous communication, in which the participants are all reading and sending messages concurrently, has proved especially successful for class discussion. The earliest use of synchronous, or "real-time," communication for class discussion took place in 1984, at Gallaudet University, in an effort to help deaf students—who because they cannot hear language, have difficulty with its written form—become proficient writers. The ENFI (Electronic Networks for Interaction[5]) project, as it was called, had students writing to each other to discuss readings and to do prewriting activities, peer editing, and other forms of collaboration. The effect of this experiment was to shift the students' attention from the teacher to each other, thus creating different audiences for the writing class and moving responsibility for learning back onto the students. It soon became apparent that electronic communication could have similar benefits for hearing students, and software—such as *Interchange* (Daedalus Corporation) and *Realtime Writer* (Realtime Learning Systems)—began to be developed for this purpose.

Today, many of our students come to us already familiar with chat rooms. Chat software, which allows for real-time communication, is widely available. In addition to refocusing class discussion away from the instructor, synchronous electronic conversations engage a far larger number of students than traditional face-to-face discussions do. Students who are shy,

[5]The acronym originally stood for "English Natural Form Instruction," but was changed as classroom-based synchronous discussion became widespread.

self-conscious about speaking with an accent or a stutter, silenced by louder or more aggressive classmates, or those who like to think about an idea before they respond—and in the process, miss their chance to speak—are especially helped by this form of discussion. Students in online forums also respond directly to one another, addressing each other's comments more often than they do in face-to-face class discussion, and they seem to respond to the instructor more often as well (Hartman, Neuwirth, Kiesler, Sproull, Cochran, Palmguist, & Zubrow, 1991). Whether addressing the instructor or a classmate, they tend to be more willing to take risks and speak more openly than they would in other contexts, to "do away with the niceties and express their opinions more readily" (Eldred, 1991).

One of the advantages of online discussions is that they are fun, and, therefore, students tend to stay with them longer than they might with a face-to-face encounter. But sometimes students get a little carried away with the freedom they experience to type whatever they like at any point in the conversation, and the dialogue can veer off topic and become silly. Although a certain amount of joking around is desirable—it gives students a chance to play with language and build a friendly classroom community—online conversations tend to dwindle into silliness more easily than face-to-face ones do. Of course, when this happens, the instructor, acting as moderator, can guide students back to the day's agenda. Still, not all online discourse is sweetness and light: Flaming and other hostile interactions or simply ignoring a classmate's post can also inhibit productive conversation. Many instructors advocate teaching students how to use this discourse to ensure that they "assume responsibility for dialectic exchange" (Hogsette, 1995). As David Hogsette points out, despite its potential for freeing student voices, online discussion can, used destructively, achieve the opposite effect:

> Students talk about what they want or what they are interested in, and if a student's ... posting ... presents a view that is radically different from other postings in that group, it will be quickly dismissed, simply ignored, or deleted from the list. When a students' post is ignored and not read, that student is silenced. (Hogsette, 1995, p. 67).

Despite these drawbacks, the majority of online discussions have tremendous creative potential. Instructors have reported that their students come to see their writing in its rhetorical context and can instantly gauge the reaction of the audience. Others praise chat for giving students a vehicle for writing in a conversational tone, developing a personal voice that can carry over into their more formal writing (Batson, 1992). And finally, proponents of classroom chat believe it provides students with "rich and valuable writing experiences":

> Students showed intelligent, creative thought and self-expression on the network that the constraints of more formal compositions... may not have encouraged them to do. (Peyton, 1990)

Many instructors link their classes with classes at other schools; students from both schools meet online to discuss a shared reading or exchange and critique drafts of papers. Students often find these exchanges eye-opening, especially when they communicate with a class in a different part of the country or world, with a demographic and world view unlike their own. Such exchanges also teach students to write for a real audience: In both their e-mail conversations and their drafts (if they're sharing them), they have to make themselves clear to someone other than their teacher. If they are vague, insensitive, overly informal, or insulting, however inadvertently, the feedback they get will let them know right away. In cross-class exchanges, online discussion lists, or Usenet groups,[6] students gain practice expressing their ideas publicly, reading messages carefully, and responding to people they cannot see or hear; because they depend entirely on words to communicate, they have an opportunity to learn to read and choose language thoughtfully. In courses where students are analyzing discourse, discussion lists can function as a resource. After subscribing to the list for a few weeks, students can study its language community: the kind of language used, the relationships among participants, the types of messages, and how these serve the purpose of the list.

FOR WRITING AND DISCUSSION

Go to the Web site Tile.net (http://www.tile.net/) or CataList (http://www.lsoft.com/catalist.html/) and find a public online discussion list or Usenet group of interest to you. Subscribe to the list or visit the Usenet group and monitor or participate in the discussion for a few weeks. Then evaluate the experience. How would you define the culture of this list?

---

[6]Discussion lists consist of groups of people with a common interest, who post messages to a list, which sends them automatically to all subscribers. Some are public, open to anyone; others are private. Usenet groups exchange messages just as members of discussion lists do, but the Usenet is like a bulletin board; rather than receive messages automatically, users get information when they visit the Usenet. There are hundreds of each kind of discussion group, on a huge variety of subjects.

What kinds of relationships do participants establish? What is the style of writing? How do participants present themselves rhetorically?

THE WORLD WIDE WEB

The World Wide Web entered the composition classroom in the early 1990s with the development of *Mosaic*, the predecessor of the Internet browsing tools Microsoft *Explorer* and Netscape *Navigator*, software that made the complex space of the Internet relatively easy to navigate and with the installation on campuses of fiber optic cable, which allowed high-speed Internet connection. The Web has offered a multitude of possibilities for composition, particularly as a rich database of information for research projects. As a source of information, the Web is both irresistible and problematic. On the one hand, it makes a vast collection of information on every subject easily available to anyone with a browser; on the other, not all this information is reliable. Regardless of whether we assign students to do Web research as a class project, students are probably going to be surfing the Net on their own, so it is a good idea to teach them how to choose and evaluate what they find there. Several Web sites have been designed for this purpose, such as "Thinking Critically about World Wide Web Resources": (http://www.library.ucla.edu/libraries/college/instruct/web/critical.htm), which pose questions for the students to consider (e.g., What is the authority behind the information? Who is the author? How up to date are the links?)[7] A helpful class assignment is to explore a few Web sites together and analyze them according to rubrics such as these. Some instructors send students on a scavenger hunt looking for 4–6 Web sites on a specified topic; or they show them how to use search engines and indexes to locate material on the topic. Afterwards, they can compare their sites and evaluate their completeness and apparent authority.

Preventing, Detecting, and Tracking Online Plagiarism

Although there is no evidence that Web-derived plagiarism is any more widespread than the traditional kind (e.g., the paper mills that operate in student residence halls), instructors are understandably concerned about the ease with which students can plagiarize, either intentionally or not. Often students lift language and information from Web sites without realizing that they need to reference these sources; other times they knowingly buy term papers from online paper vendors such as schoolsucks.com.

---

[7]A bibliography of materials on evaluating Internet resources is available at http://www.lib.vt.edu/research/libinst/evalbiblio.html/

To help them understand what plagiarism is and how to avoid it, an instructor can discuss with students sites such as "Plagiarism and the Web" (http://www.wiu.edu/users/mfbhl/wiu/plagiarism.htm) or "Cut-and-Paste Plagiarism" (http://www.lis.uiuc.edu/~janicke/plagiary.htm). To track the source of potentially plagiarized work, one can type a brief passage into a search engine such as google.com, putting the suspect passage in quotation marks.

Student Web Pages

In addition to using the Web for research, students can construct Web pages of their own: A page or set of pages can serve as a nonlinear essay on a literary work or any other topic they research. Creating a Web page can be an excellent way for students to practice researching, selecting, organizing, and focusing information; choosing an appropriate style and content for a particular audience; and establishing a consistent viewpoint on a subject. This kind of assignment also offers an opportunity to teach students how to present visual materials, a valuable skill in a world where graphic methods of communication matter as much as verbal ones. Visual literacy increasingly is being seen as essential to education at all levels. In 1997, the National Council of Teachers of English issued a statement endorsing the idea that teaching students to appreciate and create nonprint texts was essential to literacy education:

> Be it resolved, that the National Council of Teachers of English through its publications, conferences, and affiliates support professional development and promote public awareness of the role that viewing and visually representing our world have as forms of literacy. (National Council of Teachers of English, 1997)

Finally, publishing their pages on the Web also gives students a real audience other than the teacher and an incentive to make a good public impression.

Teaching students to evaluate and construct Web pages has its difficulties, however. Most composition instructors, trained in literature, linguistics, or rhetoric, are far more comfortable in a verbal medium than a visual one and may not feel they have the skills to teach Web analysis or visual literacy. And when a Web page is substituted for a traditional writing assignment, it requires new instruments for evaluation, with attention paid to links, the visual layout, and a different, nonlinear, structure. Furthermore, some class time must be devoted to teaching HTML—the language that makes a document readable on the Web—or at the very least, to using software that inserts HTML code into a document. Finding a balance between teaching technical and rhetorical skills can be tricky (Mauriello, Pagnucci, & Winner, 1999). Instructors, too, must either feel comfortable with this software or have a reliable technical consultant in the classroom. Although they may

because others on the MOO enter the class's rooms, and students visit MOO rooms other than their own.

As textual environments, MOOs are a powerful medium for writing classes: The only way to experience them is through writing. Thus, working in a MOO can help writers refine their style; users must develop verbal strategies for avoiding ambiguity, learn to convey emotion and gesture through text, ground their writing in a context, and use explanatory devices, emotes,[9] and other tools that compensate for the brevity of online discourse and the lack of face-to-face clues. In short, students are forced to write explicitly and clearly. Furthermore, when students create characters, rooms, and objects, they practice writing descriptively—using concrete, precise language and managing text in inventive, flexible ways. Even more than chat, MOOs are fun: They give students opportunities to explore and enjoy language. Serious and playful talk, and academic and personal discussion are all welcome, helping to reduce the anxiety that many students bring to first-year composition.

A MOO that has been specifically set up for teaching can function as a true online classroom. Educational MOOs provide tools such as recorders that create a printed transcript of MOO conversations, blackboards and notes that allow users to write and display information, and slides and slide projectors that allow a virtual slide show. Instructors can create virtual handouts, reserve readings in a virtual library, set up lectures with guest speakers in a virtual auditorium, assign statistical analyses in a virtual lab, and use virtual cameras, tapes, VCRs, and TV sets. Students can analyze recorded transcripts of their discussion (Day, 1996), take quizzes on virtual "notes" (Ronan, 2001), make presentations using the MOO's slide projector (Haynes, 1998), and create conversational robots ("bots") for vocabulary practice (Schweller, 1996). Although some web-based MOOs (e.g., *TappedIn*) have begun to use graphics, this is still very much a verbal world in which creating, teaching, learning, and communicating occur through words.

COURSE-MANAGEMENT SOFTWARE

Course-management software, such as *Blackboard Learning System* and *Web CT,* are web-based commercial products that provide a suite of generic tools that instructors and students can customize for their courses. These include

---

[9]An emote is a way of showing action or emotion through words.
In *Connections* MOO, if I type:

waves enthusiastically

those I'm conversing with will see:

LisaG waves enthusiastically.

There are numerous other ways to express emotion on the MOO, making it a more flexible form of expression than chat.

administrative tools, such as a grading feature that calculates a student's grade according to the value the instructor gives each assignment; a roster that allows instructors to add and drop students and keep track of each student's contribution to the course; a "dropbox," where students can submit their work; an announcements page where students and instructors can post news; and a calendar for showing the class schedule, due dates, and other events. Instructors can add content: links to other Web sites, quizzes for students to take (and instructors to grade) online, and documents uploaded from other sources—multimedia files or text (e.g., readings, student papers, exams, etc.) for students to access. These materials can be concealed and then automatically released on dates the instructor specifies. These programs also have a bulletin board for asynchronous discussion (such as e-mail) and chat rooms for real-time communication. Instructors can divide these discussion places into individual forums where small groups of students can meet, make these spaces private, so that only group members participate in or see the discussion, and organize the output of a completed discussion by subject or the name of each participant.

Advocates of these packages praise their flexibility—instructors can use as much or as little of the system as they choose and have considerable opportunities to customize both the content and physical appearance of the Web site—and their completeness, their potential to meet all a course's electronic needs, so that students and instructors don't need to acquire and learn to use several separate pieces of software (i.e., a browser, chat program, bulletin board, or grading program). Critics of course-management software deride this kind of tool as a "course in a box"; that is, they believe it is not a neutral conduit for an instructor's pedagogy, but that it molds a course toward a rigid teaching approach that discourages face-to-face contact between instructor and student, promotes lock-stop progress through a set of materials, and encourages excessive oversight over students. Course-management systems were developed primarily for large lecture classes and are often used for distance education, but many of their features (e.g., chat, customizable links) have been used successfully in face-to-face writing workshops of 15–25 students.

THE STUDY OF COMPUTERS AND COMPOSITION

Computers by themselves do not improve students' writing any more than pens, notepads, or even books do. Similarly a computer-centered pedagogy is only as effective as the instructor's composition pedagogy overall:

> Computer technology, of and by itself, does not magically change the ways in which we teach. If we believe that we should teach writing by lecture, or by oral recitation, or by large-group, offline discussion, then we will use these teaching

strategies in a computer-equipped classroom, despite the architecture and equipment of our classrooms (Klem & Moran, 1992).

What computers offer are different ways to deliver our best practices in composition teaching, many of which are described throughout this book: Pedagogy that gives students ample opportunities to write, rewrite, and talk about their writing, fosters collaboration among students, guides students while their work is in progress, supports intellectual content along with verbal proficiency, and puts the student, rather than the instructor, at the center of the course. The most effective computer-based writing instruction has been driven by research and theory in composition and rhetoric; as new technologies have emerged, practitioners have experimented to see which of them would support what we learned from composition research. Historically, the technology has been fitted to serve pedagogy, not vice versa.

But as Chris Anson has pointed out (1999), composition research may not always shape computer-based writing, as institutions feel pressure to adopt the newest technologies in multimedia, virtual reality, and distance education. Once worried about the expense of purchasing and maintaining computer labs, many schools now see the potential of technology to cut expenses. Administrators in some schools, attracted by the prospect of increasing class size without increasing resources, have requested that writing teachers teach some sections entirely over the Internet, thus calling into question the student-centered classroom, notions of a classroom community, and the relationship between student and teacher. Machine reading of student papers, once dismissed as cumbersome and unreliable, is getting a boost from new text reading computer programs seen as a solution to large class size, a problem that will increase with the anticipated growth of undergraduate enrollment throughout the first decade of this century. These programs have multiple shortcomings, and not only because they are not entirely reliable (they aren't) but also because they teach students to write to a machine, not to a human reader (Herrington & Moran, 2001).

A heavy dependence on electronic technology also increases the distance between those who have access to computers and those who do not, a difference that divides along racial and class lines. The gap between haves and have-nots concerned educators as soon as computers entered the classroom in significant numbers. This gap does not seem to have closed over time. A 1983 survey of 2209 U.S. schools conducted by Johns Hopkins University found that 66% of the affluent school districts, but only 41% of the poorest districts, had microcomputers available to their students (Janey, 1989). In 1992, the Brookings Institute reported that a child from an affluent family was twice as likely to use a computer in school as a child from a poor one (Kennedy, 1994). By the late 1990s, 73% of white students, but only 32% of African American students owned a home computer (Hoffman &

Novak, 1998). These disparities form the political climate in which we teach composition with computers, and affect decisions we make about how to deliver this kind of instruction. Charles Moran has suggested several ways to address this problem, including advocating less expensive equipment and studying the effect of technologically poor teaching environments (Moran, 1999), but like other complex problems tied to larger issues of poverty and inequity, this one may take a long time to resolve (Selfe, 1999).

Issues such as this affect the practice and theory of computers and writing. As a pedagogy and field of research, the topic of computers and composition studies addresses a wide range of concerns, among them visual literacy (Wysocki, 2000), intellectual property (Lang, 1998), gender studies (Gerrard, 1999), queer studies (Alexander, 1997), ethnic studies (Nakamura, 1995), genre (Spooner & Yancey, 1996), reading theory (Sosnoski, 1999), postmodernism (Cooper, 1999), and—as they play out in cyberspace—reconsiderations of identity (Turkle, 1995), culture (Rheingold, 2000), and even criminal behavior (Dibbell, 1998), to name a handful. It is clear that as literacy is more and more tied to computer literacy, the act of teaching writing with computers engages not only pedagogical questions but also larger social and epistemological ones.

FOR WRITING AND DISCUSSION

1. In "Beyond Imagination: The Internet and Global Digital Literacy," Lester Faigley quotes President Clinton's 1998 assertion that the Internet "has absolutely staggering possibilities to democratize, to empower people all over the world," whereas the U. S. Department of Commerce reported in 1999 that the "digital divide" between the wealthy and poor in the United States was widening. What are the implications of these apparently contradictory statements? How might it be possible to reconcile them?

2. Faigley (1998) encourages college teachers using computers to focus on learning, not on technology. What kinds of writing problems do students have, and how might you imagine using computers in ways that are not distracting, but that, instead, help students find solutions to these problems?

3. In "Like Magic, Only Real," Tari Fanderclai describes how her experience communicating on MOOs and MUDs led her to contemplate bringing this technology into her writing classes. Discuss her strategy for introducing her students to this writing strategy. What worked, what didn't work, and why?

4. Which approaches to teaching composition lend themselves well to MUDDing, and which do not?

FOR FURTHER EXPLORATION

Barker, T. (1990). Computers and the instructional context. In D. Holdstein & C. Selfe (Eds.), *Computers and writing: Theory, research, practice* (pp. 7–17). New York: MLA.

Bean, J. (1983). Computerized word processing as an aid to revision. *College Composition and Communication, 34,* 146–148.

Gruber, S. (Ed). (2000). *Weaving a virtual web: Practical approaches to new information technologies.* Urbana, IL: NCTE.

Kolko, B. (1995). Building a world with words: The narrative reality of virtual communities. *Works and Days, 13,* 105–126.

Moran, C. (1999). Access: the 'A' word in technology studies. In G. Hawisher & C. Selfe (Eds.), *Passions, pedagogies, and 21st century technologies* (pp. 205–220). Logan, UT: Utah State University Press and Urbana, IL: NCTE.

Palmquist, M. (Ed). (2000). *Transitions: Teaching writing in computer-supported and traditional classrooms.* Norwood, NJ: Ablex Press.

Sorapure, M., Inglesby P., Yatchisin, G. (1998). Web literacy: Challenges and opportunities for research in a new medium. *Computers and Composition, 14,* 409–424.

SAMPLE ASSIGNMENTS

Analyzing a Web Site That Addresses a Social Issue

1. Choose a Web site that is concerned with a social issue (e.g., censorship of the Web, AIDS research, gangbanging).

2. Divide the class into small groups to explore this site and discuss the message it communicates. Have the group respond to the following questions:
   - What is the mission of the site?
   - Who is the intended audience?
   - How would you describe the site's attitude toward its subject?
   - What are the writers worried about?
   - What social changes would they support?
   - What are some of the issues the site raises? What is the writer's stance on each issue?
   - If there are graphics, how do the visual images support or contradict the site's ideas?
   - What kinds of sites does this site link to?
   - What information does the site give, and where does this information come from?

- To what extent do you trust this information? Explain your reasons.
- Using chat, MOO, or face-to-face communication, let the groups discuss their findings with the class as a whole.

Analyzing a Short Story

Directions

1. Assign a story to the class and break the class into groups, giving each group one feature of the story to analyze.
2. Have students in each group create a brief outline of their ideas, using a word processor and an 18-point font.
3. Give each group about 5 minutes to report its findings to the class and pose questions or problems they encountered. Project their outline on a large screen as they speak.

   Group 1: Questions concerning plot.

   Group 2: Questions concerning characterization.

   Group 3: Questions concerning theme.

   Group 4: Questions concerning setting.

   Group 5: Questions concerning point of view.

   Group 6: Questions concerning irony and symbolism.

REFERENCES

Alexander, J. (1997). Out of the closet and into the network: Sexual orientation and the computerized classroom. *Computers and Composition, 14,* 207–216.

Anson, C. (1999). Teaching writing in a culture of technology. *College English, 61,* 261–280.

Apple, M. (1991). The new technology: Is it part of the solution or part of the problem in education? *Computers in the Schools, 8,* 59–77.

Barker, T. (1990). Computers and the instructional context. In D. Holdstein & C. Selfe (Eds.), *Computers and writing: Theory, research, practice* (pp. 7–17). New York: MLA.

Batson, T. (1992, May). *Findings and directions in the network-based classroom.* Paper presented at the Eighth Conference on Computers and Writing, Indianapolis, Indiana.

Bean, J. (1983). Computerized word processing as an aid to revision. *College Composition and Communication, 34,* 146–148.

Bolter, J. D. (1991). *The writing space: The computer, hypertext, and the history of writing.* Hillsdale, NJ: Lawrence Erlbaum.

Brohaugh, W. (1984). The hazards of electronic writing. *Popular Computing. 3* (131), 126–128.

Burns, H. (1979). *Stimulating rhetorical invention in English composition through computer-assisted instruction.* Unpublished doctoral dissertation, University of Texas, Austin.

Burns, H. (1984). Recollections of first-generation computer-assisted prewriting. In W. Wresch (Ed.), *The computer in composition instruction: A writer's tool* (pp. 15–33). Urbana, IL: NCTE.

Collier, R. (1983). The word processor and revision strategies. *College Composition and Communication, 34,* 149–155.

Cooper, M. (1999). Postmodern pedagogy in electronic conversations. In G. Hawisher & C. Selfe (Eds.), *Passions, pedagogies, and 21st century technologies* (pp. 140–160). Logan, UT: Utah State University Press and Urbana, IL: NCTE.

Curtis, P. (1996). MUDding: Social phenomena in text-based virtual realities. In Ludlow, P. (Ed.), *High noon on the electronic frontier: Conceptual issues in cyberspace* (pp. 347–373). Cambridge, MA: The MIT Press.

Daigon, A. (1966). Computer grading and English composition. *English Journal, 55*, 46–52.

Daiute, C. (1983). The computer as stylus and audience. *College Composition and Communication, 34*, 134–14.

Day, M. (1996). Fear and loathing in paradise: Making use of dissensus, disorientation, and discouragement on the MOO. *Kairos: A Journal for Teachers of Writing in Webbed Environments,* 2 (1). http://english.ttu.edu/kairos/1.2/coverweb/dis.html.

Dibbell, J. (1998). *My tiny life: Crime and passion in a virtual world.* New York: Henry Holt.

Elbow, P. (1973). *Writing without teachers.* New York: Oxford University Press.

Eldred, J. (1991). Pedagogy in the computer-networked classroom. *Computers and Composition, 8*, 47–61.

Engstrom, J., Whittaker, J. (1963). Improving students' spelling through automated teaching. *Psychological Reports, 12*, 125–126.

Faigley, L. (1999). Beyond imagination: The Internet & global digital literacy in *Passions, Pedagogies & 21st Century Technologies.* G. E. Hawisher & C. L. Selfe (Eds). Logan, Utah: Utah State University Press.

Fanderclai, T. L. (1996). Like magic, only real. From *Wired Women. Gender & New Realities in Cyberspace.* L. Cherny (Ed). Seattle, WA. Seal Press.

Feldman, P. (1984). Personal computers in a writing course. *Perspectives in Computing, 4*, 4–9.

Flower, L., & Hayes, J. (1977). Problem-solving strategies and the writing process. *College English, 39*, 449–461.

Gerrard, L. (1982). *Using a computerized text-editor in freshman composition.* (ERIC Document Reproduction Service No. Ed227512).

Gerrard, L. (1983). *Writing with Wylbur: Teaching freshman composition with a mainframe computer.* (ERIC Document Reproduction Service No. ED239299).

Gerrard, L. (1989). Computers and basic writers: A critical view. In G. Hawisher & C. Selfe (Eds.), *Critical perspectives on computers and composition instruction* (pp. 94–108). New York: Teachers College Press.

Gerrard, L. (1999). Feminist research in computers and composition. In K. Blair & P. Takayoshi (Eds.), *Feminist cyberscapes: Mapping gendered academic spaces* (pp. 377–400). Norwood, NJ: Ablex.

Gerrard, L., & Cohen, M. (1991). *The prewriting stacks.* San Diego, CA: Chariot Software.

Hartman, K., Neuwirth, C., Kiesler, S., Sproull, L., Cochran, C., Palmquist, M., Zubrow, D. (1991). Patterns of social interaction and learning to write: Some effects of network technologies. *Written Communication, 8* (1), 79–113.

Hayes, B. (1993). The electronic palimpsest. *The Sciences, 33* (5): 10.

Haynes, C. (1998). Help! There's a MOO in this class! In C. Haynes & J. R. Holmevik (Eds.), *High wired: On the design, use, and theory of educational MOOs* (pp. 161–191). Ann Arbor: University of Michigan Press.

Herrington, A., & Moran, C. (2001). What happens when machines read our students' writing? *College English, 63*, 480–499.

Hiller, J. H., Fisher, G. A., & Kaess, W. (1968). Opinionation vagueness, and specificity distinctiveness: Essay traits measured by computer. *American Educational Research Journal, 6*, 271–286.

Hoffman, D., & Novak, T. (1998). Bridging the racial divide on the Internet. *Science, 280,* 390–391.

Hogsette, D. (1995). Unstable conditions: Dynamics of dissent in electronic discursive communities. *Works and Days, 25* (26) 63–80.

Janey, C. B. (1989). Technology in the classroom: A chance for equity? *Equity and Choice, 5,* 32–35.

Kennedy, J. M. (1994, January 11). Ways sought to lead poor onto information highway. *Los Angeles Times,* (pp. A1, A18).

Kiefer, K. (1987). Revising on a word processor: What's happened, what's ahead. *ADE Bulletin, 87,* 24–27.

Klem, E., & Moran, C. (1992). Teachers in a strange LANd: Learning to teach in a networked writing classroom. *Computers and Composition, 9,* 5–22.

Lang, S. (1998). Who owns the course? Online composition courses in an era of changing intellectual property policies. *Computers and Composition, 15,* 215–228.

Marcus, S., & Blau, S. (1983). Not seeing is relieving: Invisible writing with computers. *Educational Technology,* 12–15.

Mauriello, N., Pagnucci, G., Winner, T. (1999). Reading between the code: The teaching of HTML and the displacement of writing instruction. *Computers and Composition, 16,* 409–419.

McDaid, J. (1991). Toward an ecology of hypermedia. In G. Hawisher & C. Selfe (Eds.), *Evolving perspectives on computers and composition studies: questions for the 1990s* (pp. 203–223). Urbana, IL: NCTE.

Murray, D. (1984). *A Writer Teaches Writing.* Boston: Houghton Mifflin.

Murray, D. M. (1978 December). *Write before writing. CCC* 29, 375–82.

Nakamura, L. (1995). Race in/for cyberspace: Identity tourism and racial passing on the Internet. *Works and Days, 13,* 181–193.

National Council of Teachers of English. (1997). On viewing and visually representing as forms of literacy. *Kairos: A Journal for Teachers of Writing in Webbed Environments, 2* (1). http://english.ttu.edu/kairos/2.1/news/briefs/nctevis.html

Nellen, T. (2000). Using the Web for high school student writers. In S. Gruber (Ed.), *Weaving a virtual web: Practical approaches to new information technologies* (pp. 219–225). Urbana, IL: NCTE.

Page, E., & Paulus, D. (1968). The analysis of essays by computer. (ERIC Document Reproduction Service No. ED028633).

Peyton, J. K. (1990). Technological innovation meets institution: Birth of creativity or murder of a great idea. *Computers and Composition, 7,* 15–32.

Rea, A., & White, D. (1999). The changing nature of writing: Prose or code in the classroom. *Computers and Composition, 16,* 421–436.

Rheingold, H. (2000). *The virtual community: Homesteading on the electronic frontier.* Cambridge, MA: The MIT Press.

Ronan, J. (2001, May). *MOOssay: Potential parameters of interpretation within a MOO essay.* Paper presented at the Seventeenth Conference on Computers and Writing, Ball State University, Muncie, Indiana.

Rose, M. (1980). Rigid rules, inflexible plans, and the stifling of language: A cognitivist's analysis of writer's block. *College Composition and Communication, 31,* 389–400.

Schweller, K. (1996). MOO educational tools. In C. Haynes & J. R. Holmevik (Eds.), *High wired: On the design, use, and theory of educational MOOs* (pp. 88–106). Ann Arbor, MI: University of Michigan Press.

Selfe, C. (1999). *Technology and literacy in the twenty-first century: The importance of paying attention.* Carbondale, IL: Southern Illinois University Press.

Slatin, J. (1990). Reading hypertext: Order and coherence in a new medium. *College English, 52,* 870–883.

Sommers, E. (1985). Integrating composing and computing. In J. Collins & E. Sommers (Eds.), *Writing on-line: Using computers in the teaching of writing* (pp. 3–10). Upper Montclair, NJ: Boynton/Cook.

Sosnoski, J. (1999). Hyper-readers and their reading engines. In G. Hawisher & C. Selfe (Eds.), *Passions, pedagogies, and 21st century technologies* (pp. 161–177). Logan, UT: Utah State University Press and Urbana, IL: NCTE.

Southwell, M. (1984). Computer assistance for teaching writing: A review of existing programs. *Collegiate Microcomputer, 2,* 193–206.

Spooner, M., & Yancey, K. (1996). Postings on a genre of email. *College Composition and Communication, 47,* 252–278.

Strassmann, P. (1983). Information systems and literacy. In R. W. Bailey, & R. M. Fosheim (Eds.), *Literacy for life.* New York: MLA.

Turkle, S. (1995). *Life on the screen: Identity in the age of the Internet.* New York: Simon & Schuster.

U.S. Department of Commerce. (1999). *Falling through the net: Defining the digital divide.* http://www.ntia.doc.gov/ntiahome/fttn99/

Vernon, A. (2000). Computerized grammar checkers 2000: Capabilities, limitations, and pedagogical possibilities. *Computers and Composition, 17,* 329–349.

Von Blum, R., & Cohen, M. (1984). WANDAH: Writing-aid AND author's helper. In W. Wresch (Ed.), *The computer in composition instruction: A writer's tool* (pp. 154–173). Urbana, Illinois: NCTE.

Walter, J. (2001). *American scholar MOO project assignment.* http://www.geocities.com/ CollegePark/1305/emerson_assignment.html/

Wresch, W. (1984). Questions, answers, and automated writing. In W. Wresch (Ed.), *The computer in composition instruction: A writer's tool* (pp. 143–153). Urbana, Illinois: NCTE.

Wysocki, A. (2000). Writing images: Using the World Wide Web in a digital photography class. In S. Gruber (Ed.), *Weaving a virtual web: Practical approaches to new information technologies* (pp. 161–175). Urbana, IL: NCTE.

Young, R. E., Becker, L., & Pike, K. L. (1970). *Rhetoric: Discovery & change.* New York: Harcourt Brace & World.

Readings

BEYOND IMAGINATION: THE INTERNET AND GLOBAL DIGITAL LITERACY

Lester Faigley

I BEGIN WITH FOUR NEWS STORIES THAT APPEARED IN NEWSPAPERS IN THE United Kingdom and Ireland during late March and early April 1996. The first story from the *Irish Times* describes a class in an isolated rural school in County Donegal that in the words of the article has "caught Internet fever" ("Drawn into the Net"). Even though the school has no computers, a first and second grade teacher, Michael McMullin, came up with the idea of teaching a unit on weather by connecting children on different continents using his home computer. McMullin identified partner schools in Alaska and Tasmania where elementary teachers had children collect weather data, and their observations were exchanged daily. Soon the children began to ask other questions. The children in Alaska wanted to know whether the water swirls down the toilet in the same direction all over the world. By comparing observations with children in Tasmania and Ireland, the children in Alaska discovered that water swirls in different directions in the Northern and Southern hemispheres. It was not long before the children began writing about other subjects, including their favorite television shows. The story ends with the teacher commenting that the project has been a good start, but the situation is far from ideal because the children are not getting hands-on experience and the school lacks funds for purchasing equipment.

The second story from *Computer Weekly* runs with the headline, "UK: A Battle for Young Hearts and Minds." It describes a large-scale give-away package to British

From *Passions, Pedagogies & 21ˢᵗ Century Technologies,* edited by Gail E. Hawisher & Cynthia L. Selfe, Utah State University Press. Logan, Utah: NCTE, 1999.

schools from Microsoft that includes software and Internet access. Mark East, a manager for Microsoft, is quoted as saying: "Microsoft does not see education as a revenue stream. We want to give children access to our products as early as possible." Until recently schools in Britain have been dominated by Acorn and Apple platforms, but the Microsoft offer is likely to direct future purchases to Intel-based computers. The article summarizes Microsoft's goals with an adaptation of the Jesuit maxim, "Give me a child of seven and I will give you a Microsoft user for life."

The third story from the *Evening Standard* concerns a television ad campaign for British Telecom office products that include Internet connections and video-conferencing (Bradshaw). The campaign runs with the slogan "Work smarter, not just harder." One of the ads depicts a bumbling male manager attempting to persuade a female secretary to stay late and type letters for a mass mailing. His inducement is an offer of cups of tea. She gently explains to him that they have a database program that can produce the letters with a simple command, and thus the commercial ends with smiles all around.

The fourth story from *The Scotsman* with the headline, "Fears of Financial Jobs Axe" begins: "Job losses in the financial services sector will rise sharply in the next three months, according to the latest survey of the sector by the Confederation of British Industry" (Stokes). It goes on to mention that huge job cuts have been announced by companies such as Barclays Bank. The results of the survey anticipate even larger cuts during the second quarter of 1996. The associate director of economic analysis for the Confederation of British Industry, Sudhir Junankar, is quoted as saying: "Firms seem determined to ease the pressure on profit margins in the current highly competitive market, and are planning to cut their costs by cutting employment and investing more heavily in information technology."

At this point you likely are thinking you have heard all these stories before set in different locations among the advanced nations of Europe, North America, and the Pacific Rim. Hundreds of articles have appeared recently about children around the world who are now connecting with other children on the Internet. Many of these articles are framed with sweeping pronouncements claiming that the Internet has become the best opportunity for improving education since the printing press (Ellsworth xxii) or even in the history of the world (Dyrli and Kinnaman 79). In spite of the hyperbole, these claims do have some justification, at least within the span of our lifetimes. According to the National Center for Education Statistics, the percentage of public schools in the United States with Internet access rose from 37% in fall 1994 to 78% in fall 1997. Schools with five or more instructional rooms increased from 25% in 1996 to 43% in 1997. And while poor and rural schools lag behind in these categories, they too have made substantial gains in connectivity. Furthermore, a little noticed provision of the Telecommunications Act of 1996 requires telephone companies to pay for wiring all schools and libraries in the United States to the Internet. By spring 1998, the Federal Communications Commission had collected $625 million to hook up

American schools and libraries with the eventual price tag expected to run much higher (Tumulty and Dickerson). If phone companies are allowed to raise rates to fund this initiative (which may be a big "if" when consumers see higher phone bills), the promise of President Clinton's Technology Literacy Challenge to connect all U.S. public schools and every instructional room (classrooms, computer labs, libraries, and media centers) to the Internet seems not only possible but inevitable.

The curiosity of the first and second graders in Michael McMullin's classroom in County Donegal suggest the potential for students creating local content and communicating worldwide. Furthermore, children connected to the Internet can use library resources on a scale that is almost beyond comprehension. Massive data bases like Lexis/Nexis offer access to thousands of periodicals, and the search tools for using these data bases are becoming increasingly easier to use. In President Clinton's words, "This phenomenon has absolutely staggering possibilities to democratize, to empower people all over the world. It could make it possible for every child with access to a computer to stretch a hand across a keyboard, to reach every book every written, every painting ever painted, every symphony ever composed." It raises the question: How does education change for a child who begins school with the potential to communicate with millions of other children and adults, to publish globally, and to explore the largest library ever assembled?

Sometimes hidden in these stories and statistics about the incredible potential of the Internet are hard facts that classroom teachers know all too well. Even though the student-to-computer ratio in American schools has risen to about 9-to-1, over half of those machines are so obsolete that they cannot be connected to the Internet. Cheap Internet access does little to help classrooms still equipped with XTs, Apple IIs, and Commodore 64s. Nearly everywhere else the situation is worse. Even in Germany, one the most technologically advanced nations in the world, the Research and Technology Minister, Juergen Ruettgers, bemoaned the fact that of the 43,000 German schools, only 500 were connected to the Internet in 1996 and only two percent of students had access to a computer in school (Boston). The ending of the County Donegal story that the school lacks funds for purchasing equipment is unfortunately the often repeated downside of children's enthusiasm for the Internet.

In rich and poor nations alike, educators are looking to the private sector to provide information networks and computers for schools. Microsoft, which now controls over eighty percent of software business worldwide, is pouring tens of millions of dollars into education. The motives of Microsoft are perhaps most clear in China, a nation that sanctions software piracy on a massive scale. Pirated copies of the latest Chinese version of Windows are sold for about five dollars before they are even announced. Nevertheless, Microsoft is spending two million dollars a year to train Chinese technicians and programmers and giving away millions more to government ministries and universities. The great irony of the massive piracy of Microsoft is that it makes Microsoft the standard with a huge base of installed customers. Microsoft figures that it will make the money back in the long run with sales of upgrades, applications, and service contracts (Engardio 1996).

The second question I want to pose is raised by the Microsoft example and its adapted slogan: "Give me a child of seven and I will give you a Microsoft user for life." Technology has brought corporate involvement in education to an extent never before seen. At a time when the level of public expenditure on education in many nations continues to decline, schools have little choice but to accept corporate support for expensive technology. Microsoft might well be commended for its largess, but the dependence on corporations to provide technology for schools is a large step toward the privatization of education. Thus my second question is: how will education be affected by the increasing presence of large corporations in making decisions about how children and adults will learn?

Finally, I want to examine the question implicit in the third and fourth news articles—the story about the ad campaign promoting the coming of digital technologies and one about corporate downsizing. Let's begin with the brutally obvious. The manager and secretary story does not have a happy ending. They are fodder for the next volley of layoffs. "Working smarter" really means cutting salaries and increasing profits.The technologically savvy secretary might be able to retrain herself, but the manager is a hopeless case. Any bean counter would identify him as a prime candidate for redundancy. The manager will be lucky to have a job drawing pints in a pub a few months from now. The question these stories present is: what sort of future will children enter in the aftermath of the massive redistribution of wealth and disruption of patterns of employment that have occurred during the last two decades?

Clearly these questions are of a scope much greater than I can address in this chapter, but I will argue that we as teachers must address them if we are to have any influence over how technology will reshape education. Times of major transition offer many possibilities as well as pitfalls, and those who can assess the terrain will be in the best positions to make convincing arguments about what roads to take. I begin with the unprecedented opportunities for education made possible by the Internet and for the moment put aside the limitations of access to equipment and willingness of teachers to enter new environments. To date there have been four primary educational functions of the Internet: communicating one-to-one, communicating in groups, publishing globally, and finding information globally.

Person-to-person communication is the most common use of computer networks big and small. The example of County Donegal is quite typical use where children exchange local information. Children learn a great deal about other countries and other cultures by communicating directly. One teacher in the United States observed: "You can't imagine how powerful it is for my kids to learn that their Malaysian counterparts speak three language, are members of a religion they never heard of, and live in a community with six racial groups" (Dyrli and

Kinnaman 79). Even more dramatic instances of one-to-one communication have occurred following natural disasters like the 1995 earthquake in Kobe, Japan, where the Internet stayed up when other lines of communications went down and the first reports came from eyewitnesses. Other major world events (e.g., the Gulf War and the fall of the Berlin Wall) have also produced vivid accounts by those on the scene.

In addition to their peers, students can communicate with members of government, professionals in various fields, and online mentors. On my campus, staff members at the Undergraduate Writing Center have been working online with students in Roma, Texas. Roma is a town with a population of about 8,500 located in the Rio Grande Valley in one of the poorest areas of the country. As part of an outreach project to introduce high school students to the expectations of college-level work, students in Roma work with consultants in the writing center who provide the students with regular online commentary on their drafts. The computers were donated to the school as part of a technology transfer program, and they are connected on a statewide network. The Roma students are enthusiastic about their online instruction and find it one of the most successful aspects of the outreach program.

The easiest and most popular way to get students started communicating online is to have them join a discussion group. Thousands of these groups exist on the Internet and on all major commercial online services. Many are specifically for children, and several others are addressed to educational and curricular issues. Besides facilitating ongoing conversions that new voices can join, network discussion groups also give many possibilities for one-to-one communication. Because individual addresses of those who post messages to discussion groups are included in the message, these individuals can be contacted one-to-one. To give one example of how students can benefit from contacting individuals, a writing instructor at Texas had his students write to individuals posting in a discussion group concerning South Africa at the time of the elections that brought Nelson Mandela to power. They were able to ask questions and obtain first-hand reports from people in South Africa.

With the development of the World Wide Web, students can now publish their work online and make it potentially available to millions of people worldwide. A typical example is Smoky Hill High in metropolitan Denver, where students have placed a virtual school on the Web. Visitors can click on click on pictures of teachers, read the parent newsletter and student newspaper, find email addresses and browse student projects. The students have also created a virtual mall where online shoppers can buy products from the student store (Bingham). There's no doubt that these and other students across the nation have put an enormous amount of effort into creating Web pages. As teachers who encourage students to publish work in print formats have found, publication itself is a strong motivating factor. Friends and parents now regularly read the work of students at all levels of education. Many of these student Websites are quite innovative in combining graphics, text, and even audio and video, taking full advantage of the multimedia capabilities of the Web.

Finally and perhaps most important, the World Wide Web already contains vast information resources. The printing press led to the widespread distribution of information, and the Web is extending that democratization, allowing anyone with an account on a Web server to become a publisher. Companies, government agencies, non-profit organizations, and individuals have been quick to publish on websites. Large libraries like those at the University of Texas have effectively put the entire reference room online along with hundreds of periodicals with full-text articles. Much information produced by the U.S. Government is available through FedWorld, extensive scientific information is on the Fisher Scientific Internet Catalog, and economic data is available on EDGAR. Conventional print publishers have also joined the rush to the Web.

Quite extraordinary kinds of learning facilitated by the Internet are happening now and no doubt will become more common in the near future. But we should remember that similar pronouncements were issued by advocates of cable television in the late 1960s and early 1970s. They envisioned two-way interactive systems that would facilitate political participation, improve education, and overcome social isolation. Seldom-viewed community-access channels are a legacy of this optimism. But as we all know the major result of cable television has been much more of the same. The Internet provides resources and opportunities for communication of a far greater magnitude than the most ambitious scheme for cable television, and therein lies the rub. Finding information on the World Wide Web has been compared to drinking from a fire hose. The quantity is overwhelming, even to experienced researchers. Finding information the World Wide Web is not magic. For those new to the Web, it is like a vast library with the card catalog scattered on the floor. You can spend hours wandering serendipitously on the Web just as you can spend hours browsing in a large library. But when you want to make a sustained inquiry, you need assistance. Libraries have very well developed tools to guide researchers. There are also powerful tools for searching the Internet, and if you want a specific piece of information such as a telephone number, a stock quote, or a train schedule, you can pull it up very fast.

But if you're looking for information that isn't so specific, such as the causes of the Cold War or the questions I began with, you will not find existing search tools nearly so helpful. Even if you can narrow down the search, you still will pull up much that isn't useful. One of the biggest problems with the Internet from a teacher's perspective is that it's not just the amount of information that is daunting to students; it's also the extreme variety. Pornography has been represented as the great danger to children who use the Internet, but a far greater danger is the amount of misinformation on the Internet. Misinformation even confounds the most literate users. Highly educated people swear to the validity of Internet-circulated urban folklore like the story of the scuba diver who was scooped out of the ocean in the water bucket of a fire-fighting helicopter and then dropped alive onto a forest fire in California.

Misinformation, of course, is a problem with print literacy also. The elaborate classification schemes of libraries, however, give many clues about the origins and reliability of information. Academic periodicals are often shelved in locations apart from popular periodicals, but such differences on the Internet are often hidden. Many discussion groups and websites purport to offer factual, neutral information but in fact contain highly biased and false information. There are Web pages that deny the Holocaust with seemingly credible references and statistics. Images likewise can be deceiving because they can be easily altered. In the past teachers have managed the information students receive by limiting the number and variety of sources. Of course, they can still impose such limitations, but at some point students need to learn how to access the vast information on the Internet and how to assess its value. Usually access is described in terms of equipment and technical skills, but information literacy will require a great deal more on the part of teachers and students. The Internet is sometimes described as a tangled information jungle, but perhaps a better metaphor is a metropolis of tribes, each with a different view of reality. Perhaps the hardest task of all is leading students to understand why the different tribes interpret reality differently.

At this point I would like to return to the issues of access I raised with my second and third questions. For those who foresee the coming the coming of a techno-utopia via the Internet, access is simply a matter of bandwidth. Expand the bandwidth by going from wires to wireless and all can communicate to their hearts' content. This vision continues a deeply embedded libertarian ideology that dates to the origins of the Internet as a Cold War project designed to maintain communications in the aftermath of a nuclear war. The ingenious solution was to flatten the lines of communication so that every node was an independent sender or receiver and messages could take any route to their destination. All that was necessary to hook up a computer to the system was a small robust set of protocols. This ease of access was celebrated in slogans like "Information wants to be free."

In fact, this vision of the Internet depended on a government-supplied communications backbone funded first by the United States Department of Defense and later by the National Science Foundation. The end of this libertarian vision of the Internet came on April 30, 1995, when the National Science Foundation unplugged its backbone and the Internet became privatized. In February 1996, the signing into law of the Telecommunications Reform Act set off a frenzy of mergers and partnerships among corporations involved in computing, communications, publishing, and entertainment—mergers that perhaps are only the beginnings of consolidation of power as the giants buy up the technology to control how we work, how we get information, how we shop, how we relax, and how we communicate with other people. The supporters of the Telecommunications Act of 1996 claimed deregulated airwaves would bring increased competition and lower prices, but to date, just the opposite has happened. The big players recognized that the biggest profits would come from the biggest market shares, and they have consolidated by merging rather than engaging in a competitive free-for-all. Prices for customers often have gone up. In November 1996 AT&T raised long-distance rates 6% for its 80 million residential customers, and some of the Baby Bells including PacTel and Bell South increased prices for high-speed ISDN Internet access.

The corporate giants are also influencing ambitious plans for higher education. Large companies such as Federal Express, Motorola, IBM, and Xerox have extensive online education programs, and state governors are looking to corporate education for models of alternatives to traditional higher education. The leaders in this movement have been Mike Leavitt, Governor of Utah, and Roy Romer, former Governor of Colorado, who have been the chief proponents of Western Governors University, that takes its name from the Denver-based Western Governors Association. Sixteen of the eighteen states in the Western Governors Association, along with Indiana, have signed on. South Dakota and California are not part of the consortium, but Pete Wilson, when he was governor, announced a similar plan for California.

Western Governors University is designed to be a virtual university without a traditional campus. Students will in enroll in courses and receive instruction online. The governors endorsed the following criteria for Western Governors University. It is to be:

- market driven, focusing on the needs of employers rather than a faculty-defined curriculum;
- degree granting, going into direct competition with community colleges, 4-year colleges and universities;
- competency-based, grounding certification on the demonstration of employer-defined competencies rather than credit hours;
- non-teaching, thus not providing direct instruction;
- cost effective, meaning that without campuses to build and maintain and large faculties to pay, it is far cheaper than traditional education;
- regional, allowing students to enroll in online courses offered at colleges and universities in any of the other states or courses offered by businesses; and
- quickly initiated, with the first associate degrees awarded in 1998.

Western Governors University is designed from an employers' perspective. Degrees from WGU are certifications of particular skills, thus in theory guaranteeing the employer that a trained worker is being hired. Companies that have contributed to WGU and sit on its Advisory Board include 3Com Corporation, AT&T, Educational Management Group (a unit of Simon and Schuster), IBM, International Thomson Publishing, MCI, and Sun Microsystems Inc. (Fahys).

One of the goals is to expand access to postsecondary education for citizens of Western states. There's no question that extensive content can be delivered by digital technologies and that it is absolutely essential for professionals in fields such as medicine, pharmacy, and engineering to have access to continuing education. But the motives of the Western governors are not solely based on expanding access. They are worried about how they will meet increasing demand for higher education when the "baby-boom echo" generation expands the traditional college age group by fifteen percent by 2008 and more adults are returning to college. This boom has been called "Tidal Wave 2," with most of the impact coming in the Western states which will see a 60% growth by 2008, in contrast to 10% in the Midwest, 21% in the Northeast, and 22% in the South (Honan).

In the late 1960s and early 1970s, in response to the surge of baby boomers, California built 42 new community colleges, 4 state colleges, and three new UC campuses. Want to bet that it will happen again? Spending on education in the Western states and especially Washington, Oregon, California, Idaho, and Nevada, is limited by voter-led tax initiatives, and elementary and secondary education is first in line for what money is available for education. In Oregon the spending on higher education has been cut by almost half in actual dollars since 1990.

The primary motive driving Western Governors University is providing higher education on the cheap. The logic is economy of scale. What can be taught to 10 can be taught to 100. What can be taught to 100 can be taught to 1,000. What can be taught to 1,000 can be taught to an infinite number.

With budgets already strained, governors and legislators are looking for cheap solutions. Online courses offered from virtual universities that do not require new buildings or faculty are going to be very popular with state legislators who want to slash faculty payrolls and abolish tenure. But if the primary motive driving distance learning is to cut costs, distance learning will be inferior learning. We've seen ambitious schemes for distance education based on economy of scale before, and they've produced a list of disappointments. You may remember Sunrise Semester, Continental Classroom, and University of Mid-America.

Not every administrator is enthusiastic about eliminating the faculty's role in teaching and defining the curriculum. Kenneth Ashworth, former Commissioner of the Texas Higher Education Board, says that Western Governors University "has enormous possibilities of harming higher education as we know it, particularly if it is largely controlled and organized to meet the demands of employers." His voice, however, is not the one of the majority.

The most immediate question for us as college teachers and administrators is how do we respond. Denial is not an option.

First, we have to keep the focus on learning and not on technology, and to do that we have to ask: What do we want students to learn? I believe we have good answers to this question. We want students to recognize and value the breadth of information available and to evaluate, analyze, and synthesize that information. We want students to construct new meaning and knowledge with technology.

We want students to be able to communicate in a variety of media for different audiences and purposes. And we want students to become responsible citizens and community members. We want them to understand the ethical, cultural, environmental and societal implications of technology and telecommunications, and develop a sense of stewardship and responsibility regarding the use of technology.

The next question is how to create the best possible environment for learning, and to answer that question, we need to query our assumptions about how people learn best. I believe that most learning is not "self-taught," most learning is not a solitary experience, and that people learn best learning with other people. From research I have read, from my experience administering a large computer-based writing program, and from ten years of teaching in networked classrooms, I offer you the following characteristics for the best possible learning environment with technology:

First, students trained in collaborative learning have higher achievement and self esteem. Even though the value of collaborative learning has been well established, many faculty still remain resistant to collaborative learning.

Second, introducing technology has made learning more student-centered, encouraged collaboration, and increased student-teacher interaction. Students who would probably not make a special trip to an instructor's office hour for a simple question will pose that question in an email message. Students likewise can work collaboratively without having to meet always face-to-face.

Third, students who use telecommunications across different geographic locations are more motivated and learn more. For one example, Wallace Fowler, professor of aerospace engineering at Texas, administers a project that joins students from historically African-American and predominantly Mexican-American colleges with students at Texas in designing actual spacecraft. He said when the project started, he feared the educational differences would be too extreme for successful collaboration, but by the end of the first year, the performance levels across institutions were comparable.

Fourth, exemplary computer-using teachers typically enjoy smaller classes and more technical support than other teachers. At Texas we have never pretended that our computer-assisted courses are cheaper than traditional courses. Instead, we have argued that our computer-assisted courses offer students opportunities that are not available traditional courses.

Fifth, teachers are more effective with training and support for integrating technology into the curriculum. While this statement seems beyond the obvious, of all the professionals who use technology, teachers are probably the most poorly supported. Training reduces anxiety and increases understanding in how to use technology.

Sixth, major change does not come overnight. I would like to end by briefly talking about my own experience. I began using mainframe computers for statistical and linguistic analyses in the mid-1970s and for word processing by the end of the 1970s. When microcomputers came on the scene in the 1980s, I like most writing teachers advocated their use because they facilitated revision. In spring 1988 I began teaching in classrooms where computers were connected in local networks. I and others have written about how these local networks led to significant changes in patterns of classroom interaction, but most of the work of students in these classes remained discussing topics which I had selected and producing essays in multiple drafts with peer reviews. If I had to plot my trajectory as a college writing teacher from my first course as a graduate assistant in 1970, I would note incremental change up to spring 1996 when I began teaching a lower-division elective course designed to give students opportunities to publish on the Internet. I had just finished teaching a practicum for new graduate student instructors, and I found myself in desperate need of a similar course. Even though I adapted most of my materials from other instructors who had taught the course before, I still spent a great deal of time preparing for the course.

Part of my difficulty was caused by shifting from essays to multimedia websites as the students' main products. I dug out books on graphic design that I had used as an undergraduate studying architecture. I went to Web publishing classes offered by my university and did independent tutorials in Photoshop. But that was only the beginning. I had to find teaching materials and figure out how to sequence activities. The biggest problem I had, however, was adjusting to a very different classroom space. We had a sense of community and we worked together well, but at the same time everything that we did involved interacting with the big world. We had throughout the semester virtual visitors from around the world who would comment on what we were doing and occasionally engage us in discussion. What I was teaching was not preparatory to interacting with the world. We were doing it from the get go.

I'm struck by the mismatch between my experience teaching with technology and visions of future of education set out in the public media and by government officials. I find the following statement nothing short of astounding:

> Academic technophobes, of course, insist that nothing will ever replace the good teacher. But even the best teacher cannot match the flexibility, the richness of resources and the ease in mastering a body of knowledge made possible by top-quality instructional software, especially for a generation often more at home on the Internet than with a textbook. (Elfin)

This quotation appeared in the lead article for *U.S. News & Word Report's* annual "Best Colleges" issue, one of the most widely read statements on higher education. I do not discount the facts that there are many academic technophobes and that many students have learned a great deal on their own by using technology. But I do not see top-quality software providing the answers for the questions I have raised nor do I see top-quality software preparing students to take active roles in public life.

Indeed, I see teachers needed more than ever before because the demands of digital literacy are greater cognitively and socially than those of print literacy. Because we have a great deal of convincing to do, I believe that teachers have to enter policy debates, even when they are not invited. We have to convince those in corporations and government and the public at large that teachers should still be allowed to determine the curriculum and be granted leadership roles in educational policy. So the downside is that we're going to have to learn a lot more and do a lot more and speak out a lot more, and we're probably not going to be directly rewarded for doing it. But if we're under-appreciated, under-loved, and underpaid, at least we're not irrelevant. And that's our big advantage in the long run.

LIKE MAGIC, ONLY REAL

Tari Lin Fanderclai

Fall 1994

The English department's tiny computer lab was packed, and at least half of the machines were taken up by my first-year composition students, all of whom were typing furiously, lines scrolling rapidly up their screens, pausing now and then to consult a handout or to scribble in a notebook. But their more obvious behaviors were giggling, poking at their neighbors, pointing to each other's screens, waving papers at each other, and talking in the tones of people who are trying to be quiet but can't quite contain themselves. I cringed a little as one of the more serious and businesslike faculty members appeared in the doorway; as manager of the computer lab, it was part of my job to see that students used our limited resources to do work for their English classes, reserving their "goofing off" for the larger, better-equipped campus computer centers. Yet there I was at the front desk with my own students having what could easily be viewed as a free-for-all while other students stood in the hallway waiting for a turn at a computer.

As the professor hesitated in the doorway, regarding the scene dubiously, one of the noisier of the crew propelled his chair across the short distance from his workstation to my desk and flopped a printout of his paper in front of me. "Hey, Tari, one of my group members from California says I should change this part of my paper," he said, and began to describe the recommended revision, clearly pleased with the suggestion, showing me how it would work and why it would be good for his essay. It was also fairly obvious that he didn't need help—he just wanted to show me the new idea, and after a couple of minutes in which he talked and I nodded a lot, he rolled back to his computer and resumed his enthusiastic typing and scribbling.

I felt a little safer—my student had demonstrated that he was indeed working. I turned to the professor, who was now standing near my desk. I could almost see her struggling to reconcile the apparent chaos before her with my student's articulate discussion of revision. Too many of us who have been trained to teach have been trained to believe that these are truths: First, that learning can be fun and a teacher should strive to make it so; and, second, that students who are having fun are not on task. And somehow the class activities we design with the first truth in mind are tempered by our belief in the second; as a result, our lessons generally hover somewhere around "more enjoyable than a dental checkup" on the fun scale. Rarely do we have to confront evidence that not only can learning be fun—it can even involve behaviors that our training tells us signal plain old goofing off. Such scenes are difficult to judge accurately—even if one has intentionally created them, the impulse is to shout for order, if only to relieve one's own cognitive dissonance.

Nervously, I began to explain: "They're using a site on the Internet to talk in real time to members of a writing class from California. We all watched the same movie and discussed it with each other online and wrote about it and then they emailed their papers to each other and now they're discussing revisions with their group members . . ." I trailed off awkwardly and went to work on the damaged disk the professor had brought with her, salvaging her files, and, I hoped, some of my reputation. In the back of my mind was the thought that maybe she'd be so relieved that her work was safe she'd forget to report to the director of composition that I was down in the computer lab encouraging bedlam.

For the chaos was necessary. My students were MUDding.

Spring 1993: The Beginning

As usual, I had stayed far too late in the computer lab, where I taught writing, administrated the network, and managed miscellaneous daily operations of the lab. I had gone in a short time from technophobe to computer addict, and I'd taken to staying long after the lab was closed. Free from users with questions and printers with paper jams, I could read manuals and tweak the network and subscribe to way too many electronic discussion lists. Recently a posting on one of those discussion lists had mentioned MediaMOO,[1] which I later discovered was a MUD operated by Amy Bruckman at Massachusetts Institute of Technology as a space for media researchers to meet and talk and collaborate with geographically distant colleagues. At the time, I knew only that a few members of a discussion list for writing teachers who use computers in their classrooms had discovered a place on the Internet where they could talk to each other in real time.

Curious, I entered the telnet address for MediaMOO and followed the directions on the welcome screen to connect to a guest character. Just like that, I was in the Lego Closet, wearing the suit of the Violet_Guest. The description of the Lego Closet reminded me of the descriptions of rooms in the text-based adventure games I was fond of, and with no better clues to go on, I tried a few of the commands from those games, pleased when they worked.

I discovered how to look around, move from room to room, and consult the online help. Shortly, I wandered into a room called the TechnoRhetorician's Bar and Grill. The room contained, among other things, a buzzword generator that when cranked emitted strings of buzzwords in nearly sensible order; a bartender who claimed to make good coffee; a boat you could really board; and several people whose names I recognized from the discussion list where I'd gotten MediaMOO's address.

I joined the conversation, a continuation of a topic that had come up that day in an asynchronous electronic forum most of us were using in conjunction with the annual Computers and Writing Conference taking place that week. Typical "newbie," I also examined and played with everything in the room. I cranked the generator over and over. I ordered all manner of things from the bartender just to see the ordered item appear in the list of things I was "carrying." I wrote on a bulletin board and petted a dog. I followed a few other characters on a tour of various areas of the MOO, fascinated with the various rooms and objects and their descriptions. I found out where to download everything from basic instruction sheets, to the MOO programming manual, to a client that would improve my interface with the MOO. After nearly two hours, I disconnected reluctantly.

The following day I obtained my own character for MediaMOO. Over the next few weeks, I obtained characters at other MUDs, and learned to build and program simple rooms and objects. And I kept returning to places like the TechnoRhetorician's Bar and Grill—spaces where those with similar interests tended to gather. For, though the virtual environment and the rooms and objects were fascinating, the main attraction for me was the ability to talk in real time to people who shared my interests. In "real life," I was at the time somewhat isolated: My department had just acquired its computer lab and network, and the school had gained Internet access relatively recently. While I was fascinated with the relationship between computers and writing instruction, as well as with the computers themselves and the resources accessible through my Internet account, most of my colleagues had other interests entirely. Many lacked the time or the inclination to learn about computers and the Internet; many were self-proclaimed technophobes and Luddites, some of them frankly alarmed at the presence of so many computers in their midst.

Though a fair number of instructors soon became competent users and made innovative uses of the capabilities of the local network in the writing classes they taught, not even a handful of them understood what I was up to alone in the lab all those nights, and fewer still ever became interested enough to join me. I soon learned not to talk much about my work or my discoveries. Trying to explain something I was excited about to someone whose eyes were glazing over was too disappointing. I often missed the sense of community I'd felt when doing work that my colleagues were interested or involved in.

Asynchronous electronic forums—discussion lists, newsgroups, bulletin boards associated with professional conferences, and so on—relieved some of my isolation, but a few key factors kept most of those forums, especially those populated by academics, from providing me with more than a superficial sense of belonging. Posters in such forums generally sign their names, with titles and affiliations—certainly a legitimate practice, but one that often helps to draw lines between the "big people" and the "little people" using the forum. It is sometimes painfully clear whose posts are to be valued and whose are to be ignored. The exchange is more like a correspondence than a conversation—members read

basic netiquette and the particular conventions of WriteMUSH. And they'd need time to get comfortable in the MUD before we asked them to work together. So, about the third week of the fall term, my classes made their first trip to WriteMUSH. We had read WriteMUSH's policies, and I'd explained the general etiquette of the place, but I knew they'd just have to get in there and look around before any of it made sense. I gave them a handout on how to get connected, get their characters described, and walk around and talk to each other, and then let them proceed at their own pace while I walked around the room helping. It was, of course, chaotic: Some students were frustrated, others were unimpressed; some seemed mildly interested, and still others stayed long after class. By the time the lab closed that day I'd already talked with a student who was certain he couldn't stand this "MUSH thing," and I'd printed sections from the MUSH programming manual for two students who wanted to learn to make their own objects (something I didn't require, but certainly encouraged among those who were interested).

We spent some more class time just practicing and playing and talking through students' questions about MUSH commands, social conventions, and so on. At this point, they did not have a formal assignment; as learning to use a MUD requires quite a bit of problem solving, I simply relied on the MUD to provide us with whatever lessons we needed. After a few days, we went on to work more specifically on the possibilities and problems of communication and discussion in a MUD. I saved the logs of our first few online discussions and put them in a shared directory on our network; we used them not only to remember what we'd come up with in the discussions, but also to examine what happens when facial expressions, tone of voice, gestures, and other elements of physical presence are removed from a conversation. Already many students were drawing conclusions about effective communication, and, as we worked, we developed strategies for keeping online discussions focused, making sure we understood each other, and so on. Many of the students found they enjoyed the free-flowing, rapid exchange of ideas on the MUD, and within a few days they were so good at online discussion that we had to break into small groups using different rooms on the MUD to keep the conversation from scrolling by so fast that no one could read it.

Just using the MUD among ourselves proved a valuable complement to our real-life discussions, for the altered environment and the comfort of being somewhat anonymous (I had invited them to choose whether to use their own names and whether to identify their characters to the rest of the class) encouraged a number of students who were silent in face-to-face discussions to contribute to the online conversations. Some of the students who seemed more willing to talk on WriteMUSH commented to me privately that when they talked online, they felt as if they were being listened to according to what they said rather than according to how they looked, how they sounded, whether they were male or female or black or white and so on. For example, two students who were not native English speakers remarked that they liked having a place to communicate where they didn't have accents; a few female students said they felt they were taken more seriously online; and a student athlete told me he was less afraid of being taken for a "dumb jock" when those he was talking to couldn't see him.

Not everyone was enjoying the experience, of course. Some said they felt silly typing to people who were right there in the room. Others complained that the MUD environment favored fast typists. But I pointed out that soon we'd be talking to people we couldn't talk to any other way, and I offered them a shareware typing tutor, and they agreed to humor me a little longer.

By this time, we were beginning to think about two categories of issues: the usefulness of MUDs as work spaces, and the differences between meeting people and communicating with them online and in person. So, for our first real project, I gave them a chance to explore those further. I invited my Netoric Project partner, Greg Siering, to meet with my students online. I told them a bit about Greg and the work we'd done together, and I asked them to prepare questions for him both about how he felt MUDs were important to his work and about the differences between MUD communication and other kinds of writing and talking. Greg told them about several projects he was working on with people he hadn't yet met except online, recounted some of his experiences with communication and miscommunication, explained some of the conventions MUDders use for making themselves clear (for example, typing :-) to represent a smiling face so that others know you're kidding), and recounted some of his experiences meeting people he already knew well online.

Following their session with Greg, I asked the students to start drafting a paper on what learning to communicate on WriteMUSH had brought to their attention about other, more familiar kinds of communication. Their discoveries included realizing how dependent they were on giving and receiving physical cues during a conversation, how disconcerted they were when they didn't know the age or gender of the person they were talking to, and how seemingly little things like punctuation can make a big difference in whether your audience understands what you intended.

A few days later, after they'd had a chance to think about what Greg had discussed with them and about the perceptions they were forming themselves, Greg drove down from Ball State to Louisville and joined my classes in person. As he continued discussing their questions with them, they were able to compare the online and in-person experiences as well as think about the differences between a person's online voice and persona and that person's real-life presence. Later I asked them what they'd expected Greg to be like. Several had thought he'd be older than he was, and pointed to places in the log of our online discussion where the way Greg had phrased his points made them think of "some old college professor with a pipe and one of those jackets with elbow patches." One student confessed that he'd pictured "a big fat greasy guy" because Greg had mentioned he was eating junk food while talking to us. By getting them to talk about such seemingly trivial misperceptions, I got the students to think about how much our communications with others are influenced by factors about that person's physical presence—so much so that when we don't have those details, we might be tempted to make them up on the basis of very little evidence.

The students' experiences talking with Greg online and in class proved valuable in several ways: They came to understand more about why we were MUDding in the first place; they were able to think more concretely about factors that influence communication and make it effective or ineffective; and they saw how a person's written words affect how that person is perceived—a point that both made them aware of the power of words to create, and gave them a healthy skepticism about what others created with words. I was impressed with the papers they wrote as a result of their initial experiences using WriteMUSH. Not only did they discuss in detail their observations about voice, tone, style, persona, context, and so on; many of them were also able to articulate ways they could apply what they'd learned to their writing and other kinds of communication. I was eager to see what would happen when we began to work with other classes.

We had already begun to exchange email with our distant classmates, introducing ourselves and working out discussion groups. One of my classes formed small groups with members of Nikki's composition class, and the other with members of Paul's introductory film class. The members of each combined class viewed a film that we would talk and write about. Nikki and I had chosen *House of Games,* and the class working with Paul's group watched *Roger and Me.* The members of each discussion group had three tasks: to use WriteMUSH and email to discuss the movie, to prepare a discussion of a topic assigned to their group and give a short oral presentation to the members of their respective real-life classes, and to exchange drafts of their papers by email and use WriteMUSH and email to give each other feedback on those drafts. We explained their goals and deadlines, but after making some suggestions about possible ways of getting things done, we left it to individual groups to work out their methods and to schedule their meetings on their own time. They could, of course, ask us for help, but we required only that each group report to us periodically on the progress it was making. This plan gave students more control over and responsibility for the collaboration, and let them experience the convenience and challenges of collaborating online.

We'd expected to have to prod people to keep up with their groups, and we did, occasionally. But mostly they prodded themselves and each other; most students took seriously the responsibility to keep up their individual contributions to their groups. Nikki, Paul, and I watched in frank amazement as students made plans, worked out schedules and solved problems; late one afternoon I logged onto MediaMOO to meet with Nikki and found her so pleased that I was sure she was actually hopping around in delight. Several groups of our students had problems that morning—WriteMUSH had been inaccessible for part of the morning, and the students also had difficulties getting email to each other (they'd made some errors using their respective mail systems, and already disconcerted by the difficulties getting to WriteMUSH, they'd had a hard time figuring out what went wrong). But instead of walking away empty-handed and blaming their problems on technical difficulties, they'd stuck it out, doing what work they could with their on-site group members and poking at the mail and the MUD periodically until they'd gotten in contact with their virtual classmates.

Nikki and I discussed what might have contributed to their willingness to solve their problems instead of taking the easy way out. Most students seemed to be enjoying MUDding and working together, and that was no doubt a motivator. In addition, that the project trusted them to work out their own methods and schedules for meeting goals and that they were responsible to people outside their own onsite classes seemed to contribute to their willingness to work out the difficulties. Given the environment we were using, there was no way for a teacher to check up on or impose control over the work they were doing; they knew that all we could do was wait for their progress reports and their products. I think that knowing they had a lot of freedom and the responsibility to use it wisely and efficiently caused them to take charge in a way they might not have in a situation where the teacher could stand over them and watch as they worked.

Students seemed to transfer those "taking charge" skills to other work in the class as well. The kinds of daily plans I was used to making were increasingly unnecessary for those classes—they much preferred to know what their goals were, what they were supposed to produce, and when they had to have it done, and to tell me what they needed to do on a day-to-day basis. They seemed far less likely than most students in my experience to bring excuses rather than work to class; if they encountered a problem in one method of getting a job done, they used another.

As I'd hoped, students in both of my classes reported that discussion with people outside their on-site classes helped them to see the film they'd watched from more than one perspective and to strengthen their own interpretations. Small classes often develop their own identities as communities, a desirable condition for a writing class, since students become more comfortable sharing their writing and working on collaborative assignments. But, like any community, the class members can also develop a shared general outlook, thus seeing only a small set of possible views on a given issue and coming rather quickly to what they consider the end of the discussion. Often they agree so thoroughly on their points that by the time they're asked to write about them, they complain there isn't anything to say that everyone doesn't already "know." Having their views expanded, challenged, and sometimes changed by their virtual classmates meant they were not so quickly satisfied (and bored) with their initial answers and solutions, and many of them carried the habit of looking at issues from unfamiliar angles with them throughout the rest of the term.

The class that worked with Paul Bowers' film class got an especially good example of the usefulness of being able to exchange ideas and information. Paul and his students gave us an introduction to looking at a film from a film studies point of view—something I couldn't give them myself. When it came time to write papers, my students got their chance to be the experts, taking charge of the draft exchange, giving useful advice about writing to their virtual classmates and showing them how to make useful comments on others' writing. Paul and I both felt that the quality of thinking and writing in the *Roger and Me* papers was in many cases exceptional, and the students attributed some of their success to the opportunities they'd had to benefit from each other's areas of expertise.

Paul, Nikki, and I found that many of our students began to think of WriteMUSH as both a playground and a resource. I often found students online building and programming, activities that I think enhanced their problem-solving skills and their willingness to be self-sufficient. Indeed, I occasionally found myself biting my lip to keep from laughing as one student would ask a question and another would say, "Look it up in the help . . . think I'm gonna spoon-feed you?" Other times, I found students on WriteMUSH deep in discussion about a topic or assignment from one of their other classes, getting ideas and input from others. As one student put it, "It helped to kick the movie around with people from outside, so I thought I'd try it for this history paper."

Figuring Out What We Learned

Of course, not everyone was thrilled about using WriteMUSH, and not everything went smoothly. For Nikki and Paul and me, one of the most fascinating and difficult parts of the project came when we tried to evaluate it. We all agreed that we'd met many of the goals we'd begun with and that many of our students had learned more than we'd hoped. But actually pinpointing successes and failures proved almost impossible. Each time we started to say, "Well, here's a part of the plan that worked," we reminded each other that that part of the plan had undergone many spontaneous changes as our students negotiated with us and with each other; each time we started to say, "Here's a part of the plan that bombed," we reminded each other of something the students had learned as they worked through the problems created by some shortsightedness in the original plan.

I think now that the main reason we had a hard time deciding whether or not those collaborations were successful is simply that we were working in such an unfamiliar way in such an unfamiliar environment. We'd placed students in a situation where they were in charge of their learning, putting in their hands many of the decisions about how to get to their goals. We'd encouraged them to build the same kind of community we felt ourselves a part of: a community of people working and learning and negotiating on an equal footing with each other. Our experiences with those communities fortunately held us back during the project when our conventional notions about what teachers are supposed to do threatened to control our actions; when one of us wanted to plan too rigidly or to interfere with a group that wasn't doing things the way we would do them, we reminded each other of the chaotic nature of our own online meetings and collaborations—the silliness, the arguments on the way to compromise, the fits and starts, the odd and unconventional ways we sometimes got from Point A to Point B. Yet for all that, when we tried to evaluate what we'd done, we found ourselves again using our old ways of thinking: We were trying to evaluate the project in terms of what we'd taught our students.

But the truth was that we hadn't taught them anything. Certainly we'd set initial goals and made the initial plan. But the students made the decisions about how to meet the goals, and they made many changes in the original plans; and as they worked they taught themselves and each other. To evaluate the experience, we had to think about what students had learned and how the entire situation, created by us and by the MUD environment, and modified by the students as they worked, had contributed to what they'd learned. The most important things we learned to do as teachers were to set clear goals, give students a variety of tools and skills to use in meeting those goals, and get out of the way while they worked through the problems on their own. Plans that didn't work and other difficulties that arose did not necessarily signify failures; when we let the students change the plans as needed and solve the problems in ways that worked for them, those would-be failures became useful learning experiences.

And thus I discovered one of the biggest values of MUDs to education. Many of us would like to create in our classrooms an environment where people can work the way that suits them best, where students have power and freedom and responsibility, where students actually take charge of their learning and develop skills they see the usefulness of and can transfer to other areas. But most teachers and students bring baggage to class that's difficult to get rid of, especially if the class is in the typical classroom at a typical school. For example, a common way of attempting to reduce the perception of teacher as authority and to put class members on equal footing is to arrange the chairs in a circle or around a table. Conventions die hard, though, and more often than not, everyone ends up directing most of their remarks to the teacher, who ends up asking most of the questions and prodding the discussion along. Given choices about how to proceed toward some goal, students often do nothing. They aren't used to making their own decisions, and they know that if they make none, the teacher will take over.

The MUD environment, however, can provide a place to shake many of the conventions of traditional education. As Nikki and Paul and I discovered, when students have a list of goals and a variety of tools they can use to meet them, and when they are placed in an environment the teacher really cannot control, the rewards are many—and sometimes unexpected.

It still isn't easy; placed in a new environment, our tendency is to look for—or create—what is familiar and comfortable, often without stopping to consider what benefits the new environment might offer as is. Certainly a MUD room can be programmed to simulate a real life classroom; in fact, in some ways it can control students better than a traditional classroom. In a face-to-face encounter, a teacher can only ask for cooperation; in a carefully programmed MUD room, the teacher can enforce, say, a request for silence by typing a command that makes it impossible for anyone to speak without being called on. Such MUD environments exist, and they perpetuate many of the other conventions and limitations of traditional education as well. You can find faithful reproductions of the typical university on any number of MUDs, complete with separate buildings for each discipline, offices for teachers, and various disciplinary bodies that spend most of their time thinking up horrible things students might do and then writing elaborate programs to stop them from doing those things (and never mind that no student thought of such a behavior before hearing there was a specific program written to prevent or punish it).

It seems to me that such MUDs cater mostly to those who want to affect innovation and novelty while maintaining the traditional authority and control of the teacher. Indeed, it is always easier to introduce a new gadget than to adopt a new philosophy. I submit, however, that little is to be gained by taking students to an online representation of a conventional classroom. I would instead encourage teachers to look at MUDs as they are: full of creativity and cleverness, playfulness and magic; brimming with multithreaded, free-flowing conversations and interesting people with various areas of expertise, and chock-full of opportunities to collaborate and invent problems and solve them. And I would ask teachers to think of ways to exploit those inherent characteristics of MUDs—not to try to override or control them. Given the chance, students make the most of alternative learning opportunities. All teachers need to do is get cut of the way more often.

Forward

Since that first online classroom experience, I've brought a number of classes to various MUDs for a variety of purposes. All have been educational experiences; many have been great fun, and some have quite frankly flopped. Often I've been pleased by the students' accomplishments, a number of which went far beyond my expectations. The Netoric Project continues, and we've hosted many successful events. I'm administrating an educational MUD where I've been given the resources and freedom to put my ideas about educational MUDding into practice. MUDding is a part of my daily work and play.

In the last couple of years I've watched the mushrooming of educational MUDs, and I've engaged in heated arguments about what kinds of educational activities MUDs are and aren't good for; indeed, I have ranted repeatedly about the uselessness of delivering a lecture in what is designed to be an interactive environment, and the irony of programs that silence people in an environment that can let everyone talk and be heard at the same time, and the silliness of separating disciplines into different buildings in an environment that could blur traditional distinctions and let us learn from all those various perspectives, and . . . well, the list goes on and on.

But I'm always ranting about the same thing. Near the end of the term, in one of those very first classes I introduced to MUDding, one of the students wrote, "It's like magic, only real, and you can figure it out and learn stuff from it that you weren't even trying to get." Later, as we talked about her paper, she pointed to that sentence and remarked, "Ugh, that's awful."

"I dunno," I said. "I like it. I think I want to remember it." She looked puzzled, then less so; then she laughed, bracketed the sentence, and handed me that page from her printout.

I still have it.

Endnote

1. MediaMOO is a MUD; MUD stands for "Multi-User Domain." MediaMOO is a MOO, which is a kind of MUD; MOO stands for "MUD, Object-Oriented." Other kinds of MUDs include MUSH, MUCK and MUSE. Although there are differences among the various kinds of MUDs, the basic idea is the same: Users connect to the MUD using telnet or any of various MUD clients. Each user connects to his or her own character (some MUDs provide guest characters for users who have not yet obtained characters of their own). Using those characters, users can move around the various rooms on a MUD, talk to other users, and interact with the various objects on the MUD. Everything a user sees on a MUD is presented in text; for example, when the user moves his or her character into a room on a MUD, he or she is presented with a text description of the room. On many MUDs, users are able to add their own rooms and objects to the MUD.

Appendix 1

Developing Effective
Writing Assignments

WRITING ASSIGNMENTS

Well-constructed writing assignments maximize the possibility for effective student writing. Therefore, it is extremely important that composition instructors devote sufficient time to developing thoughtful assignments. This section provides some suggestions for constructing and presenting quality assignments in terms of purpose, structure, audience, and sources of information.

DEVELOPING EFFECTIVE WRITING ASSIGNMENTS

Writing assignments work best when they are carefully planned, discussed thoroughly in class, and segmented into various components. The following are suggestions for developing effective assignments:

1. Introduce the topic for a writing assignment in class using exploratory writing or discussion questions, if possible.

Be sure to explain the topic carefully. Do not simply hand-out an assignment in class, or, worse, scribble the assignment on the board at the end of class.

2. Have students write responses to exploration questions.

Exploration questions enable students to become aware of what they already know or believe about the topic. They can respond to these questions either in class or at home. If there is time, students can share responses in groups.

Example exploration questions:

When you were growing up, what experiences did you have with this topic?

To what extent was the topic discussed in your home?

To what extent was the topic discussed in your high school?

Describe your feelings about this topic.

Do you think this topic is important for students to understand or explore? Why or why not?

3. Assign an initial reading(s) concerned with the topic. Students then summarize the content of these readings and/or write a response.

To use readings as springboards for writing, assign two articles on the topic, each presenting a different perspective. In preparation for class discussion, students should summarize and respond to these essays. Indicate to students that this component of the assignment will count toward the final grade.

Example assignment using summary and response:

Read Professor X's essay on the topic. In one or two paragraphs, summarize Professor X's perspective and indicate why you think that perspective is important to understand. In a second paragraph, discuss the extent to which you agree with that perspective.

Read Professor Y's essay on the topic. In one or two paragraphs, summarize Professor X's perspective and indicate why you think that perspective is important to understand. In a second paragraph, discuss the extent to which you agree with that perspective.

4. Have students create a short annotated bibliography.

Locate _____ additional articles on this topic from the (library, Internet, etc.). These articles might support the positions of Professors X and Y, take a more moderate position, or present a different position. Create an annotated bibliography in which you summarize the main positions of these articles.

5. Present the assignment in writing.

Here is an example you can use as a model. Include the following sections: background, writing task, requirements, schedule of activities and due dates.

Background:

The topic of _____ has increasingly attracted public attention, generating considerable debate among scholars. One perspective, presented in the essay by Professor X, maintains that _____.

Presenting another perspective, however, Professor Y, maintains that
_____. Moreover, other scholars, presenting less extreme
positions, have argued that _____. (Elaboration depends on the
complexity of the topic.)

Writing Task:

Consider the perspectives of both Professor X and Professor Y on the
topic of _ and those expressed in the additional articles you have
obtained. Then, in a well-organized essay of _____ pages, develop
and support a position on the topic of _____.

Requirements:

Keep in mind that this assignment requires you to develop and
support a **position**—that is, a thesis or main point that you support
throughout the essay. You should not simply summarize various
perspectives on this topic although you should acknowledge the
positions of Professors X and Y as well as those of the additional
articles you have located.

Schedule of activities and due dates:

Exploration questions due__.

Reading, summary, and response due__.

Annotated bibliography due__.

One paragraph overview due__.

Bring a paragraph to class in which you summarize the position
you plan to support in your essay. (Depending on time
constraints, students can hand these in to the instructor, or read
them aloud in small groups.)

First polished draft due__. (Depending on time constraints, the
instructor can make comments, but not assign a grade.)

Final draft due. (This is assigned a grade.)

PROBLEMS STUDENTS HAVE WITH ASSIGNMENTS

The following is a list of problems students typically have in understanding
the requirements of their assignments:

1. Students are often unaware of the necessity of having a thesis.

Students are often unaware that the assignment requires a thesis,
position, or main idea that is developed and supported throughout the
essay. As a result, they simply respond literally to the questions in the

assignment prompt without focusing their essays around a central point. For example, when students are asked to "compare and contrast" two articles on a given subject, they simply discuss one article, then the other, without realizing that they are supposed to be deriving a main point or perspective that will structure the essay as a whole. Similarly, if the assignment uses the word "describe," students assume that description is an end in itself, whereas the professor may conceive of description as a mode of presentation used to support a thesis.

2. Students often do not understand the role of definition in academic writing.

In working with assignments, students may not understand that definition can be used to provide a context for discussing other facets of the topic. For example, in a prompt that asks students to consider the extent to which television could be considered "harmful" to society, it is necessary for students to establish what they mean by "harmful."

3. Students are often confused by an assignment that asks a lot of questions. Instead of synthesizing the prompts into a central question, they attempt to answer each one separately.

Here is an assignment that asks a lot of questions

> *In the popular television show* Star Trek: Deep Space Nine, *what do the writers and producers wish to suggest about society? Do the different races of aliens have analogous groups in our contemporary society? What image does the show provide of law enforcement? Of racial tendencies? Of moral leadership? What ethical message does the show give its viewers?*

4. Students will often write a bifurcated response to an assignment with a double focus.

A question such as "Is the political correctness movement helpful or harmful to a college campus and should the rules regarding political correctness be changed?" is likely to lead to a double answer.

5. Students often do not know how to narrow an unfocused or vague assignment prompt.

A prompt that asks students to "discuss political correctness" on campus is likely to generate description and perhaps many examples, but little analysis.

TO HELP STUDENTS UNDERSTAND A WRITING ASSIGNMENT

1. Read the assignment aloud in class as students follow along. Do not simply hand-out the assignment and assume that students will study it on their own.

2. Point to key terms in the assignment that explain what students must do to write the paper. Encourage students to circle these terms.

3. Define the nature of the writing task that the assignment requires. If the paper requires a main point or thesis, provide a few examples. Caution students about latching onto a thesis too soon, before they have had time to explore the topic adequately. Explain that ideas change through the process of reading and writing.

4. Clarify terms, such as "discuss," "explicate," "trace," "examine," "analyze," that students may not understand in the context of a writing assignment

5. Discuss potential sources of information for the paper. Will the information be based primarily on personal experience or opinion? Should students locate information from the library or the Internet?

6. Clarify any implicit requirements that may not be directly stated, but are necessary for the assignment to be completed satisfactorily. For example, many college writing assignments require students to define terms, consider questions of degree, or establish a relationship between ideas.

7. If possible, identify a possible audience or audiences for this paper aside from the teacher who gave the assignment. Explain that although the teacher is, of course, going to read the paper, many college essays are written for what is ambiguously termed a "general audience." To help the students understand this concept, have them imagine that the paper has been left on a desk in the college library and read by another student. Would this student be able to understand the paper without having access to the assignment? What sort of background information on the topic is this unknown college student likely to have? What sort of information needs to be included in the paper in order for a general audience to understand it?

A useful strategy for enabling students think about audience is to have them respond to the following questions:

Before the people in my audience have read this paper, they are likely to think

_____

about this topic.

After the people in my audience have read this paper, I would like them to think

_____

about this topic.

COMPONENTS OF A WRITING ASSIGNMENT

Assignment #5 Changing the Law

Purpose: To formulate a thesis concerning a law that you think should be changed.
To support that thesis with convincing reasons.
To provide development and support for your ideas.
To demonstrate your understanding of essay structure.

Goals of the assignment are made explicit

Readings: At least three short readings that you find online.
These must be brought to class

Readings specified

Background:

A context is set for the assignment.

This assignment requires you to choose a law that exists today at the federal or local level that is currently enforced but which you believe needs to be changed. Examples can include seatbelt laws, helmet laws, drinking laws, voting laws, drug laws, cigarette laws, speed limit laws–the list is inexhaustible–but whatever you choose, it should be something that interests you, something with which you have some personal experience.

To help you develop ideas and prepare the background section of your paper, find out as much as you can about this law by answering the following questions:

Questions to generate thinking are included. But these are part of the __preparation__, not necessarily questions that must be answered within the essay itself.

Why was this law passed in the first place?
When was it passed?
Who was in favor of its passage and who was against it?
Who is most affected by it?
Who benefits from it?
What purpose did it originally serve?
Is it outdated/ Why?
What is wrong with it as it stands now?
How would society benefit if it were changed.

Writing Task:

Once you have learned as much as you can about this law, respond to the following question in a well-argued essay:

To what extent should this law be changed?

This essay will be constructed as an academic argument and therefore should be well-reasoned, supported with logic based evidence, and balanced through the inclusion of a counter-argument. Preparation for this paper must include brainstorming, a fact-idea list, and a points to make list. It should be oriented toward a general, academic audience and will be evaluated according to the grading rubric for this course.

The writing task is specified, isolated in a bolded prompt. It is desirable to have a short prompt.

Students are reminded of the type of essay this assignment requires. Audience and grading rubric are specified.

Appendix 2

Developing a Syllabus

The syllabus for your writing course serves as a contract between you and your students. It describes as comprehensively as possible the focus and structure of the course, explains course policies, and indicates responsibilities students will have to fulfill. Although many elements of syllabus will be dictated by the requirements of your program or department, your syllabus will reflect your personality as a teacher and orientation toward the teaching of writing. It is, therefore, important to reflect on what sort of persona you want to project and the philosophy of writing and writing pedagogy you want to endorse. When you distribute the syllabus, be sure to go over it carefully in class. Do not assume that students will read it at home.

Necessary components of a syllabus are listed here:

1. **Course number and contact information.**
   These include course number; classroom location; class meeting time; and instructor's name, phone number, office location, e-mail address, and office hours.

2. **Textbook Information.**
   These include author, title, publisher, edition, and any supplementary information included in the assigned readings.

3. **Overview of course and rationale.**
   This includes an overview of the course, and an explanation of its goals and the theoretical underpinnings on which they are based. Indicate how you are planning to structure the course, focusing on your primary concern of helping students develop an effective writing process and acquire a writing style appropriate to an intended audience. If you are planning to incorporate computers

into your course, provide a rationale for doing so and a schedule for helping students learn to use them.

4. **Requirements and policies.**
   Requirements include the number of essays students will be writing, the necessity for submitting multiple drafts, and other required elements such as in-class exercises, homework activities, journals, class list serves, and portfolios. Explain the format and style you require for written work; your grading policies; and your attitude toward class and group attendance, tardiness, and late papers. Be sure to address the issue of plagiarism.

5. **Additional information.**
   This might include the location of a Writing Center or services available for the disabled or handicapped.

6. **Course calendar.**
   Indicate in detail what is required for each class: readings, responses, activities, presentations, conferences, due dates for papers—including first, second, and third drafts, and portfolio submissions. Although it is important to prepare your course in advance, feel free to alter it according to the needs of your students. However, it is important to structure the submission of major essays.

The syllabi included in this section were constructed for the first-year writing course at California State University, Northridge, which focuses on academic argument.

Welcome to English 155: Freshman Composition Fall 2001

"The writer is an explorer. Every step is an advance into a new land"
Ralph Waldo Emerson.

Instructor: A   **Ticket #:** 61078
Time: MWF 8:00–9:00   **Office**: JR 219
Location: M: JR 201   **Office Hour**: M 9:00–10:00
          W: JR 248 (Lab)   **Phone**:
          F: JR 201/248   **Email**:
          (alternating Fridays in Lab)

Required Texts
Writing About Diversity, Irene L. Clark, 2nd Edition
The Writer's Harbrace Handbook, Brief Edition
Wings, 8th Edition, a collection of CSUN student essays.

Required Materials

At least 1 IBM formatted diskette

2 Bluebooks (available in the Matador Bookstore)

1 folder with 2 pockets (Don't throw anything away-you will need it for your protfolio!)

Course Description and Objectives

English 155 is a course that will prepare you for scholarly writing at the university level. You will learn and practice exploring ideas, conveying information, thinking critically about ideas in published works, and adopting a meaningful position on complex and controversial issues. You will also develop organizational and structural skills in the forming of an essay, creating a thesis and researching support to serve as evidence of an argument. Beyond these elements, you will find your own writing style, and develop it in an academic manner.

Course Requirements

Described below are the major assignments that will be required throughout the semester. Assignments are due on the date given. **NO LATE PAPERS WILL BE ACCEPTED!** Any assignments not turned in will result in a substantially lowered grade.

- 23-5 page major essays (ME) which will be multiply drafted, with topics based on class discussions, activities, assignments and readings **(10 points each)**.
- 24-6 page major essays (ME) which also will be multiply drafted, with topics based on class discussions, activities, assignments and readings **(15 points each)**.
- 2 in class timed essays, in preparation for impromptu writing and the UDWPE **(5 points each)**.
- Portfolio **(25 points)**.
- Debate **(5 points)**.
- Participation (including journals, in class activities and assignments, class discussions quizzes and attendance) **(10 points)**.
- One conference with me during the semester to discuss the class, assignments, etc.

GRADING GUIDELINES

Here is a sketch of expectations for written work.

- **A** represents a writing level of excellent polish and style, often taking an unusual or especially thoughtful or insightful position on the topic. The thesis is well-supported. The essay is also extremely well developed and organized, and the writing is not only free of grammatical problems or careless mistakes but also is rich in detail and exhibits considerable fluency and control.

B represents solid, readable writing that does what the assignment requires. The thesis is thoughtful and the paper demonstrates concrete support for the thesis, good organization, and is free of grammatical problems or careless mistakes.

C represents writing that, for the most part, satisfies all the requirements of an assignment. However, the thesis is not well-conceived and the writing lacks sufficient, concrete support needed to illustrate its assertions or prove its point. C-level writing also shows lapses in editing proficiency and contains careless errors.

D represents writing that does not adequately satisfy the requirements of an assignment. The thesis is poorly conceived or missing, and the writing lacks coherence and support. D-level writing is characterized by significant lapses in editing proficiency and many careless errors.

F represents writing that is flawed in terms of fulfilling the requirements of the assignment and supporting a thesis as well as in overall coherence and appropriateness. The writing is characterized by considerable lapses in editing and a great deal of grammatical errors.

WELCOME TO ENGLISH 155: FRESHMAN COMPOSITION
Fall 2001   Ticket # 61085

Instructor: B   *Time: Tu & Th 8:00AM – 9:15 AM*
Office Location: JR 219   *Location: Tu-JR 248(lab) Th-JR 201*
Office Hours: Th 9:30–10:30 & by appt   *Phone: (messages)*
E-Mail: *(office)*

Course Description

English 155 is an expository writing course designed for freshmen and transfer students who have not taken freshman composition elsewhere and fulfills a General Education, Basic Subjects requirement. The purpose of this course is to help you gain experience with academic reading and writing, the kind of reading and writing you will be doing in most of your courses throughout your college career. Our primary focus will be on the analysis and writing of argumentative essays: essays that are thesis driven, that make a claim, and are then supported with evidence meant to persuade or convince the audience. You will also work to develop skill in organizing an essay, using logical reasoning in support of a thesis, and expressing ideas clearly through appropriate language choices with an emphasis on multiple drafting and revision. Beyond these fundamental concerns, the course encourages you to develop a degree of grace and style that will serve to make your writing more interesting and readable. In short, this class is here to provide you with an environment to work on discovering and improving your writing process and becoming a better writer. The rest is up to you.

Required Texts and Materials

- *Writing About Diversity: An Argument Reader and Guide,* 2nd Edition, Irene Clark, 1997. **(WD)**
- *The Writer's Harbrace Handbook. Miller, Webb, Horner, Eds.* **(WHH)**
- *Wings,* 8th Edition **(W)**
- Two large blue books (available in Matador Bookstore) for in-class timed essays
- A two-pocket portfolio folder for drafts and essays. **DO NOT THROW ANY OF YOUR WRITTEN WORK AWAY; YOU WILL NEED IT FOR YOUR PORTFOLIO!**
- An IBM formatted diskette (please label with your name)
- A three-ring loose-leaf binder or file folder for your journal
- An e-mail account
- I also recommend a college dictionary and a college thesaurus

Course Requirements and Grading

Prerequisite – a CSU English Placement Test Score of 151 or better, <u>or</u> the EPT <u>and</u> a grade of Credit in English 097 and/or 098, if applicable.

Grading – You can earn a total of 100 points, divided into 3 major categories. Assignments are due at the beginning of class on their due date. NO LATE ASSIGNMENTS WILL BE ACCEPTED! For each missing assignment, your grade will be lowered.

1. Essay writing (60%) You will write four substantive, thesis-driven essays requiring multiple drafts. There will also be two, 60 minute in-class, timed essays designed to prepare you for impromptu writing and the Upper Division Writing Proficiency Exam (UDWPE).

• Essay 1	3–5 pages	10 points
• Essay 2	3–5 pages	10 points
• Essay 3	4–6 pages	15 points
• Essay 4	4–6 pages	15 points
• In-class Essay 1		5 points
• In-class Essay 2		5 points

= 60 points

2. Portfolio (25%) A final portfolio that will include your choice of your two best essay "packets", one in-class timed essay, a cover letter and a submission to <u>Wings</u>.

- Final portfolio   25 points   **= 25 points**

3. Participation (15%) Participation includes attendance, punctuality, participating in class discussions and peer review activities, journals, completing reading and homework assignments on time, bringing your books to class, and more. A word about journals: I will collect your journals 2 or 3 times throughout the semester. Although the final collection is announced on the schedule, the others will not be announced. So, please bring your journals with you to every class session and keep them current.

- Peer review sessions. Other in-class activities, reading, homework, journal writing, etc.   **= 15 points**

              TOTAL   **= 100 points**

Here is the breakdown of the grading scale and guidelines for written work. I will be using a +/− grading scale.

A	100-94	B	86-84	C	76-74	D	66-64
A−	93-90	B−	83-80	C−	73-70	D−	63-60
B+	89-87	C+	79-77	D+	69-67	F	<60

GRADING GUIDELINES:

Here is a sketch of expectations for written work

A represents a writing level of excellent polish and style, often taking an unusual or especially thoughtful or insightful position on the topic. The thesis is well supported and the writer addresses the complexity of the topic by acknowledging and then arguing skillfully against an opposing viewpoint. The essay is extremely well developed and organized, and the writing is not only free of grammatical problems or careless mistakes but is rich in detail and exhibits considerable fluency and control.

B represents solid, readable writing that does what the assignment requires. The thesis is thoughtful and the writer indicates his or her awareness of the complexity of the topic by acknowledging and then arguing against an opposing viewpoint. It demonstrates concrete support for the thesis, good organization, and is free of grammatical problems or careless mistakes.

C represents writing that, for the most part, satisfies all the requirements of an assignment. However, the thesis is not well conceived and the writing lacks sufficient, concrete support needed to illustrate its assertions or prove its point. C-level writing also shows lapses in editing proficiency and contains careless errors.

D represents writing that does not adequately satisfy the requirements of an assignment. The thesis is poorly conceived or missing, and the writing lacks coherence and support. D-level writing is characterized by significant lapses in editing proficiency and many careless errors.

F represents writing that is flawed in terms of fulfilling the requirements of the assignment and supporting a thesis, as well as in overall coherence and appropriateness. The writing is characterized by considerable lapses in editing and a great many grammatical errors.

Policies and Procedures

Attendance – This is not a lecture class. Since this course is conducted as a workshop, with in-class writing exercises, writing assignments and group activities, it is important that you come to every class prepared and on time. Because of the collaborative nature of the class, the work is difficult if not impossible to make up. For a class meeting two times a week, you are permitted no more than two absences. Anything beyond that will seriously affect your grade in this class. Missing the required class work (including discussions and peer review workshops) in 6 class meetings can result in failure. I know it's early, but class will begin promptly at 8:00 AM. At 8:05 you are considered tardy and 2 times tardy = one absence. Please don't be late as it is very disruptive to your fellow students and to me. If you must miss a class, please e-mail me or leave a message in the English Office at ahead of time. It is your responsibility to call a fellow classmate for any missed assignments.

Getting Help – We all experience problems with our writing, and there are plenty of resources available. I'm here to help! Please see me during my office hours, or schedule an appointment to meet with me. E-mail me, and I will reply within 24 hours. During the semester, you will be required to meet with me in conference, at least once. This is a mandatory meeting but it is an opportunity for us to get to know each other and for us to discuss your progress in the course. Also, you will be **required to visit the Learning Resource Center** (LRC) (located on the 4th floor of the Student Services Building) for help with at least one of your formal essays. They have experienced writing tutors ready to help you. You can schedule an appointment to work with a peer tutor by calling Monday through Friday. Walk-in appointments are also available. I strongly suggest you plan to use this resource early in the semester (on your first essay). You will be required to attach your LRC form to your essay packet as evidence of your visit to LRC.

For more information visit the LRC website at: http://www.csun.edu/~hflrc006.

Plagiarism – The act of "intentionally or knowingly representing the words, ideas, or works of another as one's own in any academic exercise" (CSUN catalog 553) will result in a failing grade on the plagiarized assignment and is grounds for disciplinary action by the university. If you are unsure about how to avoid plagiarism when incorporating other sources into your writing, please refer to *The Writer's Harbrace Handbook,* and/or meet with me. We will spend time in class reviewing how to properly cite sources. Remember, when in doubt, don't do it! You cannot become a better writer if you don't do the writing yourself.

Special Circumstances – If you require special course adaptations or accommodations because of a disability, or if you have emergency medical information to share with me, or need special arrangements in case of a building evacuation, please let me know as soon as possible.

A Few Requests – Before you come to class, please turn off anything that rings, buzzes, vibrates or otherwise distracts you and the rest of us from what we are here to do. The computer lab is a classroom. Please resist the temptation to read your e-mail or download the latest and greatest. This is not the time or place.

A Few Final Thoughts – This class is your opportunity to improve your writing skills for college work and beyond. It will not magically transform you but you will get out of this class what you put in. Most of us panic at the though of 5 blank pages that we must mysteriously turn into a well crafted, persuasive, engaging piece of writing. But the more you write, the easier it gets, and the better writer you become. You might even learn to really enjoy it! I am glad to discuss your writing with you at any time and look forward to working with you. Just ask . . . and practice, practice, practice.

Tentative Weekly Schedule
English 155 Ticket # 61085
Fall 2001 Tu/Th 8:00 – 9:15 AM

This schedule is subject to change. Read your syllabus daily, it is the key to knowing where we are. All readings and assignments are due at the beginning of class on the date assigned. Please bring all assigned materials to class for each meeting. You should bring your journal daily. SAVE ALL YOUR WRITTEN WORK!

Week #1

Aug 28th lab   Introduction to English 155 "Why write about diversity?"
Have all assigned books and materials by next class,
August 30th.
Homework – 1. Complete Confidential Information sheet.
2. Read "Judging Through Stereotypes"
3. Answer questions to Handout #2 in your journals.
Be prepared to discuss in class.

Aug 30th   In class timed writing.
Homework - 1. Read pp 1–11 in *Writing About Diversity* (WD). Answer Exploration questions page 5 and 6, #1,2,3
2. Read (WD) Chapter 1 pp. 15–41

Week #2   **The Writing Process – Negotiating Controversy in Argumentative Writing**

Sept 4th lab   **Introduction to the Writing Lab** - How I Write
Homework – 1. Read (WHH) Chapter 2 pp 29–47.

Sept 6th   **Homework – Read (WD)** Chapter 2 pp 63–84.

Week #3	**Critical Reading**
Sept 11th lab	Assign Essay #1 - Personal Experience
	Homework – 1. Read (WHH) Chapter 1 pp 3–28.
Sept 13th	Essay #1 Peer Draft #1 due. Bring 3 copies
	Peer Review Workshop
Week #4	**Form and Function in Argumentation**
Sept 18th lab	**TBA**
Sept 20th	Essay #1 Polished draft due.
Week #5	**Definition, Support and Revision**
Sept 25th lab	**TBA**
Sept 27th	Essay #1 Final draft due in portfolio folder with copies of all drafts. Points will be deducted for any missing drafts.
	In Class Essay Exam #1 – Bring Blue Book
Week #6	**CONFERENCE WEEK** – I will schedule a mandatory meeting with each of you during this week to discuss your first essay and your progress in Eng 155.
Oct 2nd lab	Assign Essay #2 - Evaluation
Oct 4th	Essay #2 Peer Draft #1 due. Bring 3 copies.
Week #7	**Library and Other Research**
Oct 9th lab	Essay #2, Polished draft due.
	Research: Finding sources. Assessing evidence and credibility
Oct 11th	Oviatt Library Presentation
Week #8	
Oct 16th lab	TBA
Oct 18th	Essay #2 Final Draft due in folder with copies of all drafts.
Week #9	
Oct 23rd lab	Assign Essay #3 – Problem Solving
Oct 25th	Essay #3 Peer draft #1 due. Bring 3 copies.
Week #10	
Oct 30th lab	Essay #3 Second draft Due.
Nov 1st	TBA
Week #11	
Nov 6th lab	TBA
Nov 8th	Essay #3 Final Draft Due in folder with copies of all drafts.
	Assign Essay #4 - Researched Topic/Argument.
Week #12	**Style Workshop**
Nov 13th lab	TBA

Nov 15th   Essay #4 Peer Draft #1 due. Bring 3 copies

Week #13   **Happy Holidays**
Nov 20th lab   Essay #4 Second draft due
Nov 22nd   Thanksgiving Holiday - No class

Week #14   **Revision and WPE strategies**
Nov 27th lab   Discuss revision and WPE strategies
Nov 29th   Essay #4 Final Draft Due in folder with copies of
                 all drafts
                 In Class Essay Exam #2 – Bring Blue Book

Week #15   **Preparing The Portfolio**
Dec 4th lab   Portfolio Workshop/Revision
Dec 6th   Portfolio Workshop

Week #16   **Semester Ends**
Dec 11th lab   Portfolios due. Wings submission due.

💻 Freshman Composition: English 155 CMP – Fall 2001 💻
"Writing is an act of faith, not a trick of grammar" – E. B. White

Ticket # 61090   Instructor:C
TTH 11:00-12:15   Office: JR 253
Class Location: T SH 304; TH JR 248   Office Hour: T 12:30-1:30 & by appt.
Email: Phone:
Class Listserv:
Class Hypernews:

Required Texts and Materials

- Scenarios for Writing, Gregory Glau, Craig Jacobsen (**SW**)
- Wings, 8th Ed, ed. Nicole Warwick, et al (**W**)
- Keys for Writers, 2nd Ed, ed. Ann Raimes (**Keys**)
- Folder with 2 pockets to hold papers and drafts; DON'T THROW ANYTHING AWAY; YOU WILL NEED IT FOR YOUR PORTFOLIO!
- One large blue book for in-class timed essay
- IBM formatted disk 💾 (SAVE your work!)
- E-mail account

Course Description

This course is intended as an aid to improve your writing skills and to prepare you for academic writing. Please note that this course will not magically transform your writing. Rather, it is an opportunity to explore the interrelationships between reading, writing, and critical thinking, and to emphasize revision as a means of developing a voice and improving writing.

Course Requirements

Following are the assignments required throughout the semester and the amount of points they count towards passing this class; there are 100 points total *(therefore, every point counts!)*.

For each missing assignment your final grade will be lowered:

- Four 4–6 page major essays **(ME)** which are multiply drafted – based on class texts/assignments/activities/workshops, and documented research **(1st essay=7 points; 2nd, 3rd, and 4th essays=14 points each)**
- One in-class timed essay designed to prepare you for impromptu writing and the UDWPE **(6 points)**
- Portfolio **(25 points)**
- Debate **(4 points)**
- E-journal **(6 points)**
- Participation (includes journals, in-class activities, workshops, discussions, and attendance) **(10 points)**

LATE WORK WILL NOT BE ACCEPTED

E-journal requirements 📧

Six responses of a *minimum* of 75 words each to any article on the Op-Ed page of the L. A. Times, sent via email to the L. A. Times (letters@latimes.com) and the class listserv (   ). Each entry is worth one point; entries must be completed by due date/time (check your syllabus) to receive credit and must contain the title, author, and publication date of the article to which you are responding.

✍TENTATIVE ASSIGNMENT SCHEDULE AND DUE DATES ✍

This schedule is subject to change. **READ YOUR SYLLABUS DAILY! Assignments *and readings* are due at the <u>beginning</u> of class on the date given; late work will not be accepted. You must bring the assigned books and/or materials needed for each class session, and SAVE ALL of your written work!**

<u>SW</u>=Scenarios for Writing

<u>W</u>=Wings

<u>Keys</u>=Keys for Writers

ME=Major Essay

💾=Bring disk to class

📧=E-journal

GETTING STARTED

Week 1	**T 8/28**	**Homework:** Have all assigned books and materials by 8/30
	TH 8/30 💾	**Reading:** <u>SW</u> chapter 1 **Due:** Assigned books and materials
Week 2	**T 9/4**	Assign ME #1 **Reading:** <u>SW</u> chapter 2
	TH 9/6 💾	**Reading:** "Auto Liberation," "Creating a Criminal" (handout) <u>**Keys**</u> 15-18, 22-34 **Due:** ME #1 source 📧 E-journal #1 by 5:00 PM
Week 3	**T 9/11**	ME #1 peer review **Reading:** (TBA) **Due:** ME #1 Peer draft/**bring 3 copies to class**

SCENARIO #1: STUDENT PRIVACY

	TH 9/13 💾	Assign ME #2 **Reading:** <u>SW</u> chapter 3, 66-75, 135-149, 151-154 **Due:** ME #1 final draft, in folder, with drafts, review sheets, and source. Missing materials = −1 point each.
Week 4	**T 9/18**	**Reading:** <u>SW</u> 201-206, 209-211, 155-201
	TH 9/20 💾	ME #2 group statements
Week 10	**T 10/30**	**Reading:** (TBA) **Due:** (TBA)
	TH 11/1 💾	**Reading:** (TBA) **Due:** ME #4 short paper ME #4 sources
Week 11	**T 11/6**	Debates **Reading:** (TBA) **Due:** 📧 E-journal #5 by 5:00 PM
	TH 11/8 💾	ME #4 peer review **Reading:** <u>**Keys**</u> 95-132 **Due:** ME #4 peer/polished draft/**bring 4 copies to class**
Week 12	**T 11/13**	Conferences – class cancelled

REVISION, REVISION, REVISION

TH 11/15 ▣   In-class essay/**bring bluebook to class**
             Reading: Keys 185-186
                       W (TBA)
             Due: ME #4 final draft, in folder, with all drafts,
             short paper, sources, and review sheets. Missing
             materials= −1 point each.

Week 13   T 11/20   Portfolio revision #1 – mandatory
          TH 11/22   Thanksgiving - enjoy!

Week 14   T 11/27   Portfolio revision #2 – mandatory
          TH 11/29 ▣ **Reading: W** (TBA)
                     Due: 📧 E-journal #6 by 5:00 PM

Week 15   T 12/4   **Due:** Portfolios/**late portfolios will not be
                     accepted**

**You can pick up your graded portfolio from my office during the scheduled
final exam time for this class.**

HAVE A GREAT BREAK!

Freshman Composition, English 155

Fall Semester, 2001   Instructor: D
Ticket #61074   Office: JR 219
Class Time: MWF 11:00-11:50   Office Hours: 12:00 – 12:50,
Class Meeting Places: MW & by appointment
JR 248, Computer Lab, **Mon. & Alternate Fri.**   Telephone:
JR 201 on **Weds. & Alternate Fri.**   Email:

Required Texts & Materials:

Writing About Diversity: An Argument Reader and Guide, 2nd ed., Irene L. Clark
The Writer's Harbrace Handbook, Brief Edition, ed. John C. Hodges
Wings, Distinguished Student Essays, 8th ed.
One 3-ring binder with dividers (for class notes, homework and journal)
At least three 2-pocket folders for journal, essay and portfolio submissions
2 blue books for in-class essays
one IBM-formatted diskette, **labeled with your name**
email account (by 3rd week of class)

Course Objectives:

English 155 is designed for freshman and transfer students. You are enrolled in
Freshman Composition because you are required to pass this course to graduate
from CSUN. Why is Freshman Composition required? In order to succeed, both in
college and out, you must be able to explore new ideas, communicate them effectively

and think analytically about what you read and hear. This course is primarily about writing, but you cannot write effectively unless you think extensively throughout the writing process. In this class, we will help each other become better writers by discussing what we read and write, by listening to each other and by offering constructive suggestions. You are here to participate in the class as an active thinker and writer.

Course Prerequisites: CSU English Placement Test score of 151 or the EPT and a grade of Credit in English 097 and/or 098, if applicable.

Course Requirements and Policies:

Assignments:

Four multiply-drafted, thesis driven essays of 4-6 pages each	40% (10% each)
Final portfolio (see "Portfolio" paragraph below)	25%
Two in-class essays in preparation for the WPE	20% (10% each)
Participation (class exercises, journals, peer group work, attendance)	15%
Total:	**100%**

I will grade using a plus/minus system and check marks for completion of journal entries, homework assignments and participation. Failing to complete assignments or not participating in required class activities will lower your grade significantly. Each student will be required to meet with me in my office at least once during the semester for an individual conference. Missing a conference will count as an absence. Each student will also be required to make at least one visit to the Computer Writing Lab in the Learning Resource Center to work on an essay.

Attendance policy: *BE HERE, BE ON TIME AND BE PREPARED*

1. *BE HERE:* This is a participation (not a lecture) course, and missing more than six classes can result in your failing the class, since you will have missed too much work.

2. *BE ON TIME:* Arriving more than 10 minutes after the scheduled class time (according to classroom clock) is considered a tardy. Two tardies equal one absence. These will also affect your grade. Obviously, in case of an emergency, call or email me ASAP.

3. *BE PREPARED:* Turn in all written work, including drafts, journal entries, homework, etc., at the beginning of class on the due date. Complete all required assignments and be ready to discuss all readings in class. Bring all necessary materials to class. All drafts *must* be turned in to receive a passing grade on each essay. Any assignments turned in late will be lowered a grade per day late.

Revision Policy: A fourth revision of each essay for a higher grade is allowed only with the following guidelines: The revision must be turned in within one week of receiving the initial grade **and** the revision must show significant changes from the third draft. Your grade may improve or it may stay the same. **Your grade will never be lowered.** I encourage you to talk to me about any grading concerns you have throughout the semester.

Class Format:

1. Class will generally begin with a warm-up exercise
2. Discussion of warm-up and homework
3. Class work (peer groups, whole class work)
4. Discussion of next class session (homework, assignments due, etc.)

Plagiarism:

In your CSUN catalog, plagiarism is defined as "intentionally or knowingly representing the words, ideas, or work of another as one's own in any academic exercise." A student who plagiarizes on an assignment will automatically receive a failing grade on that assignment, may fail the course, and may be subject to disciplinary action on the part of the university.

We will spend class time learning how to document sources correctly and avoid plagiarizing. If you ever have any questions about how to quote or document sources, please discuss them with me.

Portfolio:

The final portfolio consists of:

1. A cover letter explaining why you chose the essays you include and how they represent what you have learned in this course
2. Two essay packets containing **clean** copies of your first, second and final drafts, as well as the assignment sheet from your 4-6 page essays
3. One blue book containing an in-class essay of your choice
4. A submission to *Wings* with submission form attached

DO NOT THROW AWAY ANY ASSIGNMENTS OR DRAFTS! Maintain clean, ungraded copies of all your essays and drafts for the portfolio.

Special Needs:

If you need course adaptations or accommodations because of a disability, if you have information to share with me or if you need special arrangements in case the building must be evacuated, please let me know as soon as possible.

Mediation:

If any problems arise, you may contact me or I may contact you to discuss them. If you and I are unable to resolve the issue(s), either of us may contact the Director of Composition, Dr. Irene Clark.

TENTATIVE SCHEDULE OF READINGS AND ASSIGNMENTS

Assignments and readings must be completed by the beginning of class on the date they are listed

M (L)	8/27	Course Introduction
W	8/29	*Diversity* pps. 1–11 and 95–97
F (L)	8/31	In-class writing
		Complete questionnaire pps. 10–11
		Readings: "Are You Really a Racist?" pps 50–56;
		"Multiculturalism: Building Bridges or Burning Them?" pps. 57–59
M (L)	9/03	**LABOR DAY – NO SCHOOL**
W	9/05	*Diversity* Chapter 1, pps. 15–49
F	9/07	Complete Exploration Questions at end of *Diversity* Chapter 6, pps 365–366
		Readings: *Diversity* pps. 279-293 (Ch. 6 intro & Tan essay)
M (L)	9/10	*Diversity* Chapter 2, pps. 63–93
		Read Handbook pps. 3–17; complete Exercise #1 on page 83 of *Diversity*
W	9/12	Readings: *Diversity* pps. 337–345 (Rodriguez essay), "The Lowest Animal" (handout)
F (L)	9/14	Readings: *Diversity* pps. 322–336 (Porter essay), pps. 361–364 (Robbins essay)
M (L)	9/17	**Essay #1 First Draft due;** peer workshops – bring multiple copies!!!
W	9/19	*Diversity* Chapter 3, pps. 95-129
		Readings: *Wings* selections to be assigned
F	9/21	**Essay #1 Revised Draft due**
		Readings: selections to be assigned
M (L)	9/24	Preparation for in-class essay #1
W	9/26	**Essay #1 Final Draft due**
		Preparation for in-class essay #1
F (L)	9/28	**In-Class Essay** #1 – bring blue books!
M (L)	10/01	Complete Exploration Questions at end of *Diversity* Chapter 8
		Readings: *Diversity* Chapter 8 selections to be assigned

| W | 10/03 | Readings: *Diversity* Chapter 8 selections to be assigned; "Love is a Fallacy" (handout) |
| F | 10/05 | Readings: *Diversity* Chapter 8 selections to be assigned |

Conferences with me this week (10/8 Thru 10/12) – remember that missing a conference = missing class.

M (L)	10/08	**Essay #2 First Draft Due**; peer workshops – bring multiple copies!
W	10/10	*Diversity* Chapter 4, pps. 133–157; *Handbook* pps. 137–151
F (L)	10/12	**Essay #2 Revised Draft due**
		Readings: "Putting a Spin on the Truth..." (handout); other readings to be assigned

M (L)	10/15	Readings: *Wings* selections to be assigned
W	10/17	**Essay #2 Final Draft due**
		Readings: To be assigned
F	10/19	Library research day ... date tentative
M (L)	10/22	Readings: *Diversity* Chapter 10 to be assigned
W	10/24	Readings: *Diversity* Chapter 10 to be assigned
F (L)	10/26	Readings: *Diversity* Chapter 10 to be assigned; "A Modest Proposal;" "The Sound of Music ..." (handouts)

(L) = Class held in computer lab, JR 248

(L)	10/29	**Essay #3 1st Draft due;** peer workshops – bring multiple copies!
W	10/31	Readings: to be assigned
F	11/02	**Essay #3 Revised Draft due**
		Readings: to be assigned

M (L)	11/05	Preparation for in-class essay #2
		Readings: to be assigned
W	11/07	**Essay #3 Final Draft due**; Preparation for in-class essay #2
		Readings: *Diversity* Chapter 7 to be assigned
F (L)	11/09	**In-Class Essay #2** - bring blue books!

M (L)	11/12	**Essay #4 1st Draft due**; peer workshops - bring multiple copies!
		Readings: *Diversity* Chapter 7 to be assigned
W	11/14	Readings: *Diversity* Chapter 7 to be assigned
F	11/16	**Essay #4 Revised Draft due**
		Readings: to be assigned

M (L)	11/19	Readings: To be assigned
W	11/21	**Essay #4 Final Draft due**
		Readings: to be assigned

F	11/23	**THANKSGIVING HOLIDAY – NO SCHOOL**
M (L)	11/26	Readings: to be assigned
W	11/28	Workshop evaluations for portfolio submittal
		Readings: to be assigned
F	11/30	Portfolio preparation, cover letters
		How to write a professional letter
M (L)	12/03	**PORTFOLIOS DUE !!**
W	12/05	Last Day of Classes – something fun?

Author Index

Subject Index